Entraînez-vous

Lecture Écriture

Niveau   débutant

Jacqueline Jacquet
Michèle Pendanx

SPECIMEN

Cle international

27, rue de la Glacière 75013 paris
Vente aux enseignants : 16, rue Monsieur le Prince, 75006 Paris

© CLE INTERNATIONAL 1991 - ISBN 2.19.033335.0

Avant-propos

Cet ouvrage s'adresse aux faux débutants de français langue étrangère. Il propose un travail de lecture-analyse de l'écrit dans sa spécificité :

    – fonctions de l'écrit (écrire pour raconter, se raconter, donner des indications, exprimer des sentiments, etc.),

    – codes et conventions (comment rédiger une adresse, importance de la ponctuation, etc.),

    – grammaire de l'écrit (enchaînement narratif, reprise lexicale etc.).

Ce travail, qui débouche sur des activités d'écriture, s'effectue sur des fragments d'écrits de la vie courante dont les genres (cartes postales, catalogues, formulaires, etc.) sont classés par ordre alphabétique.

Pour chacun de ces ensembles les étapes sont les suivantes :

    – des tâches de repérage pour faciliter la lecture,

    – des activités de production dirigée demandant le plus souvent une correction collective,

    – des activités d'écriture personnelle sur de nouveaux documents plus poétiques ou fantaisistes.
Ce travail peut rester individuel ou faire l'objet d'un affichage ou d'une lecture en classe.

S'il importe que cette progression interne à chaque dossier soit respectée, l'ordre des dossiers eux-mêmes est indifférent. On y piochera selon le moment, le besoin, le plaisir.

Sommaire

utobiographie

SPORTS PRATIQUÉS

MANIES

RÊVES

LANGUES PARLÉES

NATIONALITÉ

DATE DE NAISSANCE

ÉTAT CIVIL

ADRESSE

LA PLUS GRANDE ANGOISSE

ÉTUDES EN COURS

PASSE-TEMPS FAVORI

ACTIVITÉ ARTISANALE

ÉTATS D'ÂME FRÉQUENTS

LIEU DE NAISSANCE

COULEUR PRÉFÉRÉE

PROJETS IMMÉDIATS

SENTIMENTS ACTUELS

PRINCIPAL DÉFAUT

EXPÉRIENCE PROFESSIONNELLE

FORMATION

SIGNE DU ZODIAQUE

STAGES RÉALISÉS

LE PLUS BEAU SOUVENIR

À partir des mots ci-dessus, on peut fabriquer des questionnaires pour connaître quelqu'un. Classez ces mots en deux catégories : questionnaire de données objectives, et questionnaire de données personnelles.

Questionnaire données objectives :

....
....
....
....
....
....

Questionnaire données personnelles :

....
....
....
....
....
....

● repérage ●

Autobiographie

Et maintenant, racontez-vous ! À partir des réponses que vous feriez à ces deux questionnaires, rédigez successivement :

a) un curriculum vitæ (informations sur vous et votre histoire professionnelle, destinées à un employeur, par exemple)

b) un autoportrait subjectif, fantaisiste, poétique, comique, que vous pouvez éventuellement illustrer, et qui reflète votre personnalité.

COPINE DE COLO

Je serais heureuse de retrouver une amie d'enfance qui s'appelle Patricia Berthier, elle a eu 15 ans au mois d'avril dernier, et nous sommes parties en vacances ensemble en Corse quand nous étions petites. À bientôt, j'espère.

Katia Yasmine 18, rue Paul-Bert
94240 L' Haÿ-les-Roses

Annonce

Cet avis de recherche peut donner lieu à deux lettres différentes, selon les circonstances.

Réponse 1

Ma chérie,

J'ai trouvé dans *Femmes Modernes* cet avis de recherche que je joins à ma lettre : une jeune fille recherche une certaine Patricia Berthier, qu'elle a connue autrefois en Corse. Or, je me souviens que tu es allée en colonie à Porto-Vecchio l'année de tes 8 ans.

Tu remarqueras qu'elle affirme que tu aurais eu 15 ans en avril : elle se trompe d'un an (ou est-ce une coquille?). Est-ce toi qu'elle recherche ? Tu me raconteras …

Reçois les bises de ta Tatie Madeleine.

Réponse 2

Mademoiselle,
J'ai lu la revue *Femmes Modernes* où vous avez fait paraître un avis de recherche. Je suis à peu près certaine que Patricia Berthier, que vous recherchez, est ma nièce : je me souviens qu'elle a passé un mois de vacances en Corse (à Porto-Vecchio exactement) il y a 7 ans ; mais il y a une petite différence : ma nièce a eu 16 ans le 4 avril dernier. Comme Patricia habite actuellement en Allemagne avec ses parents, je ne crois pas qu'elle ait pu lire la revue ; je vous envoie donc son adresse, afin que vous lui écriviez directement. Patricia gardait un bon souvenir de ce séjour en Corse, et je suppose qu'elle sera heureuse d'avoir de vos nouvelles.
Bonne chance !

Madeleine Sézac

Patricia Berthier - Vilandstr.17, D 6 000 FRANKFURT 90

Avis de recherche

1. Lisez le texte de l'annonce et répondez aux questions suivantes pour le résumer en deux phrases :
– qui recherche qui ? ....
– où ces deux personnes se sont-elles connues ? ....

2. Lisez les deux propositions de réponse pour remplir la grille de lecture ci-dessous :

	qui a écrit ?	à qui ?	informations présentes dans l'annonce	informations nouvelles
réponse 1				
réponse 2				

3. Résumés des deux réponses : complétez les phrases suivantes :

Réponse 1

.... écrit à ....

pour .... Mais elle se

demande ....

Réponse 2

.... répond à ....

pour .... Elle pense

que ....

Une revue publie les messages suivants :

A

Camarades de classe

J'aimerais retrouver Marianne Garcia qui était avec moi au lycée de Montpellier. Nous avons interrompu notre correspondance vers l'année 1987, et je serais vraiment heureuse de renouer cette ancienne amitié. Merci de me contacter si vous la connaissez.

Madame Ef Salah,
17, rue Bektache Nedir, 16016 Alger

B

Parente éloignée

Je recherche Solange qui habitait le faubourg Bonnefoy à Toulouse. Elle doit avoir soixante-dix ans : elle a un fils de quarante ans. Sa mère s'appelait Émilie et était apparentée à mon grand-père René Laborde. Je compte sur vous.

Madame Forsans, quartier Eslech, Route de Bayonne, 40290 Habas.

Amie du bout du monde

À cause d'une adresse égarée, je n'ai plus de nouvelles de mon amie Diane Lehmann. Nous avons fait une partie de nos études ensemble, et elle a été témoin à mon mariage, en 1978. J'ai perdu sa trace après son départ pour la Belgique. Si vous la connaissez, n'hésitez pas à prendre contact avec moi. Mille fois merci.

Éliane Guy, BP 8447 Nouméa Sud, Nouvelle-Calédonie.

C

vis de recherche

Situation d'écriture

Imaginez que vous connaissez l'une des personnes recherchées dans l'un des avis ci-contre. Écrivez-lui une lettre pour l'informer de l'avis de recherche la concernant (cf. réponse A, page 10). Vous pouvez aussi écrire à la personne qui a mis l'avis de recherche dans la revue (cf. réponse B, page 10).

Travail préalable

Répondez aux questions ci-dessous pour préparer votre texte :

qui écrit ? : ....

à qui ? : ....

informations présentes dans l'avis de recherche : ....

informations nouvelles (inventez) : ....

Réponse à l'avis de recherche n° ....

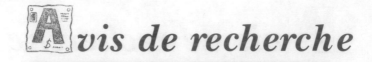

Avis de recherche

Rencontres, recherches, réponses… et rencontres

A

073. Nine, ma Nine, te souviens-tu de la rue des Tanneurs ? Tes lettres, je les avais bien cachées, j'ai été incapable de les relire depuis 1985. Et puis, la vie a fait son cours : un jour de juillet, j'ai tout relu d'un coup. Quelle émotion… Anne et Joël doivent être bien grands aujourd'hui. Moi, j'ai trente-trois ans, un an de plus que toi quand on s'est rencontrés. Habites-tu toujours à Noyon ? Travailles-tu toujours à Compiègne ? Moi, je ne quitterai plus Paris. Juste se revoir, se reparler une fois, une seule : tu ne veux pas, ma Nine ? Comment veux-tu que je t'oublie ? Si vous connaissez Aline Mazier, merci de lui faire lire cette page : elle en fera ce qu'elle voudra.

B

072. *Mystérieuse inconnue (moi) recherche mystérieux inconnu (toi). Rencontre dans un TGV direction Paris, provenance Lyon ; c'était en novembre 1989.*

Toi : jeune soldat (une vingtaine d'années) de Grenoble (je crois), les cheveux très courts, (cela va de soi), châtains il me semble : ton visage demeure flou mais une certaine émotion et un certain charme subsistent.

Moi : lycéenne, attitude et gestes bizarres (je crois me souvenir), blonde un peu frisée. Merci de m'avoir prêté ce petit bout de ton épaule que je t'ai pris de force, je le reconnais. Pourquoi ce message ? L'autre nuit, j'ai rêvé de toi par hasard… J'ai cherché dans ma mémoire, je me suis souvenue, et ça, ce n'est peut-être pas un hasard.

Si tu te reconnais, écris-moi si tu veux… Je ne connais pas ton nom et tu ne connais pas le mien non plus, alors je ne signe pas…. À bientôt, j'espère….

C

074. *Tu t'appelles Pierre Jeannet, tu as quarante-cinq ans environ, on ne s'est jamais vus, et pourtant, je te cherche car tu es responsable à 50% de ma venue sur terre. Tu es mon père. À cinq ans, déjà je te réclamais. On me répondait que tu étais en Amérique. Le 13 août, j'aurai vingt ans. Ça serait génial de fêter ça ensemble, tu ne crois pas ? Je crève d'envie de te revoir, de t'embrasser, de connaître ta vie et de te raconter la mienne. En espérant que tu lis* Les Nouvelles, *ou qu'on t'en fera part, bisous.*

Sophie Demontet
Les Nouvelles, avril 1990

Avis de recherche

1. Certaines des phrases suivantes sont l'équivalent des éléments d'information contenus dans les messages A, B et C. Lisez-les et cochez la lettre correspondante.

1. La personne recherchée :
   – une femme qui a des
      enfants   A   B   C
   – un militaire   A   B   C
   – une jeune fille   A   B   C
   – un homme d'âge mûr   A   B   C

2. L'auteur du message :
   – un homme jeune   A   B   C
   – une vieille dame   A   B   C
   – une jeune fille   A   B   C
   – une jeune femme   A   B   C

3. Où ils se sont connus :
   – dans un hôpital   A   B   C
   – à New York   A   B   C
   – dans un train   A   B   C
   – le texte ne précise pas   A   B   C

4. Quand ils se sont rencontrés :
   – 8 mois avant la publication
      de l'avis   A   B   C
   – 5 ans (minimum) avant
      la publication de l'avis   A   B   C
   – cela n'est pas précisé   A   B   C
   – en septembre 89   A   B   C

5. La relation qu'il y a eu entre eux :
   – ils se sont aimés   A   B   C
   – c'est une filiation   A   B   C
   – c'est une brève rencontre
      de hasard   A   B   C
   – ils se sont tenu compagnie   A   B   C

6. Le motif qui a provoqué l'écriture du message :
   – une date importante   A   B   C
   – des lettres relues   A   B   C
   – une maladie grave   A   B   C
   – un rêve   A   B   C

2. Relevez des mots qui montrent les sentiments et l'état d'âme de l'auteur du message.

A ....

B ....

C ....

3. Situation d'écriture :
a) À votre tour, écrivez un message pour rechercher quelqu'un que vous avez rencontré.
b) Lisez les messages écrits par vos camarades, et répondez à l'un d'entre eux.

13

A vis de recherche

RECHERCHE
PETITE CHIENNE
COCKER

PERDUE
SAMEDI
BOULEVARD
ARAGO

PELAGE NOIR FRISÉ
AGÉE DE 6 MOIS
RÉCOMPENSE ASSURÉE

47 71 60 03 - 40 12 74 26

# A vis de recherche

AVIS DE RECHERCHE

On recherche
Alain FOUQUET 9 ans,
taille : 1,30 m ; poids : 24 kg
yeux : verts
cheveux : blonds et courts.

Vêtements : pantalon jean bleu,
pull rouge, tennis Adidas,
ceinture marine, KWay rouge.

Lieu de la disparition :
RN 100 entre l'Isle-sur-la-Sorgue
et Cavaillon.

Jour de la disparition :
le 23 septembre 1990
entre 17 h et 19 h.

Alain a disparu il y a un mois,
nous vous prions de communiquer tous
renseignements à la Gendarmerie de
Cavaillon ou de votre région.

D'autre part, nous recherchons l'ensemble
des personnes qui ont emprunté
la RN 100
le dimanche 23 septembre après-midi.

Mr et Mme Fouquet,
Allée des Mimosas,
Lotissement des Bruyères,
84800 L'Isle-sur-la-Sorgue
Tél : 90 38 00 43.

Avignon infos.

Situation d'écriture :
Vous avez circulé sur la RN 100 au jour et à l'heure indiqués dans cet avis de recherche. Écrivez une très courte lettre aux parents de l'enfant disparu.

Schéma proposé :
• en-tête ;
• **introduction** : lecture de l'avis de recherche paru dans le journal ;
• vous n'avez pas vu l'enfant disparu, mais vous acceptez d'apporter votre témoignage ;
• vous donnez vos coordonnées ;
• **conclusion** : une phrase qui exprime votre sympathie, votre émotion.

lecture

écriture

A

Chère amie,
Recevez mon meilleur souvenir de Bretagne, où je passe un excellent séjour.
Toutes mes amitiés. Alain

B

Ma chère Cathie,
Le temps est parfois incertain, même sur la Côte d'Azur : ciel gris et vent frais. Mais pour moi le soleil brille ! Je te raconterai... Je t'embrasse bien fort.
Marie Lou

C

Chers enfants,
Nous voici en Turquie après un voyage sans histoires. Il fait très très chaud, mais nous tenons le coup ! Le pays est enchanteur ! Bons baisers de nous deux.
Papa   Maman

D

Un grand bonjour de Strasbourg en plein carnaval. insensé ! Délirant ! A bientôt ! Bises.
Christine

E

Venise le 4/8/90

Chers amis,
Un amical souvenir de Venise ou nous faisons un voyage d'amoureux. Il fait très beau. Nous espérons que vous passez aussi de bonnes vacances. Amitiés.

Jean-Paul   Madeleine

Monsieur et Madame DELAVIGNE

3 Allée des Mimosas

31300 MURET

FRANCE

artes postales

Voici des textes de cartes postales. Les mots en italique indiquent quels sont les sujets traités.

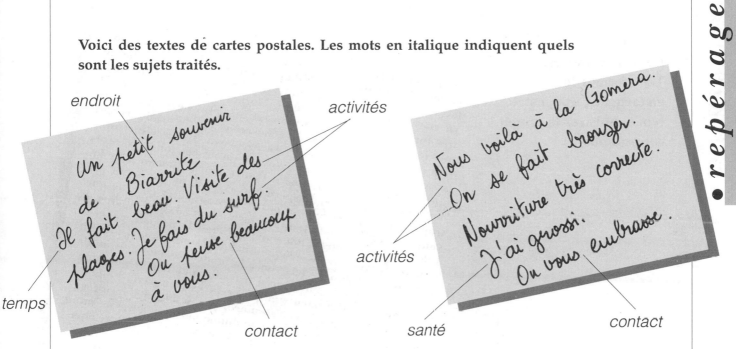

endroit

activités

Un petit souvenir de Biarritz. Il fait beau. Visite des plages. Je fais du surf. On pense beaucoup à vous.

temps

contact

Nous voilà à la Gomera. On se fait bronzer. Nourriture très correcte. J'ai grossi. On vous embrasse.

activités

santé

contact

1. Faites un relevé des formules et énoncés utilisés dans les cartes ci-contre pour parler des divers sujets :

	Carte A	Carte B	Carte C	Carte D	Carte E
Endroit visité					
Activité de l'expéditeur					
Temps qu'il fait					
Santé					
Jugement					

2. Relevez les formules de correspondance qui se trouvent au début des textes :

....

Relevez celles qui se trouvent à la fin des textes :

....

Connaissez-vous d'autres formules ?

....

Cartes postales

Voici le texte d'une
lettre de vacances.
Transformez-le
en texte de carte postale
(vous choisirez le contenu
correspondant).

"Mon cher Roch, chère Élisabeth,

Je vous envoie ce petit mot d'Italie, où je continue mon périple. Je suis passé par Milan et Bologne, et aujourd'hui je fais étape à Florence. Tu trouveras d'ailleurs dans l'enveloppe une carte postale achetée à Florence. Ici, la chaleur est très forte mais le paysage n'en est que plus beau. J'ai visité tous les monuments et tous les musées et j'ai vu pratiquement tout ce qu'il y a à voir ici. C'est très beau. J'espère que vous aurez l'occasion de faire ce voyage un de ces jours, je crois que ça vaut la peine. J'ai écrit l'autre jour à Maman pour lui donner des nouvelles. J'espère que sa sciatique ne la fait pas trop souffrir. J'espère que tout va bien de votre côté, et que vous ne souffrez pas trop de la chaleur. L'autre jour, à Milan, j'ai rencontré Emmanuel qui était là de passage avec sa femme. Nous avons évoqué quelques souvenirs. Il m'a dit qu'il comptait passer vous voir à la fin des vacances, avant de rentrer à Paris. Il paraît qu'il travaille maintenant pour une fabrique de réfrigérateurs et qu'il est très bien payé. Voilà les nouvelles. Je serai à Venise mardi prochain, et j'y resterai une quinzaine de jours. Je ne te donne pas mon adresse, mon cher Roch, parce que je sais que tu ne m'écriras pas. À bientôt donc, je vous embrasse.

Antoinette" (1)

Texte de la carte postale :

Florence
vue générale

(1) Texte de
J.M.G. Le Clézio ,
La Fièvre
© Éd. Gallimard

Cartes postales

1. Imaginez que vous êtes en vacances. Recherchez des phrases que vous pourriez écrire :

• **Sur le temps qu'il fait**

   Ex : *Il fait très beau.* ....

• **Sur l'endroit où vous êtes**

   Ex. : *On est au camping* La Baleine, ou *on a trouvé un petit hôtel très bien.*

   ....

• **Sur votre santé, votre état d'esprit**

   Ex. : *On est tous très bronzés* ou *c'est la pleine forme.*

   ....

• **Sur vos activités**

   Ex : *J'ai fait des progrès en planche à voile,* ou *il y a plein de beaux garçons dans le pays.* ....

   ....

2. À partir de ces suggestions, rédigez deux textes de cartes postales écrites le même jour, l'une adressée à votre meilleur(e) ami(e), l'autre à une personne moins proche (précisez de qui il s'agit).

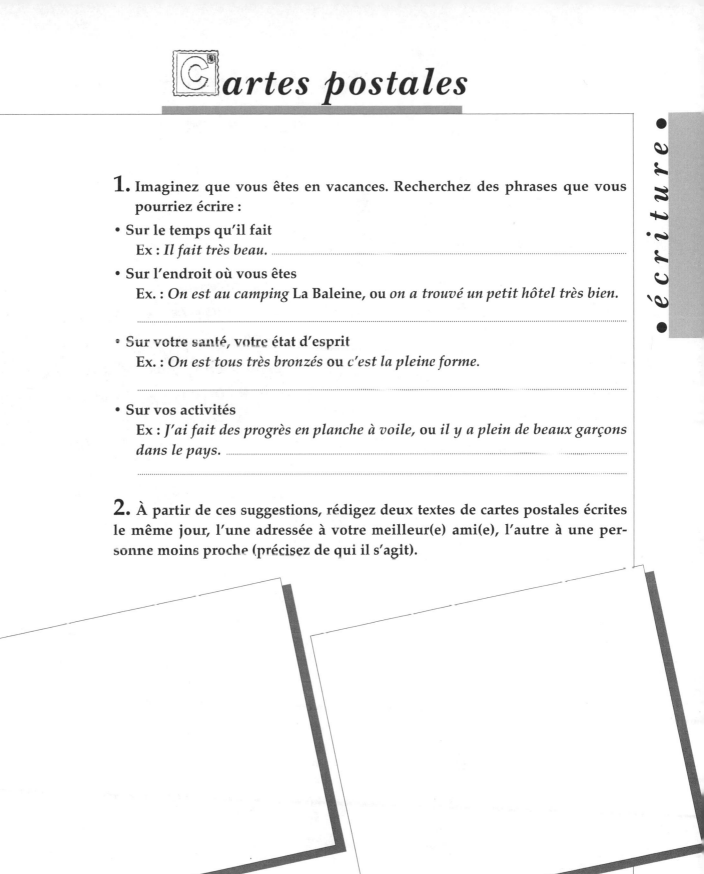

Cartes postales

A

Voilà les filles du pays ! Pas mal !... Mais encore mieux au naturel... On se baigne et on bronze.

Bises, Charles

B

Tu reconnais la fontaine ? Ça me rappelle nos balades... L'expo n'est pas terrible, mais heureusement, j'ai retrouvé une ancienne copine. Je t'embrasse avec la même tendresse.

Caroline

C

Mon jojo adoré, Qu'est-ce que tu penses de ça ? Ça ne te mets pas l'eau à la bouche ? Vivement le 23 ! Mille baisers de ta Josette qui t'attend.

D

Chère amie, J'ai choisi cette carte pour vous : vous aimeriez tant ces couleurs... L'année prochaine, peut-être ? Les gens du groupe sont charmants, et la nourriture acceptable. A bientôt, Amicalement à vous,

Antoinette

Cartes postales

Quand on écrit une carte à une personne que l'on connaît bien, on fait parfois allusion à des choses sans tout préciser. Trouvez des éléments implicites dans le texte des cartes ci-contre, et proposez une ou plusieurs significations possibles. Dans le texte de ces cartes, il est également fait allusion à l'illustration de la carte postale. Dites ce que peuvent représenter à votre avis, ces illustrations, et quels sont les mots grammaticaux employés pour faire référence à l'illustration.

	Illustration	Mots grammaticaux
Carte A	....	....
Carte B	....	....
Carte C	....	....
Carte D	....	....

Proposez plusieurs manières de faire allusion aux illustrations des cartes ci-dessous (réemployez les expressions ci-dessus).

Carte A (Paris - l'Ile de la Cité)

....
....
....

Carte B (Musée d'Orsay)

....
....
....

21

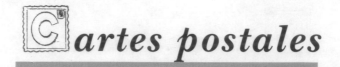

Cartes postales

écriture

Rédigez à votre tour une carte contenant une allusion à l'illustration. Déterminez votre situation d'écriture : pour cela, vous pouvez suivre la démarche suivante. Choisissez successivement :

• l'une des cartes de la page précédente :

....

• à qui vous envoyez votre carte (une personne proche) :

....

• dans quelles circonstances vous envoyez cette carte (vacances, voyage de travail, etc.) :

....

• quelles sont vos activités au moment où vous écrivez le texte de la carte :

....

Vous commencerez le texte par une allusion à la carte choisie pour votre destinataire (*).

(*) Pour écrire l'adresse, consultez la page «lecture» de ce dossier.

Cartes postales

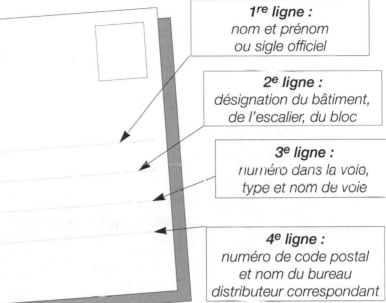

Présentation des adresses postales (*)

Les indications constituant une adresse doivent figurer sur plusieurs lignes, de façon que le lecteur aille du particulier au général.

1re ligne :
nom et prénom
ou sigle officiel

2e ligne :
désignation du bâtiment,
de l'escalier, du bloc

3e ligne :
numéro dans la voie,
type et nom de voie

4e ligne :
numéro de code postal
et nom du bureau
distributeur correspondant

lecture

Quelques conseils :

Le numéro de code postal doit obligatoirement précéder le nom du bureau distributeur, ces mentions étant séparées par un seul espace.

Madame Menaud	*Madame Menaud*
Kinésithérapeute	*Kinésithérapeute*
13, rue Saint-Saëns	*13, rue Saint-Saëns*
34500 BÉZIERS	*34500 BÉZIERS*

Ne pas séparer les deux premiers chiffres du code des trois chiffres qui suivent, ni les caractères du bureau distributeur.

Monsieur Saumon	*Monsieur Saumon*
2 rue du Docteur Maret	*2, rue du Docteur Maret*
21 000 D I J O N	*21000 DIJON*

Ne jamais utiliser sur les 2 dernières lignes de l'adresse les tirets, parenthèses, ou autre signe de ponctuation.

Madame Lefort	*Madame Lefort*
Bâtiment B	*Bâtiment B*
4, allée des Jonquilles	*4, allée des Jonquilles*
51000 – CHÂLONS S/MARNE	*51000 CHÂLONS SUR MARNE*

* Texte inspiré d'un dépliant édité par les P et T.

Série 1

C
225ᶠ

D
395ᶠ

créoles p. 222
bracelet p. 105

La Redoute

H Les bottines du Dr MAR-TENS .Dessus cuir croûte velours. Première intérieure peau et contrefort arrière. Épaisse semelle caoutchouc avec intercalaires mousse et alvéoles d'air.
• Pour hommes
marron 456 0809
noir 407 9716
6 pointures
40, 41, 42, 43, 44, 45   **395 F**
• Pour femme
marron 456 8397
noir 487 9996
5 pointures
36, 37, 38, 39, 40   **375 F**

I Le grand sac-cabas en néoprène vert fluo de PINK SODA plonge dans la mode. Dim 50 x 35 cm envir.
435 9534   **199 F**

199ᶠ

375ᶠ

LIONEL CROS
PARIS

VERTE VALLEE

E
155ᶠ

F
145ᶠ

G
395ᶠ
jean p. 129

MAGIC STREET

C Le T-shirt en lamé FRE-DERIC MOLENAC. Cintré, ras du cou. 100% polyester. Haut 54 cm env. col argent 361.9400 5 tailles
34, 36, 38, 40, 42,   **225F**

D La jupe néoprène FREDERIC MOLENAC. Doublée jersey polyami-de. Soulignée d'un galon noir, zippée dos. Long.50 cm env. noir 621 9233.
5 tailles
34, 36, 38, 40 42   **395 F**

E Le pull LIONEL CROS, long. et décolleté. En interlock pur coton, habillé d'un volant. Haut. 60 cm env. taille unique.
rouge 616 4404
blanc 616 4331
noir 616 4412
155 F

F Le caleçon moulant LIO-NEL CROS en interlock pur coton, habillé d'un volant. Taille élastiquée.
rouge 616 4528
blanc 616 4447
noir 616 4706
3 tailles
34/36, 38/40, 42/44
145 F

G La chemise western VERTE VALLEE aux pressions de nacre. Empiècement dos, 2 poches à rabat pressionné. Pur coton. Haut 75 cm env.
jaune/rouge 435 2165
2 tailles
34/38, 40/44   **395 F**

atalogues

*Acheter «sur catalogue», c'est acheter un article sans le voir
et le commander par téléphone, par Minitel
ou par correspondance. Le catalogue donne donc toutes
les précisions nécessaires sur l'article en vente :
description (photo + texte) et prix.*

1. **Relevez les mots qui servent à décrire :**

les formes	les couleurs	les compositions
cintré	argent	lamé
....	....	....
....	....	....
....	....	....
....	....	....
....	....	....
....	....	....

2. **La description de ces articles vous semble-t-elle :**

☐ précise ?   ☐ vague ?   ☐ trop détaillée ?

3. **Votre impression : ces articles ont été sélectionnés pour femmes et hommes de :**

☐ moins de 20 ans

☐ 20 à 30 ans

☐ plus de 30 ans

**À cause des couleurs ? des formes ? des matières employées ?
Justifiez votre réponse.**

....

....

....

....

....

....

....

....

....

entraînement

Série 2

REVUE DE DÉTAILS
NEWS MODE

REPÉRÉ AUX QUATRE COINS DE LA MODE, TOUT CE QUI NOUS PLAÎT. DE LA TÊTE AUX PIEDS.

D **LOOK INTELLO** En aluminium bicolore, des montures rondes et ultralégères (Alain Mikli, 1 500 F, 5 coloris).

A **ACIDULÉS** Par temps sec, ces imperméables très légers en nylon regagnent leur pochette (Figure Libre, 299 F, 3 tailles, 4 coloris).

E **VIVA ZAPATA** En coton et à pressions (Hartford, 725 F, du 38 au 44, coloris unique).

B **STYLISÉES** Chaussettes longues en coton et polyamide (Emilio Cavallini, 120 F, en bleu turquoise et en vert).

G **STRICT** En laine et polyamide, la veste est longue et ajustée, la jupe toute droite (1.2.3., 640 F et 279 F, du 36 au 42).

H **POUR VIP** Porte-documents en porc velours zippé, 21 x 29,7 cm (Didier Lavilla, 990 F, 25 coloris).

C

F ₂

I ₃

DOUILLETS (1) Gants en mouton retourné fourrés et surpiqués (Agnelle, 400 F, 4 tailles, 6 coloris). **EN VEAU VELOURS (2)** Short droit avec ceinture à passants et deux poches plaquées derrière (Sylvie Schimmel, 850 F, du 36 au 44, en marron, anis, orange, écru, noir, bleu marine, rouge). **MOTIFS EN INCRUSTATION (3)** Santiags bicolores en cuir, bout effilé et talon légèrement biseauté (Mexico Lindo, 990 F, du 36 au 44, en noir, rouge, bleu turquoise).

Informations Françoise Bernard et Caroline de Fayet. Réalisation visuelle Sandrine Aladjem et Magali Bass.

Catalogues

1. Relevez les mots qui servent à décrire :

les formes	les couleurs	les compositions
....	....	....
....	....	....
....	....	....
....	....	....
....	....	....
....	....	....
....	....	....
....	....	....

2. Y a-t-il des éléments descriptifs qui n'ont pas leur place dans ce tableau ?
Relevez-les :

....

....

....

....

....

3. Ces derniers éléments veulent faire ressortir une qualité spécifique de
l'article. Cherchez la qualité qui convient à chacun.

l'aspect pratique	le confort	l'élégance	l'originalité
article A			

4. Comparez les articles de la série 1 et ceux de la série 2 et leur description.
Que constatez-vous ?

....

....

....

....

ℰ*atalogues*

Série 3

A

E

H

B

F

I

C

J

D

G

K

28

Catalogues

Série 3

1. Voici des articles pouvant figurer dans un catalogue. Choisissez cinq articles et faites-en une description qui accompagnera leur photo dans le catalogue (modèle : série 1).

2. Ces mêmes articles (ou cinq autres de votre choix) ont été sélectionnés dans une revue pour un motif précis : prix, utilité, originalité, chic, ingéniosité, etc. Faites ressortir cet élément dans votre description (modèle : série 2).

écriture

Fragments de lettres

> " ...
> Je viens de m'acheter pour partir à Rio un ensemble terrible ! Imagine un tee-shirt brillant, en espèce de plastique, opaque, super sexy et une jupe étroite, en plastique aussi, très, très mini... Il va falloir que je soigne ma ligne ! "

> " ...
> Finalement, j'ai trouvé un cadeau pour Gontran. Une chemise ! Tu me diras que ce n'est pas très original, mais elle est superbe, à rayures de toutes les couleurs. Ça lui rappellera ses vacances au Mexique. Elle n'est pas donnée, mais c'est pas tous les jours qu'on a 20 ans ! "

1. Ces deux fragments de lettres évoquent deux articles présentés pages 24 et 26. De quels articles s'agit-il ? ....
....

2. Soulignez les mots qui vous ont mis sur la voie.

3. Vous venez d'acheter quelque chose. Vous en faites une description dans le courant d'une lettre. Vous précisez pour qui vous l'avez acheté, quels sont les motifs qui vous ont poussé à l'acheter (40 à 50 lignes).

....

....

....

....

....

....

....

....

....

Catalogues

Tandem convergent. Modèle pour fiancés

Fauteuil-radiateur. Il se branche sans aucune difficulté sur n'importe quelle installation de chauffage central. Indispensable aux personnes frileuses.

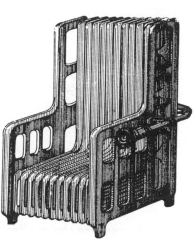

Rocking-chair latéral dit "le Roulis". Évoquera aux amoureux de la mer le doux mouvement d'une embarcation.

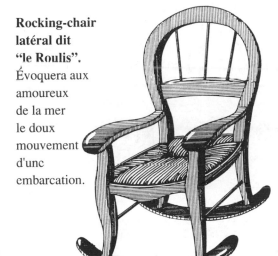

Cafetière pour masochiste. Nous pensons que le dessin est suffisamment explicite pour ne pas s'appesantir sur les détails qui pourraient s'avérer pénibles.

Miroir pour mythomane. La glace est remplacée par le portrait d'un personnage célèbre donnant ainsi à l'utilisateur l'impression qu'il est ce personnage. Très grand choix de portraits.

Ce miroir est à votre disposition. Qelle photo y mettrez-vous ?

Catalogue d'objets introuvables.
© Carelman

"Avec quels chiffres préférez-vous gagner?"

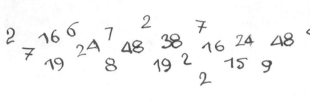

MEMO AU 30 JUIN 1990 LOTO

Numéros
Nombre de sorties*

① 140	⑩ 136	⑳ 162	㉚ 148	㊵ 161
② 147	⑪ 149	㉑ 152	㉛ 157	㊶ 138
③ 145	⑫ 151	㉒ 147	㉜ 153	㊷ 156
④ 147	⑬ 135	㉓ 146	㉝ 139	㊸ 150
⑤ 149	⑭ 149	㉔ 162	㉞ 168	㊹ 141
⑥ 154	⑮ 156	㉕ 158	㉟ 150	㊺ 162
⑦ 152	⑯ 164	㉖ 166	㊱ 160	㊻ 148
⑧ 156	⑰ 145	㉗ 156	㊲ 162	㊼ 131
⑨ 139	⑱ 166	㉘ 159	㊳ 175	㊽ 169
	⑲ 165	㉙ 140	㊴ 146	㊾ 155

* Depuis le 19 mai 1976.

POURQUOI PAS VOUS?

- Super Cagnotte du 24.12.88 : 33.456.975 F gagnés.
- 3200 personnes ont gagné plus de 1.000.000 F (dont 170 plus de 5.000.000 F).
- Plus gros gain n'ayant jamais été réclamé : 7.024.530 F, remis en jeu en 1984 à une "Super Cagnotte de l'Inconnu".

- Plus de 20.000.000 d'adultes jouent au moins une fois par an.

INFORMATIONS ET RÉSULTATS OFFICIELS  3615 LOTO

 **hiffres**

Votre chiffre préféré

1. Choisissez un chiffre de 1 à 49.

....

2. Pourquoi avez-vous choisi ce chiffre ?

....

3. Maintenant, regardez la page 32, combien de fois votre chiffre a gagné en 14 ans ?

....

Quel est le chiffre qui a le moins gagné ?

....

Quel est le chiffre qui a le plus gagné ?

....

4. Interrogez ceux qui vous entourent. Que répondent-ils à la question 2 ?

....

....

....

....

....

....

....

Que constatez-vous ?

....

....

....

....

....

Dédicaces

Des écrivains dédient leurs œuvres

1

À mes camarades
de la bataille
de Teruel.

2

À Elsa, ce livre
comme si
je ne lui avais pas
déjà donné.

3

Henri Guillaumet
mon camarade,
je te dédie ce livre.

4

À tous ceux, étudiants, amis,
auditeurs de radio,
correspondants bénévoles qui,
d'une fiche, d'un dossier
ou d'un diplôme d'études
supérieures, ont secondé mon
entreprise et contribué
à enrichir le trésor du savir
atlantique, j'offre ce résumé
de nos communs travaux.

5

Au poète impeccable,
au parfait magicien
ès lettres françaises,
à mon très cher et très
vénéré maître et ami
Théophile Gautier, avec les
sentiments de la plus
profonde humilité, je dédie
ces fleurs maladives.

Dédicaces

Voici la liste des noms d'auteurs et des œuvres d'où sont extraites ces dédicaces. Attribuez à chacune son auteur. Aidez-vous des quelques éléments d'information ci-dessous.

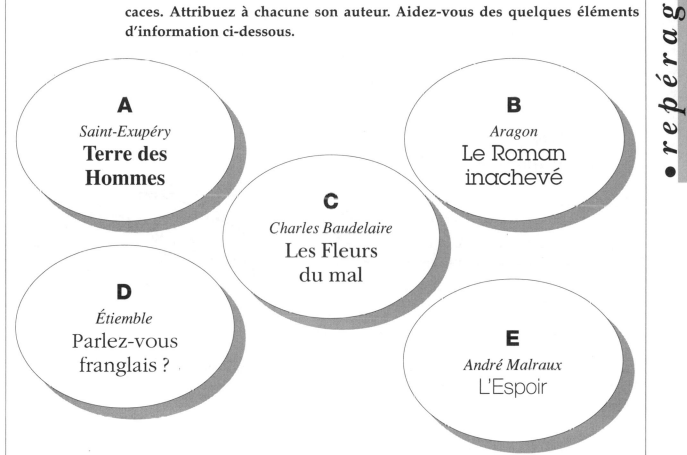

A

Saint-Exupéry
Terre des Hommes

B

Aragon
Le Roman inachevé

C

Charles Baudelaire
Les Fleurs du mal

D

Étiemble
Parlez-vous franglais ?

E

André Malraux
L'Espoir

Informations complémentaires

Aragon L. : 1897-1982 ; poète, son recueil le plus connu : Les yeux d'Elsa.

Baudelaire C. : 1821-1867 ; poète, son recueil de poèmes : Les Fleurs du mal est condamné par la justice en 1857.

Étiemble R. : né en 1909 ; essayiste et professeur à l'université.

Malraux A. : 1901-1976 ; ses romans les plus célèbres témoignent de sa participation à des conflits révolutionnaires en Chine, et en Espagne.

Saint-Exupéry A. de : 1900-1944 ; aviateur et romancier, il a chanté la fraternité humaine.

Ouvrage A : dédicace n° ....

Ouvrage D : dédicace n° ....

Ouvrage B : dédicace n° ....

Ouvrage E : dédicace n° ....

Ouvrage C : dédicace n° ....

édicaces

Voici trois dédicaces amusantes. Pouvez-vous dire pourquoi ? L'humour étant très difficile à comprendre dans une langue étrangère, nous vous donnons, ci-dessous, quelques pistes…

Aux circonstances pour qu'elles s'atténuent

Jean Vautrin
Bloody Mary

À Jean Rostand avec mes excuses

Boris Vian
Vercoquin
et le plancton

À Carmen Tessier puisqu'elle aime ma cuisine.

San Antonio,
Du poulet au menu

- *Bloody Mary* est un roman policier.
- J. Rostand était un biologiste célèbre, encore vivant lors de la publication de *Vercoquin et le plancton* qui est un roman plein de dérision.
- San Antonio est l'auteur de nombreux romans policiers remplis de jeux de mots. Sachez aussi qu'en argot «poulet» signifie «policier».

édicaces

Lorsque vous offrez un livre, vous pouvez y inscrire une dédicace. En voici un exemple.

Cette dédicace d'une jeune femme à l'une de ses amies prend tout son sens si l'on sait que dans le roman en question, plusieurs jeunes femmes se racontent leurs aventures sentimentales «à distance», par répondeur téléphonique interposé.

À qui dédicaceriez-vous les ouvrages suivants (vous pouvez choisir d'autres titres) et quelles dédicaces y inscririez-vous ?

Mariella Righini

La passion, Ginette

(roman)

Ma chère Isa,

Pour toi (pour nous)
ce mode d'emploi du
téléphone. Nous en aurons
bientôt besoin...

Bises Odile

Roland Barthes

La chambre claire

Notes sur la photographie

Jeanne Van den Brouck

Manuel à l'usage des enfants qui ont des parents difficiles

Recettes pour cuisinières nulles

Paul Lafargue

Éloge de la paresse

Françoise Dolto

Paroles pour adolescents

ou le complexe du homard

Dictionnaire des difficultés du français

écriture

vocations

L'album de photos

A

B

C

D

Quand on écrit une légende sous une photo, c'est pour se souvenir. On écrit alors l'essentiel : faits, dates, lieux. Comparez la légende qui accompagne la photo ci-contre et le commentaire oral qu'on aurait pu en faire : «C'est Amélie, dans le jardin, elle avait quinze mois, elle commençait à marcher toute seule».

Voici des phrases commentant les photos ci-contre. Trouvez la photo correspondant à chaque série de phrases.

1. «Pour mes 16 ans, Maman m'avait fait un gâteau avec de la crème et des fraises.»

2. «Tu te rappelles ? Julie et Christophe ? En ce temps-là, tout allait bien.»

3. «On partait pour Florence, 1 500 kilomètres en vélo, quand j'y pense…»

4. «C'était au Palais-Royal, il y avait un orchestre de jazz, c'était gratuit».

Premiers pas d'Amélie, avril 1975

1 : ☐   2 : ☐

3 : ☐   4 : ☐

À partir des quatre phrases, écrivez une légende pour ces quatre photos.

A ....

B ....

C ....

D ....

• repérage •

• écriture •

Le mur de Berlin

(Témoignage d'un Berlinois)

«Le mur a été construit en 1961. C'était la guerre froide : les gens de Berlin-Est passaient continuellement à Berlin-Ouest.

Pour éviter cela, le gouvernement de la RDA a construit le mur qui séparait les deux Berlin. Il était très haut et avait des kilomètres de long.

Très vite, le mur est devenu un symbole. Des artistes connus, anonymes, l'ont couvert de graffitis, de dessins. Les touristes allaient le voir, le photographiaient. C'était comme un monument. Il semblait éternel. Et puis, pendant l'été 1989, les choses ont changé.

Des milliers d'Allemands de l'Est se sont échappés en passant par la Hongrie. Alors, le gouvernement de la RDA a décidé de supprimer les contrôles entre les deux Allemagne et on a commencé à démolir le mur. Ce jour-là, le monde a pris conscience qu'une nouvelle époque commençait. Je m'en souviens : ça a été le plus beau jour de ma vie.»

J.J.R.

PLANTU
"Un vague souvenir"
Le Monde, 1990

vocations

1. Relevez les verbes correspondant aux événements ponctuels, aux actions répétées, aux descriptions, aux appréciations.

Événements ponctuels

Actions répétées

Descriptions

Appréciations

Autres

2. Observez le temps de ces verbes. Quelles constantes, quelles variantes y trouvez-vous ? Discutez-en.

3. Les connecteurs narratifs : et puis, alors, ce jour-là. À quoi servent-ils ?

Un événement historique dont vous vous souvenez, racontez.

43

Faire-part et invitations

A

Le 25 octobre 1990

Béatrice et Julien Jallu
sont heureux de vous faire part de la naissance de

Victor

51, rue Sainte-Maxence 50100 Cherbourg

C

À l'occasion de leur mariage
Béatrice et Julien

entourés de leur parents
sont heureux de vous recevoir pour un cocktail
qui se tiendra à la salle des Rochers de Pleudihen
de 17 heures à 19 heures
et au dîner à partir de 20 heures
à la Closerie des Pampres, Saint-Malo

Réponse souhaitée avant le 15 juin

B

Madame Gilbert Nerzic
son épouse

Monsieur et Madame Hervé Tsalkovitch
Monsieur et Madame Gilles Nerzic
ses enfants

Madame Adrienne Nerzic
Monsieur et Madame Julien Jallu
ses petits-enfants

Monsieur et Madame Marcel Nerzic
Monsieur Fernand Nerzic
Madame Catherine Rigout
ses frères et sœurs

Les familles
Nerzic, Gosset, Rigout et Puech
ses neveux, nièces et cousins

ont la douleur de vous part du décès de

Gilbert Nerzic
survenu le 3 octobre 1989 dans sa 85e année

Les Obsèques Civiles ont eu lieu
le vendredi 5 octobre 1990
au cimetière de Saint-Benoît,
dans la plus stricte intimité familiale.

Ni fleurs, ni couronnes

4 bis, rue de l'Église,
Saint-Benoît 86000 Poitiers.

Béatrice et Julien

ont la joie de vous annoncer la célébration de leur mariage
en l'église de Pleudihen-sur-Rance, le samedi 4 juillet 1989,
à 15 heures 30

Madame Élisabeth Delmont
Monsieur et Madame Gilbert Nerzic
Monsieur et Madame Gilles Nerzic

Hameau Kerloury, 22150 Pleudihen-sur-Rance

Leurs parents sont heureux de se joindre à eux
pour vous inviter à cette cérémonie.

Monsieur et Madame Henri Corbel
Monsieur et Madame Pierre Jallu

La Renardière, 35120 Dol-de-Bretagne

D

Faire-part et invitations

1. **Les quatre documents ci-contre sont :**

    un faire-part de deuil   un faire-part de mariage

    un faire-part de naissance   une invitation

Faites correspondre chaque document avec son nom :

A ....

B ....

C ....

D ....

2. **Ils concernent une même famille ; citez chronologiquement les événements survenus.**

....

....

....

Coll. Forgerons du Vodou - courtoisie Ulysses International

À l'occasion de la sortie du n° 1 de

FRANCE-HAÏTI,

nous vous invitons à un apéritif
de lancement du magazine

vendredi 3 novembre 1989

au **CAFÉ DES ARTS**

17, avenue de la République.

Nous espérons vous compter
parmi nous, et vous adressons
nos sentiments les meilleurs.

Manuel Augé
Éric Mercier
Xavier Sors

RSVP

Faire-part et invitations

Pour répondre à un faire-part, connaissez-vous les bonnes formules ?
Voici quelques formules toutes faites, à utiliser dans des situations
non familiales, pour répondre à un faire-part ou à une invitation.

Lisez-les et choisissez celle/celles qui conviennent :

☐ **a) vous répondez à un faire-part de mariage**

☐ **b) vous voulez souhaiter la bonne année**

☐ **c) vous avez reçu un faire-part de naissance**

☐ **d) vous voulez vous excuser de ne pouvoir accepter une invitation**

☐ **e) vous acceptez une invitation**

☐ **f) vous voulez remercier quelqu'un d'un cadeau**

☐ **g) vous avez appris la mort de quelqu'un**

1. *«Je (ou : votre nom) vous remercie infiniment de votre invitation à... et je serai (ou : et sera) très heureux/heureuse d'y assister.»*

2. *«Recevez mes meilleurs vœux.»*

3. *«Je (ou : votre nom) suis (ou : est) heureux/heureuse de la naissance de Y (le bébé) et félicite ses parents.»*

4. *«Je (ou : votre nom) regrette de ne pouvoir accepter votre aimable invitation à... .»*

5. *«Veuillez recevoir mes meilleurs vœux pour la nouvelle année.»*

6. *«Je vous adresse (ou bien : veuillez recevoir) tous mes remerciements pour le joli cadeau (ou bien : le beau livre, etc.) que vous m'avez fait parvenir.»*

7. *«Je (ou : votre nom) vous présente mes (ou : ses) plus sincères condoléances.»*

8. *«Je (ou : votre nom) vous présente tous mes (ou : ses) vœux de bonheur.»*

9. *«Je vous remercie de votre invitation ; malheureusement, je ne pourrai pas assister à... (ou bien : être des vôtres ce jour-là) : je dois, en effet (raison invoquée) ; je vous prie de bien vouloir m'en excuser ; avec mes regrets, recevez mes meilleures salutations.»*

10. *«Recevez mes sincères condoléances.»*

11. *«Je vous présente tous mes vœux pour l'année 199... .»*

46

Faire-part et invitations

CARNET DU JOUR

NAISSANCES

Évelyne Devaux et Yves Sanchez
sont heureux d'annoncer
la naissance de
Arielle
le 11 mai 1991
25, rue de la Pompe 75016 Paris

Mme Perrette Petit
est heureuse d'annoncer la naissance
de son dix-huitième petit-enfant
Laura-Andrea
au foyer de ses enfants
M. Renaud Duvivier et Mme née
Caroline Petit
Saint-Quentin, 30 avril 1991

MARIAGES

Constance Bréat
et
Jean-Marie Drouot
ont le plaisir de faire part de leur mariage, qui a été célébré dans l'intimité le 4 mai 1991.

M. et Mme Le Bihan
M. et Mme Siegfried
ont la joie de faire part du mariage de
leurs enfants
Alexandra et Karl
31, avenue Pasteur
56100 Vannes (France)
Burgstr 2 -
3400 Göttingen (Allemagne)

DÉCÈS

M. Georges Ribeiro
et ses enfants ont la douleur
de faire part du décès de
Edmond Ribeiro
son fils et leur frère, disparu subitement
à New York, le 5 mai 1991, à l'âge de
vingt-sept ans.
Priez pour lui.
64, rue de Tournon 75006 Paris

On nous prie d'annoncer le décès du
Docteur Charles Delaunay
survenu le 13 mai 1991,
dans sa 77e année
*L'incinération aura lieu le lundi 15 mai à
15 h 30, au crématorium du Père-Lachaise,
où l'on se réunira.*
Cet avis tient lieu de faire-part.

Dans la presse quotidienne, le carnet du jour présente des avis de naissances, mariages, décès ou autres.
Comparez ce carnet du jour avec les faire-part (page 44) adressés, eux, à des parents ou amis.

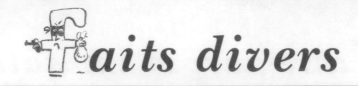

Faits divers

Série 1

Faits divers Libération/Le Figaro
Année 1989/1990

Bébé buveur

Parce qu'il dormait depuis une vingtaine d'heures, une femme a conduit lundi soir son enfant de trois ans et demi à l'hôpital de Caen (Calvados), où les médecins découvrent que le gamin a 0,70g d'alcool dans le sang. Ils en déduisent que la veille, ce taux s'élevait à plus de 2,50g. En principe, un enfant ne résiste pas à plus de 2g mais son organisme a miraculeusement supporté cette absorption massive. La mère et la grand-mère ont expliqué qu'il avait dû finir les verres qui traînaient le soir du réveillon.

Libération

1

Jean-Paul Belmondo, Pierre Vernier et toute la troupe de «Cyrano» n'en ont pas cru leurs yeux. Un couple venu assister l'autre soir à une représentation a confié au vestiaire non pas leurs manteaux mais leur bébé dans un couffin ! Des parents peu scrupuleux, certes, mais visiblement économes : le tarif pratiqué, sept francs, demeure bien modeste à côté du prix d'une baby-sitter pour plusieurs heures…

*Avec l'aimable autorisation
du Journal Le Figaro © Le Figaro, 1990*

2

Félix Blanchet, 67 ans, dit «Lariflette» a été condamné à deux ans de prison et un million de francs d'amende pour un trafic clandestin de calvados. Les gendarmes avaient découvert 350 litres d'alcool clandestin à 50 degrés planqués dans la fosse septique de son jardin à Hérouville-Saint-Clair (Calvados).

Libération

3

Baumettes : chats et rats

Aucun détenu ne s'est évadé, dimanche soir, de la prison des Baumettes à Marseille. Cette information est importante. Elle constitue un démenti cinglant aux informations mal vérifiées, qui ont provoqué au cœur de la nuit, une intense mobilisation du personnel pénitentiaire et l'intervention des forces de police. «*Un gardien a entendu du bruit dans la cuisine, a cru à une évasion et a immédiatement donné l'alerte. Il devait s'agir de rats ou de chats*», précisait-on hier de source pénitentiaire autorisée. Une fouille générale, ainsi qu'un appel et un contre-appel des détenus avaient été organisés entre 01h00 et 01h30.

Libération

4

Un mégot, vingt-cinq voitures

Vingt-cinq véhicules ont été endommagés, dont cinq détruits, à la suite d'un incendie provoqué par un mégot de cigarette, lundi soir, dans un parking à Paris (10e). Il n'y a eu aucun blessé. Selon les premiers éléments de l'enquête, un automobiliste a mis le feu au parking en jetant son mégot mal éteint dans une flaque d'huile qu'il avait prise pour de l'eau.

Libération

5

Une jeune fille de quinze ans a été retrouvée égorgée, hier, dans l'entrée de l'appartement familial à Reims. C'est son frère qui l'a découverte en rentrant de l'école. Elle aurait été frappée à la gorge par un objet tranchant.

*Avec l'aimable autorisation
du Journal Le Figaro © Le Figaro, 1990*

6

# **F**aits divers

1. Voici la définition du fait divers telle qu'elle figure dans un dictionnaire :
   FAITS DIVERS : rubrique sous laquelle
   on groupe les incidents du jour,
   accidents, crimes, suicides, etc.
   Lisez les six faits divers présentés et dites lesquels ne correspondent pas à cette définition.

....

2. Maintenant qualifiez-les à l'aide du tableau suivant :

	drôle	insolite	tragique	aurait pu être tragique
1				
2				
3				
4				
5				

3. De quels éléments linguistiques les titres des faits divers 1, 4, 5, sont-ils composés ? Remplissez le tableau par des croix.

	verbes	substantifs	déterminants	adjectifs	mots de liaison
1					
4					
5					
6					

4. Que constatez-vous ?

....

....

5. Après la lecture du titre peut-on deviner l'histoire ? Remplissez le tableau.

	oui	en partie	pas du tout
1			
4			

1. Donnez un titre aux faits divers 2, 3, 6.

2 ....

3 ....

6 ....

2. Qualifiez ce titre (drôle, insolite, tragique…).

2 ....

3 ....

6 ....

Série 2.

Faits divers Libération, Le Figaro, *années 1989, 1990.*

1

Drogue
Trafic de cocaïne en famille.

La police française a saisi 11 kilos de cocaïne et a arrêté à Paris quatre ressortissants français, dont le père, la mère et le fils, et un employé au sol d'UTA, au cours d'une enquête sur le démantèlement d'un réseau de trafiquants de drogue opérant à partir de Rio de Janeiro. Les quatre personnes ont été arrêtées samedi. Ce réseau opérait depuis un certain temps, et avait réussi à acheminer du Brésil à Paris plusieurs valises bourrées de cocaïne. Ce sont les policiers de l'office central de répression du trafic de stupéfiants (OCRTIS) qui ont mené cette opération.

*Avec l'aimable autorisation
du Journal Le Figaro © Le Figaro, 1991*

2

Route : trop

Un touriste italien, circulant à bord de son véhicule, a été grièvement blessé d'une balle de 9 mm tirée par un automobiliste qui lui reprochait de lui avoir fait une «queue de poisson», mercredi matin sur une route de Porto-Pollo (Corse du Sud).

Libération

# aits divers

Série 2

Lisez ces deux faits divers et remplissez le tableau.

	Personnages du fait divers	Lieu du fait divers	Événement qui constitue le fait divers	Événement qui précède le fait divers.
1				
2				

1. À partir des séries de mots suivantes (au choix), fabriquez une petite histoire qui pourrait être un fait divers, drôle, tragique. Vous imaginerez le lieu, la date, vous préciserez l'identité des personnages, si besoin est. Vous mettrez un titre. Avant de commencer à rédiger vous pouvez placer les différents éléments de votre fait divers dans un tableau comme le tableau ci-dessus.

Série 1	jeune garçon — mère — Coca-Cola — fusil de chasse — refuser — blesser.
Série 2	avion — couple — serpent — steward — cacher — mordre.
Série 3	dépôt municipal — femme — vide-ordures — légumes — bague — chercher — enlever — jeter.

ormulaires

Choisissez un ou plusieurs articles parmi ceux présentés dans le dossier Catalogues (page 26) et remplissez le bon de commande ci-dessous.

Vente par correspondance

BON DE COMMANDE

Pour commander le sac présenté, au dos, il vous suffit d'indiquer la référence :
310.1592 Prix : 59,90 F

ADRESSE DE LIVRAISON
(cocher la bonne case)

☐ à mon adresse
☐ à une autre adresse
que je vous donne ci-dessous.
  1. ☐ pour cette commande-ci.
  2. ☐ pour faire un cadeau.

NOM _____
PRENOM _____
ADRESSE _____

CODE POSTAL |__|__|__|__|__|
VILLE _____
☐ au Rendez-Vous Catalogue de

N° DE CLIENT |__|__|__|__|__|__|__|__| NLQ 21075
(Si vous en avez un)

A REMPLIR EN LETTRES CAPITALES

NOM _____ PRENOM _____
ADRESSE _____
_____
VILLE _____
CODE POSTAL |__|__|__|__|__|

MME ☐   MLLE ☐   M. ☐   AUTRES DENOMINATIONS ☐   TEL. _____

S.A. Redoute-Catalogue - CAP. 240.300.000F. - R.C. Roubaix B 321164/253/81 53.

DESIGNATION DES ARTICLES	REFERENCE	CODE OU TAILLE	QUANTITE	PRIX DE L'UNITE	MONTANT

🎁 *Un cadeau en plus !* Ma commande comprend 4 articles différents facturés, je reçois mon cadeau-mystère *Gratuit !*

|CL 52| N° 04294

VOTRE MODE DE PAIEMENT

A LA COMMANDE
1 ☐ MANDAT-LETTRE
2 ☐ CHEQUE POSTAL
3 ☐ CHEQUE BANCAIRE
(A L'ORDRE DE LA REDOUTE)
4 ☐ AVOIR OU CHEQUE REDOUTE
N'ENVOYEZ JAMAIS DE MANDAT-CARTE 1418, DE TIMBRES NI D'ESPECES.

AVEC VOTRE CARTE DE PAIEMENT
(n'oubliez pas d'inscrire son numéro et de signer).
Kangourou   5 ☐ CARTE KANGOUROU |__|__|__|__|__|__|__|
CB   7 ☐ CARTE BANCAIRE |__|__|__|__|__|__|__|

SIGNATURE

A LA LIVRAISON   6 ☐ ENVOI CONTRE-REMBOURSEMENT (+ frais selon taxe en vigueur).

MONTANT DE LA COMMANDE EN DATE DU _____				
PARTICIPATION AUX FRAIS D'ENVOI (PORT ET EMBALLAGE)	1	5	9	0
SI ENVOI CONTRE-REMBOURSEMENT (+ frais selon la taxe en vigueur 19.60F au 16/8/88).				
T O T A L				

$\mathcal{F}$ormulaires

1. Les formulaires contiennent souvent des indications permettant de les remplir correctement. Lisez-les, puis corrigez le premier télégramme en utilisant le second formulaire.

N° 698 TÉLÉGRAMME

Étiquettes		N° d'appel :
	Timbre à date	INDICATIONS DE TRANSMISSION

Ligne de numérotation

ZCZC N° télégraphique

Ligne pilote

Taxe principale...........

Taxes accessoires

Total . .

Bureau d'origine	Mots	Date	Heure	Mentions de service

N° de la ligne du P.V. :

Bureau de destination   Département ou Pays

Services spéciaux demandés : (voir au verso)

Inscrire en **CAPITALES** l'adresse complète (rue, n° bloc, bâtiment, escalier, etc...), le texte et la signature (une lettre par case ; **laisser une case blanche entre les mots**).

Nom et adresse M O N S I E U R É M I L E D U M A S 3 0 R U E D E
L A P A I X 3 1 0 0 0 T O U L O U S E

TEXTE et éventuellement signature très lisible I M P O S S I B L E T E J O I N D R E T E T É L É P H O N E M A
M A N H O S P I T A L I S É E B A I S E R S

Jean

Nom et adresse de l'expéditeur : ....
Pour avis en cas de non remise. - Indications transmises et taxées sur demande expresse de l'expéditeur.

TEXTE et éventuellement signature très lisible

Nom et adresse de l'expéditeur : ....
Pour avis en cas de non remise. - Indications transmises et taxées sur demande expresse de l'expéditeur.

53

entraînement

2. Voici quelques annonces publiées dans un petit journal d'informations pratiques :

DE TOUT POUR TOUS
Mannequin vend superbes
robes soirée et vêt. ville
Chanel, Kenzo, etc.
Prix intér. Tél : 48 72 38 11

Vds lave-linge Siemens
3 600 F valeur 5 200 F, récent,
2 essorages, silencieux.
Tél : 30 72 91 24

Vends 1/5 d'une jolie pouliche
de course au trot.
Frais de notaire inclus.
Tél : 39 73 84 54

COURS
Professeur d'allemand diplômé
langue maternelle, efficace
et très sérieux.
Tél : 40 92 33 53

Débutez ou poursuivez
votre formation musicale :
cours de guitare, piano,
solfège, harmonie. Sérieux
exigé. Tél : 42 40 49 67

Prof. de yoga donne
des cours gratuits
pour une meilleure maîtrise
de soi.
Tél : 43 90 58 44

AUTOS MOTOS - 2 ROUES
Audi 80 : 85 000 F modèle 90
12 000 km. Tél : 30 80 28 31

Super 5 GTS : 25 000 F, 86
gris métal. 7 CV, 5 portes,
glaces élect. expertisée
TB état. Gar. Denfert
. Tél : 44 51 90 57

Part. achète 1 scooter
Peugeot SX 80
B. état année indiff.
Paiement comptant.
Tél : 48 45 77 65

ANIMAUX
Perdu Yorkshire,
tatoué JNG 732.
Nom du chien : Davidoff `
Tél : 42 61 20 54
Récompense.

Vds chiots
toutes races,
bons prix, pédigree,
tatoués, vaccinés.
Garantie.
Crédit 200 F/MS.
Livraison gratuite
Tél : 48 25 78 78

Rédigez le texte d'une petite annonce que vous pourriez faire passer dans l'une des rubriques ci-dessus. Pour cela, inspirez-vous des annonces proposées :
- faites la sélection des éléments d'information
- présentez-les en suivant un ordre
- choisissez les mots et expressions qui conviennent
- pensez aux abréviations d'usage (suppression d'articles et de prépositions, mots abrégés, etc.) car cela diminue le prix de l'annonce.

....

....

....

....

3. Reportez ensuite le texte de votre annonce sur le formulaire page 55, et remplissez-le.

ormulaires

PASSER UNE ANNONCE C'EST SIMPLE

— soit par courrier, soit à nos bureaux —78/80 rue de la Villette 75019 Paris, M° Botzaris

Tél : 42 38 11 11 dernier délai mercredi 17 h pour parution lundi suivant

1) Choisissez et cochez votre rubrique

Mariage	Services et loisirs	De tout pour tous	Animaux	Cours
Autos/Motos	Immobilier vente	Immobilier location	Vacances	Emploi
Rencontres/ Relaxation (professionnel et particulier)			Prestations de service	

Contacts (cette rubrique doit être libellée exclusivement dans des termes ne pouvant pas choquer. Toute annonce à caractère tendancieux sera refusée. Domiciliation conseillée).

2) Rédigez votre annonce

Écrivez lisiblement (pour éviter tout risque d'erreur) votre texte : une lettre par case en laissant un espace entre chaque mot.

PARTICULIERS			DÉBUT DU TEXTE DE VOTRE ANNONCE TARIFS TTC	COMMERCIALE			
Tarifs réservés aux personnes dont l'annonce n'est pas à caractère commercial.				P. service rencontres relaxation		Autres rubriques	
1 semaine	2 semaines	4 semaines		1 semaine	4 semaines	1 semaine	4 semaines
100	170	300		500	1 800	200	720
130	220	380		600	2 160	250	900
160	270	460		700	2 520	300	1 080
190	320	540		800	2 880	350	1 260

3) Domiciliation*

1 semaine	2 semaines	4 semaines
50	80	120

☐ À garder au journal ☐ À réexpédier

* La domiciliation permet de conserver l'anonymat ou de ne pas être dérangé en permanence par des plaisantins malveillants. Terminez votre annonce par "Écr.au jnl, réf. XXX" et comptez-le dans le nombre de lignes.

4) Inscrivez vos coordonnées (Confidentiel à Paris Boum Boum)

Nom .... .Prénom ....

Adresse .... Tél ....

Libellez votre chèque à l'ordre de Paris Boum Boum. Une photocopie de la carte d'identité est obligatoire pour tout règlement par mandat ou espèces, afin de mieux vous préserver des malveillances éventuelles.

AUCUNE ANNONCE NE FERA L'OBJET D'UN REMBOURSEMENT.

UN AVOIR VOUS SERA CONSENTI (VALABLE 3 SEMAINES).

Réservé à Paris Boum Boum

☐ Chèque bancaire , CCP..

☐ Espèces ☐ Mandat N° ....

N° de parution	Nbre de parutions

4. Selon l'annonce et les modalités choisies, calculez le montant du chèque qui pourrait accompagner ce formulaire.

écriture

55

RÉPUBLIQUE FRANÇAISE

CARTE NATIONALE D'IDENTITÉ N° : 88069231028 Nationalité FRANÇAISE

Nom : BERTHIER

Prénom : CORINNE

Sexe : F Née le : 06. 12. 1965
à : PARIS 1ER (75)
Taille : 1M70

Signature
du titulaire :

IDFRABERTHIER<<<<<<<<<<<<<<<<<
8806923102858CORINNE<<<<<<<6512068F6

Adresse : 104 RUE DES FLEURS
92100 BOULOGNE-BILLANCOURT

CARTE VALABLE JUSQU'AU : 21. 06. 1998

délivrée le : 22. 06. 1988
par : SOUS-PREFECTURE DE BOULOGNE-BILLANCOURT (92)

Signature de l'autorité :

SPECIMEN

Vos papiers !
ou… vos plastiques !…

«Vos papiers !» Cette invective va-t-elle passer de mode ? «Vos plastiques !», risque-t-on d'entendre bientôt après le salut de rigueur des forces de l'ordre qui ont déjà cédé leur bon vieux képi. C'est ainsi, la carte nationale d'identité change de look et le papier de l'Imprimerie nationale s'en ira au musée des souvenirs. C'est l'ère du polyester, du polyéthylène et de la lecture optique. Il n'y a plus de métier, protesteront les faussaires pour qui le ministère de l'Intérieur a conçu de nouvelles cartes… infalsifiables ! Mais pour l'heure, nous n'en sommes encore qu'au stade expérimental et les CNI des Hauts-de-Seine devront attendre une décision politique avant de voir circuler leurs petites sœurs dans tout l'hexagone.

D'après un article de D. Pageot paru dans l'Événement du Jeudi *8/90…*

ormulaires

…et vos droits !

Un policier a-t-il le droit de vous demander vos papiers d'identité dans la rue ?

– Ne pas confondre contrôle d'identité et vérification d'identité. Le contrôle d'identité dans la rue ou dans un lieu public – cafés, cinémas, supermarchés, métro, gares ou plages – est permis chaque fois qu'un policier vous soupçonne d'avoir commis une infraction ou de vous préparer à la commettre. Ce sont des notions assez subjectives. C'est tout le problème.

La vérification d'identité s'effectue au commissariat de police, dans un car ou à la gendarmerie, si vous n'avez pas vos papiers d'identité ou si vous refusez de les montrer. Vous avez alors le droit de prévenir votre famille ou toute personne de votre choix – éventuellement votre avocat – et on ne peut pas vous garder plus de quatre heures. S'il s'agit de mineurs, (…) les policiers doivent prévenir immédiatement non seulement le procureur de la République, mais aussi et surtout les parents (…).

Le port de la carte d'identité est-il obligatoire ?

– Non, à la différence de ce qui se passe dans d'autres pays comme la Belgique, mais vous devez quand même être en mesure de justifier votre identité, soit en présentant d'autres papiers (passeport, carte de sécurité sociale, permis de conduire, carte professionnelle, etc), soit par témoins, ce qui est valable surtout dans les petites villes ou à la campagne.

Quant aux étrangers – cible privilégiée des contrôles d'identité –, ils doivent non seulement justifier leur identité, mais aussi la régularité de leur séjour. Par exemple, en France, un touriste doit avoir un passeport en règle et un travailleur immigré une carte de séjour sur lui.

D'après un article paru dans Le Nouvel Observateur, *1990, écrit par D. Langlois, avocat et auteur de :* Guide du citoyen face à la police.

1. Vous êtes un touriste étranger en France, quels papiers devez-vous avoir sur vous?

....

....

2. Si vous n'avez pas vos papiers sur vous lors d'un contrôle d'identité :
Que peut-il vous arriver ?

....

....

Quels sont vos droits ?

....

....

Lettres administratives

A

MESSIEURS RICHARD – ADMINISTRATEURS DE BIENS

39, RUE DES ÉCOLES - 75 005 PARIS

Réf. BM/CM

Dossier suivi par :

Objet :
Changement de n° code

Paris le 31 Mai 1988

Immeuble : 123, rue Amyot - Paris

Monsieur, Madame,

Par mesuré de sécurité, nous vous informons que nous avons chargé l'entreprise E.M.G.E de procéder au changement de numéro du système codé de la porte cochère.

Ce changement interviendra après le 15.06.88 et le nouveau numéro à composer sera le suivant :

0A678

Vous voudrez bien en prendre note, et vous prions d'agréer, Monsieur, Madame, l'expression de nos sentiments distingués.

Richard

B

JEAN LEFURS SA
S.A. au capital de 750 000 F.
Administrateur de Biens
33, Avenue de la République
94100 Saint-Maur
98 85 90 64 +

Réception sur rendez-vous

Saint-Maur, le 30 mars 1988

Réf. JMT/PP/Dossier 543
Résidence Rive du Lac

Madame Voisin
228, Allée de la Toison d'Or
94000 Créteil

LETTRE RECOMMANDÉE
AVEC ACCUSÉ DE RÉCEPTION

Madame,

Nous sommes saisis de plaintes signées par une grande partie des copropriétaires de votre bâtiment.

Ceux-ci se plaignent que vous ne respectez en rien le règlement de copropriété en particulier pour les bruits de musique, dégradations des parties communes et, entre autres, sauts dans la cage d'ascenseur, mégots jetés par le balcon.

Il est absolument nécessaire que le règlement de copropriété soit respecté ainsi que le règlement départemental.

Comptant sur votre compréhension,

Nous vous prions d'agréer, Madame, l'expression de nos salutations distinguées.

P⁰ J.M Toulet

58

Lettres administratives

Voici deux lettres envoyées à des locataires d'appartements à Paris.
Prenez-en connaissance.
Aucune de ces deux lettres n'exige ou ne demande de réponse ; cependant,
elles peuvent avoir donné lieu par la suite à d'autres écrits.

Exemple texte A :
a) Un petit billet fixé dans le cartable d'un enfant pour lui rappeler le nouveau
code de la porte
b) un mot que le/la locataire de l'appartement a laissé à sa femme de ménage
pour l'informer

Exemple texte B :
a) le mot adressé à la/au baby-sitter pour lui recommander une certaine dis-
crétion
b) la réponse à l'administrateur de biens pour exprimer son désaccord et pro-
tester de sa bonne foi

**Choisissez une situation pour chacun des textes et rédigez le billet corres-
pondant.**

    Texte A   Texte B

A

Le 3 juin 1986
Monsieur Dupont
8, rue Caron
75004 Paris

Monsieur,

Je vous serais reconnaissant de bien vouloir
me faire parvenir, avant la fin de ce mois,
copie du document dont nous avions parlé
l'autre jour.

Si vous pouviez, par la même occasion,
me donner l'adresse exacte de votre ami
Lucien Lenfant, cela me serait aussi
très utile.

En vous remerciant, je vous prie de croire,
Monsieur, à mes sentiments les meilleurs.

Norbert Lechat

B

Norbert Lechat
68 , bd Saint-Germain
75005 Paris

Le 3 juin 1986

Monsieur Dupont
8, rue Caron
75004 Paris

Monsieur,

Je vous serais reconnaissant de bien vouloir
me faire parvenir, avant la fin de ce mois,
copie du document dont nous avions parlé
l'autre jour.

Si vous pouviez, par la même occasion,
me donner l'adresse exacte de votre ami
Lucien Lenfant, cela me serait aussi
très utile.

En vous remerciant, je vous prie de croire,
Monsieur, à mes sentiments les meilleurs.

Norbert Lechat

C

Paris, le 3 juin 1986

Monsieur Dupont
8, rue Caron
75004 Paris

Monsieur,

Je vous serais reconnaissant de bien vouloir
me faire parvenir, avant la fin de ce mois,
copie du document dont nous avions parlé
l'autre jour.
Si vous pouviez, par la même occasion,
me donner l'adresse exacte de votre ami
Lucien Lenfant, cela me serait aussi très utile.
En vous remerciant, je vous prie de croire,
Monsieur, à mes sentiments les meilleurs.

(Signature)

Norbert Lechat
68, bd Saint-Germain
75005 Paris

D

Le 3 juin 1986

Monsieur,
Je vous serais reconnaissant de bien vouloir
me faire parvenir, avant la fin de ce mois,
copie du document dont nous avions parlé
l'autre jour.
Si vous pouviez, par la même occasion,
me donner l'adresse exacte de votre ami
Lucien Lenfant, cela me serait aussi très utile.
En vous remerciant, je vous prie de croire,
Monsieur, à mes sentiments les meilleurs.

(signature)

Monsieur Dupont
8, rue Caron
75004 Paris

Norbert Lechat
68, bd Saint-Germain
75005 Paris

Lettres administratives

Quelques normes de présentation de lettres *

Avant le texte de la lettre, trois éléments trouvent normalement place au haut de la page, mais il existe aussi plusieurs variantes, que nous allons détailler en passant ces trois éléments en revue…

• **L'adresse de l'expéditeur** se place habituellement *en haut et à gauche*, en ne laissant qu'une marge assez étroite de 2 cm environ. Les éléments suivants prennent chacun une ligne :
– prénom et nom,
– numéro et rue,
– localité,
– numéro de code postal et bureau distributeur,
– numéro de téléphone.
On obtient cette disposition :

Albert Matteau
45, rue des Pierres
Penchard
77100 Meaux
Tél. 65 63 67 18

La troisième ligne disparaît si la localité est aussi celle du bureau distributeur. Et le numéro de téléphone est loin d'être une mention obligatoire. Même si on est raccordé au réseau, on ne désire pas toujours le donner.
Ces indications peuvent éventuellement trouver place sous la signature, *en bas et à droite* de la lettre.
• **La date** de rédaction de la lettre se place *en haut et à droite*, à hauteur de la localité si l'adresse de l'expéditeur se trouve à gauche. Sinon, il est d'usage de faire précéder la date de la mention de la localité :

Penchard, le 18 avril 1985

• **L'adresse du destinataire** se place sous la date, c'est-à-dire aussi *en haut et à droite*, mais quelques centimètres plus bas. On y reprend les mêmes éléments que pour l'adresse de l'expéditeur et de la même manière, le numéro de téléphone en moins.

• Après ces trois éléments, peut venir **le texte de la lettre**, pour lequel plusieurs présentations sont possibles. Nous vous donnons deux exemples choisis parmi les plus fréquents. Une chose doit vous guider de toute manière : l'esthétique de la lettre. Votre page doit être équilibrée.
En même temps, il faut veiller à faciliter la compréhension, et donc à mettre par exemple en évidence le découpage en paragraphes. Soit en commençant chaque paragraphe en retrait, soit en laissant un espace entre chaque paragraphe.

Ces règles sont valables pour le courrier administratif. Dans les autres cas, tout est laissé à l'appréciation de l'expéditeur, qui peut tout aussi bien se contenter de noter, en haut et à droite : *ce vendredi soir*, et signer de son seul prénom sous le texte de la lettre. Évidemment, cela suppose qu'il est certain d'être reconnu…

1. Nous vous proposons, ci-contre, quatre lettres administratives : observez-les et consultez les normes ci-dessus : deux parmi ces lettres respectent les normes indiquées ; lesquelles ?

....

2. Dites en quoi les autres ne respectent pas les normes indiquées.

Lettre n° ....

Lettre n° ....

3. Les lettres acceptables présentent quelques différences entre elles, lesquelles ?

....

....

....

* *Texte tiré de* 200 modèles de lettres, *coll. Guides Marabout.*

Lettres administratives

Trois modèles de lettres administratives*

E

> Monsieur,
> Je désire me rendre, pendant les vacances d'été, dans un pays d'Afrique. Pouvez-vous me faire parvenir les prospectus de votre agence concernant ces destinations ?
> Je vous en remercie et vous prie d'agréer, Monsieur, l'expression de mes salutations distinguées.

F

> Monsieur,
> Effectuant actuellement un travail scolaire consacré à votre pays, je suis à la recherche d'une documentation portant sur les grandes entreprises industrielles nationales.
> Êtes-vous en mesure de me donner des renseignements à ce sujet ?
> À défaut, pourriez-vous m'indiquer des endroits où je pourrais en trouver ?
> Vous en remerciant, je vous prie d'agréer, Monsieur, l'expression de mes sentiments distingués.

G

> Monsieur le Directeur,
> Je souhaite compléter ma formation d'ingénieur par un approfondissement en informatique, et j'aimerais suivre ces études dans votre Centre.
> Dans quelles conditions puis-je m'inscrire à ces cours ?
> Les documents que je joins à ma lettre, qui situent plus précisément les études déjà accomplies, vous permettront de juger de mes aptitudes.
> Dans l'attente de votre réponse, veuillez agréer, Monsieur le Directeur, l'expression de mes sentiments respectueux.

* Ces lettres sont empruntées à l'ouvrage 200 modèles de lettres, coll. Guides Marabout ; il s'agit, notons-le, de lettres écrites par des particuliers.

$\mathcal{L}$ettres administratives

Pour chacune de ces lettres administratives, relevez les éléments suivants :

	1. Justification de la demande	2. Demande précise	3. Autre (éventuellement)
E			
F			
G			

Écrivez une lettre qui corresponde à un besoin que vous pouvez avoir : information pour un travail, renseignements pratiques pour un voyage, etc.

N'oubliez pas de suivre les modèles de la page 61 (normes de présentation) et de la page 62 (présentation de la demande).

LA BOÎTE A COUTURE

En bois, en plastique ou en carton fort gainé de tissu, la boîte à couture doit être suffisamment grande et munie de petits tiroirs ou de casiers pour pouvoir ranger, sans mélanger ni entasser.

LES FOURNITURES DE MERCERIE

Des aiguilles 'couture' et 'reprise' en pochette assortie ; si nécessaire, un enfile-aiguille ou des aiguilles spéciales 'vue fatiguée'.

Des épingles très fines, diamètre 0,50 mm pour tissu fin et diamètre 0,60 mm pour tissu épais.

Un aimant de couturière.

Un mètre-ruban, à porter autour du cou pour l'avoir toujours à portée de main.

Des ciseaux, un modèle 'lingère' pour petits travaux et un modèle 'coupe'.

Un dé à coudre pour pousser l'aiguille sans fatigue.

Deux craies tailleur plates, une bleue (tissu clair) et une blanche (tissu foncé) ; affiner les bords avec une lame pour tracer finement.

Un découseur : la pointe emboulée placée sous le tissu évite les accrocs.

Les fils à coudre :
• Une base de coloris courants dans les qualités Tubino, Tous Textiles et Draperie ; du Câblé noir et blanc (attention : gros fil, n°s 12, 36, fil moyen, n°s 40, 50 fil fin, n°s 60).
• Deux tresses de fils multicolores, une Coton et une Tous Textiles en dépannage.
• Du fil à bâtir, 1 blanc et 1 couleur pour bâtir sur du blanc.
• Du fil à repriser Tous Textiles et du fil à boutons en coloris classiques.
    Noter qu'il faut toujours choisir le fil en bobine très légèrement plus soutenu que le tissu pour que les piqûres soient parfaitement ton sur ton.

Listes

1. L' utilité de certains objets est précisée. Lesquels ?

....

....

....

....

2. L'utilité de certains autres semble évidente :
- des aiguilles pour ... coudre.
- des épingles pour ...
- ...

....

....

....

....

....

3. Vous partez en voyage et vous préparez une mini-boîte à couture.
Que mettrez-vous dedans ?....

....

....

....

....

....

....

....

....

....

Volcans d'Indonésie

Durée de Paris à Paris	18 jours
Prix de Paris à Paris	19 500 FF

Volcans actifs, paysages et civilisations forment la trame de ce voyage réalisé sous la conduite d'un volcanologue.

Points forts
– le dôme actif du Merapi
– les paysages du Semeru et son activité explosive
– le lac d'acide du cratère du Kawah Ijen ; randonnée
– les temples de Prambanan et Borobudur
– l'animation des quartiers d'artisans de Yogjarkata
– les villages, les temples et la danse à Bali

Aspects pratiques
Bonne condition physique et entraînement nécessaires pour réaliser 3 étapes de 4 à 6 heures de marche. Dénivelés de 400 à 800 mètres et quelques pentes raides.
– Trois nuits en bivouac. Fortes chaleurs possibles en plaine mais vêtements chauds pour les étapes d'altitude (volcans de 2 300 à 3 600 m).
Voyage réalisé en collaboration avec Fnac Voyages et le Groupe d'Étude des Volcans Actifs.

Informations complémentaires : voir encart joint

Date des départs	Ve. 27 avril 90	
	Ve. 20 juillet 90	
	Ve. 10 août 90	
Nombre de participants	10 à 15	Réf.M322

Listes

Volcans d'Indonésie
(Explorators, expéditions 1990, extrait du catalogue)

1. Répondez aux questions suivantes :
– **Dans quels endroits irez-vous ?**

....

....

– **Quel sera votre moyen de transport ?**

....

....

– **Quelles températures devrez-vous affronter ?**

....

....

2. Et maintenant, préparez votre sac à dos. Qu'emporterez-vous ?

....	....
....	....
....	....
....	....
....	....
....	....
....	....
....	....
....	....
....	....
....	....

Listes

Le jeu de la photocopieuse

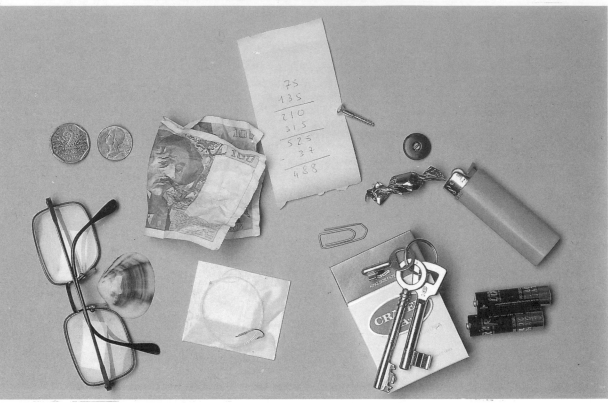

1. On peut photocopier des textes, pourquoi ne pas photocopier des objets ?
Voici la photocopie de ce qu'il y avait dans les poches d'un blouson.
Faites l'inventaire des poches du blouson.

....
....
....

2. D'après ces objets, pouvez-vous tirer quelques conclusions sur le/la propriétaire du blouson ?

....
....
....

3. Maintenant, faites la photocopie de ce que vous avez dans vos poches, dans votre sac…

 istes

Dis-moi ce qu'il y a dans ta valise…

Texte A

Depuis des mois, je suivais des inconnus dans la rue. Pour le plaisir de les suivre et non parce qu'ils m'intéressaient. Je les photographiais à leur insu, notais leurs déplacements, puis finale-ment les perdais de vue et les oubliais.

À la fin du mois de janvier 1980, dans les rues de Paris, je sui-vis un homme que je perdis quelques minutes plus tard dans la foule. Le soir même tout à fait par hasard, il me fut présenté. Je lui dis que je l'avais suivi dans l'après-midi et lui racontai pour-quoi. Au cours de la conversation, il me parla d'un projet immi-nent de voyage à Venise.

Texte B

Lundi 11 février 1980

22h. Gare de Lyon. Quai H. Départ du train en direction de Venise. Mon père m'accompagne jusqu'à la plate-forme, il agite la main.

Dans ma valise : un nécessaire de maquillage qui m'aide-ra à modifier ma physionomie, une perruque blonde coupée au carré, des chapeaux, voilettes, gants, lunettes noires, un *Leica* et un *Squintar* (cet accessoire qui se visse sur l'objectif est muni d'un jeu de miroirs permettant de prendre des photos de côté, sans viser le sujet).

Je photographie les occupants des autres couchettes et je m'endors.

Demain je verrai Venise pour la première fois.

Écrit sur l'image
Sophie Calle. *Suite vénitienne*
(Cahiers du Cinéma)

1. Lisez le texte B et d'après le contenu de la valise imaginez :
– qui est cette personne :

....

– pourquoi elle part pour Venise :

....

2. Lisez le texte A, puis dites :
– qui est cette personne:

....

– pourquoi elle part pour Venise :

....

Messages

A

MADAME ELISABETH GROS
Attachée commerciale

Vous demande de bien vouloir excuser son fils, Thierry Amaury, qui n'a pas pu se rendre au collège lundi pour raisons familiales.

12, rue Thiers   87000 Mulhouse

B

NOTRE COLLÈGUE ISABELLE SCHMITT A EU UN PETIT ARNAUD le 3 MARS

VOUS POUVEZ PASSER AU BUREAU DE Mme DEMARNE, QUI SE CHARGE DE LA COLLECTE.

C

Vendredi matin

Ma chérie,
Ton parrain est de passage à Paris. Appelle-le ce soir à 6 h à son hôtel (45.12.16.23).
Je rentre vers 11h ce soir. Ton repas est prêt (dans le plat marron). N'oublie pas de débrancher le four (le plombier n'a pas pu venir ce matin).
Ne te couche pas trop tard.   Papa qui t'embrasse

D

1) Tu vas hurler : je t'ai piqué ton pull bleu... le mien n'était pas sec... Excuse et merci quand même !
2) Tu vas être ravie : voici mes K7 d'ultramarine. Pense à la touche H pour enregistrer.
Bisous Bichette
Pour la vaisselle, c'est ton tour !!

E

Marie-Jeanne,
Cédric a une otite.
Il faut lui mettre des gouttes dans les oreilles (2g de chaque côté), à 18h et à 21h.
Vous trouverez le dîner dans le frigidaire. À ce soir.

Simone Bernard

70

Messages

1. Relevez les mots ou expressions qui permettent de déduire qui sont le ou les auteurs(s) de ces messages, et le ou les destinataire(s) à qui ils sont adressés.

	Auteur(s)	Destinataire(s) : relevez puis précisez qui est le destinataire pour l'auteur (ex. sa mère, un ami, une secrétaire, etc.)
Message A		
Message B		
Message C		
Message D		
Message E		

2. Dans chaque message, il y a une ou plusieurs demandes, et une ou plusieurs informations. Relevez-les pour chaque message.

	Demande(s)	Justification(s)
A		
B		
C		
D		
E		

71

À votre tour, écrivez quelques messages.

Message 1

Vous êtes logé(e) chez une amie francophone, et vous recevez un coup de fil qui lui est adressé.

Conversation téléphonique :

– (vous) : *Allo !*

– (votre interlocuteur) : *Allo ! C'est Anne ?*

– *Non, elle n'est pas là. C'est de la part de qui ?*

– *C'est Jean-René, un ami. Vous pouvez lui laisser un message ?*

– *Bien sûr.*

– *Dites-lui que je dois partir demain très tôt. Je pars pour toute la semaine. Je laisse deux cassettes vidéo pour elle chez son voisin Charles. Son numéro, c'est le… Vous pouvez noter ?*

– *Oui, oui.*

– *C'est le 40 14 53 34. Elle peut l'appeler vers 9 heures le soir.*

– *Oui. C'est tout ?*

– Oui, merci.

Votre message :

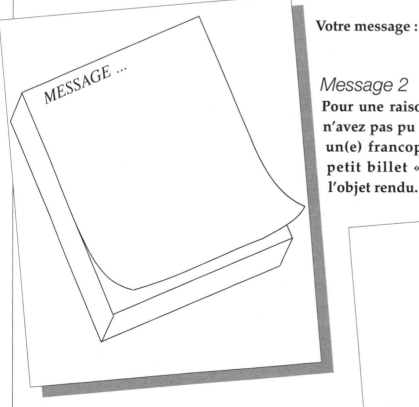

MESSAGE …

Message 2

Pour une raison quelconque (à imaginer), vous n'avez pas pu rendre à temps un objet prêté par un(e) francophone. Rédigez le contenu d'un petit billet «Post-it» que vous collerez sur l'objet rendu.

Messages

Message 3

Vous rédigez un message pour le tableau d'affichage de votre classe. Choisissez une situation.

SITUATION 1 : un professeur de français que vous connaissez veut monter un spectacle de théâtre, mais il manque d'acteurs (de 15 à 25 ans / parlant français / aimant le théâtre — expérience bienvenue — / libres les mardi et vendredi soir.

SITUATION 2 : un(e) ami(e) professeur en France vous écrit pour vous demander de trouver pour ses élèves des correspondants parmi vos camarades de classe (de 12 à 16 ans / garçons et filles / désirant échanger lettres et documents divers : revues, photos, timbres, musique éventuellement, etc.).

SITUATION 3 : vous voulez organiser une fête avec des camarades d'une autre classe que la vôtre : carnaval, fête à thème, pique-nique, etc.

Affiche que vous fixez au tableau d'affichage en classe.

Message 4

Imaginez que l'adolescente de la B.D. p. 74 accepte de faire du baby-sitting chez l'amie de sa mère. Celle-ci lui a laissé un petitmot avec les indications dont elle a besoin… Rédigez ce mot.

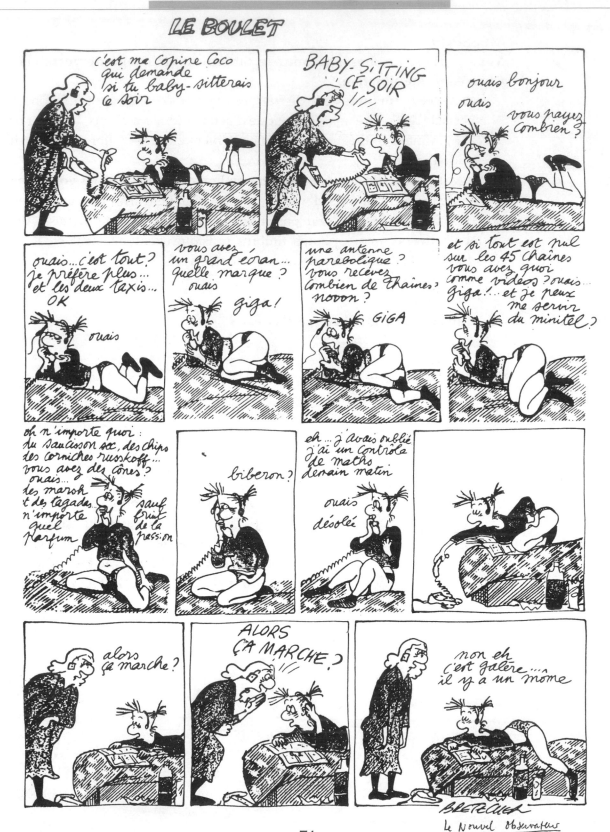

ℳessages

Messages d'autrefois et savoir-vivre...

L'Évènement du Jeudi (5.12.8<)

GALANTERIE DE SÉDUCTION

Talleyrand-Guitry (dans *Le diable boîteux*) reçoit une jeune admiratrice qui lui remet un poème. «Pardonnez-moi, lui dit-elle, je fais des fautes de français.» «Mais non, des fautes de Française», lui répond-il.

GALANTERIE EXAGÉRÉE

Envoyer des bouquets de fleurs très grands, très compliqués, très voyants, accompagnés d'une très longue missive, trois fois par semaine, à une femme intéressante, ce n'est pas raisonnable. L'excès de galanterie est formellement déconseillé : il confine à la servilité.

... et écriture d'aujourd'hui

LA CARTE DE VISITE

Vous pouvez l'utiliser pour envoyer des vœux, des félicitations, des remerciements, un cadeau, des fleurs, etc., elle vous évitera d'écrire une lettre. Mais attention vous devez la rédiger à la troisième personne. Ne la signez pas, ne la datez pas et n'écrivez pas au verso.

PRATIQUE
POST-IT-MANIA

Le papillon Post-it inventé il y a dix ans par Art Fry, un scientifique de chez 3M, compte déjà 350 millions d'utilisateurs en Europe ! Aujourd'hui, il existe en plusieurs formats et coloris ou agrémenté de messages. Nouveau : le marque-page en couleur qui, côté transparent, permet de voir le texte et d'écrire par-dessus (15 F). Et prochainement 3M va sortir un Post-it géant servant de tableau de réunion !

Madame Figaro, Maribelle Hidalgo (22.12.90)

Le blé est blond…
Le blé est blond. L'abeille est blonde.
La croûte du pain frais est blonde.
La compote, au creux du bol rond,
Et le miel sur le pain sont blonds.

Et la pluie au soleil est blonde,
Et le soleil est l'enfant blond
Qui offre en ses mains de lumière
De délicieuses choses blondes.

Comment ne serais-tu pas blonde ?

Chanson pour Caprine
© Fondation Maurice Carême
Maurice Carême (1899-1978)

Ici vous écrirez votre poème :

oèmes

1. Le poète associe l'adjectif blond/blonde successivement à :

des plantes ....

des animaux ....

des aliments ....

des éléments ....

2. Quelle est la dernière phrase du poème ?

....

3. À qui fait-elle allusion ?

....

1. Pour parler de quelqu'un on peut dire :

Il est brun, elle est brune, roux, rousse, blond, blonde,

ou bien il a les yeux bleus, elle a les yeux bleus, verts, noirs,

ou bien

....

2. Associez l'adjectif que vous aurez choisi à des animaux, des fleurs, des

choses... ....

Choisissez ceux que vous trouverez les plus tendres

les plus jolis ....

les plus fous ....

Et fabriquez un petit poème pour lui / pour elle.

....

....

....

....

....

Recopiez-le page 76

77

Sondages

Culture

Les Français sont-ils nuls ?

C'était un examen pour rire, mais les résultats sont à pleurer. Avec l'Institut Louis Harris, nous avons voulu tester les connaissances des Français. Combien font sept fois six ? Où est l'Acropole ? Qui a peint la Mona Lisa ?, etc. C'était vraiment sans malice, eh bien, c'était trop. Notre niveau est déplorable. La date du sacre de Charlemagne, passe encore. Mais Molière, Léonard de Vinci, on cherche, on bafouille et finalement… on se trompe ou on sèche. Jules Ferry cauchemarde. Ce qui a été patiemment enseigné à des générations d'élèves s'est évaporé. (Comme cette eau qui, pour 36% des Français, ne bout qu'à 100 °C !) Au fait, qui a écrit que «la culture, c'est ce qui reste quand on a tout oublié» ?

1 **Quel est le nom du Premier ministre qui a précédé Michel Rocard à la tête du gouvernement ? Réponse : Jacques Chirac : 37%. Ne savent pas : 40%.**
63% de la population a oublié qui a précédé Michel Rocard au gouvernement.

2 **Qui a peint Mona Lisa ? Réponse : Léonard de Vinci : 33%. Ne savent pas : 60%.**
Mona Lisa ? Connais pas. 66% des femmes ne savent pas qui est l'auteur du plus célèbre tableau du monde ; 54% des hommes non plus.

3 **Qui est l'auteur du «Misanthrope» ? Réponse : Molière : 41%. Ne savent pas : 57%.**
Nos classiques sont bien loin.

4 **Combien font 7 x 6 ? Réponse : 42 : 86%.**
Grande gagnante du sondage, la question qui a eu le meilleur score. Sexes, âges et professions confondus, ils sont plus de 80% à connaître leurs tables de multiplication.

5 **Qui était le père de Caïn et Abel ? Réponse : Adam : 21%. Ne savent pas : 69%.**
Catastrophe ! Le plus mauvais score.

6 **En quelle année Charlemagne a-t-il été sacré empereur ? Réponse : en l'an 800 : 25%. Ne savent pas : 56%.**
Qui a inventé l'école ? C'est ce sacré Charlemagne (dixit France Gall), mais en quelle année a-t-il été sacré, la chanson ne le dit pas.

7 **Où Bernadette Soubirous a-t-elle vu la Vierge ? Réponse : Lourdes : 71%. Ne savent pas : 23%.**
Bon score pour Lourdes, et cette fois-ci avec un plus pour les femmes. Elles sont 72% à savoir où Bernadette a vu la Vierge, pour 69% des hommes.

8 **Dans quelle ville se trouve l'Acropole ? Réponse : Athènes : 48%. Ne savent pas : 35%.**
51% des femmes ne savent pas où est l'Acropole. 2% d'entre elles la situent à Paris. 2% des hommes aussi. Mais eux, ils sont tout de même 58% à le savoir.

9 **Le Soleil tourne-t-il autour de la Terre ? Réponse : non : 66%. Ne savent pas : 3%.**
Question troublante, on en perd la boule. Eh bien non, c'est la Terre qui tourne 1) sur elle-même ; 2) autour du Soleil.

10 **À quelle température l'eau bout-elle ? Réponse : 100 ° C : 64%. Ne savent pas : 12%.**
Bon score pour les cadres (92%), les agriculteurs (78%) et les plus de 50 ans (72%).

Étude réalisée pour *Marie Claire*. Dates de réalisation les 15 et 16 décembre 1989. Sondage Louis Harris auprès d'un échantillon national représentatif de 1004 personnes âgées de 18 ans et plus selon la méthode des quotas (sexe, âge, profession du chef de famille, stratification par région et catégorie d'agglomération).

Sondages

1. Auriez-vous pu répondre aux questions proposées aux Français ?

....

2. Sous quelle rubrique placeriez-vous les 10 questions ?

art	histoire	littérature	politique	religion	sciences

3. Parmi ces 10 questions, y en a-t-il qui vous semblent spécifiquement françaises ? Lesquelles ?

....

....

....

....

4. Quelles questions mettriez-vous à leur place si vous deviez faire un sondage dans votre pays ou dans un autre pays ? (Précisez lequel.)

5. Maintenant, diffusez ce sondage autour de vous.
Que constatez-vous ?

....

....

....

ests...

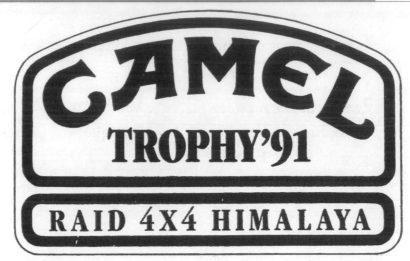

Le Camel Trophy est un raid 4x4 pas comme les autres. Ses organisateurs prennent tout en charge : la formation et les stages d'entraînement, le transport des équipages sélectionnés, les véhicules, le ravitaillement... Tout sauf l'initiative, l'imprévu, les sueurs froides, le défi, la ténacité, le coude à coude ! Le Camel Trophy est un grand rendez-vous de l'aventure où l'esprit d'équipe prédomine. En 91, dans l'Himalaya, le Camel Trophy sera gratuit. Mais comme les 11 Camel Trophy précédents, ce ne sera pas un cadeau !

ÊTES-VOUS PRÊT
POUR LE CAMEL TROPHY ?

1

Lors d'un convoi de nuit, le 4x4 qui vous précède s'enlise dans une ornière. Que faites-vous ?

A) Vous vous arrêtez pour aider l'équipage en difficulté.

B) Vous attendez qu'ils dégagent le 4x4 pour passer.

C) Vous contournez le véhicule et continuez votre route.

2

Après 12 heures de conduite périlleuse et fatigante dans la jungle, vous approchez enfin du bivouac. Une rivière en crue vous barre la route.

A) Vous décidez de longer la rivière et de trouver un passage praticable.

B) Vous hésitez et attendez l'équipe suivante pour prendre une décision.

C) Vous plantez votre tente sur place, reportant le problème au lendemain.

3

Le convoi du Camel Trophy est arrêté par un précipice. Pour le franchir, des troncs d'arbres ont été posés par les équipages. Ce pont de fortune fera-t-il l'affaire ?

A) Vous êtes volontaire pour passer le premier.

B) Vous attendez qu'un autre 4x4 soit passé avant de vous engager.

C) Vous regrettez d'être venu.

4

Au bivouac, un équipage prévoit de réparer son 4x4 endommagé pendant une partie de la nuit.

A) Débrouillard, vous proposez immédiatement votre aide.

B) Vous vous couchez en pensant à l'étape du lendemain.

C) Vous vous plaignez du bruit qui vous empêche de dormir.

Vous totalisez 3 ou 4 A : Vous avez le profil du Trophyman : vous avez l'esprit d'équipe et la volonté de vous dépasser, vous êtes tenace. Inscrivez-vous vite !

Vous totalisez 3 ou 4 B : Avec un peu plus d'assurance et d'initiative vous seriez un bon Trophyman. Inscrivez-vous, si vous êtes sélectionné, nos stages de formation et d'entraînement vous perfectionneront.

Vous totalisez 3 ou 4 C : Vous connaissez mal l'esprit du Camel Trophy. Renseignez-vous, refaites le test et posez vite votre candidature.

80

Faites le test ci-contre (même si vous n'avez pas l'esprit aventurier).

1. Ce test propose quatre situations problématiques. Remplissez le tableau suivant afin de savoir comment ces situations sont toujours délimitées dans l'espace et le temps.

	où ?	quand ?
Situation 1		
Situation 2		
Situation 3		
Situation 4		

2. Après avoir examiné les questions posées et les «bonnes» réponses, dites quelles sont les qualités que recherchaient les sélectionneurs chez les concurrents.

....

....

....

....

....

Imaginez que vous devez élaborer un test.
  – Cherchez un sujet, par exemple : avez-vous le sens de l'humour ? Savez-vous séduire ? Respectez-vous les autres ?
  – Trouvez quatre situations problématiques situées dans l'espace et le temps.
  – Proposez trois solutions : A, B, C.
  – Donnez une solution au test.

Nota : étant donné sa longueur et sa complexité, cet exercice gagnera à être fait en groupe. Le sujet sera donc choisi en commun et l'on confiera à quatre sous-groupes une seule situation et sa résolution.

Jeu-conseil
Faisons la route ensemble.

LA SÉCURITÉ ROUTIÈRE

9 CONSEILS À SUIVRE
LA SÉCURITÉ ROUTIÈRE

1. LA VITESSE. Elle constitue la cause principale des accidents. On la trouve dans 1 accident mortel sur 2. Et ce n'est pas toujours parce qu'on a dépassé les vitesses limites. Il faut adapter sa vitesse aux circonstances. Plus vous allez vite, plus vous allez vite vers l'accident.

2. L'ÉTAT DES VOITURES. Une voiture mal entretenue, c'est une voiture dangereuse. L'éclairage, les freins, les pneus sont des pièces vitales pour votre voiture mais aussi pour vous.

3. L'ALCOOL. Conduire quand on a bu, même quelques verres à table, c'est criminel. À 0,8 g d'alcoolémie, la limite légale, vous êtes déjà 10 fois plus dangereux pour vous et pour les autres. Alors pensez-y avant le premier verre.

4. LE CASQUE. En moto, sauver sa tête, ça veut vraiment dire quelque chose. Rouler les cheveux au vent, c'est supprimer la seule carrosserie que vous ayez. Même quand il fait beau et chaud, mettez votre casque.

5. EN VILLE. Il y a des enfants qui jouent au ballon, des jeunes femmes avec des poussettes et des personnes âgées qui traversent lentement. Alors respectez les autres, et ne prenez pas la ville pour un circuit, roulez calmement, c'est mieux pour tout le monde, même pour vos nerfs !

6. LA FATIGUE. Inévitable quand on fait un long trajet. Il ne suffit pas de ralentir. Le seul remède contre la fatigue, c'est de s'arrêter toutes les deux heures, marcher un peu, boire un verre d'eau ou de jus d'orange, mais jamais d'alcool ni d'excitant bien sûr.

7. LA PRIORITÉ. Respecter celle des autres, c'est bien, mais ne pas en abuser quand on l'a, c'est encore mieux. Évitez de bloquer un carrefour déjà embouteillé, même si vous pensez que c'est à vous de passer.

8. LA CEINTURE. L'attacher uniquement pour les longs trajets, ce n'est pas suffisant. Faire 1 fois 1 000 km ou 100 fois 10 km, le risque est le même. Attachez toujours votre ceinture, à l'avant comme à l'arrière. Dans tous les types d'accidents, la ceinture sauve la vie.

9. LES TRAJETS COURTS. Vous pourriez faire la route les yeux fermés, ce sont tous les jours les mêmes carrefours, et puis un jour… 2 accidents sur 3 ont lieu sur des trajets de moins de 15 km, alors ouvrez toujours les yeux.

Lisez les conseils de la Sécurité routière et faites le test ci-dessous.

VRAI OU FAUX ?
TESTEZ VOS CONNAISSANCES
Sécurité routière

	Vrai	Faux
• Un accident sur trois a lieu à moins de 15 kilomètres de chez soi.	☐	☐
• Il y a des types d'accidents où il vaut mieux ne pas avoir attaché sa ceinture.	☐	☐
• La vitesse excessive ou inappropriée est en cause dans 1 accident mortel sur 2.	☐	☐
• À 0,8 g d'alcoolémie, vous avez 2 fois plus de risques d'avoir un accident que si vous n'aviez rien bu.	☐	☐
• Il faut 135 mètres à une voiture roulant à 130 km/h pour s'arrêter.	☐	☐
• Quelle que soit la situation, quand on a la priorité, il faut en profiter.	☐	☐
• Environ 80% des personnes impliquées dans des accidents dus à l'alcool ne sont pas des «alcooliques chroniques».	☐	☐
• Attacher sa ceinture en ville est indispensable car on risque autant que sur la route.	☐	☐
• Quand on est fatigué d'avoir conduit longtemps, il suffit de ralentir.	☐	☐

rucs

*Il y a les grandes inventions
et… les petits trucs*

LE COUP DE LA BISCOTTE

Christine

– Je vais t'apprendre quelque chose dont tu te souviendras toujours : comment beurrer une biscotte sans la casser ? Tu vois : tu prends deux biscottes, tu les mets l'une sur l'autre, comme ça, et puis tu étales ton beurre. Et grâce à la biscotte du dessous, la biscotte du dessus ne se casse pas.

Antoine

– Ah, c'est bien !

Christine

– Je t'apprendrai tout ce que je sais… par exemple le coup de la biscotte… et puis toi, en échange, tu m'apprendras ce que tu sais…

Antoine

– Oui, très bien.

Extrait du film *Baisers volés* de François Truffaut.

1. Répondez aux questions suivantes :

1. Qu'est-ce qu'une biscotte ?

....

....

2. Qu'est-ce que beurrer une biscotte ?

....

....

3. Qu'est-ce qu'étaler du beurre sur une biscotte ?

....

....

....

2. Pour expliquer «le coup de la biscotte» à Antoine, Christine a décrit l'opération «Tu prends… tu mets…» (2ᵉ personne du présent de l'indicatif). Quelles autres formes linguistiques aurait-elle pu employer ?

— ....

....

— ....

....

— ....

....

3. Ce texte est écrit sous forme de dialogue, écrivez le conseil que donne Christine tel qu'il pourrait figurer dans un manuel de recettes qui pourrait s'intituler : *Mille petits trucs qui vous simplifient la vie*. Vous choisirez la forme linguistique que vous voudrez .

....

....

....

....

....

....

....

....

1. Voici une liste de verbes représentant des actions effectuées à l'aide des mains. Cherchez-en le sens dans un dictionnaire si besoin est, puis complétez la liste.

Allumer, appuyer, arracher, coudre, couper, enfoncer, éteindre, fermer, frotter, hacher, mettre, ouvrir, placer, poser, presser, soulever, tirer, tourner, visser.

....

....

....

....

....

2. Faites avec vos mains les gestes qui pourraient mimer ces actions et faites-les deviner à ceux qui vous entourent.

Pensez à un petit truc que vous connaissez (faire cuire un œuf sans le casser, ouvrir une porte dont on a perdu la clé, etc.) et rédigez-le pour le livre *Mille petits trucs qui vous simplifient la vie.*

....

....

....

....

....

....

....

....

....

....

....

Je suis presque gêné de le dire, mais j'ai un truc pour les portraits de commande. J'ai dans ma poche un petit klaxon de bicyclette (une poire qu'on presse). Si quelqu'un est revêche ou guindé, je klaxonne. Cela brise la glace, en quelque sorte. C'est bête mais ça marche.

Sauf... une fois. Je photographiais le Conseil d'administration d'une super entreprise, que je ne nommerai pas. Ils étaient assis à une grande table sombre, avec des boiseries d'acajou tout autour, sinistres, chacun plongé dans ses pensées et dans ses problèmes personnels. J'ai sorti mon klaxon et j'ai appuyé. Personne n'a bronché, sauf le chargé des relations publiques, qui avait l'air sur le point d'avoir une crise cardiaque. On ne m'a jamais rappelé. Mais ça a marché avec Khrouchtchev. Je voulais qu'il se retourne et regarde vers moi. J'ai klaxonné, il s'est tourné vers ce bruit bizarre et, clic, j'ai pris la photo. Il ne s'est pas fâché. Parfois je laisse l'objet dans ma poche, je fais «pouët-pouët» et la personne que je photographie reste perplexe. Le klaxon signifie quelque chose. Il veut dire que nous sommes conscients de la relative idiotie de ce que nous sommes en train de faire là, tous les deux ; donc autant le faire le mieux possible. C'est une connivence qui détend l'atmosphère. De toute façon, comme disait le Général Sun-Tzu : «Les réactions de l'ennemi sont imprévisibles».

Elliott Erwitt

Pouët ! Pouët !
bruit produit par une poire-klaxon.
(*Dictionnaire des bruits*, Jean-Claude Trait, Yvon Dulude. Les éditions de l'homme, Québec.)

écriture

1. Répondez aux questions en complétant la colonne de droite.

– Qui est Elliott Erwitt ?
Elliot Erwitt est ....

– Quel est le truc d'Elliott Erwitt ?
E. Erwitt a un truc, avant de ....

– Pourquoi fait-il cela ?
Il fait cela pour ....

– Le truc a-t-il toujours marché ?
Le truc a toujours marché sauf ....

– Qui devait-il photographier ce jour-là ?
Ce jour-là, il ....

– Pourquoi n'ont-ils pas réagi
devant le klaxon ?
Mais ils n'ont pas réagi ....

– Quel est le véritable sens du klaxon
pour celui qui photographie et ceux
qui sont photographiés ?
Finalement, le klaxon c'est ....

2. Maintenant, recopiez vos réponses à la suite ; que remarquez-vous ?

....

....

....

....

....

....

....

....

....

....

....

....

Corrigés

Autobiographie

Page 6

Questionnaire, données objectives :
sports pratiqués, date de naissance, signe du zodiaque, nationalité, études en cours, stages réalisés, langues parlées, adresse, expérience professionnelle, activité artistique, état civil, formation.

Questionnaire, données personnelles :
manies, musique préférée, rêves, la plus grande angoisse, couleur préférée, principal défaut, le plus beau souvenir, projets immédiats, passe-temps favori, qualité principale, états d'âme fréquents, sentiments actuels.

Avis de recherche

Page 9

1. Katia Yasmine recherche Patricia Berthier
   Elles se sont connues en Corse.

2. **Réponse 1 :**
   Tatie Danielle-Patricia Berthier/ Corse, colonie, quinze ans / Porto-Vecchio, 8 ans.

   Réponse 2 :
   Madeleine Sézac, Katia Yasmine/ Patricia Berthier, Corse / Porto-Vecchio, un mois, 16 ans, Allemagne.

3. **Réponse 1 :**
   Madeleine Sézac écrit à sa nièce pour lui envoyer un avis de recherche mais elle se demande si sa nièce est bien la personne recherchée.

   Réponse possible 2 :
   Madeleine Sézac écrit à Katia Yasmine pour lui dire qu'elle connaît la personne recherchée, elle pense que c'est sa nièce.

Page 13.

1. 1. A/B/…/C   2. A/…/B/C 3. …/…/B/A/
   4. …/…/A/B/   5. A/C/B/…   6. C/A/…/B

2. A. Ma Nine, quelle émotion, se revoir, comment veux-tu que je t'oublie ?
   B. Certaine émotion ; charme ; ce n'est peut-être pas un hasard.

C. Déjà je te réclamais, je crève d'envie.

Carte postales

Page 17

1. A. Bretagne /…/…/… / excellent souvenir
   B. Côte d'Azur/…/ gris; frais/…/ pour moi le soleil brille
   C. Turquie/…/ chaud/…/ enchanteur
   D. Strasbourg/…/…/…/ insensé, délirant
   E. Venise/voyage d'amoureux/très beaux /…/…

2. **Début :** cher, ma chère
   Fin : Toutes mes amitiés, bon baisers, je t'embrasse bien fort, amitiés, bise à bientôt.
   Autres : amicalement, cordialement, bisous …

Page 18

Réponse possible :

Cher Roch, Chère Elisabeth, je suis aujourd'hui à Florence. Il fait très chaud, mais je visite tout ce que je peux ! Venise sera la prochaine étape. Bises Elisabeth.

Page 21

A. Un groupe de filles / Voilà les filles
B. Une fontaine / la fontaine
C. Un joli paysage / ça
D. Un paysage exotique / ces couleurs.

Catalogues

Page 25

1. **Les formes :**
   cintré - ras de cou- zippée - long - décolleté - à volants - moulant - aux pressions de nacre - avec des poches - à empiècement -
   Les couleurs :
   argent , noir, blanc, rouge, jaune, marron, vert fluo.

Les compositions :
polyester, néoprène, interlock coton, pur coton, cuir, peau, caoutchouc.

2. Précise.

Page 27

1. **Les formes :**
longues, surpiqués, rondes, à pressions, droit, ajustée, à bout effilé.

Les couleurs :
turquoise, vert, 4 coloris, bicolore, marron, anis, orange, écru, noir, bleu marine, rouge.

Les compositions :
nylon, coton et polyamide, mouton retourné, aluminium, coton, veau velours.

2. Les prix, les marques, les tailles, les adjectifs de présentation (acidulés, stylisés, douillets, look intello, viva Zapata, strick, pour VIP).

On constate que ces adjectifs apportent un élément supplémentaire à la description : une appréciation.

3. **Réponses possibles :**
pratique : articles A.E.;
confort : article C;
élégance : articles B.F.G.;
originalité : articles D.H.I.

4. Les articles de la série 1 sont moins chers, les articles de la série 2 sont plus originaux ; la description des articles de la série 1 est moins technique, moins détaillée que la description des articles de la série 2, qui montre les qualités particulières de chaque article.

Page 30

1. Du T-shirt et de la chemise rayée.
2. Tee-shirt brillant, espèce de plastique, chemise, Mexique.

Chiffres

Page 32

2. Parce que c'est l'âge de mon/ma/fiancé ; c'est un porte-bonheur ; je l'ai choisi au hasard, etc.

3. C'est le 47 qui a le moins gagné - C'est le 38 qui a le plus gagné.

4. **Réponses possibles :**
Mes camarades choisissent des chiffres en relation avec les gens qu'ils aiment / Nous avons tous des chiffres fétiches / Nous sommes un peu superstitieux : il y a des chiffres que nous aimons et d'autres que nous ne jouons jamais / Les gens préfèrent certains chiffres parce qu'ils coïncident avec d'autres chiffres familiers : numéros de téléphone, de code postal, de plaque d'immatriculation de voiture, etc.

Dédicaces

Page 35

A.3. / B.2. / C.5. / D.4. / E.1.

Évocations

Page 39

Repérage
1. 1-B/. 2-D/. 3-A/ 4-C

Écriture
2. **A. Réponses possibles.** Départ pour Florence

B. Anniversaire (ou mes 16 ans, Dominique 16 ans ou le 12 mai 1985, par exemple) -
C. Palais-Royal, été 1982 -
D. Mariage de Julie et de Christophe (2 septembre 1982, par exemple).

Page 41

Repérage
Vie privée :
naissance, études, service militaire, tour de France en bateau, divers voyages, naissance des enfants, maladie, déménagements divers, divorce et remariage.

Vie professionnelle :
apprenti, commis, journaliste, vie d'écrivain : ouvrages publics, lancement d'ouvrages, choix des maisons d'édition, retraite.

Événements exceptionnels :
élection à l'Académie de Belgique, présidence de divers festivals de cinéma - tour du monde.

Page 43

1.2. Événements ponctuels :
a été construit, a construit, est devenu, ont couvert, ont changé, se sont échappés, a décidé, on a commencé, a pris conscience - (ça) a été.

Actions répétées :
allaient, photographiaient.

Descriptions :
c'était (la guerre…), passaient, séparait, il était… et avait, c'était (comme…)

Appréciations :
il semblait.

Autres :
commençait, je m'en souviens.

3. Ces mots servent à lier le récit, à créer la continuité, le déroulement de l'histoire.

Faire-part et invitations

Page 45

1. **A.** naissance **B.** deuil **C.** mariage (réception) **D.** mariage (cérémonie).

2. Mariage de Béatrice et Julien / Mort du grand-père de Julien / Naissance de Victor, fils de Béatrice et Julien.

Page 46

a) 2, 8 **b)** 2, 5, 11 **c)** 3 **d)** 4, 9 **e)** 1 **f)** 6 **g)** 7, 10

Faits divers

Page 49

1. Les faits divers 1-2-4

2. 1 : insolite - aurait pu être tragique. **2** : drôle insolite. **3** : drôle - insolite. **4** : drôle. - insolite. **5** : tragique . **6** : tragique.

3. **Verbes :** — . **Substantifs :** bébé, buveur, chats, rats, mégots, voitures. **Déterminants :** un, vingt-cinq. **Adjectifs :** — . **Mots de liaison :** et.

4. L'absence de verbes : la juxtaposition des noms.

5. 1 : oui   4 : en partie   5 : pas du tout

Page 50

1. **Réponses possibles :**
2a : Bébé au vestiaire.
2b : "Voilà le ticket de votre bébé".
3a : Alcool et parfum !
3b : Water Calva
6 : Égorgée.

2. **Réponses possibles :**
2a : insolite
2b : drôle
3a : drôle
3b : insolite
6 : tragique.

Page 51

Repérage

1. 1. Quatre ressortissants français trafiquants de drogue- Paris- l'arrestation de 4 trafiquants de drogue - avaient commencé le trafic il y a un certain temps.

2. Un touriste italien - Corse - blessé par balle - il y avait fait une "queue de poisson" (selon son agresseur).

Formulaires

Page 54

Réponse possible :
Part. vend vélo course femme B. état Prix intér. Tél. 38 15 42 43.

Page 57

1. Un passeport en règle.

2. On vous conduit dans un car, au commissariat de police ou à la gendarmerie.

3. Droit de prévenir votre famille ou votre avocat, on ne peut pas vous garder plus de 4 heures. Si vous êtes mineur, on doit prévenir vos parents.

Lettres administratives

Page 59

Réponses possibles :

A **a)** Attention ! Nouveau code : 0A678

b) Madame Ménoux, on a changé le code de la porte, c'est 0A678.

B **a)** Nadine/Alain, attention, ne faites pas de bruit le soir (télé ou musique), les voisins se sont plaints. Françoise Voisin.

b) Jean Lefurs
Administrateur de biens
33 avenue de la République
94100 Saint Maur

Le 6 avril 1988

Monsieur,

Votre lettre du 30 mars m'a surprise et indignée. Je ne suis absolument pas responsable des actes de "vandalisme" que vous m'attribuez, et je vous assure que la mauvaise foi de mes voisins est évidente.

Je vous prie d'agréer l'expression de mes sentiments distingués.

Signature
Françoise Voisin
228, allée de la Toison d'Or
94000 Créteil

Page 61

1. B et C
2. A : l'adresse de l'expéditeur ne figure pas.
   D. : l'adresse du destinataire n'est pas à la bonne place.
3. Disposition de l'adresse de l'expéditeur, disposition des paragraphes.

Page 63

Repérage

E. Voyage en Afrique / prospectus

F. Travail scolaire / documentation / autres endroits

G. Compléter formation d'ingénieur / inscription dans un centre spécialisé.

Listes

Page 65

1. Les ciseaux modèle «lingère»/ le dé à coudre/ le fil à bâtir.
2. Des épingles pour fixer deux pièces de tissu ensemble / un aimant pour ramasser les aiguilles et épingles tombées ou égarées / un mètre-ruban pour mesurer / des craies pour tracer le contour des pièces à coudre ou à découper / le découseur pour découdre.
3. **Réponses possibles :**
   des aiguilles/ des ciseaux / un dé éventuellement / une tresse de fils multicolore tous textiles.

Page 67

1. **En Indonésie :**
   visite de paysages de volcans, de temples, de quartiers d'artisans dans les villages, et de la capitale Bali – Avion (?), et randonnée ou marche. Températures extrêmes, chaudes en plaine et froides en altitude.
2. **Réponses possibles :**
   un appareil photo - un ou 2 shorts - un pantalon / une jupe - 2 ou 3 tee-shirts - un pull en laine - des lunettes de soleil - 2 ou 3 sous-vêtements - des chaussures de randonnée - 3 paires de chaussettes - une mini-trousse de toilette - des Klennex - de la crème protectrice.

Page 68

1. Une paire de lunettes - un coquillage - de l'argent (des pièces de monnaie et un billet) - un hameçon - des clés - un paquet de cigarettes - un trombone - une note de magasin -une vis - un bonbon - un briquet - 2 mini-piles - un bouton.
2. C'est probablement une personne peu ordonnée, ou qui revient de vacances ou de week-end, qui fume, qui aime la mer, etc.

Page 69

1. Une carte de téléphone - un papier de bonbon - un trousseau de clés- deux tickets de métro - une liste d'adresses- un élastique - un billet de 100 F- un

peigne - une carte avec l'adresse d'un restaurant - un petit billet de propagande commerciale.

2. C'est probablement une femme parisienne ou qui va souvent à Paris. Elle doit être assez soignée, etc.

Messages

Page 72

1. **A.** M. Elisabeth Gros / professeur / professeur de son fils.
   B. Collègue / collègues / collègues.
   C. Papa / une adolescente / sa fille.
   D. Bichette / une copine ou une sœur / la copine ou la sœur avec laquelle elle habite.
   E. Simone Bernard / Marie-Jeanne / la jeune fille qui garde son fils.

2. **A.** Excuser son fils / raisons familiales.
   B. De l'argent / Isabelle Schmitt a eu un garçon.
   C. Téléphoner au parrain / le parrain est de pas sage à Paris - Débrancher le four / le plombier n'est pas venu. / Ne pas se coucher tard.
   D. Faire la vaisselle / c'est son tour.
   E. Mettre des gouttes dans les oreilles / Cédric à une otite.

Page 73

Message 1 :
Réponse possible :

Anne, J. René a téléphoné, il part pour une semaine, il te laisse 2 cassettes vidéo chez Charles à qui tu peux téléphoner vers 9 heures du soir (40 14 53 34).

Poèmes

Page 78

Repérage

1. **Plantes :** le blé. **Animaux :** l'abeille. **Aliments :** la croûte du pain, la compote, le miel sur le pain. **Éléments :** la pluie au soleil, le soleil.

2. Comment ne serais-tu pas blonde ?

3. À une femme aimée.

Sondages

Page 80

2. **Art :** 2,8. **Histoire :** 6. **Littérature :** 3. **Politique :** 1 **Religion :** 5, 7. **Sciences :** 4, 9, 10.

3. Les questions : 1, 3 ,6 et éventuellement la 7.

Page 81

1. **Réponses possibles :**

Est-ce que tu aimes le cinéma ? Classe par ordre de préférence les types de films suivants : films de terreur, films romantiques, films comiques. Combien de fois es-tu allé au cinéma l'année dernière ? Est-ce que tu vas au cinéma à jour fixe ? - À quelle séance vas-tu de préférence ? - Pourquoi aimes-tu aller au cinéma ? - Est-ce que tu vas au cinéma : seul(e) ? / avec tes parents ? / avec des camarades ? - Classe par ordre de préférence ce qui compte le plus pour toi dans un film : les acteurs, l'histoire, etc.

Tests

Page 83

1. OÙ ? **1 :** dans une ornière. **2 :** dans la jungle . **3 :** au bord d'un précipice. **4 :** au bivouac - QUAND ? 1. 2. 3. 4 : de nuit.

2. L'esprit d'équipe, l'assurance, la ténacité, la volonté de dépassement, l'esprit d'initiative.

Page 85

F - F - V - F. Le texte ne le dit pas (vous pouvez regarder le code de la route !) - F- V -V- F.

Trucs

Page 87

1. **1.** Biscotte : tranche de pain de mie grillée industriellement.
   2. C'est étaler du beurre dessus.
   3. C'est recouvrir la biscotte d'une couche de beurre.

2. L'impératif à la deuxième personne du singulier : "prends… mets… étale…" ; le présent avec "on": "pour beurrer une biscotte sans la casser, on prend… on met… on étale"…

3. Comment beurrer une biscotte sans la casser ? On peut utiliser l'infinitif : "Prendre deux biscottes, les placer l'une sur l'autre et étaler le beurre sur celle du dessus : celle de dessous l'empêchera de se casser" : On peut également utiliser le présent avec "vous" : "vous prenez deux biscottes, etc.") : l'impératif à la deuxième personne du pluriel : "Prenez, mettez… etc." et le pronom "on" (cf. ci-dessus).

Page 88

Réponses possibles :

secouer, caresser, se gratter, pincer, agiter, saluer, etc.

Page 90 :

1. Elliot Erwitt est photographe / avant de photographier quelqu'un, il klaxonne avec un petit klaxon de bicyclette / … pour amuser ou détendre la personne qu'il veut photographier (ou : pour que la personne ait un air amusé au moment où il va la photographier) / une fois / assistait au Conseil d'administration d'une grande entreprise ; tout le monde était très sérieux / et n'ont pas semblé contents / une connivence qui détend l'atmosphère.

2. Les réponses recopiées constituent le résumé du texte.

95

Références photographiques

p.14 : Berger; p.21bg : Rapho, Mopy; p.21bd: Rapho, Baret; p.38hg: Rapho, Niepce; p.38hd: Rapho, Ohanian; p.38bg: Rapho, Fournier; p.38bd: Explorer, Roy; p.39 : Petit Format, Chaumat; p.40 : Roger Viollet; p.42: Plantu; p.56 : Atelier d'Images, Gauvreau; p.66h: Explorer, Bordes; p.66b : Explorer, Krafft; p. 68 : Gauvreau; p.69 : Gauvreau.

Composition et mise en page : EPC
Illustrations : Thierry Lamouche
Couverture : François Huertas
Recherches iconographiques : Atelier d'Images
Edition : Corinne Booth-Odot

N° d'éditeur : 10011715 II (10,5) (OSB 80) — Dépôt légal : juillet 1992
Imprimé en France par Pollina, 85400 Luçon - n° 15041

building analytical, creative,
and practical skills

CAROL CARTER   **SARAH LYMAN KRAVITS**   **PETER J. MAURIN**

Montclair State University   Mohawk College

Toronto

Dedication

This book is dedicated to the memory
of my parents Peter and Blanka Maurin.
—*Peter Maurin*

Vice-President, CMPS: Gary Bennett
Editorial Director: Claudine O'Donnell
Acquisitions Editor: David S. Le Gallais
Marketing Manager: Michelle Bish
Program Manager: Laura Pratt
Project Manager: Marissa Lok
Developmental Editor: Marissa Lok
Media Editors: Sonia Tan and Marissa Lok
Production Services: Vastavikta Sharma, Cenveo Publisher Services
Permissions Project Manager: Sue Petrykewycz
Photo Permissions Research: Marta Johnson, Lumina Datamatics
Text Permissions Research: Varoon Deo-Singh, Electronic Publishing Services
Art Director: Alex Li
Interior Designer: Anthony Leung
Cover Designer: Anthony Leung

Credits and acknowledgments for material borrowed from other sources and reproduced, with permission, in this textbook appear on the appropriate page within the text.

Original edition published by Pearson Education, Inc., Upper Saddle River, New Jersey, USA. Copyright © 2015 Pearson Education, Inc. This edition is authorized for sale only in Canada.

If you purchased this book outside the United States or Canada, you should be aware that it has been imported without the approval of the publisher or the author.

5 16

Library and Archives Canada Cataloguing in Publication

Carter, Carol, author
      Keys to success : building analytical, creative and practical skills
/ Carol Carter, Joyce Bishop, Sarah Lyman Kravits, Peter J. Maurin,
Mohawk College. — Seventh Canadian edition.

Revision of: Keys to success : building analytical, creative and
      practical skills / Carol Carter ... [et al.]. — 6th Canadian ed.
      —Toronto : Pearson Canada, 2012.
Includes bibliographical references and index.
ISBN 978-0-13-340551-4 (pbk.)

      1. College student orientation—Canada—Handbooks, manuals, etc.
2. Study skills—Handbooks, manuals, etc. 3. College students—
Canada—Life skills guides. I. Bishop, Joyce, author II. Kravits, Sarah
Lyman, author III. Maurin, Peter, author IV. Title.

LB2343.34.C3C37 2015   378.1'980971   C2014-907607-X

ISBN 978-0-13-340551-4

BRIEF CONTENTS

CONTENTS

"IT'S NOT JUST WHAT YOU KNOW;

it's what you know how to do."

Keys sets the standard for connecting academic success to success beyond school, showing students how to apply strategies within college or university, career, and life. *Keys* retains its tried-and-true emphasis on thinking skills and problem solving, re-imagined with two goals in mind: one, a **risk-and-reward** framework that reflects the demands today's students face and two, a focus on student experience specific to **institutions** with a more extensive research base. The material helps students take ownership, develop academic and transferable skills, and show the results of commitment and action so they are well equipped with the concentration, commitment, focus, and persistence necessary to succeed.

WHAT'S NEW IN THIS
edition?

- **Risk-and-reward theme.** To be rewarded with goal achievement in the fast-paced information age, students must take calculated, productive risks. The benefit of risks small (putting in the work your courses require) and large (aiming for a degree in a tough major, working toward a challenging career) is learning transferable skill building, persistence, and confidence.

- **Inspiring, motivating case studies focused on risk and reward.** Students derive motivation from reading about how others have taken risks, gotten through struggles, overcome challenges, and earned rewards. Each chapter begins with a case study focusing on a personal challenge and details the risk taken to face and surmount it. The closing section at the end of each chapter finishes the story and shows the reward earned at that time and the rewards that the person has subsequently gained from continued risk and effort. This section also relates the story to the reader's lives and challenges them to think expansively about how to make personal improvements related to the chapter.

- **Brain-based learning and metacognition.** Cites research on building intelligence, the science of learning, the changes in the brain that happen when you remember, the cost of task switching, brain development in adolescence and early adulthood, and more. This information builds student metacognition.

WHAT ELSE HAS CHANGED IN THIS
edition?

- **Successful intelligence framework.** Builds a comprehensive set of analytical, creative, practical thinking skills to empower students to strengthen their command of the problem-solving process and take practical action.

- **In-chapter exercises focused on analytical, creative, and practical thinking, and financial literacy.** These exercises give readers a chance to apply a chapter idea or skill to their personal needs and situations in a particular type of thinking.
  - *Get Analytical* builds analytical thinking skill.
  - *Get Creative* builds creative thinking skill.
  - *Get Practical* builds practical thinking skill.
  - The **NEW** exercise *Get $mart* builds financial literacy.

- **End-of-chapter exercises, each with a distinctive practical goal** targeted to develop a particular skill to have readers perform a chapter-related task that has specific personal value.
  - *Know It* builds critical thinking skill
  - *Write It* builds emotional intelligence and practical writing skill
  - *Work It* builds career readiness
- The importance of developing 21st century skills as part of one's post-secondary experience is introduced in Chapter 1 and highlighted throughout the text. This framework for 21st century learning includes Fundamental, Personal Management, and Teamwork Skills as outlined by The Conference Board of Canada's *Employability Skills 2000+*.

STUDENT
Supplements

MyStudentSuccessLab (www.mystudentsuccesslab.com): Whether face-to-face or online, MyStudentSuccessLab helps students build the skills they need through peer-led video interviews, interactive practice exercises, and activities that provide academic, life, and professionalism skills.

1. **Quick Start Connect:** Promote higher engagement and retention through real student video interviews on key issues.
2. **Practise:** Facilitate skill-building with three exercises per topic, tied to Bloom's Taxonomy, that provide interactive experience and practice.
3. **Personalize:** Students apply what they have learned and create personally relevant projects; instructors assess skill mastery.

CourseSmart for Students: CourseSmart goes beyond traditional expectations—providing instant, online access to the textbooks and course materials you need at significant savings over the printed book. With instant access from any computer and the ability to search your text, you'll find the content you need quickly, no matter where you are. And with online tools like highlighting and note-taking, you can save time and study efficiently. See all of the benefits at www.coursesmart.com/students.

peerScholar: Firmly grounded in published research, peerScholar is a powerful online pedagogical tool that helps develop your students' critical and creative thinking skills. peerScholar facilitates this through the process of creation, evaluation, and reflection. Working in stages, students begin by submitting a written assignment. peerScholar then circulates their work for others to review, a process that can be anonymous or not depending on your preference. Students receive peer feedback and evaluations immediately, reinforcing their learning and driving the development of higher-order thinking skills. Students can then resubmit revised work, again depending on your preference. Contact your Pearson sales representative to learn more about peerScholar and the research behind it.

INSTRUCTOR
Supplements

Pearson Canada is committed to preparing the best quality supplements for its textbooks. The following supplements provide an outstanding array of resources.

Instructor's Manual: Each chapter of the manual includes a chapter outline, learning objectives, facilitation questions, group exercises, and case studies. This instructor resource also contains questions and quotations that can be used in a variety of classroom activities, such as group discovery and public speaking.

PowerPoint Presentations: The PowerPoint presentation created for this text provides ready-to-use graphics and images to guide and enhance lecture presentation.

Learning Solutions Managers: Pearson's Learning Solutions Managers work with faculty and campus course designers to ensure that Pearson technology products, assessment tools, and online course materials are tailored to meet your specific needs. This highly qualified team is dedicated to helping schools take full advantage of a wide range of educational resources, by assisting in the integration of a variety of instructional materials and media formats. Your local Pearson sales representative can provide you with more details on this service program.

CourseSmart for Instructors. CourseSmart goes beyond traditional expectations—providing instant, online access to the textbooks and course materials you need at a lower cost for students. And even as students save money, you can save time and hassle with a digital eTextbook that allows you to search for the most relevant content at the very moment you need it. Whether it's evaluating textbooks or creating lecture notes to help students with difficult concepts, CourseSmart can make life a little easier. See how when you visit www.coursesmart.com/instructors.

Pearson Custom Library. For enrollments of at least 25, you can create your own textbook by combining chapters from best-selling Pearson textbooks and/or reading selections in the sequence you want. To begin building your custom text, visit www.pearsoncustomlibrary.com. You may also work with a dedicated Pearson Custom editor to create your ideal text—publishing your own original content or mixing and matching Pearson content. *Contact your Pearson representative to get started.*

Learning Solutions Managers. Pearson's Learning Solutions Managers work with faculty and campus course designers to ensure that Pearson technology products, assessment tools, and online course materials are tailored to meet your specific needs. This highly qualified team is dedicated to helping schools take full advantage of a wide range of educational resources, by assisting in the integration of a variety of instructional materials and media formats. Your local Pearson Education sales representative can provide you with more details on this service program.

ACKNOWLEDGMENTS

■ We would like to thank all those students across the country who helped us (and their fellow students) by providing *Student Profiles*: Patrick Belliveau, Sheridan College; Olivia Daub, University of Waterloo; Christian Gaumont, Sprott-Shaw Community College; Katie Hudgins, CDI College; Paige Lawson, Mohawk College; Kelcy McNally, University of Prince Edward Island; Sarah Mocherniak, Acadia University; Brandie Molley, Sprott-Shaw Community College; Tia Nguyen, Ryerson University; Dion Redgun, CDI College; James Shields, University of King's College; and Hongman Xu, Seneca College.

■ Thanks also to our reviewers, whose comments and suggestions have helped us in the preparation of this Seventh Canadian Edition: Tara Gauld, Confederation College; Sarah Hunter, Georgian College; Kim Cechetto, Fanshawe College; Debbie Cox, Conestoga College; Shaun Iles, Mohawk College; Valerie Parke, Mohawk College; and others who chose to remain anonymous.

■ Thanks to the staff at Pearson Canada: David Le Gallais, acquisitions editor; Joel Gladstone, program manager; Marissa Lok, developmental editor and project manager; Vastavikta Sharma, vendor project manager; and Charlotte Morrison-Reed, copyeditor.

■ While I am the Canadian author for this seventh Canadian edition of *Keys to Success,* the contents of this book are really the product of years of teaching (and learning) at several institutions. Thanks to my current and former students at Mohawk College and to the many former students at Brock University and Niagara College. Whether I was teaching Communications, Media, Career Planning, or Sociology, you always taught me something in the process.

■ I'd also like to thank all my colleagues at Mohawk College in Hamilton. We are an amazing team whose passion for teaching is second to none.

■ Finally, to my gifted crew at home—Kim, Sonja, and Josh: You are my "keys to success." Thanks for your love, patience, and understanding. Always remember that "I love you more."

Peter J. Maurin, M.A.

Carol Carter has spent her entire career in the business world, where she has a track record of success in corporate America, entrepreneurship, and non-profit. Her student success work is driven by firsthand knowledge of what employers expect and demand from today's graduates. As President of LifeBound, an academic and career coaching company, she drives the company's goal to help middle school and high school students become competitive in today's world, and she teaches study, interpersonal, and career skills to students as well as training and certifying adults in academic coaching skills. Carol speaks on educational topics nationally and internationally and is an expert blogger for the Huffington Post under "Impact," "College," and "Business." Carol is a co-author on many books for Pearson, including the *Keys to Success* series as well as *Keys to Business Communication* and the *Career Tool Kit*. She has also published a series of books for K-12 students through LifeBound, including *Dollars and Sense: How To Be Smart About Money* and *Majoring In the Rest of Your Life: Career Secrets for College Students*.

Sarah Lyman Kravits teaches student success at Montclair State University and has been researching and writing about student success for over 15 years. As a parent of three children (ages 14, 12, and 8), a collaborator, a co-author, and an instructor, she lives the strategies for success she writes about, striving daily for goal achievement, productive teamwork, and integrity. Sarah is a co-author on the *Keys to Success* series, including *Keys to College Success, Keys to Community College Success, Keys to College Success Compact, Keys to Effective Learning, Keys to Online Learning,* and *Keys to Success Quick*. Sarah presents workshops and trainings on student success topics such as critical thinking, risk and reward, and time management at schools all over the country. Having attended the University of Virginia as a Jefferson Scholar, she continues to manifest the Jefferson Scholars Program goals of leadership, scholarship, and citizenship with her efforts to empower college students to succeed in school and in all aspects of their lives.

Peter J. Maurin received his Masters Degree in Sociology from McMaster University in 1992, his Honours BA from Brock University in 1989, and his Diploma in Radio and Television Arts from Niagara College. He has taught at Mohawk College since 1990. He has also been an instructor at Brock University, Niagara College, and Seneca College. He is a strong advocate of blended learning and online collaboration. In 2013, Peter was honoured to receive both the Mohawk College President's Award for Excellence and the Mohawk College Award for Excellence.

Peter has been an author for Pearson Canada since 1996, co-authoring Canadian editions of both *The Media of Mass Communication* and *Keys to Success*.

In addition to his work as a freelance writer, Peter is also a broadcaster, logging over 35 years on the air for several radio stations in Ontario. He is currently the host of "Oldies Without Borders" on 101.5 The Hawk in Hamilton. It is an eclectic mix of music from all genres and interviews with singer/songwriters.

Finally, and most importantly, Peter been together since 1981 with his soul mate Kim. Together, they have two amazing children: Sonja and Josh.

MyStudentSuccessLab

Help students start strong and finish stronger.

MyStudentSuccessLab™

MyStudentSuccessLab helps students acquire the skills they need for ongoing personal and professional development. It is a learning-outcomes-based technology that helps students advance their knowledge and build critical skills for success. MyStudentSuccessLab's peer-led video interviews, interactive practice exercises, and activities foster the acquisition of academic, life, and professionalism skills.

Students have access to

- Pre- and Post-Full Course Diagnostic Assessments linked to key learning objectives

- Pre and Post # Tests dedicated to individual topics in the Learning Path

- An overview of objectives to build vocabulary and repetition

- Videos on key issues that are "by students, for students," conveniently organized by topic

- Practice exercises to improve class prep and learning

- Graded activities to build critical-thinking and problem-solving skills

- Student resources, including Finish Strong 24/7 YouTube videos, professionalism tools, research aids, writing help, and GPA, savings, budgeting, and retirement calculators

- Student inventories designed to increase self-awareness, including Golden Personality and Thinking Styles

Students using MyStudentSuccessLab may purchase a Pearson text or etext. Contact your Pearson representative for more information about these options as well as custom opportunities.

Topics and features include

- Post-Secondary Transition
- Communication
- Critical Thinking
- Financial Literacy
- Goal Setting
- Information Literacy
- Interviewing
- Job Search Strategies
- Learning Preferences
- Listening and Taking Notes in Class
- Majors/Careers and Resumes
- Memory and Studying
- Problem Solving
- Reading and Annotating
- Self-Management Skills at Work
- Stress Management
- Teamwork
- Test Taking
- Time Management
- Workplace Communication
- Workplace Etiquette

Assessment

Beyond the Pre- and Post-Full Course Diagnostic Assessments and Pre and Post # Tests within each module, additional learning-outcome-based tests can be created using a secure testing engine, and may be printed or delivered online. These tests can be customized to accommodate specific teaching needs by editing individual questions or entire tests.

Reporting

Measurement matters—and is ongoing in nature. MyStudentSuccessLab lets you determine what data you need, set up your course accordingly, and collect data via reports. The high quality and volume of test questions allows for data comparison and measurement.

Content and Functionality Training

Organized by topic, the Instructor Implementation Guide provides grading rubrics, suggestions for video use, and more to save time on course prep. Our User Guide and "How do I..." YouTube videos indicate how to use MyStudentSuccessLab, and show scenarios from getting started to utilizing the Gradebook.

Peer Support

The Student Success Community site is a place for you to connect with other educators to exchange ideas and advice on courses, content, and MyStudentSuccessLab. The site is filled with timely articles, discussions, video posts, and more. Join, share, and be inspired!

www.mystudentsuccesscommunity.com

The Faculty Advisor Network is Pearson's peer-to-peer mentoring program in which experienced MyStudentSuccessLab users share their best practices and expertise. Our Faculty Advisors are experienced in one-on-one phone and email coaching, webinars, presentations, and live training sessions. Contact your Pearson representative to connect with a Faculty Advisor or learn more about the Faculty Advisor Network.

Integration and Compliance

You can integrate our digital solutions with your learning management system in a variety of ways. For more information, or if documentation is needed for ADA compliance, contact your local Pearson representative.

1

Cable Risdon Photography

As a post-secondary student, your willingness to take targeted, productive risks will move you toward your desired reward – the achievement of the goals that spell "success" to you.

The Rewards of Post-Secondary Education

TAKING RISKS THAT MOVE YOU TOWARD SUCCESS

What Would You Risk? *Dr. Jeremy Estrada, cardiologist*

THINK ABOUT THIS SITUATION AS YOU READ, AND CONSIDER WHAT ACTION YOU WOULD TAKE. THIS CHAPTER JUMP-STARTS YOUR ENTRY INTO THE POST-SECONDARY EXPERIENCE WITH INFORMATION ON HOW TO MAKE THE TRANSITION AND GATHER THE INGREDIENTS FOR SUCCESS.

Cable Risdon Photography

Jeremy Estrada's childhood was defined by challenges. His parents separated when he was 10, and his neighbourhood was dominated by gang culture. He grew close to an older boy named Rudy, who belonged to one of the local gangs. One day as he and Rudy walked down the street, members of a rival gang drove up, jumped out of the car, and fatally stabbed Rudy on the spot. Jeremy, age 12 at the time, could only hold his best friend and watch him die.

This experience unleashed rage in Jeremy that he was unable to control. He joined the gang that Rudy had belonged to and participated in gang violence. He was repeatedly arrested for assault and battery. He went through several stints in juvenile hall and probation, eventually living in a group home for over a year. However, none of these interventions kept him from continuing to act violently on behalf of the gang.

When his stepmother discovered his gun and called the police, she disrupted Jeremy's plan to avenge the deaths of several fellow gang members. After two weeks of hiding out, he risked going to the police of his own volition. This time the intervention was different. He went to a program called Rite of Passage in the heart of the Nevada desert, where he found encouragement and motivation. A devoted teacher who worked with him sparked a desire to learn that led to his earning a high school diploma, and a counsellor helped him apply to college. He was admitted to college and started classes two days after leaving Rite of Passage. Now a new challenge loomed: How could Jeremy, a former gang member with a history of failure and violence, earn the reward of a successful college career?

To be continued . . .

In this text, you will meet people like Jeremy, who have taken risks that have helped them achieve important goals. Whether you have something in common with these people or not, they will expand your perspective and inspire you to move ahead on your own path. You'll learn more about Jeremy, and the reward resulting from his actions, within the chapter.

Notes

Today   Mar 10 8:01 AM

Working through this chapter will help you to:

statusCHECK

How Prepared Are You For Post-Secondary Life?

For each statement, circle the number that feels right to you, from 1 for "not at all true for me" to 5 for "very true for me."

1. I feel ready to handle post-secondary level work. ① ② ③ ④ ⑤
2. I can identify how post-secondary culture differs from high school and the workplace. ① ② ③ ④ ⑤
3. I am aware of what it takes to succeed in today's technology-driven, ever-changing workplace. ① ② ③ ④ ⑤
4. I believe my intelligence can increase as a result of my effort. ① ② ③ ④ ⑤
5. I use a combination of analytical, creative, and practical thinking to reach a goal. ① ② ③ ④ ⑤
6. I believe that success demands hard work and practice no matter what my talents are. ① ② ③ ④ ⑤
7. I can explain the value of acting with academic integrity in my post-secondary career. ① ② ③ ④ ⑤
8. I am able to perceive my own emotions accurately as well as those of others. ① ② ③ ④ ⑤
9. I relate effectively to others and can work successfully in a team. ① ② ③ ④ ⑤
10. I know that I will need to learn throughout my life to succeed in the workplace. ① ② ③ ④ ⑤

Each of the topics in these statements is covered in this chapter. Note the statements for which you circled a 3 or lower. Skim the chapter to see where those topics appear, and pay special attention to them as you read, learn, and apply new strategies.

REMEMBER: NO MATTER HOW PREPARED YOU ARE TO SUCCEED IN COLLEGE OR UNIVERSITY, YOU CAN IMPROVE WITH EFFORT AND PRACTICE.

WHY IS POST-SECONDARY EDUCATION A RISK, AND *what reward does it offer?*

Think about the word *risk*. What, specifically, comes to mind? There are two different ways to think about risk. One involves risky behaviour—impulsive decisions made with little or no forethought—such as substance abuse, unsafe sex, or breaking the law. The other concept is one of deliberate risk calculated to bring reward. Examples of this kind of productive risk include buying shares of stock in a new company or putting together a business plan for a new catering business that allows you to use your love of baking. This is the concept of risk that will take focus in this text, the one that will give you the power to achieve the rewards that are meaningful to you.

Post-secondary education is often seen as anti-risk, a safe choice that increases your chances of career stability. However, striving for a degree or diploma in higher education is one of the most potentially rewarding risks of your lifetime. To follow this path, you risk your most valuable resources—time, money, and yourself. You have dedicated time to learning and self-improvement. You, and anyone helping to finance your education, have committed a significant amount of money. And you have signed up

student PROFILE

Olivia Daub

UNIVERSITY OF WATERLOO,
WATERLOO, ONTARIO

About me:

I am a second-year university student at the University of Waterloo, double majoring in Psychology and English. I love working with kids, and my (current) goal for after I complete my bachelor's is to get my master's in Speech Pathology. I love to change my mind though, so who knows where I'll end up after university!

What I focus on:

I try to focus on the end of the four years, as a motivation to continue at Waterloo in my particular program. First year was frustrating because the courses were so general, and I had to take a number of breadth courses that weren't specialized. Around the mid-term point of first semester, I was wondering whether university was right for me, and whether I should transfer into something more specific, such as an Early Childhood Education program at a community college. I managed to pull through, and I chose to stay at Waterloo because I know at the end of it all my B.A. will give me more options and lead to many different career or education paths. College might be a path I explore down the road.

What will help me in the workplace:

My advice for future students is to learn time management. Know when things are due and how long you'll need to complete the assignments or study for a test. First term, I missed a lot of fun things because of either school work or my part-time job. Second term, I planned to give myself enough time for assignments, while still having a flexible enough schedule that if something came up with friends, I wouldn't miss out. This ability to balance life and work is a skill everyone will need to master.

your mind and body for years of responsibilities and challenges. It is a perfect example of a targeted risk, calculated to produce reward down the line.

Well then, why take calculated risks? Why not save your money, time, and effort? Because only with productive risk-taking (not risky behaviour) come the rewards essential to your success. Skills, intelligence, motivation, employment, growth, and advancement can be yours, but only as a result of hard work, dedication, and focus.

This text and your course are part of an experience this term that will

- show you the value of deliberate risk-taking in your day-to-day life
- allow you to discover more about how you learn and what rewards you seek
- build academic skills as well as transferable life skills
- help you set and risk pursuing your most important goals
- increase your ability to relate effectively to others and work in teams

When a high jumper or pole vaulter gets over a bar of a certain height, someone raises the bar so that the athlete can work toward a new goal. The post-secondary experience will "raise the bar" for you, with tougher instructors, demanding coursework, and fellow students whose sights are set high. You, too, can risk raising the bar, aiming for the potential rewards of jumping over it. There is potential for improvement in every life—think about how and what *you* want to improve. You don't have to have experienced brutality as a gang member, as Jeremy did, to want to make changes for the better.

First, however, begin your transition to this next stage of your life by looking at the present—the post-secondary culture, what you can expect, and what college or university expects of you. Then, consider the future—what a post-secondary education means for you in the workplace and life.

The Culture of Post-Secondary Education

Whatever your age or stage of life, knowing what to expect will help you transition more successfully. You are likely to experience most or all of the following aspects of post-secondary culture. (Spend some time with your school's student handbook to get informed about details specific to your school.)

Independent learning

Post-secondary education offers you the chance to learn with a great deal of freedom and independence. In exchange, though, instructors expect you to function without much guidance. Kirsten Somers, an academic advisor at Dalhousie University in Halifax, says, "The biggest difference is that learning is really your responsibility. That's a huge culture shift from high school. The classes are bigger; there's less class time than you're used to; and there's more independent work that needs to happen."[1] This culture requires strong self-management skills. You are expected to make the following—and more—happen on your own:

- Use syllabi or learning plans to create, and follow, a schedule for the term (see Quick Start to College and University)
- Navigate course materials electronically (if your school uses an online course management system such as Blackboard, D2L, or WebCT)
- Get to class on time with the materials you need
- Complete text and other reading with little to no in-class review of the reading
- Set up and attend study group meetings
- Turn in projects and coursework on time and be prepared for exams
- Seek help when you need it

Fast pace and increased workload

The pace of each course is typically twice as fast as high school courses and requires more papers, homework, reading, and projects. Although demanding, learning at this speed can also energize and motivate you, especially if you did not feel inspired by high school assignments. The heavy, fast-paced workload demands more study time. For each hour spent in class, plan two to three hours of study and work time outside of class. For example, if you are in class for nine hours a week, you need to spend at least twice that number each week studying and working outside of class time.

Challenging work

Although challenging, post-secondary academic work offers an enormous opportunity to learn and grow. College and university texts often have more words per page, higher-level terminology, and more abstract ideas compared to high school texts. In addition to difficult reading, post-secondary education often involves complex assignments, challenging research papers, group projects, lab work, and tests.

TIPS FOR LEARNING ONLINE

- *Be proactive.* Be sure you get any access codes or passwords for your Learning Management System (LMS) early in the term. Save them in a safe place. Once you have access to the online material, ensure that your browser is compatible and you have any plug-ins that you need. If something isn't working, contact your school's helpdesk.

- *Kick the tires.* Once you're connected, review the course material provided by your instructor. This material will include the course outline, online resources, and the learning plan. Make note of due dates for any online quizzes or chats. Just as in a traditional classroom setting, it's your responsibility to meet all online deadlines.

- *Ask for help if you need it.* Online learning is different from the traditional classroom. Don't be afraid to ask for help, whether you're asking the instructor or a teaching assistant. If you have a question or encounter a problem, the sooner you ask for help or clarification, the better off you will be.

More out-of-class time to manage

The freedom of your schedule requires strong time-management skills. On days when your classes end early, start late, or don't meet at all, you will need to use the open blocks of time effectively as you juggle other responsibilities, including perhaps a job and family.

Diverse culture

As Canada is multicultural, you will encounter different ideas and diverse people at university and college. Your fellow students may differ from you in age, life experience, ethnicity, political mindset, family obligations, values, and much more. Also, if you commute to school or attend class with others who do, you may find it challenging to connect with others.

Higher-level thinking

You'll be asked to move far beyond recall in college and university. Instead of just summarizing and taking the ideas of others at face value, you will interpret, evaluate, generate new ideas, and apply what you know to new situations (more on thinking skills later in this chapter).

You are not alone as you adjust. Look for support resources, including instructors, academic advisors, mentors, other students, or tutors; technology such as the Internet, library search engines, and electronic planning aids; and this book. (See Quick Start to College and University for more information on resources.) And to give meaning to your efforts in college or university, consider how your efforts will serve you in the workplace.

DIGITAL REVOLUTION
The change in how people communicate brought on by developments in computer systems.

KNOWLEDGE WORK
Work that is primarily concerned with information rather than manual labour.

College and University Prepare You for the Modern Workplace

Although this is likely to be one of your first courses, it can lay the foundation for career exploration and workplace skill development. You will learn to distinguish yourself in a global marketplace, in which North American workers often compete with workers from other countries. Thomas Friedman, author of *The World Is Flat*, explains how the **digital revolution** has transformed the working environment you will enter after your post-secondary education:

> It is now possible for more people than ever to collaborate and compete in real time with more other people on more different kinds of work from more different corners of the planet and on a more equal footing than in any previous time in the history of the world—using computers, e-mail, networks, teleconferencing, and dynamic new software.[2]

These developments in communication, combined with an enormous increase in **knowledge work**, such as Internet technology, and a decrease in labour-based work, such as factory jobs, mean that you may compete for information-based jobs with highly trained and motivated people from around the globe. The working world, too, has raised the bar.

What can help you achieve career goals in this new "flat" world?

Post-secondary education

As indicated in Key 1.1, statistics show that completing some level of post-secondary education increases your chances of finding and keeping a highly skilled, well-paying job. According to Human Resources and Skills Development Canada, "The benefits of learning and higher education levels include higher earnings and lower unemployment

Leah-Anne Thompson/Shutterstock

5

KEY 1.1 Education and income.

Statistics Canada compared the annual incomes of high school grads with college and university grads between 1991 and 2010. Their study, "An Investment of a Lifetime? The Long-Term Labour Market Premiums Associated with a Postsecondary Education," suggests that the more education you have, the more likely you are to make more money. For example, during that 20-year time frame:

- Men with a high school diploma: $975,000
- Men with a college diploma: $1,222,000
- Men with a university degree: $1,707,000

Meanwhile:

- Women with a high school diploma: $525,000
- Women with a college diploma: $704,000
- Women with a university degree: $973,000

In addition to better income, the study also says that individuals with post-secondary education were also less likely to be laid off.

Source: The Long Term Labour Market Premiums Associated with a Postsecondary Education. http://www.statcan.gc.ca/daily-quotidien/140227/dq140227c-eng.htm. Statistics Canada.

risks, both of which contribute to individuals' and families' financial security." In simple terms, this means not only more money per week, but also the ability to save more money and generate more retirement income.[3]

21st century skills

Taking a careful look at what the current workplace demands of workers and what it rewards, education and business leaders have founded an organization called the Partnership for 21st Century Skills. Together, these leaders developed the Framework for 21st Century Learning shown in Key 1.2, delineating the categories of knowledge and skills that successful workers need to acquire.

KEY 1.2 The framework for 21st century learning shows what you need to succeed.

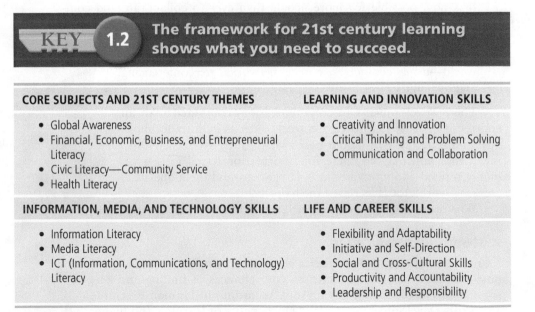

CORE SUBJECTS AND 21ST CENTURY THEMES

- Global Awareness
- Financial, Economic, Business, and Entrepreneurial Literacy
- Civic Literacy—Community Service
- Health Literacy

LEARNING AND INNOVATION SKILLS

- Creativity and Innovation
- Critical Thinking and Problem Solving
- Communication and Collaboration

INFORMATION, MEDIA, AND TECHNOLOGY SKILLS

- Information Literacy
- Media Literacy
- ICT (Information, Communications, and Technology) Literacy

LIFE AND CAREER SKILLS

- Flexibility and Adaptability
- Initiative and Self-Direction
- Social and Cross-Cultural Skills
- Productivity and Accountability
- Leadership and Responsibility

Source: Adapted from Partnership for 21st Century Skills Framework, www.p21.org/index.php?option=comcontent&task=view&id=254&Itemid=120.

TABLE 1.1 Employability skills 2000+

The skills you need to enter, stay in, and progress in the world of work—whether you work on your own or as a part of a team.

These skills can also be applied and used beyond the workplace in a range of daily activities.

Fundamental Skills	Personal Management Skills	Teamwork Skills
The skills needed as a base for further development	The personal skills, attitudes, and behaviours that drive one's potential for growth	The skills and attributes needed to contribute productively

You will be better prepared to progress in the world of work when you can:	*You will be able to offer yourself greater possibilities for achievement when you can:*	*You will be better prepared to add value to the outcomes of a task, project, or team when you can:*

Communicate
- read and understand information presented in a variety of forms (e. g., words, graphs, charts, diagrams)
- write and speak so others pay attention and understand
- listen and ask questions to understand and appreciate the points of view of others
- share information using a range of information and communications technologies (e. g., voice, e- mail, computers)
- use relevant scientific, technological, and mathematical knowledge and skills to explain or clarify ideas

Manage Information
- locate, gather, and organize information using appropriate technology and information systems
- access, analyze, and apply knowledge and skills from various disciplines (e. g., the arts, languages, science, technology, mathematics, social sciences, and the humanities)

Use Numbers
- decide what needs to be measured or calculated
- observe and record data using appropriate methods, tools, and technology
- make estimates and verify calculations

Think & Solve Problems
- assess situations and identify problems
- seek different points of view and evaluate them based on facts
- recognize the human, interpersonal, technical, scientific, and mathematical dimensions of a problem
- identify the root cause of a problem
- be creative and innovative in exploring possible solutions
- readily use science, technology, and mathematics as ways to think, gain, and share knowledge, solve problems, and make decisions
- evaluate solutions to make recommendations or decisions
- implement solutions
- check to see if a solution works, and act on opportunities for improvement

Demonstrate Positive Attitudes & Behaviours
- feel good about yourself and be confident
- deal with people, problems, and situations with honesty, integrity, and personal ethics
- recognize your own and other people's good efforts
- take care of your personal health
- show interest, initiative, and effort

Be Responsible
- set goals and priorities balancing work and personal life
- plan and manage time, money, and other resources to achieve goals
- assess, weigh, and manage risk
- be accountable for your actions and the actions of your group
- be socially responsible and contribute to your community

Be Adaptable
- work independently or as a part of a team
- carry out multiple tasks or projects
- be innovative and resourceful: identify and suggest alternative ways to achieve goals and get the job done
- be open and respond constructively to change
- learn from your mistakes and accept feedback
- cope with uncertainty

Learn Continuously
- be willing to learn and grow continuously
- assess personal strengths and areas for development
- set your own learning goals
- identify and access learning sources and opportunities
- plan for and achieve your learning goals

Work Safely
- be aware of personal and group health and safety practices and procedures, and act in accordance with these

Work with Others
- understand and work within the dynamics of a group
- ensure that a team's purpose and objectives are clear
- be flexible: respect and be open to and supportive of the thoughts, opinions, and contributions of others in a group
- recognize and respect people's diversity, individual differences, and perspectives
- accept and provide feedback in a constructive and considerate manner
- contribute to a team by sharing information and expertise
- lead or support when appropriate, motivating a group for high performance
- understand the role of conflict in a group to reach solutions
- manage and resolve conflict when appropriate

Participate in Projects & Tasks
- plan, design, or carry out a project or task from start to finish with well defined objectives and outcomes
- develop a plan, seek feedback, test, revise, and implement
- work to agreed quality standards and specifications
- select and use appropriate tools and technology for a task or project
- adapt to changing requirements and information
- continuously monitor the success of a project or task and identify ways to improve

255 Smyth Road, Ottawa
ON K1H 8M7 Canada
Tel. (613) 526-3280
Fax (613) 526-4857
Internet: www. conferenceboard. ca/nbec

lightpoet/Shutterstock

Getting through the day-to-day activities of college or university demands basic computer know-how as well as an understanding of the school's research and communication technology.

Looking at this framework, you will see that success in today's workplace requires more than just knowing skills specific to an academic area or job. Author Daniel Pink argues that the ability to create, interact interpersonally, generate ideas, and lead diverse teams—skills all found in the Framework for 21st Century Learning—will be more and more important in the workplace. Because coursework traditionally focuses more on logical and analytical skills, building your interpersonal and creative skill set will require personal initiative from you. Often, these skills can be developed through in-class collaboration and teamwork as well as volunteer work, internships, and jobs.[4]

These themes are also reflected by the CMEC (Council of Ministers of Education, Canada), a think tank of ministers of education from Canada's provinces and territories. In *Learn Canada 2020*, it states that there is a "direct link between a well-educated population and . . . a vibrant, knowledge-based economy in the 21st century, . . . a socially progressive, sustainable society, and . . . enhanced personal growth opportunities for all Canadians."[5]

This book will frequently refer to the Employability Skills 2000+ Profile developed by The Conference Board of Canada. It is a research organization whose members include Canadian corporations and the government. "Employability Skills" are defined as "the skills you need to enter, stay in and progress in the world of work—whether you want to work on your own or as part of a team."[6] Many Canadian companies helped to determine which skills were essential. These were broken down into three categories: fundamental skills, personal management skills, and teamwork skills (Table 1.1). This book will put skills learned in the classroom into the broader context of developing your employability skills.

As you read the content and complete the exercises in this seventh Canadian edition of *Keys to Success*, you will develop your skills. In fact, the three thinking skills that this book focuses on—analytical, creative, and practical—are all included within the framework. These three thinking skills will help you achieve your most important goals because they are critical to delivering what the world needs workers to do.

HOW CAN SUCCESSFUL INTELLIGENCE
help you achieve your goals?

How do you define *intelligence*? Is an intelligent person someone who excels in high-level analytical courses? A successful professional in science or law? Or a person who scores well on standardized tests such as IQ (intelligence quotient) tests? The idea of using an IQ test to gauge intelligence and predict success is based on the belief that each person is born with a fixed amount of intelligence that can be measured. However, cutting-edge researchers such as Robert Sternberg and Carol Dweck have challenged these ideas.[7]

When test anxiety caused Sternberg (a psychologist and dean of students at Tufts University) to score poorly on IQ and other standardized tests during elementary school, he delivered what was expected of him—very little. However, his fourth-grade teacher turned his life around when she expected more. Sternberg has conducted extensive research supporting his sense that traditional intelligence measurements lock people into poor performance and often do not reflect their potential.[8]

Stanford psychologist Carol Dweck also had a life-changing experience when, as a young researcher, she conducted an experiment to see how elementary school children coped with failure. She gave students a set of puzzles that grew increasingly difficult. To her surprise, certain students welcomed the tough puzzles and saw failure as an opportunity. "They knew that human qualities, such as intellectual skills, could be cultivated through effort. And that's what they were doing—getting smarter. Not only weren't they discouraged by failure, they didn't even think they were failing. They thought they were learning."[9] Dweck's research since then has focused on the potential for increasing intelligence and the attitude that fosters that potential (more on that attitude later in the chapter).

The research of Sternberg, Dweck, and others suggests that intelligence is not fixed; people have the capacity to increase intelligence. In other words, *the risk of effort and focus can produce the reward of greater brain power.* Recent brain research shows that when you are learning, your brain and nerve cells (neurons) are forming new connections (synapses) from cell to cell by growing new branches (dendrites).[10] These increased connections then enable the brain to do and learn more.

The Three Thinking Skills

How can you take productive risks that move you toward your important goals in your school, work, and life? According to Sternberg, it takes three types of thinking: analytical (critical), creative, and practical. He calls this combination *successful intelligence*,[11] and he illustrates it with a story.

Two boys are walking in a forest. They are quite different. The first boy's teachers think he is smart; his parents think he is smart; and as a result, he thinks he is smart. He has good test scores, good grades, and other good paper credentials that will get him far in his scholastic life.

Few people consider the second boy smart. His test scores are nothing great; his grades aren't so good; and his other paper credentials are, in general, marginal. At best, people would call him shrewd or street smart.

As the two boys walk along in the forest, they encounter a problem—a huge, furious, hungry-looking grizzly bear, charging straight at them. The first boy, calculating that the grizzly bear will overtake them in 17.3 seconds, panics. In this state, he looks at the second boy, who is calmly taking off his hiking boots and putting on his jogging shoes.

The first boy says to the second boy, "You must be crazy. There is no way you are going to outrun that grizzly bear!"

The second boy replies, "That's true. But all I have to do is outrun you!"[12]

This story shows that successful goal achievement and problem solving require more than book smarts. When confronted with a problem, the first boy, who used only analytical thinking, was at a disadvantage. On the contrary, the second boy *analyzed* the situation, *created* options, and took practical *action*. He knew his goal—to live to tell the tale—and he achieved it.

How Thinking Skills Move You Toward Your Goals

Sternberg explains that although those who score well on tests display strong recall and analytical skills, they are not necessarily able to put their knowledge to work.[13] No matter how high you score on a library science test, for example, as a librarian you will also need to be able to devise useful keyword searches (creative thinking) and communicate effectively with patrons and other librarians (practical thinking). Of course, having *only* practical street smarts isn't enough either. Neither boy in the bear story, if rushed to the hospital with injuries sustained in a showdown with the bear, would want to be treated by someone lacking in analytical skills.

What do each of the three thinking skills contribute to goal achievement?

Andrey Popov/Shutterstock

get analytical

DEFINE YOUR "COLLEGE/UNIVERSITY SELF"

Complete the following on paper or in digital format.

When you understand who you are as a student, you will be more able to seek out the support that will propel you toward your goals. Using the following questions as a starting point, analyze your "college/university self." Write and save your description to revisit later in the course.

- What is your student status—traditional or returning, full- or part-time?
- How long are you planning to be at your current school? Is it likely that you will transfer?
- What goal, or goals, do you aim to achieve by going to college or university?
- What family and work obligations do you have?
- What is your culture, ethnicity, gender, age, lifestyle?
- What is your current living situation?
- What do you feel are your biggest challenges in college/university?
- What do you like to study, and why does it interest you?

Analytical thinking

Commonly known as critical thinking, analytical thinking starts by engaging with information through asking questions and then proceeds to analyzing and evaluating information, often to work through a problem or decision. It often involves comparing, contrasting, and cause-and-effect thinking.

Creative thinking

Creative thinking concerns generating new and different ideas and approaches to problems and, often, viewing the world in ways that disregard convention. It often involves imagining and considering different perspectives. Creative thinking also means taking information that you already know and thinking about it in a new way.

Practical thinking

Practical thinking refers to putting what you've learned into action to solve a problem or make a decision. Practical thinking often means learning from experience and emotional intelligence (explained later in the chapter), enabling you to work effectively with others and to accomplish goals despite obstacles.

Together, these abilities move you toward a goal, as Sternberg explains:

Analytical thinking is required to solve problems and to judge the quality of ideas. Creative intelligence is required to formulate good problems and ideas in the first place. Practical intelligence is needed to use the ideas and their analysis in an effective way in one's everyday life.[14]

The following example illustrates how this works.

The goal-achieving thinking skills of Jeremy Estrada

- He **analyzed** his situation when hiding out from the police and determined that he would experience more reward from the risk of turning himself in.

Action Plan:
①
②
③

JohnKwan/Shutterstock

get $mart

ORGANIZE YOUR FINANCES

PhotoMan/Fotolia

Avoid discovering that stack of bills, statements, and receipts at mid-term time. Set yourself up to stay aware and in control of your day-to-day financial activities:

1. Find a place to store financial paperwork—perhaps a file drawer or filing box—and set up folders for each category (bank statements, tuition/financial aid, paid bills, and so on).

2. If you want to pay some or all of your bills online, set up online payments with those accounts. If you can choose due dates, cluster your due dates together at the same time of the month so you can pay bills all at once.

3. Make sure that you are set up to stay on top of tuition payments and financial aid responsibilities. Note payment or financial aid filing deadlines in your planner, phone calendar, or online calendar. Consider setting smartphone reminders and alarms.

- He **created** a vision of himself as a high school graduate and college student.
- He took **practical action** to get help from teachers and counsellors and risked time and effort to earn his high school diploma and apply for college.

Why is developing successful intelligence so important to your success?

1. *It improves understanding and achievement, increasing your value in school and on the job.* People with critical, creative, and practical thinking skills are in demand because they can apply what they know to new situations, innovate, and accomplish their goals.

2. *It boosts your motivation.* Because successful intelligence helps you understand how learning propels you toward goals and gives you ways to move toward those goals, it increases your willingness to work.

3. *It shows you where you can grow.* Students who have trouble with tests and other analytical skills can see the role that creative and practical thinking play. Students who test well but have trouble innovating or taking action can improve their creative and practical skills.

Although thinking skills provide tools with which you can achieve post-secondary education and life goals, you need **motivation** to put them to work and grow from your efforts. Explore a mindset that will motivate you to vault over that bar (and then set a higher one).

MOTIVATION
A goal-directed force that moves a person to action.

HOW CAN A GROWTH MINDSET

motivate you to persist?

Different people have different forces or *motivators*—grades, love of a subject, the drive to earn a degree—that encourage them to keep pushing ahead. Motivators can change with time and situations. Your motivation can have either an external or internal *locus of control*—meaning that you are motivated either by external factors (your parents, circumstances, luck, grades, instructors' feedback, and so on) or internal factors (values and attitudes).

11

Often, you will be motivated by some combination of external and internal factors, but internal motivation may have a greater influence on success. Why? Although you cannot control what happens around you, you *can* control your attitude, or *mindset*, and the actions that come from that mindset. Based on years of research, Carol Dweck has determined that the perception that talent and intelligence can develop with effort—what she calls a *growth mindset*—promotes success. "This view creates a love of learning and resilience that is essential for great accomplishment," reports Dweck.[15] By contrast, people with a *fixed mindset* believe that they have a set level of talent and intelligence. They think their ability to succeed matches what they've been born with, and they tend to resist effort. "In one world [that of the fixed mindset], effort is a bad thing. It . . . means you're not smart or talented. If you were, you wouldn't need effort. In the other world [growth mindset], effort is what *makes* you smart or talented."[16]

For example, two students do poorly on an anatomy mid-term. One blames the time of day of the test and her dislike of the subject, whereas the other feels that she didn't study enough. The first student couldn't change the subject or meeting time, of course, and didn't change her approach to the material (no extra effort). As you may expect, she did poorly on the final. The second student put in more study time after the mid-term (increased, focused effort) and improved her grade on the final as a result. This student knows that "smart is as smart does."

You don't have to be born with a growth mindset. *You can build one.* "You have a choice," says Dweck. "Mindsets are just beliefs. They're powerful beliefs, but they're just something in your mind, and you can change your mind."[17] One way to change your mind is through specific actions that demonstrate your beliefs. Actions that may help you change your mind include being responsible, practising academic integrity, and facing adversity with optimism.

Build Self-Esteem with Responsible Actions

You may think that you need to have a strong sense of self-esteem to take action toward your goals. In fact, the reverse is true. Taking responsible action builds strong self-esteem because it gives you something to be proud of. Your actions change your thinking. Basketball coach Rick Pitino explains, "If you have established a great work ethic and have begun the discipline that is inherent with that, you will automatically begin to feel better about yourself."[18]

SELF-ESTEEM
Belief in your value as a person that builds as you achieve your goals.

A growth mindset helps you build self-esteem because it encourages you to put forth effort. If you know you have the potential to do better, you will be more likely to try. A research study of employees taking a course in computer training supports this idea. Half the participants were told their success in the course depended on innate ability. That group lost confidence in themselves by the end of the course. In contrast, the other half, who were told their skills could develop through practice, reported *more* confidence after they had completed the same course though they made, in many cases, the same mistakes as the other group.[19]

ACADEMIC INTEGRITY
Following a code of moral values in all aspects of academic life—classes, assignments, tests, papers, projects, and relationships with students and faculty.

Even simple responsible actions can build the foundation for powerful self-esteem. What actions will you take to build your confidence? Consider using Key 1.3 as a starting point for ideas. Taking daily responsible actions such as these will help you succeed in any course. Your efforts will enable you to grow no matter what your starting point.

Practise Academic Integrity

Having academic integrity means valuing learning and ensures an education based on *ethics* (your sense of what is right to do) and hard work. Find your school's code of honour or academic integrity policy in your student handbook, on your school's website, or in your syllabus. Read it thoroughly so you know exactly what it asks of you. When you enrolled, you agreed to abide by it.

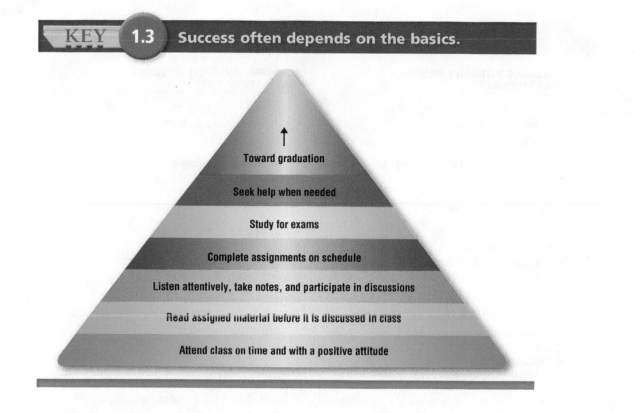

KEY 1.3 Success often depends on the basics.

↑ Toward graduation

Seek help when needed

Study for exams

Complete assignments on schedule

Listen attentively, take notes, and participate in discussions

Read assigned material before it is discussed in class

Attend class on time and with a positive attitude

The International Center for Academic Integrity (ICAI) defines *academic integrity* as a commitment to five fundamental values:[20]

- *Honesty.* Honesty defines the pursuit of knowledge and implies a search for truth in your classwork, papers, and lab reports, and teamwork with other students.
- *Trust.* Trust means being true to your word. Mutual trust—between instructor and student, as well as among students—makes the exchange of ideas possible.
- *Fairness.* Instructors must create a fair academic environment where students are judged against clear standards and in which procedures are well defined.
- *Respect.* In a respectful academic environment, both students and instructors accept and honour a wide range of opinions, even if the opinions are contrary to core beliefs.
- *Responsibility.* You are responsible for making choices that will provide you with the best education—choices that should reflect fairness and honesty.

Notice that students are not the only ones who need to act with integrity. Bill Taylor, Emeritus Professor of Political Science at Oakton Community College in Des Plaines, IL, wrote a letter to his students explaining that academic integrity makes requirements of both students and instructors, and that these requirements are in five distinct areas, as detailed in Key 1.4.[21]

The role of electronic materials

With a few clicks of a mouse, any amount of digitized text can be instantly copied and pasted into a document that a student is creating for an assignment. Furthermore, the availability of electronic information has led many students to believe that it has no author and is free to use without citation.[22] As a result of these technological developments, plagiarism has become more prevalent in recent years.

In this environment, it's easy to plagiarize without even knowing it by copying, for example, something from a web site that doesn't list an author and forgetting to go back and determine the source of the material. However, the fact that technology makes

PLAGIARISM
Using another writer's words, content, unique approach, or illustrations without crediting the author.

KEY 1.4 Academic integrity involves both students and instructors.

AREAS OF ACTION	ACADEMIC INTEGRITY REQUIRES THAT STUDENTS . . .	ACADEMIC INTEGRITY REQUIRES THAT INSTRUCTORS . . . .
Preparation for class	• Read assigned materials before class • Come up with questions • Be prepared to contribute	• Know the material they are teaching • Plan a class that is worth students' time
In class	• Treat instructors and other students with respect • Arrive and leave on time • Participate in discussions • Ask questions and pay attention	• Treat students with respect • Arrive and leave on time • Use class time well
With regard to exams	• Be as prepared as possible • Not use cheat sheets • Not copy or get help from another student • Not give help to another student	• Prepare students effectively • Create a fair exam • Be available to help students prepare • Grade fairly
With regard to written assignments	• Take the time you need to do good work • Hand in work that is entirely your own, not copied from another person's work or from work you've done in another course • Cite sources for ideas, facts, and excerpts completely and according to guidelines	• Clearly explain assignments • Create assignments that relate effectively to coursework • Evaluate carefully and grade fairly
With regard to your final grade	• Do your best on all aspects that are incorporated in your final grade • Consult the instructor if you feel your grade is unfair	• Weigh all aspects involved in the grade, as defined in the syllabus • Grade fairly

Source: William M. Taylor, Oakton Community College, Des Plaines, IL, "Academic Integrity: A Letter to My Students" (http://www.academicintegrity.org/educational_resources/pdf/LetterToMyStudentsRev2010.pdf).

plagiarism quick and easy does not make it acceptable. To avoid plagiarism, use this one general directive: *Do not submit as your own any words you did not write or any image you did not create.* Resources must be properly cited and either quoted (if used word-for-word) or paraphrased. The effort and attention required to follow this rule are no more than what are demanded for true learning.

Note that even as technology facilitates plagiarism, it also presents tools to detect it. Sites like Turnitin.com allow instructors to check student work for plagiarism; WriteCheck lets students do the same with their own work before submitting it.

Violations, regulations, and consequences

Violations of academic integrity include turning in previously submitted work, using unauthorized devices during an exam, providing unethical aid to another student, and downloading passages or whole papers from the Internet. When violations are found (often by computer programs designed for this purpose), consequences vary from school to school and can include academic integrity seminars, grade reduction or course failure, suspension, and expulsion.

When you enrolled, you agreed to abide by your school's code of honour or academic integrity policy. Find it in your student handbook, school website, or in your syllabus, and read it thoroughly so you know exactly what it asks of you. Measure the consequences of violating the policy against the risk of working hard to complete your degree with integrity. Which reward would you choose?

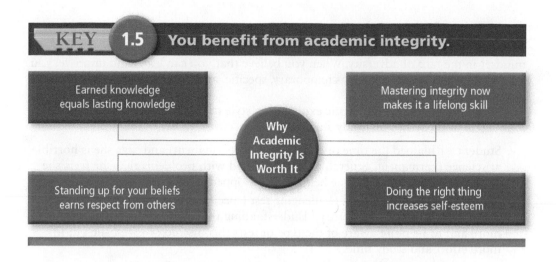

KEY 1.5 You benefit from academic integrity.

Earned knowledge equals lasting knowledge		Mastering integrity now makes it a lifelong skill
	Why Academic Integrity Is Worth It	
Standing up for your beliefs earns respect from others		Doing the right thing increases self-esteem

How academic integrity benefits you now and in the future

It may seem that a slip here and there is no big deal. However, as Professor Taylor states in his letter, "Personal integrity is … a quality of character we need to nurture, and this requires practice in both meanings of that word (as in practice the piano and practice a profession). We can only be a person of integrity if we practice it every day."[23] Finally, know that a growth mindset can help. Because academic integrity comes naturally to students who aim to grow and who see struggle and failure as opportunities to learn, maintaining a growth mindset promotes academic integrity and makes its rewards more obvious (Key 1.5).

Face Fears, Challenges, and Failures with Optimism

Every single person experiences adversity in the form of fears, challenges, and failures. Dr. Martin Seligman, a psychologist who has spent most of his career studying how and why some people persist and cope with bad things successfully while others give up and give in, has determined that optimism greatly improves one's chances for life success. He presents what he calls *learned optimism* as a skill that can be learned and used by anyone, no matter how optimistic or pessimistic a person may be naturally.[24]

Your explanatory style

Through extensive research, Dr. Seligman has determined that *explanatory style*—how you explain and think about adversity—predicts how well you are able to cope with it, learn from it, and move on. Furthermore, an optimistic explanatory style has been proven to contribute to better physical health, less depression, and more personal and professional success. Key 1.6 describes the optimistic and pessimistic sides to the three aspects of how people explain adversity.

KEY 1.6 Adversity can be explained optimistically or pessimistically.

ASPECTS OF EXPLANATORY STYLE	OPTIMISTIC PERSPECTIVE	PESSIMISTIC PERSPECTIVE
Permanence: how long the adversity will last	*Temporary:* "It's not forever; it is tough but it will pass."	*Permanent:* "It will always be like this for me."
Pervasiveness: how far ranging the effect of the adversity is	*Specific:* "This situation is bad but there are good things going on in other areas of my life."	*General:* "Every part of my life is like this. Everything is a catastrophe."
Personalization: what is to blame for the adversity	*External:* "There are some specific causes for this failure that I can examine."	*Personal:* "This is all my fault. I'm a failure."

Explanatory Style and the Growth Mindset

Using an optimistic explanatory style goes hand-in-hand with maintaining a growth mindset in the face of adversity. When you believe that you can learn and improve, you are more able to see a problem as temporary, specific, and not personal, and to manage it and move on.

How can you put an optimistic explanatory style to work for you? For an example, look again at those two anatomy students.

- Student #1 blamed the time of day of the test (permanent) and says she is horrible at science (permanent, general, personal). Faced with problems that she feels she can never change, she became helpless and stopped trying.
- Student #2 thought it was a challenging test (specific, not personal) and that she didn't study enough (temporary). Understanding that she had the power to study more and to be more aware of the type of tests this instructor gives, she put in more effort and study time.

The second student has done what an optimistic explanatory style and a growth mindset gives you the power to do—consider what you can do better, take action, and learn from the experience. Here's how you follow that lead the next time something stops you in your tracks.

- **Analyze the situation realistically.** Look carefully at the fear, challenge, or failure and what has caused it. For example, imagine that you forgot about a history paper. If your first thought is that your memory is useless, get yourself off that pessimistic path to helplessness by looking at some facts. First, you had a chemistry test on the day that the paper was due, and you spent most of that week studying for it. Second, you have not checked your calendar consistently over the week. Third, chemistry is required for an academic concentration you are considering.
- **Come up with potential actions.** You can request an appointment with the instructor to discuss the paper. You can set alarms in your planner and check due dates more regularly. Realizing that chemistry is a priority for you, you can accept that it's okay to put it first when time is short.
- **Take action and cope with consequences.** Meet with your history instructor to discuss the situation, accepting that there may be consequences for handing in your paper late. Commit to better monitoring of your planner, setting dates for individual tasks related to assignments, and trying to complete papers a day or two before they are due so you have time for last-minute corrections.

Failure approached with a growth mindset can spark motivation, showing you what you can do better and driving you to improve. Keep in mind that increased effort

Cable Risdon Photography; Shutterstock

talk risk and reward . . .

Risk asking tough questions to be rewarded with new insights. Use the following to inspire discussion with classmates, in person or online.

- Describe a dream you have that you feel is out of reach. Why does it feel impossible? Why do you still dream it? How might a growth mindset help you achieve it?
- How do you tend to respond to a challenge? Do you risk dealing with it, run away, ignore it? What tends to result from your action (or inaction)?

CONSIDER THE CASE: If you had known Jeremy Estrada in his teen years when he was a member of the gang, would you have thought that he had any hope of going to college? Moving in a new direction, for him, resulted from his stepmother's risk taking. Who believes in you, and what do they risk for you? What do they think you can achieve?

get creative

CONSIDER HOW TO CONNECT

Complete the following on paper or in digital format.

Making early connections with people and groups in your school can benefit you later on. Brainstorm how you would like to spend whatever time you have available outside of your obligations (class time, work, family). On paper or on your computer, list your ideas. Try one or more of the following questions as a starting point:

- If you had no fear of risk, what horizon-broadening experience would you sign up for?

- When you were in elementary school, what were your favourite activities? Which ones might translate into current interests and pursuits?

- What kinds of organizations, activities, groups, experiences, or people make you think, "Wow, I want to do that"?

- Think about the people that you feel bring out the best in you. What do you like to do with them? What kinds of activities are they involved with?

in the face of failure is a hallmark of successful people. Thomas Edison, one of history's most prolific inventors, and his employees tried over 3,000 different materials before finding the one they originally used as a filament in the electric bulb; his ability to see each "failure" as a step closer to the right answer enabled him to persist.

Although adversity can raise all kinds of emotional reactions, people who can manage those emotions are more likely to learn from the experience. They also demonstrate the last of this chapter's ingredients in the recipe for success—emotional intelligence.

WHY DO YOU NEED
emotional intelligence?

Success in a diverse world depends on relationships, and effective relationships demand emotional intelligence. Psychologists John Mayer, Peter Salovey, and David Caruso define *emotional intelligence* (EI) as the ability to understand "one's own and others' emotions and the ability to use this information as a guide to thinking and behavior."[25] A careful reading of this definition reveals that it isn't enough to just *understand* what you and others feel. An emotionally intelligent person uses that understanding to make choices about how to *think* and how to *act*.

In the past, and perhaps for some even today, the "head" (thought) was considered to be separate from, and perhaps more valuable than, the "heart" (emotion). However, modern science connects thought and emotion, and values both. "Emotions influence both what we think about and how we think," says Caruso. "We cannot check our emotions at the door because emotions and thought are linked—they cannot, and should not, be separated."[26]

Emotions also connect you to other people, as recent research has demonstrated. When a friend of yours is happy, sad, or fearful, you may experience similar feelings out of concern or friendship. Your brain and nervous system have cells called *mirror neurons* that mimic an observed emotion, allowing you to "participate" in the feeling even though it comes from somewhere else. An MRI brain scan would show that the

The more able you are to work and communicate with others, the more you will learn and develop teamwork skills.

same area of your friend's brain that lit up during this emotional experience lit up in your brain as well.[27]

How Emotional Intelligence Promotes Success

Two short stories illustrate the power of emotional intelligence.

- *Two applicants are competing for a job at your office.* The first applicant has every skill the job requires but doesn't respond well to your cues when you interview him. He answers questions indirectly and keeps going back to what he wants to say instead. The second applicant isn't as skilled, but you feel during the interview as though you are talking with a friend. He listens carefully, picks up on your emotional cues, and indicates that he intends to make up for any lack of skill with a willingness to learn on the job. Whom would you hire?
- *Two students are part of a group you are working with on a project.* One student always gets her share of the job done but has no patience for anyone who misses a deadline. She is quick to criticize group members. The other student is sometimes prepared, sometimes not, but always has a sense of what is going on with the group and responds to it. She works to make up for it when she hasn't gotten everything done, and when she is on top of her tasks she helps others. Which person would you want to work with again?

To be clear, skills are crucial. The most emotionally tuned-in person in the world, for example, can't perform surgery without medical training. However, the role of emotional intelligence in communication and relationships makes it a strong predictor of success in work and life, as indicated by the following conclusions of research using an assessment measuring EI.[28]

- Emotionally intelligent people are more competent in social situations and have higher quality relationships.
- Managers in the workplace with high EI have more productive working relationships and greater personal integrity.
- Employees scoring high in EI were more likely to receive both positive ratings from peers and salary raises.
- Lower levels of EI are connected to higher amounts of drug, alcohol, and tobacco use, as well as aggression and conflict in teens.

The bottom line: More emotional intelligence means stronger relationships and more goal achievement.

The Abilities of Emotional Intelligence

EI is a set of skills, or abilities, that can be described as *reasoning with emotion* (an idea illustrating how thought and emotion work together). Key 1.7 shows how you move through these skills when you reason with emotion.

EI skills allow you to create the best possible outcomes from your interactions. Given that you will interact with others in almost every aspect of school, work, and life, EI is a pretty important tool. You will see references to EI throughout the book.

How might EI fit into the rest of the skills discussed in this chapter? Think of it as *thinking skills applied to relationships.* Putting EI to work means taking in and

KEY **1.7** **Take an emotionally intelligent approach.**

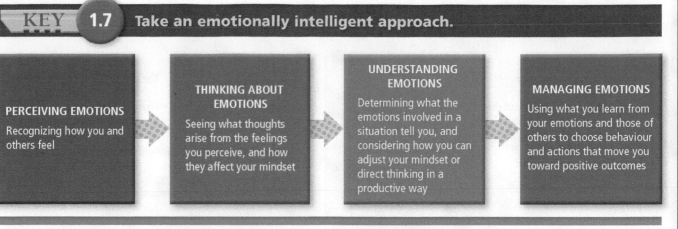

| PERCEIVING EMOTIONS | THINKING ABOUT EMOTIONS | UNDERSTANDING EMOTIONS | MANAGING EMOTIONS |

Recognizing how you and others feel → Seeing what thoughts arise from the feelings you perceive, and how they affect your mindset → Determining what the emotions involved in a situation tell you, and considering how you can adjust your mindset or direct thinking in a productive way → Using what you learn from your emotions and those of others to choose behaviour and actions that move you toward positive outcomes

Source: Adapted from John D. Mayer, Peter Salovey, and David R. Caruso, "Emotional Intelligence: New Ability or Eclectic Traits?" *American Psychologist*, 63(6), September 2008, pp. 505–507.

analyzing how you and others feel, shifting your thinking based on those feelings, and taking action in response—all with the purpose of achieving a goal.

HOW WILL YOUR WORK NOW PREPARE
you for life success?

This text is designed to help you build what you need for success in school and beyond, including thinking skills, attitudes, and emotional abilities that you can use to reach your goals. Topics will broaden your understanding, and exercises will have you putting it into action in personal and productive ways. Self-assessments and journal questions will encourage reflection. Your thinking skills will grow and transfer to any task or situation in your life.

The willingness to take calculated risks large and small is essential to your life success. You will find, threaded throughout this text, the concept of targeted, productive risk leading to a desired reward. In everything you approach in college, a reward waits in exchange for your risk.

- Risk looking confused by asking a question in class or in an online class forum for the reward of greater understanding.
- Risk the time it takes to match or exceed your abilities on a project for the reward of increased knowledge and skill (and perhaps an excellent grade).
- Risk the awkwardness of reaching out to an instructor for the reward of a relationship that can deepen your academic experience and perhaps provide career guidance.
- Risk the work required to prepare for a test rather than cheating for the reward of learning that you can use in higher-level courses or in the workplace—as well as the habit of integrity, essential for life success.
- Risk saying no to a substance or activity for the reward of greater health, even if it costs you a friend or an affiliation.
- Take a variety of day-to-day risks—speaking up in class, doing extra credit, seeking helpful resources, studying or sleeping when others are partying, setting work aside when something personal requires your energy—that earn you small but significant rewards, as well as build your risk-taking habit.

Learning for life. The signs in Key 1.8 point to the need to be a *lifelong learner*, continuing to build knowledge and skills as your career and life demand. Your work in this course will help you fulfill that need.

KEY 1.8 A changing world means learning is for life.

If you stop learning, your knowledge base will be inadequate to keep up with the changes in your career, thus affecting your marketability.

Knowledge in nearly every field is doubling every two to three years.

Technology is changing how you live and work.

The Internet and technology will shape communications and improve knowledge and productivity during the next 20 years—and will require continual learning.

In Canada and abroad, jobs are being created that ask workers to think critically to come up with solutions.

The global economy is moving from a product and service base to a knowledge and talent base.

Workers are changing jobs and careers more frequently.

Every time you decide to start a new career, you need new knowledge and skills.

revisit RISK AND REWARD

Cable Risdon Photography

What happened to Jeremy? All too aware of the consequences of falling back into anger, Jeremy risked working hard and challenged himself to sit in the front row in every class. "All the students were smarter than I was," he says, "but I worked a lot harder than they did." His work rewarded him with two years of straight A's. Jeremy completed his undergraduate degree at Pepperdine, keeping the hard work going despite failing chemistry more than once. He then earned his medical degree.

Now married, a father, and completing a fellowship in cardiology, he plans to continue taking productive risks by focusing his medical practice on disadvantaged communities similar to where he grew up.

What does this mean for you? Everyone has challenges to face with risk taking. These roadblocks can serve as opportunities to find out what you are capable of. Name a challenge or challenges that you face now. Consider what might happen if you avoid this challenge. On the other hand, consider what growth and rewards wait for you if you risk facing it with hard work. As you think the situation through, be specific about what that hard work looks like.

What risk may bring reward beyond your personal world? Part of Jeremy's mission as a successful professional is to reach out to families and young people who need him as a role model. Although you might not think of yourself as a role model, the fact that you are here, beginning your post-secondary education, says that you have something to offer. Think outside yourself and consider who looks up to you—a younger family member, a friend still in high school, someone in your neighbourhood, someone you know from an online group. Consciously act as a role model to that person. You may be surprised at how your actions can provide rewards for others.

get practical

USE EMOTIONAL INTELLIGENCE TO GET INVOLVED

Complete the following on paper or in digital format.

First, look in your student handbook at the resources and organizations your school offers. These may include some or all of the following:

Academic centres (reading, writing, and so on)	On-campus work opportunities
Academic organizations	Religious organizations
Adult education centre	School publications
Arts clubs (music, drama, dance, and so on)	School TV/radio stations
Fraternities/sororities	Sports clubs
Groups for students with disabilities	Student associations
International student groups	Student government
Minority student groups	Volunteer groups

As you read the list of possibilities, tune into your EI and take note of how different organizations or activities make you feel. What do you want to try right away . . . what makes you turn the page . . . what scares you . . . and why? Is a positive outcome possible if you try something that scares you at first?

Taking this EI feedback—as well as your analysis of yourself (Get Analytical, page 10) and your creative ideas (Get Creative, page 17)—into consideration, use the left-hand column on the chart that follows to list the three offices or organizations you plan to check out this term. Then use your school publications or online resources to fill in the next four columns of the grid. The last column requires action; fill it in when you have made contact with each office or organization. Finally, if you wish to become more involved after your initial contact, go for it.

Office or organization	Location	Hours or times of meetings	What it offers	Phone number or email	Initial contact—date and what happened

Imagine: You are sitting in class with your *growth mindset*, ready to risk and learn. You are prepared to use *analytical* and *creative* skills to examine knowledge and come up with new ideas. You are motivated to use your *practical* skills to move toward your goals. Your *emotional intelligence* has prepared you to adjust to and work with all kinds of people. The bar has been raised: Risk using *Keys to Success* to fly over it and find out just how much reward waits for you.

RISK ACTION
FOR POST-SECONDARY, CAREER, AND LIFE REWARDS

KNOW IT *Think Critically*

Activate Yourself

Robert Sternberg found that people who reach their goals successfully, despite differences in thinking and personal goals, have 20 particular characteristics in common that motivate them to grow.[29] Each of the "I" statements in the following list identifies one of the characteristics.

STEP 1 **Build basic skills.** Use this self-assessment to think about how you can get and stay motivated right now.

1	2	3	4	5
Not at All Like Me	Somewhat Unlike Me	Not Sure	Somewhat Like Me	Definitely Like Me

1. I motivate myself well.   1 2 3 4 5

2. I can control my impulses.   1 2 3 4 5

3. I know when to persevere and when to change gears.   1 2 3 4 5

4. I make the most of what I do well.   1 2 3 4 5

5. I can successfully translate my ideas into action.   1 2 3 4 5

6. I can focus effectively on my goal.   1 2 3 4 5

7. I complete tasks and have good follow-through.   1 2 3 4 5

8. I initiate action—I move people and projects ahead.   1 2 3 4 5

9. I have the courage to risk failure.   1 2 3 4 5

10. I avoid procrastination.   1 2 3 4 5

11. I accept responsibility when I make a mistake.   1 2 3 4 5

12. I don't waste time feeling sorry for myself.   1 2 3 4 5

13. I independently take responsibility for tasks.   1 2 3 4 5

14. I work hard to overcome personal difficulties.   1 2 3 4 5

15. I create an environment that helps me concentrate on my goals.   1 2 3 4 5

16. I don't take on too much work or too little.   1 2 3 4 5

17. I can delay gratification to receive the benefits.   1 2 3 4 5

18. I can see both the big picture and the details in a situation.   1 2 3 4 5

19. I am able to maintain confidence in myself.   1 2 3 4 5

20. I can balance analytical, creative, and practical thinking skills.   1 2 3 4 5

STEP 2 **Take it to the next level.** Choose five statements that focus on areas you most want to develop throughout the term. Circle or highlight them on the self-assessment. Then pretend to be an instructor recommending you for a scholarship or a job. Write a short email about how strong you are in those five areas. Save the email as a reminder of what you would like such a person to say about you.

STEP 3 **Move toward mastery.** Select one of the five statements chosen in the previous section and take action in the following ways.

1. Find the section in this book that will help you develop this ability. If you wish to procrastinate less, for example, locate the time-management information in Chapter 2.

2. Skim the book section and find one concept or strategy that catches your attention. Copy the concept or strategy onto a piece of paper or electronic file. Then, briefly describe how you plan to use it.

3. Take action in the next week based on your plan. You are on the road to growth.

In the last chapter of this book, you will revisit this self-assessment and get more specific about actions you have taken, and plan to take, to promote personal growth.

WRITE IT *Communicate*

Emotional intelligence journal: How are you feeling now? First, describe what you are feeling right now about college or university. Then, discuss what those feelings tell you about how ready you are for the experience. Last, brainstorm some actions that will help you be as prepared as possible to benefit from the experience of post-secondary education. (For example, if shyness prevents you from feeling ready to meet new people on campus, one action might be to join an organization or study group that will help you get to know people more easily.)

Real-life writing: What skills do you have now? No matter what professional goals you ultimately pursue, the skills that the 21st century workplace demands will be useful in any career area. Review The Conference Board of Canada's Employability Skills on page 7. Remind yourself of the three skill areas—and the individual skills within each category.

For each skill, write a short paragraph that contains the following elements:

- A description of your abilities in this skill area
- Specific examples, from school or work, demonstrating these abilities
- Jobs or coursework in which you have built this skill

Keep this information on hand for building your resumé. Or, if you already have a resumé, use the information to update it and to add detail that will keep your resumé current.

WORK IT *Build Your Brand*

Assess Your Successful Intelligence

A "brand" is an image or concept that people connect with a product or service. A key factor in your ability to succeed in the modern workplace is your ability to "build your brand"—identify the qualities and skills that best define you and emphasize them in how you market yourself. Seeing yourself as a product can help you work to package that product in the best possible way.

Compiling a portfolio of personal documents can help you build your brand as you work toward career exploration and planning goals. This is one of several that you may create throughout the term. Type your work and save the documents electronically in one file folder. Use loose paper so you can copy assignments that ask you to draw or make collages; also make copies of assignments that ask you to write in the text. For safekeeping, scan and save digital copies of loose or text pages to include in your portfolio file.

21st Century Learning Building Blocks

- **Initiative and self-direction**
- **Critical thinking and problem solving**

As you begin this course, use this exercise to get a big-picture look at how you perceive yourself as an analytical, creative, and practical thinker. For the statements in each of the three self-assessments, circle the number that best describes how it applies to you.

Assess Your Analytical Thinking Skills

For each statement, circle the number that feels right to you, from 1 for "not at all true for me" to 5 for "very true for me."

1. I recognize and define problems effectively.   1 2 3 4 5

2. I see myself as "a thinker," "analytical," and "studious."   1 2 3 4 5

3. When working on a problem in a group setting, I like to break down the problem into its components and evaluate them.   1 2 3 4 5

4. I need to see convincing evidence before accepting information as fact.   1 2 3 4 5

5. I weigh the pros and cons of plans and ideas before taking action.   1 2 3 4 5

6. I tend to make connections among bits of information by categorizing them.   1 2 3 4 5

7. Impulsive, spontaneous decision making worries me.   1 2 3 4 5

8. I like to analyze causes and effects when making a decision.   1 2 3 4 5

9. I monitor my progress toward goals.   1 2 3 4 5

10. Once I reach a goal, I evaluate the process to see how effective it was.   1 2 3 4 5

Total your answers here: _____

Assess Your Creative Thinking Skills

For each statement, circle the number that feels right to you, from 1 for "not at all true for me" to 5 for "very true for me."

1. I tend to question rules and regulations.   1 2 3 4 5

2. I see myself as "unique," "full of ideas," and "innovative."   1 2 3 4 5

3. When working on a problem in a group setting, I generate a lot of ideas.   1 2 3 4 5

4. I am energized when I have a brand-new experience.   1 2 3 4 5

5. If you say something is too risky, I'm ready to give it a shot.   1 2 3 4 5

6. I often wonder if there is a different way to do or see something.   1 2 3 4 5

7. Too much routine in my work or schedule drains my energy.   1 2 3 4 5

8. I tend to see connections among ideas that others do not.   1 2 3 4 5

9. I feel comfortable allowing myself to make mistakes as I test out ideas.   1 2 3 4 5

10. I'm willing to champion an idea even when others disagree with me.   1 2 3 4 5

Total your answers here: _____

Assess Your Practical Thinking Skills

For each statement, circle the number that feels right to you, from 1 for "not at all true for me" to 5 for "very true for me."

1. I can find a way around any obstacle.   1 2 3 4 5

2. I see myself as a "doer," the "go-to" person; I "make things happen."   1 2 3 4 5

3. When working on a problem in a group setting, I like to figure out who will do what and when it should be done.   1 2 3 4 5

4. I apply what I learn from experience to improve my response to similar situations.   1 2 3 4 5

5. I finish what I start and don't leave loose ends hanging.   1 2 3 4 5

6. I note my emotions about academic and social situations and use what they tell me to move toward a goal.   1 2 3 4 5

7. I can sense how people feel and can use that knowledge to interact with others effectively.   1 2 3 4 5

8. I manage my time effectively.   1 2 3 4 5

9. I adjust to the teaching styles of my instructors and the communication styles of my peers.　　1 2 3 4 5

10. When involved in a problem-solving process, I can shift gears as needed.　　1 2 3 4 5

Total your answers here:　_____

With your scores in hand, use the Wheel of Successful Intelligence to look at all the skills at once. In each of the three areas of the wheel, draw a curved line approximately at the level of your number score and fill in the wedge below that line. Look at what the wheel shows about the level of balance you perceive in your three aspects of successful intelligence. If it were a real wheel, would it roll?

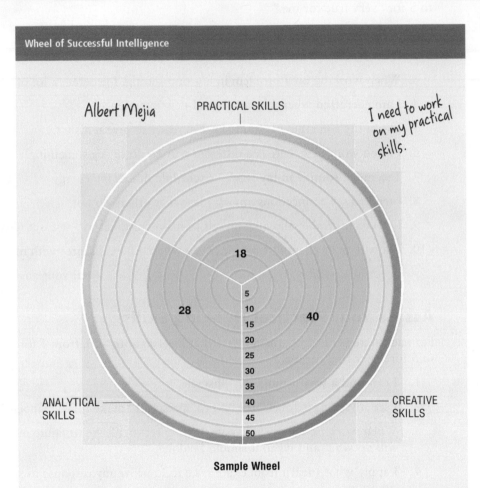

Sample Wheel

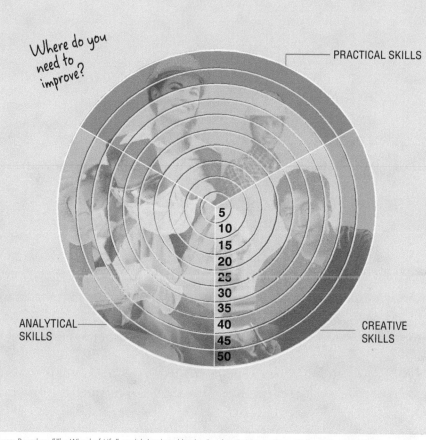

Where do you need to improve?

PRACTICAL SKILLS

ANALYTICAL SKILLS

CREATIVE SKILLS

5
10
15
20
25
30
35
40
45
50

Source: Based on "The Wheel of Life" model developed by the Coaches Training Institute. © Co-Active Space 2000.

Based on the appearance of the wheel, in which skill do you most need to build strength? Keep this goal in mind as you proceed through the term.

CHAPTER

2

LifeBound, LLC

Values are the foundation of effective goal setting and time management. You are most motivated to achieve goals and accomplish tasks that reflect what is most important to you.

Values, Goals, and Time

MANAGING YOURSELF

What Would You Risk? *Sarah Martinez*

THINK ABOUT THIS SITUATION AS YOU READ, AND CONSIDER WHAT ACTION YOU WOULD TAKE. THIS CHAPTER TAKES A CLOSER LOOK AT YOUR PERSONAL VALUES, THE GOALS YOU SET REFLECTING THOSE VALUES, AND HOW YOU MANAGE YOUR TIME TO ACHIEVE THOSE IMPORTANT GOALS.

When Sarah Martinez was five years old, she began complaining of frequent headaches. Her mother, a nurse, had been noticing how Sarah's left eye looked strange and droopy. She took her daughter to a pediatrician and, after several tests and CT scans, the doctors found that Sarah had a rare and malignant tumor called a rhabdomyosarcoma behind her left eye.

This discovery immediately catapulted Sarah and her family into the tumultuous world of cancer treatment. Sarah endured several surgeries, multiple rounds of chemotherapy, and radiation to the left side of her head. During the year over which treatment took place, Sarah spent over 100 days in the hospital. It was a difficult time for Sarah and her family. Luckily, the treatment did the job; Sarah was declared cancer-free. She did have to contend with side effects, including hearing loss and stunted growth from radiation damage. She needed growth hormone shots for five years and now wears a hearing aid in her left ear.

In remission from the cancer, Sarah moved back into a more habitual rhythm of life through the rest of her childhood. As a high school student she was involved in theatre and excelled in academics. Things changed, however, during her first year of college at Metro State University. After getting through the first semester, she found that living on her own was lonely in a way that she had never experienced before. She began to sense that the cancer had left her with more than just physical damage to contend with. Feeling depressed and burnt out, she stopped going to class and lost focus on her studies. She knew something had to change, but wasn't sure what kind of risk would help—or whether she could motivate herself to take a risk at all.

To be continued . . .

Staying motivated and connected is an essential goal for every student transitioning to college. You'll learn more about Sarah, and the reward resulting from her actions, within the chapter.

Notes

Today   Mar 10 8:01 AM

Working through this chapter will help you to:

statusCHECK

How Developed Are Your Self-Management Skills?

For each statement, circle the number that feels right to you, from 1 for "not at all true for me" to 5 for "very true for me."

1. I am aware of my values and beliefs. ① ② ③ ④ ⑤
2. I have a system for reminding myself of what my goals are. ① ② ③ ④ ⑤
3. I find ways to motivate myself when I am working toward a goal. ① ② ③ ④ ⑤
4. When I set a long-term goal, I break it down into a series of short-term goals. ① ② ③ ④ ⑤
5. I am aware of my time-related needs and preferences. ① ② ③ ④ ⑤
6. I understand my time traps and have ways to avoid them. ① ② ③ ④ ⑤
7. I know how to use the SMART approach to plan achievable goals. ① ② ③ ④ ⑤
8. When I procrastinate, I know how to get back on track. ① ② ③ ④ ⑤
9. I record tasks, events, and responsibilities in a planner of some kind and refer to it regularly. ① ② ③ ④ ⑤
10. I understand how managing my time can help reduce my level of stress. ① ② ③ ④ ⑤

Each of the topics in these statements is covered in this chapter. Note those statements for which you circled a 3 or lower. Skim the chapter to see where those topics appear, and pay special attention to them as you read, learn, and apply new strategies.

REMEMBER: NO MATTER HOW EFFECTIVELY YOU SET GOALS AND MANAGE TIME, YOU CAN IMPROVE WITH EFFORT AND PRACTICE.

CHAPTER 2

WHY IS IT IMPORTANT TO
know what you value?

You make life choices—what to do, what to believe, what to buy, how to act—based on your personal values. The choice to pursue a degree, for example, may reflect how a person values the personal and professional growth that come from a post-secondary education. If you like to be on time for classes, you may value punctuality. If you pay bills regularly and on time, you may value financial stability.

Values play a key role in your drive to achieve important goals and use your time wisely, helping you to do the following:

- *Understand what you want out of life.* Your most meaningful goals will reflect what you value most.
- *Choose how to use your valuable time.* When your day-to-day activities align with what you think is most important, you gain greater fulfillment from them.
- *Build "rules for life."* Your values form the foundation for your decisions and behaviour throughout your life. You will return repeatedly to these rules for guidance, especially in unfamiliar territory.
- *Find people who inspire you.* Spending time with people who share similar values will help you clarify how you want to live while finding support for your goals.

VALUES ←
Principles or qualities that you consider important.

MyStudentSuccessLab
Whether face-to-face or online, MyStudentSuccessLab helps students build the skills they need through peer-led video interviews, interactive practice exercises, and activities that provide academic, life, and professionalism skills.

get analytical

EXPLORE YOUR VALUES

Rate each of the listed values on a scale from 1 to 5, 1 being least important to you and 5 being most important.

___Knowing yourself   ___Being liked by others   ___Reading

___Self-improvement   ___Taking risks   ___Time to yourself

___Improving physical/mental health   ___Time for fun/relaxation   ___Lifelong learning

___Leadership and teamwork skills   ___Staying fit through exercise   ___Competing and winning

___Pursuing an education   ___Spiritual/religious life   ___Making a lot of money

___Good relationships with family   ___Community involvement   ___Creative/artistic pursuits

___Helping others   ___Keeping up with the news   ___Getting a good job

___Being organized   ___Financial stability   ___Other

Complete the following on a sheet of paper or in a digital file.

1. Write your top three values.

2. Choose one top value that is a factor in the educational choice you have made. Explain the choice and how the value was involved. Example: A student who values financial stability chooses to take a personal finance course.

3. Name an area of study that you think would help you live according to this value.

How Values Develop and Change

Your value system is complex, built piece by piece over time, and comes from many sources—such as family, friends, culture, media, school, work, neighbourhood, religious beliefs, and world events. These powerful external influences can so effectively instill values that you don't think about why you believe what you believe. However, you have a *choice* whether or not to adopt any value. Taking advantage of the power to choose requires evaluating values with questions such as the following:

- Where did the value come from?
- Is this value something from my family or culture that I have accepted without questioning, or have I truly made it my own?
- What other different values could I consider?
- What might happen as a result of adopting this value?
- Have I made a personal commitment to this choice? Have I told others about it?
- Do my life goals and day-to-day actions reflect this value?

Ant Clausen/Shutterstock

Values are not set in stone any more than your thinking power is. Your values often shift as you grow. For example, Sarah's ordeal changed and reordered her family's values. Life changes make it even more important to step back and think about what's truly important to you.

How Values Affect Your Life Experience

Because what you value often determines the choices you make, it also shapes your life experiences. For example, the fact that you value education may have led you to college or university, a practical choice that will help you build skills and persistence, choose a major and career direction, find meaningful friends and activities, and achieve learning goals.

Another example is found on Canadian college and university campuses in the growing diversity of the student body, a diversity also increasingly seen in the working population. If you value human differences, you have taken an important step on the way to working successfully with people of various cultures, at various stages of life, and with various value systems both in post-secondary education and beyond.

Values become goals when you've transformed your beliefs into something tangible and long-lasting. Not every value becomes a goal, but every goal stems from your values.

HOW DO YOU SET
and achieve goals?

GOAL
An end toward which you direct your efforts.

When you set a goal, you focus on what you want to achieve and create a path that can get you there. Setting goals involves defining your aims in both long-term and short-term time frames. *Long-term* goals are broader objectives you want to achieve over a long period of time, perhaps a year or more. *Short-term* goals move you toward a long-term goal in manageable and achievable steps (Key 2.1). Goal setting is one way to take responsibility for your life and actions. It's one of the Personal Management Skills that make up the Employability Skills 2000+.

Establish Your Personal Mission

Start with the biggest big picture: defining your *personal mission* can help you anchor your values and goals in a comprehensive view of what you want out of life. Think of a personal mission as your longest-term goal, within which all other long-term and short-term goals should fit.

KEY 2.1 **Goals reinforce one another.**

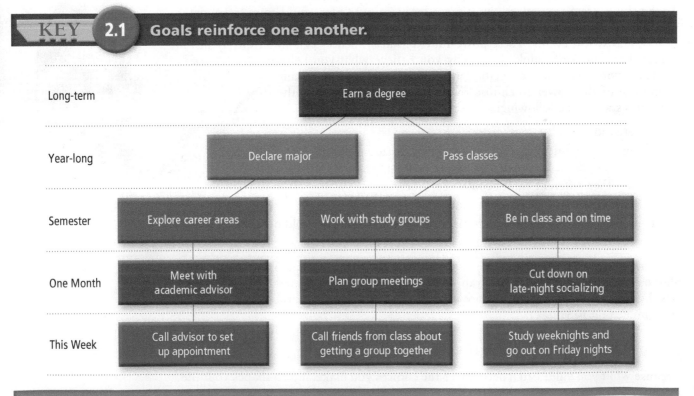

Long-term		Earn a degree	
Year-long	Declare major		Pass classes
Semester	Explore career areas	Work with study groups	Be in class and on time
One Month	Meet with academic advisor	Plan group meetings	Cut down on late-night socializing
This Week	Call advisor to set up appointment	Call friends from class about getting a group together	Study weeknights and go out on Friday nights

Dr. Stephen Covey, author of *The Seven Habits of Highly Effective People*, defines a *mission statement* as a philosophy outlining what you want to be (character), what you want to do (contributions and achievements), and the principles by which you live (your values).[1] Defining your personal mission involves creating a mission statement. The following mission statement was written by Carol Carter, one of the authors of *Keys to Success*.

My mission is to use my talents and abilities to help people of all ages, stages, backgrounds, and economic levels achieve their human potential through fully developing their minds and their talents. I aim to create opportunities for others through work, service, and family. I also aim to balance work with people in my life, understanding that my family and friends are a priority above all else.

How can you start formulating a mission statement? Try using Covey's three aspects of personal mission as a guide. Think through the following:

- *Character.* What aspects of character do you think are most valuable? When you consider the people you admire most, which of their qualities stand out?
- *Contributions and achievements.* What do you want to accomplish in your life? Where do you want to make a difference?
- *Values.* How do your values inform your life goals? What in your mission could help you live according to what you value most highly?

Goals take effort and planning to reach. This music producer spends days, and even weeks, adjusting equipment and recording tracks on the way to the production of just one song.

Because what you want out of life changes as you do, your personal mission should remain flexible and open to revision. Your mission can be the road map for your personal journey, giving meaning to your daily activities, promoting responsibility, and inspiring action. You will have a chance to craft a personal mission at the end of this chapter.

Set Long-Term Goals

What do you want your life to look like in 5 or 10 years? What degree do you want to earn? What job do you want? Where do you want to live? How do you want to live your values and activate your personal mission? Answers to questions such as these help identify long-term goals.

Long-term goals are objectives that sit out on the horizon, at least six months to a year away. They're goals that you can imagine and maybe even visualize, reflecting who you are and what is important to you, but they're too far out for you to touch. The more you know about yourself, the better able you are to set and work toward meaningful long-term goals. One way to make long-term goals real is to put them in writing, as in the following example.

My goal is to build a business in which I, as a family doctor, create opportunities to expose young people in my community to the medical field.

A student two years away from graduation who is pursuing this long-term goal might establish the following supporting set of one-year long-term goals:

Design courses for the year to make sure I am on track for pre-med course completion. Find medical practices in the area that could serve as a model for my business. Research medical schools.

To determine your long-term goals, think about the values that anchor your personal mission. For someone who values health and fitness, for example, possible

student PROFILE

Brandie Molley
SPROTT-SHAW COMMUNITY COLLEGE, PENTICTON, BRITISH COLUMBIA

About me:

I'm a mature student and a single mom.

What I focus on:

When I decided to go back to school, I really had no idea what I was signing up for! I was literally spinning in circles. Between trying to get my oldest off to school in the mornings, finding a childcare facility that was open the hours I was going to school for my youngest, and already attending school, I really wasn't sure I was going to make it. But somehow I have managed to juggle it all, and I have not yet missed a day of school.

I have learned how to make sure my time is well used. Being a single mom is hard, but when you decide to further your education it gets even harder. Making sure you get the proper amount of sleep is the key to being able to run all day and to making sure the kids stay on your timed schedule along with you. It's not always easy when there is only one of you and two of them; but, with enough energy and a schedule, everything that needs to be done gets done.

Sprott-Shaw makes going to school while caring for a family easier for me because classes don't start until later in the day. So when my oldest goes to school, after I drive a half-hour to my youngest son's daycare, I have plenty of time to study and get assignments finished before class starts. There are always computers open and classrooms available for studying. I was worried when I started that I was going to get behind, because, let's face it, if I had to do my homework or studying at home, it would never get done. Between kids screaming and dishes piling up, homework and studying is the last thing on my mind.

What will help me in the workplace:

Going to school has very much prepared me for the workforce and for working under tight timelines. I'll be using the lessons I have learned, such as scheduling everything I do as well as everything my sons do, making sure we all get good nights' sleeps, and most of all making sure I give myself extra time for "just in case" scenarios. My best advice to anyone who's feeling a little overwhelmed is take a deep breath, know that it will all be worth it in the end, and don't give up—a career is out there waiting for you.

Brandie Molley. Sprott-Shaw Community College, Penticton, British Columbia. Reprinted by permission.

long-term goals might involve working for an organic food company or training as a physical therapist. Basing your long-term goals on values increases your motivation to succeed. The stronger the link between your values and your long-term goals, the happier, more motivated, and more successful you are likely to be in setting and achieving those goals.

Set Short-Term Goals

Lasting from an hour or less to as long as several months, *short-term goals* narrow your focus and encourage progress toward long-term goals. If you have a long-term goal of graduating with a degree in nursing, for example, you may set these short-term goals for the next six months:

- I will learn the name, location, and function of every human bone and muscle.
- I will work with a study group to understand the musculoskeletal system.

These goals can be broken down into even smaller parts, such as the following one-month goals:

- I will work with onscreen tutorials of the musculoskeletal system until I understand and memorize the material.
- I will spend three hours a week with my study partners.

In addition to monthly goals, you may have short-term goals that extend for a week, a day, or even a couple of hours. To support your goal of regularly meeting with your study partners, you may set the following short-term goals:

- *By the end of today.* Text or email study partners to ask them when they might be able to meet.
- *1 week from now.* Schedule each of our weekly meetings this month.
- *2 weeks from now.* Have our first meeting.
- *3 weeks from now.* Type and distribute notes from first meeting; have second meeting.

These short-term goals might not seem risky to you. However, any action that requires energy and subjects your work to scrutiny is a risk. The smallest ways in which you "put yourself out there" can lead step by step to the greatest rewards.

Kaarsten/Shutterstock

Set Up a SMART Goal-Achievement Plan

At any given time, you are working toward goals of varying importance. First, decide which goals matter most to you and are most deserving of your focus. Then, draw up a plan to achieve those goals, using the SMART system to make your goals Specific, Measurable, Achievable, Realistic, and linked to a Time Frame.

Specific. Make your goal concrete by using as many details as possible. Focus on behaviours and events that are under your control and map out specific steps that will get you there.

Measurable. Define your goal in measurable way, and set up a progress evaluation system such as keeping a journal, setting an alarm on your phone or computer, or reporting to a friend.

Achievable. Determine if the goal aligns with your interests and values. Then, reflect on whether you have the skills or resources needed. If you're missing something, plan out how to get it.

Realistic. Make sure your risks are reasonable and calculated. Create deadlines that will help you stay on track without making you feel rushed. Avoid the struggle of a too-short timeline.

Time Frame Linked. All goals need a time frame so you have something to work toward. If a goal is "a dream with a deadline," then without the deadline, your goal is only a dream.

See Key 2.2 for a way to apply this goal-setting plan to an important objective that nearly every post-secondary student will need to achieve—declaring a major or concentration. (For the sake of simplicity, the term *major* will appear throughout the rest of the book.)

Setting goals is only the start. The real risk is in working toward them, and the real reward is in reaching them. Follow these steps, noting where your SMART system actions fit in.

> MAJOR OR CONCENTRATION
> An academic subject area chosen as a field of specialization, requiring a specific course of study.

GOAL: To decide on a major.

SMART KEY	MEANING	EXAMPLE
Specific	Name exactly how you will achieve your goal.	I will read the list of available majors, meet with my academic advisor, talk with instructors, and choose a major by the deadline.
Measurable	Find ways to measure your progress over time.	I will set alarms on my smartphone to remind me of when I should have accomplished steps. I will ask my mom to check in to make sure I'm getting somewhere.
Achievable	Set a goal that your abilities and drive can handle.	I'm driven to declare a major because I want to earn my degree, graduate, and gain work-ready skills.
Realistic	Define a goal that is workable given the resources (time and money) and other circumstances.	Because I'm starting early and already know how the process works, I should have time to think through this carefully.
Time Frame	Set up a time frame for achieving your goal and the steps toward it.	I have a year until the deadline. I will read the catalogue in the next month; I will meet with my advisor by the end of the term; I will talk with instructors at the beginning of next term; I will declare a major by the end of next term.

- *Step 1: Define an achievable, realistic goal.* **What do you want?** Write out a clear description.
- *Step 2: Define an action plan.* **How will you get there?** Brainstorm different paths. Choose one; then map out its steps. Break a long-term goal into short-term subgoals.
- *Step 3: Link your goal to a time frame.* **When do you want to accomplish your goal?** Define a realistic time frame. Create specific deadlines for each step on the path.
- *Step 4: Identify resources and support.* **What and who will keep you on track?** Use helpful websites or apps. Find people who will push you in a supportive way.
- *Step 5: Be accountable.* **How will you assess your progress?** Create a system to measure how you move toward your goal, keeping your time frame in mind.
- *Step 6: Prepare to get unstuck.* **What will you do if you hit a roadblock?** Anticipate problems and define strategies for handling them. Reach out to people who can help you. Remind yourself of the benefits of your goal.
- *Step 7: Take action.* **How will you persist?** Follow the steps in your plan until you achieve your goal.
- *Step 8: Celebrate!* **How will you recognize your accomplishments?** Appreciate your hard work with something you enjoy—a movie night, an outing with friends, something you've been wanting to buy, maybe even a long nap.

Through the process of working toward your most important goals, you will often be thinking about how well you are using your time. In fact, being able to achieve any significant goal is directly linked to effective time management.

As you work toward your most important goals, consider how well you are using your time. No matter how well you define the steps to your goals, you need to set those steps within a time frame to achieve them.

get creative

Think of a problem you frequently encounter. It could be scheduling homework around extracurricular activities, finding time to hang out with friends around studying, coming up with interesting career paths, or simply figuring out the theme of a literary work.

Now that you've defined the problem, use this visual organizer to come up with possible solutions. First, write your problem in the centre bubble. Then, begin filling in the surrounding bubbles with as many ideas as you can think of. Open your mind to risk-taking and keep writing until you've filled in every bubble with a possible solution.

When you're finished, read through all of your creative solutions. Do any of them stick out to you? Find a favourite and briefly describe here how it has the potential to reward you. _____

_____

You just got yourself unstuck. Consider using this method when faced with a tough problem. Thinking creatively can be an extremely productive (not to mention fun) way to solve any problem you may encounter. _____

_____

_____

Values, Goals, and Time

37

WHO ARE YOU AS A
time manager?

Everyone has only 24 hours in a day, and 8 or so of those hours involve sleeping (or should, if you want to remain healthy and alert enough to achieve your goals). You can't manage how time passes, but you *can* manage how you use it. That was the issue faced by Brandie Molley at Sprott-Shaw Community College. Reread her profile to find out how she was able to manage her time.

The first step in time management is to investigate your personal relationship with time. The more you're aware of your own time-related behaviours, the better you can create a schedule that maximizes your strengths, minimizes your weaknesses, and reduces stress. Determine who you are as a time manager by exploring your preferences and assessing your needs.

Identify Your Preferences

People have unique body rhythms and habits that affect how they deal with time. Some people have lots of energy late at night. Others do their best work early in the day. Some people are chronically late, while others get everything done with time to spare. The following steps will help you create a personal time profile:

- *Identify your energy patterns.* At what time of day does your energy tend to peak? When do you tend to have the least energy?
- *Notice your on-time percentage.* Do you tend to be early, on time, or late? If you are early or late, by how many minutes are you normally off schedule? Do you set your clocks five or ten minutes early to trick yourself into being on time?
- *Look at your stamina.* Do you focus more effectively if you have a long block of time in which to work? Or do you need regular breaks in order to perform effectively?
- *Evaluate the effects of your preferences.* Which of your time-related preferences are likely to have a positive impact on your success at school? Which are likely to cause problems? Which can you make adjustments for, and which will just require you to cope?
- *Establish an ideal schedule.* Describe an ideal schedule that illustrates your preferences. For example, a student studies better during the day and prefers a long block of time. His ideal schedule may read: "Classes bunched together on Mondays, Wednesdays, and Fridays. Tuesdays and Thursdays free for studying and research. Study primarily during daytime hours."

Assess Your Needs

Of course, very few people are able to perfectly align their schedules to their profile and preferences. Everyone has needs that may or may not fit into their ideal schedule. Needs include:

- Certain courses, for core requirements or for your major
- Work hours, if you have a job
- Family responsibilities, if you care for children, parents, or others

The goal is to consider your needs and your ideal schedule together, and come up with the best possible option, one that fulfills your needs but also takes your preferences into account. Consider what might happen to the student in the ideal schedule example. Looking to schedule next term's classes all on M-W-F, he finds that one class he has to take meets only on T-Th. He has a choice of 11 A.M. and 4 P.M., though, so he chooses 4 pm, because that will give him a bigger block of time to study and do research during the day prior to the class.

get $mart

Complete the following on paper or in digital format.

Imagine yourself in five years ...

1. What kind of work do you hope to be doing?

2. How much money do you hope to earn each year doing that work?

3. What type of major purchase might you make at that time?

4. How much might it cost? (*Total cost or down payment*)

5. How much money would you have to save each month to have the money to make that major purchase at the end of five years? *Monthly Savings = Total Cost ÷ (5 years × 12 months per year)*

6. Name two actions you can take to try to save that amount on a monthly basis.

Finally, remember that you will have more control over some things than others. For example, a student who functions best late at night may not have much luck finding courses that meet after 10 P.M. (unless she attends one of several colleges that have begun to schedule late-night classes to handle an overload of students).

HOW CAN YOU
schedule and prioritize?

With your preferences and needs in mind, you are ready for the central time management strategy—creating and following a schedule. An effective schedule can help you gain control of your life in two ways: it provides segments of time for goal-related tasks and it reminds you of tasks, events, due dates, responsibilities, and deadlines.

Choose a Planner

Your first step is to find a planner that will help you achieve that control that a schedule can provide. Time-management expert Paul Timm says, "rule number one in a thoughtful planning process is: use some form of a planner where you can write things down."[2]

Choose a planner that works for how you live. There are two major types:

- A *book or notebook*, showing either a day or a week at a glance, where you note your commitments. Some planners contain sections for monthly and yearly goals.

- An *electronic planner or smartphone* such as an iPhone, BlackBerry, or Android. Basic functions allow you to schedule days and weeks, note due dates, make to-do lists, perform mathematical calculations, and create and store an address book. Because most smartphone calendars have companion programs on computers, you can usually back up your schedule on a computer and view it there. You might also consider online calendars, such as Google calendar, which can communicate with your phone or other device.

Although electronic planners are handy, powerful, and capable of all kinds of functioning, on the con side they are not cheap, the software can fail, and the battery can

Terry Vine/Blend Images/Getty Images

Managing time effectively often means taking advantage of opportunities whenever they arise. This student, also a mother, fits schoolwork in during naptime.

PRIORITIZE
To arrange or deal with in order of importance.

die. Analyze your preferences and finances, and choose the best tool for you. A blank notebook, used consistently, may work as well as a top-of-the-line smartphone.

Establish Priorities

Prioritizing helps you focus the bulk of your energy and time on your most important tasks. Since many top-priority items (classes, work) occur at designated times, prioritizing helps you lock in these activities and schedule less urgent tasks around them.

Whether it's a task or goal you're scheduling, here are some basic ways to assign priorities. Think about what results your risks might bring—and what may result from taking *no* risks.

- *Priority 1.* Crucial, high-reward items that you must do, usually at a specific time. They may include attending class, working at a job, picking up a child from day care, and paying bills.
- *Priority 2.* Important items that have some flexibility in scheduling. Examples include study time and exercising.
- *Priority 3.* These are less important items that offer low-key rewards. Examples include calling a friend or downloading songs onto your iPod.

You should also prioritize long-term and short-term goals. Consider keeping high priority long-term goals visible alongside your daily schedule so you can make sure your day-to-day activities move you toward those goals. For instance, arriving at school a half hour early so you can meet with an advisor can be a step toward a long-term goal of deciding on a major.

Build a Schedule

Scheduling and goal setting work hand in hand to get you where you want to go. The most clearly defined goal won't be achieved without being put into a time frame, and the most organized schedule won't accomplish much unless it is filled with tasks related to important goals.

Be detailed and methodical about building your schedule. Follow these steps:

1. **Enter Priority 1 items in your planner first.** This means class times and days for the term, including labs and other required commitments; work hours; and essential personal responsibilities such as health-related appointments or childcare.
2. **Enter key dates from your course syllabi.** When you get your syllabi for the term, enter all dates—test and quiz dates, due dates for assignments, presentation dates for projects, holidays and breaks—in your planner right away. This will give you a big picture view of responsibilities and help you prepare for crunch times. For example, if you see that you have three tests and a presentation all in one week later in the term, you might rearrange your schedule during the preceding week to create extra study time.
3. **Enter dates of events and commitments.** Put commitments in your schedule where you can see and plan for them. Include club and organizational meetings, events you need to attend for class or for other purposes, and personal commitments such as medical appointments, family events, fitness events such as a race, or important social events.
4. **Schedule Priority 2 items around existing items.** Once you have the essentials set, put in study time, workouts, study group meetings, and other important but

flexible items. *Schedule class prep time—reading and studying, writing and working on assignments and projects—in the planner as you would any other activity.* As a rule, schedule at least two hours of preparation for every hour of class—that is, if you take 12 credits, you'll spend 24 hours or more a week on course-related activities in and out of class.

5. **Include Priority 3 items where possible.** Schedule these items, such as social time or doing errands, around the items already locked in.

When you are scheduling and evaluating the potential rewards of various tasks, be careful not to equate "reward" with "fun." They are not necessarily one and the same. For example, you might consider spending an hour on Instagram a lot more fun than studying for a test for that same hour. However, the reward for working toward a good test grade may ultimately be more desirable to you than whatever you would gain from posting and liking photos.

Link Tasks to Long-Term Goals

Linking day-to-day events in your planner to your values and broader goals will give meaning to your efforts, bring order to your schedule, and keep you motivated. Planning study time for an economics test, for example, will mean more to you if you link the hours you spend to your goal of being accepted into business school and the value you place on meaningful employment. Here is how you might translate your goal of entering business school into action steps over a year's time:

- *This year.* Complete enough courses to meet curriculum requirements for business school and maintain class standing.
- *This term.* Complete my economics class with a B average or higher.
- *This month.* Set up economics study group schedule to coincide with quizzes and tests.
- *This week.* Meet with study group; go over material for Friday's test.
- *Today.* Go over Chapter 3 in economics text.

You can then arrange this time to move you in the direction of your goal. You schedule activities that support your short-term goal of doing well on the test and write them in your planner. Achieving the overarching long-term goal of doing well in a course you need for business school is the source of your motivation.

Before each week begins, remind yourself of your long-term goals and what you can accomplish over the next seven days to move you closer to them. Additionally, every once in a while, take a hard look at your schedule to see whether you are spending time on what you most value. Key 2.3 shows parts of a daily schedule and a weekly schedule.

Make to-do Lists

When you have a cluster of tasks to accomplish, you may find it useful to create a *to-do list* and check off the items as you complete them. A to-do list can be helpful during exam week, in anticipation of an especially busy day, for a long-term or complicated assignment, or when keyed to a special event. Some people keep a separate to-do list focused on low-priority tasks.

Use a code to prioritize the items on your list so that you address the most important items first. Some people just list items in priority order and number them. Some use letters (A, B, C) and some use different-coloured pens. Others use electronic

TIPS FOR LEARNING ONLINE

- *Control your time.* For many students, time management is a greater concern when it comes to online learning. One quick check of your email can lead to hours spent online that you should have spent getting something else done. Limit your time spent emailing and try to stay focused on the task at hand.

- *Change your status.* Set your social media status to "offline" or "do not disturb" when you are studying online.

- *Set up goals and rewards.* Try doing a defined portion of your homework and then rewarding yourself with 10 minutes on your favourite social networking site.

Monday, March 14

Time	Tasks	Priority
6:00 A.M.		
7:00		
8:00	Up at 8am — finish homework	
9:00		
10:00	Business Administration	
11:00	Renew driver's license @ DMV	
12:00 P.M.		
1:00	Lunch	
2:00	Writing Seminar (peer editing to...	
3:00	↓	
4:00	check on Ms. Schwartz's office h...	
5:00	5:30 work out	
6:00	↳→ 6:30	
7:00	Dinner	
8:00	Read two chapters for	
9:00	Business Admin.	
10:00		
11:00		
12:00		

Monday, March 28

8		Call: Mike Blair		1
9	BIO 212	Financial Aid Office		2
10				3
11	CHEM 203	EMS 262	*Paramedic role-play*	4
12				5
Evening	6pm yoga class			

Tuesday, March 29

8	Finish reading assignment!	Work @ library		1
9				2
10	ENG 112	(study for quiz)		3
11	↓			4
12				5
Evening		until 7pm		

Wednesday, March 30

8		Meet w/advisor		1
9	BIO 212			2
10		EMS 262		3
11	CHEM 203 *Quiz			4
12		Pick up photos		5
Evening	6pm Dinner w/study group			

planners, choosing different highlighting or font colours. Each time you complete a task, check it off your to-do list or delete it from your electronic scheduler. This physical action can enhance the feeling of confidence that comes from getting something done.

Manage Your Schedule

The most detailed schedule won't do you any good unless you actively manage it. Here are some strategies that can help:

- *Plan regularly.* Set aside a time each day to plan your schedule (right before bed, with your morning coffee, on your commute to or from school, or whatever time and situation works best for you). Check your schedule at regular intervals throughout the day or week.

- *Use monthly and yearly calendars at home.* A standard monthly or yearly wall calendar is a great place to keep track of your major commitments. A wall calendar gives you the "big picture" overview you need. Key 2.4 shows a monthly calendar.

- *Get ahead if you can.* If you can, take the small risk of getting a task done ahead of time, get it done, and see how you appreciate the reward of avoiding pressure

MARCH

SUNDAY	MONDAY	TUESDAY	WEDNESDAY	THURSDAY	FRIDAY	SATURDAY
	1 WORK	2 Turn in English paper topic	3 Dentist 2 pm	4	5	6
				WORK		
7 Frank's birthday	8 Psych Test 9 am WORK	9	10 6:30 pm Meeting @ Acad Ctr	11 WORK	12	13 Dinner @ Ryan's
14	15 English paper due WORK	16 Western Civ paper	17	18 Library 6 pm WORK	19 Western Civ makeup class	20
21	22	23 2 pm meeting, psych group WORK	24 Start running: 2 miles	25 WORK	26 Run 2 miles	27
28 Run 3 miles	29 WORK	30 Western Civ paper due	31 Run 2 miles			

later. Focus on your growth mindset, reminding yourself that achievement requires persistent effort.

- *Schedule downtime.* It's easy to get so caught up in completing tasks that you forget to relax and breathe. Even a half-hour of downtime a day will refresh you and improve your productivity when you get back on task.

- *Schedule sleep.* Sleep-deprived bodies and minds have a hard time functioning, and research reports that one-quarter of all post-secondary students are chronically sleep-deprived.[3] Figure out how much sleep you need, and do your best to get it. With adequate rest, your mind is better able to function, which has a direct positive impact on your schoolwork.

One last overarching strategy: *Be flexible.* Sudden changes can upset your plans. Although you cannot control all the events that occur, you can control how you respond to them.

For changes that occur frequently, such as a job that tends to run into overtime, set up a backup plan (or two) ahead of time. For sudden changes such as medical emergencies and car breakdowns, or serious changes such as failing a course, use problem-solving skills to help you through. (Your course this term may include more detailed information about problem solving.) Your ability to evaluate situations, come up with creative options, and put practical plans to work will help you manage changes.

Resources at your school can help you deal with change as well as with any scheduling or time-management problem. Your academic advisor, counsellor, dean, financial aid advisor, and instructors can provide ideas and assistance.

Values, Goals, and Time

talk risk and reward . . .

Risk asking tough questions to be rewarded with new insights. Use the following to inspire discussion with classmates, in person or online.

- What time management issues do you see others face? How do they handle them? What happens when they take risks—or don't?

- When you come up against a roadblock to an important goal, how do you react— with risk-taking or retreat? What is the result? If you want to change how you "get unstuck," what adjustments would you make?

CONSIDER THE CASE: Sarah found herself in a situation where she sensed she needed to take action, but didn't know what or how. Have you ever been in a similar place, feeling paralyzed by a problem and unable to figure out the first step? If you had a friend in this type of situation, how would you motivate him or her?

Time Management Is Stress Management

If you are feeling more (stress) in your everyday life as a student, you are not alone. Stress levels among college students have increased dramatically.[4] Stress factors for college and university students include being in a new environment, having an increased workload, making difficult decisions, and juggling school, work, and personal responsibilities.

Dealing with the stress of post-secondary life is one of your biggest challenges. But here's some good news: *every time-management strategy you are reading in this chapter contributes to your ability to cope with stress*. Remember that stress refers to how you *react* to pressure. When you create and follow a schedule that gets you places on time and helps you take care of tasks and responsibilities, you reduce pressure. With less pressure comes less stress.

STRESS
Physical or mental strain or tension produced in reaction to pressure.

HOW CAN YOU

handle time traps?

Everyone experiences *time traps*—situations and activities that eat up time you could spend in a more productive way. With thought and focus, you can address and conquer time traps. Note that this doesn't mean *never* doing things like chatting with friends on Facebook or watching Funny or Die videos—it means making conscious decisions about when and how long you do certain activities so that they don't derail your most important goals. It also means thinking ahead about risks—both the risk of being unproductive as well as the risk of prioritizing work over your social life—and what rewards may or may not come from them.

Sometime traps are a part of daily life—unavoidable, but able to be managed and addressed. See Key 2.5, which lists the ones students encounter most often and offers ideas for how to take control of them. Others are linked to choices that people make. It can be risky to put out the high level of attention and focus that your work may demand, but the reward is an education that can help you fulfill your life's most significant goals. Make your most productive choices by confronting procrastination, setting effective limits, and minimizing multi-tasking.

PROCRASTINATION
The act of putting off a task until another time.

Confront Procrastination

It's human, and common for busy students, to leave difficult or undesirable tasks until later. However, if taken to the extreme, **procrastination** can develop into a habit that

	1. **Television** It's easy to just keep flipping the channels when you know you've got something due. *Take Control:* Record favourite shows by using a digital video recorder or watch a movie instead. When your program of choice is over, turn off the TV.
	2. **Commute** Though not often something you can control, the time spent commuting from one place to another can be staggering. *Take Control:* Use your time on a bus or train to do homework, study, read assignments, or work on your monthly budget.
	3. **Internet Browsing** Currently, Internet misuse in the workplace costs companies almost $200 billion per year in lost productivity. *Take Control:* If you use the Internet for research, consider subscribing to RSS feeds that can alert you when relevant information becomes available. When using the Internet for social or personal reasons, stick to a time limit.
	4. **Fatigue** Being tired can lead to below-quality work that may have to be redone and can make you feel ready to quit altogether. *Take Control:* Determine a stop time for yourself. When your stop time comes, put down the book, turn off the computer, and go to bed. During the day, when you can, take naps to recharge your battery.
	5. **Confusion** When you don't fully understand an assignment or problem, you may spend unintended time trying to figure it out. *Take Control:* The number one way to fight confusion is to ask. As the saying goes, ask early and ask often. Students who seek help show that they want to learn.

Values, Goals, and Time

causes serious problems. For example, procrastinators who don't get things done in the workplace may prevent others from doing their work, sabotage a project, or even lose a promotion or a job because of it.

If procrastination can cause such major issues, why do it? One reason people procrastinate is to avoid the truth about what they can achieve. "As long as you procrastinate, you never have to confront the real limits of your ability, whatever those limits are,"[5] say procrastination experts Jane B. Burka and Lenora Yuen, authors of *Procrastination: Why You Do It and What to Do About It*. A fixed mindset is another factor, because it naturally leads to procrastination. "I can't do it," the person with the fixed mindset thinks, "so what's the point of trying?"

Here are some strategies that can help you avoid procrastination and its negative effects.

- *Analyze the effects.* What reward will remain out of reach if you continue to put off a task? Chances are you will benefit more in the long term by facing the task head-on.
- *Set reasonable goals.* Because unreasonable goals can immobilize, take manageable risks. If you concentrate on achieving one small step at a time, the task becomes less burdensome.

get practical

CONQUER YOUR TIME TRAPS

Complete the following on paper or in digital format.

Think of two common time traps that you encounter. For each, come up with two ways to manage it effectively. Here's an example:

Time Trap: Texting

Response 1: "I'll call you in an hour. I need to finish this paper."

Response 2: "I will respond to my text messages after I've read two chapters."

1. Your turn. For each time trap of yours, name it and describe two possible responses

2. Next, for each of the two time traps you identified, name which of the two responses will most help you to take control of the situation and why.

3. Finally, what did this exercise teach you about personal time traps? Do you find yourself needing to be stricter with your time? Why and how?

- *Get started whether you "feel like it" or not.* Break the paralysis of doing nothing by doing something, anything. Most people, once they start, find it easier to continue.
- *Ask for help.* Once you identify what's holding you up, find someone to help you face the task. Another person may come up with an innovative method to get you moving again.
- *Don't expect perfection.* People learn by approaching mistakes with a growth mindset. Richard Sheridan, President of Menlo Innovations, fosters a culture of exploration by telling his employees, "Make mistakes faster."[6]
- *Acknowledge progress.* When you accomplish a task, celebrate with whatever feels like fun to you.

Set Effective Limits

Many people find it challenging to resist the pull of relaxing and fun activities such as video games, YouTube surfing, and socializing virtually or in person. However, the fun stuff can run away with your time, preventing you from taking care of responsibilities, and ultimately causing serious problems. Because technology is so much a part of modern life, it can seem risky to limit your exposure to it. However, controlling when and for how long you interface with technology will earn you the reward of its benefits minus the suffering from its drawbacks.

There is a saying that goes, "The river needs banks to flow." Within those banks—the reasonable limits that you set on activities that tend to eat up time—you can be the thriving, healthy river, flowing towards the goals most important to you. Without the banks, and without the limits, you (the river) can spill out all over, losing the power to head in any single direction.

How can you set limits that will empower you and provide balance?

- *Know what distracts you.* Be honest with yourself about what draws your attention and drains your time—chatting or texting on your cell phone, watching reality TV, visiting Facebook, managing your Twitter account, and so on.

- *Set boundaries.* Determine when, and for how long, you can perform these activities without jeopardizing your studies. Then schedule them with built-in boundaries: "I will spend ten minutes on Facebook for every 50 minutes of studying." "I will choose one TV show per day." Stick to your limits—use a cellphone alarm if you need it. You can even set up innovative browser plug-ins to block certain time-waster sites for specific periods of time. Check out LeechBlock (for Firefox) or StayFocused (for Google Chrome).

- *Think before you commit.* Whatever you are asked to do—whether it is social, family-related, in connection with a school organization, or another activity—don't say yes right away. Consider how the commitment will affect your schedule now and in the near future. If you determine the reward isn't worth the risk, say "no" respectfully but firmly.

- *Be realistic about time commitments.* Many students who combine work and school find they have to trim one or the other. Overloaded students often fall behind and experience high stress levels. Determine what is reasonable for you; you may find that taking longer to graduate is a viable option if you need to work while in school. You may also decide that you can handle easing up on work hours in order to spend more time on schoolwork.

The Myth of Multitasking

Over the years, people have come to believe that multitasking is a crucial skill. However, recent research has shown that the human brain is biologically capable of doing only one thinking task at a time—at best, it can only switch rapidly between tasks. When you think you are multitasking, you are really only "switch-tasking."[7]

This means that if you try to do two tasks at once, you can actually work on only one at a time. What you do is interrupt the first activity with the second and then switch back. The time it takes to switch from one thinking activity to another is called *switching time*. For example, suppose you're talking to a member of your study group by phone, discussing a homework assignment. If you decide to read through your email while you are on the phone, you will be unable to listen to what's being said on the phone call.

According to two researchers, David Meyer and Dr. John Medina, switching time increases errors and the amount of time it takes to finish the tasks you are working on by an average of 50 percent. This means that the more activities you juggle, the more your brain is interrupted, the more switching you do, the longer it takes to complete your activities, and the more mistakes you make.[8] The cost to the quality of your work may not be worth the juggling.

If you want to be successful at your work, consider the words of Tony Schwarz: "Difficult as it is to focus in the face of the endless distractions we all now face, it's far and away the most effective way to get work done."[9] Focusing on one task at a time will save you time, mistakes, and stress. The minor risks of managing yourself in the present will reward you with learning and accomplishment in the future—and, don't worry, you will still find time to play.

revisit RISK AND REWARD

What happened to Sarah? Compelled to find a way out of her combination of depression and severe social anxiety, Sarah took the risk to reach out for help. She went to her college's counseling center and saw both a counselor and a psychologist, both in one-on-one settings. Through these conversations she realized that she had emotional damage from her cancer experience, feelings that had been covered up but were surfacing as a result of her transition to college. As she began to feel more comfortable sharing her thoughts, she joined an "interpersonal processing group" on campus – a therapy group focused on working through issues together.

Sarah's willingness to risk and to expose her vulnerability earned her the reward of greater self-knowledge, improvement with her issues, and a bonus: A career direction. "I realized that I wasn't so different from other people, and I want to help people like me with social anxiety or depression," she says. She had chosen English as a major but had not yet connected it with a career goal. Now she plans to continue her education with a master's degree in social work.

What does this mean for you? Sarah found trust and support in the group therapy experience. Initially intimidated, she took the risk and now has a community of people that she looks forward to seeing. What group might you risk trying out at your school? It can be challenging to connect with others, and sometimes it takes a little push to get moving in a direction that could bring great reward. Set a SMART goal to find a group, whether therapeutic, social, or goal-oriented, this term. Write out your goal in terms of the SMART components and take action.

What risk may bring reward beyond your world? Sarah's idea that she could help others was cemented during a summer internship with LifeBound, a company that provides academic and career coaching to high school and college students. Observing coaching and being coached one-on-one by a student in a coaching class made her even more certain that helping people in a one-on-one environment was right for her. Set a goal to participate in an internship when you next have an opportunity. You may want to consult www.internships.com for a general overview of what's possible, and then narrow your search to local areas and specific careers. Whether you discover the perfect career area or find out an area that doesn't work out for you, you will have acquired essential information for your path toward fulfillment.

Complete the following on paper or in digital format; for time-management exercise, use the in-text grids below.

KNOW IT *Think Critically*

Discover How You Spend Your Time

Build basic skills. Everyone has exactly 168 hours in a week. How do you spend yours? Start by making guesses, or estimates, about three particular activities. In a week, how much time do you spend on the following?

_____ hours   Studying
_____ hours   Sleeping
_____ hours   Interacting with media and technology (computer, online services, cell-phone, texting, video games, TV) for non-study purposes

Now, to find out the real story, record how you spend your time for seven days. The chart on the next pages has blocks showing half-hour increments. As you go through the week, write down what you do each hour, indicating starting and stopping times. Include sleep and leisure time. Record your actual activities instead of the activities you think you should be doing. There are no wrong answers.

After a week, add up how many hours you spent on each activity (round off to half-hours—that is, mark 15 to 44 minutes of activity as a half hour and 45 to 75 minutes as one hour). Log the hours in the boxes of the chart on page 51 by using tally marks, with a full mark representing one hour and a half-size mark representing a half-hour. In the third column, total the hours for each activity, and then add the totals in that column to make sure that your grand total is approximately 168 hours. (If it isn't, go back and check your grid and calculations and fix any errors you find.) Leave the "Ideal Time in Hours" column blank for now.

Take it to the next level. Take a look at your results, paying special attention to how your estimates of sleep, study, and technology time compare with your actual logged activity hours for the week. Use a separate sheet of paper or an electronic file to answer the following questions:

- What surprises you about how you spend your time?
- Do you spend the most time on the activities representing your most important values?
- Where do you waste the most time? What do you think that is costing you?
- On which activities do you think you should spend *more* time? On which should you spend *less* time?

Move toward mastery. Go back to the Weekly Summary Chart and fill in the "Ideal Time in Hours" column. Consider the difference between actual hours and ideal hours. What changes are you willing to make to get closer to how you want to be spending your time? Write a short paragraph describing, in detail, two time-management changes you plan to make this term so that you are focusing your time more effectively on your most important goals and values.

Values, Goals, and Time

TIME	MONDAY activity	TUESDAY activity	WEDNESDAY activity	THURSDAY activity
6:00 A.M.				
6:30 A.M.				
7:00 A.M.				
7:30 A.M.				
8:00 A.M.				
8:30 A.M.				
9:00 A.M.				
9:30 A.M.				
10:00 A.M.				
10:30 A.M.				
11:00 A.M.				
11:30 A.M.				
12:00 P.M.				
12:30 P.M.				
1:00 P.M.				
1:30 P.M.				
2:00 P.M.				
2:30 P.M.				
3:00 P.M.				
3:30 P.M.				
4:00 P.M.				
4:30 P.M.				
5:00 P.M.				
5:30 P.M.				
6:00 P.M.				
6:30 P.M.				
7:00 P.M.				
7:30 P.M.				
8:00 P.M.				
8:30 P.M.				
9:00 P.M.				
9:30 P.M.				
10:00 P.M.				
10:30 P.M.				
11:00 P.M.				
11:30 P.M.				
12:00 A.M.				
12:30 A.M.				
1:00 A.M.				
1:30 A.M.				
2:00 A.M.				

Weekly Time Log

CHAPTER 2

Weekly Summary

TIME	FRIDAY activity	SATURDAY activity	SUNDAY activity
6:00 A.M.			
6:30 A.M.			
7:00 A.M.			
7:30 A.M.			
8:00 A.M.			
8:30 A.M.			
9:00 A.M.			
9:30 A.M.			
10:00 A.M.			
10:30 A.M.			
11:00 A.M.			
11:30 A.M.			
12:00 P.M.			
12:30 P.M.			
1:00 P.M.			
1:30 P.M.			
2:00 P.M.			
2:30 P.M.			
3:00 P.M.			
3:30 P.M.			
4:00 P.M.			
4:30 P.M.			
5:00 P.M.			
5:30 P.M.			
6:00 P.M.			
6:30 P.M.			
7:00 P.M.			
7:30 P.M.			
8:00 P.M.			
8:30 P.M.			
9:00 P.M.			
9:30 P.M.			
10:00 P.M.			
10:30 P.M.			
11:00 P.M.			
11:30 P.M.			
12:00 A.M.			
12:30 A.M.			
1:00 A.M.			
1:30 A.M.			
2:00 A.M.			

Values, Goals, and Time

Activity	Time Tallied Over One-Week Period	Total Time in Hours	Ideal Time in Hours
Example: Class	~~卌 卌 卌~~ ǁ	16.5	
Class			
Work			
Studying			
Sleeping			
Eating			
Family time/child care			
Commuting/traveling			
Chores and personal business			
Friends and important relationships			
Telephone time			
Leisure/entertainment			
Spiritual life			
Other			

WRITE IT *Communicate*

Build Intrapersonal and Communication Skills

Emotional intelligence journal: How you feel about your time management. Paying attention to your feelings about how you spend time can be a key step toward making time-management choices that are more in line with your values. Think, and then write, about how your most time-demanding activities make you feel. What makes you happiest, most fulfilled, or most satisfied? What makes you most anxious, frustrated, or drained? What do these feelings tell you about your day-to-day choices? Describe how you could adjust your mindset, or make different choices, to feel better about how you spend your time.

Real-life writing: Two areas of academic specialty. Use your course catalogue to identify two academic areas that look interesting. Write a short report comparing and contrasting the majors in these areas, being sure to note GPA requirements, number of courses, relevance to career areas, campus locations, "feel" of the department offices, other requirements, and any other relevant characteristics. Conclude your report with observations about how this comparison and evaluation process has refined your thinking.

WORK IT *Build Your Brand*

Explore Career Goals through a Personal Mission

21st Century Learning Building Blocks

- Initiative and self-direction
- Creativity and innovation
- Productivity and accountability

Complete the following in your electronic portfolio or separately on paper.

No matter what employment goals you ultimately pursue, a successful career will be grounded in your personal mission in one or more ways.

First, write a draft of your personal mission. Refer to the list on page 33 to remind yourself of the elements of a personal mission statement. Use these questions to get you thinking:

1. You are at your retirement dinner. You have had an esteemed career in your chosen field. Your best friend stands up and talks about the five aspects of your character that have taken you to the top. What do you think they are?

2. You are preparing for a late-in-life job change. Updating your resumé, you need to list your contributions and achievements. What would you like them to be?

3. You have been told that you have one year to live. With family or close friends, you talk about the values that mean the most to you. Based on that discussion, how do you want to spend your time in this last year? Which choices will reflect what is most important to you?

After you have a personal mission statement to provide vision and motivation, take some time to think more specifically about your working life. Spend 15 minutes brainstorming everything that you wish you could be, do, have, or experience in your career 10 years from now—the skills you want to have, money you want to earn, benefits, experiences, travel, anything you can think of. List your wishes, draw them, depict them using cut-outs from magazines, or combine ideas—whatever you like best.

Now, group your wishes in order of priority. On paper or in files labelled "Priority 1," "Priority 2," and "Priority 3," write each wish where it fits, with Priority 1 being the most important, Priority 2 the second most important, and Priority 3 the third.

Look at your priority lists. What do they tell you about what is most important to you? What fits into your personal mission, and what doesn't? Circle or highlight three high-priority wishes that mesh with your personal mission. For each, write down one action step you may have to take soon to make it come true.

You may want to look back at these materials at the end of the term to see what changes may have taken place in your priorities.

Joyce Bishop

The more you know about yourself, the more effectively you can analyze courses, evaluate partners, and decide what, how, and where to study and work. With the information you discover, you can take the risks that will prove most productive for you.

Learning How You Learn

MAKING THE MOST OF YOUR ABILITIES

What Would You Risk? *Joyce Bishop, Ph.D.*

Joyce Bishop

As a post-secondary student, author Joyce Bishop was confused by her spotty record—doing well in some classes but feeling totally lost in others, especially those that were lecture-based. She couldn't make sense of what she was hearing when she wasn't familiar with the information. If she read the material ahead of time, she could make visual pictures in her mind and look up concepts. This method helped, but there wasn't often time for it.

Joyce also had trouble in small classes because she heard voices around her as much as she heard the instructor. She would borrow classmates' notes in exchange for typing their term papers. The notes and the typing helped her to retain information. Ultimately, finding that science classes were somewhat less difficult than others, she majored in biology and managed to graduate.

Twelve years later, pursuing a master's in public health, Joyce was having trouble reading and her eye doctor was concerned about the stress it put on her eyes. He sent her to a centre that usually tests small children for learning disabilities. The therapist who tested her determined that Joyce processed language at a fourth-grade level, a condition that had not changed in her adult life. Guessing that she had not made it past the tenth grade, the therapist was shocked to hear that she was completing her master's degree. Joyce was beginning to understand what was behind so many years of mediocre grades and an intense struggle to learn.

To be continued . . .

You don't have to have a learning disability to face learning challenges. For Joyce, taking part in adventure sports, such as riding ATVs, is a way to grow from taking a risk, just as she did when working through her disability. You'll learn more about Joyce, and revisit her situation, within the chapter.

Notes

Today   Mar 10   8:01 AM

Working through this chapter will help you to:

statusCHECK

How Aware Are You of How You Learn?

For each statement, circle the number that feels right to you, from 1 for "not at all true for me" to 5 for "very true for me."

1. I believe I can develop my skills and abilities through self-knowledge and hard work. ① ② ③ ④ ⑤

2. I have a pretty clear idea of my strengths and abilities. ① ② ③ ④ ⑤

3. I understand which subjects and situations make it more difficult for me to succeed. ① ② ③ ④ ⑤

4. In my work in the classroom and out, I try to maximize what I do well. ① ② ③ ④ ⑤

5. I recognize that being comfortable with the subject matter isn't necessarily enough to succeed in a course ① ② ③ ④ ⑤

6. I assess an instructor's teaching style and make adjustments so that I can learn effectively. ① ② ③ ④ ⑤

7. I choose study techniques that tap into how I learn best. ① ② ③ ④ ⑤

8. I try to use technology that works well with how I learn. ① ② ③ ④ ⑤

9. I've taken a skills and/or interests inventory to help find a major or career area that suits me. ① ② ③ ④ ⑤

10. I understand what a learning disability is and am aware of several different types of disabilities. ① ② ③ ④ ⑤

Each of the topics in these statements is covered in this chapter. Note those statements for which you circled a 3 or lower. Skim the chapter to see where those topics appear, and pay special attention to them as you read, learn, and apply new strategies.

REMEMBER: NO MATTER HOW WELL YOU KNOW YOURSELF AS A LEARNER, YOU CAN IMPROVE WITH EFFORT AND PRACTICE.

WHY EXPLORE
who you are as a learner?

Have you thought about how you learn? Now, as you begin college or university, is the perfect time to think about how you learn, think, and function in the world. Thinking about thinking is known as *metacognition* (something you are building with each chapter-opening self-assessment). Building metacognition and self-knowledge will help you become a better student and decision maker because the more you know about yourself, the more effectively you can analyze courses, study environments, and study partners; self-knowledge can also help you come up with ideas as well as make practical choices about what, how, and where to study.

In its report entitled Employability Skills 2000+, the Conference Board of Canada recognizes the need for employees to "learn and grow continuously." It also stresses the importance of assessing one's own strengths and weaknesses as well as setting goals for learning on your own terms.[1] In other words, it is also important in the "real world" to know what your learning style is.

MyStudentSuccessLab

Whether face-to-face or online, MyStudentSuccessLab helps students build the skills they need through peer-led video interviews, interactive practice exercises, and activities that provide academic, life, and professionalism skills.

Use Assessments to Learn About Yourself

Every person is born with a unique learning style and particular levels of ability and potential in different areas. These innate raw materials combine with effort and environment to create a "recipe" for what you can achieve. Part of that recipe is the way you perceive your strengths and challenges, which comes from many different sources and starts in childhood. Maybe your mother thinks you are "the funny one" or "the quiet one." A grade school teacher may have called you "a thinker," "a slacker," "a go-getter," or "shy." These labels—from yourself and others—influence your ability to set and achieve goals.

The danger in accepting a label as truth, as Sternberg did as a child (see Chapter 1), is that it can put you in a fixed mindset and limit your potential. You are not simply stuck with what you've been given. As you read in the first chapter, brain studies show that humans of any age are able to build new neuropathways and thereby learn new ideas and skills, supporting theories that intelligence can grow over time if you work to keep learning.

Picture a bag of rubber bands of different sizes. Some are thick, and some are thin; some are long, and some are short—*but all of them can stretch.* A small rubber band, stretched out, can reach the length of a larger one that lies unstretched. In other words, with effort and focus, you can grow whatever raw material you have at the start, perhaps beyond the natural gifts of someone not making any effort. Joyce's story illustrates just how far effort can stretch a person's natural abilities.

Ask yourself: Who am I right now? Where could I be, and where would I like to be, in five years? Assessments focused on how you learn and interact with others can help you start to answer these big questions. Assessments have a different goal from tests. Where a test seeks to identify a level of performance, an assessment, as professor and psychologist Howard Gardner puts it, is "the obtaining of information about a person's skills and potentials ... providing useful feedback to the person."[2] You can think of an assessment as an exploration that, if honest, will reliably produce interesting and helpful information.

The assessments you will take in this chapter provide the questions that get you thinking actively about your strengths and challenges. (Learning disabilities—diagnosed, specific issues different from the learning challenges that all students face—are discussed at the end of the chapter.) As you search for answers, you will be gathering important information about yourself. With this information, you will be able to define your rubber band and get ready to stretch it to its limit.

> **LEARNING STYLE**
> A particular way in which the mind receives and processes information.

> **POTENTIALS**
> Abilities that may be developed.

Jelena Aloskina/Shutterstock

Use Assessments to Make Choices and to Grow

There is much about yourself, your surroundings, and your experiences that you cannot control. However, self-knowledge gives you tools to choose how you respond to circumstances. Although you cannot control, for example, the courses you are required to take or how your instructors teach, you can manage how you respond in each situation.

The two assessments in this chapter—Multiple Pathways to Learning and the Personality Spectrum—will give you greater insight into your strengths and weaknesses. The material after the assessments will help you think practically about how to maximize what you do well and compensate for challenging areas by making specific choices about what you do in class, during study time, and in the workplace.

Understanding yourself as a learner will also help you choose how to respond to others in a group situation. In a study group, classroom, or workplace, each person takes in material in a unique way. You can use what you know about how others learn to improve communication and teamwork.

Remember: An assessment is simply a snapshot of where you are at a given moment. There are no "right" answers, no "best" scores. And because many educators are aware of research that shows the benefit of learning in a variety of ways—kind of like cross-training for the brain—they will often challenge you to learn in ways that aren't as comfortable for you.

As you complete this chapter's assessments, compare the experience to trying on new glasses to correct blurred vision. The glasses will not create new paths and possibilities, but they will enable you to see more clearly the ones in front of you. Furthermore, as you gain experience, build skills, and learn more, your learning patterns are apt to change over time. You may want to take the assessments again in the future to see whether your results are different.

WHAT TOOLS CAN HELP YOU ASSESS HOW YOU
learn and interact with others?

Many different tools can help you become more aware of how you think, process information, and relate to others. Some focus on learning preferences, some on areas of potential, and some on personality type. This chapter examines two assessments in depth. The first—Multiple Pathways to Learning—is a learning preferences assessment focusing on eight areas of potential, based on Howard Gardner's multiple intelligences (MI) theory. The second—the Personality Spectrum—is a personality-type assessment based on the Myers-Briggs Type Indicator and helps you evaluate how you react to people and situations.

Following each assessment is information about the typical traits of each intelligence or Personality Spectrum dimension. As you will see from your scores, you have abilities in all areas, though some are more developed than others.

INTELLIGENCE
As defined by Howard Gardner, an ability to solve problems or create products that are of value in a culture.

Assess Your Multiple Intelligences with Pathways to Learning

In 1983, Howard Gardner changed the way people perceive intelligence and learning with his theory of multiple intelligences. Like Robert Sternberg, Gardner had developed the belief that the traditional view of intelligence—based on mathematical, logical, and verbal measurements that made up an intelligence quotient, or IQ—did not comprehensively reflect the spectrum of human ability. Where Sternberg focused on the spectrum of actions that help people achieve important goals, Gardner homed in on the idea that humans possess a number of different areas of natural ability and potential.

The theory of multiple intelligences

Gardner's research led him to believe that there are eight unique "intelligences," or areas of ability. These areas include the aptitudes traditionally associated with the term *intelligence*—logic and verbal skills—but go beyond, to encompass a wide range of potentials of the human brain.[3] These intelligences almost never function in isolation. You will almost always use several at a time for any significant role or task.[4]

Look at Key 3.1 for a description of each intelligence, along with examples of people who have unusually high levels of ability in each

Kirill Kedrinski/Fotolia

Students drawn to the sciences may find that they have strengths in logical-mathematical or naturalistic thinking.

INTELLIGENCE	DESCRIPTION	HIGH-ACHIEVING EXAMPLES
Verbal-Linguistic	Ability to communicate through language; listening, reading, writing, speaking	• Author and Nobel Prize Winner Alice Munro • Orator and American President Barack Obama
Logical-Mathematical	Ability to understand logical reasoning and problem solving; math, science, patterns, sequences	• Physicist Stephen Hawking • Mathematician Svetlana Jitomirskaya
Bodily-Kinesthetic	Ability to use the physical body skillfully and to take in knowledge through bodily sensation; coordination; working with hands	• Tennis player Eugenie Bouchard • Hockey star P.K. Subban
Visual-Spatial	Ability to understand spatial relationships and to perceive and create images; visual art, graphic design, charts and maps	• Graphic novelist Bryan Lee O'Malley • Movie director Sarah Polley
Interpersonal	Ability to relate to others, noticing their moods, motivations, and feelings; social activity, cooperative learning, teamwork	• Media personality Marilyn Denis • "Me to We" co-founder, Craig Kielburger
Intrapersonal	Ability to understand one's own behaviour and feelings; self-awareness, independence, time spent alone	• Animal researcher Jane Goodall • Philosopher Marshall McLuhan
Musical	Ability to comprehend and create meaningful sound; sensitivity to music and musical patterns	• Singer and musician Dallas Green • Composer Andrew Lloyd Webber
Naturalistic	Ability to identify, distinguish, categorize, and classify species or items, often incorporating high interest in elements of the natural environment	• Conservationist David Suzuki • Bird cataloguer John James Audubon

intelligence. Although few people will have the verbal-linguistic intelligence of William Shakespeare or the interpersonal intelligence of Oprah Winfrey, everyone has some level of ability in each intelligence. Your goal is to identify what your levels are and to work your strongest intelligences to your advantage.

Your own eight intelligences

Gardner believes that all people possess some capacity in each of the eight intelligences and that every person has developed some intelligences more fully than others. When

Learning How You Learn

you find a task or subject easy, you are probably using a more fully developed intelligence. When you have trouble, you may be using a less developed intelligence.[5]

Furthermore, Gardner believes your levels of development in the eight intelligences can grow or recede throughout your life, depending on your efforts and experiences. For example, although you will not become a world-class pianist if you have limited musical ability, you still can grow what you have with focus and work. Conversely, even a highly talented musician will lose ability without practice. These examples reflect how the brain grows with learning and becomes sluggish without it.

A related self-assessment that you may have heard of, or have already taken, is the VAK or VARK questionnaire. VAK/VARK assesses learning preferences in three (or four) areas: visual, auditory, (read/write), and kinesthetic. The multiple intelligences (MI) assessment is this book's choice because it incorporates and expands on the elements of VAK/VARK, giving you a more comprehensive picture of your abilities. For further information about VAK/VARK, go to www.vark-learn.com or search online using the keywords "VAK assessment."

A note about auditory learners who learn and remember best through listening: auditory learning is part of two MI dimensions: *verbal intelligence* (hearing words) and *musical intelligence* (associating information with sounds and rhythms). If you tend to absorb information better through listening, try study suggestions for these two intelligences. Podcasts are especially helpful to auditory learners, and an increasing number of instructors are converting their lectures into digital format for downloading.

Use the Multiple Pathways to Learning assessment to determine where you are right now in the eight intelligence areas. Then look at Key 3.2 immediately following the assessment to identify specific skills associated with each area. Finally, the Multiple Intelligence Strategies grids in Chapters 5 through 11 will help you apply your learning styles knowledge to key post-secondary success skills and to specific areas of study.

TYPOLOGY
A systematic classification or study of types.

Assess Your Style of Interaction with the Personality Spectrum

Personality assessments help you understand how you respond to the world around you, including people, work, and school. They also can help guide you as you explore majors and careers.

The concept of dividing human beings into four basic personality types, as in the Personality Spectrum, goes as far back as Aristotle and Hippocrates, ancient Greek philosophers. Modern psychologist Carl Jung focused on personality typology, defining the following parameters:[6]

- *An individual's preferred "world."* Jung said that extroverts tend to prefer the outside world of people and activities, whereas introverts tend to prefer the inner world of thoughts, feelings, and fantasies.

- *Different ways of dealing with the world, or "functions."* Jung defined four distinct interaction dimensions, which are used to different degrees: *sensing* (learning through what your senses take in), *thinking* (evaluating information rationally), *intuiting* (learning through an instinct that comes from many integrated sources of information), and *feeling* (evaluating information through emotional response).

Katharine Briggs and her daughter, Isabel Briggs Myers, developed an assessment based on Jung's typology, called the Myers-Briggs Type Inventory (MBTI; www.myersbriggs.org). One of the most widely used personality

Verbal-Linguistic		• Remembering terms easily • Mastering a foreign language • Using writing or speech to convince someone to do or believe something
Logical-Mathematical		• Recognizing abstract patterns • Using facts to support an idea and generating ideas based on evidence • Reasoning scientifically (formulating and testing a hypothesis)
Bodily-Kinesthetic		• Having a strong mind–body connection • Controlling and coordinating body movement • Using the body to create products or express emotion
Visual-Spatial		• Recognizing relationships between objects • Representing something graphically • Manipulating images
Interpersonal		• Seeing things from others' perspectives • Noticing moods, intentions, and temperaments of others • Gauging the most effective way to work with individual group members
Intrapersonal		• Accessing one's internal emotions • Understanding feelings and using them to guide behavior • Understanding self in relation to others
Musical		• Sensing tonal qualities • Being sensitive to sounds and rhythms in music and in spoken language • Using an understanding of musical patterns to hear music
Naturalistic		• Categorizing something as a member of a group or species • Understanding relationships among natural organisms • Being deeply comfortable with, and respecting, the natural world

inventories in the world, it creates 16 possible types. David Keirsey and Marilyn Bates later condensed the MBTI types into four temperaments, creating the Keirsey Sorter (found at www.keirsey.com).

When author Joyce Bishop developed the Personality Spectrum assessment in this chapter, she adapted and simplified the Keirsey Sorter and MBTI material into four personality types—Thinker, Organizer, Giver, and Adventurer. Like the

MULTIPLE PATHWAYS TO LEARNING

Each intelligence has a set of numbered statements. Consider each statement on its own. Then, on a scale from 1 (lowest) to 4 (highest), rate how closely it matches who you are right now, and write that number on the line next to the statement. Finally, total your results from each set of six questions. Enter your scores in the grid on page 63.

1. rarely   **2. sometimes**   **3. usually**   **4. always**

1. _____ I enjoy telling stories.
2. _____ I like to write.
3. _____ I like to read.
4. _____ I express myself clearly.
5. _____ I am good at negotiating.
6. _____ I like to discuss topics that interest me.
_____ **TOTAL for VERBAL-LINGUISTIC**

1. _____ I like math in school.
2. _____ I like science.
3. _____ I problem-solve well.
4. _____ I question how things work.
5. _____ I enjoy planning or designing something new.
6. _____ I am able to fix things.
_____ **TOTAL for LOGICAL–MATHEMATICAL**

1. _____ I enjoy physical activities.
2. _____ I am uncomfortable sitting still.
3. _____ I prefer to learn through doing.
4. _____ When sitting, I move my legs or hands.
5. _____ I enjoy working with my hands.
6. _____ I like to pace when I'm thinking or studying.
_____ **TOTAL for BODILY-KINESTHETIC**

1. _____ I use maps easily.
2. _____ I draw pictures/diagrams when explaining ideas.
3. _____ I can assemble items easily from diagrams.
4. _____ I enjoy drawing or photography.
5. _____ I do not like to read long paragraphs.
6. _____ I prefer a drawn map over written directions.
_____ **TOTAL for VISUAL-SPATIAL**

1. _____ I like doing a project with other people.
2. _____ People come to me to help settle conflicts.
3. _____ I like to spend time with friends.
4. _____ I am good at understanding people.
5. _____ I am good at making people feel comfortable.
6. _____ I enjoy helping others.
_____ **TOTAL for INTERPERSONAL**

1. _____ I need quiet time to think.
2. _____ I think about issues before I want to talk.
3. _____ I am interested in self-improvement.
4. _____ I understand my thoughts and feelings.
5. _____ I know what I want out of life.
6. _____ I prefer to work on projects alone.
_____ **TOTAL FOR INTRAPERSONAL**

1. _____ I listen to music.
2. _____ I move my fingers or feet when I hear music.
3. _____ I have good rhythm.
4. _____ I like to sing along with music.
5. _____ People have said I have musical talent.
6. _____ I like to express my ideas through music.
_____ **TOTAL for MUSICAL**

1. _____ I like to think about how things, ideas, or people fit into categories.
2. _____ I enjoy studying plants, animals, or oceans.
3. _____ I tend to see how things relate to, or are distinct from, one another.
4. _____ I think about having a career in the natural sciences.
5. _____ As a child, I often played with bugs and leaves.
6. _____ I like to investigate the natural world around me.
_____ **TOTAL for NATURALISTIC**

Source: Developed by Joyce Bishop, Ph.D., Golden West College, Huntington Beach, CA. Based on Howard Gardner, *Frames of Mind: The Theory of Multiple Intelligences*, New York: Harper Collins, 1993.

SCORING GRID FOR MULTIPLE PATHWAYS TO LEARNING

For each intelligence, shade the box in the row that corresponds with the range where your score falls. For example, if you scored 17 in bodily-kinesthetic intelligence, you would shade the middle box in that row; if you scored a 13 in visual-spatial, you would shade the last box in that row. When you have shaded one box for each row, you will see a "map" of your range of development at a glance.

A score of 20–24 indicates a high level of development in that particular type of intelligence, 14–19 a moderate level, and below 14 an underdeveloped intelligence.

	20–24 (HIGHLY DEVELOPED)	14–19 (MODERATELY DEVELOPED)	BELOW 14 (UNDERDEVELOPED)
Verbal-Linguistic			
Logical-Mathematical			
Bodily-Kinesthetic			
Visual-Spatial			
Interpersonal			
Intrapersonal			
Musical			
Naturalistic			

assessments on which it is based, the Personality Spectrum helps you identify the kinds of interactions that are most, and least, comfortable for you. As with the multiple intelligences, these results may change over time as you experience new things, change, and continue to learn. Key 3.3 shows skills characteristic of each personality type.

 **KEY 3.3** Particular abilities and skills are associated with each personality spectrum dimension.

Thinker		• Solving problems • Developing models and systems • Using analytical and abstract thinking
Organizer		• Being responsible and reliable • Being neat, organized, and detail-oriented • Following through on every aspect of a task
Giver		• Maintaining successful, close relationships • Making a difference in the world • Negotiating; promoting peace
Adventurer		• Being courageous and daring • Using hands-on problem solving • Possessing an active and spontaneous style

Source: Developed by Joyce Bishop, Ph.D., Golden West College, Huntington Beach, CA. Based on Howard Gardner, *Frames of Mind: The Theory of Multiple Intelligences,* New York: Harper Collins, 1993.

Learning How You Learn

PERSONALITY SPECTRUM

STEP 1 Rank-order all four responses to each question from most like you (4) to least like you (1) so that for each question you use the numbers 1, 2, 3, and 4 one time each. Place numbers on the lines next to the responses.

4. most like me　　**3. more like me**　　**2. less like me**　　**1. least like me**

1. I like instructors who
   a. _____ tell me exactly what is expected of me.
   b. _____ make learning active and exciting.
   c. _____ maintain a safe and supportive classroom.
   d. _____ challenge me to think at higher levels.

2. I learn best when the material is
   a. _____ well organized.
   b. _____ something I can work with hands-on.
   c. _____ about understanding and improving the human condition.
   d. _____ intellectually challenging.

3. A high priority in my life is to
   a. _____ keep my commitments.
   b. _____ experience as much of life as possible.
   c. _____ make a difference in the lives of others.
   d. _____ understand how things work.

4. Other people think of me as
   a. _____ dependable and loyal.
   b. _____ dynamic and creative.
   c. _____ caring and honest.
   d. _____ intelligent and inventive.

5. When I experience stress, I usually
   a. _____ do something to help me feel more in control of my life.
   b. _____ do something physical and daring.
   c. _____ talk with a friend.
   d. _____ go off by myself and think about my situation.

6. I would probably not be close friends with someone who is
   a. _____ irresponsible.
   b. _____ unwilling to try new things.
   c. _____ selfish and unkind to others.
   d. _____ an illogical thinker.

7. My vacations could be described as
   a. _____ traditional.
   b. _____ adventuresome.
   c. _____ pleasing to others.
   d. _____ a new learning experience.

8. One word that best describes me is
   a. _____ sensible.
   b. _____ spontaneous.
   c. _____ giving.
   d. _____ analytical.

STEP 2 Add up the total points for each letter.

TOTAL FOR　　a. _____ Organizer　　b. _____ Adventurer　　c. _____ Giver　　d. _____ Thinker

STEP 3 Plot these numbers on the brain diagram on page 65.

CHAPTER 3

SCORING DIAGRAM FOR PERSONALITY SPECTRUM

Write your scores from page 64 in the four coloured squares just outside the brain diagram—Thinker score at top left, Giver score at top right, Organizer score at bottom left, and Adventurer score at bottom right.

Each square has a line of numbers that go from the square to the centre of the diagram. For each of your four scores, place a dot on the appropriate number in the line near that square. For example, if you scored 15 in the Giver spectrum, you would place a dot between the 14 and 16 in the upper right-hand line of numbers. If you scored a 26 in the Organizer spectrum, you would place a dot on the 26 in the lower left-hand line of numbers.

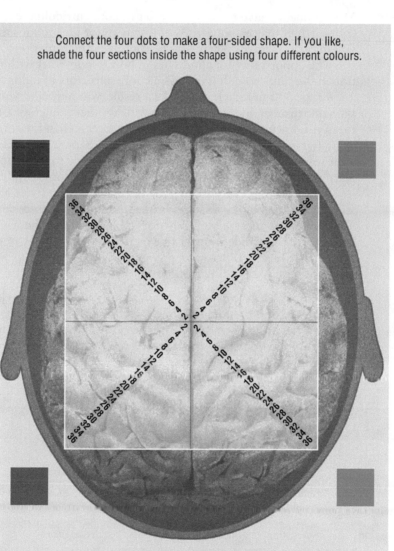

THINKER

Technical
Scientific
Mathematical
Dispassionate
Rational
Analytical
Logical
Problem Solving
Theoretical
Intellectual
Objective
Quantitative
Explicit
Realistic
Literal
Precise
Formal

GIVER

Interpersonal
Emotional
Caring
Sociable
Giving
Spiritual
Musical
Romantic
Feeling
Peacemaking
Trusting
Adaptable
Passionate
Harmonious
Idealistic
Talkative
Honest

ORGANIZER

Tactical
Planning
Detailed
Practical
Confident
Predictable
Controlled
Dependable
Systematic
Sequential
Structured
Administrative
Procedural
Organized
Conservative
Safekeeping
Disciplined

ADVENTURER

Active
Visual
Risking
Original
Artistic
Spatial
Skilful
Impulsive
Metaphoric
Experimental
Divergent
Fast-paced
Simultaneous
Competitive
Imaginative
Open-minded
Adventuresome

Connect the four dots to make a four-sided shape. If you like, shade the four sections inside the shape using four different colours.

For the Personality Spectrum,
26–36 indicates a strong tendency in that dimension,
14–25 a moderate tendency,
and below 14 a minimal tendency.

Source for brain diagram: Charles G. Morris/Pearson Education, Inc./Prentice Hall, Inc.

HOW CAN YOU USE
your self-knowledge?

In completing the assessments, you have developed a clearer picture of who you are and how you interact with others. Now use this new picture to choose effective strategies for class, study time, the workplace, or technology.

Classroom Choices

Most students have to complete a set of core curriculum courses, as well as whatever courses their majors require. As you sign up for the sections that fit into your schedule, you may be asking, "Where are the choices in this situation?"

The opportunity for choice lies in how you interact with your instructor and function in the classroom. It is impossible for instructors to tailor classroom presentation to 15, 40, or 300 unique learners. As a result, you may find yourself in a great situation with one teacher and in a mismatch with another. Sometimes, the way the class is structured can have more of an effect on your success than the subject matter.

After several class meetings, you should be able to assess each instructor's dominant teaching styles (Key 3.4) and figure out how to maximize your learning. As with learning styles, most instructors will demonstrate some combination of styles.

Although styles vary and instructors may combine styles, the word-focused lecture is still most common. For this reason, the traditional post-secondary classroom is generally a happy home for the verbal or logical learner and the Thinker and the Organizer. However, many students need to experience other modes in order to learn effectively. What can you do when your preferences don't match up with how your instructor teaches? Here are three suggestions:

- *Play to your strengths.* For example, a musical learner whose instructor delivers material in a random way might record lecture highlights digitally and listen to them on an MP3 player. (Be sure to check whether your instructor and school permit recording.) Likewise, if you are a Giver with an instructor who delivers straight lectures, you should consider setting up a study group to go over details and fill in factual gaps.

KEY 3.4 — Instructors often prefer one or more teaching styles.

TEACHING STYLE	WHAT TO EXPECT IN CLASS
Lecture, verbal focus	Instructor speaks to the class for the entire period, with little class interaction. Lesson is taught primarily through words, either spoken or written on the board, in a slide show, on handouts, or via the text.
Lecture with group discussion	Instructor presents material but encourages class discussion.
Small groups	Instructor presents material and then breaks class into small groups for discussion or project work.
Visual focus	Instructor uses visual elements such as slide shows, diagrams, photographs, drawings, transparencies, and videos.
Logical presentation	Instructor organizes material in a logical sequence, such as by steps, time, or importance.
Random presentation	Instructor tackles topics in no particular order and may jump around a lot or digress.
Conceptual presentation	Instructor spends the majority of time on the big picture, focusing on abstract concepts and umbrella ideas.
Detailed presentation	Instructor spends the majority of time, after introducing ideas, on the details and facts that underlie them.
Hands-on presentation	Instructor uses demonstrations, experiments, props, and class activities to show key points.

student PROFILE

Hongman Xu

SENECA COLLEGE, TORONTO, ONTARIO

Hongman Xu

About me:

I'm a mother of two and am originally from Jiujiang, a small and famous city in China. My mother and father are doctors. I have two sisters. Everyone in my family graduated from university in China. When my husband and I immigrated to Canada, I had 10 years of work experience in China but no idea of how to be a student in Canada. I'm enrolled in Seneca's International Transportation and Customs diploma program.

I plan to start my own customs brokerage company in the future.

What I focus on:

When I was younger, my dreams didn't include being a mature college student struggling with math in Canada. While it might be a common stereotype that Asians are good at math, it wasn't the case with me. I struggled. When I faced troubles in my studies, I was able to go to my professor for help. I also used both the textbook and online quizzes, which helped me practise over and over again. These were very useful for me and helped me study. Online studying was also helpful when my kids got sick and I couldn't get to class.

I also read the textbook step by step, a bit at a time, which helped me use what little time I had more effectively. Extra help from my professor, online quizzes, and the textbook were the keys for my success in accounting classes.

What will help me in the future:

Being able to overcome my struggles with math and accounting will help me reach my dream of starting my own customs brokerage firm. Succeeding in those classes has taught me that any problem can be solved with hard work. It's given me the confidence to succeed.

Hongman Xu. Seneca College, Toronto, Ontario. Reprinted by permission.

- *Work to strengthen weaker areas.* A visual learner reviewing notes from a structured lecture could use logical-mathematical strategies such as outlining notes or thinking about cause-and-effect relationships within the material. An Organizer, studying for a test from notes delivered by an instructor with a random presentation, could organize material by using tables and timelines.

- *Ask your instructor for help.* If you are having trouble with coursework, communicate with your instructor or teaching assistant through email or during office hours. This is especially important in large lectures in which you are anonymous unless you speak up. A visual learner, for example, might ask the instructor to recommend graphs, figures, or videos that illustrate the lecture.

No instructor of a diverse group of learners can provide exactly what each student needs. However, adjusting

Cathy Yeulet/123RF

Add a new dimension to your experience of a course and your learning by talking to your instructor outside of class time.

Learning How You Learn

get analytical

Complete the following on paper or in a digital format.

Considering what you know about yourself as a learner and about your instructors' teaching styles this term, decide which classroom situation is the most challenging for you. Use this exercise to think analytically, creatively, and practically about the situation.

1. Name the course and describe the instructor's style.

2. Analyze the problem that is making the class challenging.

3. Generate and write down three ideas about actions you can take to improve the situation.

4. Finally, choose one action and put it to practice. Briefly note what happened. Did any improvement result?

to instructors' teaching styles builds flexibility that you need for career and life success. Just as you can't hand-pick your instructors, you will rarely, if ever, be able to choose your work colleagues or their ways of working or interacting with others.

A final point: Some students try to find out more about an instructor by asking students who have already taken the course or by looking up comments online. Be careful with investigations like this. You may not know or be able to trust an anonymous poster. Even if you hear a review from a friend you do trust, every student–instructor relationship is unique, and an instructor your friend loved may turn out to be a bad match for you. Prioritize the courses that you need, and know that you will find a way to make the most of what your instructors offer, no matter who they are.

Study Choices

Start using what you have learned about yourself now to choose the best study techniques. For example, if you tend to learn successfully from a linear, logical presentation, you can look for order (for example, a *chronology*—information organized sequentially according to event dates—or a problem–solution structure) as you review notes. If you are strong in interpersonal intelligence, you can try to work in study groups whenever possible.

When faced with a task that challenges your weaknesses, use strategies that boost your ability. For example, if you are an Adventurer who does *not* respond well to linear information, you can apply your strengths to the material—for example, through a hands-on approach. Or you can focus on developing your area of weakness by trying skills that work well for Thinker-dominant learners.

When you study with others, you and the entire group will be more successful if you understand the different learning styles in the group, as in the following examples.

- An interpersonal learner could take the lead in teaching material to others.
- An organizer could coordinate the group schedule.
- A naturalistic learner might organize facts into categories that solidify concepts.

Verbal-Linguistic		• Read text; highlight selectively • Use a computer to retype and summarize notes • Outline chapters • Recite information or write scripts/debates
Logical-Mathematical		• Organize material logically; if it suits the topic, use a spreadsheet program • Explain material sequentially to someone • Develop systems and find patterns • Analyze and evaluate information
Bodily-Kinesthetic		• Move while you learn; pace and recite • Rewrite or retype notes to engage "muscle memory" • Design and play games to learn material • Act out scripts of material
Visual-Spatial		• Develop graphic organizers for new material • Draw mind maps/think links • Use a computer to develop charts and tables • Use colour in notes to organize
Interpersonal		• Study in a group • As you study, discuss information over the phone or send instant messages • Teach someone else the material • Make time to discuss assignments and tests with your instructor
Intrapersonal		• Reflect on personal meaning of information • Keep a journal • Study in quiet areas • Imagine essays or experiments before beginning
Musical		• Create rhythms out of words • Beat out rhythms with your hand or a stick while reciting concepts • Write songs/raps that help you learn concepts • Write out study material to fit into a wordless tune you have on a CD or MP3 player; chant or sing the material along with the tune as you listen
Naturalistic		• Break down information into categories • Look for ways in which items fit or don't fit together • Look for relationships among ideas, events, and facts • Study in a natural setting if it helps you focus

Look at Keys 3.5 and 3.6 for study strategies that suit each intelligence and Personality Spectrum dimension. Because you have some level of ability in each area and because there will be times that you need to boost your ability in a weaker area, you may find useful suggestions under any of the headings. Try different techniques. Pay close attention to what works best for you—you may be surprised at what is useful, as Joyce was about how typing helped her retain information.

Learning How You Learn

Thinker		• Convert material into logical charts, flow diagrams, and outlines • Reflect independently on new information • Learn through problem solving • Design new ways of approaching material or problems
Organizer		• Define tasks in concrete terms • Use a planner to schedule tasks and dates • Organize material by rewriting and summarizing class or text notes • Create, or look for, a well-structured study environment
Giver		• Study with others in person, on the phone, or via instant messages • Teach material to others • Seek out tasks, groups, and subjects that involve helping people • Connect with instructors, advisors, and tutors
Adventurer		• Look for environments or courses that encourage non-traditional approaches • Find hands-on ways to learn • Use or develop games or puzzles to help memorize terms • Fight boredom by asking to do something extra or perform a task in a more active way

Technology Choices

Technology is everywhere these days. You see it in social settings as people communicate using email, text messaging, and social networking sites. It also plays a significant role in academic settings, where you may encounter any of the following:

■ Instructors who require students to communicate via email

■ Courses that have their own websites, where you can access the syllabus and connect with resources and classmates

■ Textbooks with corresponding websites that you can, or are required to, use to complete assignments that you email to your instructor

talk risk and reward . . .

Risk asking tough questions to be rewarded with new insights. Use the following to inspire discussion with classmates, in person or online.

■ When you have trouble doing something, what is your first reaction—to risk trying again, or to give up? Do you say "I need a different approach," or "I'm no good at this"?

■ Do people perceive their own strengths accurately, or do you often see strengths in others that they don't believe they have?

CONSIDER THE CASE: Not knowing about Joyce Bishop's learning disability, what would you have assumed as an instructor of hers in college? Consider what an instructor might assume about you that is not accurate. What risk can you take to clear up that assumption?

Joyce Bishop

get $mart

PhotoMan/Fotolia

As your unique preferences affect how you learn, they also influence how you approach your finances. The Canadian Federation of Students reports that the average student debt is $27,000.[7] Based on your learning preferences, take a look at how you think about and interact with money.

1. How often do you use a credit card?
   a. Never
   b. Less than twice a month
   c. Less than twice a week
   d. Daily

2. When you see something you like at the store, what do you do?
   a. Purchase it immediately
   b. Think about it for a day or two
   c. Go to other stores to compare prices
   d. Ask your friends what they think

3. How many credit cards do you have?
   a. 0
   b. 1
   c. 2
   d. 3 or more

4. How much credit card debt do you incur each month? (In other words, how much money do you spend on credit monthly?)
   a. $0
   b. $1 to $100
   c. $101 to $500
   d. More than $500

5. How much of your credit card balance do you typically pay off each month?
   a. 100%
   b. 50% to 99%
   c. 25% to 49%
   d. Less than 24%

Now add up the number of a, b, c, and d answers:

a _____   b _____   c _____   d _____

- **Thinkers and Organizers** often have more **a and b answers** because they tend to be careful with money, thinking about the financial impact of their purchases and planning for the future.

- **Givers** may also be careful with their money but often end up helping others or giving gifts, which might give them more **c answers.**

- **Adventurers** are usually risk-takers, which means they may be willing to take on more debt. They are likely to have more **d answers.**

- Online research that takes you from website to website via links
- Projects where you create media such as a YouTube video or social media campaign

For some students, using technology such as their school's LMS or employing Google Drive to collaborate with others comes easily. For others, knowing their strengths and challenges as learners can help them make decisions about how to approach technology. Are you strong in the logical-mathematical intelligence or Thinker dimension? Working with an online tutorial may be a good choice. Are you an interpersonal learner? Find a tech-savvy classmate to help you get the hang of a new technology. An Adventurer may want to just dive in and try out the features of a book or course website in a random way. Know yourself, and make choices that can best help you demystify technology and get you up to speed.

Workplace Choices

Knowing how you learn and interact with others will help you work more effectively and make better career planning choices. How can an employee or job candidate benefit from self-awareness?

Better performance and teamwork

When you understand your strengths, you can find ways to use them on the job more readily. For tasks that take you out of your areas of strength, you will be more able to compensate and get help. In addition, you will be better able to work with others effectively. For example, a Giver might help new hires adjust to the people and environment. Or a team leader might offer an intrapersonal team member the chance to take material home to think about before a meeting.

INTERNSHIPS
Temporary work programs in which a student can gain supervised practical experience in a job and career area.

Better career planning

Exploring ways to use your strengths in school will help you make better choices about what jobs or careers will suit you. For most college and university students, internships and majors are more immediate steps on the road to a career. A strength in one or more intelligences might lead you to particular internships and majors that may make sense for you.

Key 3.7 links majors and internships to the eight intelligences. This list is by no means complete; rather, it represents only a fraction of the available opportunities. Use what you see here to inspire thought and spur investigation. If something from this list or elsewhere interests you, consider looking for an opportunity to "shadow" someone (follow the person for a day to see what he or she does) to see if the more significant commitments of internships and majoring make sense for you. See Key 12.1, in the section on careers in Chapter 12, for ideas about how intelligences may link to particular careers.

Although all students have areas of strength and weakness, challenges diagnosed as learning disabilities are more significant. These merit specific attention. Focused assistance can help students with learning disabilities manage their conditions and excel in school.

HOW CAN YOU IDENTIFY AND MANAGE
learning disabilities?

Some learning disabilities create reading problems; some produce difficulties in math; some cause issues that arise when working with others; and some make it difficult for students to process the language they hear. The following information will help you understand learning disabilities as well as the tools people use to manage them.

INTELLIGENCE	CONSIDER MAJORING IN	THINK ABOUT AN INTERNSHIP AT A
Verbal-Linguistic	• Communications • Marketing • English/Literature • Journalism • Foreign languages	• Newspaper or magazine • Public relations/marketing firm • Ad agency • Publishing house • Network TV affiliate
Logical-Mathematical	• Math • Physics • Economics • Banking/finance	• Computer science • Consulting firm • Bank • Information technology company • Research lab
Bodily-Kinesthetic	• Massage or physical therapy • Kinesiology • Construction engineering • Sports medicine	• Sports physician's office • Dance or theatre • Physical or massage therapy centre • Construction company • Dance studio or theatre company • Athletic club
Visual-Spatial	• Architecture • Visual arts • Multimedia designs • Photography	• Photo or art studio • Art history • Multimedia design firm • Architecture firm • Interior design firm • Art gallery
Interpersonal	• Education • Public relations • Nursing • Business	• Hotel or restaurant • Hotel/restaurant management • Social service agency • Public relations firm • Human resources department
Intrapersonal	• Psychology • Finance • Computer science • Biology • Philosophy	• Accounting firm • Biology lab • Pharmaceutical company • Publishing house • Computer or Internet company
Musical	• Music • Music theory • Voice • Composition • Performing arts	• Performance hall • Radio station • Record label or recording studio • Children's music camp • Orchestra or opera company
Naturalistic	• Geology • Zoology • Atmospheric sciences • Agriculture • Environmental law	• Museum • National park • Environmental law firm • Zoo • Geological research firm

Identifying a Learning Disability

The Learning Disabilities Association of Canada (LDAC) defines *learning disabilities* as "a number of disorders which may affect the acquisition, organization, retention, understanding, or use of verbal or non-verbal information. Learning disabilities result

DISABILITY OR CONDITION	WHAT ARE THE SIGNS?
Dyslexia and related reading disorders	Problems with reading (spelling, word sequencing, comprehension) and processing (translating written language to thought or the reverse)
Dyscalculia (developmental arithmetic disorders)	Difficulties in recognizing numbers and symbols, memorizing facts, understanding abstract math concepts, and applying math to life skills (time management, handling money)
Developmental writing disorders	Difficulties in composing sentences, organizing a writing assignment, or translating thoughts coherently to the page
Dysgraphia (handwriting disorders)	Disorder characterized by writing disabilities, including distorted or incorrect language, inappropriately sized and spaced letters, or wrong or misspelled words
Speech and language disorders	Problems with producing speech sounds, using spoken language to communicate, and/or understanding what others say
LD-related social issues	Problems in recognizing facial or vocal cues from others, controlling verbal and physical impulsivity, and respecting others' personal space
LD-related organizational issues	Difficulties in scheduling and in organizing personal, academic, and work-related materials

Source: LD Online: LD Basics, www.ncld.org/content/view/445/389/, 2009.

from impairments in one or more processes related to perceiving, thinking, remembering, or learning."[8]

How can you determine whether you should be evaluated for a learning disability? According to the LDAC, persistent problems in any of the following areas may indicate a problem:[9]

- Oral language (listening, speaking, understanding)
- Reading (word recognition, comprehension)
- Written language (spelling, writing)
- Mathematics (computation, problem solving)

Details on specific learning disabilities appear in Key 3.8. For an evaluation, contact your school's learning centre or student health centre for a referral to a licensed professional. Note that a professional diagnosis is required in order for a person with a learning disability to receive government-funded aid.

Managing a Learning Disability

If you are diagnosed with a learning disability, valuable information is available—information that it took Joyce until graduate school to obtain. Maximize your ability to learn by managing your disability.

Rommel Canlas/Shutterstock

- *Find information about your disability.* Search the library and the Internet—try LDAC at www.ldac-acta.ca or LD Online at www.ldonline.org. If you have an individualized education program (IEP)—a document describing your disability and recommended strategies—read it and make sure you understand what it says.

- *Seek assistance from your school.* Speak with your advisor about getting a referral to a counsellor who can help you get specific accommodations in your classes. The following services are mandated by law for students who are learning disabled:

- Extended time on tests

- Note-taking assistance (for example, having a fellow student take notes for you)
- Assistive technology devices (MP3 players, tape recorders, laptop computers)
- Modified assignments
- Alternative assessments and test formats

Other services that may be offered include tutoring, study skills assistance, and counselling.

- *Be a dedicated student.* Show up on time and pay attention in class. Read assignments before class. Sit where you can focus. Review notes soon after class. Spend extra time on assignments. Ask for help.
- *Build a positive attitude.* See your accomplishments in light of how far you have come. Rely on support from others, knowing that it will give you the best possible chance to succeed.

TIPS FOR LEARNING ONLINE

- Share. If you're comfortable, share your personality and learning style with others via Facebook or the course learning management system (LMS). You'll be able to connect with students whose weaknesses are your strengths and vice versa. Collaboratively, you'll be able to offer one another advice.

- Explore your LMS. Most LMSs are flexible and user-friendly. For example, if you are a Giver, participate in online discussion forums in which you have the opportunity to seek out other students who may need your help.

- Build an online support network. Using your favourite social networking sites, locate others with similar learning disabilities for support.

revisit RISK AND REWARD

Joyce Bishop

What happened to Joyce? Dr. Bishop now understands how her learning disability, auditory processing disorder, causes problems with understanding words she hears. Seeing how her strengths in visual-spatial, logical-mathematical, and bodily-kinesthetic intelligence served her well in science studies, she chose to study strategies for those strengths, and over time she earned her master's and doctorate degrees. Now a tenured psychology professor at Golden West College in California, Dr. Bishop has won Teacher of the Year twice at her school. She teaches both in-person and online courses and trains other teachers in online teaching strategies. She manages the challenges of her learning disability while pursuing her intention to learn throughout her life.

What does this mean for you? Getting perspective on strengths and weaknesses isn't just for those with diagnosed learning disabilities. Dr. Bishop got her wake-up call from an eye doctor and a therapist. Who can provide an outside perspective for you? Find someone who knows you well enough to have an opinion about you and who you believe will be honest and constructive. Tell this person ahead of time that you are looking for perspectives about what you do well and what challenges you. Prepare by making a short list of your three strongest and three weakest qualities. After receiving the outside perspective, compare it to your list. What matches up? What surprises you?

What effects go beyond your world? Broaden your knowledge of learning disabilities so you avoid inaccurate assumptions about people and learn how to support them in reaching their potential. Go to www.ldonline.org and read the section titled "LD Basics." Then, browse the articles at www.ldonline.org/indepth/adults to focus more closely on how adults with learning disabilities navigate school, work, and life. Finally, think about an assumption you may have made regarding someone with whom you live, work, or go to school. Address your possibly false idea by approaching that person with an open mind from this point forward, looking for strengths as well as working reasonably with challenges (and maybe even helping the person to combat them). With every person who develops a more positive attitude and understanding perspective about those with learning disabilities or other challenges, the world becomes that much more of a supportive and productive place.

Learning How You Learn

KNOW IT *Think Critically*

Link How You Learn to Your Coursework and Major

Apply what you know about yourself to some future academic planning.

STEP 1 Build basic skills. On paper or on a computer, summarize yourself as a learner in a paragraph or two. Focus on what you have learned about yourself from the chapter assessments.

STEP 2 Take it to the next level. Schedule a meeting with your academic advisor.

Name of advisor: _____

Office location/contact information: _____

Time/date of meeting: _____

Give the advisor an overview of your learning strengths and challenges, based on your summary. Ask for advice about courses that might interest you and majors that might suit you. Take notes. Based on your discussion, name two courses to consider in the next year:

1. _____

2. _____

Move toward mastery. Think about the courses you listed and other courses related to them. What majors might each of them lead you toward? Based on those courses, name two majors to investigate. Then create a separate to-do list of how you plan to explore one course offering and one major. Set a deadline for each task. Keep in mind that if you are having trouble choosing a major because of uncertainty about a career direction, you can see an advisor in the career centre for guidance.

WRITE IT *Communicate*

Build Intrapersonal and Communication Skills

Record your thoughts on a separate piece of paper, in a journal, or electronically.

Emotional Intelligence Journal: Your interactions with others. With your Personality Spectrum profile in mind, think about how you generally relate to people. Describe the type(s) of people that you tend to get along well with. How do you feel around these people? Then describe the types that tend to irk you. How do those people make you feel? Use your emotional intelligence to discuss what those feelings tell you and how you can adjust your mindset or take action to create the best possible outcome in interactions with people with whom you just don't get along.

Real-Life Writing: Support from instructors. Reach out to an instructor of a course that clashes with your learning style—in terms of the material itself, the style in which it is presented, or the way the classroom is run. Draft a friendly and respectful email requesting help that describes how you perceive yourself as a learner and details the issue you are having with the material or coverage. Include any ideas you have about how the instructor might be able to help you.

When you are done, make something happen: send the email and follow through on the response you receive.

WORK IT Build Your Brand Self-Portrait

21st Century Learning Building Blocks

- Creativity and innovation
- Initiative and self-direction

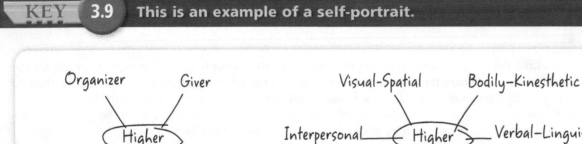

KEY 3.9 **This is an example of a self-portrait.**

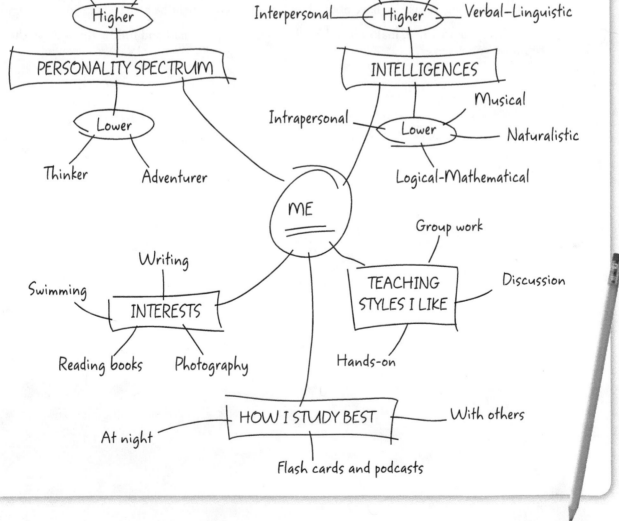

Complete the following on separate sheets of paper or electronically (if you can use a graphics program).

Because self-knowledge helps you make the best choices about your future, a self-portrait can be an important tool in your career exploration. Use this exercise to synthesize everything you have been exploring about yourself into one comprehensive "self-portrait." Design your portrait in think link (mind map) style, using words and visual shapes to describe your dominant multiple intelligences, Personality Spectrum dimensions, values, abilities and interests, personal characteristics, and anything else that you have discovered through self-exploration.

A think link is a visual construction of related ideas, similar to a map or web, representing your thought process. Ideas are written inside geometric shapes, often boxes or circles, and related ideas and facts are attached to those ideas by lines that connect the shapes. (See the note-taking section in Chapter 6 for more about think links).

If you want to use the style shown in Key 3.9, create a "wheel" of ideas coming off your central shape. Then, spreading out from each of those ideas (interests, values, and so forth), draw lines connecting the thoughts that go along with that idea. Connected to "Interests," for example, might be "singing," "stock market," and "history."

You don't have to use the wheel image, however. You might instead want to design a tree-like think link, a line of boxes with connecting thoughts, or anything else you like. Let your design reflect who you are, just as your writing does. You may want to look back at it at the end of the term to see how you have changed and grown from the self-image you have today.

Joe Martin

When you need to solve a problem or make a decision, combining analytical, creative, and practical thinking skills gives you the greatest chance of achieving your goal.

Critical, Creative, and Practical Thinking

SOLVING PROBLEMS AND MAKING DECISIONS

What Would You Risk? *Joe Martin*

THINK ABOUT THIS SITUATION AS YOU READ, AND CONSIDER WHAT ACTION YOU WOULD TAKE. THIS CHAPTER BUILDS PROBLEM-SOLVING AND DECISION-MAKING SKILLS THAT WILL HELP YOU FACE CHALLENGES IN COLLEGE AND BEYOND.

Joe Martin

Joe Martin grew up in the housing projects of Miami, Florida, in an environment in which six of his friends died—either from drug involvement or murder—by the time he was in high school. No one in his family even considered going to college. Although he had friends and family members who were in prison or caught up in crime and drugs, his mother reminded him to never accept the situation. He knew things could be different, but wasn't sure how.

Joe planned to join the military after high school. However, when he was a senior, he had a change of heart. Looking at his college-bound friends, he decided that if they could go to college, so could he. When he told the Navy recruiter he wanted to attend school, the man said he was not college material. With his low SAT scores, the recruiter said, "They won't let you drive by college, let alone get in."

This challenge made Joe determined to risk applying to colleges. Having barely passed high school, and dogged by those low SAT scores, he got turned down by so many schools he lost count. Finally he was accepted at Okaloosa Walton Junior College, thanks to open enrolment. Now he had to risk going to college with no understanding of the culture. In fact, his first day at Okaloosa was literally his first day ever on a college campus. Due to his childhood experience, he jumped when he heard noises and was nervous. He had taken on two jobs to pay for his education. Joe wasn't sure how he could handle the pressure of college and persist toward the reward of graduation and learning.

to be continued . . .

Joe's determination to move beyond the past has led him to be a powerful problem solver. You'll learn more about joe, and revisit his situation, within the chapter.

52% 🔋

Notes   +

Today   Mar 10 8:01 AM

Working through this chapter will help you to:

statusCHECK

How Developed Are Your Thinking Skills?

For each statement, circle the number that feels right to you, from 1 for "not at all true for me" to 5 for "very true for me."

1. I discover information, make decisions, and solve problems by asking and answering questions.   ① ② ③ ④ ⑤

2. I don't take everything I read or hear as fact; I question how useful, truthful, and logical it is before I decide whether I can use it.   ① ② ③ ④ ⑤

3. I look for biased perspectives when I read or listen because I am aware of how they can lead me in the wrong direction.   ① ② ③ ④ ⑤

4. Even if it seems like there is only one way to solve a problem, I brainstorm to think of other options.   ① ② ③ ④ ⑤

5. I try not to let the idea that things have always been done a certain way stop me from trying different approaches.   ① ② ③ ④ ⑤

6. When I work in a group, I try to manage my emotions and notice how I affect others.   ① ② ③ ④ ⑤

7. I think about different solutions before I choose one and take action.   ① ② ③ ④ ⑤

8. I spend time researching different possibilities before making a decision.   ① ② ③ ④ ⑤

9. I avoid making decisions on the spur of the moment.   ① ② ③ ④ ⑤

10. When I make a decision, I consider how my choice will affect others.   ① ② ③ ④ ⑤

Each of the topics in these statements is covered in this chapter. Note those statements for which you circled a 3 or lower. Skim the chapter to see where those topics appear, and pay special attention to them as you read, learn, and apply new strategies.

REMEMBER: NO MATTER HOW DEVELOPED YOUR THINKING SKILLS ARE, YOU CAN IMPROVE WITH EFFORT AND PRACTICE.

WHY IS IT IMPORTANT TO ASK
and answer questions?

What is thinking? According to experts, it is what happens when you ask questions and move toward the answers.[1] "To think through or rethink anything," says Dr. Richard Paul, director of research at the Center for Critical Thinking and Moral Critique, "one must ask questions that stimulate our thought. Questions define tasks, express problems and delineate issues. . . . [O]nly students who have questions are really thinking and learning."[2] It's human to feel as though asking questions makes you look ignorant. However, the risk of questioning is what *combats* ignorance and earns you the reward of learning. It's also an important Employability Skill. According to the Conference Board of Canada, employers underline the significance of being able to "assess situations, identify problems and then evaluate and implement solutions."[3]

MyStudentSuccessLab

Whether face-to-face or online, MyStudentSuccessLab helps students build the skills they need through peer-led video interviews, interactive practice exercises, and activities that provide academic, life, and professionalism skills.

Effective Questioning

As you answer questions, you turn information into material that you can use to achieve goals. A *Wall Street Journal* article titled "The Best Innovations Are Those That Come from Smart Questions" relays the story of a cell biology student, William Hunter, whose professor told him that "the difference between good science and great science is the quality of the questions posed." Now a physician, Dr. Hunter asks questions about new ways to use drugs. His questions have helped his company reach the goal of developing a revolutionary product—a drug-coated mesh used to strengthen diseased blood vessels.[4]

- *Know why you question.* To ask useful questions, you need to know why you are questioning. Start by defining your purpose: What am I trying to accomplish and why?

- *Want to question.* Knowing why you are questioning also helps you want to think. "Critical-thinking skills are different from critical-thinking dispositions, or a willingness to deploy these skills," says cognitive psychologist D. Alan Bensley of Frostburg State University in Maryland. In other words, having the skills isn't enough—you also need the desire to use them.[5] Having a clear understanding of your goal can help you be more willing to work to achieve it.

- *Question in different ways.*

  - Analyze (How bad is my money situation?)
  - Come up with creative ideas (How can I earn more money?)
  - Apply practical solutions (Who do I talk to about getting a job on campus?)

Your Primary Questioning Tool: The Prefrontal Cortex

One of the most significant research findings of the past decade is that your brain's prefrontal cortex, which controls your most complex thinking actions, undergoes its last and most comprehensive phase of development from around 18 to 25 years of age. During this phase, dendrites grow thicker, frequently used synapses become stronger, and nerve fibres become more heavily insulated, making "the entire brain a much faster and more sophisticated organ."[6] The prefrontal cortex controls executive function, which allows people to perceive possible future consequences of a choice, weigh pros and cons of different choices, and risk putting one to work, based on what seems to offer the greatest reward.

EXECUTIVE FUNCTION
A set of higher-order behaviours and cognitive processes involving planning, prioritizing tasks, selecting the most important information, and evaluating potential future consequences of decisions.

One key takeaway from this research is the fact that executive function is still under construction in the brains of people under the age of 25. Students who fall into this category might struggle to think through decisions and problems effectively, tend toward impulsive and physically risky actions, and make choices without anticipating pros and cons. However, the advantage is that post-secondary education, offering both academic learning and new experiences, provides exactly the training ground for thinking that a brain 18–25 years old needs at that stage.[7]

All college students have entered a different phase of life, and, for younger students, this phase involves a new level of independence. If you can apply the risk-taking tendencies your brain may exhibit now to the actions you take on behalf of your education, you may be more receptive to relationships, information, and experiences that will change and develop your mind.[8] Take advantage of your brain's useful adaptability. Your learning and experiences will build richer networks among the neurons in your brain, increasing your ability to think analytically, creatively, and practically in the service of solving problems and making decisions—your two most important and frequently-used thinking processes.

As you read and work, keep in mind your sense of where your strengths and challenges lie in the three thinking skill areas. If you are using the MyStudentSuccessLab,

Andriy Dykun/Fotolia

you may also want to complete the My Thinking Styles inventory to get a view of your thinking skills in terms of the seven styles this inventory evaluates (insightful, open-minded, timely, analytical, inquisitive, systematic, and truth seeking).

When you need to solve a problem or make a decision, combining all three thinking skills gives you the greatest chance of achieving your goal.[9] This chapter will explore each of analytical, creative, and practical thinking individually, ultimately showing how they work together to help you to solve problems and make decisions effectively. Asking questions opens the door to each thinking skill, and in each section you will find examples of the kinds of questions that drive that skill. Begin by exploring analytical thinking skills.

HOW CAN YOU IMPROVE YOUR
analytical thinking skills?

Analytical thinking is the process of gathering information, breaking it into parts, examining and evaluating those parts, and making connections for the purposes of gaining understanding, solving a problem, or making a decision.

Through the analytical process, you look for how pieces of information relate to one another, setting aside any pieces that are unclear, unrelated, unimportant, or biased. You may also form new questions that change your direction. Be open to them and to where they may lead you.

Gather Information

Information is the raw material for thinking, so to start the thinking process you must first gather your raw materials. This requires analyzing how much information you need, how much time to spend gathering it, and whether it is relevant. Say, for instance, that you have to write a paper on one aspect of the media (TV, radio, Internet) and its influence on a particular group. Here's how analyzing can help you gather information for that paper:

- Reviewing the assignment terms, you note two important items: The paper should be approximately 10 pages and describe at least three significant points of influence.

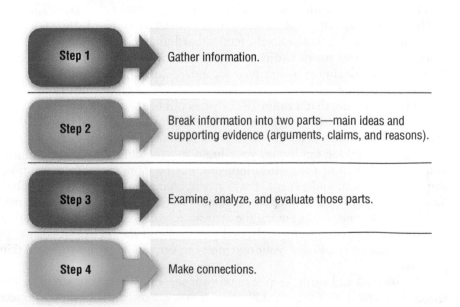

Step 1	Gather information.
Step 2	Break information into two parts—main ideas and supporting evidence (arguments, claims, and reasons).
Step 3	Examine, analyze, and evaluate those parts.
Step 4	Make connections.

- At the library and online, you find thousands of articles in this topic area. Analyzing your reaction to them and how many articles concentrate on certain aspects of the topic, you decide to focus your paper on how the Internet influences young teens (ages 13–15).
- Examining the summaries of six comprehensive articles leads you to three in-depth sources.

In this way, you achieve a subgoal—a selection of useful materials—on the way to your larger goal of writing a well-crafted paper.

Break Information into Parts

The next step is to search for the two most relevant parts of the information: the main idea or ideas (also called the *argument* or *viewpoint*) and the supporting evidence (also called *reasons* or *supporting details*).

- *Separate the ideas.* Identify each of the ideas conveyed in what you are reading. You can use lists or a mind map to visually separate ideas from one another. For instance, if you are reading about how teens ages 13 to 15 use the Internet, you could identify the goal of each method of access they use (websites, blogs, instant messaging).
- *Identify the evidence.* For each main idea, identify the evidence that supports it. For example, if an article claims that young teens rely on instant messaging three times more than on emails, note the facts, studies, or other evidence cited to support the truth of the claim.

Examine and Evaluate

The third step is by far the most significant and lies at the heart of analytical thinking. Examine the information to see whether it is going to be useful for your purposes. Keep your mind open to all useful information, even if it conflicts with your personal views. A student who thinks that the death penalty is wrong, for example, may have a hard time analyzing arguments that defend it or may focus her research on materials that support her perspective. Set aside personal prejudices when you analyze information.

The following four questions will help you examine and evaluate effectively.

Do examples support ideas?

When you encounter an idea or claim, examine how it is supported with examples or *evidence*—facts, expert opinion, research findings, personal experience, and so on. (See Key 4.1 for an illustration.) How useful an idea is to your work may depend on whether, or how well, it is backed up with solid evidence or made concrete with examples. Be critical of the information you gather; don't take it as truth without examining it.

For example, a blog written by a 12-year-old may make statements about what kids do on the Internet. The word of one person, who may or may not be telling the truth, is not adequate support. However, a study of youth technology use by the Canadian Radio-television and Telecommunications Commission (CRTC) may be more reliable.

Is the information factual and accurate, or is it opinion?

A *statement of fact* is information presented as objectively real and verifiable ("The Internet is a research tool"). In contrast, a *statement of opinion* is a belief, conclusion,

Shutterstock

Many types of work, such as the elevation drawings this engineering student is working on, involve analytical thinking.

ARGUMENT
A set of connected ideas, supported by examples, made by a writer to prove or disprove a point.

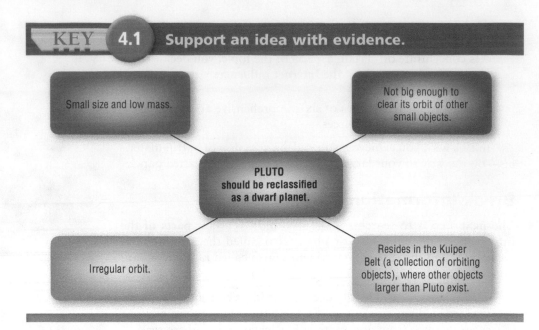

KEY 4.1 Support an idea with evidence.

Small size and low mass.

Not big enough to clear its orbit of other small objects.

PLUTO should be reclassified as a dwarf planet.

Irregular orbit.

Resides in the Kuiper Belt (a collection of orbiting objects), where other objects larger than Pluto exist.

or judgment that is inherently difficult, and sometimes impossible, to verify ("The Internet is always the best and most reliable research tool"). When you critically evaluate materials, one test of the evidence is whether it is fact or opinion. Key 4.2 defines important characteristics of fact and opinion.

KEY 4.2 Examine how fact and opinion differ.

FACTS INCLUDE STATEMENTS THAT …	OPINIONS INCLUDE STATEMENTS THAT …
• **deal with actual people, places, objects, or events.** Example: "In 2002, the European Union introduced the physical coins and banknotes of a new currency—the euro—that was designed to be used by its member nations."	• **show evaluation.** Any statement of value indicates an opinion. Words such as bad, good, pointless, and beneficial indicate value judgments. Example: "The use of the euro has been beneficial to all the states of the European Union."
• **use concrete words or measurable statistics.** Example: "The charity event raised $50,862."	• **use abstract words.** Complicated words such as misery or success usually indicate a personal opinion. Example: "The charity event was a smashing success."
• **describe current events in exact terms.** Example: "Mr. Barrett's course has 378 students enrolled this semester."	• **predict future events.** Statements about future occurrences are often opinions. Example: "Mr. Barrett's course is going to set a new enrolment record this year."
• **avoid emotional words and focus on the verifiable.** Example: "Citing dissatisfaction with the instruction, seven out of the twenty-five students in that class withdrew in September."	• **use emotional words.** Emotions are unverifiable. Words such as delightful or miserable express an opinion. Example: "That class is a miserable experience."
• **avoid absolutes.** Example: "Some students need to have a job while in school."	• **use absolutes.** Absolute qualifiers, such as all, none, never, and always, often express an opinion. Example: "All students need to have a job while in school."

Source: Adapted from Ben E. Johnson, *Stirring Up Thinking*. New York: Houghton Mifflin, 1998, pp. 268–270.

Do causes and effects link logically?

Look at the reasons given for a situation or occurrence (causes) and the explanation of its consequences (effects, both positive and negative). For example, an article might detail what causes young teens to use the Internet after school and the effects that this has on their family life. The cause-and-effect chain should make sense to you. It is also important that you analyze carefully to seek out key or "root" causes—the most significant causes of a problem or situation. For example, many factors may be involved in young teens' Internet use, including availability of service, previous experience, and education level of parents; but, on careful examination, one or two factors may be more significant than others.

Is the evidence biased?

Evidence with a bias is evidence that is slanted in a particular direction. Searching for a bias involves looking for hidden perspectives or assumptions that lie within the material.

A perspective can be broad (such as a generally optimistic or pessimistic view of life) or more focused (such as an attitude about whether students should commute or live on campus). Perspectives are associated with assumptions. For example, the perspective that people can maintain control over technology leads to assumptions such as "Parents can control children's exposure to the Internet." Having a particular experience with children and the Internet can build or reinforce such a perspective.

Assumptions often hide within questions and statements, blocking you from considering information in different ways. Take this classic puzzler as an example: "Which came first, the chicken or the egg?" Thinking about this question, most people assume that the egg is a chicken egg. If you think past that assumption and come up with a new idea—such as the egg could be a dinosaur egg—then the obvious answer is that the egg came first. Key 4.3 offers examples of how perspectives and assumptions can affect what you read or hear through the media.

Examining perspectives and assumptions helps you judge whether material is *reliable*. The less bias you can identify, the more reliable the information.

BIAS
A preference or inclination, especially one that prevents even-handed judgment.

PERSPECTIVE
A characteristic way of thinking about people, situations, events, and ideas.

ASSUMPTION
A judgment, generalization, or bias influenced by experience and values.

After the questions: What information is most useful to you?

You've examined your information, looking at its evidence, validity, perspective, and any underlying assumptions. Now, based on that examination, you evaluate whether an idea or piece of information is important or unimportant, relevant or irrelevant,

KEY 4.3 Different articles may present different perspectives on the same topic.

Topic: *How teens' grades are affected by Internet use*

STATEMENT BY A TEACHING ORGANIZATION	STATEMENT BY A PR AGENT FOR AN INTERNET SEARCH ENGINE	STATEMENT BY A PROFESSOR SPECIALIZING IN NEW MEDIA AND EDUCATION
"Too much Internet use equals failing grades and stolen papers."	"The Internet allows students access to a plethora of information, which results in better grades."	"The effects of the Internet on young students are undeniable and impossible to overlook."

get $mart

THINKING ANALYTICALLY ABOUT MONEY

Complete the following on paper or in digital format.

Analyzing potential purchases helps you decide if the pros outweigh the cons. To practise, write down your thoughts on three potential purchases and their consequences. Use this format: "If I buy [fill in the blank] for [$ amount], I will be able to [do whatever the purchase allows you to do] but I won't [sacrifice you will have to make because of the expenditure]."

Here is an example to get you started:

> **If I buy** the latest iPhone **for $700, I will** be able to access the Internet, take videos, and store music and photos, **BUT I won't** have money for my sociology books, and I won't be able to buy coffee every morning.

iStockphoto

When you think through something with others in a group, the variety of ideas gives you a better chance of finding a workable solution to a problem.

strong or weak, and why. You then set aside what is not useful and use the rest to form an opinion, possible solution, or decision.

In preparing your paper on young teens and the Internet, for example, you've analyzed a selection of information and materials to see how they apply to the goal of your paper. You then selected what you believe will be most useful in preparation for drafting.

Make Connections

The last part of analytical thinking, after you have broken information apart, is to find new and logical ways to connect pieces together. This step is crucial for research papers and essays because it is where your original ideas are born—and it is also where your creative skills get involved (more on that in the next section). When you begin to write, you focus on your new ideas, supporting them effectively with information you've learned from your analysis. Use the following techniques to make connections.

- *Compare and contrast.* Look at how ideas are similar to, or different from, each other. You might explore how different young teen subgroups (boys versus girls, for example) have different purposes for setting up pages on sites such as Facebook or Myspace.

- *Look for themes, patterns, and categories.* Note connections that form as you look at how bits of information relate to one another. For example, you might see patterns of Internet use that link young teens from particular cultures or areas of the country together into categories.

Come to new information ready to hear and read new ideas, think about them, and make informed decisions about what you believe. The process will educate you, sharpen your thinking skills, and give you more information to work with as you encounter life's problems. See Key 4.4 for some questions you can ask to build and use analytical thinking skills.

Pursuing your goals, in school and in the workplace, requires not just analyzing information but also thinking creatively about how to use what you've learned from your analysis.

KEY 4.4 Ask questions such as these to analyze.

To gather information, ask:
- What kinds of information do I need to meet my goal?
- What information is available? Where and when can I get it?
- Of the sources I found, which ones will best help me achieve my goal?

To analyze, ask:
- What are the parts of this information?
- What is similar to this information? What is different?
- What are the reasons for this? Why did this happen?
- What ideas, themes, or conclusions emerge from this material?
- How would I categorize this information?

To see whether evidence or examples support an idea, ask:
- Does the evidence make sense?
- How do the examples support the idea/claim?
- Are there examples that might disprove the idea/claim?

To distinguish fact from opinion, ask:
- Do the words in this information signal fact or opinion?
- What is the source of this information? Is the source reliable?
- If this is an opinion, is it supported by facts?

To examine perspectives and assumptions, ask:
- What perspectives might the author have, and what may be emphasized or de-emphasized as a result?
- What assumptions might lie behind this statement or material?
- How could I prove—or disprove—an assumption?
- How might my perspective affect the way I see this material?

To evaluate, ask:
- What information will support what I'm trying to prove or accomplish?
- Is this information true or false, and why?
- How important is this information?

Source: Adapted from www-ed.fnal.gov/trc/tutorial/taxonomy.html (Richard Paul, *Critical Thinking: How to Prepare Students for a Rapidly Changing World,* 1993) and from http://www.wsmc.net/pubs/WaMath/fall_2008/blooms.pdf (Barbara Fowler, Longview Community College "Using Bloom's Taxonomy to Promote Critical Reading and Thinking").

HOW CAN YOU IMPROVE YOUR
creative thinking skills?

Think of the word "creativity," and of people whom you consider to be "creative." What comes to mind? Are you thinking of music, visual arts, design, and dance? Are Arcade Fire, Zac Posen, Cate Blanchett, or Drake in your thoughts? Because creativity is often equated with visual and performing arts, many people don't grasp what this section of your text will illustrate—the range of human experience that depends on creativity. Take a look at Key 4.5 for examples of what it means to be creative.

There are many ways to define creativity. Here are a few to ponder:

- Combining existing elements in an innovative way to create a new purpose or result. (Using weak adhesive to mark pages in a book, a 3M scientist created Post-It Notes.)
- Generating new ideas from looking at how things are related. (For example, noting what ladybugs eat inspired organic farmers to bring them in to consume crop-destroying aphids.)[10]
  - The ability to make unusual connections—to view information in quirky ways that bring about unique results. (After examining how burrs stuck to his dog's fur after a walk in the woods, the inventor of Velcro imagined how a similar system of hooks and loops could make two pieces of fabric stick to each other.)

To think creatively is to generate new ideas that promote useful change, whether the change consists of world-altering communication technology or a tooth brushing technique that more effectively prevents cavities. Prepare to power up your creative thinking ability by gathering the following five ingredients.

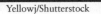

Yellowj/Shutterstock

The Five Ingredients of Creativity

This recipe produces both the mindset and the inspiration that allow you to think creatively.

1. *Belief that you can develop creativity*. Even though some people seem to have more or better ideas than others, creative thinking is a skill that can be developed. In an essay about the role of creativity in medicine, doctor of pharmacology Jennifer Gibson notes, "Creativity is not restricted to great artists, but it can be fostered by training, encouragement, and practice... Everyone has the power to be creative; while not everyone will paint a masterpiece or write a great novel, everyone can be curious, seek change and take risks."[11]

2. *Curiosity and exploration*. Seeking out new information and experiences will broaden your knowledge, giving you more raw materials with which to build creative ideas.[12] Think about what sparks your curiosity, and make a point to know more about it—take a course in it, read a book about it, check out a website or some music. If you are curious about something you don't think you'd like, explore it anyway to see if you have misjudged your reaction.

3. *Time alone*. Despite how North American society values speed (so much so that we equate being "quick" with being smart)[13] and working in teams, research indicates that creativity demands time and independent thinking.[14] Think of the stereotypes of the writer alone in a cabin or a painter alone in an attic studio. Business offers examples as well, such as Apple CEO Steve Jobs' collaborator, Steve Wozniak. Mr. Wozniak worked alone for long hours over many months to develop the personal computer that Mr. Jobs marketed so ingeniously. Comparing inventors and engineers to artists in his memoir, Mr. Wozniak provides some advice that he says "might be hard to take. That advice is: Work alone."[15]

4. *Risk taking and hard work*. Although most people think of creativity as coming in lightning flashes of inspiration, it demands that you risk time, ideas, and enormous effort in the quest for reward. "All creative geniuses work passionately

KEY **4.5** Creativity is everywhere.

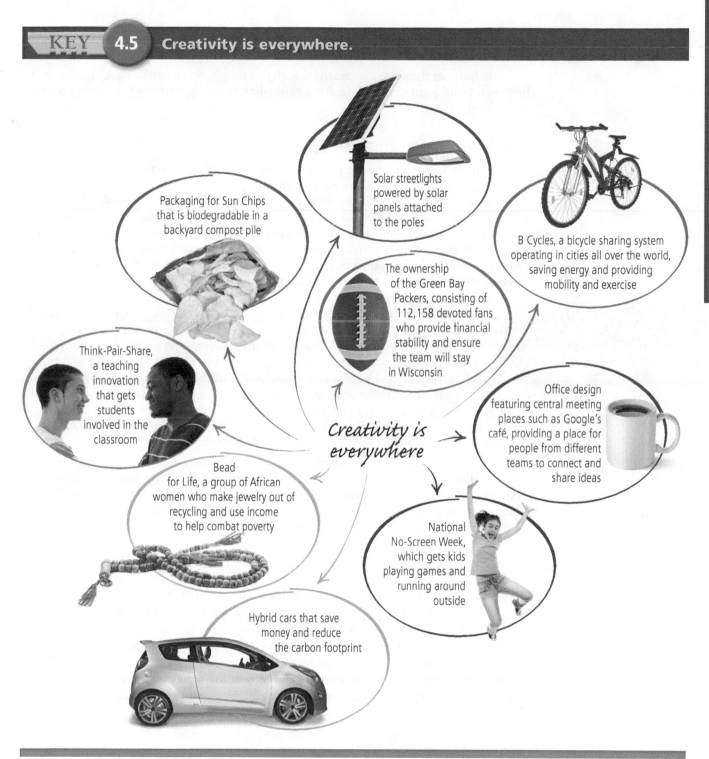

Packaging for Sun Chips that is biodegradable in a backyard compost pile

Solar streetlights powered by solar panels attached to the poles

B Cycles, a bicycle sharing system operating in cities all over the world, saving energy and providing mobility and exercise

The ownership of the Green Bay Packers, consisting of 112,158 devoted fans who provide financial stability and ensure the team will stay in Wisconsin

Think-Pair-Share, a teaching innovation that gets students involved in the classroom

Creativity is everywhere

Office design featuring central meeting places such as Google's café, providing a place for people from different teams to connect and share ideas

Bead for Life, a group of African women who make jewelry out of recycling and use income to help combat poverty

National No-Screen Week, which gets kids playing games and running around outside

Hybrid cars that save money and reduce the carbon footprint

hard and produce incredible numbers of ideas, most of which are bad," reports creativity expert Michael Michalko, recounting among other examples the fact that Picasso created more than 20,000 pieces of art.[16] He also advocates regular practice, noting that "the more times you try to get ideas, the more active your brain becomes and the more creative you become."[17] Like any other consistent action, working on ideas builds new neural pathways in your brain.

5. *Acceptance of mistakes as part of the process.* When you can risk messing up, you open yourself to ideas and promote productivity. Michalko repackages the idea of failure as a learning experience along the way to something better.

"Whenever you try to do something and do not succeed," he says, "you do not fail. You have learned something that does not work."[18]

You have set the stage for creativity with this recipe. Next, explore actions that will help you build your creative thinking skill—braingaming, shifting your perspective, and taking risks.

Go Beyond Brainstorming

You've likely heard of *brainstorming*—letting your mind free-associate to come up with different ideas or answers to a question. This longstanding creative technique demands that you generate ideas without regard to usefulness and evaluate their quality later. New research calls the value of brainstorming into question, showing that avoiding evaluating idea quality can result in fewer and less effective ideas. Researchers report that constructive criticism and dissent generate *more* ideas and promote the rethinking and refining that leads to an idea's most productive form.[19] "All these errant discussions add up," says Lehrer. "In fact, they may even be the most essential part of the creative process...It is the human friction that makes the sparks."[20]

As the Conference Board of Canada indicates as part of their Employability Skills 2000+, teamwork skills are crucial in today's workplace, and the most productive teamwork will incorporate constructive dissent and questioning. Instead of "brainstorming," think of it as *braingaming*—a term that incorporates the challenges and back-and-forth that can take groups to new heights of creativity.[21] Remember that you don't have to sacrifice civility to have a successful braingaming session. At Pixar, groups use a technique called "plussing," which refers to positive, productive criticism that includes ways of improving on the idea being discussed.[22] Keep the "plus" in mind as you contribute and evaluate.

Use these strategies to get the most out of your braingaming:

Avoid looking for one right answer. Questions may have many "right answers"—answers that have degrees of usefulness. The more possibilities you generate, the better your chance of finding the best one. Thomas Edison is said to have tried over 3,000 filaments before he found the right one for the tungsten electric bulb.

Mix collaboration with private time. Group members can become inspired by, and make creative use of, one another's ideas.[23] However, creativity also requires time alone, and working in groups can have drawbacks, including team members letting others do all the work or mimicking others' ideas out of peer pressure.[24] Consider having members generate ideas on their own before bringing them to the group. Sharing ideas electronically is often extremely productive because group members can feel independent while taking in ideas from others at the same time.

Keep recording tools at the ready. Creative ideas can fly out of your mind as quickly as they enter. Get in the habit of recording ideas as you think of them. Keep a pen and paper by your bed, your smartphone in your pocket, a notepad in your car, or a recorder in your backpack so that you can grab creative thoughts before they fade.

Shift Your Perspective

If no one ever questioned established opinion, people would still think the Sun revolved around the Earth. Here are some ways to change how you look at a situation or problem:

- *Challenge assumptions.* In the late 1960s, conventional wisdom said that school provided education and TV provided entertainment. Jim Henson, a pioneer in children's television, asked, Why can't we use TV to educate young children? From that question, the characters of *Sesame Street*, and eventually many other educational programs, were born.
- *Try on another point of view.* Try on new perspectives by asking others for their views, reading about new ways to approach situations, or deliberately going with the opposite of your first instinct.[25] Then, use those perspectives to inspire

get analytical

ANALYZE A STATEMENT

Complete the following on paper or in digital format.

Consider the statement below; then analyze it by answering the questions that follow.

> *There's no point in pursuing a career area that you love if it isn't going to earn you a living.*

1. Is this statement fact or opinion? Why?

2. What examples can you think of that support or negate this statement?

3. What perspective(s) are guiding this statement?

4. What assumption(s) underlie the statement? What negative effects might result from accepting these assumptions without investigation?

5. As a result of your critical thinking, what is your evaluation of this statement?

creativity. For a political science course, for example, you might craft a position paper for a parliamentary candidate that goes against your view of that particular issue. For a fun example of how looking at something in a new way can unearth a totally different idea, look at the perception puzzles in Key 4.6.

■ *Ask "what if" questions.* Set up imaginary environments in which new ideas can grow, such as What if I had unlimited money or time? The founders of Seeds of Peace, for example, faced with long-term conflict in the Middle East, asked, What if

---

KEY 4.6 Use perception puzzles to experience a shift in perspective.

There are two possibilities for each image. What do you see? (See page 106 for answers.)

Illustration: "Sara Nader" from the book *Mind Sights: Original Visual Illusions, Ambiguities, And Other Anomalies* by Roger N. Shepard. Copyright (c) 1990 by Roger N. Shepard. Reprinted by permission of Henry Holt and Company, LLC. All rights reserved.

93

get creative

ACTIVATE YOUR CREATIVE POWERS

Complete the following on paper or in digital format.

Think about your creativity over the past month.

1. First, describe three creative acts you performed—one in the process of studying course material, one in your personal life, and one at work or in the classroom.

2. Now think of a problem or situation that is on your mind. Generate one new idea for how to deal with it.

3. Write down a second idea, but focus on the risk-taking aspect of creativity. What would be a risky way to handle the situation? How do you hope it would pay off?

4. Finally, sit with the question—write down one more idea only after you have been away from this page for at least 24 hours.

Keep these in mind. You may want to use one soon!

Israeli and Palestinian teens met at a summer camp in Maine so that the next generation has greater understanding and respect? What if follow-up programs and reunions strengthened friendships so that relationships change the politics of the Middle East? Based on the ideas that came up, they created an organization that helps teenagers from the Middle East develop leadership and communication skills.

Take Risks

Creative breakthroughs can come from sensible risk taking.

- *Go against established ideas.* The founders of Etsy.com went against the idea that the North American consumer prefers cheap, conventional, mass-produced items. In 2005, they created an online company that allows artisans to offer one-of-a-kind, handmade products to the consumer. The site has also created a community of artists and connects each artist personally to his or her customers.

- *Risk leaving your comfort zone.* Rewards can come when you seek out new experiences and environments. Go somewhere you've never been. Play music you've never heard of. Seek out people who interest you but whom you would

Joe Martin

talk risk and reward . . .

Risk asking tough questions to be rewarded with new insights. Use the following to inspire discussion with classmates in person or online.

- What problem(s) do you see others avoid? What happens as a result?

- What problem(s) do you avoid? What do you risk when avoiding these problems? What might result from the different risk you take to address them?

CONSIDER THE CASE: What problems do you think Joe may have experienced in his first term as a college student? If you had known him at school, what risks would you have advised him to take that may have helped him adjust to college life?

KEY 4.7 Ask questions such as these to jump-start creative thinking.

To brainstorm, ask:
- What do I want to accomplish?
- What are the craziest ideas I can think of?
- What are 10 ways that I can reach my goal?
- What ideas have worked before and how can I apply them?

To shift your perspective, ask:
- How has this always been done—and what would be a different way?
- How can I approach this task or situation from a new angle?
- How would someone else do this or view this?
- What if . . . ?

To set the stage for creativity, ask:
- Where, and with whom, do I feel relaxed and inspired?
- What music helps me think out of the box?
- When in the day or night am I most likely to experience a flow of creative ideas?
- What do I think would be new and interesting to try, to see, to read?

To take risks, ask:
- What is the conventional way of doing this? What would be a totally different way?
- What would be a risky approach to this problem or question?
- What is the worst that can happen If I take this risk? What is the best?
- What have I learned from this mistake?

not normally connect with. Check out an international or independent film or documentary that is completely outside of your experience. Even small risks like these can create ideas that generate big changes.

Throughout your course, you will explore real-life, day-to-day ways that creative thinking makes a difference: Solving financial issues, deciding how to handle communication problems, finding creative ways to manage your time, and much more. Later in this chapter, you will see the starring role that creativity plays in problem solving and decision making. Your efforts to be creative will enable you to grow and change over time, adding value to your relationships and to whatever you choose to do in your life.

As with analytical thinking, asking questions powers creative thinking. See Key 4.7 for examples of the kinds of questions you can ask to get your creative juices flowing.

HOW CAN YOU IMPROVE YOUR
practical thinking skills?

Y ou've analyzed a situation. You've brainstormed ideas. Now, with your practical skill, you make things happen.

Practical thinking—also called *common sense* or *street smarts*—refers to how you adapt to your environment (both people and circumstances), or shape or change your environment to adapt to you, to pursue important goals. Think again about the successfully intelligent boy in the story in Chapter 1—he quickly sized up his environment (bear and slower boy) and adapted (got ready to run) to pursue his goal (to escape becoming the bear's dinner).

Odua Images/Shutterstock

get practical

TAKE A PRACTICAL APPROACH TO BUILDING SUCCESSFUL INTELLIGENCE

Complete the following on paper or in digital format.

Consider the three thinking skills and write the one which you most need to strengthen. (Look back at your Wheel of Successful Intelligence in Chapter 1.)

Then, name and describe two practical actions you can take that will improve your skills in that area. For example, someone who wants to be more creative could take a course focused on creativity; someone who wants to be more practical could work on paying attention to social cues; or someone who wants to be more analytical could decide to analyze one newspaper article every week. Be as specific as you can about your plans, noting what you will do, when, and how.

Another example: Your goal is to pass your first-year sociology course. You learn most successfully through visual presentations. To achieve your goal, you can use the instructor's PowerPoints or other visual media to enhance your learning (adapt to your environment) or enrol in a heavily visual Internet course (change your environment to adapt to you)—or both.

Why Practical Thinking Is Important

Real-world problems and decisions require you to add understanding of experiences and social interactions to your analytical abilities. Your success in a sociology class, for example, may depend almost as much on getting along with your instructor as on your academic work. Similarly, the way you solve a personal money problem may have more impact on your life than how you work through a problem in an accounting course.

Keep in mind, too, that in the workplace you need to use practical skills to apply academic knowledge to problems and decisions. For example, although students majoring in elementary education may successfully quote child development facts on an exam, their career success depends on the ability to evaluate and address real children's needs in the classroom. Successfully solving real-world problems demands a practical approach.

Holbox/Shutterstock

Through Experience, You Build Emotional Intelligence

You gain much of your ability to think practically from personal experience, rather than from formal training.[26] What you learn from experience answers "how" questions—how to talk, how to behave, how to proceed.[27] For example, after completing several papers for a course, you may learn what your instructor expects—or, after a few arguments with a friend or partner, you may learn how to avoid topics that cause conflict.

Emotional intelligence gives you steps you can take to promote success. For example, when Joe was told he wasn't "college material," he was angry about it. With effort, his response involved these practical and emotionally intelligent actions:

- *Perceiving emotions*: After he heard the comment, recognizing his feelings of being hurt and insulted.
- *Thinking about emotions*: Noting what perception arose from those feelings (at first, "I'm not good enough") and how it affected his mindset (at first, made him feel badly about himself).
- *Understanding emotions*: Determining that the emotions told him he was of little value and considering how to adjust that mindset to increase self-worth and determination.
- *Managing emotions*: Using what he learned, making a decision to prove the recruiter wrong, and supporting that goal with actions such as applying to colleges.

Through these actions, Joe's emotional intelligence made it more likely that he would achieve his goal of attending post secondary education and earning a degree.

If you know that social interactions are difficult for you, enlist someone to give you some informal coaching. Ask a friend to role-play the meeting with your instructor (your friend will act as if he is the instructor) and give you feedback on your words, tone, and body language. Or bring a friend with you to the actual meeting and talk later about how things went.

Practical Thinking Means Action

Action is the logical result of practical thinking. Basic student success strategies that promote action—staying motivated, making the most of your strengths, learning from failure, managing time, seeking help from instructors and advisors, and believing in yourself—will keep you moving toward your goals.[28] See Key 4.8 for some questions you can ask in order to apply practical thinking to your problems and decisions.

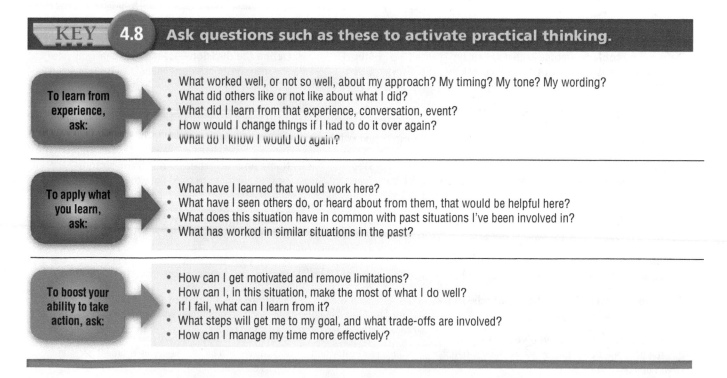

KEY 4.8 Ask questions such as these to activate practical thinking.

To learn from experience, ask:
- What worked well, or not so well, about my approach? My timing? My tone? My wording?
- What did others like or not like about what I did?
- What did I learn from that experience, conversation, event?
- How would I change things if I had to do it over again?
- What do I know I would do again?

To apply what you learn, ask:
- What have I learned that would work here?
- What have I seen others do, or heard about from them, that would be helpful here?
- What does this situation have in common with past situations I've been involved in?
- What has worked in similar situations in the past?

To boost your ability to take action, ask:
- How can I get motivated and remove limitations?
- How can I, in this situation, make the most of what I do well?
- If I fail, what can I learn from it?
- What steps will get me to my goal, and what trade-offs are involved?
- How can I manage my time more effectively?

HOW CAN YOU SOLVE PROBLEMS AND
make decisions effectively?

The best problem solvers and decision makers use their analytical, creative, and practical thinking skills together to solve problems and make decisions. Problem solving and decision making follow similar paths, both requiring you to identify and analyze a situation, generate possibilities, choose one, follow through on it, and evaluate its success. Key 4.9 gives an overview indicating the process at each step. (Keys 4.11 and 4.12 show examples of how to map out problems and decisions effectively.)

Understanding the differences between problem solving and decision making will help you know how to proceed. See Key 4.10 for more information. Remember, too, that whereas all problem solving involves decision making, not all decision making requires you to solve a problem.

Solve a Problem

The following strategies will help you move through the problem-solving process outlined in Key 4.9.

- *Use probing questions to define problems.* Ask: What is the problem? And what is causing the problem? Engage your emotional intelligence. If you determine that you are not motivated to do your work for a class, for example, you could ask questions such as these:
  - Do my feelings stem from how I interact with my instructor or classmates?
  - Is the subject matter difficult? Uninteresting?

KEY 4.9 Solve problems and make decisions by using successful intelligence.

PROBLEM SOLVING	THINKING SKILL	DECISION MAKING
Define the problem—recognize that something needs to change, identify what's happening, look for true causes.	**Step 1** Define	**Define the decision**—identify your goal (your need) and then construct a decision that will help you get it.
Analyze the problem—gather information, break it down into pieces, verify facts, look at perspectives and assumptions, evaluate information.	**Step 2** Analyze	**Examine needs and motives**—consider the layers of needs carefully, and be honest about what you really want.
Generate possible solutions—use creative strategies to think of ways you could address the causes of this problem.	**Step 3** Create	**Name and/ or generate different options**—use creative questions to come up with choices that would fulfill your needs.
Evaluate solutions—look carefully at potential pros and cons of each, and choose what seems best.	**Step 4** Analyze (Evaluate)	**Evaluate options**—look carefully at potential pros and cons of each, and choose what seems best.
Put the solution to work—persevere, focus on results, and believe in yourself as you go for your goal.	**Step 5** Take Practical Action	**Act on your decision**—go down the path and use practical strategies to stay on target.
Evaluate how well the solution worked—look at the effects of what you did.	**Step 6** Analyze (Re-evaluate)	**Evaluate the success of your decision**—look at whether it accomplished what you had hoped.
In the future, apply what you've learned—use this solution, or a better one, when a similar situation comes up again.	**Step 7** Take Practical Action	**In the future, apply what you've learned**—make this choice, or a better one, when a similar decision comes up again.

KEY **4.10** **Examine how problems and decisions differ.**

SITUATION	YOU HAVE A PROBLEM IF ...	YOU NEED TO MAKE A DECISION IF ...
Planning summer activities	Your low GPA means you need to attend summer school—and you've already accepted a summer job.	You've been accepted into two summer abroad internship programs.
Declaring a major	It's time to declare, but you don't have all the prerequisites for the major you want.	There are three majors that appeal to you and you qualify for them all.
Handling communications with instructors	You are having trouble following the lecture style of a particular instructor.	Your psychology survey course has seven sections taught by different instructors; you have to choose one.

Chances are that how you answer one or more of these questions may help you define the problem—and ultimately solve it.

- *Analyze carefully.* Gather information that will help you examine the problem. Consider how the problem is similar to, or different from, other problems. Clarify facts. Note your own perspective and look for others. Make sure your assumptions are not getting in the way.

- *Generate possible solutions based on causes, not effects.* Addressing a cause provides a lasting solution, whereas "putting a Band-Aid on" an effect cannot. Say, for example, that your shoulder hurts when you type. Getting a massage is a helpful but temporary solution, because the pain returns whenever you go back to work. Changing your keyboard height is a lasting solution to the problem, because it eliminates the cause of your pain.

- *Consider how possible solutions affect you and others.* What would suit you best? What takes other people's needs into consideration?

- *Evaluate your solution and act on it in the future.* Once you choose a solution and put it into action, ask yourself, What worked that I would do again? What didn't work that I would avoid or change in the future?

What happens if you don't work through a problem comprehensively? Take, for example, a student having an issue with an instructor. She may get into an argument with the instructor, stop showing up to class, or take a quick-and-dirty approach to assignments. Any of these choices may have negative consequences. Now look at how the student might work through this problem by using analytical, creative, and practical thinking skills. Key 4.11 shows how her effort can pay off.

Make a Decision

As you use the steps in Key 4.9 to make a decision, remember these strategies:

- *Look at the given options—then try to think of more.* Some decisions have a given set of options. For example, your school may allow you to major, double major, or major and minor. However, you may be able to brainstorm with an advisor to come up with more options, such as an interdisciplinary major. Consider similar situations you've been in or heard about, what decisions were made, and what resulted from those decisions.

- *Think about how your decision affects others.* What you choose might have an impact on friends, family, and others around you.

- *Gather perspectives.* Talk with others who have made similar decisions. If you listen carefully, you may hear ideas you haven't thought about.

- *Look at the long-term effects.* As with problem solving, it's key to examine what happens after you put the decision into action. For important decisions, do a short-term evaluation and another evaluation after a period of time. Consider whether your decision sent you in the right direction or whether you should rethink your choice.

KEY 4.11 Work through a problem relating to an instructor.

DEFINE PROBLEM HERE:	ANALYZE THE PROBLEM
I don't like my Sociology instructor	We have different styles and personality types—I am not comfortable working in groups and being vocal. I'm not interested in being there, and my grades are suffering from my lack of motivation.

Use boxes below to list possible solutions:

POTENTIAL POSITIVE EFFECTS	SOLUTION #1	POTENTIAL NEGATIVE EFFECTS
List for each solution: Don't have to deal with that instructor Less stress	Drop the course	List for each solution: Grade gets entered on my transcript I'll have to take the course eventually; it's required for my major
Getting credit for the course Feeling like I've honoured a commitment	**SOLUTION #2** Put up with it until the end of the semester	Stress every time I'm there Lowered motivation Probably not such a good final grade
A chance to express myself Could get good advice An opportunity to ask direct questions of the instructor	**SOLUTION #3** Schedule meetings with advisor and instructor	Have to face instructor one-on-one Might just make things worse

Now choose the solution you think is best—circle it and make it happen.

ACTUAL POSITIVE EFFECTS	PRACTICAL ACTION	ACTUAL NEGATIVE EFFECTS
List for chosen solution: Got some helpful advice from advisor Talking in person with the instructor actually promoted a fairly honest discussion I won't have to take the course again	I scheduled and attended meetings with both advisor and instructor and opted to stick with the course.	List for chosen solution: Still have to put up with some group work I still don't know how much learning I'll retain from this course

FINAL EVALUATION: Was it a good or bad solution?

The solution has improved things. I'll finish the course, and I got the chance to fulfill some class responsibilities on my own or with one partner. I feel more understood and more willing to put my time into the course.

student PROFILE

Katie Hudgins

CDI COLLEGE, CALGARY, ALBERTA

Katie Hudgins

About me:

I am a single mom of a child with special needs who has had a heart transplant. I have my Accounting and Payroll Administrator diploma and am currently working on my Business Administration Management diploma, both from CDI College in Calgary.

What I focus on:

Being a single mom of a child with special needs has a lot of challenges. My son has a suppressed immune system because of his heart transplant and needs to stay at home often to avoid infections. I also lost almost two months' worth of work time when my son had major surgery and was in the hospital. I had to rely on my own personal strength and determination to continue my studies while at the hospital and at home. I had to learn to balance taking care of my son's needs and my studies.

Being away from the school and teachers was a big challenge. The instructors at school were very understanding of my situation and I utilized the technology available to me to stay up to date. I used email almost daily to keep in touch with my teachers, to learn what was due, and to submit assignments.

Taking part in the ebook pilot program in which my textbooks were on an iPad was a very easy way for me to keep up with my work easily wherever I was. The ability to stay organized and keep to a schedule was paramount for me. I needed to know what was due at school and what the schedule was for my son and his doctors, as well as find the time to complete everything on time. Knowing that the goal of completing school was in the best interest for my son and myself kept me going. My motivation slipped quite a few times, but the ability to rely on the staff at my school made it possible. This support and encouragement got me through the rough times.

What will help me in the workplace:

For me, returning to school was a great challenge full of stress. I know that being able to meet tight deadlines and balance my responsibilities as a parent with a special needs child and my school responsibilities will help me meet work deadlines and balance my personal life and work. School was a great opportunity for me to learn that if I can handle these obligations while in school, then I will be able to handle them at work as well. Needing to stay organized to keep on track will help me while working in the high-stress working environments that many people face today. Also, technology played a huge part in my success and I will take the technology skills I learned with me to the workplace. School was stressful, but I now know that I can handle a busy schedule, and I look forward to continuing to balance my home life with a career.

Katie Hudgins. CDI College, Calgary, Alberta. Reprinted by permission.

What happens when you make important decisions too quickly? Consider a student trying to decide whether to transfer schools. If she makes her decision based on a reason that ultimately is not the most important one for her (for example, close friends go to the other school), she may regret her choice.

Now look at how this student might make an effective decision. Key 4.12 shows how she worked through the analytical, creative, and practical parts of the process.

Keep Your Balance

No one has equal strengths in analytical, creative, and practical thinking. However, you think and work toward goals most effectively when you combine all three. Staying as balanced as possible requires that you analyze your levels of ability in the three

KEY 4.12 Make a decision about whether to transfer schools.

DEFINE PROBLEM HERE:	EXAMINE NEEDS AND MOTIVES
Whether or not to transfer schools	My father has changed jobs and can no longer afford my tuition. My goal is to become a physical therapist, so I need a school with a full physical therapy program. My family needs to cut costs. I need to transfer credits.

Use boxes below to list possible solutions:

POTENTIAL POSITIVE EFFECTS	SOLUTION #1	POTENTIAL NEGATIVE EFFECTS
List for each solution: No need to adjust to a new place or new people Ability to continue coursework as planned	Continue at the current university	List for each solution: Need to finance most of my tuition and costs on my own Difficult to find time for a job Might not qualify for aid
Some physical therapy courses available School is close so I could live at home and save room costs Reasonable tuition; credits will transfer	**SOLUTION #2** Transfer to the community college	No personal contacts there that I know of Less independence if I live at home No bachelor's degree available
Opportunity to earn tuition money Could live at home Status should be intact	**SOLUTION #3** Stay out for a year	Could forget so much that it's hard to go back Could lose motivation A year might turn into more

Now choose the solution you think is best—circle it and make it happen.

ACTUAL POSITIVE EFFECTS	PRACTICAL ACTION	ACTUAL NEGATIVE EFFECTS
List for chosen solution: Money saved Opportunity to spend time on studies rather than on working to earn tuition money Availability of classes I need	Go to community college for two years; then transfer to a four-year school to get a B.A. and complete physical therapy course work.	List for chosen solution: Loss of some independence Cannot receive a degree in physical therapy from the college

FINAL EVALUATION: Was it a good or bad solution?

I'm satisfied with the decision. It can be hard being at home at times, but my parents are adjusting to my independence and I'm trying to respect their concerns. With fewer social distractions, I'm really getting my work done. Plus the financial aspect of the decision is ideal.

thinking areas, come up with creative ideas about how to build areas where you need to develop, and put them to use with practical action. Above all, believe in your skills as a thinker.

"Successfully intelligent people," says Sternberg, "defy negative expectations, even when these expectations arise from low scores on IQ or similar tests. They do not let other people's assessments stop them from achieving their goals. They find their path and then pursue it, realizing that there will be obstacles along the way and that surmounting these obstacles is part of the challenge."[29] Let the obstacles come, as they will for everyone, in all aspects of life. You can face and overcome them with the power of your successfully intelligent thinking.

TIPS FOR LEARNING ONLINE

- *Brainstorm.* Online learning through a learning management system (LMS) is a great way for creative minds to brainstorm solutions to problems. Use chat rooms and forums to participate in class discussions. Creative people will not only offer their own opinions but also encourage others to participate.

- *Collaborate.* Using your course LMS or other social media (such as Google Drive), your team can work together on class projects online or by using mobile devices. Dropbox or Skydrive are other options for online "cloud" collaboration.

- *Consider the source.* Determining the credibility of any information found online is critical. Look for information about the author and owner of the website or document. A good place to start is the copyright information at the bottom of the page.

revisit RISK AND REWARD

Joe Martin

What happened to Joe? The stress of what Joe had left behind motivated him to move ahead. Driven to succeed, Joe prioritized his work—and earned the reward of a 4.0 in his first term. The pressure of maintaining that success presented a different sort of challenge, to which he responded by taking two distinct risks: Putting in an enormous amount of time and effort through the rest of his experience, and refusing drink and drugs. He socialized "strategically," making friends in groups that he joined, so that he could have fun and accomplish something at the same time. He finished community college, transferred to the University of West Florida, and graduated at the top of his class with a bachelor's degree. After college, a motivational speaker helped him realize he could make a living by communicating ideas to students growing up in poverty. Now, having earned master's and doctoral degrees and spoken to more than a quarter of a million people about student success through courses, speeches, books, and recorded programs, he can reach students all over the globe through his website, Real World University. As a professor and educational consultant, he takes risks every day for the reward of helping students make the most of their gifts and talents.

What does this mean for you? Joe worked hard to move away from environments, people, and situations that he thought would not allow him to achieve the rewards he valued. Think about an environment, person, or situation that presents a problem for you and prevents you from living the way you want to live. Think through the problem. Assess its causes, determine the reward you aim for, and come up with potential risks you could take that might move you in that direction. Evaluate the pros and cons of each solution. You may not choose one right away, but commit to taking action on this problem soon.

What risk may bring reward beyond your world? One person making positive changes sets an example for others and can have an effect that stretches through many different networks of people. Joe Martin's website at www.rwuniversity.com is his way of putting his positive changes out there for others to consider. Risk making a change that your friends will notice—a change in how you spend your time, study, stay well, or anything else that can improve your day-to-day life. If anyone questions your choice, let them know what you are doing and what reward you seek. Maybe you will inspire others to think, and even to follow your lead.

CHAPTER 4

KNOW IT *Think Critically*

Make an Important Decision

Build basic skills. List the steps of the decision-making process.

Take it to the next level. Think about how you would put the decision-making process to work on something that matters to you. Write an important long-term goal that you have, and define the decision that will help you fulfill it. Example: "My goal is to become a nurse. My decision is about what to specialize in."

Move toward mastery. Using the empty flow chart (Key 4.13), apply the decision-making process to your goal. Use the following steps to organize your thinking.

- *Examine needs and concerns.* What are your needs, and how do your values come into play? What is most needed in the health market, and how can you fulfill that need? What roadblocks might be involved? List everything you come up with. For example, the prospective nurse might list the following needs: "I need to feel that I'm helping people. I intend to help with the shortage of prenatal or geriatric nurses. I need to make a good living."

- *Generate options.* Ask questions to imagine what's possible. Where might you work? What might be the schedule and pace? Who might work with you? What would you see, smell, and hear on your job? What would you do every day? Also list all the options you know of. The prospective nurse, for example, might list prenatal surgery, neonatal intensive care unit, geriatric nursing in a hospital or in a retirement community, and so on.

- *Evaluate options.* Think about how well your options will fulfill your needs. For two of your options, write potential positive and negative effects (pros and cons) of each.

- *Imagine acting on your decision.* Describe one practical course of action, based on your thinking so far, that you might follow. List the specific steps you would take. For example, the prospective nurse might list actions to help determine what type of nursing suits him best, such as interning, getting summer jobs, pursuing academic goals, and talking to working nurses.

An additional practical action is to go to an actual job site and talk to people. The prospective nurse might go to a hospital, a clinic, and a health centre at a retirement community. Get a feel for what the job is like day to day so that can be part of your decision.

KEY 4.13 Work through a problem by using this flowchart.

DEFINE PROBLEM HERE:

ANALYZE THE PROBLEM

Use boxes below to list possible solutions:

POTENTIAL POSITIVE EFFECTS		POTENTIAL NEGATIVE EFFECTS
List for each solution:	SOLUTION #1	List for each solution:
	SOLUTION #2	
	SOLUTION #3	

Now choose the solution you think is best—circle it and make it happen.

ACTUAL POSITIVE EFFECTS	PRACTICAL ACTION	ACTUAL NEGATIVE EFFECTS
List for chosen solution:		List for chosen solution:

FINAL EVALUATION: Was it a good or bad solution?

Source: Based on a heuristic created by Frank T. Lyman Jr. and George Eley, 1985.

WRITE IT *Communicate*

Emotional intelligence journal: Make a wiser choice. Think about a decision you made that you wish you had handled differently. Describe the decision and what feelings resulted from it. Then, describe what you would do if you could approach the decision again, thinking about a mindset and actions that might produce more positive feelings and a better outcome.

Real-life writing: Address a problem. Think about a problem that you are currently experiencing in school—it could be difficulty with a course, a scheduling nightmare, or a conflict with a classmate. Write a letter—to an advisor, instructor, friend, medical professional, or anyone else who may help—that asks for help with your problem. Be specific about what you want and how the person to whom you are writing can help you. After you finish, consider sending your letter via mail or email. Carefully assess the effect that it may have, and if you decide that it may help, send it. Be sure to have someone you trust review it for you before you send it.

WORK IT *Build Your Brand*

Generate Ideas for Internships

21st Century Learning Building Blocks

- Financial, economic, business, and entrepreneurial literacy
- Leadership and responsibility
- Communication and collaboration

Pursuing internships is a practical way to get experience, learn what you like and don't like, and make valuable connections. Even interning in a career area that you don't ultimately pursue can build skills that are useful in any career. The creative thinking skills you've built will help you generate ideas for where you might intern at some point during your post-secondary career.

First, use personal contacts to gather information about career fields. Note the following for each:

1. Name and contact information

2. Field

3. Why you want to interview him or her

Then, talk to the people you have listed, and take notes.

Next, look up each of these fields at "Working in Canada" (www.workingincanada.gc.ca). Take notes and compare the fields based on what you've learned.

Finally, consult someone in your school's career office about local companies that offer internships. Get specific information about internship job descriptions, timing (during the term, in the summer), and whether there is any financial compensation.

Analyze what you have learned from your reading, your interviews, and career office information. Write down the field or fields in which you would like to intern and why, and describe what practical action you plan to take to secure an internship within the next two years.

Answers to Perception Puzzles on p. 93

First puzzle: A duck or a rabbit
Second puzzle: Lines or a letter

Study Tools: *Get Ready for Exams*

Start with a Study Plan and Schedule

Because some instructors may schedule exams early and often in the semester, begin right away to develop strategies for test success. Starting off on the right foot will boost your confidence and motivate you to work even harder. The saying that "success breeds more success" couldn't be more true as you begin college or university.

The material in this Study Tools is designed to help you organize yourself as you prepare for exams. As you learn to create a pretest study plan and schedule, you will also build your ability to use your time efficiently.

When you reach Chapter 8, you will study test taking in depth, including test preparation, test anxiety, general test-taking strategies, strategies for handling different types of test questions, and learning from test mistakes.

Decide on a Study Plan

Start your test preparation by deciding what you will study. Go through your notes, texts, related primary sources, and handouts, and set aside materials you don't need. Then prioritize the remaining materials. Your goal is to focus on information that is most likely to be on the exam. Use the test preparation tips in Chapter 8 and the material on studying your text in Chapter 7 to boost your effectiveness as you prepare.

Create a Study Schedule and Checklist

Next, use the time-management and goal-setting skills from Chapter 2 to prepare a schedule. Consider all the relevant factors—your study materials, the number of days until the test, and the time you can study each day. If you establish your schedule ahead of time and write it in a planner, you are more likely to follow it.

A checklist like the one following will help you organize and stay on track as you prepare. Use a checklist to assign specific tasks to particular study times and sessions. That way, not only do you know when you have time to study, but you also have defined goals for each study session. Make extra copies of the checklist so that you can fill out a new one each time you have an exam.

Course: _____ Instructor: _____

Date, time, and place of test:_____

Type of test (is it a mid-term or a minor quiz?):_____

What the instructor said about the test, including the types of test questions, test length, and how much the test counts toward your final grade:

_____
_____

Topics to be covered on the test, in order of importance (information should also come from your instructor):

    1. _____

    2. _____

3. _____
4. _____
5. _____

Study schedule, including materials you plan to study (texts, class notes, homework problems, and so forth) and dates you plan to complete each:

MATERIAL	DATE OF COMPLETION
1. _____	_____
2. _____	_____
3. _____	_____
4. _____	_____
5. _____	_____

Materials you are expected to bring to the test (textbook, sourcebook, calculator, and so on):
_____
_____
_____

Special study arrangements (for example, plan study group meetings, ask the instructor for special help, get outside tutoring):
_____
_____
_____

Life-management issues (such as rearranging work hours):
_____
_____
_____

Source: Adapted from Ron Fry, *"Ace" Any Test*, 3rd ed., Franklin Lakes, NJ: Career Press, 1996. pp. 123–124.

Decide How Well These Techniques Work For You

After you have used these studying and scheduling techniques to prepare for a few exams, answer the following questions:

• How did this approach help you organize your time before an exam?

_____
_____
_____

• How did this approach help you organize your study material so that you remembered to cover every topic?

_____
_____
_____

• Can you think of ways to change the checklist to improve your test-prep efficiency? If you can, list the ways here and incorporate them into the checklist.

_____
_____
_____

Self-Study Quiz

Multiple choice

Circle or highlight the answer that seems to fit best.

1. A *motivator* is
   A. the ability to achieve a goal.
   B. progress toward a goal.
   C. a decision to take action.
   D. a want or need that moves a person to action.

2. **The direct benefits of responsibility include**
   A. earning the trust of others at school, work, and home.
   B. getting motivated to achieve study goals.
   C. improved ability to plan strategically.
   D. moving up at work.

3. A *learning style* is
   A. the best way to learn when attending classes.
   B. a particular way of being intelligent.
   C. an affinity for a particular job choice or career area.
   D. a way in which the mind receives and processes information.

4. **The best way to use learning style assessments is to see them as**
   A. a reference point rather than a label; a tool with which to see yourself more clearly.
   B. a road map for your life; a message that shows the paths you must take in order to be successful.
   C. a lesson about group learning; a way to find the group of learners with whom you work best.
   D. a definitive label for your working style; a clear-cut category where you fit.

5. **When choosing and evaluating your values, it is important to**
   A. set goals according to what your friends and family value.
   B. keep your values steady over time.
   C. re-evaluate values periodically as you experience change.
   D. set aside values that no one else seems to think are good for you.

6. **It is important to link daily and weekly goals with long-term goals because**
   A. the process will help you focus on the things that are most important to you.
   B. short-term goals have no meaning if they are not placed in a longer time frame.
   C. the process will help you eliminate frivolous activities.
   D. others expect you to know how everything you do relates to what you want to accomplish in life.

Fill in the blanks

Complete the following sentences with the appropriate word(s) or phrase(s) that best reflect what you learned in the chapters. Choose from the items that follow each sentence.

1. When you make a(n) _____, you do what you say you will do. (initiative, motivation, commitment)

2. Showing _____ helps you take that first step toward a goal and respond to changes in your life. (motivation, initiative, integrity)

3. One way to look at learning style is to divide it into two equally important aspects: _____ and _____. (learning preferences/personality traits, -verbal/visual, interests/abilities)

4. The best careers and majors/programs for you are ones that take into consideration your _____ and _____. (references/contacts, learning style/abilities, interests/abilities)

5. Your _____ is a philosophy outlining what you want to be, what you want to do, and the principles by which you live. (responsibility, mission, integrity)

6. Being _____ helps you cope with day-to-day changes and life changes. (organized, flexible, on time)

Essays

The following essay questions will help you organize and communicate your ideas in writing, just as you must do on an essay test. Before you begin answering a question, spend a few minutes planning. (Brainstorm possible approaches, write a thesis statement, jot down main thoughts in outline or think-link form.) To prepare yourself for actual test conditions, limit writing time to no more than 30 minutes per question.

1. Discuss habits, both good and bad. What are the effects of each? Describe a useful plan for changing a habit that is having negative effects.

2. Define *values* and *value system*. How do values develop and what effect do they have on personal choices? How are values connected to goal setting? Give an example from your life of how values have influenced a personal goal.

Gary Montrose

You live in an information age. Your future demands that you be able to read, understand, and critically evaluate information on a daily basis in school, on the job, and in life.

Reading and Information Literacy

LEARNING FROM PRINT AND ONLINE MATERIALS

What Would You Risk? *Gary Montrose*

Gary Montrose

THINK ABOUT THIS SITUATION AS YOU READ, AND CONSIDER WHAT ACTION YOU WOULD TAKE.

Gary Montrose had no idea why he struggled in public school, and neither did his family or teachers. He was the first to sit down during spelling bees and the last to turn in class exams, even though his hard work got him elected student council president while in high school. His guidance counsellor told him that he "wasn't college or university material" and should consider going straight into a job at the local Lockheed assembly plant.

Determined to persevere, Gary enrolled in college and put his nose to the grindstone. After two years, he was able to transfer to university, but the confusing struggle continued, damaging his self-confidence and requiring survival strategies developed through experience. He avoided courses with in-class timed exams—an absolute terror—and looked for classes featuring papers he could write on his own time. He gave up 90 percent of a normal college student's social life and spent hours "unpacking" textbooks by reading the table of contents, chapter headings, tables, and charts. Knowing he was unlikely to complete any reading assignment without support, he needed to develop an idea of the scope of a book.

Despite graduating with high honours and a double major, Gary still lived with his big secret, terrified about how slowly he read and wrote. Hoping for advice on what type of work he could successfully pursue, he went to the career centre while in graduate school, where a series of tests showed he was functioning at a seventh-grade reading level. From those results he learned that he had a reading disability called dyslexia that causes difficulty with recognizing and understanding words. He began to see why he needed to put in so much extra time and effort to appear normal to the outside world.

To be continued . . .

Gary's ability to move out of his comfort zone has turned learning into an adventure that he continues as a worldwide traveller. You'll learn more about Gary, and revisit his situation, within the chapter.

Notes

Today   Mar 10 8:01 AM

Working through this chapter will help you to:

How Developed Are Your Reading and Information Literacy Skills?

For each statement, circle the number that feels right to you, from 1 for "not at all true for me" to 5 for "very true for me."

1. I make choices about when and how I read that help me boost focus and comprehension. ① ② ③ ④ ⑤

2. I preview a text before studying it by skimming and scanning front matter, chapter elements, and back matter for clues about content and organization. ① ② ③ ④ ⑤

3. I develop questions to guide me before I begin to read. ① ② ③ ④ ⑤

4. I practise reciting what I've learned from the reading by working with a study partner, taking notes, using flash cards, or using some other study technique. ① ② ③ ④ ⑤

5. I use text note taking and highlighting to turn my texts into study tools. ① ② ③ ④ ⑤

6. I have a process for reading onscreen assignments and articles. ① ② ③ ④ ⑤

7. I prioritize my reading assignments so that I focus on what is most important. ① ② ③ ④ ⑤

8. When I get a research or writing assignment, I go first to general references for an overview. ① ② ③ ④ ⑤

9. I don't just rely on the Internet for research—I also consult library materials. ① ② ③ ④ ⑤

10. I evaluate every Internet source for signs of bias, validity, credibility, and reliability. ① ② ③ ④ ⑤

Each of the topics in these statements is covered in this chapter. Note those statements for which you circled a 3 or lower. Skim the chapter to see where those topics appear, and pay special attention to them as you read, learn, and apply new strategies.

REMEMBER: NO MATTER HOW DEVELOPED YOUR READING AND INFORMATION LITERACY SKILLS ARE, YOU CAN IMPROVE WITH EFFORT AND PRACTICE.

WHAT SETS YOU UP FOR
reading comprehension?

Reading comprehension is the gateway to success in school and beyond. According to the Conference Board of Canada, being able to "read and understand information presented in a variety of forms (e.g., words, graphs, charts, diagrams)"[1] is an essential fundamental skill. Why? Because if you can read and *understand* something, you can learn it and *use* it. In exchange for your risk of effort and commitment, you can earn the following rewards:

- A broad and deep range of knowledge
- A solid foundation of learning that will help you perform in advanced courses
- The ability to digest and use information on the job and to stay up-to-date on changes

MyStudentSuccessLab

Whether face-to-face or online, MyStudentSuccessLab helps students build the skills they need through peer-led video interviews, interactive practice exercises, and activities that provide academic, life, and professionalism skills.

Post-secondary reading assignments are often challenging, requiring more focus and new strategies on your part. On any given day, you may have a variety of reading assignments, such as

- An 18-page text chapter on the contributions made by First Nations peoples
- An original research study on the relationship between sleep deprivation and the development of memory problems (psychology)
- A review of *Hellgoing* by Lynn Coady, winner of the 2013 Giller Prize (Canadian literature)
- A technical manual on the design of computer antivirus programs (computer science—software design)

To face this challenge, it's helpful to use specific reading techniques. Before you open a book or log onto your computer, how can you get ready to make the most of your reading?

Define Your Reading Purpose

The first step in improving your reading comprehension is to ask yourself *why* you are reading particular material. With a clear purpose, you can decide how much time and effort to expend on your assignments. Key 5.1 shows four common reading purposes. Depending on what your instructor expects, you may have as many as three reading purposes for one assignment, such as understanding, critical evaluation, and practical application.

Use the class syllabus to help define your purpose for each assignment. For example, if the syllabus shows that inflation is the topic of your next economics class lecture, read the assigned chapter with that focus in mind: mastering the definition of inflation, evaluating historical economic events that caused inflation, and so on. And keep open the possibility that any reading assignment with purposes 1, 2, or 3 may also bring you purpose 4—enjoyment.

Take an Active and Positive Approach

Many instructors spend little or no time reviewing reading in class because they expect you to complete it independently. How can you approach difficult material actively and positively?

If you look carefully at your schedule, you may find useful segments of time in between classes. Try using such time for reading assignments.

Reading and Information Literacy

| KEY 5.1 | Establish why you are reading a given piece of material. |

WHAT'S MY PURPOSE?	EXPLANATION
1. **To understand**	Read to comprehend concepts and details. Details help explain or support general concepts, and concepts provide a framework for details.
2. **To evaluate analytically**	Read with an open mind as you examine causes and effects, evaluate ideas, and ask questions that test arguments and assumptions. Evaluation develops a level of understanding beyond basic information recall. (See pages 138–140 for more on this topic.)
3. **For practical application**	Read to find information to help reach a specific goal. For instance, when you read a lab manual for chemistry, your goal is to learn how to do the lab experiment.
4. **For pleasure**	Read for entertainment, such as "The Hockey News" website or a mystery or romance novel.

- *Start with a questioning attitude.* Consider such questions as, How can I connect the reading to what I already know? Look at the chapter headings and ask yourself questions about what the material means and why it is being presented in this way.
- *Look for order.* Use SQ3R and the critical reading strategies introduced later in this chapter to discover patterns, logic, and relationships. Text cues—how the material is organized, outlines, bold terms, and more—help you anticipate what's coming next.
- *Have an open mind.* Be careful not to prejudge assignments as impossible or boring or a waste of time before you begin.
- *Plan for multiple readings.* Don't expect to master challenging material on the first pass. Get an overview of key concepts on the first reading. Use later readings to build your understanding, relate information to what you know, and apply information elsewhere. Gary accepted multiple readings as necessary to his success.
- *Get help.* If material is tough to understand, consult resources—instructors, study group partners, tutors, related texts, and websites—for help. Build a library of texts in your major and minor areas of study, and refer to them when needed.

Choose the Right Setting

Where, when, and with whom you study has a significant effect on your success.

- *Choose locations that work.* Know yourself, and choose settings that distract you least—in your room at home, at a library, outdoors, in an empty classroom, anywhere that works. Your schedule may restrict your choices. For example, if you can study only late at night when the libraries are closed, you will probably have to work at home; if you spend a good deal of your day commuting, mass transit may be your best study spot. Evaluate how effectively you focus. If you spend too much time being distracted at a particular location, try someplace different.
- *Choose times that work.* Pay attention to your body's natural rhythms, and try to read during times when you tend to be most alert and focused. For example, although night owls are productive when everyone else is sleeping, morning people may have a hard time reading late at night. The times you choose depend, of course, on what your schedule allows.

PRIMARY SOURCES
Original documents, including academic journal articles and scientific studies.

SECONDARY SOURCES
Other writers' interpretations of primary source documents.

Learn to Concentrate

Even well-written college and university textbooks may require a lot of focus, especially when you encounter complex concepts and new terms.

Even greater focus is often necessary when assignments are from **primary sources** rather than **secondary sources**.

When you focus your attention on one thing and only one thing, you are engaged in the act of *concentration*. The following active-learning methods can help maintain focus as you study. Many involve tapping into your emotional and social intelligence.

Jose Gil/Shutterstock

- *Deal with internal distractions.* When worries come up, such as to-do list items for other projects, write them down to deal with later. Sometimes you may want to take a break to deal with something that is bothering you before continuing with your reading. For example, if you're hungry, grab a healthy snack. If you start to lose focus, an exercise break may energize you and help you concentrate.
- *Take control of technology.* Web surfing, emailing, texting, or instant messaging can distract. Plus, forcing your brain to switch back and forth between tasks can increase work time and errors. Instead, save technology for breaks or after you finish your work.
- *Structure your work session.* Set realistic goals and a specific plan for dividing your time. Tell yourself, "I'm going to read 30 pages and then go online for 30 minutes."

get $mart

PhotoMan/Fotolia

Complete the following on paper or in digital format.

Use your reading skills to make sure you understand your bank's policies about the account you use most (chequing or savings). Look up your type of account on your bank's website, and read the rules. Then answer the following questions.

1. Can you make withdrawals and deposits online without a fee? _____

2. Can you make withdrawals and deposits in the bank without a fee? _____

3. Can your transfer money electronically between accounts? _____

4. Is there a monthly fee? _____ If so, how much is it? _____

5. Is there a limit for checks, debits, or ATM transactions? _____ If so, describe:
   _____

6. Describe any other fees or rules involved (such as minimum balance).
   _____

7. What happens if a check you write bounces? Someone else's bounces?
   _____

8. What happens if you overdraw your account? If overdraft protection is available, how much does it cost?
   _____

- *Manage family obligations.* Set up activities or child care if you have kids. Tell your children, if they are old enough to understand, what your education will mean to them and to you.
- *Plan a reward.* Have something to look forward to. You deserve it!

The strongest motivation to concentrate comes from within. When you see the connection between what you study and your short- and long-term goals, you will be better able to focus, to remember, to learn, and to apply.

Expand Your Vocabulary

As reading materials become more complex, your vocabulary influences how much you comprehend—and how readily you do so. When reading a textbook, the first "dictionary" to search is the end-of-book glossary that explains technical words and concepts. The definitions there are usually limited to the meanings used in the text. Standard dictionaries provide broader information, such as word origin, pronunciation, part of speech, synonyms, antonyms, and multiple meanings. Buy a standard dictionary and investigate websites such as Dictionary.com. The suggestions in Key 5.2 will help you make the most of your dictionary.

TIPS FOR LEARNING ONLINE

- *Reading online.* To reduce eye strain while reading online, try increasing the font size, and remember to take regular short breaks.

- *Know your platform.* Before you start reading your ebook, make sure you know how to navigate the table of contents, flip pages, take notes, and highlight text.

- *Avoid distractions.* Wait for breaks or until after you finish your work to spend time checking email or texting. Schedule 10-minute breaks from studying to get caught up on your social media for every 60 minutes of study time.

Reading and Information Literacy

117

Use the word in the next 24 hours.

Not only does this demonstrate that you know how the word is used, but it also aids memorization.

Analyze word parts.

Many English words combine prefixes, roots, and suffixes. *Prefixes* are word parts added to the beginning of a root. *Suffixes* are added to the end of the root. The *root* is the central part or basis of a word around which prefixes and/or suffixes are added to produce different words. Recognizing these word parts can boost comprehension.

Read beyond the first definition.

Then think critically about which meaning suits the context of the word in question and choose the one that makes the most sense.

dic-tio-nary

Pronunciation; \'dik-shə-,ner-ē, -,ne-rē\

Function: *noun*

Inflected Form(s): *plural* **dic·tio·nar·ies**

Etymology: Medieval Latin *dictionarium*, from Late Latin *diction-*, *dictio* word, from Latin, speaking

Date: 1526

1. A reference source in print or electronic form containing words usually alphabetically arranged along with information about their forms, pronunciations, functions, etymologies, meanings, and syntactical and idiomatic uses.

2. A book giving information on particular subjects or on a particular class of words, names, or facts, usually arranged alphabetically: *a biographical dictionary; a dictionary of mathematics.*

3. (*computing*) An associative array, a data structure where each value is referenced by a particular key, analogous to words and definitions in a physical dictionary.

Say and spell new words to boost recall.

Listen to the pronunciation on a hand-held electronic or online dictionary. Then practise writing the word to verify that you know the spelling.

Restate the definition in your own words.

When you can do this with ease, you know that you understand the meaning and are not merely parroting a dictionary definition.

HOW CAN SQ3R IMPROVE
your reading?

Reading may look like a one-way street in which you, the reader, take in words the author has written. However, it is intended as an interactive communication. The author communicates ideas to you and invites your response. How can you respond? One answer is provided in the SQ3R reading strategy, which stands for *Survey, Question, Read, Recite,* and *Review.*[2] This straightforward technique helps readers take in, understand, and remember what they read. It encourages you to fulfill your side of interactive communication by asking questions, marking key ideas, introducing your own connections, and more.

As you move through the stages of SQ3R, you will skim and scan your text. **Skimming** refers to the rapid reading of such chapter elements as section introductions and conclusions, boldface or italicized terms, pictures and charts, and summaries. The goal of skimming is a quick construction of the main ideas. In contrast, scanning

SKIMMING
Rapid, superficial reading of material to determine central ideas and main elements.

SCANNING
Reading material in an investigative way to search for specific information.

multiple intelligence strategies

INTELLIGENCE	USE MI STRATEGIES TO BECOME A BETTER READER	IDENTIFY MI READING STRATEGIES THAT CAN HELP YOU IMPROVE COMPREHENSION
Verbal-Linguistic	• Use the steps in SQ3R, focusing especially on writing Q-stage questions, summaries, and so on. • Make marginal text notes as you read.	
Logical-Mathematical	• Logically connect what you are reading with what you already know. Consider similarities, differences, and cause-and-effect relationships. • Draw charts showing relationships and analyze trends.	
Bodily-Kinesthetic	• Use text highlighting to take a hands-on approach to reading. • Take a hands-on approach to learning experiments by trying to re-create them yourself.	
Visual-Spatial	• Make charts, diagrams, or think links illustrating difficult ideas you encounter as you read. • Take note of photos, tables, and other visual aids in the text.	
Interpersonal	• Discuss reading material and clarify concepts in a study group. • Talk to people who know about the topic you are studying.	
Intrapersonal	• Apply concepts to your own life; think about how you would manage. • Try to understand your personal strengths and weaknesses to lead a study group on the reading material.	
Musical	• Recite text concepts to rhythms or write a song to depict them. • Explore relevant musical links to the material.	
Naturalistic	• Tap into your ability to notice similarities and differences in objects and concepts by organizing reading materials into relevant groupings.	

Reading and Information Literacy

involves a careful search for specific information. You might use scanning during the SQ3R review phase to locate particular facts.

Just like many strategies presented to you throughout your post-secondary career, SQ3R works best if you adapt it to your own needs. Explore techniques, evaluate what works, and then make the system your own. As you become familiar with the system, keep in mind that SQ3R works best with textbook-based courses such as science, math, social sciences, and humanities. SQ3R is not recommended for literature courses.

Step 1: Survey

Surveying, the first stage in SQ3R, is the process of previewing, or prereading, a book before you study it. Compare it to looking at a map before starting a road trip; determining the route and stops along the way in advance will save time and trouble while you travel. Gary made extensive use of the survey tools that most textbooks provide, including elements that provide a big picture overview of the main ideas and themes, such as the following.

- *Front matter.* Skim the *table of contents* for the chapter titles, the main topics in each chapter and the order in which they will be covered, as well as special features. Then skim the *preface*, which is a personal note from the author that tells you what the book will cover and its point of view. For example, the preface for the American history text *Out of Many* states that it highlights "the experiences of diverse communities of Americans in the unfolding story of our country."[3] This tells you that cultural diversity is a central theme.
- *Chapter elements.* Text chapters use various devices to structure the material and highlight content.

  - *Chapter titles* establish the topic and often the author's perspective.
  - *Chapter introductions* or *outlines* generally list objectives or key topics.
  - *Level headings* (first, second, third), including those in question form, break down material into bite-size chunks.
  - *Margin materials* can include definitions, quotations, questions, and exercises.
  - *Tables, charts, photographs,* and *captions* illustrate important concepts *in a visual manner.*
  - *Sidebars* or *boxed features* are connected to text themes and introduce extra tidbits of information that supplement the text.
  - *Different styles* or *arrangements of type* (**boldface**, *italics*, underlining, larger fonts, bullet points, boxed text) can flag vocabulary or important ideas.
  - *End-of-chapter summaries* review chapter content and main ideas.
  - *Review questions and exercises* help you understand and apply content in creative and practical ways.

In Key 5.3, a typical page from the textbook *Exploring Sociology: The Concise Edition*, by Bruce Ravelli and Michelle Webber, how many elements do you recognize? How do these elements help you grasp the subject even before reading it?

- *Back matter.* Some texts include a *glossary* that defines text terms, an *index* to help you locate topics, and a *bibliography* that lists additional readings.

Step 2: Question

The next step is to ask questions about your assignment. Using the *questioning* process outlined below leads you to discover knowledge on your own by making an investment in the material and in your own memory.

176 | CHAPTER 7

professional organizations, we may be discriminating against others and not even know it. If you hire someone who went to the same university as you (but whom you do not know), are you guilty of discrimination? Are you discriminating against graduates from other schools?

The point is that we cannot always predict what people are thinking or what motivates their actions. Sociologists have known for a long time that what people think, say, and do is not always consistent (LaPierre, 1934).[1]

Explaining Prejudice and Discrimination

Both social psychologists and sociologists have offered several theories to explain prejudice and discrimination.

PSYCHOLOGICAL THEORIES

Scapegoat Theory If you sat back and considered why prejudice exists and why some people discriminate against others, how would you explain it? To many, **scapegoat theory** makes a lot of sense. Scapegoat theory asserts that prejudice and discrimination grow out of the frustrations of people who want to blame someone else for their problems. The theory originated with the work of American psychologist John Dollard (Dollard, Doob, Miller, Mowrer, & Sears, 1939), who suggested that people displace their frustrations about virtually anything onto other identifiable people whom they can target as being responsible for their problems (Weatherley, 1988, p. 88). As stated by Babad, Birnbaum, and Benne (1983, p. 83), "when there is tension and social problems seem insurmountable, find an innocent, weak and distinctive group to blame and victimize" (as cited in Gibson & Howard, 2007, p. 193). Let's say that a Canadian factory closes because cheaper products are available from China, and a laid-off worker directs his anger at his Chinese-Canadian neighbour. As you can see, victims of scapegoating rarely have anything to do with the situation at hand (Chinese Canadians have nothing to do with China's more economical production techniques), but they suffer discrimination anyway.

scapegoat theory The assertion that prejudice and discrimination originate in the frustrations of people who want to blame someone else for their problems.

Authoritarian Personality Theory According to the **authoritarian personality theory**, extreme prejudice is a personality trait linked to people who believe strongly in following cultural norms, traditions, and values. People with an authoritarian personality are generally conformists, faithfully follow instructions from their superiors, and reject those they consider to be inferior to them.

The theory is largely the result of work by researchers from what is called the **Frankfurt School**—a group of German social philosophers who worked from the conflict perspective as employed by Karl Marx and Max Weber. Fleeing the rise of the Nazi regime, this group of scholars (notably Theodor Adorno, Erich Fromm, Max Horkheimer, Leo Löwenthal, and Herbert Marcuse) travelled to the United States to pursue their work. The Frankfurt School became famous for using critical social theory to explore the role of culture and mass communication in the social reproduction of domination and oppression—clearly an attempt to understand the Nazi atrocities against Jews during World War II. Their work became increasingly focused on the psychological characteristics that predisposed certain individuals to prejudice and racial hatred (Kellner, 1990).

The theorist most responsible for developing the authoritarian personality theory was Theodor Adorno. His research found that people who show strong negative reactions toward one minority group generally feel negatively about all minorities. People with these traits

authoritarian personality theory Asserts that extreme prejudice is a personality trait of people who strongly believe in following cultural norms, traditions, and values.

Frankfurt School A group of German social philosophers dedicated to understanding the role of culture and mass communication in the Nazi regime.

Reading and Information Literacy

---

1 For a critique of LaPierre's classic study, see Dockery and Bedeian (1989).

get analytical

Practice will improve your surveying skills. Start now with this book or another you are currently using, including any etexts that your instructors may have assigned

Skim the front matter, including the table of contents and preface. What does this material tell you about the theme? About the book's approach and point of view?

_____
_____
_____

Are there unexpected topics listed in the table of contents? Are there topics you expected to see that are missing?

_____
_____

Now look at a typical chapter. List the devices that organize the structure and content of the material.

_____
_____

After skimming the chapter, what do you know about the material? What elements helped you skim quickly?

_____
_____

Finally, skim the back matter. What elements can you identify?

_____
_____

How do you plan to use each of the elements you identified in your text survey when you begin studying?

_____
_____

Ask yourself what you know

Before you begin reading, think about—and summarize in writing if you can—what, if anything, you already know about the topic. This step prepares you to apply what you know to new material. Building on current knowledge is especially important in your major, where the concepts you learn from intro courses prepare you for the higher-level material in classes to come later on.

Write questions linked to chapter headings

Next, examine the chapter headings and, on a separate page or in the text margins, write questions linked to them. When you encounter an assignment without headings, divide the material into logical sections and then develop questions based on what you think the main idea of each section is. There are no correct questions. Given the same headings, two students could create two different sets of questions. Your goal in questioning is to begin to think critically about the material.

HEADINGS	QUESTIONS
The Meaning of Freedom	What did freedom mean for both slaves and citizens in the United States?
Moving About	Where did African Americans go after they were freed from slavery?
The African American Family	How did freedom change the structure of the African American family?
African American Churches and Schools	What effect did freedom have on the formation of African American churches and schools?
Land and Labour After Slavery	How was land farmed and maintained after slaves were freed?
The Origins of African American Politics	How did the end of slavery bring about the beginning of African American political life?

Key 5.4 shows how this works. The column on the left contains primary and secondary headings from a section of *Out of Many*. The column on the right rephrases these headings in question form.

Use Bloom's Taxonomy to formulate questions

Questions can seek different types of answers and may require different levels of analytical thinking to solve. To help you understand and use different types of questions, consider the system educational psychologist Benjamin Bloom developed based on the idea that deeper learning occurs when the effort to understand is more rigorous.[4] Although some questions ask for a simple recall, said Bloom, others ask for higher thinking levels.

Key 5.5 shows the six levels of questions identified by Bloom: knowledge, understanding, application, analysis, synthesis, and evaluation. It also identifies verbs associated with each level. As you read, use these verbs to create specific questions that will help you learn. For instance, if you were to continue Key 5.4's process of creating questions based on the headings from *Out of Many*, the questions would change based on the level specified by Bloom's Taxonomy. See Key 5.6 for an example.

Step 3: Read

Your text survey and questions give you a starting point for *reading*, the first R in SQ3R. Retaining what you read requires an active approach.

- *Focus on the key points of your survey.* Pay special attention to points raised in headings, in boldface type, in the chapter objectives and summary, and in other emphasized text.
- *Focus on your Q-stage questions.* Read the material with the purpose of answering each question. Write down or highlight ideas and examples that relate to your questions.
- *Create text tabs.* Place plastic index tabs or adhesive notes at the start of each chapter so you can flip back and forth with ease.
- *Mark up your text.* Write notes in the margins, circle main ideas, or underline supporting details to focus on what's important. For an ebook, use the *Insert*

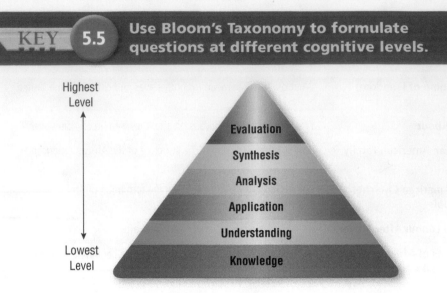

KEY 5.5 Use Bloom's Taxonomy to formulate questions at different cognitive levels.

Highest Level

Lowest Level

Evaluation
Synthesis
Analysis
Application
Understanding
Knowledge

Verbs That Indicate Each Level

1. **Knowledge:** average, define, duplicate, label, list, memorize, name, order, recall, recognize, relate, repeat, reproduce, state.

2. **Understanding:** classify, describe, discuss, explain, express, identify, indicate, locate, recognize, report, restate, review, select, translate.

3. **Application:** apply, choose, demonstrate, dramatize, employ, illustrate, interpret, operate, practise, schedule, sketch, solve, use, write.

4. **Analysis:** analyze, appraise, calculate, categorize, compare, contrast, criticize, differentiate, discriminate, distinguish, examine, experiment, question, test.

5. **Synthesis:** arrange, assemble, collect, compose, construct, create, design, develop, formulate, manage, organize, plan, prepare, propose, set up, write.

6. **Evaluation:** appraise, argue, assess, attach, choose, compare, defend, estimate, evaluate, judge, predict, rate, score, select, support, value.

Comments feature. These cues will boost memory and help you study for exams. Here are some tips for *annotating*—taking marginal notes on the pages of your text:

• Use pencil so you can erase comments or questions that are answered later.

• Write your Q questions in the margins next to text headings.

• Mark critical sections with marginal notations such as Def. for definition, e.g. for helpful example, Concept for an important concept, and so on.

• Write notes at the bottom of the page connecting the text to what you learned in class or in research. You can also attach adhesive notes with your comments.

■ *Highlight your text. Highlighting* involves the use of special markers or regular pens or pencils to flag important passages. When working with ebooks, make note of the highlighting function, which allows you to overlay a colour on important text. When used correctly, highlighting is an essential learning technique. However, experts agree that you will not learn what to highlight unless you

The Origins of African American Politics

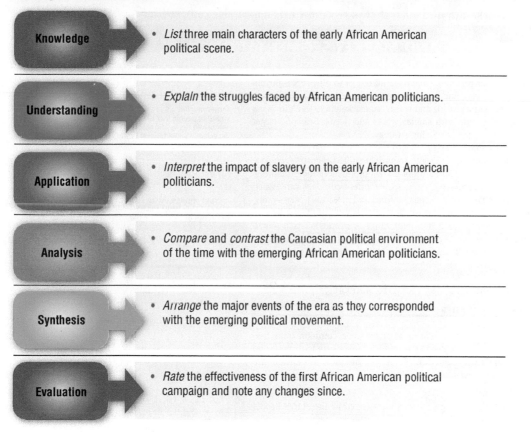

Knowledge
- *List* three main characters of the early African American political scene.

Understanding
- *Explain* the struggles faced by African American politicians.

Application
- *Interpret* the impact of slavery on the early African American politicians.

Analysis
- *Compare* and *contrast* the Caucasian political environment of the time with the emerging African American politicians.

Synthesis
- *Arrange* the major events of the era as they corresponded with the emerging political movement.

Evaluation
- *Rate* the effectiveness of the first African American political campaign and note any changes since.

interact with the material through surveying, questioning, reciting, and reviewing. Use the following tips to make highlighting a true learning tool:

- *Develop a system and stick to it.* Decide whether you will use different colours to highlight different elements, brackets for long passages, or pencil underlining.

- *Consider using a regular pencil or pen instead of a highlighter pen.* The copy will be cleaner and may look less like a colouring book.

- *Mark text carefully if you are using a rented book or a book to be resold.* Use pencil as often as possible and erase your marks at the end of the class. Write on sticky notes that you can remove. Make copies of important chapters or sections for marking. If you are renting, check with the rental service to see what it permits.

- *Read an entire paragraph before you begin to highlight, and don't start until you have a sense of what is important.* Only then put pencil or highlighter to paper as you pick out the main idea, key terms, and crucial supporting details and examples.

- *Avoid overmarking.* Too much colour can be overwhelming. Try enclosing long passages with brackets and avoid underlining entire sentences, when possible.

Key 5.7, from an introductory business textbook describing the concepts of target marketing and market segmentation, shows how to underline and take marginal notes.

How does target marketing and market segmentation help companies sell product?

■ TARGET MARKETING AND MARKET SEGMENTATION

Marketers have long known that products cannot be all things to all people. Buyers have different tastes, goals, lifestyles, and so on. The emergence of the marketing concept and the recognition of consumer needs and wants led marketers to think in terms of **target markets**—groups of people with similar wants and needs. Selecting target markets is usually the first step in the marketing strategy.

Target marketing requires **market segmentation**—dividing a market into categories of customer types or "segments." Once they have identified segments, companies may adopt a variety of strategies. Some firms market products to more than one segment. General Motors *(www.gm.com)*, for example, offers compact cars, vans, trucks, luxury cars, and sports cars with various features and at various price levels. GM's strategy is to provide an automobile for nearly every segment of the market.

In contrast, some businesses offer a narrower range of products, each aimed toward a specific segment. Note that segmentation is a strategy for analyzing consumers, not products. The process of fixing, adapting, and communicating the nature of the product itself is called *product positioning*.

Definitions

target market
Group of people that has similar wants and needs and that can be expected to show interest in the same products

← *GM eg*

market segmentation
Process of dividing a market into categories of customer types

GM makes cars for diff. market segments

How do companies identify market segments?

Identifying Market Segments

By definition, members of a market segment must share some common traits that affect their purchasing decisions. In identifying segments, researchers look at several different influences on consumer behavior. Three of the most important are *geographic, demographic,* and *psychographic variables.*

What effect does geography have on segmentation strategies?

Geographic Variables Many buying decisions are affected by the places people call home. The heavy rainfall in Washington State, for instance, means that people there buy more umbrellas than people in the Sun Belt. Urban residents don't need agricultural equipment, and sailboats sell better along the coasts than on the Great Plains. **Geographic variables** are the geographical units, from countries to neighborhoods, that may be considered in a segmentation strategy.

These patterns affect decisions about marketing mixes for a huge range of products. For example, consider a plan to market down-filled parkas in rural Minnesota. Demand will be high and price competition intense. Local newspaper ads may be

Buying decisions influenced by where people live

geographic variables
Geographical units that may be considered in developing a segmentation strategy

— good eg —
selling parkas in Minnesota

Thought
Geographical variables change with the seasons

CHAPTER 5

Find the main idea

Understanding what you read depends on your ability to recognize *main ideas* and link other ideas to them. The main idea may appear in a topic sentence at the beginning of the paragraph followed by supporting details, or at the end of the paragraph with supporting details leading up to it. Sometimes, though, it is more difficult to figure out. When the main idea of a passage is unclear, use a three-step approach to decide what it is:[5]

1. *Search for the topic of the paragraph.* The topic of the paragraph is not the same as the main idea. Rather, it is the broad subject being discussed—for example, the late CEO of Apple Steve Jobs, hate crimes on campus, or binge drinking on campus.

2. *Identify the aspect of the topic that is the paragraph's focus.* If the general topic is Steve Jobs, the author may focus on any of thousands of aspects of that topic, such as his cofounding of Apple Computer in 1976; his role at Pixar, a computer animation company; or his involvement in the development of the iPod portable music player.

3. *Find what the author wants you to know about that specific aspect.* This is the main idea or topic sentence. Whereas the topic establishes the subject, a topic sentence narrows down the purpose of the paragraph into one or two focused statements. Thus, although the topic of the paragraph might be former Apple CEO Steve Jobs, the main idea, or topic sentence, might be "In his role as CEO of Apple, Steve Jobs oversaw the creation of the iPod portable music player, which changed the way the world listens to and purchases music."

> **TOPIC SENTENCE**
> A one- or two-sentence statement describing the main idea of a paragraph.

Step 4: Recite

Once you finish reading a topic, stop and answer the questions you raised in the Q stage of SQ3R. Even if you have already done this during the reading phase, do it again now—with the purpose of learning and committing the material to memory by *reciting* the answers.

You can say each answer aloud, silently speak the answers to yourself, teach the answers to another person, or write your ideas and answers in note form. Whatever recitation method you choose, make sure you know how the ideas connect to one another and to the general concept being discussed.

Writing is often the most effective way to learn new material. Write responses to your Q-stage questions and use your own words to explain new concepts; save your writing as a study tool for review. Writing gives you immediate feedback: when it agrees with the material you are studying, you know the information. When it doesn't, you still need work with the text or a study partner.

talk risk and reward . . .

Risk asking tough questions to be rewarded with new insights. Use the following to inspire discussion with classmates in person or online.

- How can reading be a risk, and what reward would it bring? What risk do you take if you do *not* read?

- What steps do you take to ensure that you understand what you read? Have those strategies worked for you so far? Why or why not?

CONSIDER THE CASE: What step (or steps) from SQ3R were most helpful to Gary in dealing with his particular challenge? What step or steps do you think will be most helpful to *you*? Why?

Gary Montrose; Shutterstock

get practical

MARK UP A PAGE TO LEARN A PAGE

Below, the text material in Key 5.7 continues. Read it and mark it up, highlighting concepts and taking marginal notes. Compare your efforts to those of your classmates to see how each of you approached the task and what you can learn from their methods.

effective, and the best retail location may be one that is easily reached from several small towns.

Although the marketability of some products is geographically sensitive, others enjoy nearly universal acceptance. Coke, for example, gets more than 70 percent of its sales from international markets. It is the market leader in Great Britain, China, Germany, Japan, Brazil, and Spain. Pepsi's international sales are about 15 percent of Coke's. In fact, Coke's chief competitor in most countries is some local soft drink, not Pepsi, which earns 78 percent of its income at home.

demographic variables
Characteristics of populations that may be considered in developing a segmentation strategy

Demographic Variables Demographic variables describe populations by identifying such traits as age, income, gender, ethnic background, marital status, race, religion, and social class. For example, several general consumption characteristics can be attributed to certain age groups (18–25, 26–35, 36–45, and so on). A marketer can, thus, divide markets into age groups. Table 10.1 lists some possible demographic breakdowns. Depending on the marketer's purpose, a segment can be a single classification (*aged 20–34*) or a combination of categories (*aged 20–34*, *married with children*, *earning* $25,000–$34,999). Foreign competitors, for example, are gaining market share in U.S. auto sales by appealing to young buyers (under age 30) with limited incomes (under $30,000). Whereas companies such as Hyundai (*www.hyundai.net*), Kia (*www.kia.com*), and Daewoo (*www.daewoous.com*) are winning entry-level customers with high quality and generous warranties, Volkswagen (*www.vw.com*) targets under-35 buyers with its entertainment-styled VW Jetta.[4]

psychographic variables
Consumer characteristics, such as lifestyles, opinions, interests, and attitudes, that may be considered in developing a segmentation strategy

Psychographic Variables Markets can also be segmented according to such **psychographic variables** as lifestyles, interests, and attitudes. Take, for example, Burberry (*www.burberry.com*), whose raincoats have been a symbol of British tradition since 1856. Burberry has repositioned itself as a global luxury brand, like Gucci (*www.gucci.com*) and Louis Vuitton (*www.vuitton.com*). The strategy, which recently resulted in a 31-percent sales increase, calls for attracting a different type of customer—the top-of-the-line, fashion-conscious individual—who shops at such stores as Neiman Marcus and Bergdorf Goodman.[5]

Psychographics are particularly important to marketers because, unlike demographics and geographics, they can be changed by marketing efforts. For example, Polish companies have overcome consumer resistance by promoting the safety and desirability of using credit rather than depending solely on cash. One product of changing attitudes is a booming economy and the emergence of a robust middle class.

TABLE 10.1

Demographic Variables

Age	Under 5, 5–11, 12–19, 20–34, 35–49, 50–64, 65+
Education	Grade school or less, some high school, graduated high school, some college, college degree, advanced degree
Family life cycle	Young single, young married without children, young married with children, older married with children under 18, older married without children under 18, older single, other
Family size	1, 2–3, 4–5, 6+
Income	Under $9,000, $9,000–$14,999, $15,000–$24,999, $25,000–$34,999, $35,000–$45,000, over $45,000
Nationality	African, American, Asian, British, Eastern European, French, German, Irish, Italian, Latin American, Middle Eastern, Scandinavian
Race	Native American, Asian, Black, White
Religion	Buddhist, Catholic, Hindu, Jewish, Muslim, Protestant
Sex	Male, female

CHAPTER 5

Keep your learning styles in mind while exploring different strategies (see Chapter 3). For example, an intrapersonal learner may prefer writing, whereas an interpersonal learner may choose to recite answers aloud to a classmate. A logical-mathematical learner may benefit from organizing material into detailed outlines or charts, as opposed to a musical learner, who might chant information aloud to a rhythm.

When do you stop to recite? Waiting for the end of a chapter is too late; stopping at the end of one paragraph is too soon. The best plan is to recite at the end of each text section, right before a new heading. Repeat the question–read–recite cycle until you complete the chapter. If you fumble for thoughts, reread the section until you are on solid ground.

Step 5: Review

Reviewing, both immediately and periodically in the days and weeks after you read, will help you memorize, understand, and learn material. If you close the book after reading it once, chances are that you will forget almost everything, which is why students who read material for the first time right before a test don't tend to do too well. *Reviewing is your key to learning.*

Reviewing the same material in several sessions over time will also help you identify knowledge gaps. It's natural to forget material between study sessions, especially if it's complex. When you come back after a break, you can focus on where you need the most help.

Examine the following reviewing techniques (more on these in Chapter 7). Try them all, and use the ones that work best for you. Try using more than one strategy when you study—switching among several different strategies tends to strengthen learning and memory.

- Reread your notes. Then summarize them from memory.
- Review and summarize in writing the text sections you highlighted or bracketed.
- Rewrite key points and main concepts in your own words. Create written examples that will help solidify the content in your mind.
- Answer the end-of-chapter review, discussion, and application questions.
- Reread the preface, headings, tables, and summary.
- Recite important concepts to yourself, or record and play them back on an audio recorder.
- If they are available to you, listen to MP3 audio recordings of your text and other reading materials.
- Make flash cards with a word or concept on one side and a definition, examples, or other related information on the other. Test yourself.
- Quiz yourself, using the questions you raised in the Q stage.
- Discuss the concepts with a classmate or in a study group. Answer one another's Q-stage questions.
- Ask your instructor for help with difficult material.

Refreshing your knowledge is easier and faster than learning it the first time. Make a weekly review schedule and stick to it until you're sure you know everything.

Zush/Shutterstock

WHAT STRATEGIES HELP WITH SPECIFIC
subjects and formats?

If your college or university has <u>**general education requirements**</u>, you may have to take a wide variety of courses to graduate. Knowing how to approach reading materials in different academic areas will help you learn.

GENERAL EDUCATION REQUIREMENTS
Courses required for graduation in a variety of academic fields, including the humanities, social sciences, math, and science.

get creative

For this exercise, partner up with someone in your class. To begin, each of you will write a mini-biography—approximately three to five paragraphs—answering the following questions:

- Where are you from?

- How would you describe your family?

- How have they influenced the student you are today?

- What three facts or ideas about yourself would you like someone else to know?

Include a title that reflects your biography as a whole. Also, for each paragraph in the middle (not the first or last), provide a title header that tells the reader what to expect in the paragraph (for example, "My Childhood in the Ottawa Valley," "Daytime Student, Nighttime Employee," and so on).

Once you're finished, read over what you've written for spelling, punctuation, and clarity. Switch papers with your partner and read his or her biography. Using SQ3R:

1. *Survey.* Scan your partner's paper for any words that stand out or phrases that seem important. Circle or highlight anything you notice right away.

2. *Question.* Thinking about what you learned from your survey, write questions in the margins. Your questions should reflect what you expect to learn as you read.

3. *Read.* Read through the biography. Make notes in the margins when you find answers to your Q-stage questions. Use your pen to circle or underline main ideas.

4. *Recite.* Discuss what you learned from the paper with your partner. How accurate was your comprehension of the biography? Were there any areas that were not clear or that you misunderstood? If so, what might help in those cases?

5. *Review.* Summarize the biography of your partner in writing for yourself. Be sure to note any important information that relates to getting to know your partner. If there is time, solidify your review by reciting the summary aloud in front of the class. Introduce your partner to the class as if he or she had just joined, focusing on the most interesting and unique information from the biography.

Finally, discuss the impact of using SQ3R with your partner. How did it affect your comprehension of the biography? What might you try differently next time?

Math and Science

Math and science courses relate closely to one another, and almost all science courses require a base of math knowledge. Mathematical and scientific strategies help you develop thinking and problem-solving skills. In a world that is being transformed by new discoveries and technologies, a strong math and science background prepares you for tomorrow's jobs and can also help you create monthly budgets, choose auto insurance, understand illnesses, and more.

Math and science textbooks move *sequentially*. That is, your understanding of later material depends on how well you learned material in earlier chapters. Try the following strategies to get the most from your textbooks, and get extra help right away when you are confused.

student PROFILE

James Shields
UNIVERSITY OF KING'S COLLEGE, HALIFAX, NOVA SCOTIA

About me:

I grew up in Scarborough, on the outer edge of the mega city. Toronto is a great city to live in; but, when I was growing up, it always seemed like a great looming presence. After high school, I was ready to move away and see what life was like at a different pace. Halifax is no small town but compared to Toronto it seemed like a different world, just the change I was looking for.

What I focus on:

As much as I love to read, when time gets tight and assignments pile up, I find that the first thing that falls off the to-do list is assigned readings. It doesn't take long, however, for that little lapse to snowball, and pretty soon everything suffers because of it. I am often disheartened, being the slow reader that I am, when the load is heavy and reading for pleasure becomes a thing of the past.

It took me a while to find a happy medium, but the first step was to find a good space.

It can either be in your home or at a nearby coffee shop, but find somewhere that feels comfortable, which you can identify with reading and stand to be in for an extended period of time. The next step is to make a habit of spending at least some time there every day. Once it becomes routine, it will not feel like a chore and it will allow you to get out of the just-get-it-done mindset so that you can focus on the material and make sure that it registers. It is also important for me that I'm not worrying about other obligations during this time. Budgeting your time is key to staying on top of your workload, and the same principal applies to reading. If it is your designated time for reading, that should command your full attention, just as writing an exam or a paper requires your full focus and dedication.

What will help me in the workplace:

Identifying a work ethic with a workspace is not just useful at school. Making the transition from higher education to the workplace does not change the principal; it changes only the equation. The solutions can remain the same. Getting to work at 8:30 a.m. is easier some days than others, but I find that having a morning routine to help shake off the dew can put me in the right mindset for work. Similarly, organizing my workspace well and making it a comfortable place to spend the day makes a world of difference. Adding greenery, if possible, or books and little things from home that I can identify with in a work environment allows me to focus on the task at hand regardless of whether I am feeling tired or anxious on my way out the door.

Keeping up with readings at school also means that I am well versed in the topics under consideration. When it comes to writing a paper or a test, completed readings can make the difference between careful, considered responses and grasping at straws. It doesn't take much to form habits, and once I started writing papers with an arsenal of material at my disposal, I found it impossible to write from a position of relative ignorance. This thoroughness has carried over into the workplace, giving me an instinct to understand all the facets of a task before embarking upon it. Not only does it improve the quality of my work, but it has propelled me past menial entry-level tasks to more interesting, challenging work, and I am happier for it.

- *Interact with math material actively through writing.* Math textbooks are made up of problems and solutions. As you read, highlight important information and take notes on examples. Work out any missing problem steps on your pad or in the book. Draw sketches to help visualize the material. Try not to move on until you understand example problems and how they relate to the central ideas. Write down questions for your instructor or fellow students.

Reading and Information Literacy

FORMULAS
General facts, rules, or principles usually expressed in mathematical symbols.

- *Pay attention to formulas.* Math and science texts are filled with formulas. Focus on learning the main ideas behind each formula, and do problems to make sure your understanding sticks.
- *Use memory strategies to learn science.* Science textbooks are packed with vocabulary specific to the field. (For example, an environmental science text may refer to the *greenhouse effect*, *integrated waste management*, and the *law of limiting factors*.) To remember what you read, use mnemonic devices, test yourself with flash cards, and rehearse aloud or silently (Chapter 7).

Social Sciences and Humanities

Courses in the social sciences and humanities prepare you to be a well-rounded person, able and ready to fulfill your responsibilities to yourself, your family, and a free democracy. They also prepare you for 21st century jobs by focusing on critical thinking, civic and historical knowledge, and ethical reasoning. As you study these disciplines, look for themes with critical thinking as the foundation for your work. Build knowledge by using what you know to learn new material.

Themes

The National Council for the Social Studies (www.socialstudies.org) organizes the study of the social sciences and humanities under 10 themes, providing umbrellas under which you can group ideas that you encounter in different classes and reading materials:

- Culture
- Time, continuity, and change
- People, places, and environment
- Individual development and identity
- Individuals, groups, and institutions
- Power, authority, and governance
- Production, distribution, and consumption
- Science, technology, and society
- Global connections
- Ideals and practices of citizenship

Look for these themes as you read, even if they are not spelled out. For example, as you read a chapter in a political science text on federal politics, you might think of the history of federal elections or how the Internet is changing electoral politics.

Think critically

Courses in the social sciences ask hard questions about ethics, human rights and freedoms, and personal and community responsibility, looking at these topics over time and in different cultures. Critical thinking will help you maximize learning and understanding as you ask questions about what you read, think of material in terms of problems and solutions, look for evidence in arguments, consider possible bias of the writers, and examine big-picture statements for solid cause-and-effect logic.

Literature

Even if you are not an English major, you will probably take one or more literature courses, which will expose you to books that allow you to experience other times and cultures and understand how others react to the problems of daily life. Additionally, the thoughts and emotions you experience in reaction to what you read give you the opportunity to learn more about yourself.

Literature courses ask you to look at different literary elements to find meaning on various levels. As you read, use critical reading skills to consider the various aspects.

- *Character.* How do characters reveal who they are? How are the main characters similar or different? How do a character's actions change the course of the story?
- *Plot.* How would you evaluate the power of the story? Did it hold your interest?
- *Setting.* How does the setting relate to the actions of the major and minor characters?
- *Point of view.* How are the author's views expressed through characters' actions?
- *Style.* How would you describe the writing style?
- *Imagery.* How does the author use imagery as part of the theme?
- *Theme.* What is the goal of the work? What is it trying to communicate?

Visual Aids

Many textbooks use tables, charts, drawings, maps, and photographs—all types of visual aids—to show, clarify, or summarize information in a form that is easy to read and understand. Pay attention to these elements as you are reading—often they contain important information not found elsewhere. Visual learners especially may benefit from information delivered in a format other than chapter text.

Certain types of visual aids—word and data tables as well as charts/graphs (pie, bar, or line)—are designed to compare information and statistics that show the following types of information:

- *Trends over time.* For example, the number of Canadians with smartphones per household in 2015 compared to 2010
- *Relative rankings.* For example, the sizes of the advertising budgets of four major companies
- *Distributions.* For example, student performance on standardized tests by geographic area
- *Cycles.* For example, as we saw with the stock markets in 2009, the regular upward and downward movement of the nation's economy as defined by periods of prosperity and recession

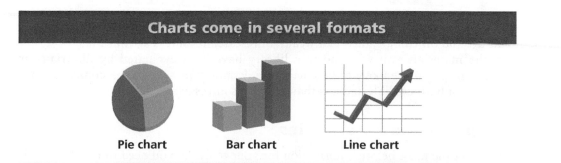

Charts come in several formats

Pie chart   Bar chart   Line chart

Online Materials

Almost any student's success in college or university depends on being able to read both printed and onscreen material effectively. For some digital natives who have grown up with technology and the Internet, screen reading comes naturally and may even be preferable to reading text on paper. Others may prefer printed materials they can hold in their hands and write on. For either group, the goal is to get the most out of what you must read online.

Screen readers tend to focus on heads and subheads, bullet points, and visuals, scanning material for the important points instead of staying focused through long paragraphs or articles.[6] They may also develop what web researcher Jakob Nielsen calls *F-pattern reading*—reading across the line at the beginning of a document, then reading less and less of the full width of the line as you move down the page, and seeing only the left-hand text by the time you reach the bottom of the document.[7]

Nielsen suggests making the most of screen reading by using a step-by-step process, which includes aspects of SQ3R:

1. *Skim through the article.* See whether it contains important ideas.
2. *Before reading in depth, save the article on your computer.* This gives you the ability to highlight and add notes, just as you would on a printed page.
3. *Survey the article.* Read the title, subtitle, headings, figures, charts, and tables.
4. *Come up with questions to guide your reading.* Ask yourself what general and specific information you want to learn from the article.
5. *Read the article in depth.* You have already judged that the material is important, so take it much slower than you would normally.
6. *Highlight and take notes.* Use the program's highlighter function and comment boxes.
7. *Print out articles you would rather study on paper.* Make sure the printouts include your highlighting and notes.
8. *Review your notes.* Combine them with your class notes and those on your printed text.

Finally, remember that "it is not so much about the tool and what it can do, but more about the purpose for using the tool," says educator Mary Beth Hertz.[8] Every choice, from the latest iPad or Galaxy Tab to a book and a pencil, has pros and cons. Evaluate on a case-by-case basis and see what works best for you, especially if you are a digital native who gravitates toward technology.

HOW CAN YOU BE AN INFORMATION-LITERATE
reader and researcher?

Although many students' first instinct is to power up the computer and start jumping around on Google, there is a wealth of research resources at your fingertips. Many of the materials you will find in a library have been evaluated by librarians and researchers and are likely to be reliable—a definite time saver when compared to the myriad of both credible and less-than-credible sources available online.

Map Out the Possibilities

To select the most helpful information for your research, you need to first know what is available to you. Sign up for a library orientation session. Familiarize yourself with the library resources shown in Key 5.8.

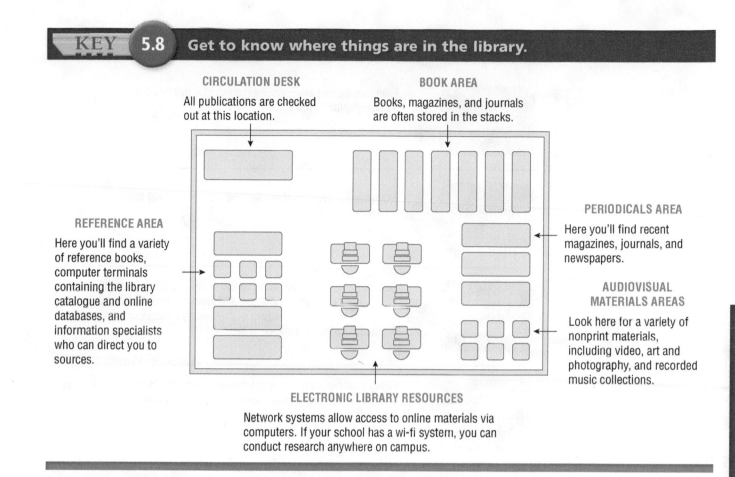

CIRCULATION DESK
All publications are checked out at this location.

BOOK AREA
Books, magazines, and journals are often stored in the stacks.

REFERENCE AREA
Here you'll find a variety of reference books, computer terminals containing the library catalogue and online databases, and information specialists who can direct you to sources.

PERIODICALS AREA
Here you'll find recent magazines, journals, and newspapers.

AUDIOVISUAL MATERIALS AREAS
Look here for a variety of nonprint materials, including video, art and photography, and recorded music collections.

ELECTRONIC LIBRARY RESOURCES
Network systems allow access to online materials via computers. If your school has a wi-fi system, you can conduct research anywhere on campus.

For a key advantage in any search for information, get to know a librarian. These professionals can assist you in locating unfamiliar or hard-to-find sources, navigating catalogues and databases, uncovering research shortcuts, and dealing with pesky equipment. Know what you want to accomplish before asking a question. At many schools, you can query a librarian via cellphone, email, or instant messaging.

Conduct an Information Search

To avoid becoming buried in the sheer magnitude of resources available, use a practical, step-by-step search method. Key 5.9 shows how you start wide and then move in for a closer look at specific sources.

When using virtual or online catalogues, you will need to adjust your research methods. Searching library databases requires that you use a keyword search—an exploration that uses a topic-related natural language word or phrase as a point of reference to locate other information. To narrow your topic and reduce the number of hits (resources pulled up by your search), add more keywords. For example, instead of searching through the broad category "art," focus on "French art" or, more specifically, "19th century French art." Key 5.10 shows how to use the keyword system to narrow searches with what is called *Boolean logic*.

Be a Critical Internet Searcher

The Internet, a worldwide computer network, can connect you to billions of information sources. Unlike your school's library collection or databases, Internet resources may not be evaluated by anyone who vouches for their quality. As a result, your research depends on critical thinking.

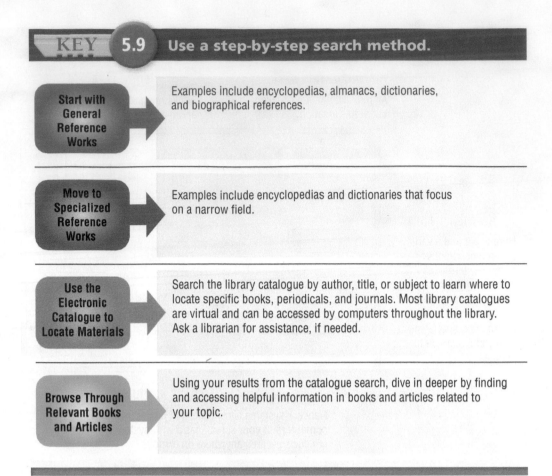

KEY 5.9 Use a step-by-step search method.

Start with General Reference Works → Examples include encyclopedias, almanacs, dictionaries, and biographical references.

Move to Specialized Reference Works → Examples include encyclopedias and dictionaries that focus on a narrow field.

Use the Electronic Catalogue to Locate Materials → Search the library catalogue by author, title, or subject to learn where to locate specific books, periodicals, and journals. Most library catalogues are virtual and can be accessed by computers throughout the library. Ask a librarian for assistance, if needed.

Browse Through Relevant Books and Articles → Using your results from the catalogue search, dive in deeper by finding and accessing helpful information in books and articles related to your topic.

KEY 5.10 Perform an effective keyword search with boolean logic.

IF YOU ARE SEARCHING FOR	DO THIS	EXAMPLE
A word	Type the word normally.	Aid
A phrase	Type the phase in its normal word order (use regular word spacing) or surround the phrase with quotation marks.	financial aid, "financial aid"
Two or more keywords without regard to order	Type the words in any order, surrounding the words with quotation marks. Use *and* to separate the words.	"financial aid" and "scholarships"
Topic A or topic B	Type the words in any order, surrounding the words with quotation marks. Use *or* to separate the words.	"financial aid" or "scholarships"
Topic A but not topic B	Type topic A first within quotation marks and then topic B within quotation marks. Use *not* to separate the words.	"financial aid" not "scholarships"

Start with search engines

Among the most popular and effective search engines are Google (www .google.ca) and Yahoo! (http://ca.yahoo.com). Search engines aimed at academic audiences include EBSCO's Canadian Reference Centre (www .ebscohost.com/public/canadian-reference-centre) and InfoMine (www .infomine.com). At these academic directories, someone has screened the sites and listed only those sources that have been determined to be reputable and regularly updated.

Additionally, your school may include access to certain nonpublic academic search engines in the cost of your tuition. Sites such as LexusNexus, InfoTrac, GaleGroup, and OneFile are known for their credibility in the academic world as well as for their vast amounts of information. Check with your school's library to see how to access these sites.

Use a search strategy

The World Wide Web has been called "the world's greatest library, with all its books on the floor." With no librarian in sight, you need to master a practical Internet search strategy.

Much, although not all, research can be done using online databases. Get to know the databases and other resources that your school provides for you.

1. *Use natural language phrases or keywords to identify what you are looking for.* University of Michigan professor Elliot Soloway recommends phrasing your search in the form of a question—for example, What vaccines are given to children before age 5? Then he advises identifying the important words in the question (*vaccines, children, before age 5*) as well as related words (*polio, shot, pediatrics,* and so on). This will give you a collection of terms to use in different combinations as you search.[9]

2. *Use a search engine to isolate valuable sites.* Enter your questions, phrases, and keywords in various combinations to generate lists of hits. Vary word order to see what you can generate. If you get too many hits, try using fewer or more specific keywords.

3. *Evaluate the list of results.* The first links in the list of search results are not always the most relevant. Often, the top hits belong to individuals or companies that have paid money to have their sites show up first. Scan through the list of results, reading the short synopsis that accompanies each. You may need to look further down the list of hits, and maybe even go the second or third page of results, to find what you need.

4. *Skim sites to evaluate what seems most useful.* Check the synopsis of the site's contents, the content providers, and the purpose of the site. Does the site seem relevant, reputable, or biased in favour of a particular point of view? A site owned by a company will want to promote its new product rather than provide unbiased consumer information. Consider the purpose—a blog is apt to focus on opinion in contrast to an article in a scholarly journal, which is likely to focus on facts and research findings.

5. *Save, or bookmark, the sites you want to focus on.* Make sure you can access them again. You may want to copy URLs and paste them into a separate document.

6. *When you think you are done, start over.* Choose another search engine and search again. Different systems access different sites.

The limitations of Internet-only research make it smart to combine Internet and library research. Search engines cannot find everything for several reasons:

- Not all sources are in digital format.
- The Internet prioritizes current information and may not find older information.

- Some digital sources may not be part of your library's subscription offerings.
- Internet searches require electricity or battery power and an online connection.

Use the Internet as a starting point to get an idea of the various documents you may want to locate in the library and read in print. When you find a blog or website that provides only a short extract of important information and then references the rest, find that original article or book and read the information in its entirety. Often, risking the time and effort that extra searching takes will reward you with more accurate, in-depth, and useful information.

Your need to be an effective researcher does not stop at graduation, especially in a workplace dominated by information and media. The skills you develop as you research school projects will serve you well in any kind of job that requires use of the Internet and other resources to find and evaluate information.

HOW CAN YOU RESPOND CRITICALLY
to what you read?

Question everything you read—books, articles, online documents, and even textbooks (which are supposed to be as accurate as possible). Think of the critical reading process as an archaeological dig. First, you excavate a site and uncover the artifacts. Then you sort what you've found, make connections among items, and judge their importance. This process of questioning, analysis, and evaluation rewards you with the ability to focus on the most important materials.

Different purposes engage different parts of critical reading. When you are reading to learn and retain information or to master a skill, you *focus on important information* (analyzing and evaluating how the ideas are structured, how they connect, and what is most crucial to remember). When you are reading to search for truth, you *ask questions to evaluate arguments* (analyzing and evaluating the author's point of view, as well as the credibility, accuracy, reliability, and relevancy of the material).

Focus on Important Information

Ronen/Fotolia

Before determining how to respond to something you've read, ask yourself what is important and what you have to remember. According to Adam Robinson, cofounder of the *Princeton Review*, "The only way you can effectively absorb the relevant information is to ignore the irrelevant information."[10] The following tips will help you determine what is most important to focus on as you study. Check to see whether the information does the following:

- Contains headings, charts, tables, captions, key terms and definitions, or an introduction or summary (for a textbook, check mid-chapter or end-of-chapter exercises)
- Offers definitions, crucial concepts, examples, an explanation of a variety or type, critical relationships or comparisons
- Sparks questions and reactions as you read
- Surprises or confuses you
- Mirrors what your instructor emphasizes in class or in assignments

When trying to figure out what to study and what to skim, ask yourself whether your instructor would expect you to know the material. If you are unsure and the topic is not on your syllabus, email your instructor and ask for clarification.

EVALUATE THE VALIDITY OF THE EVIDENCE	DETERMINE WHETHER THE EVIDENCE SUPPORTS THE CONCEPT
Is the source reliable and free of bias?	Is there enough evidence?
Who wrote this and with what intent?	Do examples and ideas logically connect?
What assumptions underlie this material?	Is the evidence convincing?
Is this argument based on opinion?	Do the examples build a strong case?
How does this evidence compare with evidence from other sources?	What different and perhaps opposing arguments seem equally valid?

Ask Questions to Evaluate Arguments

An *argument* refers to a persuasive case—a set of connected ideas supported by examples—that a writer makes to prove or disprove a point. Many scholarly books and articles, in print form or on the Internet, are organized around particular arguments. (Look for *claims*—arguments that appear to be factual but don't have adequate evidence to support them.) Critical readers evaluate arguments and claims to determine whether they are accurate and logical. When quality evidence combines with sound logic, the argument is solid.

It's easy—and common—to accept or reject an argument according to whether it fits with your point of view. If you ask questions, however, you can determine the argument's validity and understand it in greater depth (Key 5.11). Evaluating an argument involves looking at several factors:

- The quality of the evidence
- Whether the evidence fits the idea concept
- The logical connections

EVIDENCE
Facts, statistics, and other materials that are presented in support of an argument.

Approach every argument with healthy skepticism. Have an open mind to assess whether you are convinced or have serious questions.

Evaluate Every Source

Evidence examination is important for all reading materials, but especially when you research on the Internet, because online resources vary widely in reliability. In fact, your Internet research is only as strong as your critical thinking. Robert Harris, professor and web expert, has developed an easy-to-remember system for evaluating Internet information called the *CARS test for information quality* (Credibility, Accuracy, Reasonableness, Support). Use the information in Key 5.12 to question any source you find as you conduct research. You can also use it to test the reliability of non-Internet sources.

Reading is the tool you will use over and over again to acquire information in school, on the job, and in life (to understand your Registered Retirement Savings Plan, to learn about local and world news, to understand the fine print in a cellphone contract). Develop the ability to read with focus, purpose, and follow-through, and you will never stop enjoying the benefits.

CREDIBILITY	ACCURACY	REASONABLENESS	SUPPORT
Examine whether a source is believable and trustworthy.	*Examine whether information is correct—that is, factual, comprehensive, detailed, and up to date (if necessary).*	*Examine whether material is fair, objective, moderate, and consistent.*	*Examine whether a source is adequately supported with citations.*
What are the author's credentials? Look for education and experience, title or position of employment, membership in any known and respected organization, reliable contact information, biographical information, and reputation.	**Is it up to date, and is that important?** If you are searching for a work of literature, such as Shakespeare's play *Macbeth*, there is no "updated" version. However, you may want reviews of its latest productions. For most scientific research, you will need to rely on the most up-to-date information you can find.	**Does the source seem fair?** Look for a balanced argument, accurate claims, and a reasoned tone that does not appeal primarily to your emotions.	**Where does the information come from?** Look at the site, the sources used by the person or group who compiled the information, and the contact information. Make sure that the cited sources seem reliable and that statistics are documented.
Is there quality control? Look for ways in which the source may have been screened. For example, materials on an organization's website have most likely been approved by several members; information coming from an academic journal has to be screened by several people before it is published.	**Is it comprehensive?** Does the material leave out any important facts or information? Does it neglect to consider alternative views or crucial consequences? Although no one source can contain all of the available information on a topic, it should still be as comprehensive as is possible within its scope.	**Does the source seem objective?** While there is a range of objectivity in writing, you want to favour authors and organizations who can control their bias. An author with a strong political or religious agenda or an intent to sell a product may not be a source of the most truthful material.	**Is the information corroborated?** Test information by looking for other sources that confirm the facts in this information—or, if the information is opinion, sources that share that opinion and back it up with their own citations. One good strategy is to find at least three sources that corroborate one another.
Is there any posted summary or evaluation of the source? You may find abstracts of sources (summary) or a recommendation, rating, or review from a person or organization (evaluation). Either of these—or, ideally, both—can give you an idea of credibility before you decide to examine a source in depth.	**For whom is the source written, and for what purpose?** Looking at what the author wants to accomplish will help you assess whether the text has a bias. Sometimes biased information will not be useful for your purpose; sometimes your research will require that you note and evaluate bias (such as if you were to compare the diaries of Canadian and American soldiers in the War of 1812).	**Does the source seem moderate?** Do claims seem possible, or does the information seem hard to believe? Does what you read make sense when compared to what you already know? While wild claims may turn out to be truthful, you are safest to check everything out.	**Is the source externally consistent?** Most material is a mix of both current and old information. External consistency refers to whether the old information agrees with what you already know. If a source contradicts something you know to be true, chances are higher that the information new to you may be inconsistent as well.
Signals of a potential lack of credibility: Anonymous materials, negative evaluations, little or no evidence of quality control, bad grammar or misspelled words	**Signals of a potential lack of accuracy:** Lack of date or old date, generalizations, one-sided views that do not acknowledge opposing arguments	**Signals of a potential lack of reasonableness:** Extreme or emotional language, sweeping statements, conflict of interest, inconsistencies or contradictions	**Signals of a potential lack of support:** Statistics without sources, lack of documentation, lack of corroboration using other reliable sources

Source: Robert Harris, "Evaluating Internet Research Sources," December 27, 2013, VirtualSalt (www.virtualsalt.com/evalu8it.htm).

Gary Montrose

What happened to Gary? With perseverance and support, Gary has become a health-care management and strategic planning consultant whose clients include Fortune 500 insurance companies. However, he lives every day with the challenge of dyslexia. Because of the time and effort he needs to read, he has spent most of his adult life working in small private offices or a home office. He can't read directions fast enough to avoid wrong turns on highways and often makes spelling mistakes. The support of his wife, Lynne, a gifted writer and public speaker, has proven essential in his struggle to persevere. Armed with today's knowledge about learning differences, Gary and Lynne tested their children early and often and were able to provide their son with an academic environment that addressed his reading challenges. With their support, he has developed a soaring sense of self-confidence—the kind that Gary still strives for.

What does this story mean for you? Learning to be a productive member of society, with the gifts you are born with or can develop, is the name of the game. It also helps to have an understanding support system. Nearly everyone has a big secret—or perhaps a small secret—that causes challenges in school or on the job. Whether a learning disability such as dyslexia, a negative attitude about a task such as reading or math, or some other obstacle, it gets in the way as you strive for success. Think about one secret that you have, and put it in writing. Then write the name of a person whom you trust to support you. Finally, talk with this person and begin to come up with ideas of how you will address and manage your secret.

What risk may bring reward beyond your world? Reading is the essential success skill for the 21st century information-focused workplace. The more the world's citizens know how to read, the more they will be able to lead productive and successful lives. To start exploring what is happening in the promotion of literacy, read about Room to Read at www.roomtoread.org and explore what this organization is doing to build schools, stock libraries, and support education. Click on the "Get Involved" tab to see how to support its initiatives. Perhaps you will want to get involved yourself—or, if not, look into ways you can support literacy in your community, at your college or university, or even within your own family. Be a part of the solution.

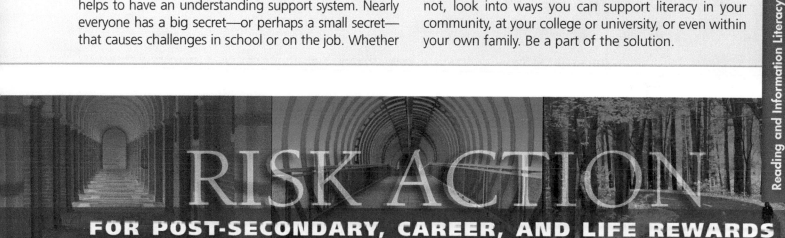

RISK ACTION

FOR POST-SECONDARY, CAREER, AND LIFE REWARDS

Reading and Information Literacy

KNOW IT *Think Critically*

Study a Text Page

Build basic skills. The following page is from the chapter "Groups and Organizations" in the sixth edition of John J. Macionis's *Sociology*.[11] Skim the excerpt. Identify the headings on the page and the relationships among them. Mark primary-level headings with a numeral 1, secondary headings with a 2, and tertiary (third-level) headings with a 3.

Take it to the next level. Analyze the headings and text by answering the following questions:

Which heading serves as an umbrella for the rest?

_____

What do the headings tell you about the content of the page?

_____

_____

_____

_____

Name three concepts that seem important to remember.

1. _____

2. _____

3. _____

Based on the three concepts you pulled out, write three study questions that you can review with an instructor, a teaching assistant, or a fellow student.

1. _____

2. _____

3. _____

Social Groups

Virtually everyone moves through life with a sense of belonging; this is the experience of group life. A social group refers to *two or more people who identify and interact with one another*. Human beings continually come together to form couples, families, circles of friends, neighbourhoods, churches, businesses, clubs, and numerous large organizations. Whatever the form, groups encompass people with shared experiences, loyalties, and interests. In short, while maintaining their individuality, the members of social groups also think of themselves as a special "we."

Groups, categories, and crowds.

People often use the term "group" imprecisely. We now distinguish the group from the similar concepts of category and crowd.

■ *Category.* A *category* refers to people who have some status in common. Women, single fathers, military recruits, homeowners, and Roman Catholics are all examples of categories.

Why are categories not considered groups? Simply because, while the individuals involved are aware that they are not the only ones to hold that particular status, the vast majority are strangers to one another.

■ *Crowd.* A *crowd* refers to a temporary cluster of individuals who may or may not interact at all. Students sitting in a lecture hall do engage one another and share some common identity as college classmates; thus, such a crowd might be called a loosely formed group. By contrast, riders hurtling along on a subway train or bathers enjoying a summer day at the beach pay little attention to one another and amount to an anonymous aggregate of people. In general, then, crowds are too transitory and impersonal to qualify as social groups.

The right circumstances, however, could turn a crowd into a group. People riding in a subway train that crashes under the city streets generally become keenly aware of their common plight and begin to help one another. Sometimes such extraordinary experiences become the basis for lasting relationships.

142

Primary and secondary groups.

Acquaintances commonly greet one another with a smile and the simple phrase, "Hi! How are you?" The response is usually a well scripted, "Just fine, thanks, how about you?" This answer, of course, is often more formal than truthful. In most cases, providing a detailed account of how you are *really* doing would prompt the other person to beat a hasty and awkward exit.

Sociologists classify social groups by measuring them against two ideal types based on members' genuine level of personal concern. This variation is the key to distinguishing *primary* from *secondary* groups.

According to Charles Horton Cooley (1864–1929), a **primary group** is *a small social group whose members share personal and enduring relationships.* Bound together by primary relationships, individuals in primary groups typically spend a great deal of time together, engage in a wide range of common activities, and feel that they know one another well. Although not without periodic conflict, members of primary groups display sincere concern for each other's welfare. The family is every society's most important primary group.

Cooley characterized these personal and tightly integrated groups as primary because they are among the first groups we experience in life. In addition, the family and early play groups also hold primary importance in the socialization process, shaping attitudes, behaviour, and social identity.

Source: John J. Macionis, *Sociology,* 6th ed., p. 145, © 1997 Prentice-Hall, Inc. Reproduced by permission of Pearson Education, Inc., Upper Saddle River, NJ.

Move toward mastery. Read the excerpt, putting SQ3R to work. Using a marker pen, highlight key phrases and sentences. Write short marginal notes to help you review the material later. After reading this page thoroughly, write a short summary paragraph.

_____

_____

_____

Source: John J. Macionis, *Sociology,* 8th Canadian ed., p. 157, ISBN 978-0-13-293553-1, © 2014 Pearson Education Canada Inc. Reproduced by permission of Pearson Education Canada Inc., Don Mills, ON.

Reading and Information Literacy

WRITE IT *Communicate*

Record your thoughts on a separate piece of paper, in a journal, or electronically.

Emotional intelligence journal: Reading challenges. Which current course presents your most difficult reading challenge? Describe what makes the reading tough—type of material, length of assignments, level of difficulty, or something else. What feelings come up for you when you read, and what effect do they have on your reading? Describe techniques you learned in this chapter that can help you get into a growth mindset to read productively.

Real-life writing: Ask for help. Self-help plans often involve reaching out to others. Draft an email to your instructor describing the difficulties in your challenging course as well as the specific help you need to move to the next step. Make sure that your message is clear and accurate, your grammar, spelling, and punctuation are correct, and your tone is appropriate. (See Quick Start to College and University for guidelines on communicating with instructors.) *Whether or not you send the email is up to you.* In either case, writing it will help you move forward in your reading improvement plan.

WORK IT *Build Your Brand*

Reading Skills on the Job

21st Century Learning Building Blocks

- Information literacy
- Media literacy
- ICT (information, communications, and technology) literacy

Excellent reading skills are a requirement for almost every 21st century job. Employers expect that you will read independently to master new skills and keep up with change. Whether in print or electronic form, on-the-job reading will challenge you just as you are challenged by college or university reading. For example, sociology courses may involve reading textbooks, journals, and case studies, but actually working in the field requires that you keep on top of case reports, government regulations, court documents, and an unending stream of work-related emails.

Prepare yourself by honestly assessing your practical skills *right now*. Use the following list to rate your ability on a scale from 1 to 10, 1 being the lowest and 10 being the highest:

- Concentrate, no matter the distractions.
- Define your reading purpose and use it to guide your focus and pace.
- Use specific vocabulary-building techniques to improve comprehension.
- Use every aspect of SQ3R to master content.

- Skim and scan.
- Use analytical thinking skills when reading.
- Use highlighting and notes to help you master content.

For the two skill areas in which you rated yourself lowest, think about how you can improve. Make a problem-solving plan for each. (You may want to use a flow chart like the one on page 105.) Check your progress in one month and at the end of the term. Finally, write down how you anticipate using the reading skills you learned in this chapter in your chosen career.

Good listening allows you to figure out what is important to write down, and taking effective notes rewards you with the ability to recall and use that information.

Listening and Note Taking

TAKING IN AND RECORDING INFORMATION

What Would You Risk? *Norton Ewart*

Norton Ewart

THINK ABOUT THIS SITUATION AS YOU READ, AND CONSIDER HOW YOU WOULD APPROACH IT. THIS CHAPTER INTRODUCES YOU TO LISTENING AND NOTE-TAKING SKILLS THAT WILL HELP YOU SUCCESSFULLY TAKE IN AND WRITE DOWN USEFUL KNOWLEDGE.

Norton Ewart struggled from Grade 4 through high school. Overwhelmed by the work and the level of independence, he avoided risk by doing the least amount of work possible. He enrolled in a local college out of a desire to please his parents. Uninterested in his courses and not ready to work for the rewards of post-secondary life, Norton hitchhiked home each weekend to work as a housepainter and left school ten weeks later. He then moved to his aunt's house in Colorado, where he skied black diamond runs, worked as a ski technician, and tried to figure out who he was and what he wanted.

After two years, Norton decided he wanted to return to school. Thinking he might follow the path of engineering, as had three generations before him, he decided to pursue a degree in math and science. Despite his newfound interest and the fun of a state-of-the-art calculator his father had given him, he could not put his inconsistent study habits behind him, and he received Cs and Ds in his calculus and physics courses during his first year.

Norton was behind, but for the first time he was determined to excel. He found himself enjoying the creativity and beauty of math and how his mind interacted with it. On the advice of an academic advisor, he spent a year in a civil technology program while retaking every calculus and physics course. Aware that he was more motivated when working with others, he risked reaching out to a group of fellow engineering students. They created a study group called the "Engineering Defense League" and met daily to work through problems, drill one another on formulas and problem solving steps, and experience the struggle together.

To be continued . . .

Skiing and working in Colorado gave Norton a sense of ownership of his success as well as a desire—and a reason—to go back to school. You'll learn more about Norton, and the reward resulting from his actions, within the chapter.

Notes

52%

Today   Mar 10 8:01 AM

Working through this chapter will help you to:

statusCHECK

How Developed Are Your Listening and Note-Taking Skills?

For each statement, circle the number that feels right to you, from 1 for "not at all true for me" to 5 for "very true for me."

1. I know and understand the stages of listening. ① ② ③ ④ ⑤

2. I arrive early for class prepared to absorb information by having read the required text ahead of time. ① ② ③ ④ ⑤

3. I ask questions during lectures and listen for verbal clues to understand important information. ① ② ③ ④ ⑤

4. I understand the differences between internal and external distractions and work to control my learning environment whenever possible. ① ② ③ ④ ⑤

5. I use different note-taking systems depending on my instructor's teaching styles and the material being taught. ① ② ③ ④ ⑤

6. I know how to use visuals in my notes to clarify tough concepts discussed in class. ① ② ③ ④ ⑤

7. I believe that good preparation is a necessary first step toward taking comprehensive notes. ① ② ③ ④ ⑤

8. I use strategies to make sense of and record large class discussions. ① ② ③ ④ ⑤

9. I review notes within 24 hours of taking them. ① ② ③ ④ ⑤

10. I use shorthand to take notes faster. ① ② ③ ④ ⑤

Each of the topics in these statements is covered in this chapter. Note those statements for which you circled a 3 or lower. Skim the chapter to see where those topics appear, and pay special attention to them as you read, learn, and apply new strategies.

REMEMBER: NO MATTER HOW DEVELOPED YOUR LISTENING AND NOTE-TAKING SKILLS ARE, YOU CAN IMPROVE WITH EFFORT AND PRACTICE.

HOW CAN YOU BECOME *a better listener?*

LISTENING
A process that involves sensing, interpreting, evaluating, and reacting to spoken messages.

The act of *hearing* is not the same as the act of listening. *Hearing* refers to sensing spoken messages and sounds from their source. You can hear all kinds of things and not understand or remember any of them. Listening, however, is a communication process that starts with hearing but also includes focused thinking about what you hear. Listening is a learnable skill that engages your analytical, creative, and practical thinking abilities and extends far beyond the classroom, enhancing your ability to relate with work and school colleagues, friends, and family.

MyStudentSuccessLab

Whether face-to-face or online, MyStudentSuccessLab helps students build the skills they need through peer-led video interviews, interactive practice exercises, and activities that provide academic, life, and professionalism skills.

Know the Stages of Listening

Listening is made up of four stages that build on one another: sensing, interpreting, evaluating, and reacting. These stages take the message from the speaker to the listener and back to the speaker (Key 6.1).

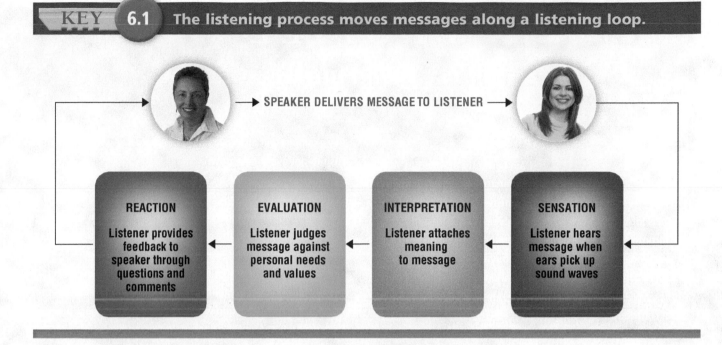

SPEAKER DELIVERS MESSAGE TO LISTENER

REACTION	EVALUATION	INTERPRETATION	SENSATION
Listener provides feedback to speaker through questions and comments	Listener judges message against personal needs and values	Listener attaches meaning to message	Listener hears message when ears pick up sound waves

- During the *sensing stage* (also known as *hearing*) your ears pick up sound waves and transmit them to the brain. For example, you are sitting in class and hear your instructor say, "The only opportunity to make up last week's test is Tuesday at 5:00 p.m."

- In the *interpretation* stage, you attach meaning to a message. You understand what is said and link it to what you already know. You relate this message to your knowledge of the test, whether you need to make it up, and what you are doing on Tuesday at 5 o'clock.

- In the *evaluating* stage, you evaluate the message as it relates to your needs and values. If the message goes against your values or does not fulfill your needs, you may reject it, stop listening, or argue in your mind with the speaker. In this example, if you need to make up the test but have to work Tuesday at 5 o'clock, you may evaluate the message in an unfavourable way.

- The final stage of listening is *reacting* to the message in the form of direct feedback. In a classroom, direct feedback often comes in the form of questions and comments. Your reaction, in this case, may be to ask the instructor whether she can schedule another test time.

You will become a better listener by learning to recognize and manage listening challenges and becoming actively involved with the material.

Become an Active Listener

On the surface, listening seems to be a passive activity. You sit back as someone else speaks. In reality, effective listening is an active process that involves the following factors.

- *Be there.* Being an active listener requires that you show up on time—preferably a few minutes before class begins. Instructors often make important announcements in the first few minutes and may also summarize the previous lecture.

Photographee.eu/Fotolia

Listening to other students can be as important as listening to instructors. These students may learn something useful from their fellow student's presentation.

student PROFILE

Sarah Mocherniak
ACADIA UNIVERSITY, WOLFVILLE, NOVA SCOTIA

About me:

I am currently enrolled at Acadia University in the School of Business Administration. My school is located in Nova Scotia; however, I was born and raised in the Toronto area. I am bilingual. Throughout my years at Acadia, I have not only worked with students but also had the opportunity to gain an alumni perspective from working in the Office of Alumni Affairs. My friends and colleagues know me best as an upbeat social contributor.

What I focus on:

At the beginning of university I came across new, unexpected challenges. My biggest challenge was note taking. Certain strategies in particular work well for me.

For example, using either the textbook or online resources posted by my professor, I make notes prior to each lecture on the material that will be discussed in that class. During the lecture, I pick up on key terms more easily because I already know the background information. Using a different-coloured pen, I add examples and other details that are not given in the book. Preparing notes before I go to class gives me the opportunity not only to add key examples but also to listen to the professor without having to rush to get every note down.

When preparing for an exam, I expand on the idea above. I divide my page into two columns. The column on the left is for the terms, equation names, or theories. The column on the right is where I write down the definitions, actual equations, explanations, or examples. This way, when I study, I can cover the right side of the page and quiz myself with the terms on the left. At the bottom of the two columns and at the end of each chapter's notes, I also have a section where I analyze and connect the terms. I go through the entire chapter's terms and examples to draw conclusions and summarize the main idea that the professor is trying to get across.

What will help me in the workplace:

It is important for me to always figure out how the material that I am learning in class relates to me or may relate to me in the future. Note taking in classes may not seem relevant for the future to some; however, it has shown to be extremely helpful in all of my jobs. For instance, knowing how to properly prepare ahead of time for a meeting and knowing how to pick up key points while in a meeting is extremely beneficial.

Sarah Mocherniak. Acadia University, Wolfville, Nova Scotia. Reprinted by permission.

- **Set purposes for listening.** Before every class, use your analytical intelligence to establish what you want to achieve, such as understanding a particular concept. Many instructors start a lecture with a statement of purpose, so listen carefully and write the purpose at the top of your notes to help you focus. If you read assignments and review previous notes before class, you may be able to follow along more easily. Come to class with ideas about how what you hear will help you achieve your goals.
- **Focus on understanding.** Rather than taking notes on everything, record information only when you can say to yourself, "I get it!" If you miss important material, leave holes in your notes and return later. Your instructor may repeat the point you missed, or another comment may help you piece it together.
- **Ask questions.** Active listeners ask analytical questions to clarify their understanding and to associate new ideas with what they already know. Questions such as "What is this part of?" or "How is it similar to yesterday's topic?" signal active involvement. Get into the habit of jotting down your questions and coming back to them during a discussion period so they don't interfere with listening.

Manage Listening Challenges

Sitting in your classes, you probably have noticed a variety of not-so-academic activities that interfere with listening. Some people may be texting or surfing the Internet; some may be talking or sleeping; and some might be daydreaming. In all of these cases, the students are probably not absorbing much—or any—of the information being provided by the instructor, and they may be distracting you from listening as well. Read on to see how to address these issues, and others, on your path to becoming a better listener.

Issue 1: Distractions that divide your attention

The common distractions that interfere with listening can be divided into *internal distractions* (worry, illness, fatigue, hunger, feeling too hot or too cold) and *external distractions* (chatting, computer use, any kind of movement or noise). Distractions such as these nip away at you while you're trying to pay attention.

Fix 1: Focus, focus, focus

First of all, tell yourself that you're in the class to learn and that you *really need* to know the material. You may even want to remind yourself of what you're paying to sit in this class. Find practical ways to minimize distractions.

- Sit near the front of the room.
- Move away from talkative classmates.
- Turn off your cellphone or put it on silent mode when in class.
- Get enough sleep to stay alert.
- Eat enough so you're not hungry—or bring small snacks, if allowed.
- Try to put your worries aside during class.

The often overwhelming pace of modern life leads students to *multitask* (do several things at once), under the impression that multitasking can help them accomplish goals effectively in less time. Although you may think you can handle distractions because you are used to multitasking, recent research shows that multitasking actually *decreases* both memory power and performance. In a study at Stanford University in the United States, low multitaskers actually outperformed high multitaskers on all tasks.[1] Try to keep your focus on one thing at a time.

Issue 2: Listening lapses

Even the most fantastic instructor can't make you listen. You and you alone can do that. If you decide that a subject is too difficult or uninteresting, you may tune out and miss what comes next. You may also focus on certain points and shut out everything else. Either way, you run the risk of not being prepared and not making the most of your time.

Fix 2: An I-can-do-it attitude

- *Start with a productive mindset.* If the class is hard, that's all the more reason to pay attention. Instructors are generally more sympathetic to, and eager to help, students who have obviously been trying even when it's tough.
- *Concentrate.* Work to take in the whole message so you will be able to read over your notes later, combine your class and text notes, and think critically about what is important. Making connections between ideas can alleviate the difficulty of the material in some cases or boredom if you are already familiar with the concepts.

SIGNALS POINTING TO KEY CONCEPTS	SIGNALS OF SUPPORT
A key point to remember . . .	A perfect example, . . .
Point 1, point 2, etc. . . .	Specifically, . . .
The impact of this was . . .	For instance, . . .
The critical stages in the process are . . .	Similarly, . . .

SIGNALS POINTING TO DIFFERENCES	SIGNALS THAT SUMMARIZE
On the contrary, . . .	From this you have learned, . . .
On the other hand, . . .	In conclusion, ...
In contrast, . . .	As a result, . . .
However, . . .	Finally, ...

VERBAL SIGNPOSTS ←
Spoken words or phrases that call attention to information that follows.

- *Refocus.* If you experience a listening lapse, try to get back into the lecture quickly instead of worrying about what you missed. After class, look at a classmate's notes to fill in the gaps.
- *Be aware.* Pay attention to verbal signposts to help organize information, connect ideas, and indicate what is important and what is not. (See Key 6.2 for examples.)

Issue 3: Rushing to judgment

It is common to stop listening when you hear something you don't agree with or don't like. You react, and then you focus on your emotions. Unfortunately, you can spend valuable class time thinking of all the reasons your instructor is wrong and miss everything else. The situation might not seem particularly bad that day, but when the test comes around, you may feel differently about having missed material.

Judgments also involve reactions to speakers themselves. If you do not like your instructors or have preconceived notions about their race, ethnicity, gender, physical characteristics, or disability, you may dismiss their ideas—and miss out on your opportunity to learn.

Fix 3: Recognize and correct your patterns

Although it can be human nature to stop paying attention when you react to a speaker or message, it can make listening a lot more difficult. College and university are about broadening your horizons and looking for what different people can teach you, even though they and their beliefs may differ from you and yours. So what do you do?

- *Recognize your pattern so you can change it.* When you feel yourself reacting to something said in a lecture, stop and take a moment to breathe. Count to 10. Take one more breath and see how you feel.
- *Know that you can't hear—and therefore can't learn anything from—others if you are filled with preconceived notions about them and their ideas.* Put yourself

in their shoes; would you want them to stop listening to you if they disagreed, or would you want to be heard completely?

- *Stop it.* It's as simple as that. Listen with an open mind even when you disagree or have a negative reaction to an instructor. Being open to the new and different, even when it makes you a bit uncomfortable, is part of what education is about.

Issue 4: Partial hearing loss and learning disabilities

If you have a hearing loss or a learning disability, listening effectively in class may prove challenging. As discussed in Chapter 3, learning disabilities can come in a variety of forms, affecting different parts of cognition.

Fix 4: Get help

If you have a hearing loss, find out about available equipment. For example, listening to a taped lecture at a higher-than-normal volume can help you hear things you missed. Ask instructors whether or not digitized recordings are available for download to a computer or MP3 player. Meeting with your instructor outside of class to clarify your notes may also help, as will sitting near the front of the room.

If you have (or think you have) a learning disability, learn what services are available. Talk to your advisor and instructor about your problem, seek out a tutor, visit academic centres that can help (such as the writing centre, if you have a writing issue), scan your school's website, or connect to the office for students with disabilities. Know that you can succeed and that people are there to help you.

Issue 5: Comprehension difficulties for speakers of other languages

If English isn't your first language, listening and understanding material in the classroom can be challenging, requiring extra concentration, dedication, and patience. Specialized vocabulary, informal language, and the rate of speech can add to the challenge.

Fix 5: Take a proactive approach to understanding

Talk to your instructor as soon as possible about your situation. Recognizing a need early and meeting to discuss it keeps your instructor informed and shows your dedication. In some cases, your professor will give you a list of key terms to review before class. During class, keep a list of unfamiliar words and phrases to look up later; but, whenever possible, don't let these terms prevent you from understanding the main ideas. Focus on the main points of the lecture and plan to meet with classmates after class to fill any gaps in your understanding. If, after several weeks, you are still having difficulties, consider enrolling in an English refresher course, getting a tutor, or visiting the campus advice centre for more assistance. Be proactive about your education.

auremar/Fotolia

Listening isn't always easy and it isn't always comfortable. As poet Robert Frost once said, "Education is the ability to listen to almost anything without losing your temper or your self-confidence." Keeping an open, engaged mind takes practice, but when excellent listening becomes second nature, you'll thank yourself for the work it took.

Post-secondary education exposes you to all kinds of facts, opinions, and ideas—and, as the Conference Board of Canada points out, the ability to "listen and ask questions to understand" is a key employability skill for the 21st Century.[2]

Effective listening skills are the basis for effective note taking—an essential and powerful study tool.

get analytical

Complete the following on paper or in digital format.

Answer the questions as you focus on your personal listening habits.

1. Analyze how present you are as a listener. Are you easily distracted, or can you focus well? Do you prefer to listen, or do you tend to talk?

2. When you are listening, what tends to distract you?

3. What happens to your listening skills when you become confused?

4. How do you react when you strongly disagree with something your instructor says—when you are convinced that you are right and your instructor is wrong?

5. Thinking about your answers, list two strategies from the chapter that will help you improve your listening skills.

HOW CAN YOU IMPROVE
your note-taking skills?

Taking notes makes you an active class participant—even when you don't say a word—and provides you with study materials. What is on the line is nothing short of your academic success.

Class notes have two primary purposes—to serve as a record of what happened in class and to use for studying, alone and in combination with your text notes. Because it is virtually impossible to take notes on everything you hear, note taking encourages you to use your analytical intelligence to critically evaluate what is worth remembering. Exploring the strategies outlined next can help you prepare and take notes in class, review notes, and take notes on reading materials.

Monkey Business Images/Shutterstock

Good listening powers note taking. When taking notes in class, stop to listen to the information before deciding what to write down.

Prepare

Showing up for class on time is just the start. Here is more about preparing to take notes:

- *Preview your reading material.* More than anything else you can do, reading assigned materials before class will give you the background to take effective notes. Check your class syllabi daily for assignment due dates and plan your reading time with these deadlines in mind.

- *Review what you know.* Taking 15 minutes before class to review your notes from the previous class and your reading assignment notes for that day will enable you to follow the lecture from the start.

- *Set up your environment.* Find a comfortable seat, away from friends if sitting with them distracts you. Use a separate notebook for each course, and start a new page for each class. If you use a laptop, open the file containing your class notes right away. Be ready to write (or type) as soon as the instructor begins speaking.
- *Gather support.* In each class, set up a support system with one or two students so you can look at their notes after an absence. Find students whose work you respect and set up a study group with them.

Record Information Effectively During Class

The following practical suggestions will help you record what is important in a format that you can review later:

- *Start a new page or section for each new topic,* especially if your instructor jumps from topic to topic during a single class.
- *Record whatever your instructor emphasizes* by paying attention to verbal and nonverbal cues.
- *Write down all key terms and definitions* so that you can refer to them easily.
- *Note relevant examples, applications, and links to other material* when you encounter difficult concepts.
- *Ask questions.* If your instructor allows questions during class, ask them. Chances are, several other students have similar queries. If your instructor prefers to answer questions at the end of class, keep a separate sheet of paper to jot down questions as you think of them.
- *Write down every question your instructor raises,* because these questions may be on a test.
- *Be organized, but not fussy.* Remember that you can always improve your notes later.
- *Leave blank spaces between points* to make it easy to see where one topic ends and another begins. (This suggestion does not apply if you are using a think link.)
- *Draw pictures and diagrams* to illustrate ideas.
- *Be consistent.* Use the same system to show importance—such as indenting, spacing, or underlining—on each page.
- *Record as much as you can if you have trouble understanding a concept.* Then leave space for an explanation and flag the margin with a large question mark. After class, try to clarify your questions by reading the text or ask a classmate or your instructor for help.
- *Consider that your class notes are only part of the picture.* You will learn best when you combine your text and class notes.
- *Go beyond the PowerPoint.* Increasingly, instructors are using computer software to present lectures in the classroom. Although it may be tempting to simply copy down what's written on the slide, realize that instructors usually show the main points, not the details that may be tested later. Take notes on what your instructor says about each main idea highlighted on a presentation slide.

Finally, don't stop taking notes when your class engages in a discussion. Even though it isn't part of the instructor's planned presentation, it often includes important information. Key 6.3 has suggestions for how to make the most of discussions.

Review and Revise

The process of note taking is not complete when you put your pen down or close your computer at the end of the class period. Notes are useful to you only if you review and revise them, and within as short a time period as you can manage. The longer you wait to review those notes, the less likely you will understand them.

- Listen to everyone; you never know when something important will be said.

- Listen for threads that weave through comments. They may signal an important point.

- Listen for ideas the instructor likes and for encouraging comments, such as "You make a great point" or "I like your idea."

- Take notes when the instructor rephrases and clarifies a point.

Class notes often have sections that are incomplete, confusing, or illegible. Review and revise your notes as soon as possible after class to fill in gaps while the material is still fresh, clarify sloppy handwriting, and raise questions. Rewriting or retyping notes is a great way to reinforce what you heard in class, review new ideas, and create easy-to-read study aids. It also prepares you for the rewarding strategy of combining class and textbook notes.

Taking Notes from Books

Note taking is not just useful in class. It can also help you decide and reinforce what is most important to remember when you read textbooks, articles, or any other materials assigned for class or used for research. You may decide to take separate notes on reading material if the book is a library copy or borrowed from a classmate. Or, you might do so when you don't have enough room to take notes in the margin. Some students simply prefer to take separate notes on reading material as a study strategy.

Start the process by identifying what you want to get from the notes. Are you looking for the basic topics from a chapter? An in-depth understanding of a particular concept? Once you've established the goal, then you can identify the best format. For instance, mind maps work well to understand broad connections, overall relationships, or how your text works in relation to your instructor's lecture. On the other hand, formal outlines make sense of complicated information in a structured way that can provide clarity. Later in the chapter, you will read about different note-taking formats and try different approaches to see which ones work for you.

After choosing a format, read and take notes on the material using the Survey, Question, and Read stages of SQ3R.

- *Survey* to get an overview of what the material can offer you.

get $mart

PhotoMan/Fotolia

Complete the following on paper or in digital format.

When you set yourself up to access financial information effectively, you will be more able to make the most of money-oriented resources on campus. Explore how you prefer to acquire financial information.

1. Which style of reading is most comfortable to you—print or electronic?

2. Rank these information sources from 1 (I respond best to this) to 7 (I respond least to this).
   a. In-person conversations
   b. Magazines/newspapers
   c. Books
   d. Websites
   e. YouTube
   f. Blog posts
   g. Twitter feeds

3. Given these preferences, identify three specific sources that will best help you stay informed. **Note:** Use the library and Internet to locate the sources.

4. What are two of your most pressing questions about personal finances right now?

5. Using the three sources you identified, find and write answers to these questions.

- *Question* to focus your attention on what is important enough to record in your notes.
- *Read* and record your notes on paper or in an electronic file.

Finally, remember that many of the in-class note-taking strategies you just explored will help you take effective notes on reading materials. For example, you can note key terms and definitions, recreate important diagrams, use consistent formatting, and flag areas of confusion with a question mark.

talk risk and reward . . .

Risk asking tough questions to be rewarded with new insights. Use the following to inspire discussion with classmates in person or online.

- Think about what typically plays on your brain's soundtrack during a class meeting—words, music, anything that streams through. Be honest—how much of it relates to the class and how much is unrelated? What effect does it have on your focus?

- When you have no interest in class material, what is the effect on your behaviour, your grades, your commitment? If you want the reward of increased focus, what are you willing to risk to be more focused in the classroom?

CONSIDER THE CASE: Come up with a risk you would advise Norton to take to help him focus on, and write down, key points in his coursework.

Norton Ewart; Shutterstock

WHAT NOTE-TAKING
systems can you use?

Now that you have gathered some useful note-taking strategies, take a look at different approaches to note taking. As you read, keep some questions in mind:

- What class or type of instruction would this system be best suited for? Why?
- How could I make use of this system?
- Which system seems most comfortable to me?
- What system might be most compatible with my learning style strengths? Why?

Outlines

Outlines use a standard structure to show how ideas interrelate. *Formal outlines* indicate idea dominance and subordination, with Roman numerals, uppercase and lowercase letters, and numbers. In contrast, *informal outlines* show the same associations but replace the formality with a system of consistent indenting and dashes.

When a lecture seems well organized, an informal outline can show how ideas and supporting details relate while also indicating levels of importance. Key 6.4 shows how the structure of an informal outline helps a student take notes on the topic of tropical rain forests. The multiple intelligences table in this chapter (page 159) is designed to help harness different learning approaches for an earth science course. Specifically, the table will suggest different note-taking strategies you can use to study the topic of tropical rain forests.

When an instructor's presentation is disorganized, it may be difficult to use an outline. Focus instead on taking down whatever information you can as you try to connect key topics. The Cornell system and other note-taking methods discussed next can be beneficial in such situations.

KEY 6.4 An informal outline is useful for taking notes in class.

Tropical Rain Forests

What are tropical rain forests?
- — Areas in South America and Africa, along the equator
- — Average temperatures between 25° and 30°C
- — Average annual rainfalls range between 250 to 400 centimetres
- — Conditions combine to create the Earth's richest, most biodiverse ecosystem.
  - – A biodiverse ecosystem has a great number of organisms coexisting within a defined area.
  - – Examples of rain forest biodiversity
    - – 2½ acres in the Amazon rain forest has 283 species of trees
    - – a 3-square-mile section of a Peruvian rain forest has more than 1300 butterfly species and 600 bird species.
    - – Compare this biodiversity to what is found in the entire U.S.—only 400 butterfly species and 700 bird species

How are humans changing the rain forest?
- — Humans have already destroyed about 40% of all rain forests.
  - – They are cutting down trees for lumber or clearing the land for ranching or agriculture.
- — Biologist Edwin O. Wilson estimates that this destruction may lead to the extinction of 27 000 species.
- — Rain forest removal is also linked to the increase in atmospheric carbon dioxide, which worsens the greenhouse effect.
  - – The greenhouse effect refers to process in which gases such as carbon dioxide trap the Sun's energy in the Earth's atmosphere as heat resulting in global warning.
- — Recognition of the crisis is growing as are conservation efforts.

Source: Teresa Audesirk, Gerald Audesirk, and Bruce E. Byers. *Life on Earth*, 2nd ed., Upper Saddle River, NJ: Prentice Hall, 2000, pp. 660–662. Printed and electronically reproduced by permission of Pearson Education, Inc., Upper Saddle River, NJ.

multiple intelligence strategies

Apply Different Intelligences to Taking Notes in Earth Science

INTELLIGENCE	USE MI STRATEGIES TO IMPROVE YOUR NOTES	APPLY MI NOTE-TAKING STRATEGIES TO THE TOPIC OF TROPICAL RAIN FORESTS FOR AN EARTH SCIENCE COURSE
Verbal-Linguistic	• Rewrite your class notes in an alternate note-taking style to see connections more clearly. • Combine class and text notes to get a complete picture.	• Rewrite and summarize your reading and lecture notes to understand the characteristics of tropical rain forests.*
Logical-Mathematical	• When reviewing or rewriting notes, put information into a logical sequence. • Create tables that show relationships.	• Create a table comparing and contrasting the different species found in a typical rain forest.
Bodily-Kinesthetic	• Think of your notes as a crafts project that enables you to see knowledge layers. Use coloured pens to texture your notes. • Study with your notes spread in sequence around you so that you can see knowledge building from left to right.	• Fill a tube with 4 metres of water to give you a physical sense of the annual rainfall in a rain forest. Or fill a bathtub with 25 centimetres of water and multiply by 16 to imagine rainfall totals. How would you react to living with so much rain? Take notes on your reaction.
Visual-Spatial	• Take notes using coloured markers or pens. • Rewrite lecture notes in think link format, focusing on the most important points.	• As part of your notes, create a chart that covers the types of vegetation that grow in a rain forest. Use a different-coloured marker for each plant species.
Interpersonal	• Try to schedule a study group right after a lecture to discuss class notes. • Review class notes with a study buddy. Compare notes to see what may have been missed.	• Interview someone you know who has visited a rain forest about what he or she saw, or interview a natural scientist at a museum about this environment. Use a different note-taking system for each person.
Intrapersonal	• Schedule some quiet time soon after a lecture to review and think about your notes. • As you review your notes, decide whether you grasp the material or need help.	• Think about the conflict between economic modernization and the preservation of rain forests in underdeveloped areas. Include your thoughts in your notes.
Musical	• To improve recall, recite concepts in your notes to rhythms. • Write a song that includes material from your class and text notes. Use the refrain to emphasize what is important.	• Use the Internet to find songs about the biodiversity of rain forests written by indigenous peoples who live in or near them. Then, use the song to remember key concepts. Take notes on what you find.
Naturalistic	• Notice similarities and differences in concepts by organizing material into natural groupings.	• If possible, visit a museum of natural history with exhibits of rain forests. Try to see common characteristics that make vegetation and species thrive in this environment. Take notes on your observations.

*For information on tropical rain forests, see Frederick Lutgens, Edward Tarbuck, and Dennis Tasa, *Foundations of Earth Science*, 5th ed., Upper Saddle River, NJ: Prentice Hall, 2008.

Listening and Note Taking

From time to time, an instructor may give you a guide, usually in outline form, to help you take notes in class. This outline, known as *guided notes*, may be on the board, projected onto a screen, or in a handout that you receive at the beginning of class. Because guided notes are usually general and sketchy, you must fill in the details.

Cornell T-note System

The *Cornell note-taking system*, also known as the *T-note system*, consists of three sections on ordinary notepaper.[3]

- *Notes*, the largest section, is on the right. Record your notes here in whatever form you choose. Skip lines between topics so you can clearly see where a section begins and ends.

KEY 6.5 The Cornell system has space for notes, comments, and a summary.

Label a sheet of paper with the date and title of the lecture.

Create the summary area by starting where the vertical line ends (about 5 centimetres from the bottom of the page) and drawing a horizontal line across the paper.

Create the cue column by drawing a vertical line about 6.5 centimetres from the left side of the paper. End the line about 5 centimetres from the bottom of the sheet.

October 3, 2010, p. 1

Understanding Employee Motivation

Why do some workers have a better attitude toward their work than others?

Some managers view workers as lazy; others view them as motivated and productive.

Maslow's Hierarchy

self-actualization needs (challenging job)
esteem needs (job title)
social needs (friends at work)
security needs (health plan)
physiological needs (pay)

Purpose of motivational theories
— To explain role of human relations in motivating employee performance
— Theories translate into how managers actually treat workers

2 specific theories
— <u>Human resources model</u>, developed by Douglas McGregor, shows that managers have radically different beliefs about motivation.
— Theory X holds that people are naturally irresponsible and uncooperative
— Theory Y holds that people are naturally responsible and self-motivated
— <u>Maslow's Hierarchy of Needs</u> says that people have needs in 5 different areas, which they attempt to satisfy in their work.
— Physiological need: need for survival, including food and shelter
— Security need: need for stability and protection
— Social need: need for friendship and companionship
— Esteem need: need for status and recognition
— Self-actualization need: need for self-fulfillment
Needs at lower levels must be met before a person tries to satisfy needs at higher levels.
— Developed by psychologist Abraham Maslow

Two motivational theories try to explain worker motivation. The human resources model includes Theory X and Theory Y. Maslow's Hierarchy of Needs suggests that people have needs in 5 different areas: physiological, security, social, esteem, and self-actualization.

- The *cue column* goes to the left of your notes. Leave it blank while you read or listen, and then fill it in later as you review. You might insert keywords or comments that highlight ideas, clarify meaning, add examples, link ideas, or draw diagrams. Many students use this column to raise questions, which they answer when they study.
- The *summary* goes at the bottom of the page. Here you reduce your notes to critical points, a process that will help you learn the material. Use this section to provide an overview of what the notes say.

Create this note-taking structure before class begins. Picture an upside-down letter T as you follow these directions:

- Start with a sheet of 8½-by-11-inch lined paper. Label it with the date and lecture title.
- To create the cue column, draw a vertical line about 6.5 centimetres from the left side of the paper. End the line about 5 centimetres from the bottom of the sheet.
- To create the summary area, start at the point where the vertical line ends (about 5 centimetres from the bottom of the page) and draw a horizontal line that spans the entire paper.

Key 6.5 shows how the Cornell system is used in a business course.

Mind Map

A *mind map*, also known as a *think link* or *word web*, is a visual form of note taking that encourages flexible thinking. When you draw a think link, you use shapes and lines to link ideas with supporting details and examples. The visual design makes the connections easy to see, and shapes and pictures extend the material beyond words.

To create a think link, start by circling or boxing your topic in the middle of the paper. Next, draw a line from the topic and write the name of one major idea at the end of the line. Circle that idea. Then jot down specific facts related to the idea, linking them to the idea with lines. Continue the process, connecting thoughts to one another with circles, lines, and words. Key 6.6, a think link on the sociological concept *stratification*, follows this structure.

Examples of think link designs include stair steps showing connected ideas that build toward a conclusion and a tree with trunk and roots as central concepts and branches as examples. Key 8.4 on page 214 shows another type of think link called a jellyfish.

A think link may be difficult to construct in class, especially if your instructor talks quickly. If this is the case, transform your notes into think link format later when you review.

Charting Method

Sometimes instructors deliver information in such quantities and at such speeds that taking detailed notes becomes nearly impossible. In such situations, when a lot of material is coming at you very quickly, the charting method might prove quite useful. It is also excellent for classes presented chronologically or sequentially.

To create charting notes, look ahead in your syllabus to determine the topics of the day's lecture. Then separate your paper into distinct columns, such as definitions, important phrases, and key themes. As you listen to the lecture, this will eliminate excessive writing, help you track dialogues that can be easy to lose, and provide quick memorization tools by splitting material into relevant categories. Shown is a partial set of charting notes for a history class:

TIME PERIOD	IMPORTANT PEOPLE	EVENTS	IMPORTANCE
1968–1972	Pierre Elliott Trudeau	October Crisis, "Just Society"	War Measures Act, Canada becomes officially bilingual, universal health care protected

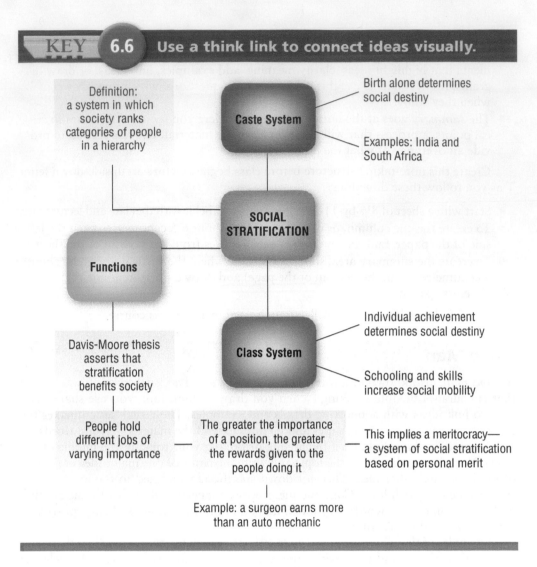

Definition: a system in which society ranks categories of people in a hierarchy

Caste System

Birth alone determines social destiny

Examples: India and South Africa

SOCIAL STRATIFICATION

Functions

Davis-Moore thesis asserts that stratification benefits society

Class System

Individual achievement determines social destiny

Schooling and skills increase social mobility

People hold different jobs of varying importance

The greater the importance of a position, the greater the rewards given to the people doing it

This implies a meritocracy—a system of social stratification based on personal merit

Example: a surgeon earns more than an auto mechanic

Other Visual Strategies

There are other strategies that help organize information for visual learners, although they may be too involved to complete during class. Use them when taking textbook notes or combining class and textbook notes for review.

- *Time lines.* Use a time line to organize information into chronological order. Draw a vertical or horizontal line on the page and place tic marks on the line in order, noting the dates and filling in basic event descriptions.
- *Tables.* Use the columns and rows of a table to organize information as you condense and summarize your class and textbook notes.
- *Branch diagrams.* This type of diagram, also called a *tree chart*, shows how items that come from a single source are related to one another. Typical examples of branch diagrams include family trees, evolutionary charts, and organizational charts (for people or files). Key 6.7 illustrates a partial branch diagram representing the structure of a Chemistry department website in a small college.
- *Flowchart.* This diagram shows a set of ordered steps that make up a process. The diagram often includes points where you have to make a decision before proceeding in a particular direction. For example, Key 6.8 illustrates a flowchart that could help you remember the steps to learning a new software program.

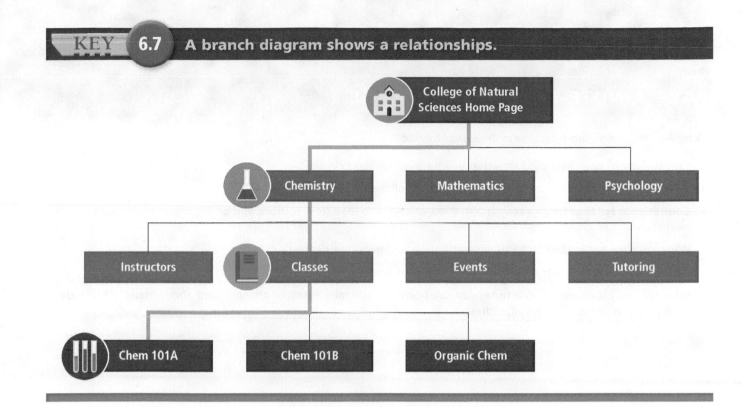

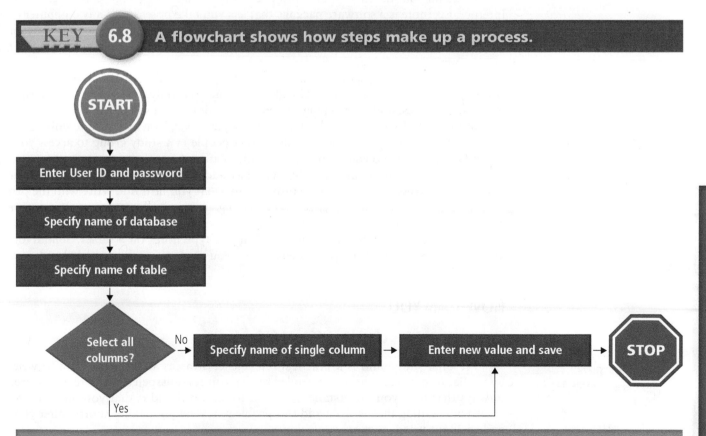

get practical

FACE A NOTE-TAKING CHALLENGE

Complete the following on paper or in digital format.

Get set to take in and record information in your most difficult class.

1. What is the name of the course that is the most challenging for you right now?
2. Consult your syllabus for this course. What do you have to read (text sections and/or other materials) before your next class?
3. Where will you sit in class to focus your attention and minimize distractions?
4. Which note-taking system is best suited for the class and why?
5. Who are two classmates whose notes you can borrow if you miss a class or are confused about material? Include their phone numbers and email addresses.

Electronic Strategies

If you take notes using an electronic device, saving them safely is essential. You can save notes on your device or on a remote server (known as *the cloud*) connected to the Internet. Evernote is a software package that lets you take notes using any computer or Android phone. These notes include text, webpage URLs and content, photographs, or voice memos—all of which can have attachments. You can save your notes on your own computer or on a special Evernote server.

GoogleDocs is another example of a documentation and note-taking tool that lets you save text to the cloud. With GoogleDocs, you need only connect to the Internet, open GoogleDocs, and start typing. When you are done, you save your work to a collection (folder) of your choice, hosted on a Google server. You can also download the file to your own computer. You can allow other people in a study group to access your file in GoogleDocs and edit it, adding new information where necessary.

Finally, recent note-taking technology has added recording capabilities to your arsenal. The Livescribe smartpen records exactly what you hear and write with the pen on a specialized notebook which saves everything electronically, enabling you to store and review the lecture and your notes on a computer. SoundNote is a similar application that works with tablet computers. When you type notes on a tablet, SoundNote will record everything you type as well as what you are hearing during the class.[4]

HOW CAN YOU
take notes faster?

SHORTHAND ←

A system of rapid handwriting that employs symbols, abbreviations, and shortened words to represent words and phrases.

Personal **shorthand** is a practical intelligence strategy that enables you to write faster. Because you are the only intended reader, you can misspell and abbreviate words in ways that only you understand. A risk of using shorthand is that you might forget what your writing means. To avoid this problem, review your notes shortly after class and spell out words that are confusing.

Another risk is forgetting to remove shorthand from work you hand in. This can happen when you use the same system for class notes as you do when talking to friends online. For example, when students take notes in text message shorthand, they may be so accustomed to omitting capitalization and punctuation, using acronyms, and replacing long words with creative contractions that they may forget to correct their final work.

The suggestions that follow will help you master shorthand. Many will be familiar and, in fact, you may already use many of them to speed up your email and text messaging.

1. Use standard abbreviations in place of complete words.

w/, w/o	with, without	cf	compare, in comparison to
ur	you are	Ff	following
→	means; resulting in	Q	question
←	as a result of	gr8	great
↑	increasing	pov	point of view
↓	decreasing	<	less than
∴	therefore	>	more than
b/c	because	=	equals
≈	approximately	b&f	back and forth
+ or &	and	Δ	change
Y	why	2	to; two; too
no. or #	number	afap	as far as possible
i.e.	that is	e.g.	for example
cos	change of subject	c/o	care of
Ng	no good	km	kilometres
p.	page	hx	history

2. Shorten words by removing middle vowels.

   Prps = purpose
   Lwyr = lawyer
   Cmptr = computer

3. Substitute word beginnings for entire words.

   Assoc = associate; association
   Info = information
   Subj = subject

4. Form plurals by adding *s* to shortened words.

   Prblms = problems
   Envlps = envelopes
   Prntrs = printers

5. Make up your own symbols and use them consistently.

   b/4 = before
   4tn = fortune
   2thake = toothache

get creative

CRAFT YOUR OWN SHORTHAND

Complete the following on paper or in digital format.

Customize your shorthand to suit your needs

1. Identify a class in which you take a lot of notes or one in which you would like to begin taking better notes.

2. Next, write 10 terms that are used often in this class. For instance, if you were creating a list for your psychology class, you might include terms such as Sigmund Freud, child development, or neuropsychology.

3. Finally, create a list of shorthand terms for the items you chose. Be creative but remember that they should be easy for you to remember and use. Thus, your shorthand should not be longer or more complex than the word itself. Use numbers, symbols, or even small images (such as a heart or smiley face). For the list of psychology terms, the shorthand might look like the following:

   - Sigmund Freud = SigFrd
   - Child development = ChDev
   - Neuropsychology = nro-psych

6. Use standard or informal abbreviations for proper nouns such as places, people, companies, scientific substances, events, and so on.

BC	=	British Columbia
H2O	=	water
Moz.	=	Wolfgang Amadeus Mozart

7. If you know that a word or phrase will be repeated, write it once and then establish an abbreviation for the rest of your notes. For example, the first time your political science instructor mentions the Iraq Study Group, the 2006 bipartisan commission that issued recommendations to the American president about the Iraq War, write the name in full. After that, use the initials ISG.

8. Write only what is essential. Include only the information nuggets you want to remember, even if your instructor says much more. Do this by paring down your writing. Say, for example, your instructor had the following to say on the subject of hate crimes.[5]

After the terrorist attacks in the United States on September 11, 2001, law enforcement officials noted a dramatic shift in the nature of hate crimes. For the first time, replacing crimes motivated by race as the leading type of hate crime were crimes that targeted religious and ethnic groups and particularly Muslims.

Your shorthand notes might look something like this:

—After 9/11 HCs ▲ focus & targeted religious and ethnic groups, esp. Muslims
—Reduction of HC based on race

TIPS FOR LEARNING ONLINE

- *Take notes.* A variety of available technologies allow you to take online notes, just as you would mark up a regular textbook. You can highlight important passages and insert your own notes (or think links) within your online ebook.

- *Listen.* If your professors make their lectures available in podcast form, either on iTunes or on the school's learning management system (LMS), download and listen to them.

- *Share.* Using Google Docs, your school's LMS, or a Facebook page, share notes with your classmates. This is useful if you miss a class or didn't quite understand the content of the lecture. While sharing notes is not a substitute for attending a class, it does offer a way to get caught up if you miss a class or two.

Norton Ewart

What happened to Norton? As a result of his increased efforts and help from his study group, Norton was rewarded with academic success and returned to the pre-engineering program, later transferring to Union College, where he graduated with a bachelor's in electrical engineering. He was hired by Hewlett-Packard after college and worked his way up to management over twenty years. After several years at a different job in the area of product management, he is back at HP. He is still an expert skier and remains just as willing to take productive risks in his personal life and career as he is on double black diamond slopes.

What does this mean for you? Every student experiences different levels of motivation and interest for different courses. Your challenge is to find a way to do the work well when your interest doesn't provide the energy. Choose the course you are taking right now that interests you the least. Make three lists with the following headers: Study Strategies That Can Help, How I Will Use What I Learn in This Course, and What Rewards Will Result If I Persist in This Course. Then fill the lists with as many items as you can and put them where you can refer to them as you make your way through the term.

What risk may bring reward beyond your world? The demands of your everyday life may be so pressing you cannot see how you will have the time to help out. Think, though, about a person, place, thing, idea, or situation that has sparked your interest and emotion. Find an organization that relates to it and investigate to see how you can help in some small way. One action now, no matter how small, can help. Who knows? Maybe you can make time for more action in the future.

RISK ACTION
FOR POST-SECONDARY, CAREER, AND LIFE REWARDS

KNOW IT *Think Critically*
Your Best Listening and Note-Taking Conditions

Build Basic Skills. Think of a recent class in which you were able to listen and take notes effectively.

1. Describe the environment (course title, classroom setting, and so on).

2. Describe the instructor's style (lecture, group discussion, Q and A).

3. Describe your level of preparation and attitude toward the class.

4. Describe the note-taking style you generally use in the class and how effective it is for you.

5. Describe any barriers to effective listening that were present.

Listening and Note Taking

Now think of a recent class in which you found it *hard to listen* and *take notes*.

1. Describe the environment (course title, classroom setting, and so on).

2. Describe the instructor's style (lecture, group discussion, Q and A).

3. Describe your level of preparation and attitude toward the class.

4. Describe the note-taking style you generally use in the class and how effective it is for you.

5. Describe any barriers to effective listening that were present.

Take it to the next level. Examine the two situations. From what you have noticed, identify three conditions that seem, for you, to be crucial for effective listening and note taking.

Move toward mastery. Think about the more difficult listening and note-taking situation. For each of the three conditions you named, describe either how you can make sure that condition occurs or how you can compensate for it if it is out of your control.

WRITE IT *Communicate*

Record your thoughts on a separate piece of paper, in a journal, or electronically.

Emotional intelligence journal: Understanding your needs and making changes. Think about a situation when you've had trouble taking effective notes. Was it the teacher's pace? The subject matter of the class? How did you feel about the situation, and what did you do? After you describe the situation, find and write three note-taking strategies discussed in this chapter that could help you in the future. How might they help you create a more positive outcome?

Real-life writing: Determining the best method for you. Over the next week, commit to trying at least two different types of note-taking systems in your classes. If possible, choose a different method for each subject. Prepare for your method before entering the class by readying your notebook with the correct formatting. Try to complete your classes by using the new method. When the week is over, reflect on which style worked best for you and which would be the most beneficial going forward.

WORK IT *Build Your Brand*

Learn More About Career Success

21st Century Learning Building Blocks

- Financial, economic, business, and entrepreneurial literacy
- Information literacy
- Media literacy

Complete the following in your electronic portfolio or separately on paper.

1. Put your listening and note-taking skills to work as you investigate what brings success in the workplace. Write down two or three potential career areas that interest you.

2. Next, visit an Internet website that hosts user-loaded videos, such as YouTube.com. Perform a search for a career interview of your choice. You might try search terms such as "marketing interview," "what's it like to be a dental technician?" or "what does a movie producer do?" When you've found a usable video (keep in mind that you are looking for credible, realistic information), practise one of the note-taking techniques discussed in this chapter.

   a. Watch the video once all the way through, concentrating on main points and overall themes

   b. Watch it again, focusing on filling in gaps, understanding key terms and concepts, and gathering interesting extras. Remember to use shorthand when necessary.

   c. After you've watched the video twice and taken thorough notes, write a one-page summary of the career for your portfolio. Include important information discussed in the video, such as the training required, salary expectations, daily duties, and so on. Keep the summary in your portfolio for future career searches.

Cindy Estrada

Whatever you study, your goal is to anchor important information in long-term memory so that you can use it – for both short-term goals like tests and long-term goals like performing effectively on the job.

Memory and Studying

RETAINING WHAT YOU LEARN

What Would You Risk? *Cindy Estrada*

Cindy Estrada

THINK ABOUT THIS SITUATION AS YOU READ, AND CONSIDER WHAT ACTION YOU WOULD TAKE. THIS CHAPTER SHOWS YOU HOW MEMORY WORKS AND THEN HELPS YOU USE IT EFFECTIVELY TO REMEMBER WHAT YOU STUDY. ALTHOUGH IT IS EASIER TO REMEMBER THINGS THAT YOU WANT TO KNOW, THE STRATEGIES YOU LEARN HERE WILL HELP YOU STUDY MATERIALS NO MATTER HOW YOU FEEL ABOUT THEM.

Cindy Estrada never knew a carefree childhood. Her father was a ground medic during the Vietnam War, and post-traumatic stress disorder took its toll on him after the war. By the time Cindy reached age 6, he was no longer a presence in the Estrada household. While her mom worked, Cindy watched over her three younger brothers. "At an early age, I was there for them after school until my mom got home in the evenings," Cindy recalls. "It was a very non-traditional household." But Cindy had plenty of ambition. She aimed for the reward of being the first member of her family get a post-secondary education, so she worked hard and explored four-year college options.

At age 17, Cindy got pregnant. Her newborn son, Jeramie, was the new joy in her life. However, she wondered how she would be able to support her new son and herself without even a high school diploma. She transferred to an alternative high school in her hometown, Cheyenne, Wyoming, to complete her high school education. But as a single mom, she knew she needed to risk more in order to provide for her son.

Cindy enrolled at Laramie County Community College while working as an operator with Mountain Bell. Two years later, she transferred to the University of Wyoming in Laramie, 50 miles away. Aiming for a telecommunications degree required her to risk balancing a full-time job with mom duties and 100 miles of daily commuting, all while retaining information from classes and study sessions.

To be continued . . .

Driven to forge a solid lifestyle for her young family, Cindy was determined to pull off an astounding juggling act. To do so, she needed to maximize study time. You'll learn more about Cindy, and the reward resulting from her actions, within the chapter.

Notes

Today   Mar 10 8:01 AM

Working through this chapter will help you to:

statusCHECK

How Developed Are Your Memory and Studying Skills?

For each statement, circle the number that feels right to you, from 1 for "not at all true for me" to 5 for "very true for me."

1. I know that not everything that I hear and read will necessarily stay in my memory for long—or at all. ① ② ③ ④ ⑤

2. When I am studying, I try to choose what is most important to remember. ① ② ③ ④ ⑤

3. Through trial and error, I have figured out study locations and times that work best for me. ① ② ③ ④ ⑤

4. After a test or presentation is over, I retain much of what I had to know. ① ② ③ ④ ⑤

5. I write, rewrite, and summarize information to remember it. ① ② ③ ④ ⑤

6. I use flash cards and other active memory strategies to remember what I study. ① ② ③ ④ ⑤

7. I create mnemonic devices with images and associations as memory hooks. ① ② ③ ④ ⑤

8. I try to review material in several sessions over time rather than cram the night before a test. ① ② ③ ④ ⑤

9. If I find myself looking something up over and over again, I make an effort to memorize it. ① ② ③ ④ ⑤

10. I know how to study class and text notes effectively to prepare for tests. ① ② ③ ④ ⑤

Each of the topics in these statements is covered in this chapter. Note those statements for which you circled a 3 or lower. Skim the chapter to see where those topics appear, and pay special attention to them as you read, learn, and apply new strategies.

REMEMBER: NO MATTER HOW DEVELOPED YOUR MEMORY AND STUDYING SKILLS ARE, YOU CAN IMPROVE WITH EFFORT AND PRACTICE.

HOW DOES *memory work?*

All learning and performance depends on memory, because all the information you remember—concepts, facts, processes, formulas, and more—is the raw material with which you think, write, create, build, and perform day-to-day in school and out. Memorization also forms a foundation for higher-level thinking, because you need to recall and understand information before you can apply, analyze, synthesize, or evaluate it.

Through the effort of studying and a positive attitude, you earn the reward of a memory that can help you move toward your goals. This chapter provides memory-improvement techniques that you can make your own. First, let us explore how memory works.

The Information Processing Model of Memory

Memory refers to the way the brain stores and recalls information or experiences that are acquired through the five senses. Although you take in thousands of pieces of

MyStudentSuccessLab

Whether face-to-face or online, MyStudentSuccessLab helps students build the skills they need through peer-led video interviews, interactive practice exercises, and activities that provide academic, life, and professionalism skills.

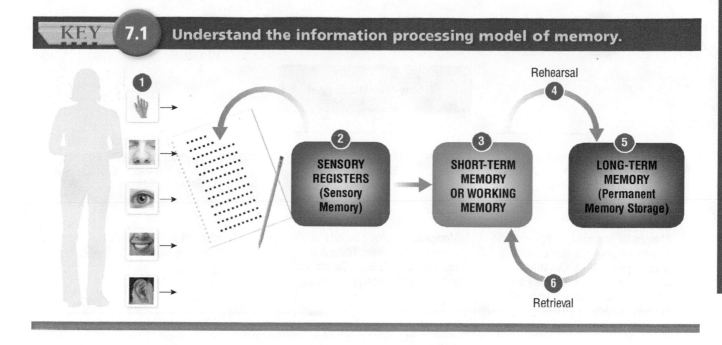

information every second—everything from the shape and colour of your chair to how your history text describes Sir John A. Macdonald's terms as prime minister—you remember few of them. Unconsciously, your brain sorts through stimuli and stores only what it considers important.

Learning and memories occur through chemical and structural changes in the brain—neurons (brain cells) growing new dendrites, strengthening synapses or forming new ones, and communicating information over those synapses using chemicals called neurotransmitters. Look at Key 7.1 as you read how the brain forms lasting memories.

1. Raw information, gathered through the five senses, reaches the brain (for example, the tune of a song you're learning in your jazz ensemble class).

2. This information enters **sensory registers**, where it stays for only seconds. (As you play the notes for the first time, the sounds stop first in your auditory register.)

3. You then choose whether to pay attention to information in the sensory register. When you selectively look, listen, smell, taste, or feel the information, you move it into **short-term memory**, also known as *working memory*, which contains what you are thinking at any moment and from where information can be made available for further processing. (The part of the song that is your responsibility, for example, the clarinet solo, will likely take up residence in your working memory.) You can temporarily keep information in short-term memory through *rote rehearsal*—the process of repeating information to yourself or even out loud.

4. Information moves to **long-term memory** through focused, active rehearsal repeated over time. (As you practise the song in class and at home, your brain stores the pitch, rhythm, and tempo in your long-term memory, where you will be able to draw on it again.) Long-term memory stores everything you know, from the dates of both World Wars to the location of your elementary school. As shown in Key 7.2, long-term memory has three separate storage houses. There are no limits to how much information long-term memory can hold or how long it is held, but most people retain memories of personal experiences and procedures longer than concepts, facts, formulas, and dates.

> **SENSORY REGISTER**
> Brain filters through which sensory information enters the brain and is sent to short-term memory.

> **SHORT-TERM MEMORY**
> The brain's temporary information storehouse, in which information remains for a limited time (from a few seconds to half a minute).

> **LONG-TERM MEMORY**
> The brain's permanent information storehouse, from which information can be retrieved.

173

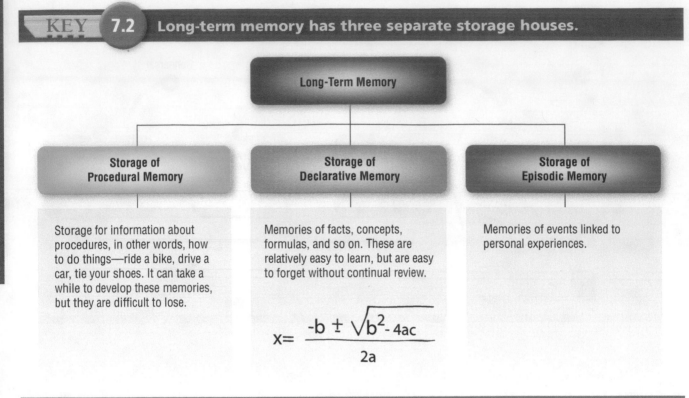

Long-Term Memory

Storage of Procedural Memory

Storage for information about procedures, in other words, how to do things—ride a bike, drive a car, tie your shoes. It can take a while to develop these memories, but they are difficult to lose.

Storage of Declarative Memory

Memories of facts, concepts, formulas, and so on. These are relatively easy to learn, but are easy to forget without continual review.

$$x = \frac{-b \pm \sqrt{b^2 - 4ac}}{2a}$$

Storage of Episodic Memory

Memories of events linked to personal experiences.

When you need a piece of information from long-term memory, the brain retrieves it and places it in short-term memory. On test day, this enables you to choose the right answer on a multiple-choice question or prepare a fact-based argument for an essay question.

The movement of information in your brain, from short-term to long-term memory and then back again, strengthens the connections among neurons (brain cells). As you read in Chapter 1, learning happens and memories are built when neurons grow new dendrites and form new synapses. When you learn an algebra formula, for example, your brain creates new connections. Every time you review it, the connections get stronger.

Syda Productions/Fotolia

Why You Forget

Issues with health, nutrition and stress can cause memory problems. Research shows that even short-term stress can interfere with cell communication in the learning and memory regions of the brain.[1] *However, the most common reason that information fails to stay in long-term memory is ineffective studying*—not doing what you should to retain what you learn.

As Key 7.3 shows, retaining information requires continual review. You are still learning information 10 minutes after you hear it for the first time. If you review the material over time—after 24 hours, a week, a month, 6 months, and more—you will retain the knowledge. If you do not review, the neural connections will weaken, and eventually you will forget. Because Cindy is in her car every day, she could benefit from recording important information and listening to it on her commute.

In a classic study conducted in 1885, researcher Hermann Ebbinghaus memorized a list of meaningless three-letter words such as *CEF* and *LAZ*. He then examined how quickly he forgot them. Within one hour, he had forgotten more than 50 percent of what he had learned; after two days, he

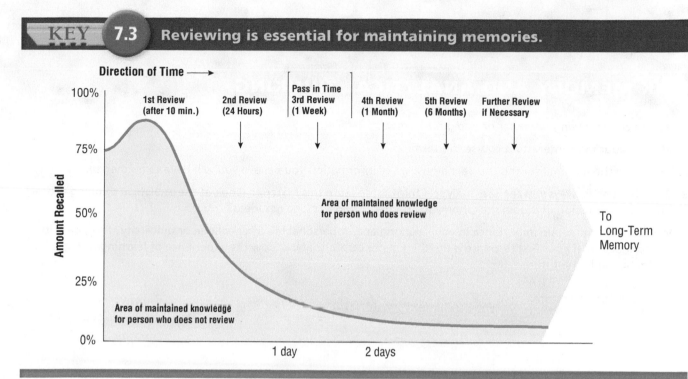

KEY 7.3 **Reviewing is essential for maintaining memories.**

Source: From Tony Buzan, *Use Both Sides of Your Brain*, copyright © 1974, 1983, 1991 by Tony Buzan. Used by permission of Dutton, a division of Penguin Group (USA) Inc., and by kind permission of Tony Buzan, www.thinkbuzan.com.

knew fewer than 30 percent of the memorized words. Although Ebbinghaus's recall of the nonsense syllables remained fairly stable after that, his experiment shows how fragile memory can be—even when you take the time and expend the energy to memorize information.[2]

Now that you know more about how memory works, get down to the business of learning how to retain the information you think is important and how to provide that information when you need it.

HOW CAN YOU REMEMBER
what you study?

Samuel Borges Photography/ Shutterstock

Whatever you study—textbooks, course materials, notes, primary sources—your goal is to anchor important information in long-term memory so that you can use it for both short-term goals, such as tests, and long-term goals, such as being an information technology specialist. Take a productive risk and try out a variety of strategies to see which will reward you with the most retention. One great way to do this is with *journalists' questions*—the six questions journalists need to answer to write an effective newspaper story.

1. *When, Where, Who.* Determine the times, places, and company (or none) that suit you.
2. *What, Why.* Choose what is important to study, and set the rest aside.
3. *How.* Find the specific tips and techniques that work best for you.

get analytical

LINK MEMORY AND ANALYTICAL THINKING

Complete the following on paper or in digital format.

1. Identify your most interesting course this term.

2. Analyzing the material for the course, name a set of information you believe you will have to memorize.

3. Describe specific ways you can use analytical thinking to learn this material. (Look at the analytical thinking procedures and discussion of Bloom's taxonomy in Chapter 5, page 125, to get ideas.)

4. Will the material retain importance in your working and/or personal life after college or university? If so, describe the connection. If your first response is no, think more carefully about how the experience of learning it might be useful to you in the future.

When, Where, and Who: Choosing Your Best Setting

Davis Barber/PhotoEdit

Figuring out the *when*, *where*, and *who* of studying is all about self-management. You analyze what works best for you, create ideas about how to put that self-knowledge to work, and use practical thinking to implement those ideas as you study.

When

The first part of *when* is *how much*. Having the right amount of time for the job is crucial. One formula for success is the simple calculation you read about earlier in this book: *for every hour you spend in the classroom each week, spend at least two to three hours preparing for the class*. For example, if you are carrying a course load of 15 credit hours, you should spend at least 30 hours a week studying outside of class. Check your syllabus for the dates reading assignments are due, and give yourself enough time to complete them.

The second part of *when* is *what time*. If two students go over their biology notes from 8:00 to 9:00 a.m., but one is a morning person who went to bed at 11:00 p.m. and the other is a night owl who hit the sack around 2:00 a.m., you can guess who has a greater chance of remembering the information.

First, determine the time available to you in between classes, work, and other commitments. Then, thinking about when you function best, choose your study times carefully. You may not always have the luxury of being free during your peak energy times, especially if, like Cindy, you have one or more children, but do the best you can.

The third part of *when* is *how close to original learning*. Because most forgetting happens right after learning, as you saw in Key 7.3, the review that helps you retain information most effectively happens close to when you first learn the material. If you can, review notes the same day you took them in class; make an organizer of important information from a text chapter shortly after you read it; or write a summary of a group study session within 24 hours of the meeting.

The study location that works for you depends on your individual needs. This student has found he can concentrate best on his physical geology material if he reads it at a table in the library.

The final part of *when* is *when to stop*. Take a break, or go to sleep, when your body is no longer responding. Forcing yourself to study when you're not focused doesn't work.

Where

Where you study matters. As with time, consider your restrictions first—there may be only so many places available to you within a reasonable travel distance that are open when you have study time free. Also, analyze previous study sessions. If you spent more than 20 percent of your time blocking out distractions at a particular location, try someplace different.

Who

Some students prefer to study alone, while some prefer pairs or groups. Many mix it up, doing some kinds of studying—first reading, close reading, creating note sets—alone, and others—test review, problem sets—with one or more people. Some find that they prefer to study certain subjects alone and others with a group. For some people, knowing they are going to work with others motivates them to be prepared, and sharing the work helps them learn.

Even students who study primarily alone can benefit by working with others from time to time. Besides the obvious benefit of greater communication and teamwork skills, group study enhances your ability to remember information in several ways:[3]

- Gets you to say what you know out loud, which solidifies your understanding
- Exposes you to the ideas of others and gets you thinking in different ways
- Increases the chance that all of the important information will be covered
- Motivates you to study in preparation for a group meeting
- Subjects you to questions about your knowledge, maybe even some challenges, that make you clarify and build on your thinking

Instructors sometimes initiate student study groups, commonly for math or science courses, as peer-assisted study sessions or supplemental instruction. However, don't wait for your instructor—or for exam crunch time—to benefit from studying with others. As you begin to get to know students in your classes, start now exchanging phone numbers and email addresses, forming groups, and scheduling meetings. Here are some strategies for study group success:

- *Limit group size.* Groups of five or fewer tend to experience the most success.
- *Set long-term and short-term goals.* At your first meeting, determine what the group wants to accomplish, and set mini-goals at the start of the first meeting.
- *Determine a regular schedule and leadership rotation.* Determine what your group needs and what the members' schedules can handle. Try to meet weekly or, at the least, every other week. Rotate leadership among members willing to lead.
- *Create study materials for one another.* Give each person a task of finding a piece of information to compile and share with the group. Teach material to one another.
- *Share the workload and pool note-taking resources.* The most important factor is a willingness to work, not knowledge level. Compare notes with group members and fill in information you don't have.
- *Know how to be an effective leader.* The leader needs to define projects, assign work, set schedules and meeting goals, and keep people focused, motivated, and moving ahead.
- *Know how to be an effective participant.* Participants are "part owners" of the team process with a responsibility for, and a stake in, the outcome. Participants need to be organized, fulfill the tasks they promise to do, and stay open to discussion.
- *Be creative with technology if it's tough to meet in person.* Use Skype, a wiki or Google Drive to collaborate.

get practical

ANSWER YOUR JOURNALIST'S QUESTIONS

Answer the following on paper or in digital format.

Think about a past study session that did not prepare you well for a test, and recall which strategies—if any—you used.

Now, plan a study session that will take place within the next seven days—one that will help you learn something important for one of your current courses. Answer the following questions to create your session:

1. *When* will you study, and for how long?

2. *Where* will you study?

3. *Who* will you study with, if anyone?

4. *What* will you study?

5. *Why* is this material important to know?

6. *How* will you study it—what strategy (or strategies) do you plan to use?

7. How do you think the journalists' questions in this structure would have helped you get more from your previous study session?

8. Final step—put this plan to work. Name the date you will use it.

One final part of *who* is dealing with *who might be distracting*. You may have friends who want you to go out. You may have young children or other family members who need you. Think carefully about your choices. Do you want to head out with a group of friends you can see any time, even if it compromises your ability to do well in an important course? Can you schedule your study time when your kids are occupied for an hour or so?

Tell your friends and family why studying is important to you. People who truly care about you are likely to support your goals. Tell your kids (if they are old enough to understand) what your education and eventual degree will mean to you—and to them. Children may be more able to cope if they see what lies at the end of the road. Key 7.4 shows some ways that parents or others caring for children can maximize their efforts.

What and Why: Evaluating Study Materials

It is impossible, inefficient, and unnecessary to study every word and bit of information. Before you study, engage your analytical thinking skills—decide *what* is important to study by examining *why* you need to know it. Here's how:

- *Choose materials to study.* Put away materials or notes you know you do not need to review. Then examine what's left. Within textbooks or other materials, which chapters or sections are important to know for your immediate goal (for example, to study for an upcoming test) and why? Thinking about the *why* highlights your purpose and can increase your focus.

- *Prioritize materials.* Determine what you need the most work on, and study that first. Almost every student has more steam at the beginning of a study session than at the end; plus, fatigue or an interruption may prevent you from covering everything.

get $mart

STAY AWARE OF YOUR MONEY

PhotoMan/Fotolia

Complete the following on paper or in digital format.

How good is your memory when it comes to bills and due dates? Find out by answering the following questions. First, create a hard copy or digital table with the headers as shown.

BILL	EST. AMOUNT	ACTUAL AMOUNT	EST. DUE DATE	ACTUAL DUE DATE

1. Off the top of your head, list your typical monthly bills, their **estimated amount** and **estimated due date**. Do this quickly and do NOT worry if you are wrong.

2. Now go through your actual bills to fill in the **actual amount** and **actual due date**.

   a. Did you forget to mention any bills?

   b. How far off were you between the estimated and actual values?

- *Set specific goals.* Look at what you need to cover and the time available, and decide what you will accomplish—for example, reading a specific section in a certain textbook, reviewing three sets of class notes, and creating a study sheet from both the book and your notes. Make a list for reference, and check things off as you go.

- *Within the sections you study, separate main points from unimportant details.* Ask yourself, What is the most important information? Highlight only the key points in your texts, and write notes in the margins about main ideas.

KEY 7.4 Manage children while studying.

STUDYING WITH CHILDREN

- **Keep them up to date on your schedule.** Kids appreciate being involved, even though they may not understand entirely. Let them know when you have a big test or project due and what they can expect of you.

- **Find help.** Know your schedule and arrange for child care if necessary. Consider hiring a sitter, using a daycare centre, or offering to help another parent in exchange for babysitting.

- **Utilize technology.** You may be able to have a study session over the phone, through instant messaging, by email, or over social networking sites. Additionally, some sites offer tools that allow multiple users to work on a document or project remotely.

- **Be prepared and keep them active.** Consider keeping some toys, activities, or books that come out only during study time. This strategy will make the time special for children.

- **Plan for family time.** Offset your time away from your children with plans to do something together, such as watch a movie or go out for ice cream. Children may be more apt to let you study when they have something to look forward to.

STUDYING WITH INFANTS

- **Utilize your baby's sleeping schedule.** Study at night if your baby goes to sleep early, or in the morning if your baby sleeps late.

- **Make time in the middle.** Study during nap times if you aren't too tired yourself.

- **Talk to your baby.** Recite your notes to the baby. The baby will appreciate the attention, and you will get work done.

- **Keep them close.** Put your baby in a safe and fun place while you study, such as a playpen, motorized swing, or jumping seat.

How: Using Study Strategies

After figuring out the *when, where, who, what,* and *why* of studying, focus on the *how*—the strategies that will anchor the information you need in your brain (Key 7.5). You may already use several of them. Try as many as you can, and keep what works.

Have purpose, intention, and emotional connection

If you can remember the lyrics to dozens of popular songs but not the functions of the pancreas, perhaps emotion is involved. When you care about something, your brain responds differently, and you learn and remember more easily.

To achieve the same results in school, try to create a purpose and will to remember through a kind of emotional involvement with what you study. For example, an accounting student might think of a friend who is running a small business and needs to keep his records in order—to pay bills on time, to record income, to meet tax payments. Putting himself in the position of his friend's accountant, the student connects learning accounting principles with making a difference in a friend's life.

Put your notes to work

It is common to let notes sit in a notebook unread until just before mid-terms or finals. Even the most comprehensive, brilliant notes won't do you any good if you don't refer to them. Regularly reread your notes in batches (for example, every one or two weeks) to build your recall of information. As you reread, do the following:

- Fill in any gaps, or get help with trouble spots.
- Mark up your notes by highlighting main ideas and key supporting points.
- Add recall or practice test questions in the margins.
- Add relevant points from homework, text, and lab work into your notes.

Shutterstock

KEY 7.5 Focus on the *how* of study success.

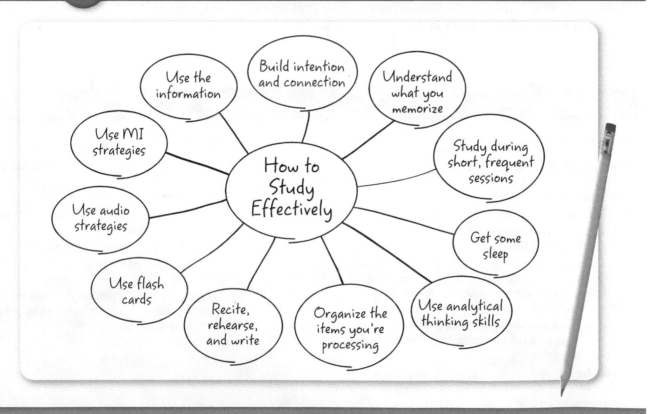

Apply Different Intelligences to Remembering Material for Psychology

INTELLIGENCE	USE MI STRATEGIES TO REMEMBER MORE EFFECTIVELY	APPLY MI MEMORY STRATEGIES TO THE TOPIC OF MOTIVATION AND EMOTION FOR A PSYCHOLOGY COURSE
Verbal-Linguistic	• Develop a story line for a mnemonic first, then work on the visual images. • Write out answers to practice essay questions.	• Answer learning objectives as though they were essay questions: What are three types of needs? What are instinct approaches to motivation?*
Logical-Mathematical	• Create logical groupings that help you memorize knowledge chunks. • When you study material in the middle, link it to what comes before and after.	• Group and compare the theories of emotion—the James–Lange theory, the Cannon–Bard theory, the Schachter–Singer cognitive arousal theory, the facial feedback hypothesis, and Lazarus's cognitive-mediational theory.
Bodily-Kinesthetic	• Re-enact concepts physically if you can, to solidify them in memory. • Record information on a digital recorder and listen as you walk between classes.	• Model facial expressions with another student and take turns guessing the emotion behind the expression.
Visual-Spatial	• Focus on visual mnemonics such as mental walks. • Use markers to add colour to the images you use in your mnemonics.	• Create a colourful mnemonic to remember maladaptive eating problems such as obesity, anorexia nervosa, and bulimia.
Interpersonal	• Do flash card drills with a study partner. • Recite important material to a study partner.	• Working with a study partner, recite and explain Maslow's hierarchy of needs to each other.
Intrapersonal	• Listen to an audio podcast that reviews test material. • Create vocabulary cartoons and test yourself on the material.	• Understand incentive approaches by considering what kind of external stimuli create incentive for you.
Musical	• Play music while you brainstorm ideas. • Create a mnemonic in the form of a musical rhyme.	• Write a rap that lists and explains the different approaches to understanding motivation.
Naturalistic	• Organize what you have to learn so you see how everything fits together. • Sit outside and go through your flash cards.	• Make a chart organizing explanatory details of the three elements of emotion—physiology, behaviour, and subjective experience.

*For information on motivation and emotion, see Saundra K. Ciccarelli and Glenn E. Meyer, *Psychology*. Upper Saddle River, NJ: Prentice Hall, 2006.

When you study for a test with a classmate, you can help each other understand difficult concepts as well as fill in the holes in each other's notes.

Shutterstock

It sounds kind of obvious—but something that has meaning is easier to recall than something that makes little sense. This basic principle applies to everything you study. Figure out logical connections, and use these connections to help you learn. For example, in a plant biology course, memorize plants in family groups; in a history course, link events in a cause-and-effect chain.

When you have trouble remembering something new, think about how the new idea fits into what you already know. A simple example: If you can't remember what a word means, look at the word's root, prefix, or suffix. Knowing that the root *bellum* means "war" and the prefix *ante* means "before" will help you recognize that *antebellum* means "before the war."

Study during short, frequent sessions

You can improve your chances of remembering material by learning it more than once. A pattern of short sessions—say, three 20-minute study sessions—followed by brief periods of rest is more effective than continual studying with little or no rest. Try studying on your own or with a classmate during breaks in your schedule. Although studying between classes isn't for everyone, you may find that it can help you remember more.

In addition, scheduling regular, frequent review sessions over time will help you retain information more effectively. If you have two weeks before a test, set up study sessions three times per week instead of putting the final two days aside for hours-long study marathons.[4]

Take care of yourself

Even though sleep may take a back seat with all you have to do in crunch times, research indicates that shortchanging your sleep during the week impairs your ability to remember and learn, even if you try to make up for it by sleeping all weekend.[5] Sleep improves your ability to remember what you studied before you went to bed. So does having a good breakfast. Even if you are running late, grab something quick so that you aren't going to class on an empty stomach.

Exercise is another key component. The latest research shows that regular exercise followed by food and rest can significantly improve the functioning of the parts of the brain most involved in memory—the cortex and hippocampus.[6] When time is tight and you have trouble scheduling workouts, remember that those workouts can improve your academic performance.

Use analytical thinking skills

Analytical, or critical, thinking encourages you to associate new information with what you already know. Imagine you have to remember information about the signing of the Treaty of Versailles, which ended World War I. How can critical thinking help?

- Recall everything that you know about the topic.
- Think about how this event is similar to other events in history.
- Consider what is different and unique about this treaty in comparison to other treaties.
- Explore the causes that led up to this event, and look at the event's effects.
- Evaluate how successful you think the treaty was.

This critical exploration makes it easier to remember the material you are studying.

Organize the items you are processing

- *Divide material into manageable sections*. Master each section, put all the sections together, and then test your memory of all the material.
- *Use the chunking strategy*. Chunking increases the capacity of short-term and long-term memory. For example, though it is hard to remember these 10 digits—4808371557—it is easier to remember them in three chunks—480 837 1557. In general, try to limit groups to 10 items or fewer. The eight-day study plan in Key 7.6 relies on chunking.

> **CHUNKING**
> Placing disconnected information into smaller units that are easier to remember.

KEY 7.6 Study plan success depends on a good memory.

DAY 8 (IN EIGHT DAYS, YOU'LL BE TAKING A TEST)

PLANNING DAY
- List everything that may be on the exam. (Check your syllabus and class notes; talk with your instructor.)
- Divide the material into four learning chunks.
- Decide on a study schedule for the next seven days—when you will study, with whom you will study, the materials you need, and so on.

DAY 7 (COUNTDOWN: SEVEN DAYS TO GO)

- Use the techniques described in this chapter and Chapter 8 to study chunk A.
- Memorize key concepts, facts, formulas, and so on that may be on the test.
- Take an active approach to learning: take practice tests, summarize what you read in your own words, and use critical thinking to connect ideas.

DAY 6 (COUNTDOWN: SIX DAYS TO GO)

- Use the same techniques to study chunk B.

DAY 5 (COUNTDOWN: FIVE DAYS TO GO)

- Use the same techniques to study chunk C.

DAY 4 (COUNTDOWN: FOUR DAYS TO GO)

- Use the same techniques to study chunk D.

DAY 3 (COUNTDOWN: THREE DAYS TO GO)

- Combine and review chunks A and B.

DAY 2 (COUNTDOWN: TWO DAYS TO GO)

- Combine and review chunks C and D.

DAY 1 (COUNTDOWN: ONE DAY TO GO)

PUT IT ALL TOGETHER: REVIEW CHUNKS A, B, C, AND D
- Take an active approach to reviewing all four chunks.
- Make sure you have committed every concept, fact, formula, process, and so on to memory.
- Take a timed practice test. Write out complete answers so that concepts and words stick in your memory.
- Create a sheet with important information to memorize (again) on test day.

TEST DAY—DO YOUR BEST WORK

- Look at your last-minute study sheet right before you enter the test room so that difficult information sticks.
- As soon as you get your test, write down critical facts on the back of the paper.

Source: Adapted from the University of Arizona, "The Eight-Day Study Plan," http://ulc.arizona.edu/documents/8day_074.pdf.

- *Use organizational tools.* Rely on an outline, a think link, or another organizational tool to record material with logical connections among the elements. (See Chapter 6 for more on note taking.)
- *Be mindful when studying more than one subject.* When studying for several tests at once, avoid studying two similar subjects back-to-back. Your memory may be more accurate when you study history after biology rather than chemistry after biology.
- *Notice what ends up in the middle—and practise it.* When studying, you tend to remember what you study first and last. The weak link is likely to be what you study midway. Knowing this, try to give this material special attention.

Recite, rehearse, and write

Repetition is a helpful memory tool. The more you can repeat, and the more ways you can repeat, the more likely you are to remember. Reciting, rehearsing, and writing help you diversify your repetition and maximize memory.

When you *recite* material, you repeat key concepts aloud, summarizing them in your own words, to aid memorization. *Rehearsing* is similar to reciting but is done silently. *Writing* is reciting on paper. The following steps represent one way to benefit from these strategies:

- Focus as you read on *main ideas*, which are usually found in the topic sentences of paragraphs. (See Chapter 5.) Then recite, rehearse, or write the ideas down.
- Convert each main idea into a keyword, phrase, or visual image—something easy to recall that will set off a chain of memories, bringing you back to the original material. Write each keyword or phrase on an index card.
- One by one, look at the keywords on your cards and recite, rehearse, or write all the associated information you can recall. Check your recall against the original material.

These steps are part of the process of consolidating and summarizing lecture and text notes as you study—a key study strategy explored later in this chapter.

Reciting, rehearsing, and writing involve more than rereading material and then parroting words out loud, in your head, or on paper. Because rereading does not necessarily require involvement, you can reread without learning. However, you cannot help but think and learn when you convert text concepts into key points, rewrite main ideas as keywords and phrases, and assess what you know and what you still need to learn.

Use flash cards

Flash cards give you short, repeated review sessions that provide immediate feedback. Either find an online site on which you can create electronic flash cards or use the front of a 3-by-5-inch index card to write a word, idea, or phrase you want to remember. Use the back for a definition, explanation, example, or other key facts. Key 7.7 shows two flash cards used to study for a psychology exam.

The following suggestions can help you make the most of your flash cards:

- *Use the cards as a self-test.* As you go through them, create two piles—the material you know and the material you are learning.
- *Carry the cards with you and review frequently.* You'll learn the most if you start using cards early in the course, well ahead of exam time.
- *Shuffle the cards and learn the information in various orders.* This method will help you avoid putting too much focus on some items and not enough on others.
- *Test yourself in both directions.* First, look at the terms and provide the definitions or explanations. Then turn the cards over and reverse the process.
- *Reduce the stack as you learn.* Eliminate cards when you know them well. As the pile shrinks, your motivation may grow. Do a final review of all the cards before the test.

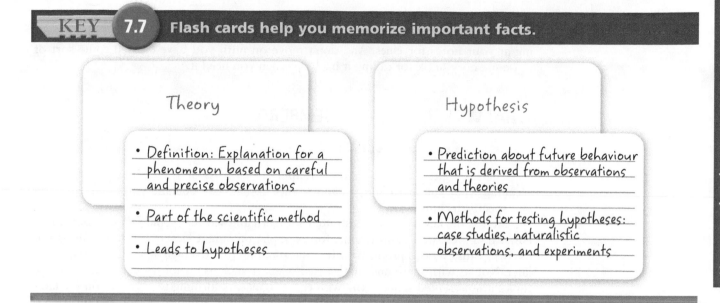

Theory

- Definition: Explanation for a phenomenon based on careful and precise observations
- Part of the scientific method
- Leads to hypotheses

Hypothesis

- Prediction about future behaviour that is derived from observations and theories
- Methods for testing hypotheses: case studies, naturalistic observations, and experiments

Use audio strategies

Although audio strategies can benefit all students, they are especially useful if you learn best through hearing.

- *Create audio flash cards.* Record short-answer study questions by leaving 10 to 15 seconds blank after questions, so you can answer out loud. Record the correct answer after the pause to give yourself immediate feedback. For example, part of a recording for a writing class might say, "Three elements that require analysis before writing are . . . [10–15-second pause] . . . topic, audience, and purpose."

- *Use podcasts.* An increasing amount of information is presented in podcasts—knowledge segments that are downloadable to your computer or MP3 player. Ask your instructors if they intend to make any lectures available in podcast format.

> **TIPS FOR LEARNING ONLINE**
>
> - *Connect with your classmates.* If your class uses a learning management system (LMS) you might be able to post course-related questions and comments in a discussion forum or a chat room. Share your class notes and acronyms or mnemonic devices with your classmates.
>
> - *Play games.* Most LMSs offer interactive games that review class material in an entertaining way. If your class doesn't have any online games, create your own by using social media or online survey tools.
>
> - *Search for apps.* Research for study applications (apps) for your smartphone and mobile devices, such as formula review sheets.

Use learning preference strategies

Thinking about any learning preference self-assessments you have completed in this course, identify your strongest areas and locate study techniques applicable for each. For example, if you scored high in bodily-kinesthetic, try reciting material aloud while standing or walking. Be open to trying something new—even if it sounds a little odd to begin with. Effective studying is about finding what works, often by any means necessary.

Mike Kemp/Getty Images

Use the information

In the days after you learn something new, try to use the information in every way you can. Apply it to new situations and link it to problems. Explain the material to a classmate. Test your knowledge to make sure the material is in long-term memory. "Don't confuse recognizing information with being able to recall it," says learning expert Adam Robinson. "Be sure you can recall the information without looking at your notes for clues. And don't move on until you have created some sort of sense-memory hook for calling it back up when you need it."[7]

WHAT WILL HELP YOU REMEMBER
math and science material?

The strategies you've just explored apply to all sorts of academic areas. However, recalling what you learn in math and science courses can demand particular attention and specific techniques.

Here is the key overarching strategy for math and science: *Avoid falling behind at all costs.* In a world religions course, for example, missing a lecture on Buddhism is not likely to cause serious problems with understanding the coverage of Taoism a few weeks later. Not so with math and math-based sciences such as chemistry and physics. These topics are presented sequentially with earlier concepts forming the foundation for later ones. You cannot effectively understand a later concept without a clear grasp of the concepts that precede it. Take calculated risks for the reward of staying on top of your work:[8]

- *Before class, read what will be covered.* You are more likely to grasp what your instructor covers if you have a baseline understanding of the concepts.
- *Read slowly and note symbols.* Go step by step through each process and description. Work to understand symbols—they are as important as numbers.
- *Stay on top of homework assignments.* Doing your homework is as important as reading when it comes to staying caught up.
- *When you have trouble, seek help fast.* Every day you wait can put you that much more behind. Consult your instructor, a tutor, or an experienced classmate.
- *Review processes and procedures.* Much of math and science work involves knowing how to work through each step of a proof, a problem-solving process, or a lab experiment. Review your class notes as soon as possible after each class. Look at your notes with the textbook alongside and compare the lecture information to the text. Fill in missing steps in the instructor's examples before you forget them. You may want to write the instructor's examples in the text next to the corresponding topics.
- *Do problems, problems, and more problems.* Working through problems provides examples that will help you understand concepts and formulas. Plus, becoming

Cindy Estrada; Shutterstock

talk risk and reward . . .

Risk asking tough questions to be rewarded with new insights. Use the following to inspire discussion with classmates in person or online.

- Every student experiences the frustration of needing to work hard to remember something that you think is completely unimportant and irrelevant to your life. How do you handle this, and what is the result? How *should* you handle it?

- What memorization techniques do you resist trying? Is it because they seem too unrelated to the information or too goofy? What would you be willing to risk to see if it works?

CONSIDER THE CASE: Whether you combine work and parenting with school or not, you have many demands on your time. Are you able to juggle it all? If not, what trips you up? If you were Cindy's advisor, how would you suggest she stay on top of her studies?

familiar with a group of problems and related formulas will help you apply what you know to similar problems on other assignments and tests.

- *Fight frustration with action.* If you are stuck on a problem, go on to another one. If you repeatedly get a wrong answer, look at the steps you've taken and see whether anything doesn't make sense. If you hit a wall, take a break to clear your head. If you have done the assigned homework but still do not feel secure, do additional problems or ask for help.

- *Work with others.* Working with one or more classmates can be particularly helpful when trying to figure out math and science problems. Do as much homework as you can on your own, and then meet to discuss it and work through additional problems. Be open to other perspectives, and ask others how they arrived at answers, especially if they used different approaches. When the work is really tough, try to meet daily, either in person or online.

- *Focus on learning preferences.* Use strategies that activate your strengths. A visual learner might draw pictures to illustrate problems, and an interpersonal learner might organize a study group. Musical learners might create songs describing math concepts. Barbara Aaker wrote 40 songs for her students at the Community College of Denver to help musical learners retain difficult concepts. Key 7.8 presents one of her algebra songs.

- *Strive for accuracy.* Complete a step of an algebra problem or biology lab project inaccurately, and your answer will be incorrect. In class, the consequences of inaccuracy are reflected in low grades. In life, the consequences could show in a patient's health or in the strength of a bridge. Check over the details of your work and always try to get it exactly right.

Because many math and science courses require you to memorize sets and lists of information, one key tool is the *mnemonic device*. As you will see next, mnemonic devices create sense-memory hooks that are difficult to forget.

KEY 7.8 Take a musical approach to math.

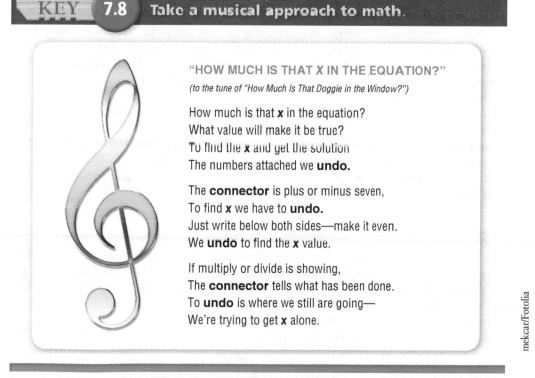

"HOW MUCH IS THAT X IN THE EQUATION?"
(to the tune of "How Much Is That Doggie in the Window?")

How much is that **x** in the equation?
What value will make it be true?
To find the **x** and get the solution
The numbers attached we **undo.**

The **connector** is plus or minus seven,
To find **x** we have to **undo.**
Just write below both sides—make it even.
We **undo** to find the **x** value.

If multiply or divide is showing,
The **connector** tells what has been done.
To **undo** is where we still are going—
We're trying to get **x** alone.

Source: Reprinted with permission. Barbara Aaker, *Mathematics: The Musical,* Denver: Crazy Broad Publishing, 1999.

187

get creative

CRAFT YOUR OWN MNEMONIC

Complete the following on paper or in digital format.

Create a mnemonic to help you remember some facts.

1. Identify a group of facts that you have to memorize—for example, the names of all the world's major religions or a series of elements in the periodic table.

2. Now create your own mnemonic to remember the grouping, using any of the devices in this chapter. Write the mnemonic out in detail.

3. Describe your mnemonic. Is it focused on images or sounds—or both? Is it humorous, ridiculous, or colourful?

4. Considering your learning style preferences, describe why you think this particular device will help you retain the information.

HOW CAN MNEMONIC DEVICES
boost recall?

Memory techniques known as mnemonic devices (pronounced neh-MAHN-ick) can help you learn and recall information. Mnemonics make information unforgettable through unusual mental associations and visual pictures. Instead of learning new facts by *rote* (repetitive practice), associations give you a hook on which to hang these facts and retrieve them later.

Because mnemonics take effort to create and motivation to remember, use them only when necessary—for instance, to distinguish confusing concepts that consistently trip you up. Also know that no matter how clever they are and how easy they are to remember, *mnemonics have nothing to do with understanding*. Their sole objective is to help you memorize.

Mnemonics all involve some combination of *imagination* (coming up with vivid images that are meaningful to you), *association* (connecting information you need to know with information you already know), and *location* (locating pieces of information in familiar places). They offer the reward of lasting memory in exchange for the risk of getting a little wacky. Here are some common types to try.

MNEMONIC DEVICES

Memory techniques that use vivid associations and acronyms to link new information to what you already know.

Stocksnapper/Fotolia

Visual Images and Associations

Turning information into mental pictures helps improve memory, especially for visual learners. To remember that the Spanish artist Picasso painted *The Three Women*, you might imagine the women in a circle dancing to a Spanish song with a pig and a donkey (*pig-asso*). The best images involve bright colours, three dimensions, action scenes, inanimate objects with human traits, and humour.

As another example, say you are trying to learn some Spanish vocabulary, including the words *carta*, *dinero*, and *libro*. Instead of relying on rote learning, you might come up with mental images, such as those described in Key 7.9.

KEY 7.9 Visual images aid recall.

SPANISH WORD	DEFINITION	MENTAL IMAGE
carta	letter	A person pushing a shopping cart filled with letters into a post office.
dinero	money	A man eating lasagna at a diner. The lasagna is made of layers of money.
libro	book	A pile of books on a table at a library.

The Method of Loci

This technique involves imagining yourself storing new ideas in familiar locations. Say, for example, that on your next biology test you have to remember the body's major endocrine glands. Think of your route to the library. You pass the theater, the science centre, the bookstore, the cafeteria, the athletic centre, and the social science building before reaching the library. At each spot along the way, you place a concept you want to learn. You then link the concept with a similar-sounding word that brings to mind a vivid image (Key 7.10):

- At the campus theatre, you imagine bumping into actor Brad *Pitt* (pituitary gland).
- At the science centre, you visualize a body builder with bulging *thighs* (thyroid gland).
- At the campus bookstore, you envision a second body builder with his *thighs* covered in *mustard* (thymus gland).
- In the cafeteria, you bump into *Dean Al* (adrenal gland).
- At the athletic centre, you think of the school team, the Panthers—nicknamed the Pans—and remember the sound of the cheer "*Pans-R-Us*" (pancreas).
- At the social science building, you imagine receiving a standing *ovation* (ovaries).
- And at the library, you visualize sitting at a table taking a *test* that is *easy* (testes).

Acronyms

Another helpful association method involves (acronyms). In history class, you can remember the Allies during World War II—Britain, America, and Russia—with the acronym *BAR*. This example is a *word acronym*, because the first letters of the items you want to remember spell a word. The word (or words) spelled don't necessarily have to be real words. See Key 7.11 for an acronym—the name *Roy G. Biv*—that will help you remember the colours of the spectrum.

> **ACRONYM**
> A word formed from the first letters of a series of words created to help you remember the series.

Other acronyms take the form of an entire sentence, in which the first letters of the words in the sentence stand for the first letters of the memorized terms. This is called a *list order acronym*. When astronomy students want to remember the list of planets in order of distance from the Sun (Mercury, Venus, Earth, Mars, Jupiter, Saturn, Uranus, and Neptune), they might learn the sentence *My very elegant mother just served us nectarines*.

Suppose you want to remember the names of the first six prime ministers of Canada. The first letters of their last names—Macdonald, Mackenzie, Abbott, Thompson, Bowell, and Tupper—together read *MMATBT*. To remember them, you

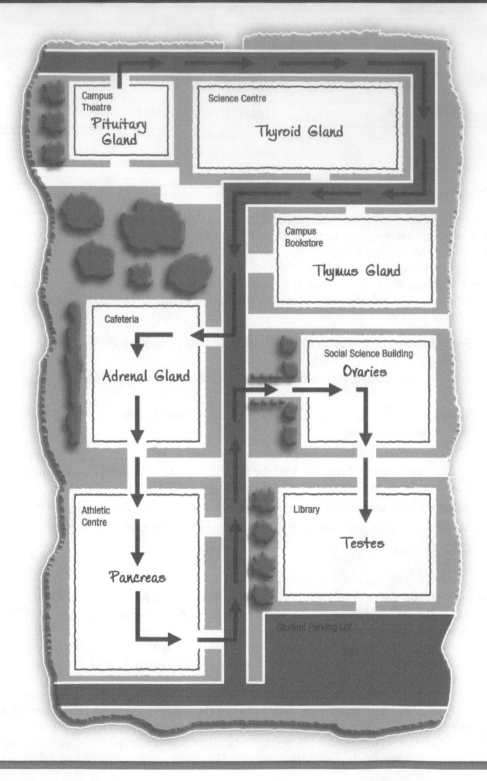

KEY 7.11 Use this acronym to remember the colours of the spectrum.

red
orange
yellow
green
blue
indigo
violet

R O Y G B I V

might add a *y* to the end and create a short nonsense word—*mmatbty*—and remember it as the word *mmat-bity*. Since there are two *t*'s in your nonsense word, just remember that alphabetically, and historically, Thompson comes before Tupper.

Songs or Rhymes

Some of the classic mnemonic devices are rhyming poems that stick in your mind. One you may have heard is the rule about the order of *i* and *e* in spelling:

> Spell i before e, except after c, or when sounded like a as in neighbour and weigh. Four exceptions if you please: either, neither, seizure, seize.

Make up your own poems or songs, linking familiar tunes or rhymes with information you want to remember. For example, to continue our earlier example, if you wanted to remember the first names, as well as the last names, of the first six Canadian prime ministers—John, Alexander, John, John, Mackenzie, and Charles—you might set the names to the tune of "Happy Birthday," or any other musical tune you know.

Improving your memory requires energy, time, and work. It also helps to master SQ3R, the textbook study technique introduced in Chapter 5. By going through the steps in SQ3R and by using the specific memory techniques described in this chapter, you will be able to learn more in less time—and remember what you learn long after exams are over. These techniques will be equally valuable when you start a career.

WHAT STUDY STRATEGIES HELP
you put it all together?

Especially in the later stages of review, strategies that help you combine and condense information are crucial. Such strategies help you relate information to what you know, connect information in new ways, and boost your ability to use it to think analytically and creatively, which is especially important for essay exams.

student PROFILE

Tia Nguyen
RYERSON UNIVERSITY, TORONTO, ONTARIO

About me:

I was born in Vietnam, in the city formerly known as Saigon. In the 1980s, my family and I escaped from Vietnam as refugees running from poverty and war. We arrived in Canada as immigrants when I was only three years old and my younger brother was learning to crawl. There was a lot of pressure on me because I was expected to do well in school and set an example for my younger brother. I struggled for a while, trying to figure out what I wanted to do before dedicating everything to my post-secondary education—I didn't want to waste time on the wrong program if I wasn't sure what I wanted to do. I decided to explore the work world to discover what options I had and what I'd enjoy doing. A few years ago, I decided to return to school and applied as a mature student. After being out of school for so long, the first semester at college was definitely a struggle for me. Three years later, I've obtained an advanced diploma in Business Administration—Marketing with honours from Seneca College. From there, I continued on as a direct-entry student to Ryerson University, where I'm working on obtaining a Bachelor of Commerce in Marketing Management with a minor in Finance. And I'm now sitting here writing about what student success means to me to encourage future post-secondary students—who knew?

What I focus on:

I am a visual learner. This learning style affected my study habits because I knew how important it was for me to attend every class. Being a visual learner meant that I needed to see the professor lecture and listen to his or her speech while watching visual presentations and words being written on the board. Sometimes, it's these exact visual memories that trigger a terminology, concept, or theory for me. Writing clear notes was helpful for me because sometimes during tests and examinations, I could recall images of sentences and paragraphs that I had written and could read them in my own script.

Recognizing my visual preference, to develop time-management skills, I invested in a huge wall calendar and notebook-size day planner. The wall calendar was organized, and entries were emphasized, with different colours to highlight important dates and grade percentages that I pulled directly from my course outline. While studying at my desk every night, I was reminded by my visual layout of the month of which days were going to be busiest and how far in advance I would need to begin certain assignments. And because I couldn't carry my enormous wall calendar around school—otherwise I might have!—I needed an 8½-by-11-inch planner for exactly the same purpose. It was a visual reminder, every moment of every day, of what I needed to do next.

Finally, during their in-class lectures, most professors will hint at what you can expect to see on class tests and final exams. If you listen carefully and take great notes, you can record these hints and then focus on these topics while studying. It'd be silly not to use this information to your advantage.

What will help me in the workplace:

My advice for students is to get started on things early! This will definitely help you in the workplace. Don't get into the habit of leaving things to the last minute. Post-secondary education is a great time for you to learn and master certain skills and habits that will help you find better jobs and keep them. On another note, be an active student and participate in events and programs that your institution offers. If you manage your time well, then you'll have more opportunities to get involved in your school's community. It's the extra experience and knowledge that you learn outside of the classroom that will help you in the work world.

Tia Nguyen. Ryerson University, Toronto, Ontario. Reprinted by permission.

Create a Summary of Reading Material

When you summarize main ideas in your own words, you engage in analytical thinking, considering what is important to include as well as how to organize and link it together. To construct a summary, focus on the main ideas and examples that support them. Don't include your own ideas or evaluations at this point. Your summary should simply condense the material, making it easier to focus on concepts and interrelationships when you review.

Use the following suggestions for creating effective summaries:

- Choose material to summarize—a textbook chapter, for example, or an article.
- Before you summarize, identify the main ideas and key supporting details by highlighting or annotating the material.
- Wherever possible, use your own words. When studying a technical subject with precise definitions, you may have little choice but to use text wording.
- Try to make your writing simple, clear, and brief. Eliminate less important details.
- Consider creating an outline of your notes or the portion of the text so you can see the interrelationship among ideas.
- Include information from tables, charts, photographs, and captions in your summary; these visual presentations may contain important information not written in the text.
- Combine word-based and visual note-taking forms that effectively condense the information, such as a concept map, time line, chart, or outline.
- Use visual strategies such as a colour-coding system to indicate different ideas or different-coloured pens to indicate levels of importance for information.

Combine Class and Reading Notes Into a Master Set

Studying from either text or class notes alone is not enough, since your instructor may present material in class that is not in your text or may gloss over topics that your text covers in depth. The process of combining class and text notes enables you to see patterns and relationships among ideas, find examples for difficult concepts, and much more. It strengthens memory and offers a cohesive and comprehensive study tool, especially useful at midterm or finals time. Follow these steps to use a **master note set:**

> **MASTER NOTE SET**
> A complete, integrated note set that contains both class and text notes.

- *Step 1: Condense to what's important.* Reduce your combined notes so they contain only main ideas and key supporting details, such as terms, dates, formulas, and examples. (Eliminating the repetition you are likely to find in your notes will also help reduce the material.) Tightening and summarizing forces you to critically evaluate which ideas are most important and to rewrite your notes with only this material. As you begin to study, move back and forth between the full set and the reduced set. Key 7.12 shows a comprehensive outline and a reduced key-term outline of the same material.

- *Step 2: Recite what you know.* As you approach exam time, use the terms in your bare-bones notes as cues for reciting what you know about a topic. Many students assume that they know concepts simply because they understand what they read. This type of passive understanding doesn't necessarily mean that they can recreate the material on an exam or apply it to problems. Make the process more active by reciting out loud during study sessions, writing your responses on paper, making flash cards, or working with a partner.

- *Step 3: Use critical thinking.* Now reflect on ideas in the following ways as you review your combined notes:

  - Brainstorm examples from other sources that illustrate central ideas. Write down new ideas or questions that come up as you review.

  - Think of ideas from your readings or from class that support or clarify your notes.

Different Views of Freedom and Equality in the American Democracy

I. U.S. democracy based on 5 core values: freedom and equality, order and stability, majority rule, protection of minority rights, and participation.

    A. U.S. would be a "perfect democracy" if it always upheld these values.

    B. U.S. is less than perfect, so it is called an "approaching democracy."

II. Freedom and Equality

    A. Historian Isaiah Berlin defines freedom as either positive or negative.

       1. Positive freedoms allow citizens to exercise rights under the Constitution, including right to vote.

       2. Negative freedoms safeguard citizens from government actions that restrict certain rights, such as the right to assemble. The 1st Amendment restricts government action by declaring that "Congress shall make no law . . ."

    B. The value of equality suggests that all people be treated equally, regardless of circumstance. Different views on what equality means and the implications for society.

       1. Equality of opportunity implies that everyone has the same chance to develop inborn talents.

          a. But life's circumstances—affected by factors like race and income—differ. This means that people start at different points and have different results. E.g., a poor, inner-city student will be less prepared for college than an affluent, suburban student.

          b. It is impossible to equalize opportunity for all Americans.

       2. Equality of result seeks to eliminate all forms of inequality, including economic differences, through wealth redistribution.

    C. Freedom and equality are in conflict, say text authors Berman and Murphy: "If your view of freedom is freedom from government intervention, then equality of any kind will be difficult to achieve. If government stays out of all citizen affairs, some people will become extremely wealthy, others will fall through the cracks, and economic inequality will multiply. On the other hand, if you wish to promote equality of result, then you will have to restrict some people's freedoms—the freedom to earn and retain an unlimited amount of money, for example."*

KEY-TERM OUTLINE OF THE SAME MATERIAL

Different Views of Freedom and Equality in the American Democracy

I. America's 5 core values: freedom and equality, order and stability, majority rule, protection of minority rights, and participation.

    A. "Perfect democracy"

    B. "Approaching democracy"

II. Value #1—Freedom and equality

    A. Positive freedoms and negative freedoms

    B. Different views of equality: equality of opportunity versus equality of result

    C. Conflict between freedom and equality centres on differing views of government's role

*Larry Berman and Bruce Allen Murphy, *Approaching Democracy: Portfolio Edition*, Upper Saddle River, NJ: Prentice Hall, 2005, pp. 6–8. Printed and electronically reproduced by permission of Pearson Education, Inc., Upper Saddle River, NJ.

- Consider how your class notes differ from your reading notes and why.

- Apply concepts to questions at the ends of text chapters, to problems posed in class, or to real-world situations.

■ *Step 4: Create study sheets.* Putting your master notes in their shortest, most manageable (and portable) form, *a study sheet* is a one-page synthesis of all key points on one theme, topic, or process. Use critical thinking skills to organize information into themes or topics that you will need to know on an exam. On an individual study sheet, include the related lecture and text page references, a quick summary, possible questions on the topic, key terms, formulas, dates, people, examples, and so on.

■ *Step 5: Review and review again.* To ensure learning and to prepare for exams, review your condensed notes, study sheets, and critical thinking questions until you know every topic cold. Try to vary your review methods, focusing on active involvement. Recite the material to yourself, have a Q and A session with a study partner, or create and take a practice test. Another helpful technique is to summarize your notes in writing from memory after reviewing them. This process will tell you whether or not you'll be able to recall the information on a test.

revisit RISK AND REWARD

Cindy Estrada

What happened to Cindy? Working nights allowed Cindy to attend college during the day. Without compromising her work duties, she was able to find time on the night shift to review that day's lessons. Writing out classroom notes in longhand helped her retain information. After graduating with her bachelor's from Wyoming, Cindy's company paid for her to get her master's degree, and ultimately her hard work earned her the reward of a promotion to senior manager. "Being a Hispanic woman was a hurdle," she says. "I needed fortitude. I had to gain the customers' trust and confidence. For me it's always been about building relationships."

Cindy's willingness to take targeted risks is evident in her recreational pursuits too. She is an accomplished marathon runner, having tackled the famed Boston Marathon as well as road treks in Honolulu and at the foot of Mount Everest. Now a director of program management at Goodman Networks, Cindy recently conquered a new challenge—breast cancer. "It's taking things one day at a time, reaching within and really discovering what type of inner strength you have," she says of beating cancer. "Believe me, it was like a hundred Everest marathons."

What does this mean for you? A strong work ethic, supportive family, and open-minded employer helped Cindy study and retain information for her coursework while holding down a job to support her young son. What are your two biggest time commitments outside of schoolwork? Name them; then, for each, identify the times you are committed to and how much time you spend per week total. Now describe how each affects your study time and your ability to retain information. Finally, determine what risks you need to take to maximize your retention—adjusting commitments, studying during work, reshuffling your schedule, and so on.

What risk may bring reward beyond your world? Everything that students accomplish in college or university owes a debt to someone who helped somewhere along the way. Even if you need support, keep in mind that your own help and expertise can offer rewards to others. Perhaps you could be the one to help someone else adjust a schedule, improve memory skills, or study more effectively. Check your school's website to see what tutoring services are offered and whether there is a peer advising or mentoring group you can consider.

RISK ACTION
FOR POST-SECONDARY, CAREER, AND LIFE REWARDS

KNOW IT *Think Critically*

Evaluate Your Memory

Build basic skills. For each of these classifications of information in long-term memory, write down an example from your personal experience:

- *Episodic memory* (events). Example: I remember the first time I conducted an experiment in chemistry class.
- *Declarative memory* (facts). Example: I know that the party that wins the most seats in a federal election forms the next government in Canada.
- *Procedural memory* (motion). Example: I know how to type without looking at the keyboard.

Take it to the next level. Answer the following:

1. Which type of information (events, facts, motion) is easiest for you to remember? Why?

2. Which type of information is hardest for you to remember? Why?

Move toward mastery. Address the type of information you find *most difficult* to remember.

1. Name an example from your life of some information in this category that you need to be able to recall and use.

2. Name two approaches from the chapter that you believe will help you strengthen it.

3. Now use both during your next study session. Afterward, identify the one that works best.

WRITE IT *Communicate*

Emotional intelligence journal: How feelings connect to study success. Think about how you were feeling when you were most able to recall and use information in a high-stress situation—a test, a workplace challenge, a group presentation. What thought, action, or situation put you in this productive mindset that helped you succeed? Did you go for a run? Talk to your best friend? Take 30 minutes for yourself? Create a list of thoughts or actions that you can call on when you will be faced with a challenge to your memory and want the best possible outcome.

Real-life writing: Combining class and text notes. Choose a course for which you have a test coming up in the next four weeks. Create a master set of notes for that course, combining one week's classes and reading assignments. (Make sure it is material you need to know for your test). Your goal is to summarize and connect all the important information covered during the period.

WORK IT *Build Your Brand*

Memory and Networking

21st Century Learning Building Blocks

- Communication and collaboration
- Social and cross-cultural skills

Your ability to remember people you meet or interact with in the workplace—their names, what they do, and other relevant information about them—is an enormous factor in your career success.

Consider this scenario: You are introduced to your supervisor's new boss, someone who is in a position to help you advance in the company, and you both exchange small talk for a few minutes. A week later you run into him outside the building. If you greet him by name and ask whether his son is over the case of the flu he had, you have made a good impression that is likely to help you in the future. If you call him by the wrong name, realize your mistake, and slink off to work, you may have set up a bit of a hurdle for yourself as you try to get ahead.

With what you know about memory strategies and what works for you, set up a system to record and retain information about people you meet whom you want to remember. For your system, decide on a tool (address book, set of notecards, electronic organizer, computer file), what to record (name, phone, email, title, how you met, important details), and how you will update the information. Choose a tool that you are most likely to use and that will be easy for you to refer to and update.

1. Name the tool of choice

2. List the information you will record for each entry

3. Describe when you will record information and how often you will check/update it.

8

Jay Dobyns

The best test preparation is learning, because the goal of a test is to see what you have learned. As you attend class, work on assignments, and participate in discussions, you become ever more ready to succeed in testing situations.

Test Taking

SHOWING WHAT YOU KNOW

What Would You Risk? *Jay Dobyns*

THINK ABOUT THIS SITUATION AS YOU READ, AND CONSIDER WHAT ACTION YOU WOULD TAKE. THIS CHAPTER HELPS YOU USE PREPARATION, PERSISTENCE, AND STRATEGY TO CONQUER TEST ANXIETY, SHOW WHAT YOU KNOW, AND LEARN FROM TEST MISTAKES.

Jay Dobyns

Raised in a solid middle-class home, Jay Dobyns had everything a boy could want—a bike, a baseball glove, and a safe place to play. His parents were great role models, blue-collar workers who inspired Jay to overachieve. By high school, Jay was taking risks calculated to bring a specific reward—being a wide receiver in the National Football League.

Never the biggest or strongest or fastest, Jay was the hardest worker on the playing field, with a "gracious confidence" that fuelled his sports aspirations. At the University of Arizona, Jay earned Pac-10 all-conference honours. Academically, Jay was uninspired but got the job done, earning a degree in public administration. "All I cared about was catching footballs and school was simply a means for me to get to do that," Jay says. The big test for him was whether he could catch a football with 70 000 people watching. As with many student–athletes, his dream was derailed by the harsh reality of professional sports.

His next test? Map out a new career. Eager for the reward of serving others in an exciting atmosphere, Jay risked embarking on a career in federal law enforcement, as an undercover officer for the Bureau of Alcohol, Tobacco, and Firearms. "As an undercover agent, every day is a test," Jay says. "They aren't written tests or multiple choice. Your instructor is the criminal. You're trying to pass the test in the eye of the criminal."

Just four days into his ATF career, Jay was taken hostage by a drug addict and was shot point blank in the back; the bullet pierced Jay's lung and exited his chest. Once an athlete destined for NFL greatness, Jay was lying in the dirt, bleeding to death. Jay's risk had presented him with the ultimate test—and no guarantee if a reward would follow.

To be continued . . .

Jay's life tests have required focus, passion, and grace under pressure. Your tests might be of a vastly different nature, but you will need skill and fortitude to pass them. You'll learn more about Jay, and the reward resulting from his actions, within the chapter.

Notes   52% ⬛   ➕

Today   Mar 10   8:01 AM

Working through this chapter will help you to:

How Prepared Are You for Taking Tests?

For each statement, circle the number that feels right to you, from 1 for "not at all true for me" to 5 for "very true for me."

1. I use strategies to help me predict what will be on tests. ① ② ③ ④ ⑤

2. I actively prepare and review before taking exams. ① ② ③ ④ ⑤

3. I do anything to avoid cramming. ① ② ③ ④ ⑤

4. When I recognize signs of test anxiety, I use relaxation methods to calm down. ① ② ③ ④ ⑤

5. I read test directions before beginning. ① ② ③ ④ ⑤

6. I use certain strategies to answer questions I'm unsure of. ① ② ③ ④ ⑤

7. I don't think cheating is worth the price. ① ② ③ ④ ⑤

8. I know the difference between objective and subjective questions and how to answer each. ① ② ③ ④ ⑤

9. I look for action verbs when answering essay questions. ① ② ③ ④ ⑤

10. I learn from my testing mistakes and actively grow from them. ① ② ③ ④ ⑤

Each of the topics in these statements is covered in this chapter. Note those statements for which you circled a 3 or lower. Skim the chapter to see where those topics appear, and pay special attention to them as you read, learn, and apply new strategies.

REMEMBER: NO MATTER HOW PREPARED YOU ARE FOR TAKING TESTS, YOU CAN IMPROVE WITH EFFORT AND PRACTICE.

HOW CAN PREPARATION IMPROVE
test performance?

Many students approach tests and exams with dread, seeing them as roadblocks, contests, or insurmountable obstacles. If you are one of these students, shift your mindset by considering this idea: *The goal of a test is to see what you have learned—and learning prepares you for tests.* As you attend class, stay on top of assignments, complete readings and projects, participate in class discussions, and generally do the day-to-day work of learning, you become ever more ready to succeed in testing situations. Re-envision the risk you are taking and the reward you seek. If learning is your reward and you are willing to risk time and energy to earn it, effective test performance is likely to come along with the package.

What makes a testing situation more challenging than demonstrating knowledge on your own terms is being required to show what you know during a pre-set period of time, in a certain setting, and with—or without—particular tools. You are generally not in charge of the circumstances. Coping with that is a crucial life skill, as it will be true

MyStudentSuccessLab

Whether face-to-face or online, MyStudentSuccessLab helps students build the skills they need through peer-led video interviews, interactive practice exercises, and activities that provide academic, life, and professionalism skills.

of most of the tests that come over the course of your life, and you often won't even know a test is coming, as was the case with Jay's life-threatening injury.

The following strategies engage your analytical, creative, and practical thinking skills and help you prepare for the challenge of test taking.

Gather Information

Test taking in school prepares you to solve problems and think, two skills listed by the Conference Board of Canada as being fundamental employability skills.[1] It's also about conquering fears, paying attention to details and learning from mistakes.

Before you begin studying, take practical steps to find out as much as you can about the test, including the following:

What type of test?

Investigate the following.

- *Types of questions.* Will the questions be objective (multiple choice with only one correct answer, multiple choice with more than one correct answer, true–false, sentence completion), subjective (essay), or a combination?
- *Test logistics.* What is the date, time, and location of the test? Is it an in-class or a take-home exam? Will you complete it in person or online?
- *Supplemental information and tools.* Is the test open-book (meaning you can use your class text)? Open-note (meaning you can use any notes you have taken)? Both? Or neither? Can you use a graphing calculator or any other tool?
- *Value of the test.* All tests are not created equal in terms of how they affect your final course grade. For example, a quiz is not as important as a midterm or final, although accumulated quiz grades do add up. Plan and prioritize your study time and energy according to the value of the quiz or test.

If you think that online tests and open book tests should be easier than traditional tests in the classroom, don't be fooled. In reality, the fact that you have access to resources usually leads instructors to create challenging tests that require more critical thinking. Don't fall into the trap of thinking you don't have to study for this type of test. If you prepare as you would any other test, chances are you will have a more successful result.

What are you expected to know?

Read your syllabus (Course Outline) and talk to your instructor to get a clear idea of the following.

- *Topics that will be covered.* Will the test cover everything since the term began or will it be more limited?
- *Material you will be tested on.* Will the test cover only what you learned in class and in the text or will it also include outside readings?

  What else can you do to predict what will be on a test?

- *Use your textbook.* Check features such as summaries, vocabulary terms, and study questions for clues about what is important to remember.
- *Listen at review sessions.* Many instructors offer review sessions before mid-terms and finals. Bring your questions to these sessions and listen to the questions others ask.
- *Make an appointment to see your instructor.* Spending a few minutes talking about the test one-on-one may clarify misunderstandings and help you focus on what to study.

- *Get information from people who already took the course.* Try to get a sense of test difficulty, whether tests focus primarily on assigned readings or class notes, what materials are usually covered, and the types of questions that are asked.
- *Examine old tests, if the instructor makes them available.* You may find old tests in class, online, or on reserve in the library. Old tests will help you answer questions like:
  - Do tests focus on examples and details, general ideas and themes, or a combination?
  - Are the questions straightforward or confusing and sometimes tricky?
  - Will you be asked to apply principles to new situations and problems?

Experience is a great teacher when it comes to test taking. After taking the first exam in a course, you will have a better idea of what to expect from that instructor over the rest of the term.

What Materials Should You Study?

With your understanding of what you need to know for the test, you can decide what to study.

- *Sort through materials.* Go through your notes, texts, related primary sources, and handouts. Choose what you need to study, and set aside materials you don't need.
- *Prioritize materials.* Arrange your chosen materials in order of priority so that you focus the bulk of your time on the information you most need to understand.

Use Time-Management Strategies to Schedule Study Time

Want to be as ready as possible for a test? Don't wait until the night before to study for it, and don't assume that paying attention during class time is enough. The most effective studying takes place in consistent segments over time. Use time-management skills to lay out a study schedule.

- *Consider relevant factors.* Note the number of days until the test, when in your days you have time available, and how much material you have to cover.
- *Schedule a series of study sessions.* If you need to, define what materials you will focus on for each session.
- *Enter study sessions in your planner.* Do this ahead of time, just as you would for a class, a work commitment, or any other important appointment. Then stick to your commitment.

Use Goal-Setting Strategies to Complete Your Plan

Here again, the skills you have built will prove essential to your success. Make getting ready for a test a SMART goal by making it:

- *Specific.* Get clear on what you will be tested on and what you need to study.
- *Measurable.* Acknowledge when you accomplish each study session.
- *Achievable.* Stay up-to-date with your coursework so that you can feel confident on test day.
- *Realistic.* Give yourself enough time and resources to get the job done.
- *Time Frame.* Anchor each step toward the test in your schedule.

student PROFILE

Kelcy McNally
UNIVERSITY OF PRINCE EDWARD ISLAND, CHARLOTTETOWN, PEI

About me:

I just successfully completed my first year at university and am looking forward to the next. While attending university I played on the varsity basketball team, which kept me on a tight schedule. I really wanted to focus on being a strong student as well as an athlete, and I believe I accomplished that by keeping my average in the 90s. Although my time was limited, I tried to do other things aside from school and basketball to have a good balance in my life. I am attending university in the hopes of getting a degree in Business Administration. After that, I plan to continue my education to become a chartered accountant.

What I focus on:

In university, I focused mainly on studying and making sure that I had a good balance of everything else in my life. Studying was difficult because of the limited amount of time I had; I was on the road almost every weekend for basketball. Also, some of the information was not interesting to me so I had to really focus in order to remember and understand it. Distractions are difficult to overcome when you are studying. To handle distractions, I usually isolate myself from anything that may cause me not to focus 100 percent. For example, I turn off my cellphone, shut off my laptop, and just focus on the subject at hand. Also, once I begin studying, I make sure to take short breaks so that I can refocus when I find it difficult to concentrate on the subject.

Knowing the way you study is also crucial. Although everyone is different, I prefer to study by thinking of possible test questions and trying to answer them to the best of my ability. I also like to create mnemonic devices in order to remember more information.

When you actually take a test, I suggest you write down what you know on the paper if you think you may forget it. Also, I would do the easy questions first, and if you come across a difficult one, mark it and then return to it later.

What will help me in the workplace:

While attending university I learned many things both inside and outside the classroom that will benefit me in the workplace. In classes, I learned fundamental skills and subject-specific knowledge. The fundamental skills included strong study habits, how to take good notes, and much more. Outside of my classes, I learned some valuable lessons about building strong relationships, working with others, and adapting to new environments. Many of these lessons were learned on the basketball team, and I know they will be useful in my future workplace.

Kelcy McNally. University of Prince Edward Island, Charlottetown, PEI. Reprinted by permission.

A comprehensive study plan will help you work SMART. Try using a plan like the one in Key 8.1. Consider making several copies and filling one out for each major test you have this term. You may prefer to create your own version, perhaps using Key 8.1 as a model and modifying it according to your specific needs. Format your version on a computer so that you can print out copies.

Review Using Study Strategies

Put your plan and schedule to work. Use what you have learned about learning, thinking, reading, memory, and studying during this course to understand and remember material:

- *Think analytically.* Post-secondary exams often ask you to analyze and apply material in more depth than you experienced in high school. For example, your

203

Complete the following checklist for each exam to define your study goals, get organized, and stay on track:

Course: _____ Instructor: _____

Date, time, and place of test: _____

Type of test (Is it a mid-term or a minor quiz?): _____

What instructor said about the test, including types of test questions, test length, and how much the test counts toward your final grade:

_____

_____

Topics to be covered on the test, in order of importance (information should also come from your instructor):

1. _____

2. _____

3. _____

4. _____

5. _____

Study schedule, including materials you plan to study (texts, class notes, homework problems, and so on) and dates you plan to complete each:

Material	**Completion Date**
1. _____	_____
2. _____	_____
3. _____	_____
4. _____	_____
5. _____	_____

Materials you are expected to bring to the test (textbook, sourcebook, calculator, and so on):

_____

_____

_____

Special study arrangements (such as planning study group meeting, asking the instructor for special help, getting outside tutoring):

_____

_____

_____

Life-management issues (such as rearranging work hours):

_____

_____

_____

Source: Adapted from Ron Fry, *"Ace" Any Test,* 3rd ed., Franklin Lakes, NJ: Career Press, 1996, pp. 123–124.

history instructor may ask you to place a primary source in its historical context. Prepare by continually asking analytical thinking questions and using the higher levels of Bloom's taxonomy.

- *Use SQ3R.* This reading method provides an excellent structure for reviewing your reading materials.
- *Consider your learning preferences.* Use study strategies that engage your strengths. When necessary, incorporate strategies that boost your areas of challenge.
- *Remember your best settings.* Use the locations, times, and company that suit you best.
- *Employ specific study strategies.* Consider your favourites. Use flash cards, audio strategies, chunking, anything that suits you and the material (see pages 191–195).
- *Create mnemonic devices.* These work exceptionally well for remembering lists or groups of items. Use mnemonics that make what you review stick.
- *Actively review your combined class and text notes.* Summaries and master sets of combined text and class notes provide comprehensive study tools.
- *Make and take a pretest.* Use end-of-chapter text questions to create a pretest. If your course does not have a text, develop questions from notes, assigned readings, and old homework problems. Some texts provide a website with online activites and pretests to help you review. Answer questions under test-like conditions—in a quiet place, with no books or notes (unless the exam is open book), and with a clock to tell you when to quit.

Part of successful test preparation is knowing when to stop. To avoid information overload, study in shorter segments over a period of time, and get the sleep you need before test day.

The Image Bank/Alvis Upitis/Getty Images

Prepare Physically

Most tests ask you to work at your best under pressure, so try to get a good night's sleep before the exam. Sleep improves your ability to remember what you studied before you went to bed.

Eating a light, well-balanced meal, including protein (eggs, milk, yogurt, meat or fish, nuts, or peanut butter) will keep you full longer than carbohydrates alone (breads, candy, or pastries). When time is short, don't skip breakfast—grab a quick meal, such as a few tablespoons of peanut butter, a banana, or a high-protein granola bar.

StockPhotosArt/Fotolia

Make the Most of Last-Minute Cramming

Cramming—studying intensively and around the clock right before an exam—often results in information going into your head and popping right back out when the exam is over. *If learning is your goal, cramming will not help you reach it.* The reality, however, is that you are likely to cram for tests, especially mid-terms and finals, from time to time in your post-secondary career. You may also cram if anxiety leads you to avoid studying. Use these hints to make the most of this study time:

- *Focus on crucial concepts.* Summarize the most important points and try to resist reviewing notes or texts page by page.
- *Create a last-minute study sheet to review right before the test.* Write down key facts, definitions, and formulas on a single sheet of paper or on flash cards.
- *Arrive early.* Review your study aids until you are asked to clear your desk.

get creative

WRITE YOUR OWN TEST

Complete the following on paper or in digital format.

Use the tips in this chapter to predict the material that will be covered, the types of questions that will be asked (multiple choice, essay, etc.), and the nature of the questions (a broad overview of the material or specific details).

Then be creative. Your goal is to write questions that your instructor is likely to ask—interesting questions that tap what you have learned and make you think about the material in different ways. Go through the following steps:

1. Write the questions you come up with on a separate sheet of paper.

2. Use what you created as a pretest. Set up test-like conditions—a quiet, timed environment—and see how you do.

3. Evaluate your pretest answers against your notes and the text. How did you do?

4. Finally, after you take the actual exam, evaluate whether you think this exercise improved your performance. Would you use this technique again? Why or why not?

Laurence Gough/Shutterstock

After the exam, evaluate how cramming affected your performance. Did it help, or did it load your mind with disconnected details? Did it increase or decrease anxiety at test time? Then evaluate how cramming affected your recall. Within a few days, you will probably remember very little—a reality that will work against you in advanced courses that build on the knowledge being tested and in careers that require it. Think ahead about how you can start studying earlier next time.

Prepare for Final Exams

Studying for final exams, which usually take place the last week of the term, is a major commitment that requires careful time management. Your college or university may schedule study days (also called a *reading period*) between the end of classes and the beginning of finals. Lasting from a day or two to several weeks, these days give you time to prepare for exams and finish papers. As tempting as it may be to blow off work for a portion of your reading period, try to take advantage of this precious study time. With classes no longer in your calendar, you have that much more time to work and prepare, and you will benefit from the extra effort.

End-of-year studying requires flexibility. Libraries are often packed, and students may need to find alternative locations. Consider outdoor settings (if weather permits), smaller libraries (many departments have their own libraries), and empty classrooms. Set up times and places that will provide the atmosphere you need.[2]

HOW CAN YOU WORK
through test anxiety?

A moderate amount of stress can be a good thing. You are alert, ready to act, and geared up to do your best. Some students, however, experience incapacitating stress before and during exams, especially mid-terms and finals. Test anxiety can cause sweating, nausea, dizziness, headaches, and fatigue. It can reduce concentration and cause you to forget everything you learned. Sufferers may get lower grades because their performance does not reflect what they know or because their fear has affected their ability to prepare effectively.

Two Sources of Test Anxiety

Test anxiety has two different sources, and students may experience one or both:[3]

- *Lack of preparation.* Not having put in the work to build knowledge of the material
- *Dislike of testing situations.* Being nervous about a test because of its very nature

For anxiety that stems from being unprepared, the answer is straightforward—get prepared. All of the information in this chapter about creating and implementing a study plan and schedule is designed to give you the best possible chance of doing well on the test. If you can stay calm as long as you feel ready, effective preparation is your key test anxiety strategy.

Unfortunately, being prepared doesn't necessarily ensure confidence. For students who dread the event no matter how prepared they are, just the fact of having a test—any test—causes anxiety. Because testing is unavoidable, this anxiety is more challenging to manage. Such students need to shift their mindset and build a positive attitude that says, "I know this material and I am ready to show it," although this is often easier said than done. To gear up for the next life test, for example, Jay had to overcome the disappointment of failing to make it in the NFL.

Anxiety is defined as an emotional disturbance, meaning that it tends to be based on an imagined risk rather than an actual one, and often leads you away from your goals rather than toward them.[4] If you experience test anxiety, analyze your situation to build a more realistic view of your risk and get back on track toward your goal of test success:

- Reconceive the negative risk and costly result you think you are facing, looking at the risk in a positive sense with a focus on the potential reward. Downplay the negative by considering the possibility that you may be more prepared than you realize, or that the test is not as important as it seems, or not as difficult as you believe it to be.

Test Taking

talk risk and reward . . .

Risk asking tough questions to be rewarded with new insights. Use the following to inspire discussion with classmates in person or online.

- What did you learn about yourself from the test-anxiety questionnaire (page 210)? If you experience test anxiety, what effect do you think it will have on your future?

- Which suggestions for reducing test-anxiety are you likely to use? How do you think they will help you feel more comfortable at test time? What other risks, however small, might reward you with better test performance?

CONSIDER THE CASE: The test that Jay faced was one of life or death. What in Jay's life before that time, do you think, prepared him to face this test? Talk about the greatest test life has given you so far. How did you handle it? What risk did you take that can inform how you can aim for rewards at test time?

Jay Dobyns; Shutterstock

- Define your goal for this test. Identify the physical and mental issues affecting your ability to reach that goal, and see which of them you can attribute to your anxiety.
- Build a realistic, positive, and productive attitude that says, "I know this material and I'm ready to show it." Key 8.2 provides several ways to do this.
- Assess your level of anxiety around test taking situations. Use the test-anxiety assessment on page 210 to determine if you have anxiety that preparation alone cannot eliminate.

Test-Time Strategies to Address Anxiety

It is test time, and you have arrived at the testing location—ideally a few minutes early—and you are waiting for the cue to begin. How can you be calm and focused? These strategies may help.

Manage your environment. Make a conscious effort to sit away from students who might distract you. If it helps, listen to relaxing music on an MP3 player while waiting for class to begin.

Reassure yourself with positive self-talk. Tell yourself that you can do well and that it is normal to feel anxious, particularly before an important exam.

Write down your feelings. Researchers have found that if students take a few minutes before an exam to put their feelings in writing, they post higher grades and have less anxiety. Without worrying about the quality of your writing, express your fears

KEY 8.2 **Use strategies to build a positive attitude and get prepared.**

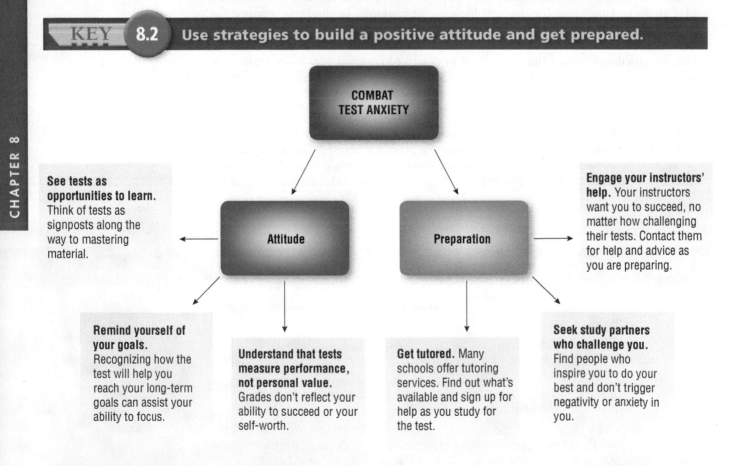

See tests as opportunities to learn. Think of tests as signposts along the way to mastering material.

Engage your instructors' help. Your instructors want you to succeed, no matter how challenging their tests. Contact them for help and advice as you are preparing.

Remind yourself of your goals. Recognizing how the test will help you reach your long-term goals can assist your ability to focus.

Understand that tests measure performance, not personal value. Grades don't reflect your ability to succeed or your self-worth.

Get tutored. Many schools offer tutoring services. Find out what's available and sign up for help as you study for the test.

Seek study partners who challenge you. Find people who inspire you to do your best and don't trigger negativity or anxiety in you.

and anxieties about the test on a piece of paper or your computer. "It's almost as if you empty the fears out of your mind," says researcher and psychology professor Sian Beilock.[5]

Practise relaxation. Close your eyes, breathe deeply and slowly, and visualize positive mental images like finishing the test with confidence. Or try a more physical tensing-and-relaxing method:[6]

1. Put your feet flat on the floor.
2. With your hands, grab underneath the chair.
3. Push down with your feet and pull up on your chair at the same time for about five seconds.
4. Relax for five to ten seconds.
5. Repeat the procedure two or three times.
6. Relax all your muscles except the ones that are actually used to take the test.

Bring a special object. If an object has special meaning for you—a photograph, a stone or crystal, a wristband, a piece of jewelry, a hat—it may provide comfort at test time. Bring it along and hold it, look at it, or wear it during the test. Let its presence settle and inspire you.

Some of these strategies may seem odd or embarassing. However, they might also make a difference for you. Consider whether you are willing to risk a little embarassment for the reward of doing well on a test. It just might be worth it.

Math Anxiety

For some students, math exams cause more anxiety than other academic areas. A form of test anxiety, *math anxiety* is often based on common misconceptions about math, such as the notion that people are born with or without an ability to think quantitatively or that men are better at math than women. Students who feel that they can't do math may give up without asking for help. At exam time, they may experience test anxiety symptoms that reduce their ability to concentrate and leave them feeling defeated.

All of the test anxiety strategies in this section will help combat math anxiety. In addition, math anxiety sufferers should focus heavily on problem solving—see the math and science study strategies on pages 229–231—and should seek help from instructors and tutors early and often.

Test Anxiety and the Returning Student

If you are returning to school after years away, you may wonder how well you will handle exams. To deal with these feelings, focus on what you have learned through life experience, including the ability to handle work and family pressures. Without even thinking about it, you may have developed many time-management, planning, organizational, and communication skills needed for college and university success.

In addition, your life experiences will give real meaning to abstract classroom ideas. For example, workplace relationships may help you understand social psychology concepts, and refinancing your home mortgage may help you grasp a key concept in economics—how the actions of the Bank of Canada influence interest rate swings.

WHAT GENERAL STRATEGIES CAN
help you succeed on tests?

Even though every test is different, certain general strategies will help you handle almost all tests, from short-answer to essay exams.

get practical

ASSESS TEST ANXIETY WITH THE WESTSIDE TEST ANXIETY SCALE

The first step toward becoming a fearless test taker is understanding your personal level of test anxiety. Answer the questions below as honestly as possible.

Rate how true each of the following is of you, from "always true" to "never true." Use the following 5-point scale. Circle your answers.

5 = always true; 4 = usually true; 3 = sometimes true; 2 = seldom true; 1 = never true

1. The closer I am to a major exam, the harder it is for me to concentrate on the material.	5 4 3 2 1
2. When I study for my exams, I worry that I will not remember the material on the exam.	5 4 3 2 1
3. During important exams, I think that I am doing awfully or that I may fail.	5 4 3 2 1
4. I lose focus on important exams, and I cannot remember material that I knew before the exam.	5 4 3 2 1
5. I remember answers to exam questions only after the exam is already over.	5 4 3 2 1
6. I worry so much before a major exam that I am too worn out to do my best on the exam.	5 4 3 2 1
7. I feel out of sorts or not really myself when I take important exams.	5 4 3 2 1
8. I find that my mind sometimes wanders when I am taking important exams.	5 4 3 2 1
9. After an exam, I worry about whether I did well enough.	5 4 3 2 1
10. I struggle with written assignments, or avoid doing them, because I want them to be perfect.	5 4 3 2 1

Sum of the 10 questions: _____

Now divide the sum by 10. Write it here. _____ This is your test anxiety score.

Compare your score against the following scale. How does your level of test anxiety rate? In general, students that score a 3.0 or higher on the scale tend to have more test anxiety than normal and may benefit from seeking additional assistance.

1.0–1.9   Comfortably low test anxiety
2.0–2.4   Normal or average test anxiety
2.5–2.9   High normal test anxiety
3.0–3.4   Moderately high (some items rated 4—high)
3.5–3.9   High test anxiety (half or more of the items rated 4—high)
4.0–5.0   Extremely high anxiety (items rated 4—high and 5—extreme)

Reflect on your results. Do they show a high level of test anxiety? A normal level? Based on what you've learned about yourself, select anxiety-reducing strategies that you will use when studying for or taking your next test. Record your plan on a sheet of paper or computer file.

Source: Used by permission of Richard Driscoll.

Apply Different Intelligences to Preparing for a Geometry Exam

INTELLIGENCE	USE MI STRATEGIES TO REMEMBER MORE EFFECTIVELY	APPLY MI TEST-PREP STRATEGIES TO STUDY FOR A TEST ON GEOMETRIC SHAPES AND MEASUREMENT*
Verbal-Linguistic	• Write test questions your instructor might ask. Answer the questions and then try rewriting them in a different format (essay, true/false, and so on). • Underline important words in review or practice questions.	• Underline important vocabulary words in the chapter. Then make a set of flash cards, with the word on one side and the definition on the other. Test yourself.
Logical-Mathematical	• Logically connect what you are studying with what you know. Consider similarities, differences, and cause-and-effect relationships. • Draw charts that show relationships and analyze trends.	• Create a table that highlights the similarities and differences among polygons, circles, and three-dimensional shapes. Use columns to note qualities such as number of sides, number of angles, measurement of angles, formulas that apply consistently, and special features (for example, in a rectangle, all angles are right angles).
Bodily-Kinesthetic	• Use text highlighting to take a hands-on approach to studying. • Create a sculpture, model, or skit to depict a tough concept that will be on the test.	• Use pencils, Popsicle sticks, pipe cleaners, containers, or other materials to create the shapes on which you will be tested.
Visual-Spatial	• Make charts, diagrams, or think links illustrating concepts. • Make drawings related to possible test topics.	• Draw illustrations that represent all of the postulates (statements assumed to be true) in the chapter.
Interpersonal	• Form a study group to prepare for your test. • In your group, come up with possible test questions. Then use the questions to test each other's knowledge.	• With a study partner, work through the exercise set on polygons and circles. Try either working through problems together or having partners teach problems to each other.
Intrapersonal	• Apply concepts to your own life; think about how you would manage. • Brainstorm test questions and then take the sample test you developed.	• Reread your text to reinforce you knowledge of geometry. Using the Internet, search for examples of geometry in the real world. Then write two additional ideas about how geometry relates to your world.
Musical	• Recite text concepts to rhythms or write a song to depict them. • Explore relevant musical links to reading material.	• Write a song that helps you remember the types of triangles and their definitions.
Naturalistic	• Try to notice similarities and differences in objects and concepts by organizing your study materials into relevant groupings.	• Create a table or visual organizer that arranges all the types of two- and three-dimensional shapes into logical groupings.

*For information on geometric shapes and measurement, see Gary L. Musser, Lynn E. Trimpe, and Vikki R. Maurer, *College Geometry: A Problem-Solving Approach with Applications*, 2nd ed., Upper Saddle River, NJ: Pearson/Prentice Hall, 2008.

Test Taking

Test-Day Strategies

Choose the right seat. Find a seat that will put you in the right frame of mind and minimize distractions. Choose a place near a window, next to a wall, or in the front row so you can look into the distance. Know yourself—for many students, it is smart to avoid sitting near friends.

Write down key facts. Before you even look at the test, write down key information, including formulas, rules, and definitions, that you don't want to forget. (Use the back of the question sheet so your instructor knows that you made these notes after the test began.)

Start with the big picture Spend a few minutes at the start of the test gathering information about the questions—how many of which types are in each section, along with their point values. Use this information to schedule your time. Take level of difficulty into account as you parcel out your time. For example, if you think you can do the short-answer questions in 45 minutes and sense that the writing section will take longer, you can budget 1 hour and 15 minutes for the essay.

Directions count, so read them. Reading test directions carefully can save you trouble. For example, you may be required to answer only one of three essay questions, or you may be penalized for incorrect responses to short-answer questions.

Mark up the questions. Mark up instructions and keywords to avoid careless errors. Circle qualifiers such as *always*, *never*, *all*, *none*, *sometimes*, and *every*; verbs that communicate specific instructions; and concepts that are tricky or need special attention.

QUALIFIERS
Words and phrases that can alter the meaning of a test question and thus require careful attention.

Be precise when taking a machine-scored test. Use the right pencil (usually a no. 2) on machine-scored tests, and mark your answer in the correct space, filling it completely. Periodically check answer numbers against question numbers to make sure they match.

Work from easy to hard. Begin with the easiest questions and answer them quickly without sacrificing accuracy. This technique will boost your confidence and leave more time for harder questions. Mark tough questions as you reach them, and return to them after answering the questions you know.

Watch the clock. If you are worried about time, you may rush through the test and have time left over. When this happens, check over your work instead of leaving early. If, on the contrary, you are falling behind, be flexible about the best use of the remaining time.

DURIS Guillaume/Fotolia

Take a strategic approach to questions you cannot answer. Key 8.3 has ideas to consider when you face questions that stump you.

Use special techniques for math tests. Use the general test-taking strategies presented in this chapter as well as the techniques in Study Tools: Slay the Math Anxiety Dragon to achieve better results on math tests.

Maintain Academic Integrity

Although cheating has the immediate gain of possibly passing a test or getting a few free answers, its long-term consequences aren't so beneficial. If you cheat, you run the risk of being caught and subsequently disciplined (which can include expulsion), not to mention

Understand what to do if you don't know the answer.

Ask for clarification. → Sometimes a simple rewording will make you realize that you do know the material.

Skip the question and come back to it later. → Letting your subconscious mind work on the question sometimes can make a difference.

Build logical connections. → Take a calculated risk by using what you already know about the topic.

Bring up a "mental map" of your notes. → Remembering where material was covered in your notes and text may jog your memory about content.

Just start writing. → The act of writing about related material may help you recall the targeted information. You may want to do this kind of writing on a spare scrap of paper, think about what you've written, and then write your final answer on the test paper or booklet.

that you probably will not actually learn the material. Cheating that goes on your record can also damage your ability to get a job. As the Conference Board of Canada states, being responsible is an important employability skill.

In recent years, cheating has become high-tech, with students putting all kinds of devices to dishonest uses. Examples include:[7]

- Texting answers from cell phones or smartphones
- Using in-phone cameras to take pictures of tests to send to friends or sell online
- Using graphing calculators to save formulas that were supposed to have been memorized
- With an online connection, finding answers on crowd-sourcing sites such as Quora
- Sharing answers on private all-student groups connected to learning management systems

Because this type of cheating can be difficult to discover when exams are administered in large lecture halls, some instructors ban all electronic devices from the room.

Valid concerns can put students under pressure: "I have to do well on the final. I am in a time crunch. I need a good grade to qualify for the next course in my major. I can't fail because I am already in debt and I have to graduate and get a job." Compounded, these worries can often drive students to thoughts of academic dishonesty. However, feeling the drive to cheat generally means you haven't learned the material. Ask yourself: Am I in college or university to learn information that I can use? Or to cheat my way to a decent GPA and breathe a sigh of relief when the term is done? Retention of knowledge is necessary both to complete future coursework and to thrive in jobs that require you to use it. Only one course of action will earn you that reward.

The risk of cheating may bring a starkly different reward than the risk of staying honest even in the face of a lack of preparation. The next time you are tempted to break the rules of academic integrity, remember: The choice is yours, and so are the consequences. Key 8.4 shows you some choices and potential consequences of cheating on a final exam.

KEY 8.4   **Think through the consequences of cheating.**

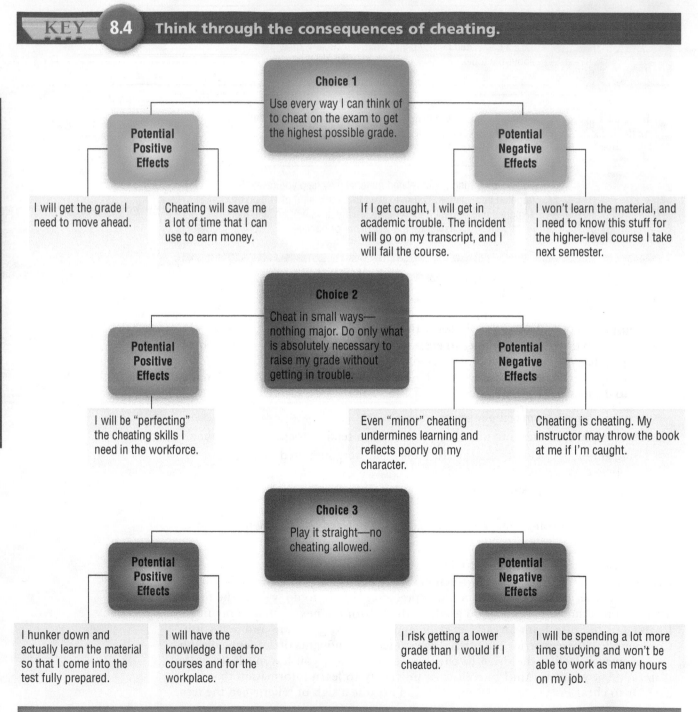

Choice 1
Use every way I can think of to cheat on the exam to get the highest possible grade.

Potential Positive Effects

I will get the grade I need to move ahead.

Cheating will save me a lot of time that I can use to earn money.

Potential Negative Effects

If I get caught, I will get in academic trouble. The incident will go on my transcript, and I will fail the course.

I won't learn the material, and I need to know this stuff for the higher-level course I take next semester.

Choice 2
Cheat in small ways—nothing major. Do only what is absolutely necessary to raise my grade without getting in trouble.

Potential Positive Effects

I will be "perfecting" the cheating skills I need in the workforce.

Potential Negative Effects

Even "minor" cheating undermines learning and reflects poorly on my character.

Cheating is cheating. My instructor may throw the book at me if I'm caught.

Choice 3
Play it straight—no cheating allowed.

Potential Positive Effects

I hunker down and actually learn the material so that I come into the test fully prepared.

I will have the knowledge I need for courses and for the workplace.

Potential Negative Effects

I risk getting a lower grade than I would if I cheated.

I will be spending a lot more time studying and won't be able to work as many hours on my job.

get $mart

PhotoMan/Fotolia

As with any academic area of study, knowledge of basic terms is a necessary foundation on which to build understanding. Test your knowledge of some financial literacy terminology with this matching exercise.

1. ____finance charge	A. A number assigned to you based on your credit activity—higher numbers are better.
2. ____net worth	B. Using more money than you have available in a bank account.
3. ____RRSP	C. Your total financial assets—cash, savings, property—minus your debt.
4. ____debit card	D. A percentage charged annually on the amount of a loan or credit card debt.
5. ____overdraft	E. A first payment on a large purchase that you cannot cover all at once.
6. ____credit score	F. When someone acquires and uses your personal information without your consent.
7. ____interest	G. When you use it, the purchase amount is subtracted from your bank account.
8. ____APR	H. A percentage that you earn on savings or pay on borrowed money or credit.
9. ____down payment	I. What it costs you to use credit; can be a percentage of what you owe, or a flat fee.
10. ____identity theft	J. An account designed to help you save money for retirement.

HOW CAN YOU MASTER DIFFERENT
types of test questions?

Every type of test question is a different way of finding out how much you know. Questions fall into two general categories.

- *Objective questions.* You generally choose or write a short answer, often selecting from a limited number of choices, for objective questions. They can include multiple-choice, fill-in-the-blank, matching, and true/false questions.
- *Subjective questions.* Demanding the same information recall as objective responses, subjective questions also require you to plan, organize, draft, and refine a response. All essay questions are subjective.

Key 8.5 shows samples of real test questions from Western civilization, macroeconomics, Spanish, and biology post-secondary texts published by Pearson Education. Included are exercises and multiple-choice, true/false, fill-in-the-blank, matching, and essay questions. Analyzing the types, formats, and complexities of these questions will help you gauge what to expect when you take your exams.

Look also at the Multiple Intelligence Strategies for Test Preparation on page 211. Harness the strategies that fit your learning strengths to prepare for geometry exams.

Note that some suggestions are repeated in the following sections in order to reinforce the importance of these suggestions and their application to different types of test questions.

Test Taking

**FROM CHAPTER 29, "THE END OF IMPERIALISM,"
IN *WESTERN CIVILIZATION: A SOCIAL AND CULTURAL HISTORY*, 2ND EDITION**

• **MULTIPLE-CHOICE QUESTION**

India's first leader after independence was:

A. Gandhi   B. Bose   C. Nehru   D. Sukharno

(answer: C)

• **FILL-IN-THE-BLANK QUESTION**

East Pakistan became the country of _____ in 1971.

A. Burma   B. East India   C. Sukharno   D. Bangladesh

(answer: D)

• **TRUE/FALSE QUESTION**

The United States initially supported Vietnamese independence.

T   F

(answer: false)

• **ESSAY QUESTION**

Answer one of the following:

1. What led to Irish independence? What conflicts continued to exist after independence?

2. How did Gandhi work to rid India of British control? What methods did he use?

**FROM CHAPTER 6, "UNEMPLOYMENT AND INFLATION," IN *MACROECONOMICS:
PRINCIPLES AND TOOLS*, 3RD EDITION**

• **MULTIPLE-CHOICE QUESTION**

If the labour force is 250 000 and the total population 16 years of age or older is 300 000, the labour-force participation rate is

A. 79.5%   B. 83.3%   C. 75.6%   D. 80.9%

(answer: B)

• **FILL-IN-THE-BLANK QUESTION**

Mike has just graduated from college and is now looking for a job, but has not yet found one. This causes the employment rate to _____ and the labour-force participation rate to _____.

A. increase; decrease   C. stay the same; stay the same
B. increase; increase   D. increase; stay the same

(answer: C)

• **TRUE/FALSE QUESTION**

The Consumer Price Index somewhat overstates changes in the cost of living because it does not allow for substitutions that consumers might make in response to price changes.   T   F   *(answer: true)*

• **ESSAY QUESTION**

During a press conference, Canada's Finance Minister notes that the unemployment rate is 5.0%. As a political opponent, how might you criticize this figure as an underestimate? In rebuttal, how might the minister argue that the reported rate is an overestimate of unemployment?

(Possible answer: The unemployment rate given by the finance minister might be considered an underestimate because discouraged workers, who have given up the job search in frustration, are not counted as unemployed. In addition, full-time workers may have been forced to work part-time. In rebuttal, the minister might note that a portion of the unemployed have voluntarily left their jobs. Most workers are unemployed only briefly and leave the ranks of the unemployed by gaining better jobs than they had previously held.)

Multiple-Choice Questions

Multiple-choice questions are the most popular type of question on standardized tests. The following analytical and practical strategies will help you answer them:

- *Read the directions carefully and try to think of the answer before looking at the choices.* Then read the choices and make your selection.

- *Underline keywords and significant phrases.* If the question is complicated, try to break it down into small sections that are easy to understand.

- *Make sure you read every word of every answer.* Focus especially on qualifying words such as *always*, *never*, *tend to*, *most*, *often*, and *frequently*. Look also for negatives in a question ("Which of the following is *not* …").

• MATCHING QUESTION

You are learning new words and your teacher asks you to think of an object similar to or related to the words he says. His words are listed below. Next to each word, write a related word from the list below.

el reloj   el cuaderno   el pupitre   una computadora

el televisor   la tiza   el lapis   la mochila

1. el escritorio _____   4. la pizarra _____

2. el bolígrafo _____   5. el libro _____

3. la videocasetera _____

(answers: 1. el pupitre; 2. el lápiz; 3. el televisor; 4. la tiza; 5. el cuaderno)

• ESSAY QUESTION

Your mother always worries about you and wants to know what you are doing with your time in Granada. Write a short letter to her describing your experience in Spain. In your letter, you should address the following points:

1. What classes you take

2. When and where you study

3. How long you study every day

4. What you do with your time (mention three activities)

5. Where you go during your free time (mention two places)

FROM CHAPTER 13, "DNA STRUCTURE AND REPLICATION," IN *BIOLOGY: A GUIDE TO THE NATURAL WORLD*, 2ND EDITION

• MULTIPLE-CHOICE QUESTION

What units are bonded together to make a strand of DNA?
A. chromatids   B. cells   C. enzymes   D. nucleotides
E. proteins   *(answer: D)*

• FILL-IN-THE-BLANK QUESTION

In a normal DNA molecule, adenine always pairs with _____ and cytosine always pairs with _____.

(answers: thymine, guanine)

• TRUE/FALSE QUESTION

Errors never occur in DNA replication, because the DNA polymerases edit out mistakes.   T   F

(answer: false)

• MATCHING QUESTIONS

Match the scientists and the approximate time frames (decades of their work) with their achievements.

Column 1	Column 2
_____ 1. Modelled the molecular structure of DNA	_____ A. George Beadle and Edward Tatum, 1930s and 1940s
_____ 2. Generated X-ray crystallography images of DNA	_____ B. James Watson and Francis Crick, 1950s
_____ 3. Correlated the production of one enzyme with one gene	_____ C. Rosalind Franklin and Maurice Wilkins, 1950s

(answers 1–B; 2–C; 3–A)

Sources: [*Western Civilization* test items] King, Margaret L., *Western Civilization: A Social & Cultural History*, 2nd Ed., (c) 2003. Reprinted and Electronically reproduced by permission of Pearson Education, Inc., Upper Saddle River, New Jersey. [*Macroeconomics* test items] O'Sullivan, Arthur; Sheffrin, Steven M., *Macroeconomics: Principles and Tools*, 3rd Ed., (c) 2003. Reprinted and Electronically reproduced by permission of Pearson Education, Inc., Upper Saddle River, New Jersey. [*Mosaicos* test items] Castells, Matilde Olivella; Guzman, Elizabeth E.; Lapuerta, Paloma E; Garcia, Carmen, *Mosaicos: Spanish As A World Language*, 3rd Ed., (c) 2002. Reprinted and Electronically reproduced by permission of Pearson Education, Inc., Upper Saddle River, New Jersey. [*Biology* test items] Krogh, David, *Biology: Guide To The Natural World*, 2nd Ed., (c) 2002. Reprinted and Electronically reproduced by permission of Pearson Education, Inc. Upper Saddle River, New Jersey.

■ *When questions are linked to a reading passage, read the questions first.* This strategy will help you focus on the information you need to answer the questions.

The following examples show the kinds of multiple-choice questions you might encounter in an introductory psychology course (the correct answer follows each question):

1. Arnold is at the company party and has had too much to drink. He releases all of his pent-up aggression by yelling at his boss, who promptly fires him. Arnold normally would not have yelled at his boss, but after drinking heavily he yelled because

Test Taking

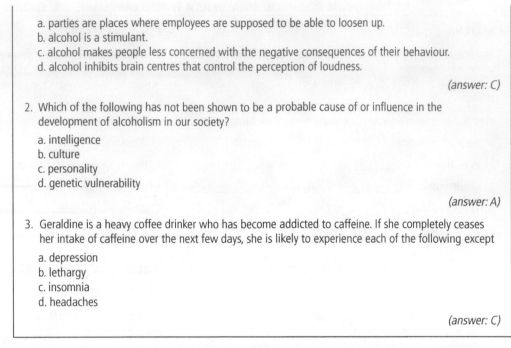

a. parties are places where employees are supposed to be able to loosen up.

b. alcohol is a stimulant.

c. alcohol makes people less concerned with the negative consequences of their behaviour.

d. alcohol inhibits brain centres that control the perception of loudness.

(answer: C)

2. Which of the following has not been shown to be a probable cause of or influence in the development of alcoholism in our society?

   a. intelligence

   b. culture

   c. personality

   d. genetic vulnerability

(answer: A)

3. Geraldine is a heavy coffee drinker who has become addicted to caffeine. If she completely ceases her intake of caffeine over the next few days, she is likely to experience each of the following except

   a. depression

   b. lethargy

   c. insomnia

   d. headaches

(answer: C)

Source: Gary W. Piggrem and Charles G. Morris, *Test Item File for Understanding Psychology*, 3rd ed., © 1996 Prentice-Hall, Inc. Reprinted by permission of Pearson Education, Inc., Upper Saddle River, NJ.

True/False Questions

Read true/false questions carefully to evaluate what they are asking. Look for absolute qualifiers (such as *all*, *only*, or *always*, which often make an otherwise true statement false) and conservative qualifiers (such as *generally*, *often*, *usually*, or *sometimes*, which often make an otherwise false statement true). For example, "The grammar rule '*i* before *e* except after *c*' is *always* true" is false, whereas "The grammar rule '*i* before *e* except after *c*' is *usually* true" is true.

Be sure to read every word of a true/false question to avoid jumping to an incorrect conclusion. Common problems in reading too quickly include missing negatives (such as *not* or *no*) that would change your response and deciding on an answer before reading the complete statement.

The following examples show the kinds of true/false questions you might encounter in an introductory psychology course (the correct answer follows each question):

Are the following questions true or false?

1. Alcohol use is clearly related to increases in hostility, aggression, violence, and abusive behaviour. *(true)*

2. Marijuana is harmless. *(false)*

3. Simply expecting a drug to produce an effect is often enough to produce the effect. *(true)*

4. Alcohol is a stimulant. *(false)*

Source: Gary W. Piggrem and Charles G. Morris, *Test Item File for Understanding Psychology*, 3rd ed., © 1996 Prentice-Hall, Inc. Reprinted by permission of Pearson Education, Inc., Upper Saddle River, NJ.

Matching Questions

Matching questions ask you to match the terms in one list with the entries in another list. For example, the directions may tell you to match a communicable disease with the microorganism that usually causes it. The following strategies will help you handle these questions.

- *Make sure you understand the directions.* The directions tell you whether each answer can be used only once (common practice) or more than once.

- *Work from the column with the longest entries.* The column on the left usually contains terms to be defined or questions to be answered, and the column on the right usually contains definitions or answers. As a result, entries on the right are usually longer than those on the left. Reading those items only once will save time.

- *Start with the matches you know.* On your first run-through, pencil in these matches. When you can use an answer only once, you may have to adjust if you rethink a choice.

- *Finally, tackle the matches you're not sure of.* Think back to your class lectures, text notes, and study sessions as you try to visualize the correct response. If one or more phrases seem to have no correct answer and you can use answers only once, consider the possibility that one of your sure-thing answers is wrong.

Fill-in-the-Blank Questions

Fill-in-the-blank questions, also known as *sentence completion questions*, ask you to supply one or more words or phrases to complete the sentence. These strategies will help you make successful choices.

- *Be logical.* Insert your answer; then reread the sentence from beginning to end to be sure it makes sense and is factually and grammatically correct.

- *Note the lengths and number of the blanks.* If two blanks appear right after each other, the instructor is probably looking for a two-word answer. If a blank is longer than usual, the correct response may require additional space.

- *If there is more than one blank and the blanks are widely separated, treat each one separately.* Answering each as if it were a separate sentence-completion question increases the likelihood that you will get at least one answer correct.

- *If you are uncertain, guess.* Have faith that after hours of studying, the correct answer is somewhere in your subconscious mind and that your guess is not completely random.

The following examples show fill-in-the-blank questions you might encounter in an introductory astronomy course (correct answers follow questions):

1. A _____ is a collection of hundreds of billions of stars. *(galaxy)*

2. Rotation is the term used to describe the motion of a body around some _____. *(axis)*

3. The solar day is measured relative to the sun; the sidereal day is measured relative to the _____. *(stars)*

4. On December 21, known as the _____ _____, the sun is at its _____ _____. *(winter solstice; southernmost point)*

Source: Eric Chaisson and Steve McMillan, *Astronomy Today*, 3rd ed., 1999. Reprinted by permission of Pearson Education, Inc., Upper Saddle River, NJ.

Essay Questions

Essay questions ask you to express your knowledge and views in a less structured way than short-answer questions. With freedom of thought and expression comes

the challenge to organize your ideas and write well under time pressure. The following steps—in part a shortened version of the writing process (see Appendix A)—will help you plan, draft, revise, and edit your responses.

1. *Read every question.* Decide which to tackle (if there is a choice). Use critical thinking to identify exactly what the question is asking.

2. *Map out your time.* Schedule how long to allot for each answer, remembering that things don't always go as planned. Above all, be flexible.

3. *Focus on action verbs.* Key 8.6 shows verbs that tell you what to do to answer the question. Underline action verbs and use them to guide your writing.

4. *Plan.* Think about what the question is asking and what you know. On scrap paper, outline or map your ideas and supporting evidence. Then develop a thesis statement that defines your content and point of view. Don't skimp on planning. Not only does planning result in a better essay, but it also reduces stress because it helps you get in control.

5. *Draft.* Note the test directions before drafting your answer. Your essay may need to be of a certain length, for example, or may need to take a certain format. Use the following guidelines as you work:

- State your thesis, and then get right to the evidence that backs it up.
- Structure your essay so that each paragraph presents an idea that supports the thesis.
- Use clear language and tight logic to link ideas to your thesis and to create transitions between paragraphs.
- Look back at your planning notes periodically to make sure you cover everything.
- Wrap it up with a short, to-the-point conclusion.

6. *Revise.* Although you may not have the time to rewrite your entire answer, you can improve it with minor changes. Check word choice, paragraph structure, and style. If you notice anything missing, use editing marks to neatly insert it into the text. When you are done, make sure your response is the best possible representation of your ideas.

As you check over your essay, ask yourself questions about it:

- Have I answered the question?
- Does my essay begin with a clear thesis statement, and does each paragraph start with a strong topic sentence that supports the thesis?
  - Have I provided the support necessary in the form of examples, statistics, and relevant facts to prove my argument, organized with tight logic?
  - Have I covered all the points in my original outline or map?
  - Is my conclusion an effective wrap-up?

7. *Edit.* Check for mistakes in grammar, spelling, punctuation, and usage. Correct language—and neat, legible handwriting—leaves a positive impression and helps your grade.

KEY 8.6 Focus on action verbs in essay tests.

ANALYZE—Break into parts and discuss each part separately.

COMPARE—Explain similarities and differences.

CONTRAST—Distinguish between items being compared by focusing on differences.

CRITICIZE—Evaluate the issue, focusing on its problems or deficiencies.

DEFINE—State the essential quality or meaning.

DESCRIBE—Paint a complete picture; provide the details of a story or the main characteristics of a situation.

DIAGRAM—Present a drawing, chart, or other visual.

DISCUSS—Examine completely, using evidence and often presenting both sides of an issue.

ELABORATE ON—Start with information presented in the question, and then add new material.

ENUMERATE/LIST/IDENTIFY—Specify items in the form of a list.

EVALUATE—Give your opinion about the value or worth of a topic and justify your conclusion.

EXPLAIN—Make meaning clear, often by discussing causes and consequences.

ILLUSTRATE—Supply examples.

INTERPRET—Explain your personal views and judgments.

JUSTIFY—Discuss the reasons for your conclusions or for the question's premise.

OUTLINE—Organize and present main and subordinate points.

PROVE—Use evidence and logic to show that a statement is true.

REFUTE—Use evidence and logic to show that a statement is not true, or tell how you disagree with it.

RELATE—Connect items mentioned in the question, showing, for example, how one item influenced another.

REVIEW—Provide an overview of ideas and establish their merits and features.

STATE—Explain clearly, simply, and concisely.

SUMMARIZE—Give the important ideas in brief, without comments.

TRACE—Present a history of a situation's development, often by showing cause and effect.

Key 8.7 shows a student's completed response to an essay question on body language, including the word changes and inserts she made while revising the draft.

To answer an essay question for a communications test, one student created the planning outline shown in Key 8.8 (page 223). Notice how abbreviations and shorthand help the student write quickly.

Test Taking

221

QUESTION: Describe three ways that body language affects interpersonal communication.

Body language plays an important role in interpersonal communication and helps shape the impression you make. Two of the most important functions of body language are to contradict and reinforce verbal statements. When body language contradicts verbal language, the message ~~conveyed~~ delivered by the body is dominant. For example, if a friend tells you that she is feeling "fine," but her posture is slumped, and her facial expression troubled, you have every reason to wonder whether she is telling the truth. If the same friend tells you that she is feeling fine and is smiling, walking with a bounce in her step, and has direct eye contact, her body language is ~~telling the truth.~~

, especially when you meet someone for the first time (margin note)

her eye contact minimal, (margin note)

accurately reflecting and reinforcing her words. (margin note)

The nonverbal cues that make up body language also have the power to add shades of meaning. Consider this statement: "This is the best idea I've heard all day." If you were to say this three different ways—in a loud voice while standing up; quietly while sitting with arms and legs crossed and looking away; and while ~~maintening~~ maintaining eye contact and taking the receiver's hand—you might send three different messages.

Finally, the impact of nonverbal cues can be greatest when you meet someone for the first time. When you meet someone, you tend to make assumptions based on nonverbal behaviour such as posture, eye contact, gestures, and speed and style of movement.

Although first impressions emerge ~~from a combination of nonverbal cues, tone of voice, and choice of words,~~ nonverbal elements (cues and tone) ~~usually come~~ across first and strongest. (margin note)

In summary, nonverbal communication plays a ~~crusial~~ crucial role in interpersonal relationships. It has the power to send an accurate message that may ~~destroy~~ belie the speaker's words, offer shades of meaning, and set the tone of a first meeting.

Neatness is crucial. No matter how good your ideas are, if your instructor can't read them, your grade will suffer. If your handwriting is a problem, try printing or skipping every other line, and be sure to write on only one side of the page. Students with illegible handwriting might ask to take the test on a computer.

The purpose of a test is to see how much you know, not merely to get a grade. Embrace this attitude to learn from your mistakes.

> Essay question: Describe three ways in which body language affects interpersonal communication.
>
> Roles of BL in IC
>   1. To contradict or reinforce words
>   —e.g., friend says "I'm fine"
>   2. To add shades of meaning
>   —saying the same sentence in 3 diff. ways
>   3. To make lasting 1st impression
>   —impact of nv cues and voice tone greater than words
>   —we assume things abt person based on posture, eye contact, etc.

WHAT CAN YOU LEARN
from test mistakes?

Congratulations! You've finished the exam, handed it in, and gone home to a well-deserved night of sleep. At the next class meeting, you've returned refreshed, rejuvenated, and ready to accept a high score. As you receive the test back from your instructor, you look wide-eyed at your grade. *How could that be?*

No one aces every test. And no one understands every piece of the material perfectly. Making mistakes on tests and learning from them is as much a part of your academic experience as studying, taking notes, working with others, and yes, even getting good grades. After all, if you never made any mistakes, what would you have to learn from?

The most important idea to remember when moving on from a bad grade is not to beat yourself up about it. Instead, benefit from it by looking realistically at what you could have done better. With exam in hand, consider the following areas to identify what you can correct—and perhaps change the way you study for, or take, your next exam.

Ask yourself global questions that may help you identify correctable patterns. Honest answers can help you change the way you study for the next exam.

- What were your biggest problems? Did you get nervous, misread the question, fail to study enough, study incorrectly, or focus on memorizing material instead of on understanding and applying it? Did your instructor's comments clarify where you slipped up? Did your answer lack specificity? Did you fail to support your thesis well? Was your analysis weak?

Sarah Lyman Kravits

Evaluating their test results will help these students understand their performance as well as learn from their mistakes.

Test Taking

223

WRITE TO THE VERB

Complete the following on paper or in digital format

Focusing on the action verbs in essay test instructions can mean the difference between giving instructors what they want and answering off the mark. Get to know action verbs a little better.

Choose three verbs from Key 8.6 that you've seen used in essay questions. List each verb. Then, for each, write out what the verb inspires you to do without reusing the verb. In other words, don't say that "describe" asks you to describe.

Now put your choices to work.

1. Name a topic you have learned about in this text—for example, the concept of successful intelligence or different barriers to listening.

2. Put yourself in the role of instructor. Write an essay question on this topic, using one of the action verbs from Key 8.6 to frame the question. For example, "List the three aspects of successful intelligence" or "Analyze the classroom-based challenges associated with internal barriers to listening."

3. Now rewrite your original question twice more, using the other two action verbs you chose, and adjusting the question to the verb each time.

4. Finally, analyze how each new verb changes the focus of the essay. Describe the goal of each essay question and note how they differ.

- Were you surprised by the questions? For example, did you expect them all to be from the lecture notes and text instead of from your notes and supplemental readings?
- Did you make careless errors? Did you misread the question or directions, blacken the wrong box on the answer sheet, skip a question, or write illegibly?
- Did you make conceptual or factual errors? Did you misunderstand a concept? Did you fail to master facts or concepts?

Rework the questions you got wrong. Based on instructor feedback, try to rewrite an essay, recalculate a math problem from the original question, or redo questions following a reading selection. If you discover a pattern of careless errors, redouble your efforts to be more careful, and save time to double-check your work.

After reviewing your mistakes, fill in your knowledge gaps. If you made mistakes because you didn't understand important concepts, develop a plan to learn the material.

Talk to your instructor. Focus on specific mistakes on objective questions or a weak essay. The fact that you care enough to review your errors will make a good impression. If you are not sure why you were marked down on an essay, ask what you could have done better. If you feel that an essay was unfairly graded, ask for a rereading. When you use your social intelligence and approach your instructor in a nondefensive way, you are likely to receive help.

Rethink the way you studied. Make changes to avoid repeating your errors. Use the varied techniques in *Keys to Success* to study more effectively so that you can show yourself and your instructors what you are capable of doing. The earlier in the term you make positive adjustments the better, so make a special effort to analyze and learn from early test mistakes.

If you fail a test, don't throw it away. Use it to review troublesome material, especially if you will be tested on it again. You might also want to keep it as a reminder that you can improve. When you compare a failure to later successes, you will see how far you have come.

A final word—tests reflect your ability to *show* what you know. They do not necessarily indicate what you know, and certainly they do not define who you are. Understand the limitations of tests. Learn from them and take from them what reward you can as you move into the greater test of life in the 21st century.

revisit RISK AND REWARD

Jay Dobyns

What happened to Jay? Saved by a skilled trauma surgeon, Jay went on to become one of the most legendary agents in ATF history. "Being shot empowered me," Jay says. "It showed me that ... I did want to be the guy that would stand up to the violence on behalf of my community." Known on the streets and in the law enforcement community as "Jaybird," he risked infiltrating the Hells Angels motorcycle gang as an undercover agent, earning the extraordinary reward of being the first law enforcement officer to defeat the gang's multilayered security measures to become a full patched member. His 2009 memoir, "No Angel: My Harrowing Undercover Journey to the Inner Circle of the Hells Angels," became a *New York Times* bestseller. Jay retired with 12 ATF Special Act Awards for excellence in criminal investigations. Now married and the father of two, Jay is a motivational speaker. "My presentations are not hero stories," Jay says. "I spend more time talking about the mistakes I made and the failures and regrets. ... I hope people listen to my stories and don't make the same mistakes I made."

What does this mean for you? To ace the test of being an undercover agent, Jay armed himself with knowledge. "I studied criminals. How they talked, walked, looked, dressed, what they drove, where they lived, how they interacted. Crime environments were my school room." Knowledge and experience are the keys to passing school tests as well as life tests such as relationships or career challenges. Risk revisiting your most recent tests. Describe how you prepared for a school test; then, list up to three things you could have done to prepare more effectively. Now do the same for a recent life test. How would you grade yourself on this test?

What risk may bring reward beyond your world? Jay's 17 years of undercover street work came at a price. "It darkened my outlook and personality. I had lost faith in people," Jay says. Jay then met Ed Harrow, the founder of Heartbeat for Africa, a faith-based nonprofit that provides clean water systems and medical care to children and orphans in the Volta Region of Ghana, West Africa. Reluctantly, Jay traveled to Africa on a Heartbeat mission, witnessing extreme poverty but encountering people full of spirit and hope. "They restored my faith in humanity," Jay says. Visit heartbeatforafrica.org to learn more about the organization's mission. Then consider how you can risk moving past your own ups and downs to create reward for someone else—locally, nationally, or internationally. What cause inspires emotions in you and makes you wish you could help? Research online and turn that wish into reality.

Test Taking

KNOW IT *Think Critically*

Prepare Effectively for Tests

Take a careful look at your performance on and preparation for a recent test.

Build basic skills. Think about how you did on the test. Were you pleased or disappointed with your performance and grade? Explain your answer.

List any of the problems you feel you experienced on this exam. If you experienced one or more problems not listed here, include them in your document. For each problem you identified, think about why you made mistakes.

- Incomplete preparation
- Fatigue
- Feeling rushed during the test
- Shaky understanding of concepts
- Poor guessing techniques
- Feeling confused about directions
- Test anxiety
- Poor essay organization or writing

Take it to the next level. Be creative about test-preparation strategies. If you had all the time and materials you needed, how would you have prepared for this test? Describe briefly what your plan would be and how it would address your problem(s).

Now think back to your actual test preparation—the techniques you used and the amount of time you spent. Describe the difference between your ideal study plan and what you actually did.

Move toward mastery. Improve your chances for success on the next exam by coming up with specific changes in your preparation.

1. Actions I took this time but do not intend to do next time:
2. Actions I did not take this time but intend to do next time:

WRITE IT *Communicate*

Record your thoughts on paper, in a journal, or electronically.

Emotional intelligence journal: Test types. What type of test do you feel most comfortable with, and what type brings up more negative feelings? Thinking of a particular situation involving the test type that challenges you, describe how it made you feel and how that feeling affected your performance. Discuss ways in which you might be able to shift your mindset in order to feel more confident about this type of test.

Real-life writing: Instructor feedback on a test. Nearly every student has been in the position of believing that a response on an essay exam was graded unfairly. The next time this happens to you—when you have no idea why you lost points or disagree with the instructor's assessment of your work—draft a respectful email to your instructor explaining your position and asking for a meeting to discuss the essay. (See the email etiquette guidelines in Quick Start to College and University.) Use clear logic to defend your work and refer to what you learned in class and in the text. It is important to specifically address any comments or criticisms the instructor made on the test paper. Before sending the email, analyze your argument: Did you make your case effectively or was the instructor correct? When you have the meeting, the work you did on the email will prepare you to defend your position.

WORK IT *Build Your Brand*

On-the-Job Testing

21st Century Learning Building Blocks

- Information literacy
- Initiative and self-direction
- Productivity and accountability

You will probably encounter different tests throughout your career. For example, if you are studying to be a nurse, you are tested on subjects such as anatomy and pharmacology. After you graduate, you will be required to take certification and recertification exams that gauge your mastery of the latest information in different aspects of nursing.

Some postgraduate tests are for entry into the field; some test proficiency on particular equipment; some move you to the next level of employment. Choose one career you are thinking about and investigate what tests are involved as you advance through different career stages.

Use the accompanying grid to organize what you find. You will be searching for the following information:

- The name of the test
- When the test is taken and if it needs to be retaken

- What it covers
- How you can prepare
- Web resources such as pretests, websites, or review materials

Test name	When Taken	What it Covers	Preparation	Web Resources

Answers to Get $mart quiz:

1. **I**
2. **C**
3. **J**
4. **G**
5. **B**
6. **A**
7. **H**
8. **D**
9. **E**
10. **F**

Study Tools: *Get Ready for Exams*

Slay the Math Anxiety Dragon

A special form of test anxiety, math anxiety is based on common misconceptions about math, such as the notion that people are born with or without an ability to think quantitatively or that men are better at math than women. Students who feel they can't do math may give up without asking for help. On exams, these students may experience a range of physical symptoms—including sweating, nausea, dizziness, headaches, and fatigue—that reduce their ability to concentrate and leave them feeling defeated.

The material in this Study Tools section is designed to help you deal with the kind of math-related anxiety that affects your grades on exams. As you learn concrete ways to calm your nerves and discover special techniques for math tests, you will feel more confident in your ability to succeed.

Use Special Techniques for Math Tests

Use the general test-taking strategies presented in this chapter as well as the techniques below to achieve better results on math exams.

- *Read through the exam first.* When you first get an exam, read through every problem quickly and make notes on how you might attempt to solve the problems.
- *Analyze problems carefully.* Categorize problems according to type. Take the givens into account, and write down any formulas, theorems, or definitions that apply before you begin. Focus on what you want to find or prove.
- *Estimate before you begin to come up with a ballpark solution.* Work the problem and check the solution against your estimate. The two answers should be close. If they are not, recheck your calculations. You may have made a calculation error.

Gauge Your Level of Math Anxiety

Use the questionnaire in Key 8.9 to get an idea of your math anxiety level.

IMPROVE YOUR MATH PERFORMANCE WITH THESE TECHNIQUES.

- Break the calculation into the smallest possible pieces. Go step by step and don't move on to the next step until you are clear about what you have done so far.
- Recall how you solved similar problems. Past experience can provide valuable clues.
- Draw a picture to help you see the problem. Visual images such as a diagram, chart, probability tree, or geometric figure may help clarify your thinking.
- Be neat. Sloppy numbers can mean the difference between a right and a wrong answer. A 4 that looks like a 9 will be marked wrong.
- Use the opposite operation to check your work. Work backward from your answer to see if you are right.
- Look back at the question to be sure you did everything. Did you answer every part of the question? Did you show all required work?

Rate each of the following statements on a scale of 1 (Strongly Disagree) to 5 (Strongly Agree).

1. _____ I cringe when I have to go to math class.

2. _____ I am uneasy when asked to go to the board in a math class.

3. _____ I am afraid to ask questions in math class.

4. _____ I am always worried about being called on in math class.

5. _____ I understand math now, but I worry that it's going to get really difficult soon.

6. _____ I tend to zone out in math class.

7. _____ I fear math tests more than any other kind.

8. _____ I don't know how to study for math tests.

9. _____ Math is clear to me in math class, but when I go home it's like I was never there.

10. _____ I'm afraid I won't be able to keep up with the rest of the class.

SCORING KEY

40–50   Sure thing, you have math anxiety.

30–39   No doubt! You're still fearful about math.

20–29   On the fence.

10–19   Wow! Loose as a goose!

Source: Freedman, Ellen. (March 1997). *Test Your Math Anxiety* [online]. Available: www.mathpower.com/anxtest.htm (May 2004).

The best way to overcome math-related anxiety is through practice. Keeping up with your homework, attending class, preparing well for tests, and doing extra problems will help you learn the material and boost your confidence.

Following are 10 additional ways to reduce math anxiety and do well on tests.

1. Overcome your negative self-image about math by remembering that even Albert Einstein wasn't perfect.

2. Ask questions of your teachers and your friends, and seek outside assistance when needed.

3. Math is a foreign language—practise it often.

4. Don't study mathematics by trying to memorize information and formulas.

5. READ your math textbook.

6. Study math according to your personal learning style.

7. Get help the same day you don't understand something.

8. Be relaxed and comfortable while studying math.

9. "TALK" mathematics. Discuss it with people in your class. Form a study group.

10. Develop a sense of responsibility for your own successes and failures.

Source: Adapted from Freedman, Ellen. *Ten Ways to Reduce Math Anxiety* [online]. Available: www.mathpower.com/reduce.htm (May 2004).

DECIDE HOW WELL THESE TECHNIQUES WORK FOR YOU. Use what you just learned about yourself and math to answer the following questions:

- What did you learn from the math anxiety questionnaire? Describe your current level of math anxiety.

_____

_____

_____

- What effect do you think your attitude toward math will have on your future?

_____

_____

_____

- Which suggestions for reducing math anxiety are you likely to use? How do you think they will help you feel more comfortable with math?

_____

_____

_____

- Which suggestions for improving your performance on math tests are you likely to use?

_____

_____

_____

- What other ways can you think of to improve your math performance?

_____

_____

_____

Self-Study Quiz

Multiple Choice

Circle or highlight the answer that seems to fit best.

1. **The activity that lies at the heart of critical thinking is**
   A. solving problems.
   B. taking in information.
   C. reasoning.
   D. asking questions.

2. *Primary sources* **are defined as**
   A. periodicals.
   B. original documents.
   C. expert opinions on experimental results.
   D. resource materials.

3. **When in class, you should choose a note-taking system that**
   A. suits the instructor's style, the course material, and your learning style.
   B. you have used in other classes successfully.
   C. matches what you use when you study outside of class.
   D. is recommended by your instructor.

4. *Association* **means**
   A. considering how information is updated.
   B. finding the differences between two sets of information.
   C. considering new information on its own terms.
   D. considering new information in relation to information you already know.

5. **A library search strategy takes you from**
   A. specific reference works to general reference works.
   B. general reference works to specific reference works.
   C. encyclopedias to almanacs.
   D. encyclopedias to the Internet.

6. **When answering an essay question on a test**
   A. spend most of your time on the introduction because the grader sees it first.
   B. skip the planning steps if your time runs short.
   C. use the four steps of the writing process but take less time for each step.
   D. write your essay and then rewrite it on another sheet or booklet.

Fill in the Blanks

Complete the following sentences with the appropriate word(s) or phrase(s) that best reflect what you learned in the chapters. Choose from the items that follow each sentence.

1. The three parts of the path of critical thinking are _____, _____, and _____. (recall/idea to example/example to idea, taking in information/asking questions about information/using information, taking in information/using information/communicating information)

2. A broad range of interests and a willingness to take risks are two common characteristics of _____. (creativity, critical thinking, cause and effect)

3. When you begin to read new material, what you already know gives you _____ that help(s) you understand and remember new ideas. (ideas, context, headers)

4. In the Cornell note-taking system, section 2 is called the _____ and is used for filling in comments and diagrams as you review. (cue column, summary area, main body)

5. A(n) _____ is a memory technique that works by connecting information you are trying to learn with simpler or familiar information. (mnemonic device, acronym, idea chain)

6. _____ encourages you to put your _____ ideas on paper and is an important part of the _____ process. (Freewriting/uncensored/planning, Editing/polished/planning, Researching/censored/editing)

Essays

The following essay questions will help you organize and communicate your ideas in writing, just as you must do on an essay test. Before you begin answering a question, spend a few minutes planning (brainstorm possible approaches; write a thesis statement; jot down main thoughts in outline or think-link form). To prepare yourself for actual test conditions, limit writing time to no more than 30 minutes per question.

1. Describe the steps of the reading strategy SQ3R. What is involved in each step? How does each step contribute to your understanding of your reading material?

2. Write an essay that supports or rejects all or part of the following statement: "The tests you take in college or university not only help ensure that you acquire important skills and knowledge, but also help prepare you for the day-to-day learning demands that are associated with 21st century careers." If possible, support your position with references to career areas that interest you.

Louise Gaile Edrozo

Much of your school and work experience will involve teamwork, both in person and virtually. Interacting effectively with all kinds of people is crucial to your success now and throughout your life.

Diversity and Communication

MAKING RELATIONSHIPS WORK

What Would You Risk? *Louise Gaile Edrozo*

Louise Gaile Edrozo

THINK ABOUT THIS PROBLEM AS YOU READ, AND CONSIDER HOW YOU WOULD APPROACH IT. THIS CHAPTER FOCUSES ON THE DIVERSITY OF TODAY'S STUDENT BODY, EFFECTIVE COMMUNICATION WITH OTHERS, AND CONNECTING WITH OTHERS.

In her native Philippines, Gaile Edrozo was on track to earn a biology degree and begin medical school. However, financial difficulties derailed her plans. Needing more opportunity to work, she and her family came to North America in 2004.

Even as Gaile got started toward a productive goal, the financial burden of her education caused excessive stress and sleepless nights. The cost of her education was too high for her family to manage, even with the many sacrifices her parents were making. Even more frightening was the possibility that Gaile would lose her immigration status if she were unable to stay in school and would have to return to the Philippines alone, without her family.

Gaile felt overcome with fear that her dream to become a nurse and have a career she loved, as well as to contribute to her family financially, would be taken away as it had been in the Philippines. She threw herself into her schoolwork, hoping to be eligible for scholarships or other aid. However, none of the scholarships she explored was available to an international student. Sensing it was time to reach out for help, Gaile took the advice of fellow students and registered for Honours 100, a course at her school for both citizens and international students that helps students explore scholarship opportunities, prepare portfolio and resumé materials, and look at four-year institutions. She hoped her instructor could help her avoid losing her dream a second time.

to be continued . . .

Connecting with others opens up possibilities and can help you live your dreams. You will learn more about Gaile, and revisit her situation, within the chapter.

Source: Adapted from Highline College Honours Scholar Program Success Stories, with permission from Louise Gaile Edrozo.

Notes

Today   Mar 10 8:01 AM

Working through this chapter will help you to:

statusCHECK

How Developed Are Your Cultural Competence and Communication Skills?

For each statement, circle the number that feels right to you, from 1 for "not at all true for me" to 5 for "very true for me."

1. I am constantly working to develop cultural competence. ① ② ③ ④ ⑤

2. I seek to incorporate diverse people and cultures into my life. ① ② ③ ④ ⑤

3. I believe even positive stereotypes can hurt my ability to get to know someone. ① ② ③ ④ ⑤

4. I understand the difference between tolerating those different from me and accepting and celebrating those differences. ① ② ③ ④ ⑤

5. I am able to adjust to different communication styles when necessary. ① ② ③ ④ ⑤

6. I pay attention to and interpret meaning from nonverbal and body language. ① ② ③ ④ ⑤

7. I use positive relationship strategies to strengthen my personal connections. ① ② ③ ④ ⑤

8. I know the warning signs of destructive or hostile relationships. ① ② ③ ④ ⑤

9. I am aware of common date rape drugs and know how to protect myself. ① ② ③ ④ ⑤

10. I manage electronic communication effectively and do not let it run my life. ① ② ③ ④ ⑤

Each of the topics in these statements is covered in this chapter. Note those statements for which you circled a 3 or lower. Skim the chapter to see where those topics appear, and pay special attention to them as you read, learn, and apply new strategies.

REMEMBER: NO MATTER HOW DEVELOPED YOUR CULTURAL COMPETENCE AND COMMUNICATION SKILLS ARE, YOU CAN IMPROVE WITH EFFORT AND PRACTICE.

HOW CAN YOU
develop cultural competence?

A century ago it was possible to live an entire lifetime surrounded only by people from your own culture. Not so today. In fact, according to Statistics Canada, by 2017, on the 150th anniversary of Confederation, upwards of 23 percent of the Canadian population will be a visible minority. Most of these Canadians will live in big cities.[1] Television, the Internet, social media, and the global marketplace have increased cultural awareness.

Being able to "recognize and respect people's diversity, individual experiences and perspectives" is highlighted in the Conference Board of Canada's Employability Skills 2000+ report.[2] Furthermore, the Canadian Charter of Rights and Freedoms guarantees everyone "freedom of thought, belief and expression." Diversity isn't just part of your academic experience, it's part of every Canadian's life.

MyStudentSuccessLab

Whether face-to-face or online, MyStudentSuccessLab helps students build the skills they need through peer-led video interviews, interactive practice exercises, and activities that provide academic, life, and professionalism skills.

What *Diversity* Means

Differences among people

On an interpersonal level, *diversity* refers to the differences among people and among groups that people are a part of. Differences in gender, skin colour, ethnicity and national origin, age, and physical characteristics are most obvious. Differences in cultural and religious beliefs and practices, education, sexual orientation, socioeconomic status, family background, and marital and parental status are less visible but no less significant.

Differences within people

Another layer of diversity lies within each person. Among the factors defining this layer are personality traits, learning style, strengths and weaknesses, and natural talents and interests. No one else has been or will ever be exactly like you.

In college or university, at work, and as you go about your daily life you are likely to meet people who reflect Canada's growing diversity. This diversity includes more than just skin colour and includes the following:

- Biracial or multiracial individuals
- People from families with more than one religious tradition
- Non-native English speakers, like Gaile, who may have emigrated from outside Canada
- Students older than the traditional 18- to 22-year-olds
- People living with various kinds of disabilities
- Gay, lesbian, bisexual, or transgender individuals
- People practising different lifestyles—often expressed in the way they dress or their interests, friends, or leisure activities

When you share goals with someone, personal differences may fade into the background. This teacher and student share a goal of repairing an internal computer component.

Davis Barber/PhotoEdit

Interacting effectively with all kinds of people is the goal of *cultural competence*—the ability to understand and appreciate differences among people and adjust behaviour in ways that enhance, rather than detract from, relationships and communication. Cultural competence is crucial to both school and life success. According to the National Center for Cultural Competence, developing cultural competence is based on five actions:[3]

1. Valuing diversity
2. Identifying and evaluating personal perceptions and attitudes
3. Being aware of what happens when different cultures interact
4. Building knowledge about other cultures
5. Using learning to adapt to diverse cultures that are encountered

In developing cultural competence, you learn practical skills that enable you to connect to others, bridging the gap between who you are and who they are.[4]

Action 1: Value Diversity

Valuing diversity means having a basic respect for the differences among people and an understanding of what is positive about those differences. No one likes everyone they meet, but if you value diversity, you treat people with tolerance and respect whether or not you like them, avoiding assumptions and granting them the right to think, feel, and believe without being judged. This attitude helps you to take emotionally intelligent actions, as shown in Key 9.1.

237

YOUR ROLE	SITUATION	CLOSED-MINDED RESPONSE	EMOTIONALLY INTELLIGENT RESPONSE
Fellow student	For an assignment, you are paired with a student old enough to be your mother.	You assume the student will be clueless about the modern world. You get ready to react against her preaching about how to do the assignment.	You acknowledge your feelings but try to get to know the student as an individual. You stay open to what you can learn from her experiences and realize you have things to offer as well.
Friend	You are invited to dinner at a friend's house. When he introduces you to his partner, you realize that he is gay.	Uncomfortable with the idea of two men in a relationship, you pretend you have a cellphone call and make an excuse to leave early. You avoid your friend after that.	You have dinner with the two men and make an effort to get to know more about them, individually and as a couple. You compare your immediate assumptions to what you learned about them at dinner.
Employee	Your new boss is of a different racial and cultural background than yours.	You assume that you and your new boss don't have much in common. Thinking he will be distant and uninterested in you, you already don't like him.	You acknowledge your stereotypes but work to set them aside so that you can build a relationship with your boss. You adapt to his style and make an effort to get to know him better.

It is important to note that valuing diversity is about more than just passive tolerance of the world around you (not causing conflict but not seeking harmony either). Moving further than that, toward acceptance, you value diversity by actively working toward teamwork and friendship, celebrating differences as an enriching part of life.

Action 2: Identify and Evaluate Personal Perceptions and Attitudes

Bringing the first and second parts of emotional intelligence into play, you identify perceptions and attitudes by noticing your feelings about others and then evaluating these attitudes by looking at the effect they have on you and others. Many who value the *concept* of diversity experience negative feelings about the *reality* of diversity in their own lives. This disconnect often reveals prejudices and stereotypes.

PREJUDICE
A preconceived judgment or opinion formed without just grounds or sufficient knowledge.

Prejudice

Almost everyone has some level of prejudice that involves prejudging others, usually on the basis of characteristics such as gender, race, sexual orientation, disability, and religion. People judge others without knowing anything about them because of factors such as the following:

- *Influence of family and culture.* Children learn attitudes—including intolerance, superiority, and hate—from their parents, peers, and community.
- *Fear of differences.* It is human to fear and make assumptions about the unfamiliar.
- *Experience.* One bad experience with a person of a particular race or religion may lead someone to condemn all people with the same background.

STEREOTYPE
A standardized mental picture that represents an oversimplified opinion or uncritical judgment.

Stereotypes

Prejudice is usually built on stereotypes—assumptions made, without proof or critical thinking, about the characteristics of a person or group of people, based on factors such as the following:

- *Desire for patterns and logic.* People often try to make sense of the world by using the labels, categories, and generalizations that stereotypes provide.

KEY 9.2 Both positive and negative stereotypes mask uniqueness.

POSITIVE STEREOTYPE	NEGATIVE STEREOTYPE
Women are nurturing.	Women are too emotional for business.
White people are successful in business.	White people are cold and power hungry.
Gay men have a great sense of style.	Gay men are overly effeminate.
People with disabilities have strength of will.	People with disabilities are bitter.
Older people are wise.	Older people are set in their ways.
Asians are good at math and science.	Asians are poor leaders.

- *Media influences.* The more people see stereotypical images—the airhead beautiful blonde, the jolly fat man—the easier it is to believe that stereotypes are universal.
- *Laziness.* Labelling group members according to a characteristic they seem to have in common takes less work than asking questions about who each individual really is.

Stereotypes derail personal connections and block effective communication; pasting a label on a person makes it hard to see the real person underneath. Even stereotypes that seem positive may be untrue and get in the way of perceiving uniqueness. Key 9.2 lists some of the positive and negative stereotypes often heard in media or conversations.

To identify attitudes that hinder cultural competence, ask analytical questions about your own ideas and beliefs:

- How do I react to differences?
- What prejudices or stereotypes come to mind when I see people, in real life or the media, who are a different colour than I am? From a different culture? Making different choices?
- Where do my prejudices and stereotypes come from?
- Are these prejudices fair? Are these stereotypes accurate?
- What harm can having these prejudices and believing these stereotypes cause?

With the knowledge you build as you answer these questions, move on to the next stage—looking carefully at what happens when people from different cultures interact.

Action 3: Be Aware of What Happens When Cultures Interact

Interaction among people from different cultures can promote learning, build mutual respect, and broaden perspectives. However, as history has shown, such interaction can also produce problems caused by lack of understanding, prejudice, and stereotypic thinking. At their mildest, these problems create roadblocks that obstruct relationships and communication. At their worst, they set the stage for acts of discrimination and hate crimes.

Discrimination

The Canadian Charter of Rights and Freedoms says that you cannot be denied basic opportunities and rights because of your race, creed, colour, age, gender, national or ethnic origin,

get creative

EXPAND YOUR PERCEPTION OF DIVERSITY

Complete the following on paper or in digital format.

The ability to respond to people as individuals requires that you become more aware of the diversity that is not always on the surface. Start by examining your own uniqueness. Brainstorm 10 words or phrases that describe you. The challenge: Keep references to your ethnicity or appearance (brunette, Italian Canadian, wheelchair dependent, and so on) to a minimum, and complete the rest of the list with characteristics that others can't see at a glance (laid-back, only child, 24 years old, drummer, marathoner, interpersonal learner, and so on).

Next, pair up with a classmate you do not know well. List on a separate sheet of paper any characteristics you know about him or her—chances are most of them will be visible. Then talk with the classmate. As you talk, you should round out your lists about each other with what you have discovered from your conversation. Finally, answer two questions.

1. What stands out to you about what you learned about your classmate, and why?

2. What about your description of yourself would you like people to focus on more often, and why?

DISCRIMINATION

Denying equal access to employment, education, or housing opportunities or treating people as second-class citizens.

religion, marital status, potential or actual pregnancy, or potential or actual illness or disability (unless the illness or disability prevents you from performing required tasks and unless accommodations are not possible). Despite these legal protections, **discrimination** is common and often appears on college and university campuses. Members of campus clubs may reject prospective members because of religious differences or race, for example, or instructors and students may judge one another according to their weight, accent, or body piercings.

Hate crimes

When prejudice turns violent, it often manifests itself in *hate crimes*—actions motivated by a hatred of a specific characteristic thought to be possessed by the victim, usually based on race, ethnicity, or religious or sexual orientation. Based on Statistics Canada data, while hate crimes are rare, they still account for 3.9 crimes per 100 000 people. In 2011, there were 1332 hate crimes reported in Canada.[5] Because hate crime statistics include only reported incidents, they tell just a part of the story—many more crimes likely go unreported by victims fearful of what might happen if they contact authorities.

Focusing on the positive aspects of intercultural interaction starts with understanding the ideas and attitudes that lead to discrimination and hate crimes. With this awareness, you will be better prepared to push past negative possibilities and open your mind to positive outcomes. Dr. Martin Luther King, Jr. believed that careful thinking could change attitudes:

> The tough-minded person always examines the facts before he reaches conclusions: in short, he postjudges. The tender-minded person reaches conclusions before he has examined the first fact; in short, he prejudges and is prejudiced. . . . There is little hope for us until we become tough minded enough to break loose from the shackles of prejudice, half-truths, and downright ignorance.[6]

Action 4: Build Cultural Knowledge

The successfully intelligent response to discrimination and hate, and the next step in your path toward cultural competence, is to gather knowledge. You have a personal responsibility to learn about people who are different from you, including those you are likely to meet on campus. What are some practical ways to begin?

- *Read* newspapers, books, magazines, and websites that expose you to different perspectives.
- *Ask questions* of all kinds of people, about themselves and their traditions.
- *Observe* how people behave, what they eat and wear, how they interact with others.
- *Travel internationally* to unfamiliar places where you can experience different ways of living.
- *Travel locally* to equally unfamiliar but close-by places where you will encounter a variety of people.
- *Build friendships* with fellow students or co-workers you would not ordinarily approach.

Some colleges and universities have international exchange programs that can help you appreciate the world's cultural diversity. Engaging with students from other countries—whether they have come to your school or you have chosen to study abroad—can provide a two-way learning experience, helping each of you learn about each other's culture.

Building knowledge also means exploring yourself. Talk with family, read, and seek experiences that educate you about your own cultural heritage; then share what you know with others.

Action 5: Adapt to Diverse Cultures

Here's where you put cultural competence to work and bring in the final stage of emotional intelligence—taking action with the intent of bringing about a positive outcome. Choose actions that feel right to you, that cause no harm, and that make a difference, however small. Let the following suggestions inspire your own creative ideas about how you can relate to others.

Junial Enterprises/Shutterstock

- *Look past external characteristics.* If you meet a woman with a disability, get to know her. She may be an accounting major, a daughter, and a mother. She may love baseball, politics, and science-fiction novels. These characteristics—not just her physical person—describe who she is.
- *Move beyond your feelings.* Engage your emotional intelligence to note what different people make you feel, and then examine the potential effect of those feelings. By working to move beyond feelings that could lead to harmful assumptions and negative outcomes, you will improve your chance for successful communication.
- *Put yourself in other people's shoes.* Ask questions about what other people feel, especially if there is a conflict. Offer friendship to someone new who is adjusting to your school community.
- *Adjust to cultural differences.* When you understand someone's way of being and put it into practice, you show respect and encourage communication. For example, if a study group member takes offense at a particular kind of language, avoid it when you meet.
- *Climb over language barriers.* When speaking with someone who is struggling with your language, choose words the person is likely to know, avoid slang expressions, be patient, and use body language to fill in what words can't say. Invite questions, and ask them yourself.
- *Help others.* There are countless ways to make a difference, from providing food or money to a neighbour in need to sending relief funds over the Internet to

Dion Redgun
CDI COLLEGE, CALGARY, ALBERTA

About me:

I am a First Nation's member from Siksika. I am the head of a family with ten grandchildren—one grand-daughter and nine grandsons. My studies are in Business Administration and Management.

What I focus on:

I own and operate a small business on Siksika Nation lands. I give back to the community by hosting youth camps and providing river floats and cultural excursions. My goal is to graduate in order to take all the teachings and knowledge back to Siksika Nation to help it utilize its natural resource, the Bow River, to promote First Nations culture through tourism. Being a mature student has

provided me with many challenges. I have suffered and lived with arthritis for over 12 years and have recently had four surgeries. Using modern technology has helped me cope with the hardship and obstacles that I have faced as a student. I am truly a product of modern technology; joint replacements, a power chair, a voice recorder, and an iPad have allowed me to continue with my journey to wellness through education.

What will help me in the workplace:

My advice to any future generations and entrepreneurs venturing out into the business industry and into new life experiences in general is don't give up. Stay focused. With discipline, courage, and education, your outlook on life will change, whether or not you have a disability.

Dion Redgun. CDI College, Calgary, Alberta. Reprinted by permission.

nations devastated by natural disasters. Every act, no matter how small, makes the world that much better. Remember Gaile's story and how she needs help to complete her education, which will enable her to help others as a nurse.

- *Stand up against prejudice, discrimination, and hate.* When you hear a prejudiced remark, notice discrimination taking place, or suspect a hate crime, ask questions about how to encourage a move in the right direction. You may choose to make a comment or to get help by approaching an authority such as an instructor or dean. Support organizations that encourage tolerance.

talk risk and reward . . .

Risk asking tough questions to be rewarded with new insights. Use the following questions to inspire discussion with classmates either in person or online.

- What stereotypes seem to stay in your head whether or not you want them to? For each one you can name, identify a person who reinforces it *and* a person who contradicts it.

- Has a point of difference ever kept you from connecting with someone? What makes you hesitate? What reward might you gain from the risk of connection?

CONSIDER THE CASE: Fellow students led Gaile to the course and person who helped her most. When have fellow students helped you? Who have you chosen to help or to avoid helping? What resulted from your choice?

- *Recognize that people everywhere have the same basic needs.* Everyone loves, thinks, hurts, hopes, fears, and plans. When you are trying to find common ground with diverse people, remember that you are united first through your essential humanity.

Just as there is diversity in skin colour and ethnicity, there is also diversity in the way people communicate. Effective communication helps people of all cultures make connections.

HOW CAN YOU
communicate effectively?

Clearly, spoken communication promotes success at school and work and in personal relationships. Thinking communicators analyze and adjust to communication styles, learn to give and receive criticism, analyze and make practical use of body language, and work through communication problems.

Communication with others is essential to every school and work goal, from team projects and study groups to on-the-job collaborations.

Shutterstock

Adjust to Communication Styles

When you speak, your goal is for listeners to receive the message as you intended. Problems arise when one person has trouble translating a message coming from someone who is using a different communication style. Your knowledge of the Personality Spectrum (Chapter 3) will help you understand and analyze the ways diverse people communicate.

Identifying your styles

Successful communication depends on understanding your personal style and becoming attuned to the styles of others. The following styles are associated with the four dimensions of the Personality Spectrum. No one style is better than another. As you read, keep in mind that these are generalizations—individuals will exhibit a range of variations within each style.

- *Thinkers communicate by focusing on facts and logic.* As speakers, they tend to rely on logical analysis to communicate ideas, and they prefer quantitative concepts to conceptual or emotional approaches. As listeners, they often do best with logical messages. Thinkers may also need time to process what they have heard before responding. Written messages—on paper or via email—are useful because creating them allows time to put ideas together logically.

- *Organizers communicate by focusing on structure and completeness.* As speakers, they tend to deliver well-thought-out, structured messages that fit into an organized plan. As listeners, they often appreciate a well-organized message that defines practical tasks in concrete terms. As with thinkers, a written format is often an effective form of communication to or from an organizer.

- *Givers communicate by focusing on concern for others.* As speakers, they tend to cultivate harmony, analyzing what will promote closeness in relationships. As listeners, they often appreciate messages that emphasize personal connection and address the emotional side of an issue. Whether speaking or listening, givers often favour in-person talks over written messages.

- *Adventurers communicate by focusing on the present.* As speakers, they focus on creative ideas, tending to convey a message as soon as the idea arises and then move on to the next activity. As listeners, they appreciate upfront, short, direct messages that don't get sidetracked. Like givers, adventurers tend to communicate and listen more effectively in person.

Diversity and Communication

What is your style? Use this information as a jumping-off point for your self-exploration. Just as people tend to demonstrate characteristics from more than one Personality Spectrum dimension, communicators may demonstrate different styles.

Put Your Knowledge of Communication Styles to Use

Compare these communication styles to your own tendencies and also consider how others seem to respond to you. Your practical thinking skills can help you figure out what works well for you. However, you are only half of any communication picture. Your creative skills will help you shift your perspective to think about the other person's thoughts and feelings and what might work best while interacting with that person's communication style.

Speakers adjust to listeners. Listeners may interpret messages in ways you never intended. Think about practical solutions to this kind of problem as you read the following interaction involving a giver (instructor) and thinker (student):

Instructor: "Your essay didn't communicate any sense of your personal voice."

Student: "What do you mean? I spent hours writing it. I thought it was on the mark."

- Without adjustment. The instructor ignores the student's need for detail and continues to generalize. Comments such as "You need to elaborate," "Try writing from the heart," or "You're not considering your audience" might confuse or discourage the student.
- With adjustment. Greater logic and detail will help. For example, the instructor might communicate more effectively by saying, "You've supported your central idea clearly, but you didn't move beyond the facts into your interpretation of what they mean. Your essay reads like a research paper. The language doesn't sound like it is coming directly from you."

Listeners adjust to speakers. As a listener, improve understanding by being aware of differences and translating messages so they make sense to you. The following example with an adventurer (employee) and an organizer (supervisor) shows how adjusting can pay off.

Employee: "I'm upset about the email you sent me. You never talked to me directly and you let the problem build into a crisis. I haven't had a chance to defend myself."

- Without adjustment. If the supervisor is annoyed by the employee's insistence on direct personal contact, he or she may become defensive: "I told you clearly what needs to be done. I don't know what else there is to discuss."
  - With adjustment. In an effort to improve communication, the supervisor responds by encouraging the in-person exchange that is best for the employee. "Let's meet after lunch so you can explain to me how you believe we can improve the situation."

Multiple intelligences can also provide clues about communication style. The multiple intelligences table in this chapter (page 245) presents different communication strategies suggested for use in a study group for a criminal justice course.

Knowing yourself is an important aspect of successful communication. However, adapting to differences between yourself and others, such as generational differences, is essential as well.

Adjust to communication styles between generations

Like other groupings of people, generations come with personal and lifestyle characteristics that can affect intergenerational communication.

multiple intelligence strategies

Apply Different Intelligences to Improve a Criminal Justice Study Group

INTELLIGENCE	USE MI STRATEGIES TO IMPROVE COMMUNICATION	APPLY MI COMMUNICATION STRATEGIES TO LEARN ABOUT THE COURT SYSTEM
Verbal-Linguistic	• Find opportunities to express your thoughts and feelings to others—either in writing or in person. • Listening to words is at least as important as speaking them.	• Divide your pair or group into two parts. One person or subgroup should teach the historical development of the provincial court system. The other should teach the historical development of the federal court system.
Logical-Mathematical	• Allow yourself time to think through a problem before discussing it. Write out an argument on paper and rehearse it. • When communicating with others whose styles are not as logic-focused, ask specific questions to learn the facts you need.	• Ask questions to evaluate the effectiveness of the federal court system: What works well? Where are the breakdowns? What improvements could you suggest?
Bodily-Kinesthetic	• Have an important talk while walking, running, or performing a task that does not involve concentration. • Work out to burn off excess energy before having an important discussion.	• Assign roles for group members to arrange a courtroom "set" in the classroom. Choose a case to recreate and perform a mock trial to illustrate an example of how a trial works in a federal court.
Visual-Spatial	• Make a drawing or diagram of points you want to communicate during an important discussion. • If you are in a formal classroom or work setting, use visual aids to explain your main points.	• In a pair or group, each individual or group half draws a diagram—one showing the structure of the provincial court system and one showing the structure of the federal court system.
Interpersonal	• If you tend to dominate group conversation, focus more on listening. • If you tend to prioritize listening to others, work on becoming more assertive about expressing your opinion.	• Select a landmark Supreme Court case. In a pair or group, each person or half of the group should argue one side of the case. Give everyone time to communicate clearly.
Intrapersonal	• Be as clear as possible when expressing what you know about yourself, and recognize that not all communicators may be self-aware. • When you have a difficult encounter, take time alone to decide how to communicate more effectively next time.	• Select the court system topic or segment that you know you will comprehend best. Suggest that you handle that topic or segment when the group divides up material for each group member to learn and present to the others.
Musical	• Before communicating difficult thoughts or feelings, work through them by writing a poem or song. • Be sensitive to the rhythms of a conversation. Sense when to voice your opinion and when to hang back.	• Create a song or rhythmic mnemonic device with a partner that helps you remember the vocabulary associated with the court system, such as *appeal*, *jurisdiction*, and *judicial review*.
Naturalistic	• Use your ability to recognize patterns to evaluate communication situations. Employ patterns that work well and avoid those that do not. • When appropriate, make an analogy from the natural world of plants or animals to clarify a point in a conversation.	• In a pair or group, talk through the process of how a trial moves from the lower provincial and military courts all the way to the Supreme Court of Canada. Make a timeline that shows the pattern of how the case progresses.

Diversity and Communication

GENERATION	COMMUNICATION STYLE	COMMUNICATION CHALLENGES	TIPS FOR COMMUNICATING
Baby Boomers (1946–1964)	• Focus on personal growth and achievement • Politically correct • Inclined to use both face-to-face and electronic communication	• Can easily misunderstand instant electronic communication (texts, IMs, blogs, and so on) • Uncomfortable with conflict • Judgmental	• Be open and direct (baby boomers are the "show me" generation) • Use face-to-face or electronic communication • Provide details
Generation X (1965–1980)	• Casual • Pragmatic • Skeptical • Unimpressed by authority • Use email	• Impatient • Cynical • Communication can be limited to email or other noninteractive forms of communication	• Use email as primary communication • Ask for feedback • Keep it short to hold attention • Use an informational style
Generation Y or Millennials (1980–1994)	• Value self-expression over self-control • Respect must be earned • Comfortable with online communication • Spend a lot of time online	• Overly focused on accessing information electronically • Teaching older generations to use technology erodes sense of respect for elders • Inexperience dealing with people	• Use email, voice mail, and texts • Communicate with visuals • Use humour • Respect their knowledge • Encourage them to break rules when thinking

Note: The majority of people from all generations prefer face-to-face communication to written or electronic communication.

Source: Some information from a table on different generations by Greg Hammil, "Mixing and Managing Four Generations of Employees." *FDU Magazine*, Winter/Spring 2005, www.fdu.edu/newspubs/magazine/05ws/generations.htm.

Being able to recognize and adapt to differences caused by generation gaps can help you communicate successfully. Key 9.3 contains helpful communication tips for interacting with people of different ages.

Know How to Give and Take Criticism

CONSTRUCTIVE CRITICISM
Criticism that promotes improvement or development.

Criticism can be either constructive or unconstructive. **Constructive criticism** is a practical problem-solving strategy, involving goodwill suggestions for improving a situation. In contrast, unconstructive criticism focuses on what went wrong, doesn't offer alternatives that might help solve the problem, and is often delivered negatively, creating bad feelings.

When offered constructively, criticism can help bring about important changes. Consider a case in which someone has continually been late to study group sessions. Which comment from the group leader would better encourage a change in behaviour?

■ *Constructive.* The group leader talks privately with the student: "I've noticed that you've been late a lot. We count on you to contribute. Is there a problem that is keeping you from being on time? Can we help?"

■ *Unconstructive.* The leader watches the student arrive late and says, in front of everyone, "If you can't start getting here on time, there's really no point in your coming."

At school, instructors criticize classwork, papers, and exams. On the job, criticism may come from supervisors, co-workers, or customers. No matter the source, constructive comments can help you grow. Be open to what you hear, and remember that most people want you to succeed.

Offering constructive criticism. Use the following strategies to increase its effectiveness:

■ *Criticize the behaviour, not the person.* Avoid personal attacks. "You've been late to five group meetings" is preferable to "You're lazy."

- *Define the specific problem.* Try to focus on the facts, backing them up with specific examples and minimizing emotions.

- *Suggest new approaches and offer help.* Talk about practical ways to handle the situation. Brainstorm creative options. Help the person feel supported.

- *Use a positive approach and hopeful language.* Express your belief that the person can turn the situation around.

Receiving criticism. When on criticism's receiving end, use the following techniques:

- *Analyze the comments.* Listen carefully and then evaluate what you hear. What does it mean? What is the intent? Try to let unconstructive comments go without responding.

- *Ask for suggestions on how to change your behaviour.* Be open to what others say.

- *Summarize the criticism and your response.* The goal is for all to understand the situation.

- *Use a specific strategy.* Apply problem-solving skills to analyze the problem, brainstorm ways to change, choose a strategy, and take practical action to make it happen.

Criticism, as well as other thoughts and feelings, may be communicated nonverbally. You will become a more effective communicator if you understand body language.

Understand Body Language

Body language has an extraordinary capacity to express people's real feelings through gestures, eye movements, facial expressions, body positioning and posture, touching behaviours, vocal tone, and use of personal space. Why is it important to know how to analyze body language?

- *Nonverbal cues shade meaning.* What you say can mean different things depending on body positioning or vocal tone. The statement "That's a great idea" sounds positive. However, said while sitting with your arms and legs crossed and looking away, it may communicate that you dislike the idea. Said sarcastically, the tone may reveal that you consider the idea a joke.

- *Cultures use body language differently.* In Canada, for example, looking away from someone may be a sign of anger or distress; in Japan, the same behaviour is usually a sign of respect.

- *Nonverbal communication strongly influences first impressions.* First impressions emerge from a combination of verbal and nonverbal cues. Nonverbal elements, including tone of voice, posture, eye contact, and speed and style of movement, usually come across first and strongest.

Shutterstock

Although reading body language is not an exact science, the following practical strategies will help you use it to improve communication.

- *Pay attention to what is said through nonverbal cues.* Focus on your tone, your body position, and whether your cues reinforce or contradict your words.

get analytical

Complete the following on paper or in digital format.

Think of a situation that could be improved if you were able to offer constructive criticism to a friend or family member.

1. Describe the situation and name the improvement you seek.

2. Imagine that you have a chance to speak to this person. First, describe the setting—time, place, atmosphere—where you think you would be most successful.

3. Now develop your script. Analyze the situation and decide on the most constructive approach. Free write what you would say. Keep in mind the goal your communication seeks to achieve.

4. Finally, if you can, make your plan a reality. Will you do it?

5. If you have the conversation, was it worth it?

Then do the same for those with whom you are speaking. Look for the level of meaning in the physical.

- *Adjust behaviour based on cultural differences.* In cross-cultural conversation, discover appropriate behaviour by paying attention to what the other person does and by noting how others react to what you do. Then consider changes based on your observations.

- *Adjust body language to the person or situation.* What body language might you use when making a presentation in class? Meeting with your advisor? Confronting an angry co-worker? Think through how to use your physicality to communicate successfully.

One of the primary goals of successful communication is to build and maintain good relationships with family, friends, and others you encounter in daily life. All the communication and cultural competence strategies you've read will contribute to that goal. Read on for more ways to navigate your relationships successfully.

Work in Teams

Much of your school and work experience will involve teamwork, both in-person and virtual. Being part of a team means knowing how to collaborate as well as how to lead.

Know how to collaborate

Collaboration means working effectively with others to achieve a common goal. It is built on trust, which can only be achieved through the following:

- *Honesty.* Team members tell one another the truth, not just what each wants to hear, so they can work together to solve problems and overcome obstacles.

- *Openness.* Team members risk saying what is on their minds and share information because they understand the reward of productivity depends on it.

- *Consistency.* Each team member works and interacts in a consistent manner, and team members consistently do what they say they will do.
- *Respect.* Team members see one another as vital parts of the team and speak, listen, and behave respectfully toward one another.

Know how to lead

You may be called upon to lead your team as well as participate in it. Being a leader is a risk, but the reward for effective leadership is getting things done. Here are some tips for being an effective leader:

- Communicate clearly so your team understands what you are trying to accomplish and why, and how they fit into your vision.
- Set goals for yourself and your team so everyone knows what to do and when.
- Be clear on the skills and talents you have and those that others have so you know how to best contribute and how to delegate the right tasks to others.
- Manage your own time and help others stay on track so your team completes tasks on time.
- Follow through to finish what you start.

Effective team meetings

To ensure you accomplish your goals during a meeting, follow good meeting etiquette:

- *Show up on time.* If you cannot avoid being late, call, text, or e-mail to let people know. Then apologize briefly when you arrive.
- *Be prepared.* Make sure you have all necessary materials. Do a tech check ahead of time to make sure your equipment is working (computer, software, and video projector).
- *Use an agenda and take notes.* Communicate the goal of the meeting, the items that will be covered, and how long it will last. Then stick to that agenda and have someone take notes.
- *Listen and don't interrupt.* Listen to what the person is saying instead of planning your response or interrupting. When it is your turn, you will appreciate not being interrupted.
- *Practice civility.* No matter how angry or frustrated you feel, do not get overly emotional. Also, if you have an issue with someone, talk to him or her privately after the meeting.
- *Avoid distractions.* If you text or take phone calls during a meeting, you will seem rude and may miss important information. Give your full attention to the meeting and your teammates.

Make an Effective Presentation

Some courses require individual students or teams of students to give a presentation at some point in the term. Many people dread this event, but if you think of a presentation as a friendly conversation with a group of people, it may be less stressful. Building this important workplace skill requires the risk of trying it over and over again. To prepare for a presentation that will resonate with your listeners, do the following:

- *Identify your audience.* Because you give a presentation to other people, you need to know who they are and why they would want to listen to you. Understanding their motivation will help you choose your topic, words, and tone.
- *Identify your goal.* Get clear on the outcome you hope to achieve. Do you want your audience to do something? Change the way they think about something?

get $mart

YOUR PERSONAL RELATIONSHIP WITH MONEY

Think about how you relate to money and why. On a separate piece of paper or in an electronic file, answer the following questions.

1. Do members of your family discuss finances? If they do, what do they talk about? If they do not discuss finances, why do you think that is?

2. Do you spend money on things you want but do not need? If and when you do, how do you feel before, during, and after the purchase? One week later?

3. How does the topic of money make you feel?

4. How often, and how regularly, do you actively manage your money?

5. What do you feel are your biggest problems with money?

6. Do you borrow money from friends or family? If so, how do you pay it back—on time or not, all at once or in smaller amounts, not at all?

7. Do you talk with friends and family about money problems? Why or why not?

8. Based on your answers, how would you summarize your relationship with money in a short paragraph?

Solve a problem? This goal becomes the purpose of the presentation and drives its content.

■ *Identify your speaking points.* To achieve your goal, what points do you need to make? Certain information will be necessary to inform, educate, or persuade your audience.

■ *Add visual aids.* Images draw people's attention, explain complicated concepts, and help people remember important information. You can use a flip chart or a white board to draw or write as you go, or use prepared slides, videos, or animations—anything that enhances your audience's understanding of the topics in the presentation.

■ *Keep text to a minimum.* If you choose to use slides, do NOT put down every word you plan to say. Simply note important points you want people to remember and then elaborate upon them with your own words. For helpful advice, check out www.presentationzen.com.

■ *Tell a story.* If you really want people to remember what you say, weave in stories throughout your presentation. People remember stories better than they remember individual facts. Give real examples. Share personal experiences. Break up your talk with humorous anecdotes. Your presentation will stick with people when you tell stories.

Whether you work by yourself, one-on-one with individuals, or in large groups, a primary goal of successful communication is to build and maintain good relationships with family, friends, and others you encounter in your daily life. All the communication and cultural competence strategies you've read will contribute to that goal. Read on for more ways to navigate your relationships successfully.

HOW DO YOU MAKE THE MOST
of personal relationships?

Shutterstock

Personal relationships with friends, classmates, spouses and partners, and parents can be sources of great satisfaction and inner peace. Good relationships can motivate you to do your best in school and on the job. When conflict arises or relationships fall apart, however, it can affect your ability to function in all areas of your life. Relationships have enormous power.

The following straightforward approaches can help make your personal relationships as good as they can be while also showing how to manage problems when things move in the wrong direction.

Use Positive Relationship Strategies

When you devote time and energy to education, work, and activities, results are more likely to be positive. The same is true of human connections. Here are a few ways to nurture relationships:

- *Approach people and conversations with emotional intelligence.* The more you can notice feelings, understand what they mean, and handle them in ways that bring people closer to you instead of pushing them away, the better your relationships will be.
- *If you want a friend, be a friend.* If you treat others with the kind of loyalty and support that you appreciate, you are likely to receive the same in return.
- *Spend time with people you respect and admire.* Life is too short to hang out with people who bring you down or encourage you to ignore your values.
- *Work through tensions.* Negative feelings can fester when left unspoken. Get to the root of a problem by discussing it, compromising, forgiving, and moving on.
- *Take risks.* It can be frightening to reveal your deepest dreams and frustrations, to devote yourself to a friend, or to fall in love. However, if you open yourself up, you stand to gain the incredible benefits of companionship, which for most people outweigh the risks.
- *Find a dating pattern that suits you.* Some students date exclusively and commit early. Some students prefer to socialize in groups. Some students date casually. Be honest with yourself—and others—about what you want in a relationship.
- *If a relationship fails, find ways to cope.* When an important relationship becomes strained or breaks up, analyze the situation and choose practical strategies to move on. Some people need time alone; others want to be with friends and family. Some need a change of scene, whereas others let off steam with exercise or other activities. Whatever you do, believe that in time you will emerge stronger from the experience.

Plug into Communication Technology Without Losing Touch

Modern technology has revolutionized the way people communicate. You can call or text on a mobile phone; write a note via e-mail, instant message, or Twitter; communicate through blogs and chat rooms; and catch up on social networking sites such as Facebook. Although communication technologies allow you to communicate faster, more frequently, and with more people than ever before, it has its drawbacks. Key 9.4 shows some positive and negative aspects of communication technology.

As freeing and convenient as it may be to communicate electronically in a faceless environment, its low-risk feeling matches its limited potential for reward. Real life

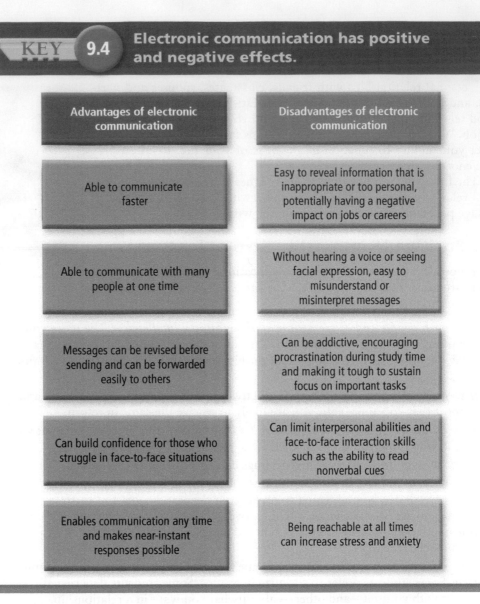

KEY 9.4 Electronic communication has positive and negative effects.

Advantages of electronic communication	Disadvantages of electronic communication
Able to communicate faster	Easy to reveal information that is inappropriate or too personal, potentially having a negative impact on jobs or careers
Able to communicate with many people at one time	Without hearing a voice or seeing facial expression, easy to misunderstand or misinterpret messages
Messages can be revised before sending and can be forwarded easily to others	Can be addictive, encouraging procrastination during study time and making it tough to sustain focus on important tasks
Can build confidence for those who struggle in face-to-face situations	Can limit interpersonal abilities and face-to-face interaction skills such as the ability to read nonverbal cues
Enables communication any time and makes near-instant responses possible	Being reachable at all times can increase stress and anxiety

demands that people interact effectively face to face. It's important to keep up your interpersonal communication skills and fine-tune your ability to read non-verbal cues. It is also crucial to make sure that you don't prioritize electronic communication over in-person real-time interaction. (Think about how you feel when a friend you are with spends half your time together texting.) Additionally, electronic communication can compromise your privacy. See Key 9.5 for ten strategies for safeguarding your privacy and personal information.

Aim for electronic communication to *enhance* real-time interaction rather than *replace* it. Ask questions to develop your own personal communication recipe: How do you prefer to communicate with others? What forms of communication do you use, and what are the effects? Consider keeping a time journal. Whenever you use an electronic device, log the time you start and the time you stop. Review the log after a week, think about the results, and consider whether you need to make changes to improve the balance in your life.

Whether online or in person, conflict occurs within nearly every relationship, and it can cause anger. With effort, you can manage both conflict and anger (and stay away from those who cannot).

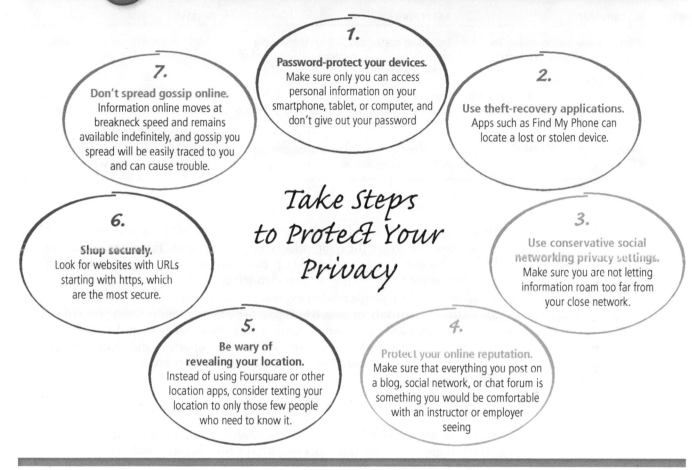

1. Password-protect your devices. Make sure only you can access personal information on your smartphone, tablet, or computer, and don't give out your password

2. Use theft-recovery applications. Apps such as Find My Phone can locate a lost or stolen device.

3. Use conservative social networking privacy settings. Make sure you are not letting information roam too far from your close network.

4. Protect your online reputation. Make sure that everything you post on a blog, social network, or chat forum is something you would be comfortable with an instructor or employer seeing

5. Be wary of revealing your location. Instead of using Foursquare or other location apps, consider texting your location to only those few people who need to know it.

6. Shop securely. Look for websites with URLs starting with https, which are the most secure.

7. Don't spread gossip online. Information online moves at breakneck speed and remains available indefinitely, and gossip you spread will be easily traced to you and can cause trouble.

Take Steps to Protect Your Privacy

Source: Maier, Fran. "Back to School: 10 Privacy Tips for the Connected Student" (Retitled: "Take Steps to Protect Your Privacy"). *Mashable,* September 7, 2011. From http://mashable.com/2011/09/07/privacy-back-to-school. Copyright (c) 2011 by Fran Maier. Used by Permission of Fran Maier.

Manage Conflict

Conflicts, both large and small, arise when ideas or interests clash. You may have small conflicts with a housemate over a door left unlocked. You may have major conflicts with your partner about finances or with an instructor about a failing grade. Conflict, as unpleasant as it can be, is a natural element in the dynamic of getting along with others. Prevent it when you can—and when you can't, use problem-solving strategies to resolve it.

Conflict-prevention strategies

Some strategies can help you to prevent conflict from starting in the first place.

- *Send "I" messages.* "I" messages communicate your needs rather than attacking someone else. Creating these messages involves some

TIPS FOR LEARNING ONLINE

- *Interact without bias.* Communicating via your course learning management system allows you to relate to other students based on who they are. It allows you to be open-minded and prevents you from prejudging them based on cultural differences.

- *Meet face to face when appropriate.* While more learning takes place online, it can't replace the benefits of meeting face to face. Use online learning to enhance your personal relationships, not replace them.

- *Control your temper.* Wait, and think, before you post on emotional topics. Forums can turn into hostile environments. Snarky tweets and updates can come back to haunt you if they are viewed by potential employers, instructors, or others who may judge you by them or potentially cause conflict.

Diversity and Communication

253

AGGRESSIVE	ASSERTIVE	PASSIVE
Blaming, name-calling, and verbal insults: "You created this mess!"	Expressing oneself and letting others do the same: "I have thoughts about this—first, what is your opinion?"	Feeling that one has no right to express anger: "No, I'm fine."
Escalating arguments: "You'll do it my way, no matter what it takes."	Using "I" statements to defuse arguments: "I am uncomfortable with that choice and want to discuss it."	Avoiding arguments: "Whatever you want to do is fine."
Being demanding: "Do this."	Asking and giving reasons: "Please consider doing it this way, and here's why ..."	Being noncommittal: "I'm not sure what the best way to handle this is."

simple rephrasing: "You didn't lock the door!" becomes "I was worried when I came home and found the door unlocked." "I" statements soften the conflict by highlighting the effects that the other person's actions have on you, rather than focusing on the person or the actions themselves.

■ *Be assertive.* Most people tend to express themselves in one of three ways— aggressively, assertively, or passively. Aggressive communicators focus primarily on their own needs and can become impatient when these needs are not satisfied. Passive communicators focus primarily on the needs of others and often deny themselves power, causing frustration. Assertive communicators are able to declare and affirm their opinions while respecting the rights of others to do the same. Assertive behaviour strikes a balance between aggression and passivity and promotes the most productive communication. Key 9.6 contrasts these three communication styles.

What can aggressive and passive communicators do to move toward a more assertive style? Aggressive communicators might take time before speaking, use "I" statements, listen to others, and avoid giving orders. Passive communicators might acknowledge anger, express opinions, exercise the right to make requests, and know that their ideas and feelings are important.

Conflict resolution

All too often, people deal with conflict through avoidance (a passive tactic that shuts down communication) or escalation (an aggressive tactic that often leads to fighting). Conflict resolution demands calm communication, motivation, and careful thinking. Use analytical, creative, and practical thinking skills to apply the problem-solving plan from Chapter 4 (page 98) when things heat up.

Trying to calm anger is an important part of resolving conflict. All people get angry at times—at people, events, and themselves. However, excessive anger can contaminate relationships, stifle communication, and turn friends and family away.

Manage Anger

Strong emotions can get in the way of happiness and success. It is hard to concentrate on Canadian history when you are raging over a nasty email or a bad grade. Psychologists report that angry outbursts may actually make things worse. When you feel yourself losing control, try some of these practical anger management techniques.

■ *Try to calm down.* Breathe. Slowly repeat a phrase such as "Take it easy" or "Relax."
■ *Change your environment.* Take a break from what is upsetting you. Take a walk, go to the gym, or see a movie. Come up with a creative idea that will help you settle down.

get practical

CONFLICT-PREVENTION STRATEGIES

Complete the following on paper or in digital format.

1. List two ways to manage conflict that seem effective to you.

2. Think of a conflict you were involved in over the past year—one that was not resolved well. Choose which of the two listed strategies you believe would have helped you prevent it or at least manage it more effectively. In the space below, describe the impact you think the strategy would have had on the situation. What might the other party's reaction have been?

3. Now, ask yourself why the technique would have been beneficial. What issue in the conflict does this technique address or improve?

4. Name two other situations where it might prove useful, and describe how you think it would play out.

revisit RISK AND REWARD

Louise Gaile Edrozo

What happened to Gaile? Gaile's Honors 100 course instructor Dr. Barbara Clinton, also the head of the Highline honors program, helped her express her strengths in her portfolio and resumé and take productive risks toward the rewards she sought. After Gaile shared her financial concerns, Dr. Clinton helped her find and win scholarships for which she was eligible. With newfound confidence, Gaile took risks that rewarded her with employment authorization from the Immigration and Naturalization Service and a job as a critical care nurse technician. She graduated in 2007 and started working as a registered nurse. She has completed a B.A. in nursing from the University of Washington at Tacoma, and will soon have permanent resident status.[7]

What does this mean for you? Everyone needs a person who can be a resource for life, like Dr. Clinton was for Gaile. This person can help bring out strengths and provide support and encouragement as you take risks. Who could be your resource for life? Make two lists, each with at least five people's names (friends, family, faculty, work acquaintances, anyone you know personally). One list identifies people who you know well, who already support you and care about you. The other list identifies people you don't know as well but that you admire and feel you could learn from. Choose one person from each list and brainstorm a short paragraph about what you think you need from that person as a mentor.

What risk may bring reward beyond your world? Your needs are important and so are the needs of others. Risk reaching beyond your world to mentor someone who could use your help. Check out www.mentoring .org as a start to find out more about what mentoring involves and what kinds of programs are already in place for people who want to mentor others. Look into a program from that website, a program at your college or in your community, or start making more regular contact with someone in need on your own. Your presence will reward the person you mentor as well as yourself.

- *Think before you speak.* When angry, people tend to say the first thing that comes to mind, even if it's hurtful. Instead, wait until you are in control before you say something.
- *Problem-solve.* Instead of blowing up, analyze a challenging situation, make a plan, and begin. Even if it doesn't work, making the effort may help cool your anger.
- *Get help if you need it.* If you can't keep your anger in check, you may need the help of a counsellor. Many schools provide professional mental health services to students.

RISK ACTION

FOR POST SECONDARY, CAREER, AND LIFE REWARDS

KNOW IT *Think Critically*

Build basic skills. Review the five actions for cultural competence earlier in this section. Re-read the suggestions for Action 5: Adapt to Diverse Cultures on pages 241–243. For the four strategies listed here, give a real-life version (something you have done or know someone else has done). For example, by choosing to wear a blindfold for an entire day as part of a "Blind for a Day" experience, students put themselves in other people's shoes.

Look past external characteristics: _____
_____

Put yourself in other people's shoes: _____
_____

Adjust to cultural differences: _____
_____

Help others in need: _____
_____

Take it to the next level. Make these three strategies into personal plans. Rewrite them as specific actions you are willing to take in the next six months. For example, "Help others in need" might become "Sign up as a tutor for the Writing Centre."

1. _____
2. _____
3. _____

Move toward mastery. Choose one of the three plans to put into action in the next 30 days (or even tomorrow, if you can). Choose wisely—recall your knowledge of SMART goals, and pick the one that is most attainable and realistic. Circle your choice. Describe your goal, with this action—how you want to make a difference.

_____
_____
_____
_____
_____

☐   Finally, do it. Check the checkbox when you can honestly say you have taken your planned action.

WRITE IT *Communicate*

Record your thoughts on a separate piece of paper, in a journal, or electronically.

Emotional Intelligence Journal: Your experience with prejudice. Have you ever been discriminated against or experienced any other type of prejudice? Have you been on the other end and acted with prejudice yourself? Describe what happened and your feelings about the situation. If you have no personal experience, describe a situation you have seen or heard about. Outline an emotionally intelligent response that you feel would bring something positive or helpful out of the situation.

Real-Life Writing: Improve communication. Few students make use of the wealth of ideas and experience that academic advisors can offer. Think of a question you have regarding a specific course, major, or academic situation that your advisor might help you answer. Craft an email in appropriate language to your advisor, and send it. Then, to stretch your communication skills, rewrite the same email twice more: once in a format you would send to an instructor, and once in a format appropriate for a friend. Send either or both of these if you think the response would be valuable to you.

DO IT   *Build Your Brand*

Write a Job Interview Cover Letter

21st Century Learning Building Blocks

- Communication and collaboration
- Financial, economic, business, and entrepreneurial literacy
- Leadership and responsibility

257

Complete the following in your electronic portfolio or on separate sheets of paper.

To secure a job interview, you will have to create a cover letter to accompany your resumé. With this key communication tool, you can pull out your best selling points from your resumé and highlight them to a potential employer so the employer wants to continue on to read your resumé.

Write a one-page, three-paragraph cover letter to a prospective employer, describing your background and explaining your value to the company. Be creative—you may use fictitious names, but select a career and industry that interest you. Use the format shown in Key 9.7.

- *Introductory paragraph:* Start with a statement that convinces the employer to read on. You might name a person the employer knows who suggested that you write to this employer, or refer to something positive about the company that you read in the newspaper paper or on the Internet. Identify the position for which you are applying, and tell the employer why you are interested in working for the company.
- *Middle paragraph:* Sell your value. Try to convince the employer that hiring you will help the company in some way. Centre your sales effort on your experience in school and the work-place. If possible, tie your qualifications to the needs of the company. Refer indirectly to your enclosed resumé.
- *Final paragraph:* Close with a call to action. Ask the employer to call you or tell the employer to expect your call to arrange an interview.

Exchange your first draft of the cover letter with a classmate. Read each other's letter and make marginal notes to improve impact and persuasiveness, writing style, grammar, punctuation, and spelling. Discuss and then make corrections. Create a final draft for your portfolio.

First name Last name
1234 Your Street
City, Province, Postal Code

November 1, 2011

Ms. Prospective Employer
Prospective Company
5432 Their Street
City, Province, Postal Code

Dear Ms. Employer:

On the advice of Mr. X, career centre advisor at Y college/university, I am writing to inquire about the position of production assistant at CPJM Radio. I read the description of the job and your company on the career centre's employment-opportunity bulletin board, and I would like to apply for the position.

I am in my final year at college/ university and will graduate this spring with a degree in communications. Since I declared my major, I have wanted to pursue a career in radio. For the last year I have worked as a production intern at the college's/university's station, and have occasionally a filled in as a disc jockey on the evening news show. I enjoy being on the air, but my primary interest is production and programming. My enclosed resumé will tell you more about my background and experience.

I would be pleased to talk with you in person about the position. You can reach me anytime by calling 555-555–5555 or by emailing xxxx@xx.com. Thank you for your consideration, and I look forward to meeting you.

Sincerely,

Sign Your Name Here

First name Last name

Enclosure(s) [Use this notation if you have included a resumé or other item with your letter.]

Kelly Addington and Becca Tieder

Because stress and health are linked, every action you take to improve your physical and mental health can also increase your ability to cope with stress.

Wellness and Stress Management

STAYING HEALTHY IN MIND AND BODY

What Would You Risk? *Kelly Addington and Becca Tieder*

Kelly Addington and Becca Tieder

THINK ABOUT THIS SITUATION AS YOU READ, AND CONSIDER HOW YOU WOULD APPROACH IT. THIS CHAPTER EXAMINES WAYS TO MANAGE STRESS THROUGH HEALTH MAINTENANCE, TO HANDLE PHYSICAL AND MENTAL HEALTH ISSUES, AND TO MAKE EFFECTIVE DECISIONS ABOUT SUBSTANCES AND SEX.

Kelly and Becca were typical students and close friends. They studied hard and enjoyed the non-academic side of the college experience. One Saturday night, they were socializing and drinking moderately at a local beach bar. Kelly accepted a ride home from a designated driver, a male friend with whom she felt secure.

The next morning, Kelly felt ill with what she thought was simply a hangover. She couldn't remember what had happened the previous night. But the headaches persisted, and she had nightmares and visions of someone on top of her and of feeling suffocated. She took a pregnancy test and it was positive, even though she had not had sexual intercourse in a year. After confiding in Becca, Kelly took another pregnancy test to be sure. It, too, was positive.

Becca and Kelly put the pieces together: Kelly was a victim of date rape. Her male friend had slipped a date rape drug into her drink, then sexually assaulted her. She called the friend, who claimed that Kelly was begging for sex that night. "I had a lot of trust issues from that," Kelly says, "because this is someone I cared about and someone I thought I could trust."

Kelly later suffered a miscarriage. Physically, she would recover. Mentally, however, she was shaken and vulnerable. Did she do something to deserve this? What would her parents think? What would she need to risk to be able to have healthy self-esteem or a positive sexual relationship? "Within six months to a year after being sexually assaulted," Kelly says, "the only thing I was trying to do was forget what happened."

To be continued . . .

Kelly and Becca's determination to learn from their ordeal has led them to discover personal empowerment and deliver a powerful message to the post-secondary population. You will learn more about Kelly and Becca, and the rewards resulting from their actions, within the chapter.

Notes

52%

statusCHECK

How Effectively Do You Maintain Your Personal Wellness?

For each statement, circle the number that feels right to you, from 1 for "not at all true for me" to 5 for "very true for me."

1. I know that my health is a major factor in my success as a post-secondary school student. ① ② ③ ④ ⑤

2. I am comfortable delaying gratification when I know the reward is worth it. ① ② ③ ④ ⑤

3. I actively balance and moderate my diet. ① ② ③ ④ ⑤

4. I make it a point to exercise in some way regularly. ① ② ③ ④ ⑤

5. I consistently get the sleep that I need. ① ② ③ ④ ⑤

6. I recognize when I am feeling out of it, and I have methods to elevate my mood. ① ② ③ ④ ⑤

7. I know the ways in which addiction can affect my life. ① ② ③ ④ ⑤

8. I understand the risks involved with substance use and incorporate that knowledge into my choices regularly. ① ② ③ ④ ⑤

9. I feel comfortable taking a stand about my sexual activity and sticking to it. ① ② ③ ④ ⑤

10. I know the risks involved with becoming sexually active and consciously work to stay safe. ① ② ③ ④ ⑤

Each of the topics in these statements is covered in this chapter. Note those statements for which you circled a 3 or lower. Skim the chapter to see where those topics appear, and pay special attention to them as you read, learn, and apply new strategies.

REMEMBER: NO MATTER HOW WELL YOU TAKE CARE OF YOURSELF, YOU CAN IMPROVE WITH EFFORT AND PRACTICE.

HOW CAN FOCUSING ON HEALTH
help you manage stress?

If you are feeling high levels of **stress**—the physical or mental strain that occurs when your body reacts to pressure—you are not alone. Stress levels tend to be high among post-secondary students, who are frequently overloaded with activities and responsibilities. A 2013 survey revealed that 89% of Canadian post-secondary students often feel overwhemed by all the responsiblities of young adulthood.[1] The greater your stress, the greater the toll it may take on your health and on your ability to achieve your goals. Moderate stress can actually be helpful, motivating you to do well on tests, finish assignments on time, and prepare for presentations. While some stress can be good and help you be productive, too much can actually affect your productivity. Research by Robert M. Yerkes and John E. Dodson, two doctors who study stress, indicates that stress can be helpful or harmful, depending on how much you experience. They found that level of performance or efficiency increased, reached a peak, and then decreased as the level of stress or anxiety increased. The highest performance level was achieved with a moderate amount of stress. The key is to find the "right" amount of stress that works for you and knowing when and how to manage your stress levels.

MyStudentSuccessLab

Whether face-to-face or online, MyStudentSuccessLab helps students build the skills they need through peer-led video interviews, interactive practice exercises, and activities that provide academic, life, and professionalism skills.

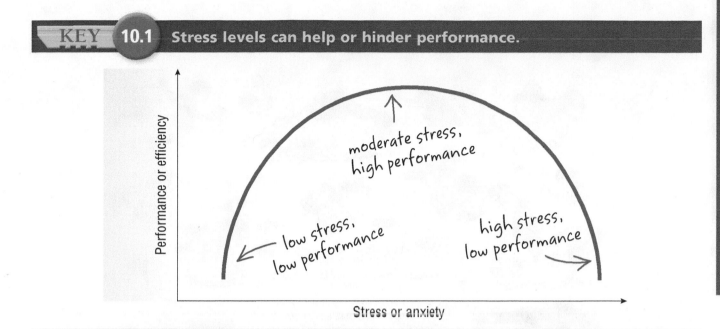

KEY 10.1 Stress levels can help or hinder performance.

moderate stress, high performance

low stress, low performance

high stress, low performance

Performance or efficiency

Stress or anxiety

Source. From *Your Maximum Mind* by Herbert Benson M.D., copyright © 1987 by Random House, Inc. Used by permission of Crown Publishers, a division of Random House, Inc.

Your ability to manage stress depends in part on your understanding of how it affects you. Certain assessments look at your level of exposure to stressors. In the Get Practical exercise in this chapter, you will fill an assessment that asks you how much a series of experiences have been part of your life recently. With the information it provides, you will have a better idea of how stressed you are and what factors cause the most stress for you. This is also an important tool that you will use after graduation. The Conference Board of Canada lists the ability to "take care of your personal health" as an important Personal Management Skill.[2]

Although you cannot always control what happens to you, you can control your response. Being as physically and mentally health as possible is crucial to responding productively to stress. In fact, you are on your way to becoming more healthy by simply being in school. Scientists and researchers who study aging report that more education is linked to a longer life, perhaps because education teaches cause-and-effect thinking that helps people make better choices. Another link could be that educated people tend to be more able to **delay gratification,** which helps you to avoid harmful habits.[3]

DELAY GRATIFICATION
To delay an immediate pleasure or reward to gain a more substantial one later.

No one is able to make healthy choices and delay gratification all the time. However, you can pledge to do your best to maintain your health. As you consider the range of choices, think through what risks you are willing to take to earn the reward of a healthy body and mind. Also think about stress-management techniques that may relate to different intelligences. (See the Multiple Intelligence Strategies for Stress Management on p. 270 for ideas.)

Eat Well

Making intelligent choices about what you eat can lead to more energy, better general health, and an improved quality of life. However, this is easier said than done, for two reasons in particular. One is that the *food environment* in which most people live—characterized by an overabundance of unhealthful food choices, combined with the cheaper pricing of many of the worst alternatives—does not support people's efforts to choose well.[4]

Day-to-day post-secondary life can make it tough to eat right. Students spend hours sitting in class or studying and tend to eat on the run; students may also build social events around food or eat as a reaction to stress. Many new students find that

KEY 10.2 Create positive food habits.

- Vary what you eat, focusing on fruits and vegetables
- Choose foods with limited fat, cholesterol, and trans fats
- Replace sugary snacks with fresh or dried fruit
- Keep healthy snacks within reach
- Limit calorie-heavy alcoholic drinks and sugar-heavy soda
- Notice and reduce portion sizes
- Plan meals and minimize late-night eating sprees
- Substitute other activities for stress-related eating
- Get help from weight-loss organizations and on-campus support

Giuseppe Porzani/Fotolia

the freshman 15—referring to the 15 pounds (6.8 kilograms) that first-year students tend to gain in the first year of school—is an unpleasant reality.

Healthful eating requires *balance* (varying your diet) and *moderation* (eating reasonable amounts). Key 10.2 presents some ways to incorporate both into your life.

To get a good picture of where you are and where you want to be, evaluate your eating habits, understand obesity and its effects, and target your ideal weight.

Subbotina Anna/Shutterstock

Evaluate your eating habits. Keep a food log for a week, writing down what you eat and when you eat it each day. Look over the log. What kinds of food are you eating? What time of day are you eating the most? Do you eat when you are hungry? Worried? Nervous? Are you eating more than you need? See Key 10.3 for some healthy alternatives to common foods you might be eating. If you consistently have trouble with a certain type of food, consult a doctor. You may have a condition such as celiac disease, lactose intolerance, or a food allergy that requires you to change how you eat.

KEY 10.3 Explore healthier alternatives.

CREATE POSITIVE FOOD HABITS

UNHEALTHY FOOD CALORIES AND NUTRIENT CONTENT	HEALTHY ALTERNATIVE CALORIES AND NUTRIENT CONTENT	BENEFITS OF HEALTHY ALTERNATIVE
Large cheeseburger from fast food restaurant (550 calories)	Whole grain sandwich with tuna fish, chopped celery, and tomato (390 calories)	More fiber, vitamins (B and E), and high-quality protein; less salt and fat
Fruit-flavored candy (80–100 calories)	Fresh or dried fruit such as organic apples, peaches, apricots, and strawberries (50–90 calories)	More fiber and vitamins (A and C); less sugar
Can of soda (90 calories)	Fresh juice from fruits or vegetables, such as apple, orange, or carrot juice (64–80 calories)	More vitamins and antioxidents (vitamins A and C); less sugar and phosphorous (phosphorous can leach calcium from your teeth and bones)
Milk shake from a fast food restaurant (750–1000 calories)	Fruit smoothie, glass of milk (cow, goat, soy, or rice), or yogurt (100–250 calories)	More protein, calcium, and magnesium; less sugar and fat
Canned vegetable soup (120–150 calories)	Fresh, lightly steamed, or stir-fried vegetables, such as spinach, chard, broccoli, carrots, or beets (50 calories)	More vitamins (A and B), more iron, and more fiber; much less salt
French fries from fast food restaurant (230 calories)	Baked potato (60 calories)	More vitamin C and fiber; much less fat and salt

Source: "The Fast Food Explorer." 2011. Retrieved October 28, 2011, from http://www.fatcalories.com.

Eat a variety of foods. For guidance about the different types and amounts of food you should be eating, explore the information provided by Canada's Food Guide at www.hc-sc.gc.ca/fn-an/alt_formats/hpfb-dgpsa/pdf/food-guide-aliment/view_eatwell_vue_bienmang-eng.pdf. For example, half of your daily food intake should be fruits and vegetables—ideally, 8–10 servings a day. However, research has found that the average student barely managed five servings of fruits and vegetables a week.[5] Work to balance your diet so that you get the nutrients you need.

Evaluate your food sources. Do you buy your food at a convenience store? The dining hall? A supermarket? A local farmer's market? Eat the highest quality food you can find (and afford). Your body breaks your food down into nutrients that allow you to think, move, and live. If the food is poor quality, your body won't get what it needs to keep you going.

Understand the effects of obesity. The term *obese* refers to having a **Body Mass Index (BMI)** of 30 or more (*overweight* refers to having a BMI of 25 to 29). According to the Canadian Medical Association, obesity rates in Canada have tripled since 1985. Their report, published in 2014, estimates that 18 percent of Canadians have a BMI of more than 30.[6] Obesity is a major risk factor in the development of adult-onset diabetes, coronary heart disease, high blood pressure, stroke, cancer, and other illnesses. Additionally, studies have shown that overweight job applicants tend to be reviewed more negatively during interviews and that overweight employees tend to be paid less than normal weight people in the same jobs and have a reduced chance of promotion.[7]

> BODY MASS INDEX (BMI)
> The ratio of your weight to your height.

Target your ideal weight. The Centers for Disease Control has information about weight ranges.

The BMI calculator at www.cdc.gov/healthyweight/assessing/bmi/index.html can help you see whether you fall within a healthy range or are considered over-weight or obese. If you want to lose weight, set a reasonable goal and work toward it at a pace of approximately 1 to 2 pounds (0.45 to 0.9 kilograms) a week. You may

student PROFILE

Paige Lawson
MOHAWK COLLEGE, HAMILTON, ONTARIO

Paige Lawson

About me:

I am a second-year Television Broadcasting student at Mohawk College. At the age of 12, I was diagnosed with generalized anxiety disorder and panic disorder, which negatively impacted my performance in a school environment. One year after my high school graduation, I developed a mental health anti-stigma program for high school students in London, Ontario, and was selected as a Top 20 Under 20 Award recipient in 2010. At the age of 19, I returned to a school environment at Mohawk College after a three-year break. Entering college for the first time has made me face new anxieties and stressors that I am learning to cope with through various techniques and stress busters.

What I focus on:

Attending college can be a stressful time for any student, but for those challenged by an anxiety disorder, it can be even more difficult. I have had to learn to focus on getting proper amounts of exercise, eating balanced meals, staying organized and focused on my studies, and finding time to rest. I make sure to take full advantage of the exercise programs and gym memberships available at my school throughout the year. Exercising helps give my body the energy it needs to achieve my other lifestyle goals. I organize a chart at the beginning of each semester that outlines my upcoming assignments, exams, and workshops so that I can establish time to dedicate to my other goals and reduce any stress by efficiently scheduling time to work on my various assignments. Most importantly, I find time to rest and participate in activities that I enjoy.

Finding a lifestyle balance of work and play has helped me achieve a stress-free school year!

What will help me in the workplace:

Establishing positive relationships within my workplace, staying organized, and integrating my lifestyle goals with my work goals will help me in my future workplace. Developing strong communication skills within a workplace will be useful in reducing stress caused by overwhelming workloads and will assist in creating stress-free teamwork environments. Committing to an organized schedule will keep me on track and provide me with the free time I need to relax and stay involved in activities that lower my stress and anxiety levels. I look forward to joining my future workplace and maintaining a stress-free lifestyle—something that I believe everyone can achieve.

---

also want to consult health professionals, enrol in a reputable and reasonable weight-loss program, and incorporate regular exercise into your life. Striving for the goal of reducing your BMI will improve not only your physical well-being but your mental health as well.

Get Exercise

Evidence increasingly points to exercise as a key element of your health. The Mayo Clinic reports numerous positive effects of exercise including easing depression, warding off illnesses, reducing fatigue, and maintaining a healthy weight.[8] During physical activity, the brain releases endorphins, chemical compounds that have a positive and calming effect on the body. Additionally, regular exercise builds discipline, time management, and motivation that can also contribute to academic success. Risking the time and effort to exercise brings enormous rewards.

Types of exercise

There are three general categories of exercise: cardiovascular, strength, and flexibility (Key 10.4). The type you choose depends on your exercise goals, available equipment, your time and fitness level, and other factors.

Some exercises, such as lifting weights or biking, fall primarily into one category. Others, such as power yoga or Pilates, combine elements of two or all three. For maximum benefit, try alternating exercise methods through *cross-training* (alternating types of exercise and combining elements from different types of exercise). For example, if you lift weights, use a stationary bike for cardiovascular work and build stretching into your workout.

Always check with a physician before beginning an exercise program, and adjust your program to your physical needs and fitness level. If you don't currently exercise, walking daily is a good way to begin. Start with a 10-minute walk and increase your time gradually. Walking is gentle on your joints, burns calories, helps your heart, and can improve your mood as well.

How much exercise do you need? Try to do both aerobic and muscle-strengthening activities and spread out your activity through the week. You may want to break it into smaller chunks of time throughout the day. Even 10 minutes at a time is just fine.[9] Dr. Mike Evans has a video on YouTube identifying 30 minutes of exercise a day as a more significant health intervention than any other. He asks a question: "Can you limit your sitting and sleeping to just 23 ½ hours a day?" When you think about it, that's a pretty minimal risk for a significant reward.[10]

KEY 10.4 Vary your exercise activities among these three types of training.

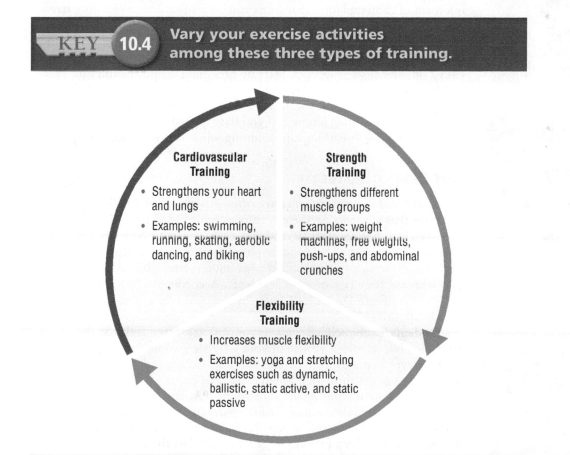

Cardiovascular Training
- Strengthens your heart and lungs
- Examples: swimming, running, skating, aerobic dancing, and biking

Strength Training
- Strengthens different muscle groups
- Examples: weight machines, free weights, push-ups, and abdominal crunches

Flexibility Training
- Increases muscle flexibility
- Examples: yoga and stretching exercises such as dynamic, ballistic, static active, and static passive

Make exercise a priority

Busy students often have trouble getting to the gym, even when there is a fully equipped athletic centre on campus. Use these ideas to help make exercise a priority, even in your busiest weeks.

- Walk to classes and meetings. When you reach your building, use the stairs.
- Use your school's fitness facilities.
- Ride your bike or walk instead of driving.
- Play team recreational sports at school or in your community.
- Find activities you can do outside of a club, such as running, pickup basketball, or road hockey.
- Take walks or bike rides for study breaks.
- Work out with friends or family to combine socializing and exercise.
- Do a routine on your own with a DVD/Blu-Ray or an on-demand exercise program.

Being fit is a lifelong pursuit that is never done. Furthermore, because your body is constantly changing, re-evaluate your exercise program on a regular basis to maximize its benefits. Finally, remember that being healthy is part of your personal responsibility. Think preventatively about your well-being, and take charge of your choices.

Increase Stability and Focus with Mindfulness Meditation

Many people's minds are overwhelmed with thoughts and worries on a daily basis. *Mindfulness* refers to paying focused attention, and meditation is a form of contemplation that helps you create that focus, reducing stress and anxiety and the damage they cause to your body.

Pick a quiet time of day and a location where you can be alone and comfortable. Sit on a cushion or in a chair. Rest your hands in your lap, palms up, and close your eyes. Start by breathing deeply, in and out, preferably through your nose. Listen to your breathing. Some people like to count as they inhale and exhale. When thoughts come up, let them pass by as if you were watching a movie. If you have a hard time sitting still, try an active meditation, breathing and counting while you walk, bike, or swim.

Get Enough Sleep

University and college students are often sleep deprived. While research indicates that students need eight to nine hours of sleep a night to function well, studies show that students average six to seven hours—and often get much less.[11] Inadequate sleep hinders your ability to concentrate, raises stress levels, and makes you more susceptible to illness. It can also increase your risk of auto accidents. According to Dr. Tracy Kuo at the Stanford Sleep Disorders Clinic, "A sleepy driver is just as dangerous as a drunk driver."[12]

Students, overwhelmed with responsibilities, often feel that they have no choice but to prioritize schoolwork over sleep. Some stay up regularly until the wee hours of the morning to study. Others pull all-nighters from time to time to get through a tough project or paper.

For the sake of your health and your GPA, find a way to get enough sleep. Look for telltale symptoms of sleep deprivation such as being groggy in the morning, dozing off during the day, or needing caffeine to make it through the day. Sleep expert Gregg D. Jacobs has the following practical suggestions for improving sleep habits:[13]

Shutterstock

If you overload on caffeine, it can become less effective and may disrupt your sleep patterns. Choose your coffee breaks carefully and try to avoid drinking caffeine late at night.

- *Reduce consumption of alcohol and caffeine.* Caffeine may keep you awake, especially if you drink it late. Alcohol causes you to sleep lightly, making you feel less rested when you awaken.

- *Exercise regularly.* Regular exercise, especially in the afternoon or early evening, promotes sleep.

- *Take naps.* Taking short afternoon naps can reduce the effects of sleep deprivation.

- *Be consistent.* Try to establish somewhat regular times to wake up and go to bed.

- *Create a ritual.* Wind down and transition from work to sleep with a bedtime ritual. Read a book, listen to calming music, or drink a cup of herbal tea.

- *Manage your environment.* Wear something comfortable, turn down the lights, and keep the room cool. Use earplugs, soft music, or white noise if you are dealing with outside distractions.

TIPS FOR LEARNING ONLINE

- *Reach out.* The nature of online education can lead to feelings of isolation. Make sure to participate in chat rooms and discussion boards, and make an effort to connect with other students both online and offline.

- *Be wary of dangers online.* Don't give out personal information online to people whom you don't know well. If you have a Facebook page, update your privacy settings and be careful about the text and photos you post. If you feel that someone is harassing you via email or IM, contact an advisor or counsellor who can help you address the problem.

- *Limit your online time.* Whether you are online for learning or for personal use, be sure to take regularly scheduled breaks.

Address Mental Health Issues

Staying positive about who you are, making hopeful plans for the future, and building resilience to cope with setbacks will all help you target positive mental health. However, some people experience emotional disorders that make it more difficult than usual to cope with life's stressful situations. If you recognize yourself in any of the following descriptions, take practical steps to improve your health. Most student health centres and campus counselling centres provide both medical and psychological help or referrals for students with emotional disorders. Although asking for help may feel like a risk, most who do it find it is well worth the reward of feeling better and functioning more effectively. You won't be alone. Statistics Canada reports that in 2012, about 5 million Canadians (almost 1 out of every 5 Canadians) felt they needed help with a mental health issue. Luckily, of those 5 million, two-thirds were able to find the help they needed.[14]

Depression

Almost everyone has experienced sadness after setbacks such as the end of a relationship or the failure of a course. However, a depressive disorder is an illness—a whole-body illness, involving your body, mood, and thoughts—not a mental state that can be escaped by trying to snap out of it.

The Canadian Mental Health Association says depression isn't just someone feeling blue. It is a person "grappling with feelings of severe despair over an extended period of time. Almost every aspect of their life can be affected, including their emotions, physical health, relationships, and work. For people with depression, it does not feel like there is a light at the end of the tunnel—there is just a long, dark tunnel."[15]

It is also fairly common among college and university students. Sociologist Dr. Andrée Demers of the Université de Montréal says students who suffer with mental health issues "tend to exhibit lack of concentration, absenteeism and many leave school before they graduate."[16]

Shutterstock

269

multiple intelligence strategies

FOR STRESS MANAGEMENT

Apply Different Intelligences to Reduce the Stress of Writing a Final Paper in Human Development

INTELLIGENCE	USE MI STRATEGIES TO MANAGE STRESS	APPLY MI STRESS MANAGEMENT STRATEGIES TO HANDLE A FINAL PAPER ON THE STAGES OF PHYSICAL DEVELOPMENT IN INFANCY*
Verbal-Linguistic	• Keep a journal of what situations, people, or events cause you stress. • Write letters or email friends about your problems.	• Early in the writing process, summarize the different reflex reactions common in normal newborns.
Logical-Mathematical	• Think through problems by using a problem-solving process, and devise a detailed plan. • Analyze the negative and positive effects that may result from a stressful situation.	• Analyze the functions of each of the six different states of being in infants: crying, waking activity, alert activity, drowsiness, irregular sleep, and regular sleep.
Bodily-Kinesthetic	• Choose a physical activity that helps you release tension—running, yoga, team sports—and do it regularly. • Plan physical activities during free time—go for a hike, take a bike ride, go dancing with friends.	• When you need a break from writing or research, re-create the classic experiment to test infants' depth perception, known as the *visual cliff*.
Visual-Spatial	• Enjoy things that appeal to you visually—visit an exhibit, see an art film, shoot photos with your camera. • Use a visual organizer to plan a solution to a stressful problem.	• Create a visual aid comparing the development of a full-term infant with that of a premature infant.
Interpersonal	• Talk with people who care about you and are supportive. • Shift your focus by being a good listener to others who need to talk about their stresses.	• Interview the parents of a premature infant to learn about the special challenges the family faced during the first year.
Intrapersonal	• Schedule downtime when you can think through what is causing stress. • Allow yourself five minutes a day of meditation during which you visualize a positive way in which you want a stressful situation to resolve.	• Separate your scheduled working times over a period of weeks so that you have time to contemplate individual development topics between sessions.
Musical	• Listen to music that relaxes, inspires, and/or energizes you. • Write a song about what is bothering you.	• Listen to lullabies from different countries. Compare and contrast melody and rhythm. Link observations to what you know about infants' auditory systems.
Naturalistic	• See whether the things that cause you stress fall into categories that can give you helpful ideas about how to handle situations. • If nature is calming for you, interact with it—spend time outdoors, watch nature-focused TV, read books or articles on nature or science.	• Visit the newborns at your local hospital during visiting hours. Search for common characteristics—for example, reflex responses and states of wakefulness or sleep. Create a chart to report your findings.

*For information on the newborn, see Robert S. Feldman, *Child Development*, 4th ed., Upper Saddle River, NJ: Prentice Hall, 2007.

get practical

POST-SECONDARY STRESS EXPLORATION

All sorts of situations and experiences can cause stress during college or university. Furthermore, everyone has a unique response to any potential stressor. One way to assess your individual situation is to look at the different areas of your life, and rate how much stress you are experiencing in each at the current time. Use a scale from 1 to 10, with 1 being the lowest possible level of stress, and 10 being the highest possible.

_____ 1. Increased independence and responsibility

_____ 2. Family relationships

_____ 3. Friend relationships

_____ 4. Academic relationships (instructors, student peers, administration, etc.)

_____ 5. Boyfriend/girlfriend/spouse relationships

_____ 6. Managing time and schedule

_____ 7. Managing money

_____ 8. Performance on assignments

_____ 9. Performance on tests

_____ 10. Physical health and fitness

_____ 11. Mental health and balance

_____ 12. Academic planning (major, etc.)

_____ 13. Career planning and vision for future

_____ 14. Work situation, if you have a job on or off campus

_____ 15. Current living situation (home, dorm, etc.)

Total your points here: _____

The lowest possible score is 15, and the highest possible 150. The higher your score, the more stress you perceive you are experiencing currently. Things to think about:

- Ponder what your total score says about your life at the moment. A score over 100 may indicate that reducing stress should be a top priority for you right now. A score under 50 may indicate that you are currently experiencing tolerable, and even productive, levels of stress.

- Take a look at how you rated each item, and consider putting particular energy into the areas that you rated the highest. There are two ways to determine where your energy would serve you best: One, focus on any area that you rated a 7 or higher. Two, focus on the five areas that you rated highest, no matter what number you gave them.

School and community resources can help you manage whatever level of stress you are experiencing. Write down names, locations, hours, phone numbers, URLs, and any other pertinent information for the following:

- Free counselling offered to students

- Exercise facility

- Sexual assault centre

- Other resources

Adapted in part from "The Inventory of College Students Recent Life Experiences: A Decontaminated Hassles Scale for a Special Population," by P.M. Kohn, K. Lafreniere, and M. Gurevich, *Journal of Behavioral Medicine*, 13(6), 1990, 619–630.

Key 10.5 shows possible causes of depression as well as some typical symptoms. If you recognize some of these symptoms in yourself, seek help from a professional. Depression requires a medical evaluation and is treatable. Most student health centres and campus counselling centres provide both medical and psychological help or referrals for students with emotional disorders. For some people, adequate sleep, a regular exercise program, a healthful diet, and the passage of time are enough to lessen stress and ease the disorder. For others, medication is important.

KEY 10.5 Know the causes and symptoms of depression.

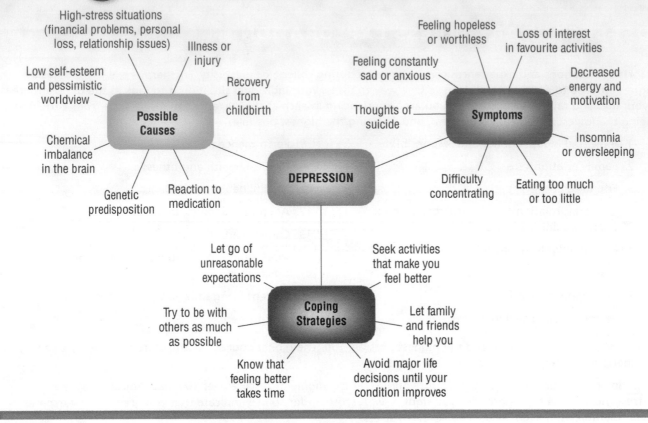

Source: Depression, National Institutes of Health publication 02-3561, National Institutes of Health, 2002.

At its worst, depression can lead to suicide. SAVE (Suicide Awareness Voices of Education) lists these suicide warning signs:[17]

- Statements about hopelessness or worthlessness: "The world would be better without me."
- Loss of interest in people, things, or activities.
- Preoccupation with suicide or death.
- Visiting or calling family and friends and giving things away.
- Sudden sense of happiness or calm. (A decision to commit suicide often brings a sense of relief that convinces others that the person seemed to be on an upswing.)

If you recognize these symptoms in someone you know, begin talking with the person about his or her feelings. Then do everything you can to convince the individual to see a doctor or mental health professional. Don't keep your concerns a secret; sound an alarm that may save a life. If you recognize these symptoms in yourself, know that you can find help if you reach out.

Anxiety disorders

As with depression, anxiety disorders have been on the rise among college and university students over the past decade. Potential causes include the struggling economy and job market, being constantly available via communication technology, and information overload—both in general, as well as specifically regarding what everyone around you is doing and accomplishing. If factors like these cause a high stress response that won't settle down, an anxiety disorder can result.

Types of anxiety disorders include:

- Generalized anxiety disorder (GAD), referring to a nearly constant state of worry that is difficult to control and not always related to a cause
- Obsessive-compulsive disorder (OCD), characterized by obsessive thoughts that lead to compulsive behaviours
- Post-traumatic stress disorder (PTSD), especially common in war veterans or survivors of abuse, involving flashbacks, avoidance, and heightened emotion and awareness
- Panic disorder, characterized by panic attacks that feature increased heart and breathing rates, dizziness, and a sense of impending doom

Shutterstock

Recognizing an anxiety disorder can be challenging. In fact, many students who ultimately are diagnosed do not initially believe they have a medical problem, figuring that the anxiety they are experiencing is normal. This is especially true for students who have experienced high levels of anxiety all of their lives up until this point without any medical intervention. Any student who feels that anxiety is affecting the ability to function in or out of class should consult with a professional to see whether an anxiety disorder is to blame.

Eating disorders

Every year, millions of people develop serious and sometimes life-threatening *eating disorders*, including anorexia nervosa, bulimia, and binge eating disorder. Negative effects of these disorders range from fertility and obesity issues to digestive tract and other organ damage, heart failure, and even death. There are three basic types of eating disorders:[18]

- *Anorexia nervosa.* People with anorexia nervosa restrict their eating and become dangerously underweight. They may also engage in over exercising, vomiting, and abuse of diuretics and laxatives. Anorexia nervosa is often linked to excessive anxiety and perfectionism.
- *Bulimia nervosa.* People with bulimia engage in *binge episodes*, which involve eating excessive amounts of foods and feeling out of control. Following the binge, the person feels remorseful and attempts to purge the calories through self-induced vomiting, laxative abuse, excessive exercise, or fasting.
- *Binge eating disorder.* Binge eating disorder is the most common eating disorder. People with this condition eat large amounts of food and feel out of control, similar to those with bulimia, but they do not purge after a binge episode. They also tend to eat unusually fast, eat in secret, eat until they feel uncomfortably full, and feel ashamed of their eating behaviour.

The stresses of life lead some students to experiment with alcohol, tobacco, and other potentially addictive substances. Although these substances may alleviate stress temporarily, they have potentially serious consequences.

HOW CAN YOU MAKE EFFECTIVE
decisions about alcohol, tobacco, and drugs?

Abusing alcohol, tobacco, and drugs adds significantly to stress levels and can cause financial struggles, emotional traumas, family and financial upheaval, health problems, and even death. As you read the information in this section, think about the effects of your actions on yourself and others, and continually look for new and better ways to make positive, life-affirming choices.

Jeffrey Greenberg/Science Source

CHAPTER 10

When you can take a break, try out different ways to have fun. These students escape to some open space for a picnic.

The frontal lobe of your brain is responsible for *if-then* thinking and impulse control. It's the part that asks, Is this really a good idea? What will happen if I take this action? However, the frontal lobe does not reach full development until around the age of 25. This means that people under 25 are more likely to act without considering potential consequences than people over 25, including decisions to take drugs.[19] Worse, those drugs are more likely to impair brain development and result in addiction in a younger person than in an older one.[20] Consider the information in this section.

Alcohol

Alcohol is a depressant and the most frequently abused drug on campus. Even a few drinks affect thinking and muscle coordination. Heavy drinking can damage the liver, the digestive system, and brain cells, and also impair the central nervous system. Prolonged use can lead to addiction, making it seem impossible to quit. Statistics Canada reports that while drinking among post-secondary students has decreased somewhat since 2004,[21] people between the ages of 18 and 34 were more likely to be heavy drinkers.[22] Heavy drinking is defined as consuming five or more drinks at one sitting.

According to the Centers for Disease Control (CDC), your tolerance and reaction to alcohol can depend on a variety of factors, including, but not limited to, age, gender, race or ethnicity, physical condition, the amount of food consumed before drinking, how quickly alcohol is consumed, use of drugs or prescription medications, and family history.[23] Key 10.6 shows the varying levels of drinking behaviours defined by the CDC.

Of all alcohol consumption, binge drinking (Key 10.6) is associated with the greatest problems. Consistently an issue on post-secondary campuses, students who binge

ADDICTION
The compulsive need for a habit-forming substance.

KEY 10.6 Understand levels of alcohol consumption.

		Men	Women
Moderate Drinking	Lower-risk drinking pattern equalling "having no more than 1 drink per day for women and no more than 2 drinks per day for men."	per day	per day
Heavy Drinking	For men, heavy drinking is typically defined as consuming an average of more than 2 drinks per day. For women, heavy drinking is typically defined as consuming an average of more than 1 drink per day.	per day	per day
Binge Drinking	"A pattern of alcohol consumption that brings the blood alcohol concentration (BAC) level to 0.08% or above . . . usually corresponds to 5 or more drinks on a single occasion for men or 4 or more drinks on a single occasion for women, generally within about 2 hours."	in 2 hrs	in 2 hrs

Source: www.cdc.gov/alcohol/index.htm. Reprinted by permission of The Center for Disease Control and Prevention.

talk risk and reward . . .

Risk asking tough questions to be rewarded with new insights. Use the following to inspire discussion with classmates in person or online.

- When a friend has a substance problem or abusive tendencies, trying to help can be risky. How can you reach out without insulting the person? What reward do you think is possible?

- The vulnerability that comes from close friendship is a risk that can bring great reward. However, it also has the potential to hurt. Have you experienced losing your trust in a friend? What happened, and what changed as a result?

CONSIDER THE CASE: Imagine you are one of Kelly's best friends and you hear what happened to her. How would you help her cope and move ahead? Discuss a risk you would advise her to take and what reward she might earn from it.

Kelly Addington and Becca Tieder; Shutterstock

drink are more likely to miss classes, perform poorly, experience physical problems (memory loss, headache, stomach issues), become depressed, and engage in unplanned or unsafe sex.[24]

If you drink, think carefully about the effects on your health, safety, and academic performance. The Get Analytical exercise on page 276, a self-test, will help you analyze your habits.

Tobacco

The good news is that smoking is on the decline in Canada. This decrease may be due to public education or to smoking bans becoming more common. However, the bad news is that about 4.6 million Canadians over 15 years of age still smoke. However, according to Health Canada's 2012 Canadian Tobacco Use Monitoring Survey, people aged 20–24 are more likely to smoke than any other group.[25]

Many students use tobacco as a stress reliever and then become hooked on nicotine, a highly addictive drug found in all tobacco products. Nicotine's immediate effects may include an increase in blood pressure and heart rate, sweating, and throat irritation. Long-term effects may include high blood pressure, bronchitis and emphysema, stomach ulcers, heart disease, and cancer.

In recent years, the health dangers of **secondhand smoke** have been recognized. Living with smokers or being around them on a regular basis is linked to lung cancer and heart disease in nonsmokers.[26] This awareness has led many colleges, universities, and some towns/cities to ban smoking not only in classrooms and other public spaces, but also around entranceways to public buildings. More and more companies, aware of the risk, are banning smoking or even refusing to hire people who smoke.[27]

> **SECONDHAND SMOKE**
> Smoke in the air exhaled by smokers or given off by cigarettes, cigars, or pipes.

If you smoke regularly, you can quit with motivation, perseverance, and outside help. The following tips provide practical suggestions for quitting:[28]

- Try a nicotine patch or nicotine gum, and be sure to use them consistently.
- Get support and encouragement from a health care provider, a quit-smoking program, a support group, and friends and family.
- Avoid situations that increase your desire to smoke, such as being around other smokers and drinking heavily.
- Find other ways to lower stress, such as exercise or other activities you enjoy.
- Set goals. Set a quit date and tell friends and family. Make and keep medical appointments.

get analytical

EVALUATE YOUR SUBSTANCE USE

Even one yes answer may indicate a need to look carefully at your habits. Three or more yes answers indicate that you may benefit from discussing your use with a counsellor.

Within the last year:

Y N 1. Have you tried to stop drinking or taking drugs but found that you couldn't do so for long?

Y N 2. Do you get tired of people telling you they are concerned about your drinking or drug use?

Y N 3. Have you felt guilty about your drinking or drug use?

Y N 4. Have you felt that you needed a drink or drugs in the morning—as an eye-opener—in order to cope with a hangover?

Y N 5. Do you drink or use drugs alone?

Y N 6. Do you drink or use drugs every day?

Y N 7. Have you found yourself regularly thinking or saying "I need" a drink or any type of drug?

Y N 8. Have you lied about or concealed your drinking or drug use?

Y N 9. Do you drink or use drugs to escape worries, problems, mistakes, or shyness?

Y N 10. Do you find you need increasingly larger amounts of drugs or alcohol in order to achieve a desired effect?

Y N 11. Have you forgotten what happened while drinking or using drugs because you had a blackout?

Y N 12. Have you spent a lot of time, energy, or money getting alcohol or drugs?

Y N 13. Has your drinking or drug use caused you to neglect friends, your partner, your children, or other family members, or caused other problems at home?

Y N 14. Have you gotten into an argument or a fight that was alcohol or drug related?

Y N 15. Has your drinking or drug use caused you to miss class, fail a test, or ignore schoolwork?

Y N 16. Have you been choosing to drink or use drugs instead of attending social events or performing other activities you used to enjoy?

Y N 17. Has your drinking or drug use affected your efficiency on the job or caused you to fail to show up at work?

Y N 18. Have you continued to drink or use drugs despite any physical problems or health risks that your use has caused or made worse?

Y N 19. Have you driven a car or performed any other potentially dangerous tasks while under the influence of alcohol or drugs?

Y N 20. Have you had a drug- or alcohol-related legal problem or arrest (for example, possession, use, disorderly conduct, driving while intoxicated)?

Source: Adapted from the Criteria for Substance Dependence and Criteria for Substance Abuse in the *Diagnostic and Statistical Manual of Mental Disorders*, Fourth Edition, published by the American Psychiatric Association, Washington, D.C., and from materials titled "Are You an Alcoholic?" developed by Johns Hopkins University.

The positive effects of quitting—increased life expectancy, lung capacity, and energy, as well as significant financial savings—may inspire any smoker to make a lifestyle change. If you are interested in quitting, the Canadian Lung Association provides a website with quitting resources at www.lung.ca/protect-protegez/tobacco-tabagisme/quitting-cesser/how-comment_e.php.

To assess the level of your potential addiction, you may want to take the self-test in the exercise on this page, replacing the words *alcohol* or *drugs* with *cigarettes* or *smoking*. Think about your results, weigh your options, and make a responsible choice.

Drugs

Although alcohol remains the drug most abused by young people in Canada, use of illicit drugs is also a problem. Drug users rarely think through the possible effects when choosing to take a drug. However, many of the so-called rewards of drug abuse are empty. Drug-using peers may accept you for your drug use and not for who you are.

Illicit drug use is a perennial problem on college and university campuses. The National Survey on Drug Use and Health (NSDUH) reports that more than 37 percent of post-secondary students surveyed had used illicit drugs in the year prior to the survey.[29] Students may use drugs to relieve stress, to be accepted by peers, or just to try something new.

In most cases, the negative consequences of drug use outweigh any temporary high. Drug use violates the law, and you may be arrested, tried, and imprisoned for possessing even a small amount of drugs. You can jeopardize your reputation, your student status, and your ability to get a job if you are caught using drugs or if drug use impairs your performance. Finally, long-term drug use can damage your body and mind. Key 10.7 has comprehensive information about the most commonly used illicit drugs.

KEY 10.7 Drugs have potent effects on the user.

DRUG	DRUG CATEGORY	USERS' EFFECTS	POTENTIAL PHYSICAL EFFECTS, SHORT-TERM AND LONG-TERM	DANGER OF DEPENDENCE
Cocaine (also called *coke, blow, snow*) **and crack cocaine** (also called *crack or rock*)	Stimulant	Alert, stimulated, excited, energetic, confident	Nervousness, mood swings, sexual problems, stroke or convulsions, psychoses, paranoia, coma at large doses	Strong
Alcohol	Depressant	Sedated, relaxed, loose	Impaired brain function; impaired reflexes and judgment; cirrhosis; impaired blood production; greater risk of cancer, heart attack, and stroke	Strong with regular, heavy use
Marijuana and hashish (also called *pot, weed, herb*)	Cannabinol	Euphoric, mellow, little sensation of time, paranoid	Impaired judgment and coordination, bronchitis and asthma, lung and throat cancers, anxiety, lack of energy and motivation, hormone and fertility problems	Moderate
Heroin (also called *smack, dope, horse*) **and codeine**	Opiates	Warm, relaxed, without pain, without anxiety	Infection of organs, inflammation of the heart, convulsions, abscesses, risk of needle-transmitted diseases such as hepatitis and HIV	Strong with heavy use
Lysergic acid diethylamide (LSD) (also called *acid, blotter, trips*)	Hallucinogen	Heightened sensual perception, hallucinations, distortions of sight and sound, little sense of time	Impaired brain function, paranoia, agitation and confusion, flashbacks	Insubstantial
Hallucinogenic mushrooms (psilocybin mushrooms or *Amanita muscaria*) (also called *shrooms, magic mushrooms*)	Hallucinogen	Strong emotions, hallucinations, distortions of sight and sound, out-of-body experience	Paranoia, agitation, poisoning	Insubstantial

(Continued)

KEY 10.7 Drugs have potent effects on the user. (Continued)

DRUG	DRUG CATEGORY	USERS' EFFECTS	POTENTIAL PHYSICAL EFFECTS, SHORT-TERM AND LONG-TERM	DANGER OF DEPENDENCE
Glue, aerosols (also called *whippets, poppers, rush*)	Inhalants	Giddy, lightheaded, dizzy, excited	Damage to brain, liver, lungs, and kidneys; suffocation; heart failure	Insubstantial
Ecstasy (also called *X, XTC, vitamin E*)	Stimulant	Heightened sensual perception, relaxed, clear, fearless	Fatigue, anxiety, depression, heart arrhythmia, hyperthermia from lack of fluid intake during use	Insubstantial
Ephedrine (also called *chi powder, zest*)	Stimulant	Energetic	Anxiety, elevated blood pressure, heart palpitations, memory loss, stroke, psychosis, insomnia	Strong
Gamma hydroxy butyrate (GHB) (also called *G, liquid ecstasy, goop*)	Depressant	Uninhibited, relaxed, euphoric	Anxiety, vertigo, increased heart rate, delirium, agitation	Strong
Ketamine (also called *K, Special K, vitamin K*)	Anaesthetic	Dreamy, floating, having an out-of-body sensation, numb	Neuroses, disruptions in consciousness, reduced ability to move	Strong
OxyContin (also called *Oxy, OC, legal heroin*)	Analgesic (containing opiate)	Relaxed, detached, without pain or anxiety	Overdose death can result when users ingest or inhale crushed time-release pills, or take them in conjunction with alcohol or narcotics	Moderate, with long-term use
Anabolic steroids (also called *roids, juice, hype*)	Steroid	Increased muscle strength and physical performance, energetic	Stunted growth, mood swings, male-pattern baldness, breast development (in men) or body hair development (in women), mood swings, liver damage, insomnia, aggression, irritability	Insubstantial
Methamphetamine (also called *meth, speed, crank*)	Stimulant	Euphoric, confident, alert, energetic	Seizures, heart attack, strokes, vein damage (if injected), sleeplessness, hallucinations, high blood pressure, paranoia, psychoses, depression, anxiety, loss of appetite	Strong, especially if taken by smoking

Source: SafetyFirst, Drug Policy Alliance (www.safety1st.org/drugfacts.html).

Shutterstock

You are responsible for analyzing the potential consequences of what you introduce into your body. Ask questions such as the following:

- What reward am I receiving from taking this risk, and is it worthwhile?
- Am I taking drugs to escape from other problems?
- What positive and negative effects might my behaviour have?
- Why do others want me to take drugs, and what do I really think of these people?
- How would my drug use affect the people in my life?

Use the self-test on page 276 to assess your relationship with drugs. If you believe you have a problem, read the following section on steps that can help you get your life back on track.

Facing Addiction

If you think you may be addicted, seek help through counselling and medical services, detoxification centres, and support groups. Because substances often cause physical changes and psychological dependence, habits are tough to break, and quitting may involve a painful withdrawal. Asking for help isn't an admission of failure but a courageous move to reclaim your life.

Working through substance abuse problems can lead to restored health and self-respect. Helpful resources can provide guidance for generating options and developing practical plans for recovery.

- *Counselling and medical care.* You can find help from school-based, private, government-funded, or workplace-sponsored resources. Ask your school's counselling or health centre, your personal physician, or a local hospital for a referral.
- *Detoxification (detox) centres.* If you have a severe addiction, you may need a controlled environment where you can separate yourself completely from drugs or alcohol.
- *Support groups.* The effectiveness of Alcoholics Anonymous (AA) has led to other support groups for addicts such as Overeaters Anonymous (OA) and Narcotics Anonymous (NA).

HOW CAN YOU MAKE EFFECTIVE
decisions about sex?

What sexuality means to you and the role it plays in your life are personal choices. However, the physical act of sex can go beyond the private realm. Individual sexual conduct can result in an unexpected pregnancy or exposure to *sexually transmitted diseases* or *infections* (STDs and STIs). These consequences affect everyone involved in the sexual act and, often, their families.

Just as your success in school depends on your ability to manage time, your success in school can also depend on making choices that maintain health and safety—yours as well as those of the person with whom you are involved. Analyze sexual issues carefully, weighing the positive and negative effects of your choices. Ask questions such as the following:

- Is this what I really want? Does it fit with my values?
- Do I feel ready or do I feel pressured? Does this choice cause stress for me?
- Is this the right person/moment/situation? Does my partner truly care for me and not just for what we might be doing? Will this enhance or damage our emotional relationship?
- Do I have what I need to prevent pregnancy and exposure to STIs? If not, is having unprotected sex worth the risk?

Birth Control

Using birth control is a choice that helps you decide when and if you want to be a parent. However, it is not for everyone. For some, using any kind of birth control goes against religious or personal beliefs. Others may want to have children. But many sexually active people who do not want children at the moment choose one or more methods of birth control.

Evaluate the pros and cons of each option for yourself and your partner. Consider cost, ease of use, reliability, comfort, and protection against STIs. Communicate with your partner and together make a choice that is comfortable for both of you. For more information, check your library, the Internet, or a bookstore; talk to

Shutterstock

get creative

FIND MORE FUN

Complete the following on paper or in digital format.

Sometimes students get involved in potentially unsafe activities because it seems like there isn't anything else to do. Use your creativity to find enjoyable activities to choose from when you hang out with friends. Check your resources: What possibilities can you find at your student union, student activities centre, school or local arts organizations, athletic organizations, various clubs, nature groups? Could you go hiking? Take a walk or bike ride? Paint pottery? Check out a hockey game? Run a 5K? Try a new kind of cuisine? Volunteer at a children's hospital ward? See a play? Read a book? Watch a movie? List 10 specific activities available to you.

your doctor; or ask a counsellor at the student health centre. Key 10.8 describes established methods, with effectiveness percentages and STI prevention based on proper and regular use.

Sexually Transmitted Infections

STIs spread through sexual contact (intercourse or other sexual activity that involves contact with the genitals). All are highly contagious. The only birth control methods that offer protection are the male and female condoms (latex or polyurethane only), which prevent skin-to-skin contact. Have a doctor examine any irregularity or discomfort as soon as you detect it. Key 10.9 describes common STIs.

KEY 10.8 Make an educated decision about birth control.

METHOD	APPROXIMATE EFFECTIVENESS	PREVENTS STIS?	DESCRIPTION
Abstinence	100%	Only if no sexual activity occurs	Just saying no. No intercourse means no risk of pregnancy. However, alternative modes of sexual activity can still spread STIs.
Condom	85% (95% with spermicide)	Yes, if made of latex	A sheath that fits over the penis or within the vagina and prevents sperm from entering the vagina.
Diaphragm, cervical cap, or shield	85%	No	A bendable rubber cap that fits over the cervix and pelvic bone inside the vagina. (The cervical cap and shield are smaller and fit over the cervix only.) The diaphragm and cervical cap must be fitted initially by a gynecologist. All must be used with a spermicide.
Oral contraceptives (the Pill)	99% with perfect use, 92% for typical users	No	A dosage of hormones taken daily by a woman, preventing the ovaries from releasing eggs. Side effects can include headaches, weight gain, and increased chances of blood clotting. Various brands and dosages; must be prescribed by a doctor.
Injectable contraceptives (Depo-Provera)	97%	No	An injection that a woman must receive from a doctor every few months. Possible side effects may resemble those of oral contraceptives.
Vaginal ring (NuvaRing)	92%	No	A ring inserted into the vagina that releases hormones. Must be replaced monthly. Possible side effects may resemble those of oral contraceptives.

Continued

KEY 10.8 Make an educated decision about birth control. (Continued)

Spermicidal foams, jellies, inserts	71% if used alone	No	Usually used with diaphragms or condoms to enhance effectiveness, they have an ingredient that kills sperm cells (but not STIs). They stay effective for a limited period of time after insertion.
Intrauterine device (IUD)	99%	No	A small coil of wire inserted into the uterus by a gynecologist (who must also remove it). Prevents fertilized eggs from implanting in the uterine wall. May or may not have a hormone component. Possible side effects include increased or abnormal bleeding.
Tubal ligation	Nearly 100%	No	Surgery for women that cuts and ties the fallopian tubes, preventing eggs from travelling to the uterus. Difficult and expensive to reverse. Recommended for those who do not want any, or any more, children.
Vasectomy	Nearly 100%	No	Surgery for men that blocks the tube that delivers sperm to the penis. Like tubal ligation, difficult to reverse and recommended only for those who don't want any, or any more, children.
Rhythm method	Variable	No	Abstaining from intercourse during the ovulation segment of the woman's menstrual cycle. Can be difficult to time and may not account for cycle irregularities.
Withdrawal	Variable	No	Pulling the penis out of the vagina before ejaculation. Unreliable, because some sperm can escape in the fluid released prior to ejaculation. Dependent on a controlled partner.

Source: MayoClinic.com (www.mayoclinic.com/health/birth-control/BI99999/PAGE=BI00020)

KEY 10.9 To stay safe, know these facts about sexually transmitted infections.

DISEASE	SYMPTOMS	HEALTH PROBLEMS IF UNTREATED	TREATMENTS
Chlamydia	Discharge, painful urination, swollen or painful joints, change in menstrual periods for women	Can cause pelvic inflammatory disease (PID) in women, which can lead to sterility or ectopic pregnancies; infection; miscarriage or premature birth.	Curable with full course of antibiotics; avoid sex until treatment is complete.
Gonorrhea	Discharge, burning while urinating	Can cause PID, swelling of testicles and penis, arthritis, skin problems, infections.	Usually curable with antibiotics; however, certain strains are becoming resistant to medication.
Genital herpes	Blisterlike itchy sores in the genital area, headache, fever, chills	Symptoms may subside and then reoccur, often in response to high stress levels; carriers can transmit the virus even when it is dormant.	No cure; some medications, such as Acyclovir, reduce and help heal the sores and may shorten recurring outbreaks.
Syphilis	A genital sore lasting one to five weeks, followed by a rash, fatigue, fever, sore throat, headaches, swollen glands	If it lasts more than four years, it can cause blindness, destruction of bone, insanity, or heart failure; can cause death or deformity of a child born to an infected woman.	Curable with full course of antibiotics.
Human papillomavirus (HPV, or genital warts)	Genital itching and irritation, small clusters of warts	Can increase risk of cervical cancer in women; virus may remain in body and cause recurrences even when warts are removed.	Treatable with drugs applied to warts or various kinds of wart removal surgery. Vaccine (Gardasil) newly available; most effective when given to women before exposure to HPV.
Hepatitis B	Fatigue, poor appetite, vomiting, jaundice, hives	Some carriers will have few symptoms; others may develop chronic liver disease that may lead to other diseases of the liver.	No cure; some will recover, some will not. Bedrest may help ease symptoms. Vaccine is available.

PhotoMan/Fotolia

get $mart

THE RELATIONSHIP BETWEEN WELLNESS AND FINANCIAL FITNESS

Wellness has its costs—fitness fees and healthy food often aren't cheap, although they can save you medical costs down the line. Track health-related expenses (both positive and negative) for one week (note that "Food +" is healthy food, and "Food –" is junk food) and enter your daily and weekly totals in the grid below. For monthly fees such as fitness memberships, divide by four and enter your result in the TOTAL box for fitness.

ITEM	MON	TUES	WED	THURS	FRI	SAT	SUN	TOTAL
Food +								
Food –								
Alcohol								
Tobacco								
Fitness								
Other								

1. Approximately how much did you spend on items that increase wellness?
2. Approximately how much did you spend on items that decrease wellness?
3. Are you spending more to increase or decrease wellness?

If you want to change how you spend money related to your wellness, describe your desired change here and be specific about how you plan to put it into action.

AIDS and HIV

Shutterstock

The most serious STI is AIDS (acquired immune deficiency syndrome), which is caused by the human immunodeficiency virus (HIV). AIDS can result in death. Medical science continues to develop drugs to combat AIDS and related illnesses. Although the drugs can slow the progression of the infection and extend life expectancy, there is currently no known cure.

People acquire HIV through sexual relations, by sharing hypodermic needles for drug use, and by receiving infected blood transfusions. You cannot become infected except through blood, semen, or vaginal fluid contact with one of your own fluids. Breast milk is the only other fluid that can carry the disease. Therefore, it is unlikely you can contract HIV from toilet seats, hugging, kissing, or sharing a glass. Other than not having sex at all, condoms are the best defense against AIDS. Always use a latex condom, because natural skin condoms may let the virus pass through. Avoid petroleum jelly, which can destroy latex. Be wary of *safe sex fatigue*, which leads young and healthy people to be less vigilant about using condoms for every sexual encounter. Although some people dislike using condoms, avoiding them is not worth the risk. The reward is preserving your life.

To be safe, have an HIV test done at your doctor's office or at a clinic. Your school's health department may also administer HIV tests, and home HIV tests are available over the counter. Consider requiring that any sexual partner be tested as well. If you are infected, inform all sexual partners and seek medical assistance. If you're interested, contact a support organization in your area.

HOW CAN YOU STAY SAFE AND
avoid sexual assault?

Staying safe is part of staying well and reducing stress. Crime is a reality on campus as it is in any community. Alcohol and drug-related offenses may occur more frequently than other crimes on campus. College- and university-age females are particularly vulnerable to sexual assault. By law, post-secondary schools are required to report crime statistics yearly.

Personal Safety Strategies

Making intelligent choices is a crucial part of staying safe. Take these practical measures to prevent incidents that jeopardize your well-being.

Be aware of safety issues. Every school has its particular issues—problematic areas of the campus, particular celebrations that get out of hand, bad habits such as students propping open security doors. With awareness, you can steer clear of problems and even work to improve them.

Avoid situations that present clear dangers. Don't walk or exercise alone at night, especially in isolated areas. Don't work or study alone in a building. If a person looks suspicious, contact someone who can help.

Avoid drugs or overuse of alcohol. Anything that impairs judgment makes you vulnerable to assault. Avoid driving while impaired or riding with someone who has taken drugs or alcohol. Avoid attending large parties where people are binge drinking. It is too easy for rape to occur when someone is inebriated.

Avoid people who make you uneasy. If you feel threatened by anyone inside or outside of classes, tell an instructor or campus security. If you feel uncomfortable with someone, trust your intuition and get away from him or her. Stay alert and make no assumptions. As Kelly found out, danger can lurk even with a friend whom you think you can trust.

Be wary of dangers online. Don't give out personal information online to people whom you don't know well. If you have a MySpace or Facebook page, be careful about the text and photos you post. If you feel that someone is harassing you by email or IM, contact an advisor or counsellor. (You may want to save the messages as proof of harassment.)

Review your immunizations. Your success in college or university also depends on your ability to fight off infections and diseases. Post-secondary students living on campus should pay particular attention to the meningococcal meningitis vaccine (which protects you against an infection that results in the swelling and inflammation of the spinal cord and brain), and women under 26 should look into the HPV (human papillomavirus) vaccine (which protects you against an infection that attacks the skin and mucous membranes, often causing cervical cancer).

Take Steps to Avoid Sexual Assault

One in four females is likely to be sexually assaulted in her lifetime, as is one in six males. Females between the ages of 18 and 24 are more likely to be stalked, harassed, or sexually assaulted than any other age group. In fact, most sexual assaults among that age range occur on college or university campuses or on dates.[30]

Sexual assault includes a wide range of behaviours, often called the *sexual violence continuum*, ranging from obscene phone calls or to exhibitionism to actual penetration or forced prostitution.[31] Unfortunately, many behaviours bordering on or involving sexual assault are actually advertised or condoned by society and the media. Kelly and Becca's program, One Student, provides resources, facts, and programs for students on campuses around the nation, aiming to educate students and create a future where sexual assaults no longer occur.

Rape is not about sex, it's about one person exerting power over another. Rape is not caused by the victim's behaviour or clothing, any more than auto theft is caused by the owner of the car. Rape is about one person having non-consensual sex (without permission) with another. It can happen on a date, at home, or at a party. And it is a crime.

If you find yourself in a situation where you feel powerless or threatened, leave immediately. If you feel afraid to leave by yourself, call a friend or call a cab. And if you see someone being inappropriate or offensive toward another, show your disapproval and publicly interrupt the behaviour as best you can. If necessary, call for help.

If you are assaulted, tell someone you trust, right away. Call the Rape and Incest National Network (RAINN) hotline to find the phone number of a local rape crisis centre so you can talk to someone. They are also online at https://www.rainn.org/get-help/sexual-assault-and-rape-international-resources. It offers information on Canadian Rape Crisis Centres.

If you want to report the assault to the police, you can do that as well, preferably with a supportive person accompanying you. Get ongoing counselling to help you deal with your feelings and eventually move from being a victim to becoming a survivor. Rape-crisis centres specialize in this type of counselling.

revisit RISK AND REWARD

Kelly Addington and Becca Tieder

What happened to Kelly and Becca? With Becca's guidance, Kelly came to grips with the sexual assault. "Being a great leader is a choice," says Becca. "We were very average people who chose to respond to something in a way that was earnest." Choosing the risk of leading through education and communication, they founded *Let's Talk About "IT"* to uncover the truths about sexual assault and show how friendship and empathy help the recovery process. They decode the toxic language surrounding sex, and their work rewards students with innovative ways to address alcohol, sex under the influence, and date rape drugs.

Kelly and Becca continue to take risks that have brought great reward to students all over the country. They created the Sexversations card game to foster conversations about intimacy, sexuality, and sexual assault. In 2010, they founded *One Student* to combat sexual violence. They also created a public awareness campaign—the *No Woman Left Behind* initiative. They have shared their story and insight on more than 300 post-secondary campuses, taking special satisfaction when someone confides in them. Best of friends now for two decades, they have achieved personal fulfillment in relationships with loving husbands and supportive parents.

What does this mean for you? Most people think that sexual assault, like being struck by lightning, will never happen to them. Planning ahead and promoting a safe community can help. What are some specific steps you can take to reduce the likelihood that you will be a victim of, or be involved in, sexual assault? Kelly and Becca's case illustrates the importance of communication in the prevention and recovery process. Who are some people in your life you could risk talking to about sexual assault? Are there other resources in your school, family, or community to which you can turn?

What risk may bring reward beyond your world? One Student's slogan is "One sexual assault is too many. One student can make a difference." Go to the website onestudent.org to learn how to take action. Then choose one or more risks that you think will bring rewards at your school. Consider ordering the free posters and post them in strategic locations, organizing a wristband campaign to symbolize a united front against sexual violence, or using the video "Take the First Step" to get a dialogue going with classmates, administrators, teachers, and parents. "We don't see the snow and the lack of life. We see the first blades of grass and the first blossom of flowers," Becca says. "Those are the students we hear from and their stories… we don't see the lack of success, we see the opportunity."

KNOW IT *Think Critically*

Move toward better health

Build basic skills. Pick a behaviour—eating, drinking, sleeping, sexual activity—that holds some kind of issue for you. Describe your behaviour and your attitude toward what you do.

Example

Issue: binge drinking

Behaviour: I binge drink probably once a week.

Attitude: I don't think it's any big deal. I like using it to escape.

Your turn

Issue:

_____

_____

Behaviour:

_____

_____

Attitude:

_____

_____

Question to think about: Is it worth it?

Take it to the next level. Examine whether your behaviour is a problem by noting positive and negative effects. To continue the example above:

Positive effects: I have fun with my friends. I feel confident, accepted, social.

Negative effects: I feel foggy the next day. I miss class. I'm irritable.

Your turn

Positive effects:

_____

_____

Negative effects:

_____

_____

Move toward mastery. Based on the effects of your behaviour, think about where you want to make a difference, and why. Then come up with changes you could make. For example, the binge drinker might consider cutting back on one drinking outing a week and investigating one new social activity that does not involve drinking.

How you might change your behaviour:

_____

_____

_____

How you might change your attitude:

_____

_____

_____

Positive effects you think these changes would have:

_____

_____

_____

Choose two actions to take—one that would improve your attitude and one that would improve your behaviour—that you think would have the most positive effect for you. Commit to these actions with specific plans and put positive change in motion.

Attitude improvement plan:

_____

_____

_____

Behaviour improvement plan:

_____

_____

_____

WRITE IT *Communicate*

Record your thoughts on a separate piece of paper, in a journal, or electronically.

Emotional intelligence journal: Addiction. Discuss how you feel about addiction in any form—to alcohol, drugs, food, sex, the Internet, gambling—whether or not you have had direct or indirect experience with it. Imagine that a close friend or family member has a dangerous addiction of some kind. Use your emotional intelligence to describe how you would address the problem with that person to produce the best possible outcome.

Real-life writing: Health on campus. Think about what you consider the most significant health issue at your school—personal safety, alcohol or drug abuse, smoking, weight management, and so on. Write a 500-word editorial for your school paper on the topic, describing the details of the problem and proposing one or more solutions. For example, if weight control is a problem, you might suggest changing the contents of the drink vending machines. When you are done, consider submitting your editorial to the paper. (Have an instructor or peer review it before you send it in.)

DO IT

Build Your Brand

Wellness at Work

21st Century Learning Building Blocks:

- **Initiative and self-direction**
- **Critical thinking and problem solving**
- **Information literacy**

Complete the following in your electronic portfolio or on separate sheets of paper.

Taking responsibility for your health can make you a more valuable employee, in part because many companies are putting pressure on their employees to do more in less time. Increased work burdens, late nights, and work calls during weekends or off-hours create a great deal of stress for workers. In addition, health care costs are on the rise for companies.

Part of your responsibility involves getting routine screenings from a doctor or health clinic. Below is a list of health items commonly tested during screening. Using the Internet or your library, research the listed items. For each, describe 1) What the item is and why it is important to your overall health; 2) What the normal range is for the item and what numbers (high, low, or both) indicate a concern; and 3) What to do if you have abnormal results for this item.

- Hemoglobin
- Hematocrit
- Glucose
- Potassium
- Magnesium
- Calcium
- Iron
- Cholesterol

11

Torian Richardson

When you understand the values and perspectives that lie behind your financial decisions, you will be more able to take productive action toward financial goals that are meaningful to you.

Managing Money

LIVING BELOW YOUR MEANS

What Would You Risk? *Torian Richardson*

Torian Richardson

THINK ABOUT THIS SITUATION AS YOU READ, AND CONSIDER WHAT ACTION YOU WOULD TAKE. THIS CHAPTER HELPS YOU GET TO KNOW YOURSELF AS A MONEY MANAGER. IT OFFERS STRATEGIES FOR USING MONEY WISELY IN THE PRESENT SO THAT YOU HAVE MORE FINANCIAL STABILITY IN THE FUTURE.

Despite growing up in a mentally, physically, and emotionally abusive, working-class household on the South Side of Chicago, Torian Richardson developed strong work habits early on. His dad drove a bus and his mom worked at the post office to help send Torian and his sister to better schools. "Although my parents didn't have a college education—they always talked about the value of education," he says.

Although a lackadaisical student in high school, Torian remained curious about how to overcome challenges, escape cycles of abuse, and succeed. Always observant and aware, he asked friends how they handled certain situations. To escape stress at home, he spent time on the playing fields, excelling in football, wrestling, and track. When he was 16, he moved from living with his mother on the South Side to living with his father in the western suburbs of the city. He became aware of who had money and who didn't, and what budgeting was all about.

Torian earned a partial sports scholarship to college, and his grandmother helped cover expenses, but he struggled and was put on academic probation. Less than a year later, Torian lost that scholarship and transferred to a community college. He worked part-time at a fast-food drive-through, trying to scrape together enough money to pay his tuition on his own. Friends and classmates who once looked up to him and anticipated his success in college saw the apparent lack of progress he had made, and his self-esteem took a hit. He doubted that he could take the risks needed to earn the reward of graduating from college and supporting his athletic pursuits on his own.

to be continued . . .

Economic challenges and rapidly developing technology have changed how people manage money, and paying for post-secondary school continues to be a challenge. You will learn more about Torian, and the reward resulting from his actions, within the chapter.

Notes

Today   Mar 10   8:01 AM

Working through this chapter will help you to:

statusCHECK

How Effectively Do You Manage Money?

For each statement, circle the number that feels right to you, from 1 for "not at all true for me" to 5 for "very true for me."

1. I am aware of my personal views on money, spending, and saving. ① ② ③ ④ ⑤

2. I know how much money I have to spend each month. ① ② ③ ④ ⑤

3. I know the difference between things that I want and things that I need, and I shop accordingly. ① ② ③ ④ ⑤

4. I control my spending by using a monthly budget. ① ② ③ ④ ⑤

5. I successfully balance my responsibilities at work and at school. ① ② ③ ④ ⑤

6. I understand the benefits and responsibilities of financial aid. ① ② ③ ④ ⑤

7. I know the current interest rates on my credit cards. ① ② ③ ④ ⑤

8. I know my credit rating and its potential effect on my financial future. ① ② ③ ④ ⑤

9. I add to a savings account regularly. ① ② ③ ④ ⑤

10. I have begun planning for my retirement. ① ② ③ ④ ⑤

Each of the topics in these statements is covered in this chapter. Note those statements for which you circled a 3 or lower. Skim the chapter to see where those topics appear, and pay special attention to them as you read, learn, and apply new strategies.

REMEMBER: NO MATTER HOW EFFECTIVELY YOU MANAGE YOUR MONEY, YOU CAN IMPROVE WITH EFFORT AND PRACTICE.

WHAT DOES MONEY
A *mean in your life?*

study by Sun Life Financial suggests that 72% of Canadians experience "excessive levels of anxiety" over their finances. [1] Adding the high cost of college or university tuition to the normal list of financial obligations means that, for the vast majority of post-secondary students, money is tight. This situation is especially true for self-supporting students, who may have to cover living and family expenses in addition to funds for tuition, books, and other school fees.

Thinking analytically, creatively, and practically about money management can help relieve money-related stress and increase control. Start first by analyzing who you are as a money manager and examining the relationship between your money and your time.

How You Perceive and Use Money

How you interact with money is unique. Some people spend earnings right away, some save for the future. Some charge everything, some make cash purchases only, others do

MyStudentSuccessLab

Whether face-to-face or online, MyStudentSuccessLab helps students build the skills they need through peer-led video interviews, interactive practice exercises, and activities that provide academic, life, and professionalism skills.

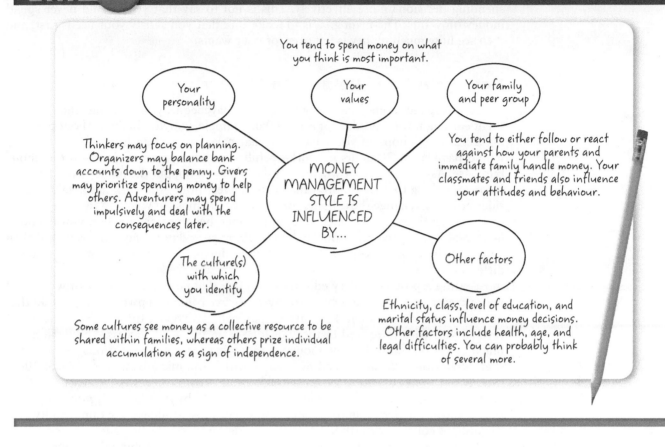

You tend to spend money on what you think is most important.

Your personality

Your values

Your family and peer group

MONEY MANAGEMENT STYLE IS INFLUENCED BY...

Thinkers may focus on planning. Organizers may balance bank accounts down to the penny. Givers may prioritize spending money to help others. Adventurers may spend impulsively and deal with the consequences later.

You tend to either follow or react against how your parents and immediate family handle money. Your classmates and friends also influence your attitudes and behaviour.

The culture(s) with which you identify

Other factors

Some cultures see money as a collective resource to be shared within families, whereas others prize individual accumulation as a sign of independence.

Ethnicity, class, level of education, and marital status influence money decisions. Other factors include health, age, and legal difficulties. You can probably think of several more.

something in between. Some pay bills online and others mail cheques. Some rewards that people seek are measured in dollar amounts and others in non-material terms. Your spending and saving behaviour tends to reflect your values and goals. As you analyze who you are as a money manager, consider the influences in Key 11.1.

Money coach Connie Kilmark notes that you cannot change how you handle money until you analyze your attitudes and behaviours. "If managing money was just about math and the numbers, everyone would know how to manage their finances sometime around the fifth grade," she says.[2] When you take an honest look at how you feel about money, you can make more effective financial decisions based on what works best for you.

Needs Versus Wants

People often confuse what they need with what they want. True needs are few and basic: food, water, air, shelter (rent or mortgage as well as home maintenance costs and utilities), family and friends, and some mode of transportation. Everything else is technically a want—something you would like to have but can live without. When people spend money on those wants, they often find that they don't have enough cash available for needs. You may want to spend $1,000 on a flat-screen TV, but you might regret the purchase if your car suddenly breaks down and needs a $1,000 transmission repair.

Check your spending for purpose. What do you buy with your money? Are the items you purchase necessary? When you do spend on a want rather than a need, are you doing so thoughtfully by planning the added expense into your monthly budget? If you get a clear idea of what you want and what you need, you can think through spending decisions more effectively. This is not to say that you should never spend money on wants. The main goal is to make sure that you satisfy your needs first, and then see how much money is left over for your wants.

How Your Time Relates to Money

When you spend money that came to you in a paycheque, you exchange the time you spent earning it for a product or service. For example, you are thinking about purchasing a $200 cellphone. If you have a job that pays you $10 an hour after taxes, you would have spent 20 hours of work—a full week at a part-time job—on the phone purchase. Ask yourself: Is it worth it? If the answer is no, put the money away and use it for something that is of more value to you. Every hour you work has a value—consider how to exchange those hours for what matters most to you.

The relationship between time and money becomes clear when you examine how long it takes to earn money while tracking your day-to-day expenses, and then compare the results. Key 11.2 shows how reducing regular expenses can make a difference.

Getting a post-secondary education is a risk that costs many hours of work, and will increase your student debt. A four-year degree can cost upwards of $80,000 that takes the average student 14 years to pay off.[3] However, tuition and time spent reward you with improved chances of long-term financial success. "Education is a much better reason to borrow money than buying cars or McMansions," reports the *Wall Street Journal*, "and it endows people with economic advantages... As of 2009, the annual pre-tax income of households headed by people with at least a college degree exceeded that of less-educated households by 101%."[4] *Opportunity cost* refers to what you give up to get something. For most students, the opportunity cost of going to college is worth it.

With more of an idea of what values and perspectives lie behind the financial decisions you make, you will be more able to choose and take productive risks that move you toward meaningful financial goals. Start with creating a budget.

KEY 11.2 Put your wallet away today, and earn money for tomorrow.

DAY-TO-DAY EXPENSE	APPROXIMATE COST	POTENTIAL SAVINGS
Gourmet coffee	$4 per day, 5 days a week, totals $20 per week	$80 per month; $960 for the year. Invested in a 5-percent interest account for a year, the total would amount to more than $1,000.
Alcohol	Two drinks plus tip total about $20 per night; 2 nights per week amounts to $40 per week	$160 per month; $1,920 for the year. Invested in a 5-percent interest account for a year, the total would amount to more than $2,000.
Ordering in meals	$15 per meal, twice per week, totals $30 per week	$120 per month; $1,440 for the year. Invested in a 5-percent interest account for a year, the total would amount to nearly $1,550.

HOW CAN YOU CREATE
and use a budget?

Everything you will read about money management in this chapter falls under the umbrella of one central concept: *Live below your means* or, in other words, spend less than you earn whenever possible. When money in is more than money out, you will have extra to save or spend.

How can you find out the difference between what you spend and what you earn? Track your spending and earning, and create a **budget** that balances both. Because many expenses are billed monthly, most people use a month as a unit of time. Creating a budget involves several steps:

> **BUDGET**
> A plan to coordinate resources and expenditures; a set of goals regarding money.

1. *Gather information* about what you earn (money flowing in).
2. *Figure out* your expenditures (money flowing out).
3. *Analyze* the difference between earnings and expenditures.
4. Come up with *creative ideas* about how you can make changes.
5. Take *practical action* to adjust spending or earning so you come out even or ahead.

Your biggest expense right now is probably the cost of your education, including tuition and perhaps room and board. However, that expense may not hit you fully until after you graduate and begin to pay back your student loans. (Financial aid options will be explored later in the chapter.) For now, include in your budget only the part of the cost of your education you are paying while you are in school.

Figure Out What You Earn

To determine what is available to you on a monthly basis, start with the money you earn in a month's time at any regular job. Then, if you have savings set aside for your education or any other source of income, determine how much of it you can spend each month and add that amount. If you have a grant for the entire year, for example, divide it by 12 (or by how many months you are in school over the course of a year) to see how much you can use each month.

Figure Out What You Spend

First, note regular monthly expenses like rent, phone, and cable. (Look at past cheques and electronic debits to estimate what the month's bills will be.) Some expenses, like automobile and health insurance, may be billed only once or twice a year. In these cases, divide the yearly cost by 12 to see how much you spend every month. Then, over a month's time, keep a spending log in a small notebook to record each day's cash or debit card expenditures. Be sure to count smaller purchases if they are frequent. (For example, one or two pricey coffees a day add up over time.) By the end of the month, you will have a good idea of where your dollars go.

Key 11.3 lists common sources of income as well as expenses for students. Use the total of all your monthly expenses as a baseline for other months, realizing that spending will vary depending on events in your life or factors such as seasons. For example, if you pay for heating, that cost will be far greater in cold weather.

Personal finance software programs, such as Quicken, can help you track spending and saving and categorize expenses. With software, you can create reports about how much you spend on groceries in a one-month period or how much you earned from work in a

Shutterstock

Common Sources of Income

- Take-home pay from a full-time or part-time job
- Take-home pay from summer and holiday employment
- Money earned from work-study or paid internship
- Money from parents or other relatives
- Scholarships
- Grants
- Loans

Common Expenses

- Rent or mortgage
- Tuition you are paying now
- Books and other course materials
- Utilities (electricity, gas, oil, water)
- Telephone (cellphone and/or land line)
- Food
- Clothing, toiletries, household supplies
- Child care
- Transportation and auto expenses (gas, maintenance, service)
- Credit cards and other payments on credit (car payment)
- Insurance (health, auto, homeowner's or renter's, life)
- Entertainment (cable TV, movies, eating out, books and magazines, music downloads)
- Computer-related expenses, including online service costs
- Miscellaneous expenses

year's time. Also, if you manage bank and credit accounts online, you can easily access information about what you are earning and spending over a period of time.

Evaluate the Difference

Once you know what you earn and what you spend, calculate the difference—subtract your monthly expenses from your monthly income. Ideally, you have money left over to save or spend. However, if you are spending more than you take in, examine these areas of your budget.

- *Expenses.* Did you forget to budget for recurring expenses such as the cost for semi-annual dental visits? Or was your budget derailed by an emergency expense?
- *Spending patterns and priorities.* Did you spend money wisely during the month, or did you overspend on luxuries?
- *Income.* Do you bring in enough money? Do you need another source?

Adjust expenses or earnings

If you spend more than you are earning, you can either earn more or spend less, or better yet, do both. You will explore ways to increase income through jobs and/or financial aid in the next section.

There are many ways to decrease spending. Perhaps the most important one is thinking before you buy: Do I really need this? Is the expense worth it? Just answering those questions will reduce unnecessary purchases. Other ways to manage spending include:

Set up automatic payments. If you set up electronic monthly payments for bills and tuition and schedule regular automatic transfers of small amounts into your savings, you will take care of your needs first without thinking about it. Then you can look at what is left over and decide how you want to spend or save it.

Comparison shop. Again, think before you buy. If you are in the market for an expensive item such as a cellphone, computer, or car, research prices at stores and online. Use websites such as ShopBot, PriceBat, and Price Finder to comparision shop. You can also find deals on WagJag or Groupon. Consider purchasing used items at Value Village or other second-hand shops.

Show your student ID. Your student identification card is your ticket to savings for a variety of items such as movies, shows, concerts, restaurant meals and take out, book and clothing stores, travel services, electronics, and much more.

Finally, work to save money on a day-to-day basis. The effort of saving small amounts regularly can eventually bring significant reward. Key 11.4 has some suggestions.

Call on your dominant multiple intelligences when planning your budget. For example, logical-mathematical learners may choose a classic detail-oriented budgeting plan, visual learners may want to create a budget chart, and bodily-kinesthetic learners may want to make budgeting more tangible by dumping receipts into a big jar and tallying them at the end of the month. Personal finance software can accommodate different types of learners with features such as written reports (verbal-linguistic, logical-mathematical) and graphical reports (visual). See the Multiple Intelligence Strategies for Financial Management (page 306) for more MI-based ideas on how to manage your money.

KEY 11.4 Look for ways to trim your spending.

- Share living space.
- Rent movies or borrow them from friends or the library.
- Eat at home more often.
- Use grocery and clothing coupons from the paper or online.
- Take advantage of sales, buy store brands, and buy in bulk.
- Find play and concert tickets that are discounted for students.
- Walk or use public transportation.
- Bring lunch from home.
- Shop in secondhand or consignment stores or swap clothing with friends.
- Communicate via email or snail mail.
- Ask a relative to help with child care, or create a babysitting co-op.
- Reduce electricity costs by cutting back on air conditioning and switching to compact fluorescent bulbs (CFLs) in your lamps at home.

get practical

MAP OUT YOUR BUDGET

Use this exercise to see what you take in and what you spend. Then decide what adjustments you need to make. Consider using an online calculator for this task, such as www.calculatorweb.com.

Before You Begin: Keep a spending log for one week to one month (whatever you have time for). Make sure to note all purchases made by cash, cheque, debit card, and credit card.

Step 1: Expenses. Based on your spending log, estimate your current expenses in dollars per month, using the following table. The grand total is your total monthly expenses. If any expense comes only once a year, enter it in the *Annual Expenses* column and divide by 12 to get your *Monthly Expenses* figure for that item.

EXPENSES	MONTHLY EXPENSES	ANNUAL EXPENSES
School supplies including books and technology		
Tuition and fees		
Housing: dorm, rent, or mortgage		
Phone (cell and/or landline)		
Cable TV, Internet		
Gas and electricity, water		
Car costs: monthly payment, auto insurance, maintenance, repairs, registration, inspections		
Travel costs: gas, public transportation, parking permits, tolls		
Vacations, trips home		
Food: Groceries, meal plan cafeteria, eating out, snacks		
Health insurance		
Health maintenance costs: gym, equipment, sports fees, classes		
Medical costs: doctor and dentists visits, vision, prescriptions, counselling		
Entertainment: movies, music purchases, socializing		
Laundry costs: supplies, service		
Clothing purchases		
Household supplies		
Payments on credit card debt		
Student loan or other loan repayment		
Donations to charitable organizations		
Childcare		
Other: emergencies, hobbies, gifts		
TOTAL EXPECTED EXPENSES		

get practical

Step 2: Gross Income. Calculate your average monthly income. As with expenses, if any source of income arrives only once a year, enter it in the *Annual* column and divide by 12 to get the monthly figure. For example, if you have a $6,000 scholarship for the year, your monthly income would be $500 ($6,000 divided by 12).

INCOME/RESOURCES	MONTHLY INCOME	ANNUAL
Employment (after federal/provincial taxes)		
Family contribution		
Financial assistance: grants, federal and other loans		
Scholarships		
Interest and dividends		
Other gifts, income, and contributions		
Total Expected Income		

Step 3: Net Income (Cash Flow). Subtract the grand total of your monthly expenses from the grand total of your monthly income.

INCOME PER MONTH	
Total expected expenses	
Total expected income	
NET INCOME (INCOME – EXPENSES)	

Source: Adapted from Julie Stein, California State University, East Bay.

Step 4: Adjustments. If you have a negative cash flow, what would you change? Examine your budget and spending log to look for problem areas. Remember, you can increase income, decrease spending, or do both. List two ideas about how to get your cash flow back in the black.

HOW CAN YOU INCREASE INCOME
through work and financial aid?

If you reduce your spending and still come up short, as countless people do, you may need to look at ways to increase your income. The rising cost of education leads most students to seek additional money through work, financial aid, or both.

- According to a 2007 survey, nearly 50 percent of first-year post-secondary students added a job to their scheduled weekly responsibilities to earn money for tuition.[5]
- Statistics Canada's *The Daily*, reports that almost 6 out of every 10 students needed student loans to help them complete their post-secondary degree/diploma.[6]

Read on to find ways to get as much help as possible from these income sources.

Managing Money

297

Juggle Work and School

If you want or need a job, try to work in a way that doesn't completely derail you from your academic work and goals. Think analytically and creatively, and come up with a practical plan that suits your situation.

Establish your needs

Think about what you need from a job. Ask questions such as the following:

- How much money do I need to make—weekly, per term, for the year?
- What time of day is best for me? Should I consider night or weekend work?
- Can my schedule handle a full-time job, or should I look for part-time work?
- Do I want hands-on experience in a particular field?
- How flexible a job do I need?
- Can I, or should I, find work at my school or as part of a work-study program?

Analyze the impact

Working while in school has positive and negative effects. Think through these pros and cons when considering or evaluating any job:

PROS OF WORKING WHILE IN SCHOOL	CONS OF WORKING WHILE IN SCHOOL
• General and career-specific experience	• Time commitment that reduces available study time
• Developing contacts	• Reduced opportunity for social and extracurricular activities
• Enhanced school performance (although full-time work can be problematic, working up to 15 hours a week may actually improve efficiency)	• Having to shift gears mentally from work to classroom
• Money earned	• Stretching yourself too thin; fatigue

Create and choose options

With the information you have gathered and analyzed, you can look carefully at what is available on and off campus, and apply for the job or jobs that suit your needs best. Continue to evaluate after you start a job. If it doesn't benefit you as much as you had anticipated, consider making a change, either in that job or by changing jobs.

Your goal is to earn the money you need without derailing your education. If you make careful choices about work and about how to schedule your life around work, you can reach that goal.

talk risk and reward . . .

Torian Richardson

Risk asking tough questions to be rewarded with new insights. Use the following questions to inspire discussion with classmates, either in person or online.

- What obstacles, reasonable or not, have kept you from applying for financial aid? Identify a risk you can take today to earn the reward of overcoming one or more of them.
- How good are you at differentiating between needs and wants? At prioritizing needs?
- Everyone has coping strategies that involve spending: some people like new clothes, others like expensive restaurants. What can you do to make the reward of saving money seem worth the risk of feeling deprived?

CONSIDER THE CASE: Torian had a sudden change in his finances when he lost his athletic scholarship. Are you prepared to handle a sudden drain on your bank account or loss of financial support from your family? What could you do to be ready? If you have experienced a financial crisis, how did you get through it?

get $mart

PhotoMan/Fotolia

Examine your current financial lifestyle with a few short questions:

1. Which do you typically spend money on first?
   a. needs
   b. wants

2. Where do you tend to find yourself at the end of the month?
   a. With a little bit of spending money
   b. Down to zero

3. How do you typically use credit cards?
   a. only when I know I can pay off the balance at the end of the month
   b. frequently, and I pay the minimum each month

4. How aware are you of money coming in and going out?
   a. I check my finances regularly and stay aware
   b. I don't pay much attention to my finances

5. Where do you keep money that you've saved?
   a. in a chequing or savings account
   b. I don't have savings

Add up the number of a's and b's: a_____ b_____

More a's than b's indicates *more* financial stability. More b's than a's indicates *less* financial stability. Whether you tend to be more or less stable is not a judgment on you, but an opportunity to assess the effects of your financial lifestyle and decide if you want to adjust it in order to increase your stability. What is your reaction to this small look at your habits?

Managing Money

Explore and Apply for Financial Aid

Let's face it: post-secondary education in Canada is not cheap. As a result, many students need some sort of financial help. Most sources of financial aid don't seek out recipients. It is up to you to learn how you (or you and your parents, if they currently help to support you) can finance your education. Visit your school's financial aid office, research what is available, weigh the pros and cons of each option, decide what works best, and then apply early. Above all, think critically. Never assume that you are not eligible for aid. The types of aid available are student loans, grants, and scholarships.

Student loans

As the recipient of a student loan, you are responsible for paying back the amount you borrow, plus interest, according to a predetermined payment schedule that may stretch over a number of years. The amount you borrow is known as the loan *principal*, and *interest* is the fee that you pay for the privilege of using money that belongs to someone else.

The federal government administers or oversees most student loans. To receive aid from any federal program, you must be a citizen or eligible noncitizen and be enrolled in a program that meets government requirements. The federal government recently took over control of the Canada Student Loans Program. Applying for

student PROFILE

Christian Gaumont
SPROTT-SHAW COMMUNITY COLLEGE, BRITISH COLUMBIA

Christian Gaumont

About me:

I'm a single dad of French Canadian descent on the cusp of turning 40. My shoes are worn thin from walking many, many avenues of life. I live with passion, lead by example, and cultivate compromise rather than despise it. Every day, for me, is a privilege and an adventure.

What I focus on:

For me, managing money starts with managing myself. It's about attitudes and emotions, self-control and priorities. If I am to dress for success, the fabric of my suit must be tightly woven with all these threads. Once the self is well managed, it becomes much easier to apply and properly execute a financial plan, or any plans for that matter; that's my way of doing. I entered this current academic year with just enough money to cover tuition fees and a few groceries. From the very beginning, the order was tall: coordinate studies, work, and family. I can say that hardship builds character and hunger prompts action. I know what the phrase "starving student" means now; my only food comes from what my children leave on their plates after each meal. Money is that tight, but my motto is to not complain.

I find my present lifestyle resembling in many ways the lifestyle of those who faced great adversity during the Great Depression. Just like them, I am developing a strong aversion to waste and unnecessary luxuries. Yes, hardship builds character.

What will help me in the workplace:

This school year I have learned more than textbook material. I have learned to strengthen myself and humble my soul, while also learning the real value of money. Essentially, I will carry these things with me forever in all my future quests for success.

Christian Gaumont. Sprott-Shaw Community College, British Columbia. Reprinted by permission.

assistance, no matter what province you live in, is done with a single application form. Your application is evaluated for eligibility for several programs, including the Canada Millennium Scholarship Program, provincial loans, plus any bursaries and grants you may be entitled to. For information regarding student loans in Canada, get an application form from your school. You can also contact the Canada Student Loans Program, administered through Human Resources and Skills Development Canada, by calling 1-800-O CANADA (1-800-622-6232), or you can find the latest information available by going to www.canlearn.ca. There are many helpful online references for student loans, some of which even enable you to apply online. Be sure to apply early. Get your application completed at least two to three months prior to the start of your studies to ensure it will have time to be processed.

Grants and scholarships

Unlike student loans, neither grants nor scholarships require repayment. *Grants*, funded by governments as well as private organizations, are awarded to students who show financial need. *Scholarships* may be financed by government or private organizations, schools, or individuals, and are awarded to students who show talent or ability in specified areas.

Even if you did not receive a grant or scholarship in your first year, you may be eligible for opportunities in other years of study. These opportunities are often based on grades and campus leadership and may be given by individual departments.

get creative

Complete the following on paper or in digital format.

Think about all the ways you spend money in a month's time. Where can you trim a bit? What expense can you do without? Where can you look for savings or discounts? Can you barter a product or service for one that a friend can provide? Create a list of five to ten workable ideas.

Give these a try and see how they can help you put some money toward your savings. To make the experiment tangible, put cash into a jar daily or weekly in the amounts that these changes are saving you. See what you have accumulated at the end of one month—and bank it.

If you are receiving aid from your school, follow all the rules and regulations, including meeting application deadlines and remaining in good academic standing. In most cases, you will be required to reapply for aid every year.

■ *Scholarships.* Scholarships are given for various abilities and talents. They may reward academic achievement, exceptional abilities in sports or the arts, citizenship, or leadership. Certain scholarships are sponsored by government agencies. If you display exceptional ability and are disabled, female, of an ethnic background classified as a minority, or a child of someone who draws government benefits, you might find federal scholarship opportunities geared toward you.

All kinds of organizations offer scholarships. You may receive scholarships from individual departments at your school or from your school's independent scholarship funds, local organizations such as the Rotary Club, or privately operated aid foundations. Labour unions and companies may offer scholarships for children of employees. Membership groups, such as Scouting organizations or the YMCA/YWCA, might offer scholarships, and religious organizations are another source of money.

■ *Researching grants and scholarships.* It can take work to locate scholarships and work-study programs because many are not widely advertised. Start digging at your financial aid office and visit your library, bookstore, and the Internet. Two good places to start looking are www.studentawards.com and http://www.scholarshipscanada.com/.

WHAT WILL HELP YOU
use credit cards wisely?

The typical college or university student receives dozens of credit card offers. These offers—and the cards that go along with them—are a double-edged sword. They are a handy alternative to cash and can help build a strong credit history if used appropriately, but they also can plunge you into a hole of debt.

The majority of Canadians have some level of debt, and many people go through periods when they have a hard time keeping up with their bills. Falling behind on payments, however, could result in a poor credit rating that makes it difficult for you to make large purchases or take out loans. If you are having trouble keeping up with your payments, seek out the advice of a credit counsellor. Their services are often free.

David Thompson, a credit counsellor in Ottawa, says students need to be careful when using credit cards. Abusing credit cards can damage your credit rating, which can

Managing Money

affect you when applying for jobs in the future. Two companies in Canada track and collect credit information: Equifax Canada and TransUnion Canada. They document your credit history, including your payment history and any missed payments.[7]

How Credit Cards Work

To charge means to create a debt that must be repaid. The credit card issuer earns money by charging interest, often 18 percent or higher, on unpaid balances. Here is an example—say you have a $3,000 unpaid balance on your card at an annual interest rate of 18 percent. If you make the $60 minimum payment every month, it will take eight years to pay off your debt, assuming that you make no other purchases. The effect on your wallet is staggering:

Original debt	$3,000
Cost to repay credit card loan at an annual interest rate of 18 percent for 8 years	$5,760
Cost of using credit	**$2,760**
	($5,760 − $3,000)

By the time you finish, you will have repaid nearly twice your original debt.

Keep in mind that credit card companies are in business to make money and do not have your financial best interests at heart. Focusing on what's best for your finances is your job, and the first step is to know as much as you can about credit cards. Start with the important concepts presented in Key 11.5, and make sure you read the fine print of any card you are considering so that you know what you are getting into.

Watch For Problems

In response to recent economic changes, credit card disclaimers and policies can cause problems unless you stay alert. Here are a few you should note, both when seeking a new card and when looking at existing card statements:[8]

- *New fees.* In addition to annual fees becoming once again common, a card may charge fees for reward programs, paying your bill by phone, or even checking your balance.
- *Shrinking or disappearing grace periods.* In the past, a *grace period* of a few days may have given you a chance to pay late but avoid fees. Now, even just slightly late payments will usually result in a fee charged to your card.
- *Reward program changes.* Even with a reward program you have enjoyed for a while, such as airline miles or cash back, keep checking your statements. Cards may charge for reward programs or may change or remove them if you are late with a payment.
- *Fee harvesting cards.* Some cards feature low credit limits and come loaded with extra fees. After the fees are tacked onto the low credit limit, very little is left to spend and consumers often end up going over their limit—resulting in more fees.
- *The universal default clause.* This increasingly common policy allows creditors to increase your interest rates if you make a late payment to any account, not just those that you have with them. This means that if you are late on your payment for an unrelated loan, your creditors can increase your credit card interest rate. You can avoid this situation by paying your bills on time

The best way to avoid mishaps is to read the fine print and to attempt to pay your bills on time as often as possible. Keep a schedule of bill due dates and check your balances regularly. Prevention is the best line of defence.

Manage Credit Card Debt

To avoid excessive debt, ask yourself questions before charging: Would I buy it if I had to pay cash? Can I pay off the balance in full at the end of the billing cycle? If I buy this, what purchases will I have to put off or give up altogether? Even if you limit your card use to needs, you can still get into trouble. Many students put books and tuition on

WHAT TO KNOW ABOUT	. . . AND HOW TO USE WHAT YOU KNOW
Account balance—a dollar amount that includes any unpaid balance, new purchases and cash advances, finance charges, and fees. Updated monthly.	Charge only what you can afford to pay at the end of the month. Keep track of your balance. Hold on to receipts and call customer service if you have questions.
Annual fee—the yearly cost that some companies charge for owning a card.	Look for cards without an annual fee or, if you have paid your bills on time, ask your current company to waive the fee.
Annual percentage rate (APR)—the amount of interest charged on your unpaid balance (that is, the cost of credit if you carry a balance in any given month). The higher the APR, the more you pay in finance charges.	Shop around for the best rate available for students. Also, watch out for low, but temporary, introductory rates that skyrocket to more than 20 percent after a few months. Look for fixed rates (guaranteed not to change).
Available credit—the unused portion of your credit line, updated monthly on your bill.	It is important to have credit available for emergencies, so avoid charging to the limit.
Cash advance—an immediate loan, in the form of cash, from the credit card company. You are charged interest immediately and may also pay a separate transaction fee.	Use a cash advance only in emergencies because the finance charges start as soon as you complete the transaction. It is a very expensive way to borrow money.
Credit limit—the debt ceiling the card company places on your account (for example, $1,500). The total owed, including purchases, cash advances, finance charges, and fees, cannot exceed this limit.	Credit card companies generally set low credit limits for college and university students. Many students get around this limit by owning more than one card, which increases the credit available but most likely increases problems as well.
Delinquent account—an account that is not paid on time or for which the minimum payment has not been met.	Avoid having a delinquent account at all costs. Not only will you be charged substantial late fees, but you also risk losing your good credit rating, affecting your ability to borrow in the future. Delinquent accounts remain part of your credit record for many years.
Due date—the date your payment must be received and after which you will be charged a late fee.	Avoid late fees and finance charges by setting up your online payment to come out of your account the day before the bill is due.
Finance charges—the total cost of credit, including interest and service and transaction fees.	The only way to avoid finance charges is to pay your balance in full by the due date.
Minimum payment—the smallest amount you can pay by the statement due date. The amount is set by the credit card company.	Making only the minimum payment each month can result in disaster if you charge more than you can afford. When you make a purchase, think in terms of total cost.
Outstanding balance—the total amount you owe on your card.	If you carry a balance over several months, additional purchases are hit with finance charges. Pay cash instead.
Past due—your account is considered *past due* when you fail to pay the minimum required payment on schedule.	Two credit bureaus note past-due accounts on your credit history: TransUnion and Equifax. You can contact each bureau for a copy of your credit report to make sure there are no errors.

Managing Money

their cards, and if you add items such as clothing, food, and car repairs, your debt can escalate quickly and can even lead to personal bankruptcy—a major blot on your credit that can last for years and should be avoided at all costs.

A few basics will help you stay in control.

- *Choose your card wisely.* Look for a card with a low interest rate, no annual fee, a rewards program, and a grace period (a week or two to pay your bill without having to pay interest).

- *Pay bills regularly and on time, and always make at least the minimum payment.* Set up a reminder system that activates a week or so before the due date. You can create an email alert through your card account, make a note in your planner, or set an alarm on your electronic planner.

- *If you get into trouble, call the credit company and ask to set up a payment plan.* Then, going forward, try to avoid the same mistakes. If you still need help, contact any local organization that features credit/debt counselling.

get analytical

EXAMINE CREDIT CARD USE

Complete the following on paper or in digital format.

Take a careful look at who you are as a credit consumer. Gather your most recent credit card statements in preparation for this exercise. Answer questions 1 through 5 separately on paper or your computer, because they contain personal information.

1. How many credit cards do you have? List the names. For each, indicate the following:
   - Current interest rate
   - Current balance
   - Amount due as late fee if you do not pay on time
   - Approximate date card payment is due each month

2. Add your balances together. This total is your current credit debt.

3. How much did you pay last month in finance charges? Total your finance charges from the most recent statements of all cards.

4. Do you pay on time, do you tend to pay late, or is it variable?

5. Estimate how many times in a year you have to pay a late fee. Looking at how much your cards charge for late fees, estimate how much money you have spent in the last year on late fees.

When you've gathered all your information, analyze how effectively you currently use credit. If you are satisfied with your habits, keep up the good work. If your evaluation indicates that you need to make some changes, don't waste any time. Write specific plans here and start now to change your habits.

CREDIT SCORE
A measure of credit risk calculated from a credit report by using a standardized formula.

- *Use your card only for emergencies if you can.*
- *Shred credit cards if and when you have closed an account* or if you feel you have too many. However, remember that even though you have destroyed the card, the debt attached to it remains until you have paid it off in full and sent a written statement to the company indicating your request to close the account.

Build a Good Credit Score

Many people go through periods when they have a hard time paying bills. Falling behind on payments, however, could result in a poor credit score (also referred to as a *credit rating*) that can make it tough to get a loan or finance a large purchase. Your credit score is a prediction of your ability to pay back debt. If you have ever bought a car, signed up for a credit card, or purchased insurance, the deal you got was related to your credit score. If you are looking to rent an apartment, sign up for a new cellphone plan, connect utilities at your home, or even start a job in which you may be required to handle money, someone will be examining your credit score.

Most credit scores are determined from a credit-scoring scale. The scale, which can run anywhere from 300 to 850,

To keep track of where your money goes, keep credit card receipts and include those expenses in your budget.

Sarah Lyman Kravits

will give creditors an idea of how reliable you are. In general, having a higher score is related to getting better interest rates. For instance, if a person with a score of 500 and a person with a score of 700 both had a $100,000 25-year mortgage, the lower-scoring person would have a higher APR (annual percentage rate) on the loan and would ultimately pay tens of thousands of dollars in additional interest charges.[9]

CREDITOR
A company or person to whom a debt, usually money, is owed.

If you're trying to keep your score in good shape, or if you need to get your score back on track, look at Key 11.6 to get an idea of what affects your credit.

Having a poor credit rating can have several negative effects. Most notably, it means increased rates of interest, which can cost you more money in the long run. Additional effects may include the following:

- An indication to a potential employer that you may be unfit to run a department or less trustworthy in security situations or when handling money
- Difficulty in getting a loan for a home or car
- Higher premiums with insurance companies, which believe that people with lower credit scores are more likely to file a claim
- Obstacle to renting an apartment if it appears to the landlord that you may have trouble paying your bills
- Extra charges from utilities such as a requirement to pay a deposit when opening a new account

KEY 11.6 Different factors determine your credit rating.

35% How You Pay Your Bills	Remember: Always paying your bills on time is great; always paying them late is bad. Declaring bankruptcy is worse.
30% Amount of Money You Owe and the Amount of Available Credit	Statistically, people who have a lot of credit available tend to use it, which makes them a less attractive credit risk.
15% Length of Credit History	In general, the longer you've had credit, the more points you get.
10% Mix of Credit	Statistically, people with a variety of credit types usually understand how to use credit better. Thus, having different types of credit—such as credit cards, loans, and mortgages—looks better to creditors.
10% New Credit Applications	Depending on the length and overall health of your credit history, applying for new lines of credit can indicate certain behaviours signalling your reliability to lenders. Usually, multiple applications are less favourable when seen on shorter histories.

multiple intelligence strategies

Apply Different Intelligences to the Concept of Opportunity Cost in Economics

INTELLIGENCE	USE MI STRATEGIES TO MANAGE YOUR MONEY	APPLY MI BUDGETING STRATEGIES TO LEARN ABOUT OPPORTUNITY COST*
Verbal-Linguistic	• Talk over your financial situation with someone you trust. • Write out a detailed budget outline. If you can, store it on a computer file so you can update it regularly.	• Clarify the concept of opportunity cost (what you sacrifice to get something) with two personal examples: the opportunity cost of a course you are taking and of a purchase you have made or plan to make.
Logical-Mathematical	• Focus on the numbers; using a calculator and amounts as exact as possible, determine your income and spending. • Calculate how much money you will have in 10 years if, starting now, you put $2,000 in a 5-percent interest-bearing account each year.	• Compute the estimated opportunity cost of one year of your post-secondary education by comparing it to working full time for the year. Consider all education-related expenses in your computation. Analyze your results.
Bodily-Kinesthetic	• Consider putting money, or a slip with a dollar amount, each month in envelopes for various budget items—rent, dining out, and so on. When the envelope is empty or the number is reduced to zero, spending stops.	• On slips of paper, write opportunity costs of a choice—for example, buying a new car—and put the slips in a pile. Then, write the benefits of the choice on more slips, and put them in a separate pile. Compare your piles—does the benefit outweigh the cost?
Visual-Spatial	• Set up a budgeting system that includes colour-coded folders and coloured charts. • Create colour-coded folders for papers related to financial and retirement goals—investments, accounts, and so on.	• To see what combination of work time and school time is ideal for you, design a production-possibilities curve that shows all of the possible combinations.
Interpersonal	• Whenever money problems come up, discuss them right away with a family member, partner, or roommate. • Brainstorm a five-year financial plan with one of your friends.	• Meet with a friend to discuss the opportunity cost of different ways to spend your discretionary income (money available after you pay your monthly fixed expenses).
Intrapersonal	• Schedule quiet time to plan how to develop, follow, and update your budget. Consider financial management software, such as Quicken. • Think through where your money should go to best achieve your long-term financial goals.	• Schedule downtime to think about the opportunity cost of an extracurricular activity with which you are involved. Overall, do you benefit from this experience? If you decide that the cost is too high, change your level of involvement.
Musical	• Include a category of music-related purchases in your budget—going to concerts, buying CDs—but keep an eye on it to make sure you don't go overboard.	• Look at what you spend on music-related purchases throughout one term. Thinking about other ways you could use that money, calculate the opportunity cost of that expense.
Naturalistic	• Analyze your spending by using a system of categories. Your system may be based on time (when payments are due), priority (must-pay bills versus extras), or spending type (monthly bills, education, family expenses).	• Choose a category and total your spending in that category throughout the year. Think about something else that you would like to do with that amount of money. Is there a more favourable choice you could make in the future?

*For information on opportunity cost, see Arthur O'Sullivan, Steven M. Sheffrin, and Stephen J. Perez, *Survey of Economics: Principles*, Applications, and Tools, Upper Saddle River, NJ: Prentice Hall, 2008.

HOW CAN YOU PLAN FOR A
solid financial future?

Being able to achieve long-term financial goals—buying a car or house, having money for expenses that go beyond everyday costs, saving money for retirement and for emergencies—requires that you think critically about what you do with your money for the long term. Effective budgeting, working while in school, managing credit use, and finding financial aid contribute to your long-term goals because they help you spend wisely and maximize your savings.

Save and Invest Your Money

Having financial security requires that you spend less than you earn. Then the money accumulated can go into savings accounts and investments, helping you with regular expenses, long-term financial plans, and emergencies (financial advisors recommend, if at all possible, to keep enough cash in an emergency fund to cover three to six months' expenses). Savings and money market accounts are basic tools to help your money grow. If you manage them online, be cautious about the websites you use, emails you receive, and how you protect your personal information.

Savings accounts. The most basic and flexible place to save money is in an account that earns compound interest. Most savings accounts have a variable, albeit low, rate of interest, which is a sum paid for the use of your money while it is in the bank. Here is how compound interest works: If you put $1,000 in an account that carries 5-percent interest, you will earn $50 over the course of the first year. Your account then holds $1,050. From that point on, interest is calculated on that $1,050, not just on the original $1,000. Imagine this: If you invested that $1,000 at the age of 22 and put a mere $50 in the account each month, by the time you turned 62 you would have more than $100,000.

Chequing accounts. Most banks offer more than one chequing plan. Some accounts include cheque-writing fees, a small charge on every cheque you write or on any cheques above a certain number per month. Some accounts have free chequing, meaning unlimited cheque writing without extra fees—but you often have to maintain a minimum balance in your account to qualify. Some accounts charge a monthly fee that is standard or varies according to your balance. Chequing accounts pay you a low rate of interest, although you may have to keep a certain balance or have a savings account at the same bank.

> **COMPOUND INTEREST**
> Interest calculated on the principal (original investment) as well as the interest already added to the account.

The Canadian Press Images/
Mario Beauregard

Begin Saving For Retirement

With so many workers switching jobs frequently and working freelance, fewer people are retiring with guaranteed retirement income other than their Canada Pension Plan. As more and more large and small employers are reducing or eliminating pension benefits, it is up to individual workers to put away as much money as they can for retirement. Starting your *Registered Retirement Savings Plan* (RRSP) early and continuing on a yearly basis gives you the benefit of growth over time. Key 11.7 shows the earning potential of an **RRSP**.

Managing Money

revisit RISK AND REWARD

Torian Richardson

What happened to Torian? Torian came to see that year of juggling community college and his job as a turning point. "I knew if I didn't buckle down and put some structure into my life, I wouldn't reach my goals." The risks he took to refocus earned him the reward of a 3.7 grade-point average that year. He transferred to Benedictine University, which would meet his athletic and academic needs without putting him in loan debt. After earning his bachelor's in business administration, Torian embarked on a fast-rising career in finance, sales, and growth strategies for publishing industry leaders Houghton Mifflin and Pearson Education, working most recently as business solutions director for Pearson's Africa division. His latest risk involves working toward his master's in public administration and learning to speak Mandarin at Tsinghua University in Beijing, China, while maintaining his investment company, Torianite, Inc.

What does this mean for you? "I've done quite well over the past 10 years, but I've made it a point to keep budgeting," says Torian. "I haven't changed the way I live." Torian advises students to stick to a budget, avoid impulse purchases, keep debt low, and evaluate high-cost items by including interest payments in your analysis. How can you emulate Torian's financial restraint? Name one action you are willing to take in each area—sticking to a budget, avoiding impulse purchases, and keeping debt low—to work toward the reward of financial stability.

What risk may bring reward beyond your world? Torian's career has taken him to Africa, the Middle East, and Asia. Working in villages where food, water, and electricity are scarce, he has learned firsthand about the contrast between the opportunities that people have in the U.S. and the lack of opportunities elsewhere. You too can fight poverty, and in ways that won't jeopardize a college student's budget. Check out you-think.worldbank.org and click on the Get Involved tab; then explore the Resource Center. The site lists dozens of volunteer, internship, and activism opportunities. Find a cause that has appeals to you, then brainstorm cost-effective ways for you to make a difference.

KEY 11.7 Use an RRSP to grow your retirement investment.

Initial investment and contributions	Investment growth, based on 10% return, after . . .		
	10 years	25 years	40 years
$5,000 one-time investment	$12,969	$54,174	$226,296
$2,000 investment plus $2,000 annual contribution	$37,062	$218,364	$975,704

Note: Calculations based on 10-percent average annual S & P Index growth from 1926 to present, as per "Investment Intelligence," Legg Mason Investor Services, 2007 (http://investorservices.leggmason.com/doc_library/1730.pdf?seq=11).

KNOW IT *Think Critically*

Your Relationship With Money

Getting a handle on money anxiety starts with an honest examination of how you relate to money.

Build basic skills. Analyze yourself as a money manager. Look back at page 291 for a description of what influences the way people handle money. Make some notes about your personal specifics in the following areas.

I most value spending money on _____

_____

I manage my money by _____

_____

My culture tends to view money as_____

_____

My family and friends tend to handle money by _____

_____

Take it to the next level. Generate ideas about what you want to do with your money. If you had enough money for your expenses and then some, what would you do with the extra? Would you save it, spend it, do a little of both? Imagine what you would do if you had an extra $10,000 to spend this year. Describe your plan on a separate sheet of paper.

Move toward mastery. Look for practical ways to move toward the scenario you imagined. Realistically, how can you make that $10,000 a reality over time? You may need to change how you operate as a money manager. You may need to make some sacrifices in the short term. Come up with two specific plans here about changes and sacrifices that will move you toward your goal.

1. _____
2. _____

When you put these ideas to work, save or invest the money to reach for your goal.

Managing Money

309

WRITE IT *Communicate*

Record your thoughts on a separate piece of paper, in a journal, or electronically.

Emotional intelligence journal: You and credit. First, describe yourself as a credit card user. Do you pay in full or run up a balance? Pay on time or pay late? Restrict use to emergencies or use your credit card (or cards) all the time? Describe how using credit cards makes you feel. Examine those feelings and their effect on how you use credit. Then describe a change in your thinking you could make that would help you handle money more wisely.

Real-life writing: Apply for aid. Use the Internet or library resources to find two non-federally funded scholarships, available through your college or university, for which you are eligible. They can be linked to academic areas of interest, associated with particular talents you have, or offered by a group to which you or members of your family belong. Get applications for each and fill them out. Jot down notes about your personality, skills, talent, achievements, dreams, and contributions to others. Use the information from those notes to write a one-page cover letter for each application, telling the committee why you should receive this scholarship. Have someone proofread your work, send the applications, and see what happens.

WORK IT *Build Your Brand*

Be Specific About Your Job Needs

21st Century Learning Building Blocks

- Business literacy
- Initiative and self-direction

Complete the following in your electronic portfolio or on separate sheets of paper.

As you consider specific job directions and opportunities, begin thinking about a variety of job-related factors that may affect your job experience and personal life. These factors include the following:

- Benefits, including health insurance, vacation, pension
- Integrity of company (its reputation)
- How the company deals with employees
- Promotion prospects (your chances for advancement)
- Job stability
- Training and educational opportunities (Does the company offer in-house training or fund job-related coursework?)
- Starting salary
- Quality of employees and physical environment
- Quality of management
- Nature of the work you will be doing (Will you be required to travel extensively? Will you be expected to work long hours? Will you be working in an office or in the field?)

- Your relationship with the company (Will you be a full-time or part-time employee or an independent contractor?)
- Job title
- Location of your primary workplace
- Company size
- Company's financial performance over time

Think about how important each factor is in your job choice. Then rate each on a scale of 1 to 10, with 1 being the least important and 10 being the most important. As you consider each factor, keep in mind that even if you consider something very important, you may not get it right away if you are just beginning your career.

Finally, consider the results of a survey of post-secondary students conducted by the National Association of Colleges and Employers. According to students, their top two reasons for choosing an employer are: *integrity of organization in its dealings with employees* as number one and *job stability* as number two. How do these top choices compare to your own?[10]

Joe Chielli

Post-secondary education provides an extraordinary opportunity to explore yourself and the knowledge available to you. The earlier you risk thinking about career goals, the greater reward you can receive from your educational resources, which can prepare you for work in both job-specific and general ways.

Careers and More

BUILDING A SUCCESSFUL FUTURE

What Would You Risk? *Kelly Carson*

Joe Chielli

THINK ABOUT THIS PROBLEM AS YOU READ, AND CONSIDER HOW YOU WOULD APPROACH IT. THIS CHAPTER FOCUSES FIRST ON HOW TO PREPARE FOR SUCCESS ON THE JOB. THEN IT HELPS YOU ANALYZE HOW YOU FARED THIS TERM. FINALLY, IT PROVIDES TOOLS TO HELP YOU APPLY THE POWER OF SUCCESSFUL INTELLIGENCE TO YOUR LIFE NOW AND AFTER COLLEGE OR UNIVERSITY.

When Kelly Carson first stepped into her seventh-grade Spanish class, she felt a sense of potential in the idea that soon she would be able to speak to a whole new group of people. When she got home that day, she told her mother that she wanted to major in Spanish at university.

Continuing to take Spanish in high school, Kelly asked her teacher how she could practise outside the classroom. The teacher recommended her to the English as a second language (ESL) program at a local elementary school. Her first tutoring session was with a third-grade girl who spoke only a few words of English. When the girl discovered Kelly spoke Spanish, the words came pouring out, and she talked about how none of the students talked to her, she never understood the teacher, and she sat through class every day staring at a book. As Kelly worked with her, the English the girl learned transformed her into an active member of the class, and Kelly began to see how she could harness communication skills to solve problems.

Kelly entered university determined to continue teaching ESL. During her first year, she tutored a Mexican immigrant, Diana, a few days a week. Word spread that there was a free English teacher in Diana's building, and more and more of her friends showed up. Kelly was amazed at the need for English teachers when hundreds of university students were learning languages a few blocks away. Overwhelmed by the demand, she wanted to figure out a way to solve this problem in a way that involved her school and its students.

To be continued . . .

If you know yourself well and take advantage of opportunities that present themselves, you are likely to discover the start of a rewarding career blueprint. You will learn more about Kelly, and the reward resulting from her actions, within the chapter.

Notes

52%

Today   Mar 10 8:01 AM

Working through this chapter will help you to

statusCHECK

HOW CAN YOU PREPARE
for career success?

Every student is in a unique position when it comes to preparing for a productive career. Some already have a work history, and others none; some have known for a while exactly what they want to do, others have no idea at all, and still others are in the middle, with some thoughts but no focus yet. Know three things as you begin this chapter:

Your starting point is not better or worse than anyone else's. Knowing exactly what you want is not better than having no clue—it is just different. Different starting points require different risks. Someone driven to pursue engineering, for example, may take risks that lead them toward specialization, while someone who has not yet pinpointed an area of interest may focus on risks that help clarify personal passions and abilities.

Sarah Lyman Kravits

The modern workplace is defined by change. The working world today shifts more rapidly than at any other time in history, responding to technological developments, global competition, economic change, and other factors. Although this brings a risk of frequent job changes, it also offers the reward of myriad opportunities to learn and reinvent yourself throughout your career. It also increases the importance of strong transferable skills such as thinking, teamwork, writing, goal setting, and more, which can make choosing a major a little less stressful. This is why the Conference Board of Canada says that employees need to be adaptable and "be open and respond constructively to change" in its Employability Skills 2000+ Profile.[1]

Now is the time to start thinking about careers. Postsecondary education provides a once-in-a-lifetime opportunity to explore yourself and the knowledge available to you. The earlier you take the risk to consider career goals, the greater reward you can receive from your education and college resources, which can prepare you for work in both job-specific and general ways.

Taking courses in an area of interest can help you see how well a job in this area might suit you. These students get hands-on experience in respiratory therapy as well as advice from an experienced instructor.

Ideally, your career will reflect your values and talents and reward you with the income you need. The right career means something different to everyone, and what you think is best at one point may not be the path you ultimately take. With your work on the Work It: Build Your Brand exercises, you are already on the road to discovering what makes the most sense for you. Read on about more career preparation strategies including considering your personality and strengths, exploring majors, investigating career paths, building knowledge and experience, knowing what employers want, and creating a strategic plan.

Consider Your Personality and Strengths

Because who you are as a learner relates closely to who you are as a worker, your assessment results from Chapter 3 will give you helpful clues in the search for the right career. The multiple intelligences assessment (Multiple Pathways to Learning) points to information about your natural strengths and challenges, which can lead you to careers that involve these strengths. Review Key 3.7 on page 73 to see majors and internships that tend to suit different intelligences, and look at Key 12.1 to see how those intelligences may link up with various careers.

The Personality Spectrum assessment is equally significant, because it focuses on how you work best with others, and career success depends in large part on your ability to function in a team. Key 12.2 focuses the four dimensions of the Personality Spectrum on career ideas and strategies. Look for your strengths and decide what you may want to keep in mind as you search. Look also at areas of challenge, and try to identify ways to boost your abilities in those areas. Even the most ideal job involves some tasks that are not in your area of comfort.

Use the information in Key 12.2 as a guide, not a label. Although you may not have all the strengths and challenges indicated by your dominant area, thinking through them will still help you clarify your abilities and interests.

In addition, remember that you are capable of change, and with focus and effort you can develop your abilities. Use ideas about strengths and challenges as a starting point for your goals concerning how you would like to grow.

Finally, one other way to investigate how your personality and strengths may inform your career choice is to take an inventory based on the Holland theory. Psychologist John Holland theorized that personality was related to career choice, and he came up with six different types that identify both personality and career

Careers and More

MULTIPLE INTELLIGENCE	CAREERS
Verbal-Linguistic	• Author or journalist • TV/radio producer • Literature or language teacher • Business executive • Copywriter or editor
Logical-Mathematical	• Doctor or dentist • Accountant • Attorney • Chemist • Investment banker
Bodily-Kinesthetic	• Carpenter or draftsman • Physical therapist • Mechanical engineer • Dancer or actor • Exercise physiologist
Visual-Spatial	• Graphic artist or illustrator • Photographer • Architect or interior designer • Art museum curator • Art teacher • Set or retail stylist
Interpersonal	• Social worker • Public relations or human resources rep • Sociologist • Teacher • Nurse
Intrapersonal	• Research scientist • Computer engineer • Psychologist • Economist • Author
Musical	• Singer or voice coach • Music teacher • Record executive • Musician or conductor • Radio DJ or sound engineer
Naturalistic	• Biochemical engineer • Natural scientist (geologist, ecologist, etymologist) • Paleontologist • Position with environmental group • Farmer or farm management

area: Realistic, Investigative, Artistic, Social, Enterprising, and Conventional (together known as *RIASEC*).[2] Holland developed two interest surveys that allow people to identify their order of preference for the six types and help them link their stronger types to career areas. Ask your career centre about these surveys: the Vocational Preference Inventory (VPI) and the Self-Directed Search (SDS).

DIMENSION	JOB STRENGTHS	JOB CHALLENGES	WHAT TO LOOK FOR IN JOBS/CAREER
Thinker	• Problem solving • Development of ideas • Keen analysis of situations • Fairness to others • Efficiency in working through tasks • Innovation of plans and systems • Ability to look strategically at the future	• A need for private time to think and work • A need, at times, to move away from established rules • A dislike of sameness—systems that don't change, repetitive tasks • Not always being open to expressing thoughts and feelings to others	• Some level of solo work/think time • Problem solving • Opportunity for innovation • Freedom to think creatively and to bend the rules • Technical work • Big picture strategic planning
Organizer	• High level of responsibility • Enthusiastic support of social structures • Order and reliability • Loyalty • Ability to follow through on tasks according to requirements • Detailed planning skills with competent follow-through • Neatness and efficiency	• A need for tasks to be clearly, concretely defined • A need for structure and stability • A preference for less rapid change • A need for frequent feedback • A need for tangible appreciation • Low tolerance for people who don't conform to rules and regulations	• Clear, well-laid-out tasks and plans • Stable environment with consistent, repeated tasks • Organized supervisors • Clear structure of how employees interact and report to one another • Value of, and reward for, loyalty
Giver	• Honesty and integrity • Commitment to putting energy toward close relationships with others • Finding ways to bring out the best in self and others • Peacemaker and mediator • Ability to listen well, respect opinions, and prioritize the needs of co-workers	• Difficulty in handling conflict, either personal or between others in the work environment • Strong need for appreciation and praise • Low tolerance for perceived dishonesty or deception • Avoidance of people perceived as hostile, cold, or indifferent	• Emphasis on teamwork and relationship building • Indications of strong and open lines of communication among workers • Encouragement of personal expression in the workplace (arrangement of personal space, tolerance of personal celebrations, and so on)
Adventurer	• Skillfulness in many different areas • Willingness to try new things • Ability to take action • Hands-on problem-solving skills • Initiative and energy • Ability to negotiate • Spontaneity and creativity	• Intolerance of being kept waiting • Lack of detail focus • Impulsiveness • Dislike of sameness and authority • Need for freedom, constant change, and constant action • Tendency not to consider consequences of actions	• A spontaneous atmosphere • Less structure, more freedom • Adventuresome tasks • Situations involving change • Encouragement of hands-on problem solving • Travel and physical activity • Support of creative ideas and endeavours

Investigate Career Paths

Career possibilities extend far beyond what you can imagine. Talk to instructors, relatives, mentors, and fellow students about careers. Explore job listings, occupation lists, assessments, and other information at your school's career centre. Check online or at your library for biographies of people who worked in fields that interest you. Visit job search and information websites such as Job Bank; Job Bank provides information about education and skills required for particular occupations, on-the-job tasks, possible salaries and more. Look at Key 12.3 for the questions you might ask yourself as you conduct your research. Job Bank also offers insight into which careers are expected to grow over time. If you have an interest in a growing career area, you will have a better chance of finding a job.

What can I do in this area that I like and do well?	Do I respect the company or the industry? The product or service?
What are the educational requirements (certificates or degrees, courses)?	Does this company or industry accommodate special needs (child care, sick days, flextime)?
What skills are necessary?	Do I need to belong to a union? What does union membership involve?
What wage or salary and benefits can I expect?	Are there opportunities near where I live (or want to live)?
What personality types are best suited to this kind of work?	What other expectations exist (travel, overtime, and so on)?
What are the prospects for moving up to higher-level positions?	Do I prefer the service or production end of this industry?

Keep the following in mind as you investigate careers:

A wide array of job possibilities exists for most career fields. For example, the medical world consists of more than doctors and nurses. Administrators run hospitals, researchers test drugs, pharmacists prepare prescriptions, security experts ensure patient and visitor safety, and so on.

Within each job, there are a variety of tasks to perform. For instance, you may know that an instructor teaches, but you may not think about the fact that instructors may also write, research, study, design courses, give presentations, counsel, and coach. Take your career exploration beyond first impressions to get an accurate picture of the careers that interest you.

Explore Majors

You probably have explored majors at other times during this course, perhaps while choosing a major as related to goal setting and self-knowledge. Look to previous ideas and work for guidance as you continue and extend your exploration.

Focus on your interests and abilities. Countless sources of career advice make the point that pursuing a passion is a key element of career success. This doesn't mean that you will love every aspect or every day of your job—no one does. However, you improve your chances of thriving if you spend the bulk of your job doing work that interests you and taps into your strengths.

Examine what your school offers. Unless you plan to transfer, the majors that your school offers are an important aspect of your exploration. Look for them online and in your school's course calendar. Meet with an advisor to discuss the options and find out what flexibility you may have (double majors, minoring, interdisciplinary majors, or, potentially, designing your own major).

Consider career interests. If you are interested in one or more careers, investigate majors that may link to them—but don't narrow the field too much. An advisor can help you define which careers need specific majors and which are accessible from a broader range of educational backgrounds. For example, students going into medical professions usually need to major in a science or pre-med area, while students planning to pursue careers in law might major in anything from history to philosophy. Business owners are becoming more aware of how liberal arts majors bring value to the workplace through skills such as problem solving and writing.[3]

Build Knowledge and Experience

Even after comprehensive investigation, it is hard to choose the right career path without knowledge or experience. Courses, internships, jobs, and volunteering are risks that promote those rewards

Courses. Take a course or two in your areas of interest to determine whether you like the material and can excel. Find out what courses are required for a major in those areas and decide whether or not you are willing to study this material during college or university. Check out your school's course calendar for detailed information on the courses involved. Also, consider talking with the department chair or a senior level student to gain more insight into the field.

Internships. An internship gives you a chance to work in your chosen field to see how you like it. Your career centre may list summer or year-round internship opportunities. For more comprehensive guides, check out Services for Youth (www.youth.gc.ca/eng/topics/career_planning/internships.shtml) or Career Edge (careeredge.ca).

Jobs. You may discover career opportunities while earning money during a part-time job. Someone who takes a legal proofreading job to make extra cash might discover an interest in law. Someone who answers phones for a newspaper company might be drawn into journalism.

Volunteering. Helping others in need can introduce you to careers and increase your experience, as Kelly discovered. Many schools establish committees to organize volunteering opportunities or sponsor their own groups. You may even be able to find opportunities that mesh with an area of interest. For example, if you are studying accounting, donating your time as a part-time bookkeeper in a shelter will increase your skills while you help those less fortunate than you. Many employers look favourably on volunteering. Check out Volunteer Canada (volunteer.ca) or Canada World Youth (canadaworldyouth.org/.

Service learning. The goal of service learning is to provide the community with service and students with knowledge gained from hands-on experience.[4] Students in service learning programs often enrol in for-credit courses in which volunteer service and related assignments are required. Taking the risk of service learning can reward you with a sense of civic responsibility, opportunity to apply what you learn in the classroom, and personal growth. If you are interested, talk to your advisor about whether your school offers service learning programs.

Know What Employers Want

If you want to enter the job market or are already in it, know that prospective employers (regardless of the occupation) look for particular skills and qualities that mark you as a promising candidate. Most employers require you to have a skill set that includes specific technical know-how, but in this rapidly changing workplace, general life skills and emotional intelligence may be even more crucial to your success.

Transferable skills

In the modern workplace, workers will hold an average of 11 jobs through their productive working years.[5] The high rate of job and workplace change means that abilities such as successful thinking and teamwork are crucial to workplace success. Many of these general skills can also be described as *transferable skills*—general skills learned through job or life experience that you can use with (or transfer to) a new and different job or career. For example, you will need teamwork and writing skills for almost any job. Key 12.4 describes transferable skills that employers look for. Note how

INTERNSHIP
A temporary work program in which a student can gain supervised practical experience in a particular professional field.

SKILL SET
A combination of the knowledge, talent, and abilities that are needed to perform a specific job.

Shutterstock

KEY 12.4 Employers look for candidates with these important skills.

SKILL	WHY IS IT USEFUL?
Communication	Good listening, speaking, and writing skills are key to working with others, as is being able to adjust to different communication styles.
Analytical thinking	An employee who can analyze choices and challenges, as well as assess the value of new ideas, stands out.
Creativity	The ability to come up with new concepts, plans, and products helps companies improve and innovate.
Practical thinking	No job gets done without employees who can think through a plan for achieving a goal, put it into action, and complete it successfully.
Teamwork	All workers interact with others on the job. Working well with others is essential for achieving workplace goals.
Goal setting	Teams fail if goals are unclear or unreasonable. Employees and the company benefit from setting realistic, specific goals and achieving them reliably.
Cultural competence	The workplace is increasingly diverse. An employee who can work with, adjust to, and respect people from different backgrounds and cultures is valuable.
Leadership	The ability to influence and motivate others in a positive way earns respect and career advancement.
Positive attitude	Other employees will gladly work with, and often advance, someone who completes tasks with positive, upbeat energy.
Integrity	Acting with integrity at work—communicating promptly, being truthful and honest, following rules, giving proper notice—enhances value.
Flexibility	The most valuable employees understand the constancy of change and have developed the skills to adapt to its challenge.
Continual learning	The most valuable employees take personal responsibility to stay current in their fields.

these skills echo the Conference Board of Canada's list of Fundamental, Personal Management and Teamwork Skills that were introduced in Chapter 1 and highlighted through the text.

Emotional intelligence

Employers are also drawn to emotionally intelligent job candidates, as you learned in Chapter 1. Your emotional intelligence has an impact on your effectiveness. Consider this scenario: You arrive at work distracted by a personal problem and tired from studying late the night before. Your supervisor is overloaded with a major project due that day. The person you work most closely with is arriving late because of a car problem. In other words, everyone is strung out. What does an emotionally intelligent person do? Remember the three actions of emotional intelligence:

- *Tune in to everyone's emotions first.* You: tired and distracted. Your co-worker: worried about the car and about being late. Your supervisor: agitated about the project.

get creative

Complete the following on paper or in digital format.

Considering your self-knowledge, experience, possible career paths, and understanding of the workplace, create a practical five-year timeline as a strategic plan to achieve a career goal. First, describe where to you want to be in five years. For each of the following time frames, write in the steps you think you will need to take toward that five-year goal. Include anything you envision in your path toward a career, such as steps related to declaring a major or transfer to another school to pursue additional education.

- One month from now...

- Three months from now...

- Six months from now...

- One year from now...

- Two years from now...

- Three years from now...

- Four years from now...

Finally, create a timeline version of your plan using a visual format you like and adding smaller goals as necessary. Keep your timeline where you can refer to and revise it, since changes in the world and in your knowledge and experience may require adjustments in your plan.

- *Understand what the emotions are telling you.* Making the deadline that day might be more challenging than anticipated. Everyone is going to need to set aside distracted, negative thinking and maintain an extra-focused and positive state of mind to get through it.
- *Take action toward positive outcomes.* You come up with several ideas.

  - Prioritize your task list so that you can concentrate on what is most pressing.
  - Put a memo on your supervisor's desk saying that you are available to support her as she nails down the loose ends on her urgent project.
  - Call your co-worker on his cellphone while he settles the car problem and let him know the status at work, preparing him to prioritize and to support the supervisor.
  - Ask another co-worker to bring in a favourite mid-morning snack to keep everyone going on what looks to be a long day.

The current emphasis on teamwork has highlighted emotional intelligence in the workplace. The more adept you are at working with others, the more likely you are to succeed.

Create a Strategic Plan

After you establish your time frame, focus on details. Decide what risks will help you pursue the jobs or careers that have piqued your interest. Establish whom you will talk

student PROFILE

Patrick Belliveau
SHERIDAN COLLEGE, TORONTO, ONTARIO

About me:

I am a third-year business student who has changed his mind about careers and educational paths numerous times. I started in an honours psychology program at a prominent university, but after a year and a half I decided it was not right for me. The electrical field seemed to be my dream career, so I completed a one-year pre-apprentice program and began working. After one year of working as an electrical apprentice, I was laid off during the turbulent economic time of 2008. That was the motivation I needed to go back to school and complete a degree that I now know was the one I should have chosen from the start. However, without trying different programs, I would have never been sure of the right path for me.

What I focus on:

My biggest focus, other than academic work, is networking. I try to create meaningful relationships with individuals who have already completed a business career in my field of interest. Asking questions about how they succeeded or how they approach decision making helps me build my own decision-making model. The biggest lesson I've learned in networking is that a person will form an initial opinion of you starting from your opening sentence. Therefore, you want to make sure you have a well-thought-out opening sentence that will intrigue or at least generate some interest in who you are and what you have to say.

Remember: if the individual is successful in business, you are neither the first nor the last to speak to him or her about their career. This means it is crucial to captivate the person's attention and make him or her remember you!

What will help me in the workplace:

In the business world, any worthy opponent will likely have a fairly similar degree to yours, or perhaps even the same one. Therefore, experience will be what sets you apart from the competition. Try to join as many different clubs as you can without interfering with your schoolwork. However, I suggest waiting until the second semester to join any club, as adjusting to post-secondary school will be hard enough without any added stress.

Patrick Belliveau. Sheridan College, Toronto, Ontario. Reprinted by permission.

to, what courses you will take, what skills you will work on, what jobs or internships you will investigate, and any other tasks. Be proactive in finding opportunities. But keep your plan flexible, seeing it as a structure to guide your actions, and knowing that there may be possibilities yet unknown to you.

With your knowledge of general workplace success strategies, you can search effectively for a job in a career area that works for you.

HOW CAN YOU CONDUCT
an effective job search?

Whether you are looking for a job now or planning ahead for a search closer to graduation, you have choices about how to proceed. Maximize your success by using the resources available to you, knowing the basics about resumés and interviews, and planning strategically.

Use Available Resources

Use your school's career planning and placement office, your networking skills, classified ads, and online services to help you explore possibilities for career areas or specific jobs.

Your school's career planning and placement office

Generally, the career planning and placement office deals with post-graduation job opportunities, whereas the student employment office, along with the financial aid office, has information about working during school. At either location you might find job listings, interview sign-up sheets, and company contact information. The career office may hold frequent informational sessions on different topics. Your school may also sponsor job or career fairs that give you a chance to explore job opportunities. Get acquainted with the career office early in your post-secondary career.

Networking

The most basic type of networking—talking to people about fields and jobs that interest you—is one of the most important job-hunting strategies. Networking contacts can answer questions regarding job hunting, occupational responsibilities and challenges, and salary expectations. For example, you can network with friends and family members, instructors, administrators, counsellors, alumni, employers, co-workers, and people you meet through extracurricular activities.

Online social networking can also help you in your job search. Tools such as Facebook, Twitter, and LinkedIn allow members to create personalized pages and connect with other individuals through groups, fan pages, and similar interests. During a job search, these sites can be used to meet potential employers through your contacts and showcase portfolio pieces. A word of caution though—your online presence is public. Before you post anything, remember that if you wouldn't want a potential employer (or your parents, instructor, or religious leader) to see it, don't put it online.

Informational interviews and the hidden job market

When you find someone who is doing the job you want to do, teaching in your field of interest, or responsible for hiring in that field, try to set up an *informational interview* with this person—an opportunity for you to ask questions about what they do, how they got into the job, what they like or don't like, and who they know. Since you are asking the questions and there is less at stake than in a traditional interview, you are likely to feel less nervous. Despite the lower risk, there is still potential for reward in the form of information and networking contacts.

To set up an interview, call or email the person. Introduce yourself and make it clear you are not looking for a job, just advice and support. Ask for 30 minutes of the person's time—find out when he or she is available and then suggest a meeting by phone, in the office, or at a coffee shop, whatever is most convenient. Ahead of time, prepare a set of questions for the person you will be interviewing, about things that matter to you. See Key 12.5 for a good list of informational interview questions.

On the day of the informational interview, dress professionally and arrive early. Have a copy of your resumé in case the person you are interviewing wants to see it. Take

NETWORKING
The exchange of information or services among individuals, groups, or institutions.

CONTACTS
People who serve as carriers or sources of information.

Take advantage of career fairs sponsored by your school. These career fair attendees pick up useful information and applications from different employers.

Careers and More

1.	How did you find out about the job you are now in?
2.	What skills do you have that are useful on the job?
3.	Did you have those skills when you first started?
4.	What are you good at?
5.	Tell me about your typical day—what you do and who you work with.
6.	What are your manager and co-workers like?
7.	What's the communication style at your workplace?
8.	What do you like about your job?
9.	What makes your job difficult?
10.	What is your educational and job background? Have you found it useful on the job?
11.	What kind of education or experience do you recommend to get a job like the one you have?
12.	What are the most important abilities you think someone needs to do your job well?
13.	What is the starting salary range in your field?
14.	About how many hours a week do you work?
15.	Does your job have any benefits?
16.	What do you think would prepare someone for your type of work?
17.	Is there anything else you would like to share with me about your job?
18.	Can you think of anyone else I should talk to?

notes during the interview, and consider writing by hand so you do not distract the interviewee by typing. When you finish, express appreciation and ask if you can keep in touch. Provide your contact information (or a business card, if you have one) and ask for his or her card. Follow up with a personal thank-you note and send it by mail—handwritten notes get remembered. Then type up your notes and think about what they tell you about the job or career area you are investigating.

Through informational interviewing, you tap the hidden job market—unadvertised jobs that are filled through networking. More than 80 percent of new jobs are unadvertised.[6] Most companies would rather find a qualified person through word of mouth or a referral by one of their own employees. And the best way to get referred is to meet some of those employees through informational interviewing.

Online services and classified ads

When jobs get advertised, they generate a lot of competition. However, it doesn't hurt to look at job advertisements. Although classified ads are still helpful when looking locally, the Internet is capable of storing tonnes of information without any paper and ink costs. Therefore, more employers post through online job boards, and those listings are often more detailed than the two- or three-sentence ads you find in a newspaper. In addition to a job description and salary information, most online postings will contain company information and a link to where you can submit an application. To make the most of your virtual resources:

■ look up career-focused and job-listing websites such as Canadianjobs.com, Canadajobs.com, or Monster.ca. Many sites offer resources on career areas, resumés, and online job searching, in addition to listings of employment openings.

- check the webpages of individual associations and companies, which may post job listings and descriptions.

If nothing happens right away, keep at it. New job postings appear, and new people sign on to look at your resumé. Plus, sites change all the time. Search using the key-words "job sites" or "job search" to see what sites come up.

Use an Organized, Consistent Strategy

Organize your approach according to what you need to do and when you have to do it. Do you plan to make three phone calls per day? Will you fill out one job application each week? Keep a record—on 3-by-5-inch cards, in a computer file or smartphone, or in a notebook—of the following:

- People you contact plus contact information and method of contact (email, snail mail, phone)
- Companies to which you apply
- Jobs for which you apply, including any results (for example, a job that becomes unavailable)
- Responses to communications (phone calls to you, interviews, written communications), information about the person who contacted you (name, title), and the times and dates of contact

Keeping accurate records enables you to both chart your progress and maintain a clear picture of the process. If you don't get a job now but another opens up at the same company in a few months, well-kept records will enable you to contact key personnel quickly and efficiently.

Your Resumé, Cover Letter, and Interview

How-to information on resumés, cover letters, and interviews fills entire books. To get you started, here are a few basic tips on giving yourself the best possible chance.

Cover letter and resumé

Cover letters and resumés are how you introduce yourself to prospective employers on paper so they will want to meet you in person. The purpose of the cover letter is to get the reader's attention so he or she will read your resumé. And the purpose of your resumé is to get the reader interested enough to call you in for an interview.

Keep your cover letter short but attention-getting. Make sure it is focused on the job and company you are interested in. A good cover letter usually covers four main points:

1. The position you are applying for and how you learned about it
2. Why you are the best person for the job (your abilities)
3. Why you want to work for the employer
4. A call to action (how you plan to follow up)

Design your resumé neatly, using a current and acceptable format (books or your career office can show you some standard formats). Make sure the information is accurate and truthful. Proofread it for errors and have someone else proofread it as well. Type or print it on high-quality paper (a heavier bond paper than is used for ordinary copies). Include a brief, to-the-point cover letter along with your resumé that tells the employer what job you are interested in and why he or she should hire you.

Here are some general tips for writing a resumé:

- Always put your name and contact information at the top. Make it stand out.
- State an objective whenever possible. If your focus is narrow or you are designing this resumé for a particular interview or career area, keep your objective specific; otherwise, keep the objective more general.

Désirée Williams

237 Custer Street, San Francisco, CA 94101 • (415) 555-5252 (W) or (415) 555-7865 (H)
• email: desiree@comcast.net • website: www.DesireCulture.com

OBJECTIVE

Use my language, cross-cultural, and web skills to help children in an educational or corporate setting.

EDUCATION

2012 to present	San Francisco State University, San Francisco, CA
	Pursuing a B.A. in the Spanish BCLAD (Bilingual, Cross-Cultural Language Acquisition Development) Education and Multiple Subject Credential Program.
	Expected graduation: June 2016

SKILLS SUMMARY

Languages:	Fluent in Spanish and English.
	Proficient in Italian and Shona (majority language of Zimbabwe).
Computer:	Programming ability in HTML, PHP, Javascript, .Net, and Silverlight.
	Multimedia design expertise in Adobe Photoshop, Netobjects Fusion, Adobe Premiere, Macromedia Flash, and other visual design programs.
Personal:	Perform professionally in Mary Schmary, a women's a cappela quartet.
	Climbed Mt. Kilimanjaro.

PROFESSIONAL EMPLOYMENT

Sept. 2013 to present	**Research Assistant, Knowledge Media Lab**
	San Francisco State University, San Francisco, CA
	Develop ways for teachers to share their teaching practices online, in a collaborative, multimedia environment.
June 2013 to present	**Webmaster/web Designer**
	Quake Net, San Mateo, CA (Internet service provider and Web commerce)
	Designed several sites for the University of California, Berkeley, Graduate School of Education, as well as private clients, such as A Body of Work and Yoga Forever
Sept. 2012 to June 2013	**Literacy Coordinator (internship)**
	Prescott School, Oakland, CA
	Coordinated, advised, and created literacy curriculum for an America Reads literacy project.
	Worked with nonreader 4th graders on writing and publishing, incorporating digital photography, Internet resources, and graphic design.
June 2012 to August 2012	**Bilingual Educational Consultant (volunteer)**
	Children's Television Workshop, San Francisco, CA
	Field-tested bilingual materials. With a research team, designed bilingual educational materials for an ecotourism project run by an indigenous rain forest community in Ecuador.
June 2009 to Sept. 2009	**Children's Recreation Director: After-School Program**
	San Francisco Recreation and Parks Department
	Performed playground supervision, taught arts and cultural activities, provided homework assistance, and managed summer reading program.
	Worked primarily with low-income, Hispanic children, grades 1 to 5.

References and Portfolio of Work

Available upon request

- Provide a *core competencies* section that lists your key skills.
- List your post secondary education, starting from the latest and working backward. This may include summer school, night school, seminars, and accreditations.
- List jobs in reverse chronological order (most recent job first). Include all types of work experience (full-time, part-time, volunteer, internship, and so on).
- When you describe your work experience, use action verbs and focus on what you have accomplished. Some use the P + A = R formula when writing their job tasks; they identify a problem, the action they took to solve it, and the results. For example: "Organized randomly filed client records in alphabetical and date order, reducing the time to access them by 80 percent."
- Always make sure the descriptions in your job history demonstrate the skills listed in your core competencies section and relate to the job you are applying for.
- Include keywords that are linked to jobs for which you will be applying.
- List references on a separate sheet (names, titles, companies, and contact information). You may want to put "References upon request" at the bottom of your resumé.
- Use professional formatting and bullets to help the important information stand out. Stick with one font family for the body of the resumé and one for the headings (usually larger and bolded). Use italics sparingly because they are hard to read.
- Get several people to look at your resumé before you send it out. Other readers will have ideas that you haven't thought of and may find errors that you have missed.

Key 12.6 shows a professional resumé that accompanies the previous cover letter.

Prospective employers often use a computer to scan resumés, selecting the ones that contain *keywords* relating to the job opening or industry. Resumés without enough keywords probably won't even make it to the human resources desk. When you construct your resumé, make sure to include relevant keywords. For example, if you are seeking a computer-related job, list computer programs you use and other specific technical proficiencies. To figure out what keywords you need, use the ones found in the job descriptions and job postings.[7]

Interview

Be clean, neat, and appropriately dressed. Choose a nice pair of shoes—people notice. Bring an extra copy of your resumé and any other materials that you want to show the interviewer. Avoid chewing gum or smoking. Offer a confident handshake. Make eye contact. Show your integrity by speaking honestly about yourself. After the interview, no matter what the outcome, follow up right away with a formal but pleasant thank-you note.

Being on time to your interview makes a positive impression—and being late will almost certainly be held against you. If you are from a culture that does not consider being late a sign of disrespect, remember that your interviewer may not agree.

HOW CAN YOU CONTINUE TO GROW
as a risk taker and thinker?

Much as finding a job is the beginning of your career adventure, finishing this course is the beginning of your life as a calculated risk taker and successfully intelligent learner. How can you stay motivated to keep thinking and risking? Earlier in this text, you may have completed a self-assessment to examine your levels of development in twenty characteristics that promote action and productive risks. According to Robert Sternberg, successfully intelligent people do the following:[8]

get practical

FIND USEFUL KEYWORDS

Complete the following on paper or in digital format.

Name two career fields that you would consider pursuing. Then, research resumé keywords that employers in these fields look for. On your chosen search engine, enter the words keyword, resumé, and a word or phrase related to the field (for example, chemical engineering, criminal justice). Fill in the list with 10 keywords for each field. Keep them on hand to tailor your resumé for a job in either one of these fields.

1. *Motivate themselves.* They make things happen, spurred on by a desire to succeed and a love of what they are doing.

2. *Learn to control their impulses.* Instead of going with their first quick response, they sit with a question or problem. They allow time for thinking and let ideas surface before making a decision.

3. *Know when to persevere.* When it makes sense, they push past frustration and stay on course, confident that success is in their sights. They also are able to see when they've hit a dead end—and, in those cases, to stop pushing.

4. *Know how to make the most of their abilities.* They understand what they do well and capitalize on it in school and work.

5. *Translate thought into action.* Not only do they have good ideas, but they are able to turn those ideas into practical actions that bring ideas to fruition.

6. *Have a product orientation.* They want results; they focus on what they are aiming for rather than on how they are getting there.

7. *Complete tasks and follow through.* With determination, they finish what they start. They also follow through to make sure all the loose ends are tied and the goal has been achieved.

8. *Are initiators.* They commit to people, projects, and ideas. They make things happen rather than sitting back and waiting for things to happen to them.

9. *Are not afraid to risk failure.* Because they take risks and sometimes fail, they often enjoy greater success and build their intellectual capacity. Like everyone, they make mistakes—but they tend not to make the same mistake twice.

10. *Don't procrastinate.* They are aware of the negative effects of putting things off, and they avoid them. They create schedules that allow them to accomplish what is important on time.

11. *Accept fair blame.* They strike a balance between never accepting blame and taking the blame for everything. If something is their fault, they accept responsibility and don't make excuses.

12. *Reject self-pity.* When something goes wrong, they find a way to solve the problem. They don't get caught in the energy drain of feeling sorry for themselves.

13. *Are independent.* They can work on their own and think for themselves. They take responsibility for their own schedule and tasks.

14. *Seek to surmount personal difficulties.* They keep things in perspective, looking for ways to remedy personal problems and separate them from their professional lives.

get analytical

EVALUATE YOUR SELF-ACTIVATORS

To see how you use successful intelligence in your daily life, assess your perceived development on Sternberg's activators. Circle the number that best represents your answer, with "1" being "not like me at all" to "5" being "definitely like me."

1. I motivate myself well.		1 2 3 4 5
2. I can control my impulses.		1 2 3 4 5
3. I know when to persevere and when to change gears.		1 2 3 4 5
4. I make the most of what I do well.		1 2 3 4 5
5. I can successfully translate my ideas into action.		1 2 3 4 5
6. I can focus effectively on my goal.		1 2 3 4 5
7. I complete tasks and have good follow through.		1 2 3 4 5
8. I initiate action—I move people and projects ahead.		1 2 3 4 5
9. I have the courage to risk failure.		1 2 3 4 5
10. I avoid procrastination.		1 2 3 4 5
11. I accept responsibility when I make a mistake.		1 2 3 4 5
12. I don't waste time feeling sorry for myself.		1 2 3 4 5
13. I independently take responsibility for tasks.		1 2 3 4 5
14. I work hard to overcome personal difficulties.		1 2 3 4 5
15. I create an environment that helps me concentrate on my goals.		1 2 3 4 5
16. I don't take on too much or too little work.		1 2 3 4 5
17. I can delay gratification in order to receive the benefits.		1 2 3 4 5
18. I can see both the big picture and the details in a situation.		1 2 3 4 5
19. I am able to maintain confidence in myself.		1 2 3 4 5
20. I balance my analytical, creative, and practical thinking skills.		1 2 3 4 5

If you completed this self-assessment at the beginning of the course, look back at your original scores. Describe three changes over the course of the term that feel significant to you.

Finally, choose one self-activator that you feel still needs work. Analyze the specific reasons why it remains a challenge. For example, if you are still taking on too much work, is it because you want to please others? Write a brief analysis here, and let this analysis guide you as you work to build your strength in this area.

15. *Focus and concentrate to achieve their goals.* They create an environment in which they can best avoid distraction to focus steadily on their work.
16. *Spread themselves neither too thin nor too thick.* They strike a balance between doing too many things, which results in little progress on any of them, and too few things, which can reduce the level of accomplishment.

get $mart

FIND WORK THAT COMBINES EARNINGS AND FULFILLMENT

Complete the following on paper or in digital format.

Investigate which jobs in your areas of interest can earn you what you need.

1. What are your most significant interests and skills?

2. What are three possible careers you feel would suit your interests and skills?

3. Identify three people you could talk to who work in, or know about, any of these careers. For each, write down the name, career, and contact information.

4. Contact an individual from the list to set up an informational interview. *Note:* Refer to the "Informational Interviews and the Hidden Job Market" section in this chapter for assistance.

5. Develop a list of questions to ask the individual about his or her job, making sure to focus on the question of how to balance passion and earnings. Save the list on a computer and print it.

6. Attend the informational interview, taking notes on your printed list. Send a follow-up thank-you note. If you can, repeat the informational interview process with the other two people.

17. *Have the ability to delay gratification.* Although they enjoy the smaller rewards that require less energy, they focus the bulk of their work on the goals that take more time but promise the most gratification.

18. *Have the ability to see the forest and the trees.* They are able to see the big picture and avoid getting bogged down in tiny details.

19. *Have a reasonable level of self-confidence and a belief in their ability to accomplish their goals.* They believe in themselves enough to get through the tough times, while avoiding the kind of overconfidence that stalls learning and growth.

20. *Balance analytical, creative, and practical thinking.* They sense what to use and when to use it. When problems arise, they combine all three skills to arrive at solutions.

These characteristics are your personal motivational tools. Consult them when you need a way to get moving. You may even want to post them somewhere in your home, in the front of a notebook, or as a note in your smartphone.

Lifelong Learning and the Growth Mindset

Knowledge in many fields is doubling every two to three years, and your personal interests and needs are changing all the time. With a growth mindset—the attitude that you can always grow and learn—you are as ready to achieve the goals you set out for yourself today as you are to achieve future goals you cannot yet anticipate.

Risk asking tough questions to be rewarded with new insights. Use the following to inspire discussion with classmates in person or online.

- As one saying goes, "Do what you love and the money will follow." Do you agree that this risk will bring financial reward, or disagree? Support your opinion with examples.

- People who work freelance jobs make their own schedules but need to be careful money managers in order to save and pay taxes. People who are employed by companies may have less freedom but are more likely to enjoy benefits such as insurance, savings plans, and having taxes taken out. Which suits you better?

- Have you had a job application rejected, failed to get a job after an interview, or been fired from a job? How did you cope? What reward resulted from your risk taking?

CONSIDER THE CASE: Kelly saw a problem and was driven to try to solve it. If you knew her, would you advise her to take the risk to begin freelancing as an ESL teacher? Starting a new business can be demanding but also rewarding. How has making a difference for someone else in your life had a positive effect on you?

Joe Chielli, Shutterstock

You leave this course with a set of tools—skills and attitudes—that open the door to success in the 21st century. Throughout the term, you have built skills and knowledge in each quadrant of the 21st Century Learning grid. As you continue your education, you will further develop these tools that benefit you in everything you do. See Key 12.7 for details.

What risks will reward you with learning throughout your life? Here are some:

- *Spend time with interesting people.* When you meet someone new who inspires you and makes you think, keep in touch. Form a book club, get a pickup basketball game together, or join a local volunteer organization. Learn something new from everyone you meet.

- *Talk to people from different generations.* Younger people can learn from the broad perspective of those from older generations; older people can learn from the fresh perspective of youth. Communication builds mutual respect.

- *Investigate new interests.* When information and events catch your attention, take your interest one step further and find out more. Instead of dreaming about it, just do it.

- *Read, read, read.* Reading expert Jim Trelease says that people who don't read "base their future decisions on what they used to know. If you don't read much, you really don't know much."[9] Open a world of knowledge and perspectives through reading. Ask friends which books have changed their lives. Keep up with local, national, and world news through newspapers, magazines, and Internet sources.

- *Keep on top of changes in your career.* After graduation, continue your education both in your field and in the realm of general knowledge. Stay on top of ideas, developments, and new technology in your field by seeking out continuing education courses. Sign up for career-related seminars. Some companies offer additional on-the-job training or pay for their employees to take courses that will improve their knowledge and skills.

CONTINUING EDUCATION
Courses that students can take without needing to be part of a degree or diploma program.

Shutterstock

Careers and More

Attitudes and skills acquired in college and university are tools for lifelong success.

ACQUIRED SKILL	IN COLLEGE/UNIVERSITY, YOU WILL USE IT TO . . .	IN CAREER AND LIFE, YOU WILL USE IT TO . . .
Investigating resources	. . . find who and what can help you have the post-secondary experience you want.	. . . get acclimated at a new job or in a new town—find the people, resources, and services that can help you succeed.
Knowing and using your learning styles	. . . select study strategies that make the most of your learning styles.	. . . select jobs, career areas, and other pursuits that suit what you do best.
Setting goals and managing stress	. . . complete assignments and achieve educational goals; reduce stress by being in control.	. . . accomplish tasks and reach career and personal goals; reduce stress by being in control.
Managing time	. . . get to classes on time, juggle school and work, turn in assignments when they are due, and plan study time.	. . . finish work tasks on time or before they are due, and balance duties on the job and at home.
Analytical, creative, and practical thinking	. . . think through writing assignments, solve math problems, analyze academic readings, brainstorm paper topics, work through academic issues, and work effectively on team projects.	. . . find ways to improve product design, increase market share, present ideas to customers; analyze life issues, come up with ideas, and take practical action.
Reading	. . . read course texts and other materials.	. . . read operating manuals, work guidebooks, media materials in your field; read for practical purposes, for learning, and for pleasure at home.
Note taking	. . . take notes in class, in study groups, during studying, and during research.	. . . take notes in work and community meetings and during important phone calls.
Test taking	. . . take quizzes, tests, and final exams.	. . . take tests for certification in particular work skills and for continuing education courses.
Writing	. . . write essays and reports.	. . . write work-related documents, including emails, reports, proposals, and speeches; write personal letters and journal entries.
Building successful relationships	. . . get along with instructors, students, and student groups.	. . . get along with supervisors, co-workers, team members, friends, and family members.
Staying healthy	. . . stay physically and mentally healthy so that you can make the most of school.	. . . stay physically and mentally healthy so that you can be at your best at work and at home.
Managing money	. . . stay on top of school costs and make decisions that earn and save you the money you need.	. . . budget the money you earn so that you can pay your bills and save for the future.
Establishing and maintaining a personal mission	. . . develop a big picture idea of what you want from your education, and make choices that guide you toward those goals.	. . . develop a big picture idea of what you wish to accomplish in life, and make choices that guide you toward those goals.

- *Delve into other cultures.* Invite a friend over who has grown up in a culture different from your own. Eat food from a country you have never visited. Initiate conversations with people of different races, religions, values, and ethnic backgrounds. Travel internationally and locally. Take a course that deals with cultural diversity. Try a term or year abroad. Learn a new language. Kelly's experience with other cultures broadened her horizons and has led her on a path toward a fulfilling career.

- *Nurture a spiritual life.* Wherever you find spirituality—in organized religion, family, friendship, nature, music, or anywhere else—it will help you find balance and meaning.

- *Experience the arts.* Art is "a means of knowing the world" (Angela Carter, author), "a lie that makes us realize truth" (Pablo Picasso, painter), a revealer of "our most secret self" (Jean-Luc Godard, filmmaker). Through art, you can discover new ideas and shed light on old ones. Seek out whatever moves you—music, visual arts, theatre, photography, dance, performance art, film and television, poetry, prose, and more.

- *Be creative.* Take a class in drawing, writing, or quilting. Learn to play an instrument. Write poems for your friends or stories to read to your children. Concoct a new recipe. Design and build something for your home. Express yourself, and learn more about yourself, through art.

Lifelong learning is the master key that unlocks so many of the doors you encounter on your journey. If you keep it firmly in your hand, you will discover worlds of knowledge—and a place for yourself to continue growing within them.

Learned Optimism Will Help You Cope with Change and Challenge

As a citizen of the 21st century, you are likely to move in and out of school, jobs, and careers in the years ahead. You are also likely to experience important personal changes. How you react to change, especially if it is unexpected and difficult, is almost as important as the changes themselves in determining your future success. The ability to make lemonade from lemons is the hallmark of people who are able to hang on to hope.

Use your optimistic explanatory style to analyze situations, brainstorm solutions, and take practical action. With this skill you can

Shutterstock

- *see adversity as temporary.* Consider losing a job, for example, as a step along the way to a better one.

- *see the limited scope of your problems.* One issue does not make your entire life a disaster.

- *avoid the personal.* If you look for explanation in the details of a situation instead of seeing yourself as incompetent, you can keep your self-esteem and creative energy alive.

With successful intelligence, a growth mindset, and learned optimism, you will always have a new direction in which to grow. Your willingness to take calculated, productive risks will allow you to put these valuable tools to work and reward you with the achievement of your most valued goals. Risk being true to yourself, a respectful friend and family member, a focused student who believes in the power of learning, a productive employee, and a contributing member of society, to earn the ultimate reward of a meaningful life—a life that can change the world.

Careers and More

revisit RISK AND REWARD

Joe Chielli

What happened to Kelly? Kelly came up with an idea for a nonprofit program, Project Bridge, that would recruit university students learning Spanish to teach ESL in-home to local residents, giving the resident a free tutor and the tutor a chance to practise Spanish and help the community. Within a year, Project Bridge grew to more than 50 student–teacher partnerships, and it is still thriving. She then applied to business schools, hoping to further her understanding of the problem-solving capabilities of communication so that she could make a difference for organizations. She is now working toward her MBA.

What does this mean for you? Doing something to improve the life of even one person in your community has ripple effects that can bring positive change to many people. You don't need to start an entire organization to be able to make a difference, of course. Use your analytical thinking skills to look carefully at what is going on around you. Think creatively to come up with ideas about what you could do.

Don't rule out any idea, however small it seems. Finally, take practical action and make it happen. Involve others if you can.

What risk may bring reward beyond your world? Kelly's organization, in addition to providing a service to people, also bridges a gap between cultures. You may have opportunities to make cross-cultural connections locally, if you live in a diverse area. However, even if you don't, you can look further for a chance to connect. An organization called Cross-Cultural Solutions (www.crossculturalsolutions.org) provides volunteer opportunities all over the world in areas such as teaching, health care, and community development. Time frames are flexible, with placements from 2 to 12 weeks and even some 1-week opportunities. Explore the site. Even if you don't want to travel, it may give you ideas about other ways to make a better world.

RISK ACTION

FOR POST SECONDARY, CAREER, AND LIFE REWARDS

KNOW IT *Think Critically*

Become a Better Interviewee

Build basic skills. Make a list of questions that a job applicant would typically hear in an entry-level interview. Recall questions from job interviews you have had; look up questions using online sources such as www.quintcareers.com; or consult books on job interviews. On a separate sheet of paper, list 15 to 20 questions.

Take it to the next level. Imagine yourself as the interviewer, and brainstorm some more creative questions to add to your list. Think about learning styles, life experiences, learning from failure, role models, and more as you ponder. Write five additional questions.

Move toward mastery. Pair up with a student in your class and interview each other. Person A interviews Person B for 5 to 10 minutes and takes notes. Then switch roles: Person B interviews Person A and takes notes. Each person uses the set of questions developed in the first and second parts of the exercise.

When you are done, share with each other what interesting ideas stand out from the interviews. If you have suggestions, offer constructive criticism to each other about interview skills.

Write a brief analysis and summary of your experience, including what you learned and would keep in mind for a real interview—both the good and the bad.

WRITE IT *Communicate*

Record your thoughts on a separate piece of paper, in a journal, or electronically.

Emotional intelligence journal: Revisit your personal mission. If you drafted a personal mission and/or established career priorities earlier this term, look back at what you wrote. Think about how you feel now at the end of the term. Consider what has changed about the outcomes you originally wanted to make happen in your life, and write an updated version of your mission. Incorporate one or more of those career priorities into your mission statement.

Real-life writing: Create a resumé. On one electronic page or sheet of paper, list information about your education (where and when you have studied, degrees or certificates you have earned) and your skills (what you know how to do, such as use a computer program or operate a type of equipment). On another, list job experience. For each job, record the job title (if you had one), dates of employment, and tasks performed. Include tasks that demonstrate skills. Be as detailed as possible. When you compile your resumé, you will make this material more concise. Keep this list and update it periodically as you gain experience and accomplishments.

Using the information you have gathered and Key 12.6 as your guide, draft a resumé. There are many ways to construct a resumé; consult resources for different styles (try www.resume-help. org or www.howtowritearesume.net). You may want to format your resumé according to a style that your career counsellor or instructor recommends. Also, certain career areas may favour a particular style of resumé. (Check with your career counsellor or an instructor in that area.)

Keep this resumé draft in hard copy and on a computer hard drive or disk. When you need to submit a resumé with a job application, update the draft and print it out on high-quality paper. For electronic submission, convert your resumé file to PDF format.

WORK IT *Build Your Brand*
Revisit the Wheel of Successful Intelligence

21st Century Learning Building Blocks:

- Initiative and self-direction
- Critical thinking and problem solving

Complete the following in your electronic portfolio or on separate sheets of paper. When you finish, read through your entire career portfolio. You have gathered a lot of information to turn to on your path to a fulfilling, successful career.

Without looking at any previously completed versions of these assessments or the wheel, analyze where you are after completing this course by taking the three assessments.

Assess Your Analytical Thinking Skills

For each statement, circle the number that feels right to you, from 1 for "not at all true for me" to 5 for "very true for me."

1. I recognize and define problems effectively.   1 2 3 4 5

2. I see myself as *analytical, studious,* and a *thinker*.   1 2 3 4 5

3. When working on a problem in a group setting, I like to break down the problem into its components and evaluate them.   1 2 3 4 5

4. I need to see convincing evidence before accepting information as fact.   1 2 3 4 5

5. I weigh the pros and cons of plans and ideas before taking action.   1 2 3 4 5

6. I tend to make connections among pieces of information by categorizing them.   1 2 3 4 5

7. Impulsive, spontaneous decision-making worries me.   1 2 3 4 5

8. I monitor my progress toward goals.   1 2 3 4 5

9. Once I reach a goal, I evaluate the process to see how effective it was.   1 2 3 4 5

10. When something goes wrong, I work to find out why.   1 2 3 4 5

Total your answers here: _____

Assess Your Creative Thinking Skills

For each statement, circle the number that feels right to you, from 1 for "not at all true for me" to 5 for "very true for me."

1. I tend to question rules and regulations.   1 2 3 4 5

2. I see myself as *unique, full of ideas,* and *innovative*.   1 2 3 4 5

3. When working on a problem in a group setting, I generate a lot of ideas.   1 2 3 4 5

4. I am energized when I have a brand-new experience.   1 2 3 4 5

5. If you say something is too risky, I am ready to give it a shot.   1 2 3 4 5

6. I often wonder if there is a different way to do or see something.   1 2 3 4 5

7. Too much routine in my work or schedule drains my energy.   1 2 3 4 5

8. I tend to see connections among ideas that others do not.   1 2 3 4 5

9. I feel comfortable allowing myself to make mistakes as I test out ideas.   1 2 3 4 5

10. I am willing to champion an idea even when others disagree with me.   1 2 3 4 5

Total your answers here: _____

Assess Your Practical Thinking Skills

For each statement, circle the number that feels right to you, from 1 for "not at all true for me" to 5 for "very true for me."

1. I can find a way around any obstacle.   1 2 3 4 5

2. I see myself as a *doer*, the *go-to person*, and *I make things happen*.   1 2 3 4 5

3. When working on a problem in a group setting, I like to set up the plan and monitor how it is carried out.   1 2 3 4 5

4. Because I learn well from experience, I don't tend to repeat a mistake.   1 2 3 4 5

5. I finish what I start and don't leave loose ends hanging.   1 2 3 4 5

6. I pay attention to my emotions in academic and social situations to see if they help or hurt me as I move toward a goal.   1 2 3 4 5

7. I can sense how people feel, and can use that knowledge to interact with others effectively in order to achieve a goal.   1 2 3 4 5

8. I manage my time effectively.   1 2 3 4 5

9. I find ways to adjust to the teaching styles of my instructors and the communication styles of my peers.   1 2 3 4 5

10. When involved in a problem solving process, I can see when I am headed in an ineffective direction and I can shift gears.   1 2 3 4 5

Total your answers here: _____

After you finish, fill in your new scores in the blank Wheel of Successful Intelligence in Key 12.8. If you completed a wheel at the start of term, compare it to this wheel and look at the changes. Complete the following on paper or in digital format:

- Note the areas where you see the most change. Where have you grown, and how has your self-perception evolved?
- Note three *creative ideas* you came up with over the term that aided your exploration or development.
- Note three *practical actions* that you took that moved you toward your goals.

Let what you learn from this new wheel inform you about what you have accomplished and what you plan to accomplish. Continue to grow your analytical, creative, and practical skills and use them to manage the changes that await you in the future.

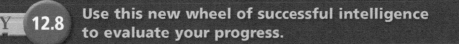

KEY 12.8 Use this new wheel of successful intelligence to evaluate your progress.

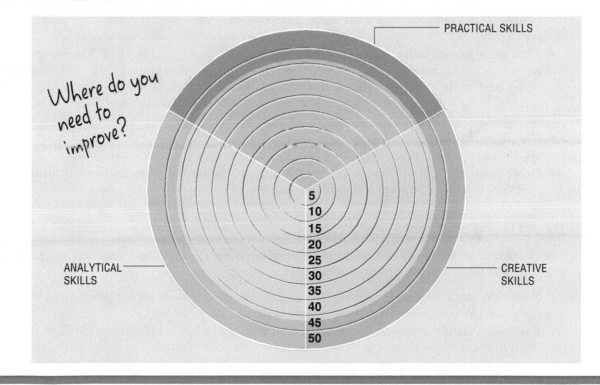

Study Tools: *Get Ready for Exams*

Demonstrate What You Know in an Oral Exam

In an oral exam, your instructor asks you to verbally present your responses to exam questions or to discuss a pre-assigned topic. Oral exam questions may be similar to essay questions on written exams. They may be broad and general, or they may focus on a narrow topic that you are expected to explore in depth.

The material in this Study Tools is designed to help you master the skills you need to perform well during an oral exam. These skills have life-long benefits. The more comfortable you are speaking in front of instructors, the more prepared you will be for any kind of public speaking situation—in school, in the community, and at work.

Keep in mind that if you have a documented learning disability that limits your ability to express yourself effectively in writing, you may need to take all your exams orally. Speak with your advisor and instructors to set up an oral exam schedule.

Preparation strategies

Because oral exams require that you speak logically and keep to the point, your instructors will often give you the exam topic in advance and may even allow you to bring your notes to the exam room. Other instructors ask you to study a specified topic and they then ask questions about the topic during the exam.

Speaking in front of others—even an audience of one, your instructor—involves developing a presentation strategy before you enter the exam room:

- *Learn your topic.* Study for the exam until you have mastered the material. Nothing can replace subject mastery as a confidence booster.
- *Plan your presentation.* Dive into the details. Brainstorm your topic if it is pre-assigned, narrow it with prewriting strategies (Appendix A), determine your central idea or argument, and write an outline that will be the basis of your talk. If the exam uses a Q and A format, make a list of the most likely questions, and formulate the key points of your response.
- *Use clear thinking.* Make sure your logic is solid and that your evidence supports your thesis. Work on an effective beginning and ending that focus on the exam topic.
- *Draft your thoughts.* To get your thoughts organized for the exam, make a draft using "trigger" words or phrases that will remind you of what you want to say.

Practise your presentation

The element of performance distinguishes speaking from writing. As in any performance, practice is essential. Use the following strategies to guide your efforts:

- *Know the parameters.* How long do you have to present your topic? Where will you be speaking? Will you have access to a podium, table, chair, or whiteboard?
- *Use index cards or notes.* If your instructor doesn't object, bring note cards to the presentation. Keep them out of your face, however; it's tempting to hide behind them.

- *Pay attention to the physical.* Your body positioning, voice, eye contact, and what you wear contribute to the impression you make; therefore, try to look good and sound good.
- *Time your practice sessions to determine whether you should add or cut material.* If you are given your topic in advance, make sure you can state your points in the allotted time. During the exam, make sure you don't speak too quickly.
- *Try to be natural.* Use words you are comfortable with to express concepts you know. Be yourself as you show your knowledge and enthusiasm for the topic.

Be prepared for questions

After your formal presentation, your instructor may ask you topic-related questions. Your responses and the way you handle the questions will affect your grade. Here are some strategies for answering questions effectively:

- *Take the questions seriously.* The exam is not over until the Q and A period ends.
- *Jot down keywords from the questions.* This strategy is especially important if the question has several parts, and you intend to address one part at a time.
- *Ask for clarification.* Ask the instructor to rephrase a question you don't understand.
- *Think before you speak.* Take a moment to organize your thoughts and to write down keywords for the points you want to cover.
- *Answer only part of a question if that's all you can do.* Emphasize what you know best, and impress the instructor with your depth of knowledge. If you draw a blank, simply tell the instructor that you don't know the answer.

Control your nerves during an exam

If you are nervous, there are things you can do to help yourself:

- *Keep your mind on your presentation, not yourself.* Focus on what you want to say and how you want to say it.
- *Take deep breaths right before you begin, and carry a bottle of water.* Deep breathing will calm you, and the water will ease a dry mouth.
- *Visualize your own success.* Create a powerful mental picture of yourself acing the exam. Then visualize yourself speaking with knowledge, confidence, and poise.
- *Establish eye contact with your instructor and realize that he or she wants you to succeed.* You'll relax when you feel that your instructor is on your side.

Decide how well these techniques work for you

Practice makes perfect, especially when it comes to public speaking. Gauge your ability to speak effectively during an oral exam with the following team exercise:

- Team up with another student to prepare for a written essay, and then quiz each other as if you were taking an actual oral exam. How did your partner evaluate your presentation? What were your strengths? Your weaknesses?
- Do you think that your answers demonstrated all you know about the subject or that you could have done better in writing? If you answered the latter, what obstacles prevented you from doing your best in your oral presentation?
- Describe three actions you will take to improve your next presentation.

1. _____
2. _____
3. _____

Self-Study Quiz

Multiple choice

Circle or highlight the answer that seems to fit best.

1. **Students who experience stereotyping may**
   A. call attention to themselves as members of a minority group.
   B. be self-conscious because they see themselves as underachievers.
   C. feel superior to others because of their minority status.
   D. distance themselves from the qualities they think others associate with their group and avoid asking for help because they fear perpetuating a group stereotype.

2. **The goal of stress management is to**
   A. eliminate all stress from your life.
   B. focus only on school-related stress.
   C. learn to blame all stressful situations on others.
   D. develop strategies for handling the stresses that are an inevitable part of life.

3. **Which of the following regarding body weight is FALSE?**
   A. Your BMI is the ratio of your height to your weight.
   B. Losing 1 to 2 pounds (0.45 to 0.9 kilograms) per week is considered a healthy rate of weight loss.
   C. A BMI of 25 is considered obese.

D. Obesity is a key factor in adult-onset diabetes.

4. ***Networking* can be defined as**
   A. visiting your instructor during office hours.
   B. the exchange of information or services among individuals, groups, or institutions.
   C. discovering your ideal career.
   D. making a strategic plan.

5. **Being flexible in the face of change involves**
   A. changing your direction when you encounter obstacles in your life and work.
   B. acknowledging the change and assessing what new needs it brings.
   C. reacting in a way that you have seen work for others.
   D. focusing on an aspect of your life not affected by the change.

6. **To be open to unpredictability,**
   A. put your energy into building existing relationships.
   B. make a plan and stick with it even in the face of change.
   C. focus on what is rather than on what is supposed to be.
   D. don't let surprises throw you off.

Fill in the blanks

Complete the following sentences with the appropriate word(s) or phrase(s) that best reflect what you have learned in the chapters. Choose from the items that follow each sentence.

1. _____ factors play an important role in how _____ are interpreted. (Personal/body movements, Biological/verbal cues, Cultural/nonverbal cues)

2. _____ criticism involves goodwill suggestions for improvement. (Nonconstructive, Direct, Constructive)

3. The three most common eating disorders are _____, _____, and _____. (anorexia nervosa/food allergies/binge drinking; anorexia nervosa/bulimia/binge eating; constant dieting/eating too much fat/bulimia)

4. Two effective ways to build career knowledge and experience are _____ and _____. (job hunting/networking, internships/volunteering, learning style/critical thinking)

5. The debt ceiling a credit card company places on your account is called a _____. (cash advance, account balance, credit limit)

Essays

The following essay questions will help you organize and communicate your ideas in writing, just as you must do on an essay test. Before you begin answering a question, spend a few minutes planning (brainstorm possible approaches, write a thesis statement, jot down main thoughts in outline or think-link form). To prepare yourself for actual test conditions, limit writing time to no more than 30 minutes per question.

1. Discuss the mind–body connection—specifically, the impact of diet, exercise, sleep, and medical care on the development and management of stress. Describe the changes you hope to make in your stress-management plan as a result of the information you have read in this book.

2. Choose three important skills you have developed during this course. Explain how they will contribute to your success for the remainder of your post-secondary experience and beyond.

Answer Key: *For Self-Study Quizzes*

Chapter 4, pages 109–111

MULTIPLE CHOICE	FILL IN THE BLANKS
1. D	1. commitment
2. A	2. initiative
3. D	3. learning preferences/personality traits
4. A	4. interests/abilities
5. C	5. mission
6. A	6. flexible

Chapter 8, pages 232–233

MULTIPLE CHOICE	FILL IN THE BLANKS
1. D	1. taking in information/asking questions about-information/using information
2. B	
3. A	2. creativity
4. D	3. context
5. B	4. cue column
6. C	5. mnemonic device
	6. Freewriting/uncensored/planning

Chapter 12, pages 340–341

MULTIPLE CHOICE	FILL IN THE BLANKS
1. D	1. Cultural/nonverbal cues
2. D	2. Constructive
3. C	3. anorexia nervosa/bulimia/binge eating
4. B	4. internships/volunteering
5. B	5. credit limit
6. C	

The Writing Process

Writing a research paper or essay involves planning, drafting, revising, and editing.

Planning

The planning process involves six steps that help you think about the assignment:

Pay Attention to Logistics

These practical questions will help you decide on a topic and depth of coverage:

1. *How much depth does my instructor expect and how long should the paper be?*
2. *How much time do I have?* Consider your other courses and responsibilities.
3. *What kind of research is needed?* Your topic and purpose may determine this.
4. *Is it a team project?* If you are working with others, determine what each person will do.

Generate Topic Ideas

Start the process of choosing a paper topic by creatively generating ideas within the boundaries your instructor has set (see Chapter 5):

- Begin by writing down anything on the assigned subject that comes to mind, in no particular order. Tap your multiple intelligences for creative ideas. To jump-start your thoughts, scan your text and notes, check library or Internet references, or meet with your instructor to discuss ideas.
- Next, organize that list into an outline or think link so you can see different possibilities.

Use Prewriting Strategies to Narrow Your Topic

Prewriting strategies, such as brainstorming, freewriting, and asking journalists' questions,[1] help you decide which possible topic you would most like to pursue. Use them to narrow your topic, focusing on the specific sub-ideas and examples from your brainstorming session.

- *Generating Ideas.* The same creative process you used to generate ideas will help you narrow your topic. Write down your thoughts about the possibilities you have chosen, do some more research, and then organize your thoughts into categories, noticing patterns that appear.
- *Freewriting.* When you *freewrite*, you jot down whatever comes to mind without censoring ideas or worrying about grammar, spelling, punctuation, or organization.
- *Asking journalists' questions.* When journalists start working on a story, they ask Who? What? Where? When? Why? How? Asking these questions will help you choose a specific topic.

Prewriting helps you develop a topic that is broad enough for investigation but narrow enough to handle. Prewriting also helps you identify what you know and what you don't know. If an assignment involves more than you already know, you need to do research.

Conduct Research and Take Notes

Research develops in stages as you narrow and refine your ideas. In the first brainstorming-for-ideas stage, look for an overview that can lead to a working thesis statement. In the second stage, track down information that fills in gaps. Ultimately, you will have a body of information that you can evaluate to develop and implement your final thesis.

As you research, create source and content notes to organize your work, keep track of your sources, and avoid plagiarism.

Source notes. Source notes, written on index cards, are preliminary notes that should include the author's name; the title of the work; the edition (if any); the publisher, year, and city of publication; the issue and/or volume number when applicable (such as for a magazine); and the page numbers consulted. Notes on Internet sources should reference the website's complete name and address, including the universal resource locator (URL)—the string of text and numbers that identifies an Internet site. Include a short summary and critical evaluation for each source.

Content notes. Content notes, written on large index cards, in a notebook, or on your computer, are taken during a thorough reading and provide an in-depth look at source material. Use them to record needed information. To supplement your content notes, make notations—marginal notes, highlighting, and underlining—directly on photocopies of sources.

Write a Working Thesis Statement

Next, organize your research and write a *thesis statement*—the organizing principle of your paper. The thesis declares your specific subject and point of view and reflects your writing purpose (to inform or persuade) and audience (your intended readers).

Consider this your *working* thesis—it may change as you continue your research and develop your draft. Be ready and willing to rework your writing—and your thesis—one or more times before handing in your paper.

Write a Working Outline or Think Link

The final planning step is to create a working outline or think link to guide your writing.

Drafting

You may write many versions of the assignment until you are satisfied. Each version moves you closer to saying exactly what you want in the way you want to say it. You face the following main challenges at the first-draft stage:

- Finalizing your thesis
- Defining an organizational structure
- Integrating source material into the body of the paper to fit your structure
- Finding additional sources to strengthen your presentation
- Choosing the right words, phrases, and general tone

- Connecting ideas with logical transitions
- Creating an effective introduction and conclusion
- Checking for plagiarism
- Producing a list of works cited

Don't aim for perfection in a first draft. Trying to get every detail right too early may shut the door on ideas before you even know they are there.

Freewriting Your Draft

Use everything that you developed in the planning stage as the raw material for freewriting a draft. For now, don't think about your introduction, conclusion, or organizational structure. Simply focus on what you want to say. Only after you have thoughts down should you begin to shape your work.

Writing an Introduction

The introduction tells readers what the paper contains and includes a thesis statement, which is often found at the end of the introduction.

Creating the Body of a Paper

The body of the paper contains your central ideas and supporting evidence, which underpins your thesis with facts, statistics, examples, and expert opinions. Try to find a structure that helps you organize your ideas and evidence into a clear pattern, such as one of the several organizational options presented in Key A.1.

 **KEY A.1** **Find the best way to organize the body of the paper.**

ORGANIZATIONAL STRUCTURE	WHAT TO DO
Arrange ideas by time.	Describe events in order or in reverse order.
Arrange ideas according to importance.	Start with the idea that carries the most weight and move to less important ideas. Or move from the least to the most important ideas.
Arrange ideas by problem and solution.	Start with a problem and then discuss solutions.
Arrange ideas to present an argument.	Present one or both sides of an issue.
Arrange ideas in list form.	Group a series of items.
Arrange ideas according to cause and effect.	Show how events, situations, or ideas cause subsequent events, situations, or ideas.
Arrange ideas through the use of comparisons.	Compare and contrast the characteristics of events, people, situations, or ideas.
Arrange by process.	Go through the steps in a process: a how-to approach.
Arrange by category.	Divide topics into categories and analyze each in order.

Writing the Conclusion

A conclusion brings your paper to a natural ending by summarizing your main points, showing the significance of your thesis and how it relates to larger issues, and calling the reader to action or looking to the future. Let the ideas in the body of the paper speak for themselves as you wrap up.

Avoiding Plagiarism: Crediting Authors and Sources

Using another writer's words, content, unique approach, or illustrations without crediting the author is called *plagiarism* and is illegal and unethical. The following techniques will help you properly credit sources and avoid plagiarism:

Make source notes as you go. Plagiarism often begins accidentally during research. You may forget to include quotation marks around a quotation, or you may intend to cite or paraphrase a source but never do. To avoid forgetting, write detailed source and content notes as you research.

Learn the difference between a quotation and a paraphrase. A *quotation* repeats a source's exact words and uses quotation marks to set them off from the rest of the text. A paraphrase (a restatement of the quotation in your own words) requires that you completely rewrite the idea, not just remove or replace a few words.

Use a citation even for an acceptable paraphrase. Credit every source that you quote, paraphrase, or use as evidence (except when the material is considered common knowledge). To credit a source, write a footnote or endnote that describes it, using the format preferred by your instructor.

Understand that lifting material off the Internet is plagiarism. Words in electronic form belong to the writer just as words in print form do. If you cut and paste sections from a source document into your draft, you are probably committing plagiarism.

Key A.2 will help you identify the types of material that instructors regard as plagiarized work.

Students who plagiarize place their academic careers at risk, in part because cheating is easy to discover. Increasingly, instructors are using antiplagiarism software, such as Turnitin, to investigate whether strings of words in student papers match material in a database. Make a commitment to hand in your own work and uphold the highest standards of academic integrity.

KEY A.2 Plagiarism takes many forms.

Instructors consider the following types of work to be plagiarized:

- Submitting a paper from a website that sells or gives away research papers
- Handing in a paper written by a fellow student or family member
- Copying material in a paper directly from a source without proper quotation marks or source citation
- Paraphrasing material in a paper from a source without proper source citation
- Submitting the same paper in more than one class, even if the classes are in different terms or even different years

Citing Sources

You may be asked to submit different kinds of source lists when you hand in your paper:

- *References list.* Only the sources actually cited in your paper (also called a List of Works Cited)
- *Bibliography.* All the sources you consulted, whether or not they were cited in the paper
- *Annotated bibliography.* All the sources you consulted as well as an explanation or critique of each source

Your instructor will tell you which documentation style to use (commonly one of the following):

- The Modern Language Association (MLA) format is generally used in the humanities, including history, literature, the arts, and philosophy.
- The American Psychological Association (APA) style is the appropriate format in psychology, sociology, business, economics, nursing, criminology, and social work.

Consult your college's or university's student handbook for an overview of these documentation styles, or read about them online at www.mla.org and www.apa.org.

Get Feedback

Talk with your instructor about your draft, or ask a study partner to read it and answer specific questions. Be open-minded about the comments you receive. Consider each carefully, and then make a decision about what to change.

Revising

When you *revise*, you critically evaluate the content, organization, word choice, paragraph structure, and style of your first draft. You evaluate the strength of your thesis and whether your evidence proves it, looking for logical holes. You can do anything you want at this point to change your work. You can turn things around and present information from the end of your paper at its beginning, tweak your thesis to reflect the evidence presented, or choose a different organizational structure.

Engage your critical thinking skills to evaluate the content and form of your paper. Ask yourself these questions as you revise:

- Does the paper fulfill the requirements of the assignment?
- Do I prove my thesis?
- Is each idea and argument developed, explained, and supported by examples?
- Does the introduction prepare the reader and capture attention?
- Is the body of the paper organized effectively?
- Does each paragraph have a topic sentence that is supported by the rest of the paragraph?
- Are my ideas connected to one another through logical transitions?
- Do I have a clear, concise writing style?
- Does the conclusion provide a natural ending without introducing new ideas?

Check for Clarity

Now check for sense, continuity, and clarity. Also focus on tightening your prose and eliminating wordy phrases. Examine once again how paragraphs flow into one another by evaluating the effectiveness of your *transitions*—the words, phrases, or sentences that connect ideas.

Editing

Editing involves correcting technical mistakes in spelling, grammar, and punctuation, as well as checking for consistency in such elements as abbreviations and capitalization. If you use a computer, start with the grammar-check and spell-check to find mistakes, realizing that you still need to check your work manually. Look also for *sexist language,* which characterizes people according to gender stereotypes and often involves the male pronouns *he, his,* or *him.*

Proofreading, the last editing stage, involves reading every word for accuracy. Look for technical mistakes, run-on sentences, spelling errors, and sentence fragments. Look for incorrect word usage and unclear references. A great way to check your work is to read it out loud.

Your final paper reflects all the hard work you put in during the writing process. Ideally, when you are finished, you have a piece of work that shows your researching, writing, and thinking ability.

Social Networking and Media

Social networking refers to interacting with a community of people through an online network such as Facebook, Twitter, forums (message boards), or chat rooms. Social media are the types of media people use to share information online (for example, web logs/blogs, podcasts, websites, videos, and news feeds). Social media allows participation through comments and ratings. The people who provide social media content range from experts to amateurs, which means the content will not always be accurate or trustworthy.

In general, social networking and media make three things possible:

1. Communicating information about yourself to others
2. Connecting with people who have similar interests
3. Networking with others to accomplish goals

Social networking has grown rapidly worldwide through sites such as the following:

- *Facebook* enables users to set up personal profiles and communicate with other users through profile updates, public or private messages, games, and photos.
- *Twitter* enables users to send or receive short text updates, or tweets, to other users signed up on their accounts.
- *Skype* enables users to make calls over the Internet.

HOW SOCIAL NETWORKING AND MEDIA CAN HELP
you in college or university

Use social networking and media to do the following:

- *Connect with peers to achieve academic goals.* Students might create groups that correspond to courses, study together on an Internet call, or post course-related questions and comments on a message board or chat room used by the class (e.g., Facebook or Skype).
- *Manage coursework and projects.* Particular sites can help you search for information, study, and ask questions. When doing a group project, social networking can help you collaborate in an online format (e.g., Evernote, Google Docs, EtherPad, or Wikidot).
- *Network with students who have shared interests.* A student might start a blog on an academic topic and hope to attract interested readers, or look for groups or Internet forums (e.g., Facebook, Tumblr, or Pinterest).
- *Adjust to college/university.* Ask other students at your school about local issues (bus schedules, library hours), or ask students anywhere in the world about more general concerns (test anxiety). You can even use social media to stay organized. (e.g., Twitter, Facebook, GradeMate, or Backpack).
- *Focus on career development.* Put your qualifications and career goals out there for others to peruse, and build a network that may lead you to job opportunities (e.g., LinkedIn or Zumeo).
- *Stay connected with loved ones.* Students might tweet or blog happenings to family and old friends, post updates, or make free phone calls. A budgeting

bonus—most social networking tools cost nothing to use as long as you have Internet access (e.g., Twitter, Facebook, or Skype).

- *Share your opinion.* Blogs allow you to communicate to an audience on a regular basis, and creating a blog is usually free. Another tool, the forum or message board, encourages individuals to come together and discuss a common knowledge or experience (e.g., Blogger or Myspace).

TEN STRATEGIES
for success

Follow these guidelines to get the most from your time and energy on social networks and with social media.

1. *Control your personal information.* Read the privacy policy of any network you join. Adjust security settings that indicate what information, photos, and so on you want to be visible or invisible. Know what will always be visible to users.

2. *Control your time.* One quick check of your email can lead to hours spent online that you should have spent getting something else done. To stay focused and in control,

   - Create a separate email account for alerts from your social networking sites.
   - Set your status to *offline* or *do not disturb* when you are studying.
   - Set up goals and rewards. Try doing a defined portion of your homework and then rewarding yourself with 10 minutes on your favourite social networking site.

3. *Be an information-literate critical thinker.* Evaluate what you read on social networking sites or social media with a critical eye. Use the CARS test (page 140) to check the Credibility, Accuracy, Reasonableness, and Support of any source or statement.

4. *Keep career goals in mind.* With anything you write, think: How will this look to others who may evaluate me in the future? Also, choose and post photographs carefully, because some employers use social networking sites for background checks.

5. *Use caution with forums and chat rooms.* There is no way to know who is posting on a forum or in a chat room. Consider using a name that differs from your legal name or regular email address. Remember, too, that everything you write can be copied and saved.

6. *Watch your temper.* Wait, and think, before you post on emotional topics. Forums can turn into hostile environments. Snarky tweets and updates can come back to haunt you if they are viewed by potential employers, instructors, or others who may judge you by them.

7. *Separate the personal and the academic/professional.* You probably don't want an employer seeing that crass video your cousin posted on your page. Consider having two profiles on a network if you want to use one to communicate with students or advance your career.

8. *Show restraint.* Although it is easy to get carried away, keep your purpose in mind. For example, if one goal is to keep up with friends by using Facebook, you are defeating your purpose if you have so many friends that you can't possibly stay up to date with them.

9. *Understand what a blog or website requires.* Blogs need updating at least weekly if not more often, and require time and motivation. Websites can be even more labour intensive.

10. *Network with integrity.* Treat others with respect. Search for, and use, information legitimately. Cite sources honestly.

CHAPTER 1

1. Shelley White, "Are You Ready for University?" *Canadian University Report 2014, Globe and Mail,* p. 6.

2. Thomas Friedman, *The World Is Flat,* New York: Farrar, Straus & Giroux, 2006, p. 8.

3. Human Resources and Skills Development Canada, *Special Reports: What Difference Does Learning Make to Financial Security?* January 2008, www4.hrsdc.gc.ca/.3ndic.1t.4r@-eng.jsp?iid=54.

4. Daniel Pink, "Revenge of the Right Brain," *Wired Magazine,* February 2005, www.wired.com/wired/archive/13.02/brain.html?pg=1&topic=brain&topic_set=.

5. Council of Ministers of Education Canada, *Learn Canada 2020,* April 15, 2008, www.cmec.ca/Publications/Lists/Publications/Attachments/187/CMEC-2020-DECLARATION.en.pdf.

6. Conference Board of Canada, "Employability Skills 2000+," www.conferenceboard.ca/topics/education/learning-tools/employability-skills.aspx.

7. Robert J. Sternberg, *Successful Intelligence: How Practical and Creative Intelligence Determine Success in Life,* New York: Plume, 1997, pp. 85–90; Carol S. Dweck, *Mindset: The New Psychology of Success,* New York: Random House, 2006, p. 5; and Susanne Jaeggi, Martin Buschkuehl, John Jonides, and Walter J. Perrig, "Improving Fluid Intelligence with Training on Working Memory," 2008, *Proceedings of the National Academy of Sciences USA,* 105, pp. 6829–6833.

8. Sternberg, *Successful Intelligence,* p. 11.

9. Dweck, *Mindset,* pp. 3–4.

10. The Society for Neuroscience, *Brain Facts: A Primer on the Brain and Neurosystem,* Washington, DC: The Society for Neuroscience, 2008, pp. 34–35.

11. Sternberg, *Successful Intelligence,* p. 12.

12. Ibid., p. 127.

13. Ibid., p. 11.

14. Ibid., pp. 127–128.

15. Carol Dweck, "The Mindsets," 2006, www.mind-setonline.com/whatisit/themindsets/index.html.

16. Dweck, *Mindset,* p. 16.

17. Ibid.

18. Rick Pitino, *Success Is a Choice,* New York: Broadway Books, 1997, p. 40.

19. Dweck, *Mindset,* p. 51.

20. Center for Academic Integrity, Kenan Institute for Ethics, Duke University, "The Fundamental Values of Academic Integrity," October 1999, www.academicintegrity.org/fundamental_values_project/pdf/FVProject.pdf.

21. Taylor, William M. "Academic Integrity: A Letter to My Students," Oakton Community College, Des Plaines, IL. From http://www.academicintegrity.org/educational_resources/pdf/LetterToMyStudentsRev2010.pdf.

22. Gabriel, Trip. "Plagiarism Lines Blur for Students in Digital Age" *New York Times,* August 1, 2010. From http://www.nytimes.com/2010/08/02/education/02cheat.html?pagewanted=all.

23. Taylor, "Academic Integrity."

24. John D. Mayer, Peter Salovey, and David R. Caruso, "Emotional Intelligence: New Ability or Eclectic Traits?" September 2008, *American Psychologist,* 63, no. 6, p. 503.

25. David R. Caruso, "Zero In on Knowledge: A Practical Guide to the MSCEIT," *Multi-Health Systems,* 2008, p. 3.

26. Sandra Blakeslee, "Cells That Read Minds," January 10, 2006, *New York Times,* www.nytimes.com/2006/01/10/science/10mirr.html.

27. Mayer, Salovey, and Caruso, pp. 510–512.

28. List and descriptions based on Sternberg, *Successful Intelligence,* pp. 251–268.

CHAPTER 2

1. Stephen Covey, *The Seven Habits of Highly Effective People,* New York: Simon & Schuster, 1989, pp. 70–144, 309–318.

2. Paul Timm, *Successful Self-Management: A Psychologically Sound Approach to Personal Effectiveness,* Los Altos, CA: Crisp Publications, 1987, pp. 22–41.

3. Jane E. Brody, "At Every Age, Feeling the Effects of Too Little Sleep," *New York Times,* October 23, 2007, www.nytimes.com/2007/10/23/health/23brod.html.

4. Trish Crawford, "Stress Takes Trouble Toll on Students in University," *Toronto Star*, September 3, 2009, www.healthzone.ca/health/mindmood/article/689929—stress-takes-troubling-toll-on-students-in-university.

5. Jane B. Burka and Lenora M. Yuen, *Procrastination: Why You Do It, What to Do About It*, Reading, MA: Perseus Books, 1983, pp. 21–22.

6. Sheridan, Richard, and Lisamarie Babik. "Breaking Down Walls, Building Bridges, and Taking Out the Trash." InfoQ, December 22, 2010. From http://www.infoq.com/articles/agile-team-spaces.

7. Schwarz, Tony. "Four Destructive Myths Most Companies Still Live By." *Harvard Business Review,* November 1, 2011. From http://blogs.hbr.org/schwartz/2011/11/four-destructive-myths-most-co.html.

8. Takeaways and quotes from Dr. John Medina's "Brain Rules for PowerPoint and Keynote Presenters". Slideshare presentation, Slide 79. From http://www.presentationzen.com/presentationzen/2008/05/brain-rules-for.html.

9. Schwarz.

CHAPTER 3

1. Conference Board of Canada, "Employability Skills 2000+," www.conferenceboard.ca/topics/education/learning-tools/employability-skills.aspx.

2. Howard Gardner, *Multiple Intelligences: New Horizons*, New York: Basic Books, 2006, p. 180.

3. Howard Gardner, *Multiple Intelligences: The Theory in Practice,* New York: HarperCollins, 1993, pp. 5–49.

4. Gardner, *Multiple Intelligences: New Horizons*, p. 8.

5. Gardner, *Multiple Intelligences: The Theory in Practice*, p. 7.

6. C. George Boeree, "Carl Jung," 2006, http://webspace.ship.edu/cgboer/jung.html.

7. BMO Financial Group, "Students Demonstrating Restraint With Credit Card Use," http://newsroom.bmo.com/press-releases/students-demonstrating-restraint-with-credit-card-tsx-bmo-201210310829577001.

8. Learning Disabilities Association of Canada, "Official Definition of Learning Disabilities," www.ldac-acta.ca/learn-more/ld-defined/official-definition-of-learning-disabilities.html.

9. Ibid.

CHAPTER 4

1. Vincent Ruggiero, *The Art of Thinking,* 2001, quoted in "Critical Thinking," http://success.oregonstate.edu/criticalthinking.html.

2. Richard Paul, "The Role of Questions in Thinking, Teaching, and Learning," 1995, www.criticalthinking.org/resources/articles/the-role-of-questions.shtml.

3. Conference Board of Canada, "Employability Skills 2000+," www.conferenceboard.ca/topics/education/learning-tools/employability-skills.aspx.

4. "The Best Innovations Are Those That Come from Smart Questions," *Wall Street Journal*, April 12, 2004, p. B1.

5. Sharon Begley, "Critical Thinking: Part Skill, Part Mindset and Totally Up to You," *Wall Street Journal*, October 20, 2006, p. B1.

6. David Dobbs, "Beautiful Brains." *National Geographic,* October 2011. From http://ngm.nationalgeographic.com/print/2011/10/teenagebrains/dobbs-text.

7. Ibid.

8. Ibid.

9. Matt Thomas, "What Is Higher-Order Thinking and Critical/Creative/Constructive Thinking?" n.d., Center for Studies in Higher-Order Literacy, http://a-s.clayton.edu/tparks/What is Higher Order Thinking.doc.

10. Charles Cave, "Definitions of Creativity," August 1999, http://members.optusnet.com.au/~charles57/Creative/Basics/definitions.htm.

11. Jennifer Gibson, "The Art of Medicine." *Brain Blogger,* October 31, 2010. From http://brainblogger.com/2010/10/31/the-art-of-medicine.

12. Adapted from T. Z. Tardif and R. J. Sternberg, "What Do We Know About Creativity?" in *The Nature of Creativity*, ed. R. J. Sternberg, London: Cambridge University Press, 1988.

13. Sternberg, p. 212.

14. Susan Cain, "The Rise of the New Groupthink," *New York Times,* January 13, 2012. From http://www.nytimes.com/2012/01/15/opinion/sunday/the-rise-of-the-new-groupthink.html?pagewanted=1&_r=1&smid=fb-nytimes.

15. Ibid.

16. Michael Michalko, "Twelve Things You Were Not Taught in School About Creative Thinking," *Psychology Today,* December 2, 2011. From http://www.psychologytoday.com/blog/creative-thinkering/201112/twelve-things-you-were-nottaught-in-school-about-creative-thinking.

17. Ibid.

18. Ibid.

19. Jonah Lehrer, "Groupthink," *The New Yorker,* January 30, 2012. From http://www.newyorker.com/reporting/2012/01/30/120130fa_fact_lehrer?currentPage=3.

20. Ibid.

21. Conference Board of Canada, "Employability Skills."

22. Sarah Lyman Kravits, 2012.

23. Jonah Lehrer, Jonah. *Imagine: How Creativity Works*. New York: Houghton Mifflin Harcourt, 2012, pp. 163–164.

24. Dennis Coon, *Introduction to Psychology: Exploration and Application,* 6th ed. St. Paul: West, 1992, p. 295.

25. Cain.

26. Sternberg, p. 236.

27. J. R. Hayes, *Cognitive Psychology: Thinking and Creating*. Homewood, IL: Dorsey, 1978.

28. Robert J. Sternberg, and Elena L. Grigorenko. "Practical Intelligence and the Principal," Yale University: Publication Series No. 2, 2001, p. 5.

29. Sternberg, pp. 251–269.

CHAPTER 5

1. Conference Board of Canada, "Employability Skills 2000+," www.conferenceboard.ca/topics/education/learning-tools/employability-skills.aspx.

2. Francis P. Robinson, *Effective Behavior*, New York: Harper & Row, 1941.

3. John Mack Faragher, Mari Jo Buhle, Daniel Czitrom, and Susan H. Armitage, *Out of Many: A History of the American People*, 5th ed., Upper Saddle River, NJ: Prentice Hall, 2005, p. xxxvii.

4. Benjamin S. Bloom, *Taxonomy of Educational Objectives, Handbook I: The Cognitive Domain*, New York: McKay, 1956.

5. Ophelia H. Hancock, *Reading Skills for College Students*, 5th ed., Upper Saddle River, NJ: Prentice Hall, 2001, pp. 54–59.

6. Mark Bauerlein, "Online Literacy Is a Lesser Kind," *The Chronicle of Higher Education*, September 19, 2008, http://chronicle.com/article/Online-Literacy-Is-a-Lesser/28307.

7. Ibid.

8. Mary Beth Hertz, "The Right Technology May Be a Pencil." Edutopia.com, November 29, 2011. From http://www.edutopia.org/blog/technologyintegration-classroom-mary-beth-hertz?utm_source=facebook&utm_medium=post&utm_content=blog&utm_campaign=techisapencil.

9. Lori Leibovich, "Choosing Quick Hits over the Card Catalog," *New York Times*, August 10, 2001, p. 1.

10. Adam Robinson, *What Smart Students Know: Maximum Grades, Optimum Learning, Minimum Time*, New York: Three Rivers Press, 1993, p. 82.

11. John J. Macionis, *Sociology*, 6th ed., Upper Saddle River, NJ: Prentice Hall, 1997, p. 174.

CHAPTER 6

1. Conference Board of Canada, "Employability Skills 2000+," www.conferenceboard.ca/topics/education/learning-tools/employability-skills.aspx.

2. Alina Tugend, "Multitasking Can Make You Lose . . . Um . . . Focus," *New York Times*, October 25, 2008, p. B7.

3. System developed by Cornell professor Walter Pauk. See Walter Pauk, *How to Study in College*, 10th ed., Boston: Houghton Mifflin, 2011, pp. 236–241.

4. Ezra Klein, "Better Note-Taking Through Technology." *The Washington Post,* May 16, 2011. From http://www.washingtonpost.com/blogs/ezra-klein/post/better-note-takingthrough-technology/2011/05/09/AFMs8z4G_blog.html.

5. Information from Frank Schmalleger, *Criminal Justice Today*, 8th ed., Upper Saddle River, NJ: Prentice-Hall, 2005, p. 71.

CHAPTER 7

1. University of California–Irvine, "Short-Term Stress Can Affect Learning and Memory," *ScienceDaily*, March 13, 2008, www.sciencedaily.com/releases/2008/03/080311182434.htm.

2. Herman Ebbinghaus, *Memory: A Contribution to Experimental Psychology,* trans. H. A. Ruger and C. E. Bussenius, New York: Teachers College, Columbia University, 1885.

3. Bullet points from Kenneth C. Petress, "The Benefits of Group Study," 2004, *Education*, 124, www.questia.com/googleScholar.qst;jsessionid=L4TDXZJvQmb4whQFL7v1mjGfBgp4YGzjJyg0mL3g1SJKyjvXK4h,/N!-747430471!743789914?docId=5006987606.

4. Dartmouth College Academic Skills Center, "How to Avoid Cramming for Tests," 2001, www.dartmouth.edu/~acskills/handouts.html.

5. "Study Shows How Sleep Improves Memory," *Science Daily*, June 29, 2005, www.sciencedaily.com/releases/2005/06/050629070337.htm.

6. Gretchen Reynolds, "How Exercise Fuels the Brain," *New York Times*, February 12, 2012. From http://well.blogs.nytimes.com/2012/02/22/how-exercise-fuels-the-brain.

7. Adam Robinson, *What Smart Students Know: Maximum Grades, Optimum Learning, Minimum Time*, New York: Three Rivers Press, 1993, p. 118.

8. These strategies from Student Counseling Service, Division of Student Affairs, "Self-Help: Math Study Skills," Texas A & M University, 2012. Adapted from William C. Resnick and David H. Heller. *On Your Own in College.* From http://scs.tamu.edu/?q=node/92.

CHAPTER 8

1. Conference Board of Canada, "Employability Skills 2000+," www.conferenceboard.ca/topics/education/learning-tools/employability-skills.aspx.

2. Ben Gose, "Notes from Academe: Living It Up on the Dead Days," *The Chronicle of Higher Education*, June 8, 2002, http://chronicle.com/article/Living-It-Up-on-the-Dead-Days/8983.

3. Barbara J. Speidel, "Overcoming Test Anxiety," Academic Success Center of Southwestern College. From http://www.swccd.edu/~asc/lrnglinks/test_anxiety.html.

4. "Anxiety Management," Michigan Technological University, www.counseling.mtu.edu/anxiety_management.html.

5. Peter Gwynne, "The Write Way to Reduce Test Anxiety," Inside Science News Service, January 14, 2011. From http://www.usnews.com/science/articles/2011/01/14/the-write-way-to-reduce-test-anxiety.

6. Paul D. Nolting, *Math Study Skills Workbook: Your Guide to Reducing Test Anxiety and Improving Study Strategies,* Boston: Houghton Mifflin, 2000. Cited in "Test Anxiety," West Virginia University at Parkersburg, http://www.wvup.edu/wp-content/uploads/2013/01/TEST-ANXIETY.pdf.

7. Jill Duffy, "How Students Use Technology to Cheat and How Their Teachers Catch Them," PCMag.com, March 25, 2011. From http://www.pcmag.com/slideshow/story/262232/how-students-use-technology-to-cheat.

CHAPTER 9

1. Statistics Canada, "Study: Canada's Visible Minority Population in 2017," *The Daily,* March 22, 2005, www.statcan.gc.ca/daily-quotidien/050322/dq050322b-eng.htm.

2. Conference Board of Canada, "Employability Skills 2000+," www.conferenceboard.ca/topics/education/learning-tools/employability-skills.aspx.

3. "Conceptual Frameworks/Models, Guiding Values and Principles," National Center for Cultural Competence, 2002, http://gucchd.georgetown.edu//nccc/framework.html.

4. Information in the sections on the five stages of building competency is based on Mark A. King, Anthony Sims, and David Osher, "How Is Cultural Competence Integrated in Education?" *Cultural Competence,* www.air.org/cecp/cultural/Q_integrated.htm#def.

5. Statistics Canada, "Police-Reported Hate Crimes," *The Daily,* July 11, 2013, http://www.statcan.gc.ca/pub/85-002-x/2013001/article/11822-eng.htm.

6. Martin Luther King Jr., from his sermon "A Tough Mind and a Tender Heart," *Strength in Love,* Philadelphia: Fortress Press, 1986, p. 14.

7. This section and chapter opener story from Highline College Honors Scholar Program Success Stories (adapted with permission from original story, online at http://flightline.highline.edu/honors/success/gaile.htm).

CHAPTER 10

1. Patty Winsa, "National Survey of Post-Secondary Students in Canada Show Stress and Anxiety Are Major Factors in Mental Health," *The Toronto Star*, June 17, 2013. From http://www.thestar.com/news/gta/2013/06/17/national_survey_of_postsecondary_students_in_canada_shows_stress_and_anxiety_are_major_factors_in_mental_health.html.

2. Conference Board of Canada, "Employability Skills 2000+," www.conferenceboard.ca/topics/education/learning-tools/employability-skills.aspx.

3. Gina Kolata, "A Surprising Secret to a Long Life: Stay in School," *New York Times*, January 3, 2007, pp. A1, A16.

4. Information in this section based on materials from Dr. Marlene Schwartz of the Rudd Center for Food Policy and Obesity at Yale University.

5. Beth Fontenot, "College Students Get a Failing Grade on Their Eating Habits." *The Atlantic*, September 24, 2011. From http://www.theatlantic.com/health/archive/2011/09/college-students-get-a-failing-grade-on-their-eating-habits/245296.

6. CMAJ, "Current and predicted prevalence of obesity in Canada: a trend analysis," http://www.cmajopen.ca/content/2/1/E18.

7. Rudd Center for Food Policy and Obesity, "Employment," 2005, www.yaleruddcenter.org/default.aspx?id=77.

8. Mayo Clinic, "Aerobic Exercise: Top 10 Reasons to Get Physical," Mayoclinic.com, 2012. From http://www.mayoclinic.com/health/aerobic-exercise/EP00002/NSECTIONGROUP=2.

9. Centers for Disease Control and Prevention. "How Much Physical Activity Do Adults Need?" CDC website, March 30, 2011. From http://www.cdc.gov/physicalactivity/everyone/guidelines/adults.html.

10. Mike Evans, "23½ hours," YouTube, December 2, 2011. From http://www.youtube.com/watch?v=aUaInS6HIGo.

11. CBS News, "Help for Sleep-Deprived Students," April 19, 2004, www.cbsnews.com/stories/2004/04/19/health/main612476.shtml.

12. "College Students' Sleep Habits Harmful to Health, Study Finds," The Daily Orange—Feature Issue, September 25, 2002, www.dailyorange.com/news/2002/09/25/Feature/College.Students.Sleep.Habits.Harmful.To.Health.Study.Finds-280340.shtml.

13. Herbert Benson, Eileen M. Stuart, et al., The Wellness Book, New York: Simon & Schuster, 1992, p. 292; and Gregg Jacobs, "Insomnia Corner," Talk About Sleep, 2004, www.talkaboutsleep.com/sleepdisorders/insomnia_corner.htm.

14. Statistics Canada, "Canadian Community Health Survey: Mental Health 2012," http://www.statcan.gc.ca/daily-quotidien/130918/dq130918a-eng.htm.

15. Centre for Addiction and Mental Health (CAMH), "Depression," http://www.cmha.ca/mental-health/understanding-mental-illness/depression/.

16. Centre for Addiction and Mental Health, "Heavy Drinking, Levels of Stress High among University Students—Canadian Campus Survey," September 15, 2005, http://www.camh.ca/en/research/research_areas/community_and_population_health/Pages/population_health_surveys.aspx.

17. SAVE (Suicide Awareness Voices of Education), "Symptoms of Major Depression," 2010, www.save.org/index.cfm?fuseaction=home.viewPage&page_id=A806E240-95E6-44BB-C2D6C47399E9EFDB.

18. National Eating Disorders Association, "Learning Basic Terms and Information on a Variety of Eating Disorder Topics," 2010, www.nationaleatingdisorders.org/information-resources/general-information.php#facts-statistics.

19. Richard Knox, "The Teen Brain: It's Just Not Grown Up Yet," NPR.org, March 1, 2010. From http://www.npr.org/templates/story/story.php?storyId=124119468.

20. Linda Foster, "Teen Alcoholism and Drug Addiction." EverydayHealth.com, April 20, 2009. From http://www.everydayhealth.com/addiction/addiction-in-adolescence.aspx.

21. Jeremiah Rodriguez, "Canada sixth in alcohol consumption," The Gazette, March 8, 2013. From http://www.westerngazette.ca/2013/03/08/canada-sixth-in-alcohol-consumption/.

22. Statistics Canada, "Heavy Drinking: 2012," http://www.statcan.gc.ca/pub/82-625-x/2013001/article/11838-eng.htm.

23. Centers for Disease Control and Prevention, "Alcohol and Public Health," September 3, 2008, www.cdc.gov/alcohol/index.htm.

24. Joel Seguine, "Students Report Negative Consequences of Binge Drinking in New Survey," The University Record, University of Michigan, October 25, 1999, www.umich.edu/~urecord/9900/Oct25_99/7.htm.

25. Health Canada, "Canadian Tobacco Use Monitoring Survey," http://www.hc-sc.gc.ca/hc-ps/tobac-tabac/research-recherche/stat/ctums-esutc_2012-eng.php.

26. "Secondhand Smoke," October 1, 2009, American Cancer Society, www.cancer.org/docroot/PED/content/PED_10_2X_Secondhand_Smoke-Clean_Indoor_Air.asp.

27. Hilary Smith, "The High Cost of Smoking," 2007, MSN Money, http://moneycentral.msn.com/content/Insurance/Insureyourhealth/P100291.asp.

28. National Institutes of Health, "Clearing the Air: Quit Smoking Today," National Cancer Institute, Publication No. 08-1647, October, 2008, pp. 10–24.

29. National Survey on Drug Use and Health (NSDUH), "The NSDUH Report: College Enrollment Status and Past Year Illicit Drug Use Among Young Adults: 2002, 2003, and 2004," October 21, 2005, http://oas.samhsa.gov/2k5/College/college.htm.

30. Rape Abuse and Incest National Network. "Statistics." From http://www.rainn.org/statistics.

31. "The Sexual Assault Continuum." Sexual Assault Victim Advocate (SAVA) Center: Fort Collins, CO, 2011.

CHAPTER 11

1. Rob Carrick, "Money Stress Catches Up With Canadians," http://www.theglobeandmail.com/globe-investor/personal-finance/household-finances/money-stress-catches-up-with-canadians/article5221810/#dashboard/follows/.

2. Jim Hanson, "Your Money Personality: It's All in Your Head," University Credit Union, December 25, 2006, http://hffo.cuna.org/012433/article/1440/html.

3. Jeff Lagerquist, "Student debt: Average payback takes 14 years," *Financial Post,* September 4, 1012, http://business.financialpost.com/2012/09/04/student-debt-average-payback-takes-14-years/.

4. Mark Whitehouse, "Number of the Week: Class of 2011, Most Indebted Ever," *Wall Street Journal,* May 7, 2011. From http://blogs.wsj.com/economics/2011/05/07/number-of-the-week-classof-2011-most-indebted-ever.

5. "Attitudes and Characteristics of Freshmen at 4-Year Colleges, Fall 2007," Chronicle of Higher Education.

6. Statistics Canada, "Study: The Financial Impact of Student Loans," *The Daily,* January 29, 2010, www.statcan.gc.ca/daily-quotidien/100129/dq100129c-eng.htm.

7. Colin Campbell, "The Danger of Debt," www.carleton.ca/ottawainsight/2002/pfinance/s4.html.

8. Most items in bullet list based on Michael Bowler, "Watch Out for Credit Card Traps," *The Lucrative Investor,* 2009, www.thelucrativeinvestor.com/watch-credit-card-traps; and Chris Arnold, "Credit Card Companies Abuse the Unwitting," November 6, 2007, NPR, www.npr.org/templates/story/story.php?storyId=16035323.

9. Pat Curry, "How Credit Scores Work, How a Score Is Calculated," Bankrate.com, November 8, 2006, www.bankrate.com/brm/news/credit-scoring/20031104a1.asp.

10. The University of Arizona, "Young Adults Financial Capability: APLUS Arizona Pathways to Life Success for University Students Wave 2," September 2011, p. 29. From http://aplus.arizona.edu/Wave-2-Report.pdf.

CHAPTER 12

1. Conference Board of Canada, "Employability Skills 2000+," www.conferenceboard.ca/topics/education/learning-tools/employability-skills.aspx.

2. Self-Directed Search, www.self-directed-search.com.

3. Kevin May, "Humanities and Liberal Arts Majors Are Going into Business," *The BYU Daily Universe,* December 14, 2011. From http://universe.byu.edu/index.php/2011/12/14/humanities-andliberal-arts-majors-are-going-into-business.

4. National Service Learning Clearinghouse, "Service Learning Is. . . ," May 2004, www.servicelearning.org/article/archive/35.

5. U.S. Department of Labor, Bureau of Labor Statistics, "Number of Jobs Held, Labor Market Activity, and Earnings Growth Among the Youngest Baby Boomers: Results from a Longitudinal Survey," August 25, 2006, www.bls.gov/news.release/pdf/nlsoy.pdf.

6. Jessica Dickler, CNN Money, June 10, 2009. Accessed on October 1, 2011, from http://money.cnn.com/2009/06/09/news/economy/hidden_jobs.

7. Job Interview and Career Guide, "Resume: Keywords for Resumes—Keywords List," December 8, 2009. From http://www.job-interview-site.com/resume-keywords-for-resumes-keywords-list.html.

8. List and descriptions based on Sternberg, pp. 251–269.

9. Quoted in Linton Weeks, "The No-Book Report: Skim It and Weep," *Washington Post,* May 14, 2001, p. C8.

APPENDIX A

1. Analysis based on Lynn Quitman Troyka, *Simon & Schuster Handbook for Writers,* Upper Saddle River, NJ: Prentice Hall, 1996, pp. 22–23.

NAME INDEX

Mochermak, Sarah, 150
Molley, Brandie, 34, 38
Montrose, Gary, 113
Morris, Charles G., 218*n*
Mosaicos: Spanish as a World Language, 217*n*
Murphy, Bruce Allen, 194*n*
Musser, Gary L., 211*n*

N

Nguyen, Tia, 192
Nielsen, Jakob, 134

O

O'Sullivan, Arthur, 217*n*, 306*n*

P

Partnership for 21st Century Skills Framework, 6*n*
Paul, Dr. Richard, 89*n*
Perez, Stephen J., 306*n*
Peterson, Dolores Davison, 217*n*
Picasso, Pablo, 91
Piggrem, Gary W., 218*n*
Pink, Daniel, 8
Pitino, Rick, 12
Posen, Zac, 90
Psychology, 181*n*

R

Ravelli, Bruce, 121*n*
Redgun, Dion, 242
Richardson, Torian, 289, 308
Robinson, Adam, 138

S

Salovey, Peter, 19*n*
Schwarz, Tony, 47
Seligman, Dr. Martin, 15
Shakespeare, William, 59
Sheffrin, Steven M., 217*n*, 306*n*
Sheridan Richard, 46
Soloway, Elliot, 137
Somers, Kirsten, 4
Sternberg, Robert, 8, 9, 57, 58, 103, 327, 329
Stirring Up Thinking, 86*n*
Survey of Economics: Principles, Applications and Tools, 306*n*

T

Tarbuck, Edward, 159*n*
Tasa, Dennis, 159*n*
Taylor, William M., 14*n*
Thompson, David, 301
Tieder, Becca, 261, 284
Timm, Paul, 39
Trimpe, Lynn E., 211*n*

U

Use Both Sides of Your Brain, 175*n*
"Using Bloom's Taxonomy to Promote Critical Reading and Thinking", 89*n*

V

W

Webber, Michelle, 121*n*
Western Civilization: A Social and Cultural History, 217*n*
"Wheel of Life, The", 27*n*
Wilson, Edwin O., 158
Winfrey, Oprah, 59
Wozniak, Steve, 90

X

Xu, Hongman, 67

Y

Your Maximum Mind, 263*n*
Yuen, Lenora, 45

SUBJECT INDEX

communication (Cont.)
 organizational style of, 243
 passive, 254
 speakers adjust to listeners in, 244
 technology, 251–252
 thinking style of, 243
community service, 6
compound interest, 307
computerized tomography (CT)
  scan, 29
Conference Board of Canada, 7, 8, 56,
  82, 92, 114, 153, 213, 236, 263,
  315, 320
conflicts, 253
 prevention strategies, 253–254,
  255–256
 resolution, 254
constructive criticism, 246–247
contacts, 323
continuing education, 331
continuous learning, 7
Cornell system of note-taking (T-note
  system), 158, 160–161
Council of Ministers of Education,
  Canada (CMEC), 8
Covey, Dr. Stephen, 33
cramming, 205–206
creative thinking, 9, 10
 asking what if questions in, 93–94
 braingaming in, 92
 challenging assumptions in, 92
 improving, 90–91
 perspective shifting as, 92–93
 risk taking in, 94–95
creativity,
 belief ingredient of, 90
 curiosity and exploration ingredient
  of, 90
 definitions of, 90
 failure as learning ingredient of,
  91–92
 risk taking and hard work
  ingredient of, 90–91
 time alone ingredient of, 90
Credibility, Accuracy, Reasonableness,
  Support (CARS) test for
  information quality, 139, 350
credit score (rating), 304
 factors determining, 305
creditors, 305
critical reading, 138
 argument evaluation during, 139
 evidence evaluation during, 139
 focusing during, 138
critical thinking, 10
 skills, 182–184
 social science reading and, 132
criticism,
 constructed, 246–247
 receiving, 247
 unconstructed, 246

Cross-Cultural Solutions, 334
cultural competence, 236–238
 awareness of culture interaction as
  action base for, 237, 239–240
 emotional intelligence (EI)
  and, 241
 evaluating personal perceptions and
  attitudes as action base for, 237,
  238–239
 knowledge of other cultures as
  action base for, 237, 241
 learning to adapt to diversity as
  action base for, 237, 241–243
 value diversity as action base for,
  237–238

D

Daily, The, 297
Dalhousie University, 4
Daub, Olivia, 3
decision making,
 balance keeping in, 101, 103
 effective, 98–99
 strategies for, 99, 101
delay gratification, 263
depression, 269–270
 causes of, 272
 suicide and, 272
 symptoms of, 271–272
dictionaries, 117–118
digital revolution, 5
discrimination, 239–240, 242
diversity, 236–237
 among people, 237
 definitions of, 237
 in Canada, 237
 valuing, 237–238
 within people, 237
Drake, 90
drug abuse, 273–274, 277–278
Dweck, Carol, 8, 9, 12
dyslexia, 113

E

eating disorders, 273
Ebbinghaus, Hermann, 174, 175
ecstasy, 278
Edison, Thomas, 17, 92
electronic communications, 251
 advantages of, 251–252
 disadvantages of, 251–252
 privacy protection in, 253
electronic materials, 13–14
Elton B. Stephens Company (EBSCO)
  Canadian Reference Centre, 137
emotional intelligence (EI),
 abilities of, 18–19
 career planning and, 320–321
 cultural competence and, 241

definitions of, 17
experience builds, 96–97
power of, 18
role of, 18
skills, 18–19
steps for success in, 97
success and, 18
emotions, 17, 19
Employability Skills 2000+ Profile, 8,
  32, 56, 92, 236, 315
employability skills, 7, 8
ephedrine, 278
Equifax Canada, 302
essays, 219–222
Estrada, Dr. Jeremy, 1, 10, 16
ethics, 12
Evernote software, 164
evidence, 139
Ewart, Norton, 145
executive functions (of brain), 83
explanatory style, 15
 aspects of, 15
 growth mindset and, 16
 optimistic perspective, 15, 16
 pessimistic perspective, 15
*Exploring Sociology: The Concise
  Edition,* 120, 121

F

F-pattern reading, 134
fact *vs.* opinion, 85–86
fairness, 13
financial management, 290–292
 achieving long-term goals, 307–308
 budgeting, 293–294
 calculating income and expenditures,
  293–294
 credit cards, 301–304
 credit scores (ratings), 304–305
 factors affecting, 290–291
 grants, 300
 multiple intelligence factors, 306
 needs *vs.* wants, 291–292
 retirement savings, 307
 scholarships, 300–301
 strategies for decreasing spending, 295
 strategies for increasing income,
  298–299
 student loans, 299–300
 time and money relationship, 292
financial security, 307–308
First Nations peoples, 115
fixed mindset, 12
Framework for 21st Century Learning,
  7, 8
 critical thinking building block for,
  24
 initiative and self-direction building
  blocks for, 24
 problem solving building block for, 24

successful intelligence, 9
  attitudes and tools for lifelong, 332
  importance of, 11
Suicide Awareness Voices of Education
  (SAVE), 272
suicide, 272
Sun Life Financial, 290
Survey, Question, Read, Recite, and
  Review (SQ3R) reading strategy,
  118–120, 205
  note-taking and, 156–157
  online materials and, 134
  question step in, 120–123
  reading materials in different
    academic fields, 129, 130
  reading step in, 123–125, 127
  recite step in, 127, 129
  review step in, 129
  surveying step in, 120

T

task participation, 7
Taylor, William M., 13, 15
team meetings, 249
teamwork, 248
technology choices, 70, 72
teleconferencing, 5
test anxiety, 206–207
  comfort article to address, 209
  definition of, 207
  dislike of testing as source of, 207
  in mathematics, 209
  lack of preparation as source of, 207
  relaxation to address, 209
  returning student and, 209
  situation analysis to help address,
    207–208
  test time strategies to address,
    208–209
test mistakes, 223–225
test performance, 199, 200
  academic integrity in, 212–214
  anxiety and, 206–207
  cramming for, 205–206
  end-of-year studying, 206
  expectations, 201–202
  goal-setting strategies for, 202–203
  goals, 200
  information gathering preparations,
    201–202
  physical preparation for, 205
  preparations for, 200–202
  SMART strategies for, 202–203
  SQ3R and, 205
  strategies for success in, 210–212
  study strategies for, 203, 205
  test-day strategies, 212
  time management strategies for, 202
  types of, 201

test questions,
  analyze real previous tests, 216
  essays, 219–222
  fill-in-the-blank, 219
  matching, 218–219
  multiple-choice, 216–217
  objective, 215
  subjective, 215
  true/false, 218
thinking skills,
  analytical, 8, 10
  creative, 8, 10
  critical, 10
  goals and, 9–10
  practical, 8, 10
  See also skills
  types of, 9
Thompson, David, 301
Tieder, Becca, 261, 284
time management, 3, 5
  central strategy for, 39–40
  ideal schedule step in, 38
  needs assessment step in, 38
  planner choice for, 39–40
  preference identification
    step in, 38
  prioritizing for, 40
  procrastination and, 44–45
  schedule study time in, 202
  scheduling for, 40
  strategies for test preparation, 202
  stress management and, 44
  time traps and, 44
  to-do lists for, 41–42
time traps, 44
Timm, Paul, 39
to-do lists, 41–42
tobacco abuse, 273, 275–276
topic sentence, 127
TransUnion Canada, 302
trust, 13
Tsinghua University, 308
Tufts University, 8
twenty-first century skills, 6

U

unconstructive criticism, 246
Université de Montréal, 269
University of Arizona, 199
University of Michigan, 137
University of Prince Edward Island,
  PEI, 203
University of Waterloo, 3
use of numbers, 7

V

VAK (or VARK) questionnaire, 60
values and value system, 30, 31
  choices of, 31

external influences on, 31
goals and, 30, 32
life experiences and, 31–32
personal mission statement
  and, 33
sources of, 31
verbal signposts, 152
Vocational Preference Inventory (VPI),
  317
volunteering, 319

W

Wall Street Journal, 83, 292
Webber, Michelle, 120
Westside Test Anxiety Scale, 210
Wheel of Successful Intelligence, 26
Wilson, Edwin O., 158
Winfrey, Oprah, 59
work safely, 7
work socially, 7
workload, 5
workplace choices, 72
World is Flat, The, 5
World Wide Web (WWW), 137
Wozniak, Steve, 90
writing process,
  clarity revising, 347
  conclusion drafting, 346
  drafting, 344–345
  editing, 348
  feedback drafting, 347
  freewriting drafting, 345
  introduction drafting, 343
  logistics planning, 343
  paper body drafting, 345
  plagiarism avoidance drafting, 346
  prewriting strategy planning, 343–
    344
  research planning, 344
  revising, 347
  source citing drafting, 347
  topics planning, 343
  working outline planning, 344
  working thesis planning, 344

X

Xu, Hongman, 67

Y

Young Men's Christian Association
  (YMCA), 301
Young Women's Christian Association
  (YWCA), 301
Yuen, Lenora, 45